D1434234

The firstwriter.com
Writers' Handbook
2019

01 223 · 355098

15th July
602

The firstwriter.com

Writers' Handbook

2019

EDITOR
J. PAUL DYSON

Published in 2018 by JP&A Dyson
27 Old Gloucester Street, London WC1N 3AX, United Kingdom
Copyright JP&A Dyson

https://www.jpandadyson.com
https://www.firstwriter.com

ISBN 978-1-909935-24-2

**Registered with the IP Rights Office
Copyright Registration Service
Ref: 3105545464**

Foreword

The firstwriter.com Writers' Handbook returns for its 2019 edition with over 1,300 listings of literary agents, publishers, and magazines, updated in firstwriter.com's online databases between 2016 and 2018, including revised and updated listings from the previous edition and over 30% new entries.

Previous editions of this handbook have been bought by writers across the United States, Canada, and Europe; and ranked in the United Kingdom as the number one bestselling writing and publishing directory on Amazon. The 2019 edition continues this international outlook, giving writers all over the English-speaking world access to the global publishing markets.

The handbook also provides free online access to the entire current firstwriter.com databases, including over 2,300 magazines, over 750 literary agencies, over 1,900 book publishers that don't charge fees, and constantly updated listings of current writing competitions, with typically more than 50 added each month.

For details on how to claim your free access please see the back of this book.

Included in the subscription
A subscription to the full website is not only free with this book, but comes packed with all the following features:

Advanced search features

- Save searches and save time – set up to 15 search parameters specific to your work, save them, and then access the search results with a single click whenever you log in. You can even save multiple different searches if you have different types of work you are looking to place.
- Add personal notes to listings, visible only to you and fully searchable – helping you to organise your actions.
- Set reminders on listings to notify you when to submit your work, when to follow up, when to expect a reply, or any other custom action.
- Track which listings you've viewed and when, to help you organise your search – any listings which have changed since you last viewed them will be highlighted for your attention.

Daily email updates
As a subscriber you will be able to take advantage of our email alert service, meaning you can specify your particular interests and we'll send you automatic email updates when we change or add a listing that matches them. So if you're interested in agents dealing in romantic fiction

in the United States you can have us send you emails with the latest updates about them – keeping you up to date without even having to log in.

User feedback

Our agent, publisher, and magazine databases all include a user feedback feature that allows our subscribers to leave feedback on each listing – giving you not only the chance to have your say about the markets you contact, but giving a unique authors' perspective on the listings.

Save on copyright protection fees

If you're sending your work away to publishers, competitions, or literary agents, it's vital that you first protect your copyright. As a subscriber to firstwriter.com you can do this through our site and save 10% on the copyright registration fees normally payable for protecting your work internationally through the Intellectual Property Rights Office (https://www.Copyright RegistrationService.com).

firstwriter.magazine

firstwriter.magazine showcases the best in new poetry and fiction from around the world. If you're interested in writing and want to get published, the most important thing you can do is read contemporary writing that's getting into print now. Our magazine helps you do that.

Monthly newsletter

When you subscribe to firstwriter.com you also receive our monthly email newsletter – described by one publishing company as "the best in the business" – including articles, news, and interviews for writers. And the best part is that you can continue to receive the newsletter even after you stop your paid subscription – at no cost!

For details on how to claim your free access please see the back of this book.

Contents

Publishers

Free Access

Glossary of Terms

This section explains common terms used in this handbook, and in the publishing industry more generally.

Academic

Listings in this book will be marked as targeting the academic market only if they publish material of an academic nature; e.g. academic theses, scientific papers, etc. The term is not used to indicate publications that publish general material aimed at people who happen to be in academia, or who are described as academic by virtue of being educated.

Adult

In publishing, "adult" simply refers to books that are aimed at adults, as opposed to books that are aimed at children, or young adults, etc. It is not a euphemism for pornographic or erotic content. Nor does it necessarily refer to content which is unsuitable for children; it is just not targeted at them. In this book, most ordinary mainstream publishers will be described as "adult", unless their books are specifically targeted at other groups (such as children, professionals, etc.).

Advance

Advances are up-front payments made by traditional publishers to authors, which are off-set against future royalties.

Agented

An *agented* submission is one which is submitted by a literary agent. If a publisher accepts only *agented* submissions then you will need a literary agent to submit the work on your behalf.

Author bio

A brief description of you and your life – normally in relation to your writing activity, but if intended for publication (particularly in magazines) may be broader in scope. May be similar to *Curriculum Vitae* (CV) or résumé, depending on context.

Bio

See *Author bio*.

Curriculum Vitae

A brief description of you, your qualifications, and accomplishments – normally in this context in relation to writing (any previous publications, or awards, etc.), but in the case of nonfiction proposals may also include relevant experience that qualifies you to write on the subject. Commonly abbreviated to "CV". May also be referred to as a résumé. May be similar to *Author bio*, depending on context.

CV

See *Curriculum Vitae*.

International Reply Coupon

When submitting material overseas you may be required to enclose *International Reply Coupons*, which will enable the recipient to send a response and/or return your material at your cost. Not applicable/available in all countries, so check with your local Post Office for more information.

IRC

See *International Reply Coupon*.

Manuscript

Your complete piece of work – be it a novel, short story, or article, etc. – will be referred to as your manuscript. Commonly abbreviated to "ms" (singular) or "mss" (plural).

MS

See *Manuscript*.

MSS

See *Manuscript*.

Professional

Listings in this book will be marked as targeting the professional market if they publish material serving a particular profession: e.g. legal journals, medical journals, etc. The term is not used to indicate publications that publish general material aimed at a notional "professional class".

Proposal

A proposal is normally requested for nonfiction projects (where the book may not yet have been completed, or even begun). Proposals can consist of a number of components, such as an outline, table of contents, CV, marketing information, etc. but the exact requirements will vary from one publisher to another.

Query

Many agents and publishers will prefer to receive a query in the first instance, rather than your full *manuscript*. A query will typically consist of a cover letter accompanied by a *synopsis* and/or sample chapter(s). Specific requirements will vary, however, so always check on a case by case basis.

Recommendation

If an agent is only accepting approaches by recommendation this means that they will only consider your work if it comes with a recommendation from an established professional in the industry, or an existing client.

RoW

Rest of world.

SAE

See *Stamped Addressed Envelope*. Can also be referred to as SASE.

SASE

Self-Addressed Stamped Envelope. Variation of SAE. See *Stamped Addressed Envelope*.

Simultaneous submission

A simultaneous submission is one which is sent to more than one market at the same time. Normally you will be sending your work to numerous different magazines, agents, and publishers at the same time, but some demand the right to consider it exclusively – i.e. they don't accept simultaneous submissions.

Stamped Addressed Envelope

Commonly abbreviated to "SAE". Can also be referred to as Self-Addressed Stamped Envelope, or SASE. When supplying an SAE, ensure that the envelope and postage is adequate for a reply or the return of your material, as required. If you are submitting overseas, remember that postage from your own country will not be accepted, and you may need to provide an *International Reply Coupon*.

Synopsis

A short outline of your story. This should cover all the main characters and events, including the ending. It is not the kind of "teaser" found on a book's back cover. The length of synopsis required can vary, but is generally between one and three pages.

TOC

Table of Contents. These are often requested as part of nonfiction proposals.

Unagented

An unagented submission is one which is not submitted through a literary agent. If a publisher accepts unagented submissions then you can approach them directly.

Unsolicited mss

A manuscript which has not been requested. Many agents and publishers will not accept unsolicited mss, but this does not necessarily mean they are closed to approaches – many will prefer to receive a short *query* in the first instance. If they like the idea, they will request the full work, which will then be a solicited manuscript.

Youth

The term "Youth" in this book is used to indicate the Young Adult market.

The Writer's Roadmap

With most objectives in life, people recognise that there is a path to follow. Whether it is career progression, developing a relationship, or chasing your dreams, we normally understand that there are foundations to lay and baby steps to take before we'll be ready for the main event.

But for some reason, with writing (perhaps because so much of the journey of a writer happens in private, behind closed doors), people often overlook the process involved. They often have a plan of action which runs something like this:

1. Write novel.

2. Get novel published.

This is a bit like having a plan for success in tennis which runs:

1. Buy tennis racket.

2. Win Wimbledon.

It misses out all the practice that is going to be required; the competing in the minor competitions and the learning of the craft that will be needed in order to succeed in the major events; the time that will need to be spent gaining reputation and experience.

In this roadmap we'll be laying out what we think is the best path to follow to try and give yourself the best shot of success in the world of writing. You don't necessarily have to jump through all the hoops, and there will always be people who, like Pop Idol or reality TV contestants, get a lucky break that propels them to stardom without laying any of the foundations laid out below, but the aim here is to limit your reliance on luck and maximise your ability to shape your destiny yourself.

1: Write short material

Writers will very often start off by writing a novel. We would advise strongly against this. It's like leaving school one day and applying for a job as a CEO of an international corporation the next. Novels are the big league. They are expensive to produce, market, and distribute. They require significant investment and pose a significant financial risk to publishers. They are not a good place for new writers to try and cut their teeth. If you've already written your novel that's great – it's great experience and you'll have learned a lot – but we'd recommend shelving it for now (you can always come back to it later) and getting stuck into writing some short form material, such as poetry and short fiction.

Claim your free access to **www.firstwriter.com**: See p.389

This is what novelist George R. R. Martin, author of *A Game of Thrones*, has to say on the subject:

> "I would also suggest that any aspiring writer begin with short stories. These days, I meet far too many young writers who try to start off with a novel right off, or a trilogy, or even a nine-book series. That's like starting in at rock climbing by tackling Mt Everest. Short stories help you learn your craft."

You will find that writing short material will improve your writing no end. Writing short fiction allows you to play with lots of different stories and characters very quickly. Because you will probably only spend a few days on any given story you will quickly gain a lot of experience with plotting stories and will learn a lot about what works, what doesn't work, and what you personally are good at. When you write a novel, by contrast, you may spend years on a single story and one set of characters, making this learning process much slower.

Your writing will also be improved by the need to stick to a word limit. Writers who start their career by writing a novel often produce huge epics, the word counts of which they wear as a badge of honour, as if they demonstrate their commitment to and enthusiasm for writing. What they actually demonstrate is a naivety about the realities of getting published. The odds are already stacked against new writers getting a novel published, because of the cost and financial risk of publishing a novel. The bigger the novel, the more it will cost to print, warehouse, and distribute. Publishers will not look at a large word count and be impressed – they will be terrified. The longer the novel, the less chance it has of getting published.

A lengthy first novel also suggests that the writer has yet to learn one of the most critical skills a writer must possess to succeed: brevity. By writing short stories that fit the limits imposed by competitions and magazines you will learn this critical skill. You will learn to remove unnecessary words and passages, and you will find that your writing becomes leaner, more engaging, and more exciting as a result. Lengthy first novels are often rambling and sometimes boring – but once you've been forced to learn how to "trim the fat" by writing short stories, the good habits you've got into will transfer across when you start writing long form works, allowing you to write novels that are pacier and better to read. They will stand a better chance of publication not just because they are shorter and cheaper to produce, but they are also likely to be better written.

2: Get a professional critique

It's a good idea to get some professional feedback on your work at some point, and it's probably better to do this sooner, rather than later. There's no point spending a long time doing something that doesn't quite work if a little advice early on could have got you on the right track sooner. It's also a lot cheaper to get a short story critiqued than a whole novel, and if you can learn the necessary lessons now it will both minimise the cost and maximise the benefit of the advice.

Should you protect the copyright of short works before showing them to anyone?

This is a matter of personal preference. We'd suggest that it certainly isn't as important to register short works as full novels, as your short works are unlikely to be of much financial value to you. Having said that, films do sometimes get made which are based on short stories, in which case you'd want to have all your rights in order. If you do choose to register your short works this can be done for a relatively small amount online at https://www. copyrightregistrationservice.com/register.

3: Submit to competitions and magazines, and build a list of writing credits

Once you have got some short works that you are happy with you can start submitting them to competitions and small magazines. You can search for competitions at https://www. firstwriter.com/competitions and magazines at https://www.firstwriter.com/magazines. Prize money may not be huge, and you probably won't be paid for having your work appear in the kind of small literary magazines you will probably be approaching at first, but the objective here is to build up a list of writing credits to give you more credibility when approaching agents and publishers. You'll be much more likely to grab their attention if you can reel off a list of places where you have already been published, or prizes you have won.

4: Finish your novel and protect your copyright

Okay – so you've built up a list of writing credits, and you've decided it's time to either write a novel, or go back to the one you had already started (in which case you'll probably find yourself cutting out large chunks and making it a lot shorter!). Once you've got your novel to the point where you're happy to start submitting it for publication you should get it registered for copyright. Unlike the registration of short works, which we think is a matter of personal preference, we'd definitely recommend registering a novel, and doing so before you show it to anybody. That *includes* family and friends. Don't worry that you might want to change it – as long as you don't rewrite it to the point where it's not recognisable it will still be protected – the important thing is to get it registered without delay. You can protect it online at https:// www. copyrightregistrationservice.com/register.

If you've already shown it to other people then just register it as soon as you can. Proving a claim to copyright is all about proving you had a copy of the work before anyone else, so time is of the essence.

5: Editing

These days, agents and publishers increasingly seem to expect manuscripts to have been professionally edited before being submitted to them – and no, getting your husband / wife / friend / relative to do it doesn't count. Ideally, you should have the whole manuscript professionally edited, but this can be expensive. Since most agents and publishers aren't going to want to see the whole manuscript in the first instance you can probably get away with just having the first three chapters edited. It may also be worth having your query letter and synopsis edited at the same time.

6: Submit to literary agents

There will be many publishers out there who will accept your submission directly, and on the face of it that might seem like a good idea, since you won't have to pay an agent 15% of your earnings.

However, all the biggest publishers are generally closed to direct submissions from authors, meaning that if you want the chance of getting a top publisher you're going to need a literary agent. You'll also probably find that their 15% fee is more than offset by the higher earnings you'll be likely to achieve.

To search for literary agents go to https://www.firstwriter.com/Agents. Start by being as specific in your search as possible. So if you've written a historical romance select "Fiction", "Romance", and "Historical". Once you've approached all the agents that specifically mention all three elements broaden your search to just "Fiction" and "Romance". As long as the new results don't specifically say they don't handle historical romance, these are still valid markets to approach. Finally, search for just "Fiction", as there are many agents who are willing to consider all kinds of fiction but don't specifically mention romance or historical.

Don't limit your approaches to just agents in your own country. With more and more agents accepting electronic queries it's now as easy to approach agents in other countries as in your own, and if you're ignoring either London or New York (the two main centres of English language publishing) you're cutting your chances of success in two.

7: Submit directly to publishers

Once you're certain that you've exhausted all potential agents for your work, you can start looking for publishers to submit your work directly to. You can search for publishers at https://www.firstwriter.com/publishers. Apply the same filtering as when you were searching for agents: start specific and gradually broaden, until you've exchausted all possibilities.

8: Self-publishing

In the past, once you got to the point where you'd submitted to all the publishers and agents who might be interested in your book, it would be time to pack away the manuscript in the attic, chalk it up to experience, and start writing another. However, these days writers have the option to take their book directly to market by publishing it themselves.

Before you decide to switch to self-publishing you must be sure that you've exhausted all traditional publishing possibilities – because once you've self-published your book you're unlikely to be able to submit it to agents and publishers. It will probably take a few years of exploring the world of traditional publishing to reach this point, but if you do then you've nothing to lose by giving self-publishing a shot. See our guide to self-publishing for details on how to proceed.

Why Choose Traditional Publishing

When **firstwriter.com** first started, back in 2001, there were only two games in town when it came to getting your book published: traditional publishing, and vanity publishing – and which you should pick was a no-brainer. Vanity publishing was little more than a scam that would leave you with an empty bank account and a house full of unsold books. If you were serious about being a writer, you had to follow the traditional publishing path.

Since then, there has been a self-publishing revolution, with new technologies and new printing methods giving writers a genuine opportunity to get their books into the market by themselves. So, is there still a reason for writers to choose traditional publishing?

The benefits of traditional publishing

Despite the allure and apparent ease of self-publishing, the traditional path still offers you the best chance of making a success of being a writer. There are rare cases where self-published writers make staggering fortunes and become internationally renowned on the back of their self-published books, but these cases are few and far between, and a tiny drop in the rapidly expanding ocean of self-published works. The vast majority of successful books – and the vast majority of successful writers – have their homes firmly in the established publishing houses. Even those self-published authors who find success usually end up moving to a traditional publisher in the end.

This is because the traditional publishers have the systems, the market presence, and the financial clout to *make* a book a bestseller. While successful self-published authors often owe their success in no small part to a decent dose of luck (a social media comment that goes viral; the right mention on the right media outlet at the right time), traditional publishers are in the business of engineering that success. They might not always succeed, but they have the marketing budgets and the distribution channels in place to give themselves, and the book they are promoting, the best possible chance.

And it's not just the marketing and the distribution. Getting signed with a traditional publisher brings a whole team of people with a wealth of expertise that will all work towards the success of the book. It will provide you with an editor who may have experience of working on previous bestsellers, who will not only help you get rid of mistakes in your work but may also help you refine it into a better book. They will help make sure that the quality of your content is good enough to make it in the marketplace.

The publishers will source a professional cover designer who will make your book look the part on the shelves and on the pages of the bookselling websites. They will have accountants who will handle the technicalities of tax regimes both home and abroad. They will have overseas contacts for establishing foreign publishing rights; translations; etc. They may even have contacts in the film industry, should there be a prospect of a movie adaptation. They will have experts working on every aspect of your book, right down to the printing and the warehousing and the shipping of the physical products. They will have people to manage the

*Claim your free access to **www.firstwriter.com**: See p.389*

ebook conversion and the electronic distribution. As an author, you don't need to worry about any of this.

This means you get more time to simply be a writer. You may have to go on book tours, but even these will be organised for you by PR experts, who will also be handling all the press releases, etc.

And then there's the advances. Advances are up-front payments made by traditional publishers to authors, which are off-set against future royalties. So, an author might receive a $5,000 advance before their book is published. When the royalties start coming in, the publisher keeps the first $5,000 to off-set the advance. The good news for the author is that if the book flops and doesn't make $5,000 in royalties they still get to keep the full advance. In an uncertain profession, the security of an advance can be invaluable for an author – and of course it's not something available to self-published authors.

The drawbacks of traditional publishing

The main downside of traditional publishing is just that it's so hard to get into. If you choose to self-publish then – provided you have enough perseverance, the right help and advice, and perhaps a little bit of money – you are guaranteed to succeed and see your book in print and for sale. With traditional publishing, the cold hard fact is that most people who try will not succeed.

And for many of those people who fail it may not even be their fault. That aspect of traditional publishing which can bring so many benefits as compared to self-publishing – that of being part of a team – can also be part of its biggest drawback. It means that you have to get other people to buy into your book. It means that you have to rely on other people being competent enough to spot a bestseller. Many failed to spot the potential of the Harry Potter books. How many potential bestsellers never make it into print just because none of the professionals at the publishers' gates manage to recognise their potential?

So if you choose traditional publishing your destiny is not in your own hands – and for some writers the lack of exclusive control can also be a problem. Sometimes writers get defensive when editors try to tinker with their work, or annoyed when cover artists don't realise their vision the way they expect. But this is hardly a fair criticism of traditional publishing, as most writers (particularly when they are starting out) will benefit from advice from experienced professionals in the field, and will often only be shooting themselves in the foot if they insist on ignoring it.

The final main drawback with traditional publishing is that less of the sale price of each copy makes it to the writer. A typical royalty contract will give the writer 15%. With a self-published book, the author can expect to receive much more. So, all other things being equal, the self-published route can be more profitable – but, of course, all things are not equal. If self-publishing means lower sales (as is likely), then you will probably make less money overall. Remember, it's better to have 15% of something than 50% of nothing.

Conclusion

In conclusion, our advice to writers would be to aim for traditional publishing first. It might be a long shot, but if it works then you stand a much better chance of being successful. If you don't manage to get signed by an agent or a publisher then you still have the option of self-publishing, but make sure you don't get tempted to resort to self-publishing too soon – most agents and publishers won't consider self-published works, so this is a one-way street. Once you've self-published your work, you probably won't be able to change your mind and go back to the traditional publishers with your book unless it becomes a huge hit without them. It's therefore important that you exhaust all your traditional publishing options before making the leap to self-publishing. Be prepared for this to take perhaps a few years (lots of agents and publishers can take six months just to respond), and make sure you've submitted to everyone you can on *both* sides of the Atlantic (publishing is a global game these days, and you need to concentrate on the two main centres of English-language publishing (New York and London) equally) before you make the decision to self-publish instead.

Formatting Your Manuscript

Before submitting a manuscript to an agent, magazine, or publisher, it's important that you get the formatting right. There are industry norms covering everything from the size of your margins to the font you choose – get them wrong and you'll be marking yourself out as an amateur. Get them right, and agents and editors will be far more likely to take you seriously.

Fonts

Don't be tempted to "make your book stand out" by using fancy fonts. It *will* stand out, but not for any reason you'd want. Your entire manuscript should be in a monospaced font like Courier (not a proportional font, like Times Roman) at 12 points. (A monospaced font is one where each character takes up the same amount of space; a proportional font is where the letter "i" takes up less space than the letter "m".)

This goes for your text, your headings, your title, your name – everything. Your objective is to produce a manuscript that looks like it has been produced on a simple typewriter.

Italics / bold

Your job as the author is to indicate words that require emphasis, not to pick particular styles of font. This will be determined by the house style of the publisher in question. You indicate emphasis by underlining text; the publisher will decide whether they will use bold or italic to achieve this emphasis – you shouldn't use either in your text.

Margins

You should have a one inch (2.5 centimetre) margin around your entire page: top, bottom, left, and right.

Spacing

In terms of line spacing, your entire manuscript should be double spaced. Your word processor should provide an option for this, so you don't have to insert blank lines manually.

While line spacing should be double, spaces after punctuation should be single. If you're in the habit of putting two spaces after full stops this is the time to get out of that habit, and remove them from your manuscript. You're just creating extra work for the editor who will have to strip them all out.

Do not put blank lines between paragraphs. Start every paragraph (even those at the start of chapters) with an indent equivalent to five spaces. If you want a scene break then create a line with the "#" character centred in the middle. You don't need blank lines above or below this line.

Word count

You will need to provide an estimated word count on the front page of your manuscript. Tempting as it will be to simply use the word processor's word counting function to tell you exactly how many words there are in your manuscript, this is not what you should do. Instead, you should work out the maximum number of characters on a line, divide this number by six, and then multiply by the total number of lines in your manuscript.

Once you have got your estimated word count you need to round it to an approximate value. How you round will depend on the overall length of your manuscript:

- up to 1,500 words: round to the nearest 100;
- 1,500–10,000 words: round to the nearest 500;
- 10,000–25,000 words: round to the nearest 1,000;
- Over 25,000 words: round to the nearest 5,000.

The reason an agent or editor will need to know your word count is so that they can estimate how many pages it will make. Since actual pages include varying amounts of white space due to breaks in paragraphs, sections of speech, etc. the formula above will actually provide a better idea of how many pages will be required than an exact word count would.

And – perhaps more importantly – providing an exact word count will highlight you immediately as an amateur.

Layout of the front page

On the first page of the manuscript, place your name, address, and any other relevant contact details (such as phone number, email address, etc.) in the top left-hand corner. In the top right-hand corner write your approximate word count.

If you have registered your work for copyright protection, place the reference number two single lines (one double line) beneath your contact details. Since your manuscript will only be seen by agents or editors, not the public, this should be done as discreetly as possible, and you should refrain from using any official seal you may have been granted permissions to use. (For information on registering for copyright protection see "Protecting Your Copyright", below.)

Place your title halfway down the front page. Your title should be centred and would normally be in capital letters. You can make it bold or underlined if you want, but it should be the same size as the rest of the text.

From your title, go down two single lines (or one double line) and insert your byline. This should be centred and start with the word "By", followed by the name you are writing under. This can be your name or a pen name, but should be the name you want the work published under. However, make sure that the name in the top left-hand corner is your real, legal name.

From your byline, go down four single lines (or two double lines) and begin your manuscript.

Layout of the text

Print on only one side of the paper, even if your printer can print on both sides.

In the top right-hand corner of all pages except the first should be your running head. This should be comprised of the surname used in your byline; a keyword from your title, and the page number, e.g. "Myname / Mynovel Page 5".

Text should be left-aligned, *not* justified. This means that you should have a ragged right-hand edge to the text, with lines ending at different points. Make sure you don't have any sort of hyphenation function switched on in your word processor: if a word is too long to fit on a line it should be taken over to the next.

Start each new chapter a third of the way down the page with the centred chapter number / title, underlined. Drop down four single lines (two double lines) to the main text.

At the end of the manuscript you do not need to indicate the ending in any way: you don't need to write "The End", or "Ends", etc. The only exception to this is if your manuscript happens to end at the bottom of a page, in which case you can handwrite the word "End" at the bottom of the last page, after you have printed it out.

Protecting Your Copyright

Protecting your copyright is by no means a requirement before submitting your work, but you may feel that it is a prudent step that you would like to take before allowing strangers to see your material.

These days, you can register your work for copyright protection quickly and easily online. The Intellectual Property Rights Office operates a website called the "Copyright Registration Service" which allows you to do this:

- *https://www.CopyrightRegistrationService.com*

This website can be used for material created in any nation signed up to the Berne Convention. This includes the United States, United Kingdom, Canada, Australia, Ireland, New Zealand, and most other countries. There are around 180 countries in the world, and over 160 of them are part of the Berne Convention.

Provided you created your work in one of the Berne Convention nations, your work should be protected by copyright in all other Berne Convention nations. You can therefore protect your copyright around most of the world with a single registration, and because the process is entirely online you can have your work protected in a matter of minutes, without having to print and post a copy of your manuscript.

What is copyright?

Copyright is a form of intellectual property (often referred to as "IP"). Other forms of intellectual property include trade marks, designs, and patents. These categories refer to different kinds of ideas which may not exist in a physical form that can be owned as property in the traditional sense, but may nonetheless have value to the people who created them. These forms of intellectual property can be owned in the same way that physical property is owned, but – as with physical property – they can be subject to dispute and proper documentation is required to prove ownership.

The different types of intellectual property divide into these categories as follows:

- **Copyright:** copyright protects creative output such as books, poems, pictures, drawings, music, films, etc. Any work which can be recorded in some way can be protected by copyright, as long as it is original and of sufficient length. Copyright does not cover short phrases or names.

- **Trade marks:** trade marks cover words and/or images which distinguish the goods or services of one trader from another. Unlike copyright, trade marks can cover names and short phrases.

- **Designs:** designs cover the overall visual appearance of a product, such as its shape, etc.

- **Patents:** patents protect the technical or functional aspects of designs or inventions.

The specifics of the legal protection surrounding these various forms of intellectual property will vary from nation to nation, but there are also generally international conventions to which a lot if not most of the nations of the world subscribe. The information provided below outlines the common situation in many countries but you should be aware that this may not reflect the exact situation in every territory.

The two types of intellectual property most relevant to writers are copyright and trade marks. If a writer has written a novel, a short story, a poem, a script, or any other piece of writing then the contents themselves can be protected by copyright. The title, however, cannot be protected by copyright as it is a name. An author may therefore feel that they wish to consider protecting the title of their work by registering it as a trade mark, if they feel that it is particularly important and/or more valuable in itself than the cost of registering a trade mark.

If a writer wants to register the copyright for their work, or register the title of their work as a trade mark, there are generally registration fees to be paid. Despite the fact that copyright covers long works that could be hundreds of thousands of words long, while trade marks cover single words and short phrases, the cost for registering a trade mark is likely to be many times higher than that for registering a work for copyright protection. This is because trade marks must be unique and are checked against existing trade marks for potential conflicts. While works to be registered for copyright must also not infringe existing works, it is not practical to check the huge volume of new works to be registered for copyright against the even larger volume of all previously copyrighted works. Copyright registration therefore tends to simply archive the work in question as proof of the date at which the person registering the work was in possession of it.

In the case of both copyright and trade marks the law generally provides some protection even without any kind of registration, but registration provides the owner of the intellectual property with greater and more enforceable protection. In the case of copyright, the creator of a work usually automatically owns the copyright as soon as the work is recorded in some way (i.e. by writing it down or recording it electronically, etc.), however these rights can be difficult to prove if disputed, and therefore many countries (such as the United States) also offer an internal country-specific means of registering works. Some countries, like the United Kingdom, do not offer any such means of registration, however an international registration is available through the Intellectual Property Rights Office's Copyright Registration Service, and can be used regardless of any country-specific provisions. This can help protect copyright in all of the nations which are signatories of the Berne Convention.

In the case of trade marks, the symbol "™" can be applied to any mark which is being used as a trade mark, however greater protection is provided if this mark is registered, in which case the symbol "®" can be applied to the mark. It is often illegal to apply the "®" symbol to a trade mark which has not been registered. There are also options for international registrations of trade marks, which are administered by the World Intellectual Property Organization, however applications cannot be made to the WIPO directly – applications must be made through the relevant office of the applicant's country.

Copyright law and its history

The modern concept of copyright can be traced back to 1710 and the "Statute of Anne", which applied to England, Scotland, and Wales. Prior to this Act, governments had granted monopoly rights to publishers to produce works, but the 1710 Act was the first time that a right of ownership was acknowledged for the actual creator of a work.

From the outset, the attempt to protect the creator's rights was beset with problems due to the local nature of the laws, which applied in Britain only. This meant that lots of copyrighted works were reproduced without the permission of the author in Ireland, America, and in European countries. This not only hindered the ability of the London publishers to sell their legitimate copies of their books in these territories, but the unauthorised reproductions would also find their way into Britain, harming the home market as well.

A natural progression for copyright law was therefore its internationalisation, beginning in 1846 with a reciprocal agreement between Britain and Prussia, and culminating in a series of international treaties, the principal of which is the Berne Convention, which applies to over 160 countries.

Traditionally in the United Kingdom and the United States there has been a requirement to register a work with an official body in order to be able to claim copyright over it (Stationers Hall and the US Library of Congress respectively), however this has been changed by the Berne Convention, which requires signatory countries to grant copyright as an automatic right: i.e. the creator of a work immediately owns its copyright by virtue of creating it and recording it in some physical way (for instance by writing it down or making a recording of it, etc.). The United Kingdom and the United States have both been slow to fully adopt this approach. Though the United Kingdom signed the Berne Convention in 1887, it took 100 years for it to be fully implemented by the Copyright Designs and Patents Act 1988. The United States did not even sign the convention until 1989.

In the United States the US Library of Congress continues to provide archiving services for the purposes of copyright protection, but these are now optional. US citizens no longer need to register their work in order to be able to claim copyright over it. It is necessary, however, to be able to prove when the person who created it did so, and this is essentially the purpose of the registration today. In the United Kingdom, Stationers Hall has ceased to exist, and there is no longer any state-run means of registering the copyright to unpublished works, leaving the only available options as independent and/or international solutions such as the copyright registration service provided by the IP Rights Office.

Registering your work for copyright protection

Registering your work for copyright protection can help you protect your rights in relation to your work. Generally (particularly if you live in a Berne Convention country, as most people do) registration will not be compulsory in order to have rights over your work. Any time you create a unique original work you will in theory own the copyright over it, however you will need to be able to prove when you created it, which is the purpose of registering your work for copyright protection. There are other ways in which you might attempt to prove this, but registration provides better evidence than most other forms.

There are a range of different options for protecting your copyright that vary depending on where you live and the kind of coverage you want. Some countries, like the United States, provide internal means of registering the copyright of unpublished works, however the scope of these will tend to be restricted to the country in question. Other countries, like the United

Kingdom, do not offer any specific government-sponsored system for registering the copyright of unpublished works. An international option is provided by the Intellectual Property Rights Office, which is not affiliated to any particular government or country. As long as you live in a Berne Convention country you should be able to benefit from using their Copyright Registration Service. You can register your work with the Intellectual Property Rights Office regardless of whether or not there are any specific arrangements in your home country (you may even choose to register with both to offer your work greater protection). Registration with the Intellectual Property Rights Office should provide you with protection throughout the area covered by the Berne Convention, which is most of the world.

Registering your work for copyright protection through the Intellectual Property Rights Office is an online process that can be completed in a few minutes, provided you have your file in an accepted format and your file isn't too large (if your file is too large and cannot be reduced you may have to split it and take out two or more registrations covering it). There is a registration fee to pay ($45 / £25 / €40 at the time of writing) per file for registration, however if you are a subscriber to **firstwriter.com** you can benefit from a 10% discount when you start the registration process on our site.

When registering your work, you will need to give some consideration to what your work actually consists of. This is a straightforward question if your work is a novel, or a screenplay, but if it is a collection of poetry or short stories then the issue is more difficult. Should you register your collection as one file, or register each poem separately, which would be more expensive? Usually, you can answer this question by asking yourself what you propose to do with your collection. Do you intend to submit it to publishers as a collection only? Or do you intend to send the constituent parts separately to individual magazines? If the former is the case, then register the collection as a single work under the title of the collection. If the latter is the case then this could be unwise, as your copyright registration certificate will give the name of the collection only – which will not match the names of the individual poems or stories. If you can afford to, you should therefore register them separately. If you have so many poems and / or stories to register that you cannot afford to register them all separately, then registering them as a collection will be better than nothing.

Proper use of the copyright symbol

The first thing to note is that for copyright there is only one form of the symbol (©), unlike trade marks, where there is a symbol for registered trade marks (®) and a symbol for unregistered trade marks (™).

To qualify for use of the registered trade mark symbol (®) you must register your trade mark with the appropriate authority in your country, whereas the trade mark symbol (™) can be applied to any symbol you are using as a trade mark. Use of the copyright symbol is more similar to use of the trade mark symbol, as work does not need to be registered in order to use it.

You can place the copyright symbol on any original piece of work you have created. The normal format would be to include alongside the copyright symbol the year of first publication and the name of the copyright holder, however there are no particular legal requirements regarding this. While it has historically been a requirement in some jurisdictions to include a copyright notice on a work in order to be able to claim copyright over it, the Berne Convention does not allow such restrictions, and so any country signed up to the convention no longer has this requirement. However, in some jurisdictions failure to include such a notice can affect the damages you may be able to claim if anyone infringes your copyright.

A similar situation exists in relation to the phrase "All Rights Reserved". This phrase was a requirement in order to claim international copyright protection in countries signed up to the 1910 Buenos Aires Convention. However, since all countries signed up to the Buenos Aires Convention are now also signed up to the Berne Convention (which grants automatic copyright) this phrase has become superfluous. The phrase continues to be used frequently but is unlikely to have any legal consequences.

The Berne Convention

The Berne Convention covers 162 of the approximately 190 countries in the world, including most major nations. Countries which are signed up to the convention are compelled to offer the same protection to works created in other signatory nations as they would to works created in their own. Nations not signed up to the Berne Convention may have their own arrangements regarding copyright protection.

You can check if your country is signed up to the Berne Convention at the following website:

- *https://www.CopyrightRegistrationService.com*

The status of your country should be shown automatically on the right side of the screen. If not, you can select your country manually from the drop-down menu near the top right of the page.

Should You Self-Publish?

Over recent years there has been an explosion in self-published books, as it has become easier and easier to publish your book yourself. This poses writers with a new quandary: continue to pursue publication through the traditional means, or jump into the world of self-publishing? As the rejections from traditional publishers pile up it can be tempting to reach for the control and certainty of self-publishing. Should you give into the temptation, or stick to your guns?

Isn't it just vanity publishing?

Modern self-publishing is quite different from the vanity publishing of times gone by. A vanity publisher would often pose or at least seek to appear to be a traditional publisher, inviting submissions and issuing congratulatory letters of acceptance to everyone who submitted – only slowly revealing the large fees the author would have to pay to cover the cost of printing the books.

Once the books were printed, the vanity publisher would deliver them to the author then cut and run. The author would be left with a big hole in their pocket and a mountain of boxes of books that they would be unlikely to ever sell a fraction of.

Modern self-publishing, on the other hand, is provided not by shady dealers but by some of the biggest companies involved in the publishing industry, including Penguin and Amazon. It doesn't have the large fees that vanity publishing did (depending on the path you choose and your own knowledge and technical ability it can cost almost nothing to get your book published); it *does* offer a viable means of selling your books (they can appear on the biggest bookselling websites around the world); and it *doesn't* leave you with a house full of unwanted books, because modern technology means that a copy of your book only gets printed when it's actually ordered.

That isn't to say that there aren't still shady characters out there trying to take advantage of authors' vanity by charging them enormous fees for publishing a book that stands very little chance of success, but it does mean that self-publishing – done right – can be a viable and cost effective way of an author taking their book to market.

The benefits of self-publishing

The main benefit of self-publishing, of course, is that the author gets control of whether their book is published or not. There is no need to spend years submitting to countless agents and publishers, building up countless heartbreaking rejection letters, and possibly accepting in the end that your dreams of publication will never come true – you can make them come true.

And this need not be pure vanity on the author's part. Almost every successful book – even such massive hits as *Harry Potter* – usually build up a string of rejections before someone finally accepts them. The professionals that authors rely on when going through the traditional publishing process – the literary agents and the editors – are often, it seems, just not that good at spotting what the public are going to buy. How many potential bestsellers might languish forever in the slush pile, just because agents and editors fail to spot them? What if your book is one of them? The traditional publishing process forces you to rely on the good judgment of others, but the self-publishing process enables you to sidestep that barrier and take your book directly to the public, so that readers can decide for themselves.

Self-publishing also allows you to keep control in other areas. You won't have an editor trying to change your text, and you'll have complete control over what kind of cover your book receives.

Finally, with no publisher or team of editors and accountants taking their slice, you'll probably get to keep a lot more of the retail price of every book you sell. So if you can sell the same amount of books as if you were traditionally published, you'll stand to make a lot more money.

The drawbacks of self-publishing

While self-publishing can guarantee that your book will be available for sale, it cannot guarantee that it will actually sell. Your self-published book will probably have a much lower chance of achieving significant sales than if it had been published traditionally, because it will lack the support that a mainstream publisher could bring. You will have no marketing support, no established position in the marketplace, and no PR – unless you do it yourself. You will have to arrange your own book tours; you will have to do your own sales pitches; you will have to set your own pricing structure; and you will have to manage your own accounts and tax affairs. If you're selling through Amazon or Smashwords or Apple (and if you're not, then why did you bother self-publishing in the first place?) you're going to need to fill in the relevant forms with the IRS (the US tax office) – whether you're a US citizen or not. If you're not a US citizen then you'll have to register with the IRS and complete the necessary tax forms, and potentially other forms for claiming treaty benefits so that you don't get taxed twice (in the US and your home country). And then of course you'll also have to register for tax purposes in your home nation and complete your own tax return there (though you would also have to do this as a traditionally published author).

It can all get very complicated, very confusing, and very lonely. Instead of being able to just be a writer you can find yourself writing less and less and becoming more and more embroiled in the business of publishing a book.

And while it's great to have control over your text and your cover, you'd be ill advised to ignore the value that professionals such as editors and cover designers can bring. It's tempting to think that you don't need an editor – that you've checked the book and had a friend or family member check it too, so it's probably fine – but a professional editor brings a totally different mindset to the process and will check things that won't have even occurred to you and your reader. Without a professional editor, you will almost certainly end up publishing a book which is full of embarrassing mistakes, and trust me – there is no feeling quite as deflating as opening up the first copy of your freshly printed book to see an obvious error jump out – or, even worse, to have it pointed out in an Amazon review, for all to see.

The cover is also incredibly important. Whether for sale on the shelf or on a website, the cover is normally the first point of contact your potential reader has with your book, and will cause them to form immediate opinions about it. A good cover can help a book sell well, but a bad one can kill its chances – and all too often self-published books have amateurish covers that will have readers flicking past them without a second glance.

Finally, the financial benefits of self-publishing can often be illusory. For starters, getting a higher proportion of the retail price is pretty irrelevant if you don't sell any copies. Fifty per cent of nothing is still nothing. Far better to have 15% of something. And then there's the advances. Advances are up-front payments made by traditional publishers to authors, which are off-set against future royalties. So, an author might receive a $5,000 advance before their book is published. When the royalties start coming in, the publisher keeps the first $5,000 to off-set the advance. The good news for the author is that if the book flops and doesn't make $5,000 in royalties they still get to keep the full advance. In an uncertain profession, the security of an advance can be invaluable for an author – and of course it's not something available to self-published authors.

Conclusion

Self-publishing can seem like a tempting shortcut to publication, but in reality it has its own challenges and difficulties. For the moment at least, traditional publishing still offers you the best shot of not only financial success, but also quality of life as a writer. With other people to handle all the other elements of publishing, you get to concentrate on doing what you love.

So we think that writers should always aim for traditional publishing first. It might be a long shot, but if it works then you stand a much better chance of being successful. If you don't manage to get signed by an agent or a publisher then you still have the option of self-publishing, but make sure you don't get tempted to resort to self-publishing too soon – most agents and publishers won't consider self-published works, so this is a one-way street. Once you've self-published your work, you probably won't be able to change your mind and go back to the traditional publishers with your book unless it becomes a huge hit without them. It's therefore important that you exhaust all your traditional publishing options before making the leap to self-publishing. Be prepared for this to take perhaps a few years (lots of agents and publishers can take six months just to respond), and make sure you've submitted to everyone you can on *both* sides of the Atlantic (publishing is a global game these days, and you need to concentrate on the two main centres of English-language publishing (New York and London) equally) before you make the decision to self-publish instead.

However, once you have exhausted all options for traditional publishing, modern self-publishing does offer a genuine alternative path to success, and there are a growing number of self-published authors who have managed to sell millions of copies of their books. If you don't think traditional publishing is going to be an option, we definitely think you should give self-publishing a shot.

For directions on your path through the traditional publishing process see our Writers' Roadmap, above.

If you're sure you've already exhausted all your options for traditional publishing then see below for our quick guide to the self-publishing process.

The Self-Publishing Process

Thinking about self-publishing your book? Make sure you go through all these steps first – and in the right order! Do them the wrong way round and you could find yourself wasting time and/or money.

1. Be sure you want to self-publish

You need to be 100% sure that you want to self-publish, because after you've done it there is no going back. Publishers and literary agents will not normally consider books that have been self-published, so if you wanted to get your book to print the old fashioned way you should stop now and rethink. Make absolutely sure that you've exhausted every possible opportunity for traditional publishing before you head down the self-publishing path.

For more information, see "Why choose traditional publishing?" and "Should you self-publish?", above.

2. Protect your copyright

Authors often wonder about what stage in the process they should protect their copyright – often thinking that it's best to leave it till the end so that there are no more changes to make to the book after it is registered.

However, this isn't the case. The key thing is to protect your work before you let other people see it – or, if you've already let other people see it, as soon as possible thereafter.

Don't worry about making small changes to your work after registering it – as long as the work is still recognisable as the same piece of work it will still be protected. Obviously, if you completely change everything you've written then you're going to need another registration, as it will effectively be a different book, but if you've just edited it and made minor alterations this won't affect your protection.

You can register you copyright online at https://www.copyrightregistrationservice.com.

3. Get your work edited

Editing is a vital step often overlooked by authors who self-publish. The result can often be an amateurish book littered with embarrassing mistakes. Any professionally published book will go through an editing process, and it's important that the same applies to your self-published book. It's also important to complete the editing process before beginning the layout, or you could find yourself having to start the layout again from scratch.

4. Choose your self-publishing path

Before you can go any further you are going to need to choose a size for your book, and in order to do that you are going to need to choose a self-publishing path.

There are various different ways of getting self-published, but in general these range from the expensive hands off approach, where you pay a company to do the hard work for you, to the cheap DIY approach, where you do as much as you can yourself.

At the top end, the hands off approach can cost you thousands. At the bottom end, the DIY approach allows you to publish your book for almost nothing.

5. Finalise your layout / typesetting

Before you can finalise your layout (often referred to in the industry as "typesetting") you need to be sure that you've finalised your content – which means having your full work professionally edited and all the necessary changes made. If you decide to make changes after this point it will be difficult and potentially costly, and will require you to go through many of the following steps all over again.

You also need to have selected your path to publication, so that you know what page sizes are available to you, and what page margins you are going to need to apply. If you create a layout that doesn't meet printing requirements (for instance, includes text too close to the edge of the page) then you will have to start the typesetting process all over again.

6. Organise your ISBN

Your book needs to have an ISBN. If you are using a self-publishing service then they may provide you with one of their own, but it is likely to come with restrictions, and the international record for your book will show your self-publishing service as the publisher.

You can acquire your own ISBNs directly from the ISBN issuer, but they do not sell them individually, so you will end up spending quite a lot of money buying more ISBNs than you need. You will, however, have control of the ISBN, and you will be shown as the publisher.

Alternatively, you can purchase a single ISBN at a lower price from an ISBN retailer. This should give you control over the ISBN, however the record for the book will show the ISBN retailer as the publisher, which you may not consider to be ideal.

Whatever you choose, you need to arrange your ISBN no later than this point, because it needs to appear in the preliminary pages (prelims) of your book.

7. Compile your prelims

Your prelims may include a variety of pages, but should always include a title page, a half title page, and an imprint/copyright page. You might then also include other elements, such as a foreword, table of contents, etc. You can only compile your table of contents at this stage, because you need to know your ISBN (this will be included on the copyright/imprint page) and the page numbers for your table of contents. You therefore need to make sure that you are happy with the typesetting and have no further changes to make before compiling your prelims.

8. Create your final press proof

Depending on the self-publishing path you have chosen, you may be able to use a Word file as your final document. However, you need to be careful. In order to print your book it will have to be converted into a press-ready PDF at some point. If a self-publishing service is doing this for you then you will probably find that they own the PDF file that is created, meaning you don't have control over your own press files. Some services will impose hefty charges (hundreds or even more than a thousand dollars) to release these press files.

It might also be the case that you won't get to see the final PDF, and therefore won't get chance to check it for any errors introduced by the conversion process. If it's an automated system, it may also be difficult to control the output you get from it.

We'd suggest that it's best to produce your own PDF files if possible. To do this you will need a copy of Adobe Acrobat Professional, and you will need to be familiar with the correct settings for creating print ready PDFs. Be careful to embed all fonts and make sure that all images are at 300 DPI.

9. Create your cover

Only once your press proof is finalised can you complete your cover design. That's because your cover includes not only the front cover and the back cover, but also (critically) the spine – and the width of the spine will vary according to the number of pages in your final press proof. In order to complete your cover design you therefore need to know your page size, your page count (including all prelims), and your ISBN, as this will appear on the back cover. You also need to get a barcode for your ISBN.

10. Produce your book

Once your cover and press proof are ready you can go through whichever self-publishing path you have chosen to create your book. With some pathways the production of a print proof can be an optional extra that is only available at an extra cost – but we'd recommend standing that cost and getting a print version of your book to check. You never know exactly how it's going to come out until you have a physical copy in your hand.

If you're happy with the proof you can clear your book for release. You don't need to do anything to get it on online retailers like Amazon – they will automatically pick up the ISBN and add your book to their websites themselves.

11. Create an ebook version

In the modern day, having an ebook version of your book is imperative. Ebooks account for a significant proportion of all book sales and are a particularly effective vehicle for unknown and self-published authors.

There are various different file formats used by the different platforms, but .epub is emerging as a standard, and having your book in .epub format should enable you to access all the platforms with a single file.

12. Distribute your ebook

Unlike with print books, you will need to act yourself to get your ebooks into sales channels. At a minimum, you need to ensure that you get your ebook available for sale through Amazon, Apple, and Google Play.

US Magazines

For the most up-to-date listings of these and hundreds of other magazines, visit https://www.firstwriter.com/magazines

*To claim your **free** access to the site, please see the back of this book.*

AARP Bulletin

601 E Street, NW
Washington DC 20049
Tel: +1 (877) 434-7598
Email: member@aarp.org
Website: http://www.aarp.org

Publishes: Articles; Essays; News; Nonfiction; *Areas:* Health; Lifestyle; Politics; *Markets:* Adult

Publishes material relating to health, social security, and consumer protection. No unsolicited mss.

Abramelin

Email: nessaralindaran@aol.com
Website: http://thegiantgilamonsters.com/abramelin

Publishes: Poetry; *Markets:* Adult; *Treatments:* Literary

Editors: Vanessa Kittle

Publishes modern, literary poetry. Send submissions by email, but no attachments. See website for full guidelines.

The Account

Email: poetryprosethought@gmail.com
Website: http://theaccountmagazine.com

Publishes: Essays; Fiction; Nonfiction; Poetry; *Areas:* Short Stories; *Markets:* Adult; *Treatments:* Literary

Editors: Tyler Mills, Editor-in-Chief; Christina Stoddard, Managing Editor/Publicist; Brianna Noll, Poetry Editor; Jennifer Hawe, Nonfiction Editor; M. Milks, Fiction Editor

Accepts poetry, fiction, and creative nonfiction, between May 1 and September 1, annually. Send 3-5 poems, essays up to 6,000 words, or fiction between 1,000 and 6,000 words, through online submission system. Each piece of work must be accompanied by an account between 150 and 500 words, giving voice to the artist's approach.

Adelaide Literary Magazine

1340 Stratford Avenue, Suite 3K
Bronx, NY 10472
Tel: +35 918 635 457
Email: info@adelaidemagazine.org
Website: http://www.adelaidemagazine.org

Publishes: Articles; Essays; Fiction; Interviews; News; Nonfiction; Poetry; Reviews; *Areas:* Arts; Criticism; Culture; Literature; Media; Short Stories; *Markets:* Academic; Adult; Professional; *Treatments:* Contemporary; Literary

Editors: Stevan V. Nikolic, Adelaide Franco Nikolic

An independent international quarterly publication, based in New York and Lisbon. Founded in 2015, the magazine'€™s aim is to publish quality poetry, fiction, nonfiction, artwork, and photography, as well as interviews, articles, and book reviews, written in English and Portuguese. Most of our content comes from unsolicited submissions.

We publish print, digital, and online editions of our magazine four times a year, in Fall (September), Winter (December), Spring (March), and Summer (June). The online edition is updated continuously. There are no charges for reading the magazine online.

Adornment
Website: http://www.jewelryandrelatedarts.com

Publishes: Nonfiction; *Areas:* Antiques; *Markets:* Adult; Professional

Quarterly electronic magazine delivered to association members. Publishes material for collectors of and professionals involved with jewellery.

Advisor Today
2901 Telestar Court
Falls Church, VA 22042
Tel: +1 (703) 770-8204
Email: amseka@naifa.org
Website: https://www.advisortoday.com

Publishes: Articles; Features; News; Nonfiction; *Areas:* Business; Finance; *Markets:* Professional

Editors: Ayo Mseka

Magazine for insurance and financial planning advisors.

After Happy Hour Review
4750 Centre Avenue
Apt 60
Pittsburgh, PA 15213
Email: hourafterhappyhour@gmail.com
Website: https://afterhappyhourreview.com/

Publishes: Fiction; Nonfiction; Poetry; *Markets:* Adult; *Treatments:* Contemporary; Dark; Experimental; Light; Literary; Mainstream; Progressive; Traditional

Editors: Mike Good, Jason Peck

An online journal. We gravitate towards work that is quirky, accessible, and unconventional. An ideal piece might cover a subject few people write about or cover familiar subjects from an unexpected angle.

Air Force Times
Sightline Media Group
1919 Gallows Road, 4th Floor
Vienna, VA 22182
Email: mtan@militarytimes.com
Website: https://www.airforcetimes.com

Publishes: Articles; News; Nonfiction; *Areas:* Military; *Markets:* Professional

Editors: Michelle Tan

Magazine for those serving in the Air Force, and their families.

Alabama Heritage
Box 870342
Tuscaloosa, AL 35487-0342
Tel: +1 (205) 348-7467
Fax: +1 (205) 348-7473
Email: alabama.heritage@ua.edu
Website: http://www.alabamaheritage.com

Publishes: Articles; Features; Nonfiction; *Areas:* Culture; Historical; *Markets:* Adult

Publishes stories of the history and culture of Alabama and the South.

Alebrijes
Email: alebrijesliterature@gmail.com
Website: http://www.alebrijeslit.org

Publishes: Essays; Fiction; Nonfiction; Poetry; *Markets:* Adult; *Treatments:* Experimental; Literary

Editors: Franco Strong; Anna Torres; Tiffany Ameline Zhu; Tyler Grinham

Publishes fiction, poetry, and lyrical essays. Particularly interested in pieces that play with form and structure, and surreal themes. In each reading period send up to one piece of fiction, one essay, or up to three poems, as Word file attachments. See website for full submission guidelines.

All Animals
Email: allanimals@humanesociety.org
Website: http://www.humanesociety.org

Publishes: Articles; News; Nonfiction;
Areas: Nature; *Markets:* Adult

Publishes material relating to animal welfare
and the humane movement, including
profiles of people on the front lines, tips for
pet owners and wildlife watchers, tales of
rescue and rehab, actions readers can take,
and more.

Alternative Therapies in Health and Medicine
1400 Corporate Center Curve Suite 130
Eagan MN 55121
Tel: +1 (877) 904-7951
Fax: +1 (651) 344-0774
Email: athmsubmissions@
innovisionhm.com
Website: http://www.alternative-
therapies.com

Publishes: Articles; Nonfiction; *Areas:*
Health; Medicine; *Markets:* Academic;
Professional

Editors: Craig Gustafson

International scientific forum for the
dissemination of peer-reviewed information
indexed in the National Library of Medicine
to healthcare professionals regarding the use
of complementary and alternative therapies
in promoting health and healing.

America's Pharmacist
National Community Pharmacists
Association
100 Daingerfield Road
Alexandria, VA 22314
Tel: +1 (703) 683-8200
Fax: +1 (703) 683-3619
Website: http://www.ncpanet.org/newsroom/
america's-pharmacist

Publishes: Articles; News; Nonfiction;
Areas: Business; Health; *Markets:*
Professional

Magazine aimed at independent community
pharmacists, publishing articles on business,
management, and the latest legal and
regulatory information.

American Baby
Meredith Corporation
125 Park Avenue, 6th Floor
New York, NY 10017
Website: http://www.americanbaby.com

Publishes: Articles; Nonfiction; *Areas:*
Health; Medicine; *Markets:* Adult

Magazine for new and expectant parents.

American History
1919 Gallows Road, Suite 400
Vienna, VA 22182
Email: americanhistory@historynet.com
Website: http://www.historynet.com

Publishes: Articles; Features; Nonfiction;
Areas: Historical; *Markets:* Adult

Magazine of American history for a general
readership. Send stories or ideas by post or
by email. See website for full guidelines.

American Quarter Horse Journal
American Quarter Horse Association
1600 Quarter Horse Drive
Amarillo, TX 79104
Tel: +1 (806) 376-4811
Website: https://www.aqha.com

Publishes: Articles; Nonfiction; *Areas:*
Business; How-to; Lifestyle; Nature;
Markets: Adult

Magazine covering horse ownership, horse
breeding, and Western lifestyle. Send query
with published clips.

American Snowmobiler
Email: editor@amsnow.com
Website: http://www.amsnow.com

Publishes: Articles; Nonfiction; *Areas:*
Hobbies; How-to; Leisure; Technology;
Travel; *Markets:* Adult

Magazine publishing material relating to
snowmobiles, their use and modification, etc.

Send query or complete ms by email. See website for full guidelines.

AntiqueWeek

PO Box 90
27 North Jefferson Street
Knightstown, IN 46148-0090
Tel: +1 (765) 345-5133
Email: cswaim@antiqueweek.com
Website: http://www.antiqueweek.com

Publishes: Articles; Nonfiction; *Areas:* Antiques; *Markets:* Adult; Professional

Editors: Connie Swaim

Publishes articles on antiques for collectors, dealers, and auctioneers.

Aphelion: The Webzine of Science Fiction and Fantasy

Alpharetta, GA
Email: editor@aphelion-webzine.com
Website: http://www.aphelion-webzine.com

Publishes: Essays; Features; Fiction; Interviews; Nonfiction; Poetry; Reviews; *Areas:* Adventure; Fantasy; Gothic; Horror; Humour; Literature; Sci-Fi; Short Stories; Suspense; Thrillers; *Markets:* Family; Professional; *Treatments:* Commercial; Contemporary; Cynical; Dark; Experimental; In-depth; Light; Literary; Mainstream; Niche; Popular; Positive; Progressive; Satirical; Serious; Traditional

Editors: Dan Hollifield, Nate Kailhofer, Curtis Manges, Iain Muir, Rob Wynne

Published since 1997. Free Science Fiction, Fantasy, and Horror Webzine which offers original fiction by new and established writers published on the first Sunday of every month except January. There is a double issue in December. The magazine includes poetry, short stories, serials and novellas, flash fiction, and reviews of interest to science fiction, fantasy, and horror fans. New writers are encouraged to submit their work to the webzine, and feedback to the authors is encouraged through the forum.

APICS Magazine

8430 West Bryn Mawr Avenue, Suite 1000
Chicago, IL 60631
Email: editorial@apics.org
Website: http://www.apics.org

Publishes: Articles; Nonfiction; *Areas:* Business; *Markets:* Professional

Publishes articles on supply chain management.

Architectural Record

350 5th Ave, Suite 6000
New York, NY 10118
Tel: +1 (646) 849-7100
Fax: +1 (646) 849-7148
Email: mcguiganc@bnpmedia.com
Website: https://www.architecturalrecord.com

Publishes: Articles; Nonfiction; *Areas:* Architecture; Design; *Markets:* Professional

Magazine for architects and designers.

Arizona Wildlife Views

Arizona Game and Fish Department
5000 W. Carefree Highway
Phoenix, AZ 85086-5000
Tel: +1 (623) 236-7216
Email: hrayment@azgfd.gov
Website: https://www.azgfd.com/media/magazine/

Publishes: Articles; Nonfiction; *Areas:* How-to; Leisure; Nature; *Markets:* Adult

Editors: Heidi Rayment

Publishes articles on the wildlife and outdoors or Arizona, including general interest, how-to, photo features, popularized technical material on Arizona wildlife and wildlife management, habitat issues, outdoor recreation (involving wildlife, boating, fishing, hunting, bird watching, animal observation, off-highway vehicle use, etc.), and historical articles about wildlife and wildlife management. No "me and Joe" articles, anthropomorphism of wildlife or opinionated pieces not based on confirmable facts.

Arthritis Today

1355 Peachtree St NE, 6th Floor
Atlanta, GA 30309
Tel: +1 (404) 872-7100
Website: https://www.arthritis.org

Publishes: Articles; News; Nonfiction;
Areas: Health; Medicine; *Markets:* Adult

Consumer health magazine aimed at
sufferers of arthritis.

Athletic Business

22 E. Mifflin St., Suite 910
Madison, WI 53703
Email: editors@athleticbusiness.com
Website: https://www.athleticbusiness.com

Publishes: Articles; Nonfiction; *Areas:*
Health; Leisure; Sport; *Markets:*
Professional

Magazine for Athletic, Fitness and
Recreation Professionals.

Aviation History

1919 Gallows Road, Ste 400
Vienna, VA 22182
Email: aviationhistory@historynet.com
Website: http://www.historynet.com/
aviation-history

Publishes: Articles; Features; Nonfiction;
Areas: Historical; Military; Travel; *Markets:*
Adult

Publishes articles on the history of military
and civil aviation.

Bartender

PO Box 157
Spring Lake, NJ 07762
Tel: +1 (732) 449-4499
Email: barmag2@gmail.com
Website: https://bartender.com

Publishes: Articles; Features; News;
Nonfiction; *Areas:* Business; Leisure;
Markets: Professional

Editors: Jackie Foley

Magazine for establishments which mix
drinks on site.

BedTimes

501 Wythe Street
Alexandria, VA 22314
Tel: +1 (703) 683-8371
Fax: +1 (703) 683-4503
Email: mbest@sleepproducts.org
Website: https://bedtimesmagazine.com

Publishes: Articles; News; Nonfiction;
Areas: Business; *Markets:* Professional

Editors: Mary Best

Publishes news, trends and issues of interest
to mattress manufacturers and their
suppliers, as well as more general business
stories. Send queries, CV, and writing
samples by email.

Bella Grace New Generation

Stampington & Company
22992 Mill Creek Drive, Suite B
Laguna Hills, CA 92653
Tel: +1 (949) 380-7318
Fax: +1 (949) 380-9355
Email: bellagrace@stampington.com
Website: https://stampington.com

Publishes: Articles; Nonfiction; *Areas:*
Women's Interests; *Markets:* Youth;
Treatments: Positive

Inspirational magazine for young women
aged 12-19, devoted to "discovering magic
in the ordinary". Interested in hearing from
writers and photographers who fall within
the target age range; young women aged 12
to 19 interested in being part of a special
focus group where they will help generate
ideas for content as well as provide feedback
on potential topics, designs, and stories;
parents of young women in this age range
willing to share what kinds of content they
would like their daughters to read; and
parents who can write thoughtful, reflective
articles geared toward young women in this
age group.

Better Than Starbucks

7711 Ashwood Lane
Lake Worth, FL 33467
Tel: +1 (561) 719-8627
Email: betterthanstarbucks2@gmail.com
Website: http://www.betterthanstarbucks.org

Publishes: Fiction; Interviews; Poetry; *Areas:* Short Stories; Translations; *Markets:* Adult; Youth; *Treatments:* Contemporary; Literary; Popular; Traditional

Editors: Vera Ignatowitsch

Monthly online literary magazine. Founded 1995, renamed 1998, revived in May 2016. While based in US, The editors are based in the US and three other countries.

The journal publishes original poetry, poetry reviews and interviews with established poets or translators. As of August 2017, the publication has seven poetry sections, each with its own page editor. Each of the various page editors also occasionally contribute an interview, as well as helping select the featured poem and nominees for various awards. There is also both a fiction section as well as nonfiction, and the publisher's monthly column on things poetic and sometimes not so poetic.

At this point, the publication is strictly online (older issues are archived on site).

Big Fiction

Email: info@bigfictionmagazine.com
Website: http://www.bigfictionmagazine.com

Publishes: Fiction; *Areas:* Short Stories; *Markets:* Adult; *Treatments:* Literary

Closed to submissions until January 1, 2019

Literary magazine devoted to longer short fiction, between 7,500 and 30,000 words. Accepts submissions online via competition ($20 entry fee).

BizTimes Milwaukee

126 N. Jefferson St., Suite 403
Milwaukee, WI 53202
Tel: +1 (414) 336-7120
Fax: +1 (414) 277-8191
Website: https://www.biztimes.com

Publishes: Articles; News; Nonfiction; *Areas:* Business; *Markets:* Professional

Publishes news and analysis for business leaders in southeastern Wisconsin.

BoxOffice Magazine

63 Copps Hill Road
Ridgefield, CT 06877
Tel: +1 (203) 438-8389
Email: ken@boxoffice.com
Website: https://pro.boxoffice.com

Publishes: Articles; News; Nonfiction; *Areas:* Business; Entertainment; Film; Media; *Markets:* Professional

Editors: Kenneth James Bacon

Magazine for professionals in the film industry.

Bugle

Rocky Mountain Elk Foundation
5705 Grant Creek
Missoula, MT 59808
Tel: (800) 225-5355
Email: bugle@rmef.org
Website: http://www.rmef.org/NewsandMedia/BugleMagazine.aspx

Publishes: Articles; Essays; Fiction; Nonfiction; Poetry; *Areas:* Adventure; Historical; Hobbies; Humour; Nature; *Markets:* Adult

Editors: PJ DelHomme

Magazine of elk hunting and conservation. Publishes relevant articles, essays, and also fiction and poetry on the subject.

Bust

253 36th Street, Suite C307
Brooklyn, NY 11232
Email: submissions@bust.com
Website: http://bust.com

Publishes: Articles; Features; Fiction; News; Nonfiction; *Areas:* Beauty and Fashion; Cookery; Crafts; Culture; Erotic; Health; Music; Travel; Women's Interests; *Markets:* Adult

Editors: Debbie Stoller

Magazine for women, publishing a variety of nonfiction, plus erotic fiction. No poetry or other forms of fiction considered. See website for full details and submission guidelines.

Cadaverous Magazine
Email: cadaverousmagazine@gmail.com
Website: https://cadaverousmagazine.wixsite.com/litmag

Publishes: Fiction; Poetry; *Areas:* Horror; *Markets:* Academic; Adult; Youth; *Treatments:* Dark; Literary

Editors: Alexa Findlay

A not-for-profit online supernatural horror (global) literary magazine. We feature: poetry, prose, fiction, flash fiction, art and photography. We accept submissions from writers and artists of all ages from all across the globe. They must be at least 13 years old.

Cadet Quest
PO Box 7259
Grand Rapids, MI 49510-7259
Tel: +1 (616) 241-5616
Email: submissions@calvinistcadets.org
Website: http://www.calvinistcadets.org

Publishes: Articles; Fiction; Nonfiction; *Areas:* Adventure; Hobbies; Humour; Religious; Short Stories; *Markets:* Children's

Editors: G. Richard Broene

Publishes fiction and nonfiction for boys aged 9-14, presenting Christian life and helping boys relate to Christian values in their own lives. Issues are themed. View website for details or send request with SASE. Submit complete ms. Do not query first.

The Cafe Irreal
Email: editors@cafeirreal.com
Website: http://www.cafeirreal.com

Publishes: Fiction; *Areas:* Short Stories; *Markets:* Adult; *Treatments:* Literary

Quarterly webzine publishing fantastic fiction resembling the work of writers such as Franz Kafka and Jorge Luis Borges. Send stories up to 2,000 in the body of an email. No simultaneous submissions.

Cahoodaloodaling
Email: cahoodaloodaling@gmail.com
Website: http://cahoodaloodaling.com

Publishes: Articles; Essays; Fiction; Interviews; Nonfiction; Poetry; Reviews; *Markets:* Adult; *Treatments:* Literary

Editors: Raquel Thorne

Themed quarterly journal, publishing poetry, fiction, and articles and essays that are either about writing and publishing, or match the current submission call. See website for upcoming themes, and to submit via online submission system. If you would like your book reviewing, query by email with a brief sample.

Callaloo
249 Blocker Hall, 4212 TAMU
College Station, TX 77843-4212
Tel: +1 (979) 458-3108
Fax: +1 (979) 458-3275
Email: callaloo@tamu.edu
Website: http://callaloo.tamu.edu

Publishes: Articles; Essays; Fiction; Interviews; Nonfiction; Poetry; Reviews; *Areas:* Arts; Culture; Literature; Short Stories; *Markets:* Academic; Adult; *Treatments:* Literary

Editors: Charles H. Rowell

Literary journal devoted to creative work by and critical studies of the work of African Americans and peoples of African descent throughout the African Diaspora. Submit via online submission system.

Camas
Email: camas@mso.umt.edu
Website: http://www.camasmagazine.org

Publishes: Essays; Fiction; Nonfiction; Poetry; *Areas:* Nature; *Markets:* Adult; *Treatments:* Literary

Publishes fiction, essays, and poetry that examines the relationships between individuals, communities, and the natural world in the American West. Issues are themed: see website for current theme and to submit via online submission system.

The Carolina Quarterly

510 Greenlaw Hall
CB# 3520
The University of North Carolina at Chapel
Hill
Chapel Hill, NC 27599-3520
Tel: +1 (919) 408-7786
Email: carolina.quarterly@gmail.com
Website: http://thecarolinaquarterly.com

Publishes: Essays; Fiction; Nonfiction;
Poetry; *Areas:* Autobiography; Short Stories;
Travel; *Markets:* Adult; *Treatments:* Literary

Publishes poetry, fiction, nonfiction, and
visual art. Submit by post or through online
submission system from September to May.
Send up to 6 poems, or one piece of prose.
As well as fiction, increasingly looking for
nonfiction, including personal essays, travel
writing, memoirs, and other forms of
creative nonfiction. Novel excerpts
acceptable if self-contained.

Catster

535 Connecticut Avenue
Norwalk, CT 06854-1713
Email: catstermag@belvoir.com
Website: http://www.catster.com

Publishes: Articles; Features; Nonfiction;
Areas: Health; How-to; Lifestyle; Nature;
Markets: Adult

Magazine covering the subjects of cats and
cat ownership. No completed articles. Send
query by email with details of your
background and a link to writing samples
online. Response only if interested.

Caveat Lector

400 Hyde St. #606
San Francisco, CA 94109
Email: caveatlectormagazine@gmail.com
Website: http://www.caveat-lector.org

Publishes: Essays; Fiction; Nonfiction;
Poetry; *Areas:* Arts; Criticism; Literature;
Short Stories; *Markets:* Adult; *Treatments:*
Literary

Online magazine dedicated to literature,
social and cultural criticism, philosophy, and
the arts. Send poetry submissions by post
only, between February 1 and June 30.

Prose, art, and multimedia accepted year-
round by post or by email (up to 5MB).
Postal submissions should include brief bio
and SASE.

The Chaffin Journal

Department of English
467 Case Annex
Eastern Kentucky University
Richmond, KY 40475
Email: robert.witt@eku.edu
Website: http://english.eku.edu/chaffin-
journal

Publishes: Fiction; Poetry; *Areas:* Short
Stories; *Markets:* Adult; *Treatments:*
Literary

Editors: Robert W. Witt

Annual literary journal, open to all forms,
subjects, schools, and styles. Send 3-5
poems, or short fiction up to 10,000 words,
by post.

Chantarelle's Notebook

Email: chantarellesnotebook@yahoo.com
Website: http://www.
chantarellesnotebook.com

Publishes: Poetry; *Markets:* Adult;
Treatments: Literary

Poetry ezine. Submit 3-5 poems per reading
period, pasted into the body of an email (no
attachments) with cover letter and bio, up to
75 words.

Charleston Magazine

PO Box 1794
Mount Pleasant, SC 29465-1794
Tel: +1 (888) 242-7624
Email: dshankland@charlestonmag.com
Website: http://charlestonmag.com

Publishes: Articles; News; Nonfiction;
Areas: Arts; Culture; Current Affairs;
Gardening; Leisure; Lifestyle; Travel;
Markets: Adult

Editors: Darcy Shankland

Magazine covering the city of Charleston
and surrounding areas.

Charleston Style and Design Magazine

Email: editor@
charlestonstyleanddesign.com
Website: https://www.
charlestonstyleanddesign.com

Publishes: Articles; Nonfiction; *Areas:* Antiques; Architecture; Arts; Beauty and Fashion; Design; Health; Lifestyle; Travel; *Markets:* Adult

Editors: Mary Love

Design and lifestyle magazine for the Lowcountry, covering architects, designers and builders, home projects, lifestyle trends, restaurants, wines, fashions, art galleries, and travel destinations. Experienced writers should send their resume and writing samples by email, with "writer" in the subject line.

The Chattahoochee Review

Georgia State University's Perimeter College
555 North Indian Creek Drive
Clarkston, GA 30021
Email: gpccr@gpc.edu
Website: http://thechattahoocheereview.
gpc.edu

Publishes: Essays; Fiction; Interviews; Nonfiction; Poetry; Reviews; *Areas:* Arts; Short Stories; Translations; *Markets:* Adult; *Treatments:* Literary

Editors: Anna Schachner

Publishes fiction, poetry, reviews, essays, interviews, translations, and visual art. See website for details and for online submission system. No paper submissions.

Chicago Quarterly Review

517 Sherman Avenue
Evanston, IL 60202
Email: cqr@icogitate.com
Website: http://www.
chicagoquarterlyreview.com

Publishes: Essays; Fiction; Nonfiction; Poetry; *Areas:* Short Stories; *Markets:* Adult; *Treatments:* Literary

Editors: S. Afzal Haider; Elizabeth McKenzie

Submit fiction or personal essays up to 5,000 words, or 3-5 poems, via online submission system.

Chicago Review

935 East 60th Street
Chicago, IL 60637
Email: chicagoreviewmail@gmail.com
Website: http://chicagoreview.org

Publishes: Essays; Fiction; Nonfiction; Poetry; Reviews; *Areas:* Criticism; Literature; Short Stories; *Markets:* Adult; *Treatments:* Literary

Send fiction up to 5,000 words, or poetry of any length (prefers to see at least three pages). Also publishes critical essays, books reviews, and review essays, but query by email before submitting nonfiction.

The Christian Science Monitor

210 Massachusetts Avenue
Boston, MA 02115
Tel: +1 (617) 450-2300
Website: https://www.csmonitor.com

Publishes: Articles; Essays; News; Nonfiction; *Areas:* Culture; Current Affairs; Finance; Literature; Nature; Religious; Science; *Markets:* Adult

Editors: Mark Sappenfield

Accepts new writers' work on spec only. Approach via contact forms on website.

Cimarron Review

205 Morrill Hall
English Department
Oklahoma State University
Stillwater, OK 74078
Email: cimarronreview@okstate.edu
Website: https://cimarronreview.com

Publishes: Fiction; Poetry; *Areas:* Short Stories; *Markets:* Adult; *Treatments:* Literary

Editors: Toni Graham

Submit 3-6 poems or one piece of fiction by post or through online submission system.

No fixed length restrictions, but rarely publishes short shorts or fiction over 25 pages. See website for full submission guidelines.

Classical Singer
PO Box 1710
Draper, UT 84020
Email: support@csmusic.net
Website: https://csmusic.net

Publishes: Articles; News; Nonfiction; *Areas:* Music; *Markets:* Professional

Magazine for professional classical singers.

Cloud Rodeo
Email: submit@cloudrodeo.org
Website: https://cloudrodeo.org

Publishes: Fiction; Nonfiction; Poetry; *Markets:* Adult; *Treatments:* Experimental; Literary

Editors: Jake Syersak

Describes itself as a journal of the irregular. Send 3-5 short pieces or one longer piece of fiction, nonfiction, or poetry, as a Word or PDF attachment by email.

Cloudbank
PO Box 610,
Corvallis, OR 97339-0610
Tel: +1 (877) 782-6762
Email: michael@cloudbankbooks.com
Website: http://www.cloudbankbooks.com

Publishes: Fiction; Poetry; *Areas:* Short Stories; *Markets:* Adult; *Treatments:* Literary

Editors: Michael Malan

Publishes poetry and flash fiction. Submit up to five poems or up to five pieces of flash fiction by post or via online submission system. Online submissions require payment of a $3 fee.

Coal City Review
English Department
University of Kansas
Lawrence KS, 66045

Email: briandal@ku.edu
Website: https://coalcitypress.com

Publishes: Fiction; Poetry; *Areas:* Short Stories; *Markets:* Adult; *Treatments:* Literary

Editors: Brian Daldorph

Publishes poetry, short stories, and flash fiction. Send up to 6 poems, or one story up to 4,000 words, per year. Submissions by post only, with SASE for reply.

Cold Mountain Review
Attn: Poetry/Nonfiction/Fiction/Art
Submission
Department of English
ASU Box 32052
Boone, NC 28608-2052
Email: coldmountain@appstate.edu
Website: http://coldmountain.appstate.edu

Publishes: Essays; Fiction; Interviews; Nonfiction; Poetry; *Areas:* Autobiography; Short Stories; *Markets:* Adult; *Treatments:* Literary

Send up to five poems, creative nonfiction up to 6,000 words, interviews up to five double-spaced pages, or fiction up to 6,000 words, by post or via online submission system. See website for full details and to submit.

The Collagist
Email: fiction@thecollagist.com
Website: http://thecollagist.com

Publishes: Essays; Fiction; Nonfiction; Poetry; Reviews; *Areas:* Literature; Short Stories; *Markets:* Adult; *Treatments:* Literary

Editors: Gabriel Blackwell (fiction and excerpts); Matthew Olzmann (poetry and nonfiction)

Online journal publishing short fiction, poetry, essays, book reviews, and excerpts from novels. Reads submissions from March 1-August 31 and from October 1-January 31. Poetry and nonfiction submissions closed until summer 2016.

Colorado Review
9105 Campus Delivery
Department of English
Colorado State University
Fort Collins, CO 80523-9105
Tel: +1 (970) 491-5449
Fax: +1 (970) 491-0283
Email: creview@colostate.edu
Website: http://coloradoreview.colostate.edu/
colorado-review/

Publishes: Essays; Fiction; Nonfiction;
Poetry; Reviews; *Areas:* Short Stories;
Markets: Adult; *Treatments:* Literary

Send full MSS with cover letter through
online submission system ($3 charge) or by
post with SASE. Poetry and fiction read
between August 1 and April 30 only.
Nonfiction read year-round. No specific
word limit, but generally publishes short
stories and essays between 15 and 25
manuscript pages. Submit up to five poems
in any style at one time. No unsolicited book
reviews – query first. Simultaneous
submissions are accepted if immediate
notification is given of acceptance
elsewhere. No previously published material.

Columbia: A Journal of Literature and Art
Email: info@columbiajournal.org
Website: http://columbiajournal.org

Publishes: Essays; Fiction; Poetry; *Areas:*
Arts; Film; Music; Short Stories;
Translations; *Markets:* Adult; *Treatments:*
Literary

Publishes poetry, fiction, nonfiction,
translations, art, film, and music. Submit via
online submission system. Send up to 5
pages of poetry, or up to 7,500 words of
prose. See website for details of specific
reading periods for print and online editions.

Compose
Email: editor@composejournal.com
Website: http://composejournal.com

Publishes: Articles; Fiction; Interviews;
Nonfiction; Poetry; *Areas:* How-to;
Literature; Short Stories; *Markets:* Adult;
Treatments: Literary

Online journal publishing fiction, poetry,
creative nonfiction, articles on the craft of
writing (both practical and inspirational),
interviews with established writers, literary
agents, editors, etc. excerpts from
traditionally published works, photography
and artwork. Submit online via website.

Conduit
788 Osceola Avenue
St Paul, MN 55105
Email: waltz@conduit.org
Website: http://www.conduit.org

Publishes: Fiction; Poetry; *Areas:* Short
Stories; *Markets:* Adult; *Treatments:*
Literary

Editors: William D. Waltz; Brett Astor

Publishes previously unpublished poetry and
prose that demonstrates originality,
intelligence, courage, irreverence, and
humanity. Send 3-5 poems or 1 prose piece
up to 3500 words with SASE. No online
submissions.

Confrontation Magazine
English Department
LIU Post
Brookville, NY 11548
Email: confrontationmag@gmail.com
Website: http://confrontationmagazine.org

Publishes: Essays; Fiction; Nonfiction;
Poetry; *Areas:* Autobiography; Culture;
Politics; Short Stories; *Markets:* Adult;
Treatments: Literary

Editors: Jonna G. Semeiks

Submit fiction up to 7,500 words; up to six
pieces of flash fiction up to 500 words per
piece; up to six poems up to two pages each;
or cultural, political, or other types of essays
or self-contained sections of memoirs up to
5,000 words. Will consider genre fiction if it
has literary merit. Accepts email submissions
from writers outside the US only.

Connecticut River Review
PO Box 516
Cheshire, CT 06410
Email: connpoetry@comcast.net

Website: http://www.ctpoetry.net/
publications.html

Publishes: Poetry; *Markets:* Adult;
Treatments: Literary

Editors: Pat Mottola

Poetry magazine accepting submissions
nationally and internationally during the
annual reading period from January 1 to
April 15. Send 3-5 original unpublished
poems on any topic (5 pages maximum) with
SASE for response only (no poems will be
returned). See website for full details.

Connotation Press

Website: http://www.connotationpress.com

Publishes: Fiction; Interviews; Nonfiction;
Poetry; Reviews; Scripts; *Areas:* Drama;
Literature; Music; Short Stories; *Markets:*
Adult; *Treatments:* Literary

Editors: Ken Robidoux

Online journal publishing poetry, fiction,
creative nonfiction, playwriting, screenplays,
interviews, book reviews and music reviews.
Send 3-5 poems, one story or chapter, 1-5
flash fiction pieces, one piece of creative
nonfiction, or one script. Accepts unsolicited
reviews, but also welcomes initial enquiries.
For interviews, submit short treatment. See
website for full guidelines.

Construction Equipment Guide

470 Maryland Drive
Fort Washington, PA 19034
Tel: +1 (800) 523-2200
Email: cmongeau@cegltd.com
Website: https://www.
constructionequipmentguide.com

Publishes: News; Nonfiction; *Areas:*
Business; Technology; *Markets:* Professional

Editors: Craig Mongeau; Christine Allen

Covers the United States with four regional
newspapers offering construction industry
news and information, and new and used
construction equipment for sale.

Contemporary Haibun Online

Email: bob.lucky01@yahoo.com
Website: http://www.
contemporaryhaibunonline.com

Publishes: Poetry; *Markets:* Adult;
Treatments: Literary

Editors: Bob Lucky (Content Editor); Ray
Rasmussen (Technical Editor)

Quarterly journal publishing haibun and
tanka prose only. Send submissions by email
during the following submission windows
only:

Oct 15 – Nov 30
Jan 15 – Feb 28
April 15 – May 31
July 15 – Aug 31

Coping with Cancer Magazine

PO Box 682268
Franklin, TN 37068-2268
Tel: +1 (615) 790-2400
Email: info@copingmag.com
Website: https://www.copingmag.com

Publishes: Articles; Nonfiction; Poetry;
Areas: Health; Medicine; *Markets:* Adult;
Treatments: Positive

Publishes articles, poems, reflections, and
professional advice relating to cancer. See
website for full submission guidelines.

Cottonwood

Room 400 Kansas Union
1301 Jayhawk Boulevard
University of Kansas
Lawrence, KS 66045
Email: tlorenz@ku.edu
Website: http://englishcw.ku.edu/cottonwood

Publishes: Essays; Fiction; Nonfiction;
Poetry; *Areas:* Short Stories; *Markets:* Adult;
Treatments: Literary

Editors: Tom Lorenz (Prose); Phil Wedge
(Poetry)

Nationally circulated literary review. Send 4-
6 poems or essays or short stories up to
8,500 words. Address material to appropriate
editor.

Crab Creek Review
P.O. Box 840
Vashon, WA 98070
Tel: +1 (206) 463-5668
Email: crabcreekreview@gmail.com
Website: http://www.crabcreekreview.org

Publishes: Essays; Fiction; Nonfiction; Poetry; *Areas:* Short Stories; *Markets:* Adult; *Treatments:* Literary

Editors: Jenifer Lawrence

Submit fiction or creative nonfiction up to 3,500 words, or up to four poems, up to eight pages total, via online submission system. Only accepts material during specific reading periods. See website for details.

Creative Knitting
Website: https://www.creativeknittingmagazine.com

Publishes: Nonfiction; *Areas:* Crafts; Design; Hobbies; *Markets:* Adult

Knitting magazine, featuring clear instructions for classic and current trends in knitting design.

Crucible
Email: crucible@barton.edu
Website: https://www.barton.edu/crucible/

Publishes: Fiction; Poetry; *Areas:* Short Stories; *Markets:* Adult; *Treatments:* Literary

Send up to 5 poems or fiction up to 8,000 words by email. All submissions entered into poetry or fiction contest, with $150 prize and $100 runner-up prize in each.

The Cumberland River Review
Trevecca Nazarene University
Department of English
333 Murfreesboro Road
Nashville, TN 37210
Email: crr@trevecca.edu
Website: http://crr.trevecca.edu

Publishes: Essays; Fiction; Nonfiction; Poetry; *Areas:* Short Stories; *Markets:* Adult; *Treatments:* Literary

Quarterly online publication of new poetry, fiction, essays, and art. Submit 3-5 poems or one short story or one essay up to 5,000 words, between September and April only. Submissions accepted by post with SASE, but encourages submissions through online submission system via website.

The Daily Tea
Media40
1000 Germantown Pike, Suite F2
Plymouth Meeting, PA 19462
Tel: +1 (484) 688-0299
Email: alexis@thedailytea.com
Website: http://thedailytea.com

Publishes: Articles; Essays; Features; Interviews; Nonfiction; *Areas:* Historical; How-to; Humour; Travel; *Markets:* Adult

Magazine publishing material relating to tea. Send query with proposal or complete ms.

The Dark
Email: thedarkmagazine@gmail.com
Website: http://thedarkmagazine.com

Publishes: Fiction; *Areas:* Fantasy; Horror; *Markets:* Adult; *Treatments:* Dark

Publishes horror and dark fantasy stories between 2,000 and 6,000 words. No graphic, violent horror. Send submissions by email as .doc or .rtf attachment. See website for full guidelines.

Darkling
Darkling Publications
28780 318th Avenue
Colome, SD 57528
Email: darkling@mitchelltelecom.net
Website: http://darklingpublications.com

Publishes: Poetry; *Markets:* Adult; *Treatments:* Dark; Literary

Editors: James C. Van Oort

Open to submissions of dark poetry between October and May 15, annually. Submit up to 8 poems of any length by post with SASE or by email, either in the body of the email or as an attachment.

The Dead Mule School of Southern Literature

Email: deadmule@gmail.com
Website: http://www.deadmule.com

Publishes: Essays; Fiction; Nonfiction; Poetry; *Areas:* Short Stories; *Markets:* Adult; *Treatments:* Literary

Online journal of Southern literature. Submit online via website.

december Magazine

PO Box 16130
St. Louis, MO 63130
Tel: +1 (314) 956-9210
Email: jenniferg@decembermag.org
Website: http://decembermag.org

Publishes: Essays; Fiction; Nonfiction; Poetry; *Areas:* Arts; Autobiography; Biography; Culture; Entertainment; Humour; Literature; Short Stories; Women's Interests; *Markets:* Adult; *Treatments:* Experimental; Literary; Progressive; Satirical

Editors: Jennifer Goldring

An independent non-profit literary journal that is published twice a year. We publish poetry, fiction, creative nonfiction, and art. We accept submissions from October 1 to May 15 through our submission portal online. We charge a small administrative fee ($2.50) to help cover our cost for the submission manager. You may also submit for free via USPS. Our complete submission guidelines are on our website. We do not read full manuscripts. We read short stories and essays of any length and we will read up to 5 poems at a time.

Denver Quarterly

University of Denver
Department of English
2000 E. Asbury
Denver, CO 80208
Email: denverquarterly@gmail.com
Website: http://www.du.edu/denverquarterly

Publishes: Essays; Fiction; Interviews; Nonfiction; Poetry; Reviews; *Areas:* Short Stories; *Markets:* Adult; *Treatments:* Literary

Editors: Laird Hunt

Submit prose up to 15 pages, or 3-5 poems, between September 15 and May 15 annually, by post with SASE or via online submission system on website.

The Deronda Review

P.O. Box 55164
Madison, WI 53705
Email: derondareview@att.net
Website: http://www.derondareview.org

Publishes: Poetry; *Markets:* Adult; *Treatments:* Literary

Editors: Esther Cameron; Mindy Aber Barad (Co-editor for Israel)

Literary magazine publishing mainly poetry, but will consider reflective prose up to 500 words (especially expository blank verse). First-time contributors (unless in Israel) should submit by post with SASE.

Devil's Lake

600 North Park Street, Suite 6195
Madison, WI 53706
Email: devilslake.editor@gmail.com
Website: https://english.wisc.edu/devilslake

Publishes: Fiction; Nonfiction; Poetry; *Areas:* Short Stories; *Markets:* Adult; *Treatments:* Literary

Submit 3-5 poems, or fiction or nonfiction up to 4,500 words, via online submission system only. See website for full details, and to submit.

Diagram

Dept of English, PO Box 210067
University of Arizona
Tucson, AZ 85721-0067
Email: editor@thediagram.com
Website: http://thediagram.com

Publishes: Fiction; Nonfiction; Poetry; Reviews; *Areas:* Short Stories; *Markets:* Adult; *Treatments:* Literary

Editors: Ander Monson

Online literary journal publishing text, images, and new media. No material previously published in print or online (except personal websites). Submit material online through submission manager, or (if necessary) by post. See website for full guidelines.

The Dos Passos Review

Longwood University
Department of English and Modern Languages
201 High Street
Farmville, VA 23909
Email: dospassosreview@gmail.com
Website: https://brierycreekpress.
wordpress.com/the-dos-passos-review/

Publishes: Fiction; Nonfiction; Poetry; *Markets:* Adult; *Treatments:* Literary

Publishes unpublished literary fiction, creative nonfiction, and poetry; particularly writing that explores specifically American themes. No genre fiction, experimentation for the sake of experimentation, or scholarly or critical nonfiction. Send submissions by email as Word attachments between April 1 and July 31, or between February 1 and May 31. See website for full details.

Down in the Dirt

Email: dirt@scars.tv
Website: http://scars.tv

Publishes: Essays; Fiction; Nonfiction; Poetry; *Areas:* Short Stories; *Markets:* Adult; *Treatments:* Literary

Editors: Janet Kuypers

Online and print magazine publishing poetry, prose, essays, and art work. Send submissions by email as .rtf or Word file attachments. No PDFs.

Dressing Room Poetry Journal

Email: dressingroompoetryjournal@
gmail.com
Website: http://www.
dressingroompoetryjournal.com

Publishes: Poetry; *Markets:* Adult; *Treatments:* Literary

Send 3-7 poems by email as an attachment.

Ducts

Email: vents@ducts.org
Website: http://www.ducts.org

Publishes: Fiction; Nonfiction; Poetry; *Areas:* Autobiography; Humour; Short Stories; *Markets:* Adult; *Treatments:* Literary; Satirical

Editors: Voichita Nachescu (Essays); Julie Wilkerson (Fiction); Mary Cool (Humour); Lisa Kirchner (Memoir); Amy Lemmon (Poetry)

Free online journal. Accepts submissions by email only. Send 3-5 poems, personal essays up to 3,000 words, fiction or humour (including satire and humorous short stories) up to 4,000 words, or memoir between 900 and 2,000 words. See website for specific submission email addresses and full submission guidelines.

Déraciné

Email: deracinemagazine@gmail.com
Website: http://deracinemagazine.
wordpress.com

Publishes: Fiction; Poetry; *Areas:* Gothic; Literature; *Markets:* Adult; Professional; Youth; *Treatments:* Contemporary; Cynical; Dark; Experimental; In-depth; Literary; Serious

Editors: Victoria Elghasen and Michelle Baleka

A literary magazine featuring dark, psychological fiction, poetry, and art. Started in 2017, we are a nonprofit publication. Our goal is to share literature that raises awareness of and expresses psychological issues and feelings of displacement through the literary gothic. We're open to a variety of styles, including writing that is minimalistic or that has elements of fantasy or horror, so long as it fits within our theme.

Earthshine

C/O Ruminations
PO Box 245
Hummelstown, PA 17036
Email: poetry@earthshinepoetry.org
Website: http://www.earthshinepoetry.org

Publishes: Poetry; *Markets:* Adult;
Treatments: Literary

Editors: Sally Zaino; Julie Moffitt

Poetry magazine with a voice of
"illumination, compassion, humanity, and
reason", publishing continually online and
sporadically in print when a volume is full.
Send submissions by post with SASE or by
email (preferably pasted into the body of the
email). See website for full guidelines.

Ellery Queen Mystery Magazine

Tel: +1 (212) 686-7188 x 675
Email: elleryqueenmm@dellmagazines.com
Website: http://www.
elleryqueenmysterymagazine.com

Publishes: Fiction; *Areas:* Crime; Mystery;
Short Stories; *Markets:* Adult

Mystery magazine, publishing every kind of
mystery short story: psychological suspense;
deductive puzzle; private eye case; realistic
to imaginative; hard-boiled to "cozies".
However, no explicit sex or violence, or true
crime. Always seeking original detective
stories, and especially happy to review first
stories by authors who have never before
published fiction professionally (submit to
the "Department of First Stories). No need to
send query – unsolicited MSS welcome.
Submit through online system (see website
for details). Accepts postal submissions only
from those with a prior publishing history
with the magazine.

Empty Mirror

Email: mirror@emptymirrorbooks.com
Website: http://www.emptymirrorbooks.com

Publishes: Articles; Essays; Features;
Interviews; Nonfiction; Poetry; Reviews;
Areas: Arts; Criticism; Culture; Literature;
Music; *Markets:* Adult; *Treatments:*
Experimental; In-depth; Literary

Editors: Denise Enck

We accept features, articles, criticism and
essays on literary or art-related topics, for
instance, essays about authors or artists,
styles or periods, places, movements, or

some aspect of writing or art. Scholarly
papers are sometimes accepted. Book
reviews and interviews are welcome.

We occasionally accept previously published
nonfiction.

For personal essays, we especially like to
some connection to art or literature or to
cultural or societal issues.

Special interests include art and literature
outside the mainstream, the Beat Generation,
Surrealism, and countercultural movements.

We also publish poetry and are very open to
experimental poetry and visual poetry.

Emrys Journal

The Emrys Foundation
PO Box 8813
Greenville, SC 29604
Email: emrys.info@gmail.com
Website: http://www.emrys.org

Publishes: Fiction; Nonfiction; Poetry;
Areas: Short Stories; *Markets:* Adult;
Treatments: Literary

Editors: Katherine Burgess

Literary journal publishing fiction, poetry,
and creative nonfiction. Submit up to three
poems or prose up to 5,000 words between
August 1 and November 1 annually, via
online submission system. No postal
submissions. $250 awarded to one piece
selected from each category.

Enchanted Tales Literary Magazine

Email: enchantedtaleslitmag@gmail.com
Website: http://
enchantedtalesliterarymagazine.weebly.com

Publishes: Fiction; Poetry; *Areas:* Fantasy;
Romance; Short Stories; *Markets:*
Academic; *Treatments:* Literary

Editors: Alexa Findlay

A not-for-profit online global literary
magazine. Our mission is to create a space
for writers and artists to share their passion
and love for fairy tales as much as we do.

We are dedicated to publishing new fairy tales as well as re-told classic fairy tales.

Essence
241 37th Street, 4th floor
Brooklyn, NY 11232
Email: toletters@essence.com
Website: http://www.essence.com

Publishes: Articles; Nonfiction; *Areas:* Beauty and Fashion; Culture; Entertainment; Health; Lifestyle; Politics; *Markets:* Adult

Magazine of black culture.

The Evansville Review
University of Evansville Creative Writing Department
Room 416A, Olmsted Administration Hall
1800 Lincoln Avenue
Evansville, IN 47722
Tel: +1 (812) 488-2963
Email: evvreview@evansville.edu
Website: https://www.evansville.edu/majors/creativewriting/evansvilleReview.cfm

Publishes: Fiction; Interviews; Nonfiction; Poetry; Scripts; *Areas:* Drama; Short Stories; *Markets:* Adult; *Treatments:* Experimental; Literary; Traditional

Publishes poetry, fiction, nonfiction, plays, and interviews by a wide range of authors, from emerging writers to Nobel Prize recipients. Accepts submissions between September 1 and October 31 annually, through online submission system.

failbetter.com
2022 Grove Avenue
Richmond, VA 23220
Email: editor@failbetter.com
Website: http://failbetter.com

Publishes: Fiction; Poetry; *Areas:* Short Stories; *Markets:* Adult; *Treatments:* Literary

Online literary journal. Publishes poetry, short stories, self-contained novel excerpts, and novellas. Send one piece of prose or between 4 and 6 poems at a time via online submission system.

Feminist Studies
4237 Susquehannna Hall
4200 Lehigh Road
University of Maryland
College Park, MD 20742
Tel: +1 (301) 405-7415
Fax: +1 (301) 405-8395
Email: info@feministstudies.org
Website: http://www.feministstudies.org

Publishes: Essays; Fiction; Nonfiction; Poetry; *Areas:* Criticism; Short Stories; Women's Interests; *Markets:* Academic; Adult

Feminist journal publishing research and criticism, creative writing, art, essays, and other forms of writing and visual expression. See website for submission guidelines and specific submission email addresses.

The Fifth Di...
Email: thefifthdi@yahoo.com
Website: http://www.nomadicdeliriumpress.com/fifth.htm

Publishes: Fiction; *Areas:* Fantasy; Sci-Fi; Short Stories; *Markets:* Adult

Publishes science fiction and fantasy stories up to 10,000 words. No horror or poetry. Flash fiction is unlikely to find favour unless exceptional. Send submissions by email as RTF attachments. No Word files. See website for full guidelines.

Five:2:One
Website: http://five2onemagazine.com

Publishes: Essays; Fiction; Nonfiction; Poetry; *Areas:* Short Stories; *Markets:* Adult; *Treatments:* Experimental; Literary

Publishes fiction of 1,000 words or more; visual / experimental / written poetry of 120 words or more; and nonfiction / essays / manifestos of 1,000 words or more. Submit online through website.

Flint Hills Review
Dept. of English, Modern Languages, and Journalism
Emporia State University
1 Kellogg Circle

Emporia, KS 66801
Email: bluestem@emporia.edu
Website: http://www.emporia.edu/fhr

Publishes: Fiction; Nonfiction; Poetry;
Scripts; *Areas:* Drama; Short Stories;
Markets: Adult; *Treatments:* Literary

Annual literary magazine, publishing poetry, short stories, short plays, and creative nonfiction. Send 3-6 poems, short fiction 2,000-5,000 words (or one or two short pieces of flash fiction between 500 and 1,500 words), play scripts up to 10 minutes, or creative nonfiction between 2,000 and 5,000 words. Accepts work both by post and by email. See website for full details.

Flyway: Journal of Writing & Environment

Email: flywayjournal@gmail.com
Website: https://flyway.org

Publishes: Essays; Fiction; Nonfiction; Poetry; *Areas:* Nature; Short Stories; *Markets:* Adult; *Treatments:* Literary

Online journal publishing poetry, fiction, nonfiction, and visual art that explores the many complicated facets of the word "environment". Submit online between August 15 and May 1 each year.

Fogged Clarity

Email: submissions@foggedclarity.com
Website: http://foggedclarity.com

Publishes: Essays; Fiction; Nonfiction; Poetry; Reviews; *Markets:* Adult; *Treatments:* Literary

Online journal publishing poetry, fiction, essays, reviews and visual art. Send up to five poems, or up to two pieces of prose up to 8,000 words, or one review between 300 and 1,000 words.

Fourteen Hills

Fourteen Hills Press
Department of Creative Writing
San Francisco State University
1600 Holloway Avenue
San Francisco, CA 94137

Email: hills@sfsu.edu
Website: http://www.14hills.net

Publishes: Fiction; Nonfiction; Poetry; *Areas:* Short Stories; *Markets:* Adult; *Treatments:* Literary

Publishes poetry, fiction, and creative nonfiction. Submit 1-3 poems (up to 7 pages max); or one short story or novel excerpt, or piece of creative nonfiction (up to 20 pages or 6,000 words). Submit via website using online submission system ($2 charge for non-subscribers). Accepts submissions between September 1 and December 1, and between March 1 and June 1, annually.

Fugue

Email: fugue@uidaho.edu
Website: http://www.fuguejournal.com

Publishes: Essays; Fiction; Nonfiction; Poetry; *Areas:* Short Stories; *Markets:* Adult; *Treatments:* Literary

Editors: Corey Oglesby, Editor-in-Chief; Lauren Yarnall, Managing Editor

Submit up to 5 poems, up to two short shorts, one story, or one essay per submission. Accepts submissions online only, between September 1 and May 1. Submission service charges $3 per submission.

Garbled Transmissions

Email: editor@garbledtransmission.com
Website: http://garbledtransmission.com

Publishes: Fiction; News; Nonfiction; Reviews; *Areas:* Fantasy; Film; Sci-Fi; *Markets:* Adult; *Treatments:* Dark

Editors: James Robert Payne

Online magazine publishing science fiction and fantasy short stories between 500 and 15,000 words, and book, movie, and comic book reviews and news, slanted towards the science fiction and fantasy genres, between 500 and 3,000 words. Submit by email as .doc or OpenOffice documents. Responds in a month to all serious enquiries. Accepts simultaneous submissions, but no multiple submissions.

A Gathering of the Tribes
PO Box 20693
Tompkins Square Station
New York, NY 10009
Tel: +1 (212) 777-2038
Email: gatheringofthetribes@gmail.com
Website: http://www.tribes.org

Publishes: Essays; Fiction; Interviews;
Nonfiction; Poetry; *Areas:* Arts; Short
Stories; *Markets:* Adult; *Treatments:*
Literary

Magazine focusing on excellence in the arts
from a diverse perspective.

Gertrude
Email: EditorGertrudePress@gmail.com
Website: http://www.gertrudepress.org

Publishes: Essays; Fiction; Interviews;
Nonfiction; Poetry; Reviews; *Markets:*
Adult; *Treatments:* Literary

Editors: Tammy

**Closed to fiction submissions as at May
2018. Check website for current status.**

Online LGBTQA journal publishing fiction,
poetry, and creative nonfiction. Subject
matter need not be LGBTQA-specific, and
writers from all backgrounds are welcomed.
Submit fiction or creative nonfiction up to
3,000 words, or up to five poems (no line
limit, but under 40 lines preferred), via
online submission system. For book reviews
and interviews, email editor with proposal.
See website for full guidelines.

The Gettysburg Review
Gettysburg College
300 N. Washington Street
Gettysburg, PA 17325-1491
Tel: +1 (717) 337-6770
Email: mdrew@gettysburg.edu
Website: http://www.gettysburgreview.com

Publishes: Essays; Fiction; Poetry; Reviews;
Areas: Short Stories; *Markets:* Adult;
Treatments: Literary

Editors: Mark Drew, Editor

Send submission by post with SASE for
return, or through online submission system

(small admin charge). Accepts submissions
from September 1 to May 31 only:
submissions received between June 1 and
August 31 are returned unread. For poetry,
submit up to five poems. Accepts both short
poetry and longer narrative verse. Fiction is
usually short stories, but will consider longer
pieces for serialisation. No length limit.
Accepts essays on any subject, so long as
treated in a literary fashion. Simultaneous
submissions accepted if immediate
notification of acceptance elsewhere is
given. No previously published material or
submissions by fax or email.

Grasslimb
PO Box 420816
San Diego, CA 92142
Email: editor@grasslimb.com
Website: http://www.grasslimb.com

Publishes: Fiction; Nonfiction; Poetry;
Reviews; *Areas:* Short Stories; *Markets:*
Adult; *Treatments:* Literary

Editors: Valerie Polichar

Submit 4-6 poems, or prose up to 2,500
words, by email or by post. No submissions
via links/downloads. See website for full
details.

Green Hills Literary Lantern
Dept of English and Linguistics
Truman State University
Kirksville, MO 63501
Email: adavis@truman.edu
Website: http://ghll.truman.edu

Publishes: Fiction; Poetry; *Areas:* Short
Stories; *Markets:* Adult; *Treatments:*
Literary

Editors: Adam Brooke Davis; Joe Benevento

Online, open-access journal. Submit 3-7
poems, a short story or excerpt from a novel
(15-18 double-spaced pages), or up to three
short shorts, by email as a .doc, .rtf, or .txt
attachment; or by post with SASE if return is
required. See website for full details.

Green Mountains Review (GMR)
Johnson, VT 05656
Email: gmr@jsc.edu
Website: http://greenmountainsreview.com

Publishes: Essays; Fiction; Interviews; Nonfiction; Poetry; Reviews; *Areas:* Short Stories; *Markets:* Adult; *Treatments:* Literary

Editors: Jessica Hendry Nelson

Literary magazine publishing poetry, fiction, creative nonfiction, literary essays, interviews, and book reviews by both well-known writers and promising newcomers. Submit up to 5 poems, or prose up to 25 pages, via online submission system ($3 charge per submission).

GUD Magazine
Email: mike@ktf-design.com
Website: http://www.gudmagazine.com

Publishes: Articles; Essays; Features; Fiction; Interviews; Nonfiction; Poetry; *Areas:* Arts; Fantasy; Historical; Horror; Humour; Mystery; Romance; Sci-Fi; Short Stories; Suspense; *Markets:* Adult; *Treatments:* Literary

Editors: Kaolin Fire, Mike Coombes, Sue Miller, Sal Coraccio

Note: Closed to submissions as at November 2016. See website for current status.

What you've been looking for in a magazine. Published two times a year, we provoke with words and art. We bring you stories that engage. Essays and interviews that make you think harder. Poetry that bares reality, more subtly interprets what it means to be human.

We're aiming to make each issue roughly two hundred pages of content, 450 words (or a single poem or piece of art) per page.

Information for how to subscribe will be available shortly. Subscribe and discover a new magazine that looks good, feels good in the hand, and delivers content that will make you hungry for more.

Guernica
447 Broadway, 2nd Floor
New York, NY 10013
Email: editors@guernicamag.com
Website: https://www.guernicamag.com

Publishes: Essays; Fiction; Interviews; News; Nonfiction; Poetry; Reviews; *Areas:* Arts; Autobiography; Politics; Short Stories; Translations; *Markets:* Adult; *Treatments:* Literary

Editors: Hillary Brenhouse; Rachel Riederer

Non-profit online magazine focused on the intersection of arts and politics. Prefers work with a diverse international outlook – or, if it's American, from an underrepresented or alternative perspective. No stories about American tourists in other countries. Submit fiction between 1,200 and 4,500 words; up to five poems of any length (translations welcome); news, reviews, Q&A, and commentary up to 2,500 words; or memoirs, essays, reportage, or interviews between 2,500 and 7,500 words. Submit via online form on website only.

Gulf Coast: A Journal of Literature and Fine Arts
4800 Calhoun Road
Houston, TX 77204-3013
Email: gulfcoastea@gmail.com
Website: http://www.gulfcoastmag.org

Publishes: Essays; Fiction; Interviews; Nonfiction; Poetry; Reviews; *Markets:* Adult; *Treatments:* Literary

Editors: Luisa Muradyan Tannahill

Submit up to five poems, or fiction or essays up to 7,000 words, by post or via online submission manager. For other material, send query by email to address on website. $2.50 submission fee. Accepts material September 1 to March 1, annually.

Gulf Stream Magazine
FIU English Dept. AC 1 338
3000 NE 151 St.
North Miami, FL 33181
Email: gulfstreamlitmag@gmail.com
Website: https://gulfstreamlitmag.com

Publishes: Fiction; Interviews; Nonfiction; Poetry; Reviews; *Markets:* Adult; *Treatments:* Literary

Editors: Ariel Francisco

A print magazine until 2008, now publishes two online issues a year. Publishes fiction up to 5,000 words; nonfiction; poetry; artwork; and graphic narratives. Submit via online submission system or by post. No submissions by email. Reading periods run from September 1 to November 1, and January 15 to April 1. No work by current or former students of the university.

Haight Ashbury Literary Journal

558 Joost Avenue
San Francisco, CA 94127
Email: haljeditor@gmail.com
Website: https://haightashburyliteraryjournal.
wordpress.com

Publishes: Fiction; Poetry; *Areas:* Short Stories; *Markets:* Adult; *Treatments:* Literary

Publishes poetry and fiction – often by people who have been marginalised, oppressed, or abused. Submit up to 6 poems and/or 1-3 short stories or one long story. Submit by post with SASE. Email submissions from overseas authors only.

Hanging Loose

231 Wyckoff Street
Brooklyn, NY 11217
Tel: +1 (317) 529-4738
Fax: +1 (347) 227-8215
Email: print225@aol.com
Website: http://hangingloosepress.com

Publishes: Fiction; Poetry; *Markets:* Adult; *Treatments:* Literary

Send up to six poems or one story at a time. Potential contributors should familiarise themselves with the magazine before submitting. Includes regular section of High School writers. Send submissions by post with SASE. Allow up to three months for a response.

Hawai'i Pacific Review

Website: https://hawaiipacificreview.org

Publishes: Essays; Fiction; Nonfiction; Poetry; *Markets:* Adult; *Treatments:* Experimental; Literary

Editors: Tyler McMahon

Literary journal founded in 1987, publishing online only as of 2013. Publishes poetry and prose by authors from Hawai'i, the mainland, and around the world, on a rolling basis. Accepts poetry, short fiction, and personal essays. Encourages experimental narrative techniques and poetic styles. Send up to three poems or fiction or nonfiction up to 4,000 words, via online submission system.

Hawai'i Review

Hemenway Hall 107
2445 Campus Road
Honolulu, HI 96822
Tel: +1 (808) 956-3030
Fax: +1 (808) 956-3083
Email: managing@hawaiireview.org
Website: http://hawaiireview.org

Publishes: Essays; Fiction; Nonfiction; Poetry; Scripts; *Areas:* Arts; Autobiography; Fantasy; Music; Science; Sci-Fi; Short Stories; Translations; *Markets:* Adult; *Treatments:* Literary

Editors: LynleyShimat Lys; Sashily Kling; Marley Aiu; Tina Togafau

Accepts Prose (Fiction, Creative Nonfiction, Lyric Essay); Poetry; Theatre and Drama; Visual and Performing Arts; Hybrid and Multimedia Work; Translation, Creative Translation, and Multilingual Work; and Educational Materials. Submit through online submission system.

Hayden's Ferry Review

Box 870302
Arizona State University
Tempe, AZ 85287
Email: hfr@asu.edu
Website: http://www.haydensferryreview.org

Publishes: Essays; Fiction; Nonfiction; Poetry; *Areas:* Short Stories; *Markets:* Adult; *Treatments:* Literary

Submit up to six poems or one essay or piece of fiction per submission only, via online submission system. See website.

The Helix

Email: helixmagazine@gmail.com
Website: https://helixmagazine.org

Publishes: Essays; Fiction; Nonfiction; Poetry; Scripts; *Areas:* Drama; Short Stories; *Markets:* Adult; *Treatments:* Literary

Editors: Victoria-Lynn Bell

Closed to submissions until September 1, 2018.

Publishes fiction, creative nonfiction, poetry, plays, and art. Submit up to four pieces of prose up to 3,000 words each, or up to four poems.

HelloHorror

Email: submissions@hellohorror.com
Website: http://www.hellohorror.com

Publishes: Fiction; Nonfiction; Poetry; *Areas:* Horror; Psychology; Short Stories; *Markets:* Adult

Online magazine, publishing fiction, short stories, micros, flash fiction, nonfiction, and poetry, in the horror genre. Aims to offer something new within the genre, with a focus on the psychological aspects of horror. See website for full submission guidelines.

Hennen's Observer

Email: moderator@hennensobserver.com
Website: https://www.hennensobserver.com

Publishes: Articles; Fiction; Nonfiction; Poetry; *Areas:* Arts; Entertainment; Short Stories; *Markets:* Adult; *Treatments:* Literary

Literary magazine and website that supports artists taking their first steps in the world of publishing. Join online community for free in order to submit work. Selected works from those submitted to the online community will be chosen for print publication and receive payment. Also runs competitions.

Hoot

Email: info@hootreview.com
Website: http://www.hootreview.com

Publishes: Fiction; Nonfiction; Poetry; Reviews; *Areas:* Autobiography; *Markets:* Adult; *Treatments:* Literary

Publishes a postcard each month featuring one piece of fiction or nonfiction up to 150 words, or one poem, up to 10 lines. Publishes four pieces in each online issue. Accepts fiction, nonfiction, memoir, poetry, and book reviews year-round. Graphic fiction / nonfiction also welcome, but it must fit on a postcard. Submit via online submission system.

Iconoclast

1675 Amazon Road
Mohegan Lake, NY 10547-1804
Website: http://www.iconoclastliterarymagazine.com

Publishes: Fiction; Poetry; *Areas:* Short Stories; *Markets:* Adult; *Treatments:* Literary

Editors: Phil Wagner

Publishes poetry and prose from authors interested in the creation, sharing, and transmission of ideas, imaginings, and experiences. Send prose up to 3,500 words or poetry up to two pages with SASE. See website for full guidelines.

Idaho Review

Boise State University
1910 University Drive
Boise, Idaho 83725
Email: mwieland@boisestate.edu
Website: http://idahoreview.org

Publishes: Fiction; Poetry; *Areas:* Short Stories; *Markets:* Adult; *Treatments:* Literary

Annual literary journal publishing poetry and fiction. No specific limit for fiction, but most of the stories accepted are under 25 double-spaced pages. For poetry, submit up to five poems. Reading period runs from September to March (see website for specific dates for this year). Accepts submissions by post with SASE, but prefers submissions through online submission system ($3 fee).

Indefinite Space
PO Box 40101
Pasadena, CA 91114
Email: indefinitespace@yahoo.com
Website: http://www.indefinitespace.net

Publishes: Poetry; *Markets:* Adult; *Treatments:* Experimental; Literary

Literary journal publishing innovative, imagistic, philosophical, and experimental poetry, drawings, collage, photography and paintings. Reads year round.

Indiana Review
Indiana University
Ballantine Hall 529
1020 E. Kirkwood Avenue
Indiana University
Bloomington, IN 47405-7103
Tel: +1 (812) 855-3439
Email: inreview@indiana.edu
Website: http://www.indiana.edu/~inreview

Publishes: Essays; Fiction; Nonfiction; Reviews; *Areas:* Short Stories; Translations; *Markets:* Adult; *Treatments:* Literary

Editors: Tessa Yang

Closed to submissions until September 2018. See website for current status.

Send fiction or nonfiction up 8,000 words or 3-6 poems per submission, during specific submission windows only (see website for details). No submissions by post or by email – all submissions must be made through online submission manager ($3 fee). See website for full guidelines, and to submit.

Infinite Rust
Texas Southern University, Dept. of English
3100 Cleburne St.
Houston, TX 77004
Email: editor@infiniterust.com
Website: http://www.infiniterust.com

Publishes: Essays; Fiction; Nonfiction; Poetry; *Areas:* Arts; Autobiography; Culture; Current Affairs; Historical; Literature; Media; Philosophy; Photography; Politics; Science; Short Stories; Sociology; Travel; *Markets:* Academic; Adult; Professional; *Treatments:* Contemporary; Experimental; Literary; Popular; Progressive; Satirical; Traditional

Editors: Marjorie Ward

University-affiliated quarterly online literary arts journal showcasing creative work. We publish short fiction, poetry, creative nonfiction, and essays, as well as art and photography. The goal of our publication is to assemble a variety of literary and artistic styles and a broad range of voices, perspectives, and life experiences.

The theme of our Fall 2018 issue is "Home".€ We are interested in your perspective relating to ideas such as the meaning of home, immigration, marginalization, nationalism, ownership, comfort, security, displacement, boundaries, and identity.

Please include a brief author bio of no more than 100 words. Limit submissions to no more than 2,500 words of prose, five poems, or five artworks or photographic images. Works previously published elsewhere cannot be submitted. Simultaneous and multiple submissions are fine. Please notify if work gets accepted for publication elsewhere.

For additional guidelines and to submit, please visit our website.

InJoy Magazine
2302 Noblewood Road
Edgewater, MD 21037
Tel: +1 (660) 281-4488
Email: cjsmith@injoymagazine.com
Website: http://www.injoymagazine.com

Publishes: Articles; Features; Fiction; Poetry; Reviews; *Areas:* Arts; Beauty and Fashion; Culture; Entertainment; Hobbies; How-to; Humour; Romance; Short Stories; Spiritual; Women's Interests; *Markets:* Family; *Treatments:* Positive

Editors: Crystal Smith

Provides a collaborative platform for art, encouragement and enjoying life. Our target audience is Women in all walks of life seeking to connect with others, share stories and laugh.

The Iowa Review

The University of Iowa
308 English-Philosophy Building
Iowa City, IA 52242
Tel: +1 (319) 335-0462
Fax: +1 (319) 335-2535
Email: iowa-review@uiowa.edu
Website: http://www.iowareview.org

Publishes: Essays; Fiction; Poetry; Reviews; *Areas:* Short Stories; Translations; *Markets:* Adult; *Treatments:* Literary

Editors: Harilaos Stecopoulos

Publishes poetry, fiction, and nonfiction. Submit in September, October, and November only, via online submission system ($4 charge for non-subscribers) or by post with SASE. Accepts prose up to 25 pages and poetry up to 8 pages (query by email if your poem is longer). Do not mix genres in a single envelope. Work must be unpublished. Simultaneous submissions accepted if immediate notification of acceptance elsewhere is given.

Josephine Quarterly

Website: https://www.josephinequarterly.com

Publishes: Poetry; *Markets:* Adult; *Treatments:* Literary

Online poetry journal. Submit up to five poems of any length via online submission system.

Kaimana: Literary Arts Hawai'i

Email: reimersa001@hawaii.rr.com
Website: http://www.hawaii.edu/hlac/kaimana.htm

Publishes: Fiction; Poetry; *Areas:* Short Stories; *Markets:* Adult; *Treatments:* Literary

Publishes poetry and fiction, with a particular (but not exclusive) interest in work which makes reference to the Pacific / Asia / Polynesia / Hawai'i. Send complete ms with SASE. No submissions by email.

Little Rose Magazine

460 N 50 E
Apt 460
Orem, UT 84057
Email: littlerosemagazine@gmail.com
Website: https://littlerosemagazine.weebly.com/

Publishes: Articles; Essays; Fiction; Interviews; Nonfiction; Poetry; *Areas:* Arts; Autobiography; Culture; Current Affairs; Entertainment; Lifestyle; Literature; Photography; Politics; Psychology; Religious; Self-Help; Short Stories; Sociology; Spiritual; Technology; *Markets:* Academic; Adult; Family; Professional; Youth; *Treatments:* Contemporary; Experimental; Literary; Progressive; Serious; Traditional

Editors: Kendra Nuttall

A Utah-based online magazine of literature and art, aiming to confront issues of identity, such as gender, race, class, religion, intersectionality, internet identity, and culture. We want to give artists and authors a space to reveal everything about the human experience – the good, bad, ugly, and everything in between.

Long Life Magazine

Cryonics Institute
24355 Sorrentino Court
Clinton Township, MI 48035
Tel: +1 (586) 791-5961
Email: info@cryonics.org
Website: http://www.cryonics.org/resources/long-life-magazine

Publishes: Articles; Essays; Fiction; Nonfiction; Poetry; *Areas:* Science; Short Stories; Technology; *Markets:* Adult; *Treatments:* Positive

Magazine on the subject of cryonics, publishing articles and essays covering the various aspects and challenges of being frozen and then re-animated. Welcomes poetry and occasionally accepts fiction, provided cryonics are central. No horror or stories portraying a dismal future.

Longshot Island
Eugene, OR
Email: contact@longshotisland.com
Website: http://www.longshotisland.com

Publishes: Fiction; *Markets:* Adult; Youth; *Treatments:* Literary; Mainstream; Traditional

Editors: D. S. White

We are a small independent publisher. We create ebooks, paperbacks and magazines. Read more in our blog.

Work submitted that is considered good is published on the website as our 'short list'. From the website, we pick the best of the best and put those stories in a quarterly magazine. At the end of the year, we pick the best stories from the magazines and put them in a book. Everything gets sent off to various competitions. The magazines go to the O. Henry Awards and the best stories in the book go to the Pushcart Prizes.

Louisiana Literature
SLU Box 10792
Hammond, LA 70402
Email: lalit@selu.edu
Website: http://www.louisianaliterature.org

Publishes: Fiction; Nonfiction; Poetry; *Areas:* Short Stories; *Markets:* Adult; *Treatments:* Literary

Editors: Dr Jack Bedell

Literary journal publishing fiction, poetry, and creative nonfiction. Submit via online system available at the website.

The Lyric
PO Box 110
Jericho, VT 05465
Email: themuse@thelyricmagazine.com
Website: https://thelyricmagazine.com

Publishes: Poetry; *Markets:* Adult; *Treatments:* Literary; Traditional

Editors: Jean Mellichamp Milliken

Publishes rhymed verse in traditional forms, with an occasional piece of blank or free verse. Poems must be original, unpublished, and not under consideration elsewhere. Send submissions by post with SASE if return required (not necessary if email response is sufficient). No submissions by email unless from outside the US.

Midway Journal
Email: editors@midwayjournal.com
Website: http://midwayjournal.com

Publishes: Fiction; Nonfiction; Poetry; *Markets:* Adult; *Treatments:* Literary

Editors: Ralph Pennel (Fiction Editor); Paige Riehl (Poetry Editor); Christopher Lowe (Nonfiction Editor)

Accepts submissions of fiction, poetry, and creative nonfiction via online submission system between January 1 and May 1 each year. Seeks aesthetically ambitious work that invokes the colliding and converging energies of the fairgrounds. See website for full guidelines.

The Mystic Blue Review
Email: themysticbluereview@gmail.com
Website: http://themysticbluereview. weebly.com/

Publishes: Articles; Fiction; Nonfiction; Poetry; *Areas:* Adventure; Arts; Crime; Fantasy; Gothic; Horror; Humour; Mystery; Photography; Romance; Sci-Fi; Short Stories; Suspense; Thrillers; *Markets:* Academic; Adult; Youth; *Treatments:* Literary

Editors: Alexa Findlay

A not-for-profit online global literary magazine.

Our mission is to create a space for writers and artists to share their mystic creativity. We like work that makes us wish fairytales were real, that sends a chill down our spine, that keeps us on the edge of our seat, etc. We want to bring forth the those that are hiding in the shadows. We like the unusual.

Every writer has a distinct voice and we want to hear it.

We accept submissions from writers and artists of all ages from all across the globe. High school and college (undergraduate and graduate) students are encouraged to submit. You must be at least 13 years old.

NFPA Journal

Tel: +1 (617) 770-3000
Email: nfpajournal@nfpa.org
Website: http://www.nfpa.org

Publishes: Articles; Features; News; Nonfiction; *Markets:* Professional

Association magazine covering fire protection and suppression.

Niche

3000 Chestnut Avenue, Suite 104
Baltimore, MD 21211
Tel: +1 (410) 889-3093
Email: info@nichemagazine.com
Website: http://www.nichemagazine.com/

Publishes: Articles; Nonfiction; *Areas:* Arts; Business; Crafts; Finance; *Markets:* Professional

Editors: Hope Daniels

Trade magazine aimed at craft gallery retailers. Send query with published clips.

Nob Hill Gazette

Fairmont Hotel
950 Mason Street, Mezzanine Level
San Francisco, CA 94108
Tel: +1 (415) 227-0190
Email: fred@nobhillgazette.com
Website: http://www.nobhillgazette.com

Publishes: Articles; Nonfiction; *Areas:* Arts; Beauty and Fashion; Cookery; Design; Finance; Health; Historical; Lifestyle; Travel; *Markets:* Adult

Editors: Fred Albert

Upscale lifestyle magazine for the San Francisco Bay area. Send query with published clips.

Nostalgia Magazine

PO Box 8466
Spokane, WA 99203
Email: editor@nostalgiamagazine.net

Publishes: Essays; Nonfiction; *Areas:* Historical; *Markets:* Adult

Publishes nostalgic personal essays, illustrated with interesting photographs. At least one photo per 400 words. Accepts submissions in any format, but prefers stories and photos by email.

Nurseweek

Email: editor@nurse.com
Website: http://www.nurse.com

Publishes: Articles; Nonfiction; *Areas:* Medicine; *Markets:* Professional

Magazine provided free to registered nurses living in the United States.

NY Literary Magazine

Email: nyliterarymag@gmail.com
Website: https://nyliterarymagazine.com

Publishes: Articles; News; Poetry; *Areas:* Arts; *Markets:* Adult; Professional; Youth

Editors: Elizabeth Harding, Sandra Reynolds, Amanda Graham, Lara Wilson

Publishes the finest literary achievements in modern poetry. We are searching for outstanding talent, a beautiful play of words, emotionally stirring poems that have deep meaning and will withstand the test of time.

We strive to highlight talent and bring to light gifted poets of all ages and nationalities. Publishes both poetry as well as striking visual art.

Our bimonthly magazine is available both as a free digital edition and in print.

OfficePro

10502 N Ambassador Drive, Suite 100
Kansas City, MO 64153
Tel: +1 (816) 891-6600
Fax: +1 (816) 891-9118
Email: john.naatz@iaap-hq.org

Website: http://www.iaap-hq.org/page/
OfficeProMagazine

Publishes: Articles; News; Nonfiction;
Areas: Business; *Markets:* Professional

Editors: John Naatz

Publishes stories related to office life, from
office politics to new software. Send query
by email.

Old Red Kimono
Georgia Highlands College
3175 Cedartown Hwy SE
Rome, GA 30161
Email: napplega@highlands.edu
Website: https://www2.highlands.edu/site/
ork

Publishes: Fiction; Poetry; *Areas:* Short
Stories; *Markets:* Adult; *Treatments:*
Literary

Editors: Steven Godfrey

Annual student-edited literary magazine.
Send 3-5 poems or short stories up to 1,500
words by post or by email. Submissions from
contributors outside the university are
considered between October and February
each year.

Opera News
70 Lincoln Center Plaza, 6th Floor
New York, NY 10023-6593
Tel: +1 (212) 769-7080
Fax: +1 (212) 769-8500
Email: info@operanews.com
Website: http://www.operanews.com

Publishes: Articles; News; Nonfiction;
Areas: Music; *Markets:* Adult; Professional

Editors: Kitty March

Magazine for opera professionals and
enthusiasts. Send queries, proposals, and
unsolicited mss with published writing clips
by email.

Organic Life
400 South 10th Street
Emmaus, PA 18049
Email: ROLsubmissions@rodale.com
Website: http://www.rodalesorganiclife.com

Publishes: Articles; Nonfiction; *Areas:*
Gardening; Health; Lifestyle; Nature;
Markets: Adult

Publishes articles that address some aspect of
the magazine's focus on living naturally in
the modern world.

Orson Scott Card's InterGalactic Medicine Show
Website: http://www.
intergalacticmedicineshow.com

Publishes: Fiction; *Areas:* Fantasy; Sci-Fi;
Short Stories; *Markets:* Adult; Youth

Online magazine publishing fantasy and
science fiction of any length. Submit via
online submission form.

Overtime
PO Box 250382
Plano, TX 75025-0382
Email: overtime@workerswritejournal.com
Website: http://www.
workerswritejournal.com/overtime.htm

Publishes: Fiction; *Areas:* Short Stories;
Markets: Adult; *Treatments:* Literary

Editors: David LaBounty

A series of one-story chapbooks, publishing
stories between 5,000 and 10,000 words,
where work is a central theme.

Pediatric Annals
Healio.com, c/o SLACK Incorporated
6900 Grove Road, Thorofare, NJ 08086
Tel: +1 (856) 848-1000
Fax: +1 (800) 257-8290
Email: editor@healio.com
Website: http://www.healio.com/pediatrics/
journals/pedann

Publishes: Articles; News; Nonfiction;
Areas: Medicine; *Markets:* Professional

Monthly online medical journal providing
pediatricians and other clinicians with
practical information on the diagnosis and
treatment of pediatric diseases and disorders.

Pentecostal Evangel
1445 N. Boonville Avenue
Springfield, MO 65802
Email: pe@ag.org
Website: http://www.pe.ag.org

Publishes: Articles; Nonfiction; *Areas:* Religious; *Markets:* Adult

Christian magazine publishing inspirational articles. Prefers submissions by email. See website for full guidelines.

Pentecostal Messenger
701 Brown Trail
Bedford, TX 76021
Email: Communications@pcg.org
Website: http://www.pcg.org

Publishes: Articles; Essays; Nonfiction; *Areas:* Religious; *Markets:* Adult

Christian magazine acting as the official voice of the Pentecostal Church.

Pest Management Professional
North Coast Media
1360 E. 9th Street, Suite 1070
Cleveland, OH 44114
Tel: +1 (216) 706-3766
Fax: +1 (216) 706-3712
Email: mwhitford@northcoastmedia.net
Website: http://www.mypmp.net

Publishes: Articles; News; Nonfiction; *Areas:* Nature; *Markets:* Professional

Editors: Marty Whitford, Publisher & Editorial Director

Magazine for professionals working in the pest management industry. Send query by email with news or ideas for stories.

Philly Weekly
1617 JFK Boulevard, Suite 1005
Philadelphia, PA 19103
Tel: +1 (215) 563-7400
Fax: +1 (215) 563-6799
Email: mail@phillyweekly.com
Website: http://philadelphiaweekly.com

Publishes: News; Nonfiction; *Areas:* Arts; Current Affairs; Entertainment; *Markets:* Adult

Editors: Anastasia Barbalios

Local magazine publishing arts and entertainment news, dining reviews, and provocative current affairs coverage relating to Philadelphia.

Phoenix Magazine
15169 North Scottsdale Road, Suite 310
Scottsdale, AZ 85254
Website: http://www.phoenixmag.com

Publishes: Articles; Features; News; Nonfiction; *Areas:* Beauty and Fashion; Cookery; Finance; Health; Lifestyle; Travel; *Markets:* Adult

Publishes material of interest to the local area only. Send query by email with published clips.

Photonics & Imaging Technology
Tech Briefs Media Group
261 Fifth Avenue, Suite 1901
New York, NY 10016
Tel: +1 (212) 490-3999
Website: http://www. techbriefsmediagroup.com

Publishes: Articles; Nonfiction; *Areas:* Science; Technology; *Markets:* Academic; Professional

Technical magazine for the photonics / optics industry. Send query or submit complete ms.

Pirene's Fountain
Email: pirenesfountain@gmail.com
Website: http://pirenesfountain.com

Publishes: Poetry; *Markets:* Adult; *Treatments:* Literary

Send between three and eight previously unpublished poems in the body of an email with a brief bio, between May 1 and August 1 annually.

Pizza Today
908 South 8th Street, Suite 200
Louisville, KY 40203
Tel: +1 (502) 736-9500
Email: jwhite@pizzatoday.com
Website: http://www.pizzatoday.com

Publishes: Articles; Features; News;
Nonfiction; *Areas:* Business; Cookery;
Markets: Professional

Editors: Jeremy White

Magazine aimed at the pizza industry. Send
query by email, post, or fax.

Plain Truth Magazine
Plain Truth Ministries
Pasadena, CA 91129
Tel: +1 (800) 309-4466
Email: managing.editor@ptm.org
Website: http://www.ptm.org

Publishes: Articles; Interviews; Nonfiction;
Areas: Religious; *Markets:* Adult

Christian magazine promoting a direct
relationship with God, disintermediated by
religion. Send query with SASE and
published clips.

Play & Playground Magazine
Playground Professionals, LLC
10 North Bridge Street
Saint Anthony, ID 83445
Tel: +1 (208) 569-9189
Website: http://www.
playgroundprofessionals.com

Publishes: Articles; Features; News;
Nonfiction; *Areas:* Design; How-to; Leisure;
Technology; *Markets:* Professional

Trade journal publishing material of
relevance to the play and playground
industry.

PN (Paraplegia News)
PVA Publications
2111 East Highland Avenue, Suite 180
Phoenix, AZ 85016-4702
Tel: +1 (602) 224-0500
Fax: +1 (602) 224-0507
Email: richard@pvamag.com
Website: http://pvamag.com/pn/

Publishes: Articles; Nonfiction; *Areas:*
Health; Leisure; Lifestyle; Sport; *Markets:*
Adult

Editors: Richard Hoover

Monthly magazine for people with spinal-
cord injuries, family members and
caregivers.

Poetica Magazine
5215 Colley Avenue #138
Norfolk, VA 23508
Email: poeticapublishing@aol.com
Website: http://www.poeticamagazine.com

Publishes: Poetry; *Markets:* Adult;
Treatments: Contemporary; Literary

Editors: Michal (Mitak) Mahgerefteh

Publishes contemporary Jewish poetry.
Submit via online submission manager.

Police and Security News
1208 Juniper Street
Quakertown, PA 18951-1520
Tel: +1 (215) 538-1240
Fax: +1 (215) 538-1208
Email: dyaw@policeandsecuritynews.com
Website: http://policeandsecuritynews.com

Publishes: Articles; News; Nonfiction;
Areas: How-to; Legal; *Markets:* Professional

Magazine for law enforcement professionals,
covering new technology; training and
tactics; new weaponry; management ideas;
and more. Send query by email or through
online form.

Popular Science
2 Park Avenue, 9th Floor
New York, NY 10016
Email: queries@popsci.com
Website: http://www.popsci.com

Publishes: Articles; News; Nonfiction;
Areas: Science; Technology; *Markets:*
Adult; *Treatments:* Popular

Magazine covering science and technology
for a general adult readership. Welcomes
queries by email. Send pitch with brief
summary and links to past work, if available.
No submission by post.

PracticeLink Magazine
415 2nd Avenue
Hinton, WV 25951
Tel: +1 (800) 776-8383
Email: HelpDesk@PracticeLink.com
Website: http://www.practicelink.com

Publishes: Nonfiction; *Areas:* Medicine;
Markets: Professional

Career advancement resource for physicians.

Preservation in Print
The Leeds-Davis Building
923 Tchoupitoulas Street
New Orleans, LA 70130
Tel: +1 (504) 636-3043
Email: ddelsol@prcno.org
Website: http://www.prcno.org

Publishes: Articles; Essays; Interviews;
Nonfiction; *Areas:* Architecture; Historical;
Markets: Adult

Editors: Danielle Del Sol

Louisiana publication covering architectural
preservation and neighbourhood
revitalisation issues.

The Produce News
800 Kinderkamack Road, Suite 100
Oradell, NJ 07649
Tel: +1 (201) 986-7990
Fax: +1 (201) 986-7996
Email: groh@theproducenews.com
Website: http://www.theproducenews.com

Publishes: Articles; News; Nonfiction;
Markets: Professional

Editors: John Groh

Magazine for professionals in the fresh fruits
and vegetables industry.

Properties Magazine
3826 W. 158th St.
Cleveland, OH 44111
Tel: +1 (216) 251-0035
Fax: +1 (216) 251-2655
Email: mwatt@propertiesmag.com
Website: http://www.propertiesmag.com

Publishes: Articles; News; Nonfiction;
Areas: Architecture; Business; Design;
Markets: Professional

Editors: Mark Watt, Managing Editor/Art
Director

Monthly publication dedicated to realty,
construction and architecture in Northeast
Ohio.

QSR
Tel: +1 (919) 945-0703
Email: sam@qsrmagazine.com
Website: https://www.qsrmagazine.com

Publishes: Articles; News; Nonfiction;
Areas: Business; Cookery; *Markets:*
Professional

Editors: Sam Oches

Magazine for the limited-service restaurant
industry.

Quill
3909 N. Meridian St.
Indianapolis, IN 46208
Tel: +1 (317) 927-8000 x211
Fax: +1 (317) 920-4789
Email: quill@spj.org
Website: http://www.spj.org/quillabout.asp

Publishes: Articles; Nonfiction; *Markets:*
Professional

Editors: Scott Leadingham

Magazine covering professional journalism.
Accepts unsolicited mss if sent by email
only, but prefers topic pitches and queries to
the editor.

Rain Taxi
PO Box 3840
Minneapolis, MN 55403
Email: info@raintaxi.com
Website: http://www.raintaxi.com

Publishes: Essays; Interviews; Nonfiction;
Reviews; *Areas:* Culture; Literature;
Markets: Adult; *Treatments:* Literary

Journal of literary culture. Publishes reviews,
interviews, and essays. Prefers submissions
by email, but will accept submissions by

post, with SASE or email address for response. See website for full submission guidelines.

Real Simple

Time Inc.
1271 Avenue of the Americas
New York, NY 10020
Tel: +1 (212)522-1212
Fax: +1 (212)467-1392
Email: publishing@realsimple.com
Website: http://www.realsimple.com

Publishes: Articles; Nonfiction; *Areas:* Cookery; Lifestyle; Women's Interests; *Markets:* Adult

Women's interest magazine. Send query in first instance.

Recommend Magazine

5979 NW 151st Street, Suite 120
Miami Lakes, FL 33014
Tel: +1 (305) 828-0123
Fax: +1 (305) 826-6950
Email: paloma@recommend.com
Website: http://www.recommend.com

Publishes: Articles; News; Nonfiction; *Areas:* Travel; *Markets:* Professional

Editors: Paloma Villaverde de Rico

Magazine for travel agents.

Referee

2017 Lathrop Avenue
Racine, WI 53405
Tel: +1 (800) 733-6100
Fax: +1 (262) 632-5460
Email: submissions@referee.com
Website: http://www.referee.com

Publishes: Articles; News; Nonfiction; *Areas:* Sport; *Markets:* Adult; Professional

Magazine for sports officiators from youth to professional level.

Remodeling

One Thomas Circle, N.W., Suite 600
Washington, DC 20005
Tel: +1 (202) 452-0800
Fax: +1 (202) 785-1974

Email: cwebb@hanleywood.com
Website: http://www.remodeling.hw.net

Publishes: Articles; Features; Interviews; News; Nonfiction; *Areas:* Business; Design; How-to; *Markets:* Professional

Editors: Craig Webb

Magazine publishing material relating to residential and light commercial remodelling.

Rider Magazine

1227 Flynn Road, Suite 304
Camarillo, CA 93012
Tel: +1 (763) 383-4400
Email: rider@ridermagazine.com
Website: http://ridermagazine.com

Publishes: Articles; Interviews; Nonfiction; *Areas:* How-to; Technology; Travel; *Markets:* Adult

Magazine written for, and by, mature, affluent and discerning motorcyclists. Query by email in first instance. Only buys stories with photos.

Ripcord.

Email: ndowney@ripcordmagazine.org
Website: https://www.ripcordmagazine.org

Publishes: Essays; Fiction; Poetry; *Areas:* Short Stories; *Markets:* Adult; *Treatments:* Experimental; Literary; Progressive

Editors: Noelle Downey

An online multimedia literary magazine where we celebrate stories in all their forms, no matter how bizarre or unconventional those forms may be. We want to create a platform that embraces diverse, exciting, and inventive narratives. Whether it's a poem, a short story, a photo set, a performance piece, or something even weirder, if it's quality and has a narrative we can sink our teeth into, it's for us. We help tell the stories that would otherwise be lost, and yours could be next. Send us something that helps us see the world in a new way.

River Heron Review

PO Box 543
New Hope, PA 18953
Email: riverheronreview@gmail.com
Website: http://www.riverheronreview.com

Publishes: Poetry; *Markets:* Adult;
Treatments: Contemporary; Experimental;
Literary; Satirical; Serious; Traditional

Editors: Robbin Farr, Judith Lagana

Established to support the arts through the
sharing of poetry in our online journal, at
readings, workshops and by making public
the transformative power of poetic
expression.

We hope to contribute to the expansion of a
community of poets, to establish a creative
outlet that does not discriminate by age, race,
or sexual orientation in order to offer voice
to all and to represent poetry in its many
forms, styles, perspectives, and intentions.

The Road Not Taken: The Journal of Formal Poetry

Email: TheRoadNotTakenJournal@
gmail.com
Website: http://www.
journalformalpoetry.com

Publishes: Poetry; *Markets:* Adult;
Treatments: Literary

Editors: Kathryn Jacobs; Rachel Jacobs

Publishes metrical poetry in modern English.
See website for previous issues and full
guidelines. Submit 3-5 poems by email
during specific reading periods (August 15 –
October 15; January 15 – March 15; and
April 1 – June 15).

Rochester Business Journal

45 East Avenue, Suite 500
Rochester, NY 14604
Tel: +1 (585) 546-8303
Fax: +1 (585) 546-3398
Email: rbj@rbj.net
Website: http://www.rbj.net

Publishes: Articles; News; Nonfiction;
Areas: Business; *Markets:* Professional

Local business magazine aimed at small
business owners and corporate executives in
the Rochester area. Send query with
published clips.

Runner's World

400 South Tenth Street
Emmaus, PA 18098-0099
Tel: +1 (610) 967-8441
Fax: +1 (610) 967-8883
Email: rwedit@rodale.com
Website: http://www.runnersworld.com

Publishes: Articles; Interviews; Nonfiction;
Areas: How-to; Leisure; Sport; *Markets:*
Adult

Magazine for runners. Query in first
instance.

San Diego Family Magazine

1475 6th Avenue, 5th Floor
San Diego, CA 92101-3200
Tel: +1 (619) 685-6970
Fax: +1 (619) 685-6978
Email: editor@sandiegofamily.com
Website: http://www.sandiegofamily.com

Publishes: Articles; Features; Nonfiction;
Areas: Lifestyle; *Markets:* Adult

Magazine on parenting for caregivers in the
San Diego area. Send articles by email with
"Article submission" in the subject line. See
website for full details.

Santa Barbara Magazine

2064 Alameda Padre Serra, Suite 120
Santa Barbara, CA 93103
Tel: +1 (805) 965-5999
Fax: +1 (805) 965-7627
Email: editorial@sbmag.com
Website: http://sbmag.com

Publishes: Articles; Nonfiction; *Areas:*
Architecture; Arts; Gardening; Historical;
Lifestyle; *Markets:* Adult

Magazine publishing articles on Santa
Barbara lifestyle, people, homes, gardens,
architecture, history, and more.

School Bus Fleet
3520 Challenger Street
Torrance, CA 90503
Tel: +1 (310) 533-2587
Email: info@schoolbusfleet.com
Website: http://www.schoolbusfleet.com

Publishes: Articles; News; Nonfiction;
Areas: Travel; *Markets:* Professional

Editors: Nicole Schlosser

Magazine for school transportation
professionals in the US and Canada. Query
in first instance.

Scifaikuest
Email: gatrix65@yahoo.com
Website: https://www.
albanlakepublishing.com/scifaikuest

Publishes: Articles; Nonfiction; Poetry;
Areas: Horror; Sci-Fi; *Markets:* Adult;
Treatments: Literary

Print and online magazine publishing science
fiction and horror poetry in forms such as
scifaiku, haibun, senryu, and tanka. Also
publishes articles. See website for full
submission guidelines.

Scouting
1325 W. Walnut Hill Lane
PO Box 152401
Irving, TX 75015-2401
Tel: +1 (866) 584-6589
Website: http://scoutingmagazine.org

Publishes: Articles; Features; Interviews;
Nonfiction; *Areas:* Adventure; Hobbies;
Leisure; Nature; Travel; *Markets:* Adult

Magazine for scout leaders. Query with
SASE.

Screen Printing
ST Media Group International
11262 Cornell Park Drive
Cincinnati, OH 45242
Email: kiersten.wones@stmediagroup.com
Website: http://www.screenweb.com

Publishes: Articles; Features; News;
Nonfiction; *Areas:* Technology; *Markets:*
Professional

Magazine for commercial and industrial
screen printers. Query in first instance.

Self
Conde Nast
1 World Trade Center
New York, NY 10007
Tel: +1 (212) 286-2860
Email: letters@self.com
Website: http://www.self.com

Publishes: Articles; Nonfiction; *Areas:*
Beauty and Fashion; Finance; Health;
Lifestyle; Women's Interests; *Markets:*
Adult

Women's healthy lifestyle magazine
promoting self-expression and self-
compassion as part of a path to personal
well-being. Send query with published clips
in first instance.

Seshat Literary Magazine
Email: seshatlitmag@gmail.com
Website: http://seshatlitmag.wordpress.com

Publishes: Fiction; Nonfiction; Poetry;
Areas: Adventure; Fantasy; Historical;
Literature; Mystery; Nature; Romance; Sci-
Fi; Short Stories; *Markets:* Adult; Family;
Youth; *Treatments:* Contemporary; Literary

Editors: Maribel C. Pagan

This literary journal is dedicated to mostly
young writers who are homeschooled or
have been homeschooled in the past.
However, all ages (13+) are encouraged to
submit to this journal. Literary fiction,
speculative fiction, creative non-fiction, and
poetry, are all welcome here.

Sew Simple
741 Corporate Circle, Suite A
Golden, CO 80401
Email: sewnews@sewnews.com
Website: http://www.sewsimple.com

Publishes: Articles; Nonfiction; *Areas:*
Crafts; Hobbies; How-to; *Markets:* Youth

Editors: Beth Bradley, Associate Editor

Sewing magazine for younger stitchers,
providing fun ideas and quick, easy projects.

Shutterbug
PO Box 7
Titusville, FL 32781
Tel: +1 (321) 269-3212
Fax: +1 (321) 225-3146
Email: dhavlik@enthusiastnetwork.com
Website: http://www.shutterbug.com

Publishes: Articles; Features; News;
Nonfiction; Reviews; *Areas:* How-to;
Photography; Technology; *Markets:* Adult;
Professional

Photography magazine for amateurs and
professionals. No unsolicited mss. Send
query by post or by email.

SignCraft Publishing Co., Inc.
PO Box 60031
Fort Myers, FL 33906
Tel: +1 (239) 939-4644
Fax: +1 (239) 939-0607
Email: signcraft@signcraft.com
Website: https://www.signcraft.com

Publishes: Articles; Interviews; News;
Nonfiction; *Areas:* Business; How-to;
Markets: Professional

Magazine for the sign industry. Welcomes
photos, tips, article submissions, ideas, and
suggestions.

Sinister Wisdom
2333 McIntosh Road
Dover, FL 33527
Tel: +1 (813) 502-5549
Email: julie@sinisterwisdom.org
Website: http://www.sinisterwisdom.org

Publishes: Essays; Fiction; Nonfiction;
Poetry; *Areas:* Arts; Culture; Short Stories;
Women's Interests; *Markets:* Adult

Editors: Julie R. Enszer

Multicultural lesbian literary and art journal.
Material may be in any style or form, or
combination of forms. Submit five poems,
two short stories or essays, OR one longer
piece of up to 5,000 words, via online
submission system.

Ski Patrol Magazine
133 South Van Gordon Street, Suite 100
Lakewood, CO 80228
Tel: +1 (303) 988-1111
Email: chorgan@nsp.org
Website: http://www.nsp.org

Publishes: Articles; Nonfiction; *Areas:*
Health; Sport; Travel; *Markets:* Professional

Editors: Candace Horgan

Magazine covering mountain rescue, skiing,
snowboarding, and related sports.

Southern Boating
330 N. Andrews Ave, Suite 200
Fort Lauderdale, FL 33301
Tel: +1 (954) 522-5515
Fax: +1 (954) 522-2260
Email: liz@southernboating.com
Website: https://southernboating.com

Publishes: Articles; Nonfiction; Reviews;
Areas: Hobbies; How-to; Leisure; Lifestyle;
Sport; Travel; *Markets:* Adult

Magazine for boating and yachting
enthusiasts, focused on the Southeast of the
United States, Caribbean, Bahamas, and Gulf
of Mexico.

Spin Off
F+W Media/Interweave Press
Attention: Spin Off
4868 Innovation Dr
Ft. Collins, CO 80525-5576
Email: spinoff@interweave.com
Website: http://www.interweave.com/
spinning/

Publishes: Articles; Nonfiction; *Areas:*
Crafts; Hobbies; *Markets:* Adult

Magazine covering a variety of spindles and
spindle techniques.

SQL Server Pro
Penton Media
221 East 29th Street
Loveland, CO 80538
Email: articles@sqlmag.com
Website: http://sqlmag.com

Publishes: Articles; Features; News; Nonfiction; *Areas:* Technology; *Markets:* Professional

Magazine for SQL Server database administrators, developers, and architects, as well as BI professionals.

St Anthony Messenger
28 West Liberty Street
Cincinnati, OH 45202
Tel: +1 (513) 241-5615
Email: MagazineEditors@
FranciscanMedia.org
Website: http://www.americancatholic.org

Publishes: Articles; Fiction; Interviews; Nonfiction; Poetry; *Areas:* How-to; Humour; Lifestyle; Religious; Short Stories; *Markets:* Adult; Family; *Treatments:* Mainstream

Catholic magazine publishing fiction, poetry, and nonfiction relating to the Catholic faith. Send query (nonfiction) or submissions (fiction and poetry) by email only. See website for full guidelines.

St Petersburg Review
Email: annejjames@gmail.com
Website: http://www.stpetersburgreview.com

Publishes: Essays; Fiction; Nonfiction; Poetry; Scripts; *Areas:* Short Stories; Theatre; *Markets:* Adult; *Treatments:* Literary

Send submissions of up to four poems, fiction, essays, or creative nonfiction up to 7,500 words, or plays up to 30 pages, via online submission system. Accepts submissions between September 1 and January 1 annually.

The Stampers' Sampler
22992 Mill Creek Drive
Laguna Hills, CA 92653
Email: thestamperssampler@
stampington.com
Website: https://stampington.com/the-stampers-sampler

Publishes: Features; Nonfiction; *Areas:* Crafts; Hobbies; *Markets:* Adult

Rubber stamping magazine, publishing stamped project ideas.

State Journal
324 Hewes Avenue PO Box 2000
Clarksburg, WV 26301
Tel: +1 (800) 982-6034
Email: news@theet.com
Website: http://www.theet.com/statejournal/

Publishes: Articles; News; Nonfiction; *Areas:* Business; *Markets:* Professional

Magazine aimed at the West Virginia business community.

Stone World
2401 W. Big Beaver Rd., Suite 700
Troy, MI 48084-3333
Tel: +1 (248) 362-3700
Fax: +1 (248) 362-0317
Email: info@stoneworld.com
Website: http://www.stoneworld.com

Publishes: Articles; News; Nonfiction; *Areas:* Architecture; Design; Technology; *Markets:* Professional

Editors: Jennifer Richinelli

Magazine for professionals working with natural building stone.

Stormwater
Forester Media Inc.
PO Box 3100
Santa Barbara, CA 93130
Email: asantiago@forester.net
Website: http://foresternetwork.com/magazines/stormwater/

Publishes: Articles; Features; Interviews; News; Nonfiction; *Areas:* Architecture; Business; Design; *Markets:* Professional

Magazine aimed at professionals concerned with storm water management. Send query by email.

StoryNews
Email: jess@storynews.net
Website: https://www.storynews.net

Publishes: Essays; Nonfiction; *Areas:* Arts; Culture; Current Affairs; Literature; Media; Politics; *Markets:* Adult

Editors: Jess Millman

An online literary journal committed to showcasing the human stories behind headlines. We're seeking nonfiction writing as well as visual, audio, and multimedia art that tells a true story in response to news articles, capturing something unique, special, and personal about the way you see the world.

Our mission isn't to convert folks to new political ideologies, but to give people of all backgrounds insights into each other's worldviews for the sake of understanding and more open dialogues, both personally and globally. All stories are welcome – so long as they are honest, thoughtful, vulnerable, and free of hate speech or bigotry.

Our full submission guidelines are accessible on our website.

SuCasa
Bella Media, LLC
4100 Wolcott Avenue. NE, Suite B
Albuquerque, NM 87109
Tel: +1 (505) 344-1783
Fax: +1 (505) 345-3795
Email: amygross@sucasamagazine.com
Website: http://www.sucasamagazine.com

Publishes: Articles; Nonfiction; *Areas:* Architecture; Design; *Markets:* Adult; *Treatments:* Contemporary

Editors: Amy Gross

Magazine on contemporary home building in the South West. Send query with published clips.

Sunshine Artist
N7528 Aanstad Road
PO Box 5000
Iola, WI 54945
Tel: +1 (800) 597-2573
Email: editor@sunshineartist.com
Website: http://www.sunshineartist.com

Publishes: Nonfiction; Reviews; *Areas:* Arts; Crafts; *Markets:* Professional

Editors: Stephanie Hintz

Publishes reviews of fine art fairs, festivals, events, and small craft shows around the country, for professionals making a living through art shows.

Susquehanna Life
217 Market Street
Lewisburg, PA 17837
Tel: +1 (800) 232-1670
Fax: +1 (570) 524-7796
Email: susquehannalife@gmail.com
Website: http://www.susquehannalife.com

Publishes: Articles; Nonfiction; *Areas:* Arts; Beauty and Fashion; Business; Entertainment; Gardening; Health; Lifestyle; Nature; Travel; *Markets:* Adult

Lifestyle magazine covering central Pennsylvania.

Tallahassee Magazine
Rowland Publishing, Inc.
1932 Miccosukee Road
Tallahassee, FL 32308
Tel: +1 (850) 878-0554
Email: info@rowlandpublishing.com
Website: http://www.
tallahasseemagazine.com

Publishes: Articles; Features; Interviews; Nonfiction; *Areas:* Business; Entertainment; Historical; Lifestyle; Sport; Travel; *Markets:* Adult

Publishes material for visitors to and residents of Florida's capital city. Send query with published clips.

Tech Directions
251 Jackson Plaza, Suite A
Ann Arbor, MI 48103-1955
Tel: +1 (734) 975-2800
Fax: +1 (734) 975-2787
Email: vanessa@techdirections.com
Website: http://www.techdirections.com

Publishes: Articles; Nonfiction; *Areas:* Science; Technology; *Markets:* Professional

Editors: Vanessa Revelli

Publishes articles about what is going on in the career-technical and STEM education fields; ideas teachers can use in the classroom; and anything that can help prepare students for a career. See website for submission guidelines.

Texas Co-op Power

1122 Colorado Street, 24th Floor
Austin, TX 78701
Email: info@texascooppower.com
Website: http://www.texascooppower.com

Publishes: Articles; Nonfiction; *Areas:* Technology; *Markets:* Adult

Magazine which aims to improve the quality of life of electric co-operative member-customers in Texas in an informative and engaging format. Potential contributors should familiarise themselves with the magazine, then submit query by email.

This Is Bill Gorton

Hacienda Publishing
300 State Street
PO Box 92951
Southlake, TX 76092
Tel: +1 (936) 468-5759
Email: thisisbillgorton@gmail.com
Website: http://thisisbillgorton.org

Publishes: Fiction; Nonfiction; *Areas:* Short Stories; *Markets:* Adult; *Treatments:* Literary

Editors: Andrew Brininstool; Joshua Hines

Accepts fiction and nonfiction of any length. Submit via online submission system.

This Old House

262 Harbor Drive
Stamford, CT 06902
Tel: +1 (475) 209-8665
Email: contact@thisoldhouse.com
Website: https://www.thisoldhouse.com

Publishes: Articles; Features; Nonfiction; *Areas:* Design; How-to; *Markets:* Adult

Home improvement magazine. Send query with published clips.

TimberWest

PO Box 610
Edmonds, WA 98020
Tel: +1 (425) 778-3388
Fax: +1 (425) 771-3623
Email: timberwest@forestnet.com
Website: http://forestnet.com/TimberWest.php

Publishes: Articles; Interviews; Nonfiction; *Areas:* Business; Historical; *Markets:* Professional

Magazine covering the logging industry in the Northwest. No material that puts a negative slant on the industry.

Tobacco International

Lockwood Publications, Inc.
3743 Crescent Street, 2nd Floor
Long Island City, NY 11101
Tel: +1 (212) 391-2060
Fax: +1 (212) 827-0945
Email: editor@tobaccointernational.com
Website: http://www.tobaccointernational.com

Publishes: Articles; News; Nonfiction; *Areas:* Business; *Markets:* Professional

Magazine publishing material relating to the tobacco industry.

Trailer Life Magazine

2750 Park View Ct., Suite 240
Oxnard, CA, 93036
Tel: +1 (800) 765-1912
Email: info@trailerlife.com
Website: http://www.trailerlife.com

Publishes: Articles; Features; News; Nonfiction; *Areas:* Hobbies; Leisure; Technology; Travel; *Markets:* Adult

Magazine written for, and by, mature and discerning RVers. No unsolicited submissions, or queries by email. Send queries by post only.

TravelWorld International Magazine

3579 Foothill Boulevard, #744
Pasadena, CA 91107
Tel: +1 (626) 376-9754

Fax: +1 (626) 628-1854
Website: http://www.
travelworldmagazine.com

Publishes: Articles; Nonfiction; *Areas:*
Travel; *Markets:* Adult

Editors: Dennis A. Britton

Travel magazine. Contributors must be
members of NATJA.

Tropical Fish Hobbyist Magazine
Email: associateeditor@tfh.com
Website: http://www.tfhmagazine.com

Publishes: Articles; Nonfiction; *Areas:*
Hobbies; Nature; *Markets:* Adult

Publishes articles of interest to keepers of
tropical fish. Articles are normally between
10,000 and 20,000 words. See website for
full submission guidelines.

Underground Construction
Oildom Publishing Company of Texas, Inc.
1160 Dairy Ashford Road, Suite 610
Houston, TX 77079
Tel: +1 (281) 558-6930
Email: rcarpenter@oildom.com
Website: https://ucononline.com

Publishes: Articles; News; Nonfiction;
Areas: Business; Design; How-to; *Markets:*
Professional

Publishes material for industries involved in
the construction and maintenance of
underground pipelines. Send query with
published clips in first instance.

US Glass Magazine
Key Communications Inc.
20 PGA Drive, Suite 201
Stafford, VA 22554
Tel: +1 (540) 720-5584
Fax: +1 (540) 720-5687
Email: info@usglassmag.com
Website: http://www.usglassmag.com

Publishes: Articles; Nonfiction; *Areas:*
Architecture; Business; *Markets:*
Professional

Editors: Ellen Rogers

Magazine aimed at companies involved in
the architectural class industry. Send query
with published clips.

Vegetable Growers News Magazine
Great American Media Services
PO Box 128
Sparta, Michigan 49345
Tel: +1 (616) 887-9008
Fax: +1 (616) 887-2666
Email: vgnedit@vegetablegrowersnews.com
Website: http://vegetablegrowersnews.com

Publishes: Articles; Interviews; News;
Nonfiction; Reviews; *Areas:* Nature;
Markets: Professional

Magazine for professional vegetable
growers. Send query with published clips
and author CV.

VFW (Veterans of Foreign Wars) Magazine
406 West 34th Street
Kansas City, MO 64111
Tel: +1 (816) 756-3390
Email: magazine@vfw.org
Website: http://www.vfwmagazine.org

Publishes: Articles; News; Nonfiction;
Areas: Current Affairs; Historical; Military;
Markets: Adult

Magazine aimed at veterans of US overseas
conflicts. Send query by email with
published clips. No poetry, fiction, op-eds,
reprints or book reviews.

Vogue Patterns
The McCall Pattern Company
Attn: Customer Service
120 Broadway, 34th floor
New York, New York 10271
Email: editor@voguepatterns.com
Website: https://voguepatterns.mccall.com

Publishes: Articles; Nonfiction; *Areas:*
Crafts; Hobbies; How-to; *Markets:* Adult

Publishes sewing articles and patterns.

Walls & Ceilings
2401 West Big Beaver Road, Suite 700
Troy, MI 48084-3333
Tel: +1 (248) 362-3700
Fax: +1 (248) 362-5103
Email: wyattj@bnpmedia.com
Website: http://www.wconline.com

Publishes: Nonfiction; *Areas:* Architecture;
Design; How-to; *Markets:* Professional

Editors: John Wyatt

Magazine aimed at interior and exterior wall
and ceiling contractors, architects,
manufacturers, suppliers and distributors.
Send query or complete ms.

The Washington Pastime
Email: paulkaraffa@washingtonpastime.com
Website: http://www.
washingtonpastime.com

Publishes: Articles; Essays; Fiction;
Nonfiction; Poetry; *Areas:* Adventure;
Crime; Drama; Entertainment; Fantasy;
Gothic; Horror; Humour; Literature;
Mystery; Romance; Sci-Fi; Short Stories;
Suspense; Thrillers; Westerns; *Markets:*
Adult; Children's; Family; Professional;
Youth; *Treatments:* Commercial;
Contemporary; Cynical; Dark; Experimental;
In-depth; Light; Literary; Mainstream;
Niche; Popular; Positive; Progressive;
Satirical; Serious; Traditional

Editors: Paul Karaffa, Laura Bolt

Note: Not accepting submissions as at
November 2016. Check website for current
status.

In 2010 a study from Central Connecticut
State University found that the Washington
DC area was the most well-read urban city in
the United States. But Washington, DC did
not have a professional literary magazine in
the city representing its stake in
contemporary American literature.

This magazine was founded as an electronic
and print publication based in Washington,
DC committed to publishing the best in
literary and genre fiction. Work featured here
will push literary limitations and take a new
look at antiquated perspectives.

Authors will find a home here from all
around the world, and in turn find
themselves burrowing a place into the hearts
of the readership in the United States, and
specifically the DC metropolitan area.

Water Well Journal
National Ground Water Association
Attn: Water Well Journal
601 Dempsey Road
Westerville, OH 43081-8978
Email: tplumley@ngwa.org
Website: http://waterwelljournal.com

Publishes: Articles; Features; Interviews;
Nonfiction; *Areas:* Business; How-to;
Technology; *Markets:* Professional

Editors: Thad Plumley

Magazine serving the water well drilling
industry. Send query with published clips.

Welding Design & Fabrication
1300 E. 9th St.
Cleveland, OH 44114-1503
Tel: +1 (216) 696-7000
Fax: +1 (216) 931-9524
Email: Robert.brooks@penton.com
Website: http://weldingdesign.com

Publishes: Articles; News; Nonfiction;
Areas: Business; How-to; Technology;
Markets: Professional

Magazine for welders, and those involved in
the welding industry.

Western & Eastern Treasures
PO Box 647
Pacific Grove, CA 93950-0647
Tel: +1 (831) 920-2426
Email: editor@wetreasures.com
Website: http://www.wetreasures.com

Publishes: Articles; Nonfiction; *Areas:*
Hobbies; Leisure; Sport; *Markets:* Adult

Magazine for metal detectorists, covering
every aspect of the hobby. Articles must be
between 1,500 and 2,500 words and must be
accompanied by digital photos of at least 300
dpi.

Western Outdoor News
Email: pat@wonews.com
Website: http://www.wonews.com

Publishes: Articles; Nonfiction; *Areas:* Hobbies; Leisure; Sport; *Markets:* Adult

Editors: Pat McDonell

Magazine serving the interests of fishermen and hunters living in and around California. Submit articles via website or by email. See website for full details.

The Wholesaler
6201 West Howard Street, Suite 201
Niles, IL 60714
Email: danielle@tmbpublishing.com
Website: http://www.thewholesaler.com

Publishes: Articles; News; Nonfiction; *Areas:* Business; How-to; *Markets:* Professional

Editors: Danielle Galian

Publishes news, trends, developments and management how-to for wholesalers and distributors in the plumbing, heating, air conditioning and industrial piping marketplace.

Willow and Sage
22992 Mill Creek, Suite B
Laguna Hills, CA 92653
Email: willowandsage@stampington.com
Website: https://stampington.com/willow-and-sage

Publishes: Articles; Nonfiction; *Areas:* Crafts; How-to; *Markets:* Adult

Publishes recipes, uses, and packaging ideas for homemade bath and body products. Send submissions by post or email.

Window Fashion Vision
4756 Banning Avenue, Suite 206
St. Paul, MN 55110
Tel: +1 (651) 330-0574
Fax: +1 (651) 756-8141
Email: susan@wf-vision.com
Website: https://www.wf-vision.com

Publishes: Articles; Interviews; Nonfiction; *Areas:* Design; How-to; *Markets:* Professional

Editors: Susan Schultz

Magazine serving the window fashions industry. Send query or complete ms.

Wire Rope News & Sling Technology
VS Enterprises
PO Box 871
Clark, New Jersey 07067-0871
Email: info@wireropenews.com
Website: http://www.wireropenews.com

Publishes: Articles; Interviews; News; Nonfiction; *Areas:* Business; Technology; *Markets:* Professional

Publishes articles of interest to those in the wire rope industry. Send ideas by email or by post.

Wisconsin Natural Resources Magazine
P.O. Box 7921
Madison, WI 53707-7921
Tel: +1 (608) 266-2625
Email: kathryn.kahler@wisconsin.gov
Website: http://dnr.wi.gov/wnrmag/

Publishes: Articles; Essays; Features; Nonfiction; *Areas:* How-to; Leisure; Nature; *Markets:* Adult

Editors: Kathryn Kahler, Acting Editor

Publishes features on Wisconsin resources, environmental issues, observation and research, and outdoor activities. Contact editor with ideas before starting a story. See website for full guidelines.

Women's Health Magazine
400 South 10th Street
Emmaus, PA 18098
Tel: +1 (800) 324-1731
Email: whsubmissions@rodale.com
Website: http://www.womenshealthmag.com

Publishes: Articles; Nonfiction; *Areas:* Health; Women's Interests; *Markets:* Adult

Women's health magazine for women who want to reach a healthy, attractive weight.

WoodmenLife Magazine

Woodmen Tower
1700 Farnam Street
Omaha, NE 68102
Tel: +1 (402) 342-1890
Fax: +1 (402) 271-7269
Email: service@woodmen.com
Website: https://www.woodmenlife.org

Publishes: Articles; News; Nonfiction; *Markets:* Adult

Magazine for members of non-profit insurance company.

World War II

1919 Gallows Road, Suite 400
Vienna, VA 22182
Email: worldwar2@historynet.com
Website: http://www.historynet.com

Publishes: Articles; Features; Nonfiction; *Areas:* Historical; Military; *Markets:* Adult

Publishes material relating to the second world war. No unsolicited mss. Send query by post or by email in first instance.

Yes! Magazine

PO Box 10818
Bainbridge Island, WA 98110
Email: editors@yesmagazine.org
Website: http://www.yesmagazine.org

Publishes: Articles; Nonfiction; *Areas:* Current Affairs; Nature; Politics; *Markets:* Adult; *Treatments:* Positive

Magazine reframing the biggest problems of our time in terms of their solutions.

Zoning Practice

American Planning Association
205 North Michigan Avenue, Suite 1200
Chicago, IL 60601-5927
Tel: +1 (312) 431-9100
Fax: +1 (312) 786-6700
Email: zoningpractice@planning.org
Website: https://www.planning.org/zoningpractice

Publishes: Articles; Features; Nonfiction; *Areas:* Architecture; Politics; *Markets:* Professional

Professional magazine covering planning and land use.

UK Magazines

For the most up-to-date listings of these and hundreds of other magazines, visit https://www.firstwriter.com/magazines

*To claim your **free** access to the site, please see the back of this book.*

Acumen

6 The Mount
Higher Furzeham
Brixham
South Devon
TQ5 8QY
Tel: +44 (0) 1803 851098
Email: patriciaoxley6@gmail.com
Website: http://www.acumen-poetry.co.uk

Publishes: Articles; Features; Nonfiction; Poetry; Reviews; *Areas:* Criticism; Literature; *Markets:* Adult; *Treatments:* Literary

Editors: Patricia Oxley

Magazine publishing poetry and articles, features, and reviews connected to poetry. Send submissions with SAE and author details on each page, or submit by email as Word attachment. See website for full submission guidelines.

Aeroplane

Key Publishing Ltd
PO BOX 100
Stamford
PE9 1XQ
Tel: +44 (0) 1780 755131
Fax: +44 (0) 1780 751323
Email: ben.dunnell@keypublishing.com
Website: http://www.aeroplanemonthly.com

Publishes: Features; News; Nonfiction; *Areas:* Historical; Technology; *Markets:* Adult

Editors: Ben Dunnell

Publishes news and features relating to historic aviation and aircraft preservation, up to the 1960s. Send query by post or email. Features must be illustrated with good quality photographs.

Aesthetica: A Review of Contemporary Artists

PO Box 371
York
YO23 1WL
Tel: +44 (0) 1904 629137
Email: info@aestheticamagazine.com
Website: http://www.aestheticamagazine.com

Publishes: Articles; Essays; Features; Interviews; News; Nonfiction; Reviews; *Areas:* Arts; Culture; Current Affairs; Drama; Film; Humour; Literature; Music; Theatre; Women's Interests; *Markets:* Adult; *Treatments:* Literary

Editors: Cherie Federico

I am the founder and editor of a literary and arts magazine that I actually began with my MA fee money (I eventually paid the fees and received my MA). I started the magazine because I believe that there are too many closed doors in the literary and art world. I believe in making the arts accessible and available for all. My convictions are deep because I believe that in this modern, some say, post-modern world that we live in it is important to remember the essentials about being human. There are too many reality TV shows that mock existence. As a culture we are slipping away from the arts. Writing has too many stigmas attached and people believe that there are too many rules. My aim was to bring a magazine to life that would challenge some of these notions and make a difference.

This writing and artistic platform is spreading across the UK and making it to places like Israel, Italy, Ireland, New Zealand, Australia, America, Canada, Bulgaria, and Switzerland. We started in York and are now selling at Borders in York, Leeds, Brighton, Islington, and Oxford Street as well as in some local York bookshops and direct either from the website or by post.

I believe that art and literature is something that is found within all of us. We need to believe in ourselves and see the beauty of the moment to take this concept further. With my literary magazine I have created a space for new ideas and fresh opinions. I believe in creativity, diversity, and equality.

Africa Confidential
37 John's Mews
London
WC1N 2NS
Tel: +44 (0) 20 7831 3511
Email: andrew@africa-confidential.com
Website: http://www.africa-confidential.com

Publishes: Articles; News; Nonfiction; *Areas:* Finance; Politics; *Markets:* Adult

Editors: Andrew Weir, Deputy Editor

Magazine publishing news and articles on African politics and economics. Welcomes unsolicited mss.

Agenda
Harts Cottage
Stonehurst Lane
Five Ashes
Mayfield
East Sussex
TN20 6LL
Tel: +44 (0) 1825 831994
Email: submissions@agendapoetry.co.uk
Website: http://www.agendapoetry.co.uk

Publishes: Essays; Poetry; Reviews; *Areas:* Criticism; Literature; *Markets:* Adult; *Treatments:* Literary

Editors: Patricia McCarthy

Publishes poems, critical essays, and reviews. Send up to five poems or up to two essays / reviews with email address, age, and short bio. No previously published material. Submit by email only, with each piece in a separate Word attachment. Accepts work only during specific submission windows – see website for current status.

All Out Cricket
TriNorth Ltd
Fourth Floor
Bedser Stand
Kia Oval
Kennington
London
SE11 5SS
Tel: +44 (0) 20 3696 5732
Email: comments@alloutcricket.com
Website: http://www.alloutcricket.com

Publishes: Articles; Interviews; News; Nonfiction; *Areas:* Sport; *Markets:* Adult

Editors: Phil Walker

Cricket magazine. Send query by email in first instance.

Amateur Gardening
Westover House
West Quay Road
Poole
BH15 1JG
Tel: +44 (0) 1202 440840
Fax: +44 (0) 1202 440860
Email: amateurgardening@timeinc.com
Website: http://www.amateurgardening.com

Publishes: Articles; Features; News; Nonfiction; *Areas:* Gardening; *Markets:* Adult

Editors: Garry Coward-Williams

Publishes news items, articles, and features relating to gardening.

Amazing! Magazine
Amazing Publishing Limited
4 Old Park Lane
Mayfair
London
W1K 1QW
Tel: +44 (0) 20 3633 2531
Email: hello@amazing.org.uk
Website: https://amazing.org.uk

Publishes: Nonfiction; *Markets:* Children's

Editors: Yousuf Aslam

Monthly printed magazine for children aged 6-12 that makes learning fun. Each issue covers maths, english, science, history, geography, and more. Inside are articles, facts, stories, debates, activities, puzzles, and jokes.

Ambit
Staithe House
Main Road
Brancaster Staithe
Norfolk
PE31 8BP
Tel: +44 (0) 7503 633601
Email: contact@ambitmagazine.co.uk
Website: http://ambitmagazine.co.uk

Publishes: Fiction; Poetry; *Areas:* Arts; Short Stories; *Markets:* Adult; *Treatments:* Literary

An international magazine. Potential contributors are advised to read a copy before submitting work. Send up to 5 poems, a story up to 5,000 words, or flash fiction up to 1,000 words. Submit via online portal on website, or by post (see website for full details). No submissions by email. Accepts submission only during specific submission windows – see website for details.

Amethyst Review
Email: Sarah.Poet@gmail.com
Website: https://amethystmagazine.org

Publishes: Fiction; Nonfiction; Poetry; *Areas:* Religious; Short Stories; Spiritual; *Markets:* Adult

Editors: Sarah Law

Publishes work that engages in some way with spirituality or the sacred. Submit up to five poems (of any length) and / or prose pieces of up to 2,000 words. Simultaneous submissions if notification of acceptance elsewhere is provided. No previously published work. Send submissions by email with author bio of around 50 words. See website for full guidelines.

Angler's Mail
Pinehurst 2
Pinehurst Road
Farnborough Business Park
Farnborough
Hampshire
GU14 7BF
Tel: +44 (0) 1252 555055
Email: anglersmail@timeinc.com
Website: http://www.anglersmail.co.uk

Publishes: Features; News; Nonfiction; *Areas:* Hobbies; Sport; *Markets:* Adult

Publishes pictures, stories, and features relating to angling news and matches.

Architectural Design
Email: architecturaldesign@wiley.com
Website: http://wileyactual.com/architect-design/

Publishes: Articles; Nonfiction; *Areas:* Architecture; Design; *Markets:* Professional

Editors: Helen Castle

Prestigious magazine of architecture and design.

Areté
8 New College Lane
Oxford
OX1 3BN
Tel: +44 (0) 1865 289193
Fax: +44 (0) 1865 289194
Email: craigraine@aretemagazine.co.uk
Website: http://www.aretemagazine.com

Publishes: Fiction; Poetry; Reviews; *Areas:* Drama; Short Stories; *Markets:* Adult

Editors: Craig Raine

Arts magazine publishing fiction, poetry, reportage, and reviews. Previous contributors have included TS Eliot, William Golding, Harold Pinter, Ian McEwan, Martin Amis, Simon Armitage, Rosemary Hill, Ralph Fiennes, and many more.

Send hard copy only. Unsolicited MSS should be accompanied by an SAE or email address for response. No International Reply Coupons, and no submissions by email.

Art Quarterly

Art Fund
2 Granary Square
King's Cross
London
N1C 4BH
Tel: +44 (0) 20 7225 4800
Email: artquarterly@artfund.org
Website: https://www.artfund.org/about-us/art-quarterly

Publishes: Articles; Features; Nonfiction; *Areas:* Arts; *Markets:* Adult

Arts magazine publishing features on artists, galleries and museums.

ARTEMISpoetry

3 Springfield Close
East Preston
West Sussex
BN16 2SZ
Email: editor@poetrypf.co.uk
Website: http://www.secondlightlive.co.uk/artemis.shtml

Publishes: Poetry; *Markets:* Adult; *Treatments:* Literary

Editors: Dilys Wood; Katherine Gallagher; Anne Stewart

For poems by women. Submit up to four poems, up to 200 lines total, by post only. Poems must be unpublished and not out for submission elsewhere. See website for full guidelines.

ArtReview

1 Honduras Street
London
EC1Y 0TH
Tel: +44 (0) 20 7490 8138
Email: artreview@abacusemedia.com
Website: http://artreview.com

Publishes: Articles; News; Nonfiction; Reviews; *Areas:* Arts; Criticism; *Markets:* Adult; *Treatments:* Contemporary

International contemporary art magazine, dedicated to expanding contemporary art's audience and reach.

The Author

84 Drayton Gardens
London
SW10 9SB
Tel: +44 (0) 207 7373 6642
Email: theauthor@societyofauthors.org
Website: http://www.societyofauthors.org

Publishes: Articles; Nonfiction; *Areas:* Business; How-to; Legal; *Markets:* Professional

Editors: James McConnachie

Magazine covering all aspects of the writing profession, including legal, technical, and commercial considerations. Query in writing in first instance.

Banipal

1 Gough Square
London
EC4A 3DE
Tel: +44 (0) 20 7832 1350
Email: editor@banipal.co.uk
Website: http://www.banipal.co.uk

Publishes: Features; Fiction; Poetry; Reviews; *Areas:* Short Stories; Translations; *Markets:* Adult

Editors: Margaret Obank

Contemporary Arab authors in English translations. Publishes new and established writers, and diverse material including translations, poetry, short stories, novel excerpts, profiles, interviews, appreciations, book reviews, reports of literary festivals, conferences, and prizes. Welcomes submissions by post, but queries only by email. Unsolicited email submissions with attachments will be automatically deleted. Response in 3-6 months.

BBC Countryfile Magazine
9th Floor
Tower House
Fairfax Street
Bristol
BS1 3BN
Tel: +44 (0) 1173 147399
Email: joe.pontin@immediate.co.uk
Website: http://www.countryfile.com

Publishes: Articles; Features; Nonfiction; *Areas:* Nature; *Markets:* Adult

Editors: Fergus Collins; Joe Pontin (Features Editor)

Magazine on British countryside and rural life. Send queries with ideas by email. No unsolicited mss.

BBC Wildlife Magazine
4th Floor
Tower House
Fairfax St
Bristol
BS1 3BN
Tel: +44 (0) 1173 147366
Email: wildlifemagazine@immediate.co.uk
Website: http://www.discoverwildlife.com

Publishes: Articles; Features; News; Nonfiction; *Areas:* Nature; *Markets:* Adult

Editors: Ben Hoare

Magazine publishing news, articles, and features covering the natural world.

Black Static
TTA Press
5 Martins Lane
Witcham
Ely
Cambs
CB6 2LB
Website: http://ttapress.com

Publishes: Fiction; *Areas:* Fantasy; Horror; Short Stories; *Markets:* Adult; *Treatments:* Dark

Editors: Andy Cox

Publishes short stories of horror and dark fantasy. See website for full guidelines and online submission system.

Blithe Spirit
Email: teamblithespirit@gmail.com
Website: http://britishhaikusociety.org.uk

Publishes: Poetry; *Markets:* Adult

Editors: Colin Blundell (haiku), Karen Hoy (tanka), Alan Summers (haibun), David Jacobs (reviews) and Caroline Skanne (co-ordinator and cover design)

Primarily a membership magazine featuring haiku and related forms, however members do not enjoy an automatic right to publication – quality is key. Non-members may appear as featured writers. All work must be original. Submissions should be sent by email with a covering note. Alternatively, send by post with SAE or IRCs for reply.

Boat International
First Floor
41-47 Hartfield Road
London
SW19 3RQ
Tel: +44 (0) 20 8545 9330
Fax: +44 (0) 20 8545 9333
Email: stewart.campbell@ boatinternationalmedia.com
Website: https://www.boatinternational.com

Publishes: Articles; News; Nonfiction; *Areas:* Design; Lifestyle; Technology; Travel; *Markets:* Adult

Editors: Stewart Campbell

Magazine celebrating superyachts and the life that comes with them.

British Birds
4 Harlequin Gardens
St Leonards on Sea
East Sussex
TN37 7PF

EDITORIAL
Spindrift
Eastshore

Virkie
Shetland
ZE3 9JS
Tel: +44 (0) 1424 755155
Fax: +44 (0) 1424 755155
Email: editor@britishbirds.co.uk
Website: https://britishbirds.co.uk

Publishes: Articles; Nonfiction; *Areas:*
Nature; *Markets:* Adult

Editors: Roger Riddington

Magazine for birdwatchers, publishing
articles on behaviour, conservation,
distribution, identification, status and
taxonomy.

British Journalism Review
SAGE Publications
1 Oliver's Yard
55 City Road
London
EC1Y 1SP
Tel: +44 (0) 20 7324 8500
Fax: 20 7324 8600
Email: editor@bjr.org.uk
Website: http://www.bjr.org.uk

Publishes: Articles; Nonfiction; *Areas:*
Media; *Markets:* Academic

Editors: Kim Fletcher

Quarterly peer-reviewed academic journal
covering the field of journalism. Welcomes
letters and articles, by post or by email.

Brittle Star
Diversity House
72 Nottingham Road
Arnold
Nottingham
NG5 6LF
Tel: +44 (0) 20 8802 1507
Email: post@brittlestar.org.uk
Website: http://www.brittlestar.org.uk

Publishes: Fiction; Poetry; *Areas:* Short
Stories; *Markets:* Adult

Editors: Louise Hooper

Publishes original and unpublished poetry
and short stories. Send 1-4 poems or 1-2
stories of up to 2,000 words each. Include

short bio of up to 40 words. No simultaneous
submissions.

Broadcast
Media Business Insight
Zetland House
5-25 Scrutton Street
London
EC2A 4HJ
Tel: +44 (0) 20 8102 0900
Email: chris.curtis@broadcastnow.co.uk
Website: https://www.broadcastnow.co.uk

Publishes: Features; News; Nonfiction;
Areas: Business; Entertainment;
Technology; TV; *Markets:* Adult;
Professional

Editors: Chris Curtis

Publishes news and features relating to
broadcasting.

Building Design
Email: bdonline@ubm.com
Website: https://www.bdonline.co.uk

Publishes: Articles; Features; News;
Nonfiction; *Areas:* Architecture; Design;
Markets: Professional

Editors: Thomas Lane

Publishes news, comment, and reviews of
interest to architects.

Bunbury Magazine
Email: submissions@bunburymagazine.com
Website: https://bunburymagazine.com

Publishes: Articles; Fiction; Nonfiction;
Poetry; Reviews; *Areas:* Short Stories;
Markets: Adult; *Treatments:* Literary

Online literary magazine. Publishes anything
from poetry to artwork, flash fiction to
graphic story, life writing to photography,
plus reviews and articles. Send submissions
by email. See website for full guidelines, and
for current issue theme.

The Burnt Candle
Hamilton House
Nottingham

NG5 1AE
Email: theburntcandle@compsncalls.com
Website: https://www.compsncalls.com/
burntcandle.html

Publishes: Fiction; Poetry; *Areas:* Crime;
Drama; Erotic; Fantasy; Literature; Mystery;
Romance; Short Stories; Suspense; Thrillers;
Markets: Adult; *Treatments:* Dark; Literary;
Mainstream; Popular; Serious

Editors: Judith Darcey-Blake

Magazine looking for original, well-written,
powerful and emotional stories. Also open
for poetry. New and up-and-coming writers
are just as welcome as established writers.

Cambridge Magazine

Winship Road
Milton
Cambridge
Cambridgeshire
CB24 6BQ
Tel: +44 (0) 01223 434419
Email: alice.ryan@cambridge-news.co.uk
Website: http://www.cambridge-news.co.uk/
CambridgeMagazine.html

Publishes: Features; Interviews; Nonfiction;
Areas: Arts; Beauty and Fashion; Culture;
Gardening; Lifestyle; Technology; *Markets:*
Adult

Editors: Alice Ryan

Magazine covering Cambridge, including
food and drink, arts and culture, homes and
gardens, fashion and beauty, and gears and
gadgets.

The Casket of Fictional Delights

Email: joanna@thecasket.co.uk
Website: http://www.thecasket.co.uk

Publishes: Fiction; *Areas:* Short Stories;
Markets: Adult

Editors: Joanna Sterling

Online magazine publishing flash fiction up
to 300 words and short stories between 1,200
and 3,000 words. Submissions by invitation
and recommendation only.

The Caterer

Travel Weekly Group Ltd
52 Grosvenor Gardens
London
SW1W 0AU
Tel: +44 (0) 20 7881 4803
Email: info@thecaterer.com
Website: https://www.thecaterer.com

Publishes: Articles; News; Nonfiction;
Areas: Business; *Markets:* Professional

Editors: Amanda Afiya

Magazine for hotel, restaurant, foodservice
and pub and bar operators.

Catholic Pictorial

Media House
Mann Island
Liverpool
L3 1DG
Tel: +44 (0) 1512 362191
Fax: +44 (0) 1512 362216
Email: catherine@merseymirror.com
Website: http://www.catholicpic.co.uk

Publishes: Features; News; Nonfiction;
Areas: Religious; *Markets:* Adult

Publishes news and photo features of relating
to Catholicism and Merseyside.

Catholic Universe

The Universe Media Group Ltd
Guardian Print Centre
Parkway
Longbridge Road
Trafford Park
M17 1SN
Tel: +44 (0) 1619 085301
Website: http://www.
thecatholicuniverse.com

Publishes: Articles; Features; News;
Nonfiction; *Areas:* Religious; *Markets:*
Adult

Catholic Sunday newspaper. Launched in
1860 and based in Manchester.

Central and Eastern European London Review

Email: ceel.org@gmail.com
Website: http://ceel.org.uk

Publishes: Articles; Nonfiction; Reviews;
Areas: Arts; Culture; Film; Literature;
Music; Theatre; Travel; *Markets:* Adult

Editors: Robin Ashenden

Online magazine covering all aspects of
Central and Eastern European life in London.
Send submissions by email.

Climb Magazine

Greenshires Publishing
160-164 Barkby Road
Leicester
LE16 8FZ
Tel: +44 (0) 1162 022600
Fax: +44 (0) 1162 769002
Email: climbmagazine@gmail.com
Website: http://www.climbmagazine.com

Publishes: Articles; Nonfiction; *Areas:*
Hobbies; Leisure; Sport; *Markets:* Adult

Editors: David Pickford

Magazine aimed at climbers. Query editor in
first instance.

Climber

Email: climbereditorial@gmail.com
Website: https://www.climber.co.uk

Publishes: Articles; Nonfiction; *Areas:*
Sport; *Markets:* Adult

Monthly climbing magazine for experienced
climbers, boulderers, mountaineers, and
those who are just starting out. Query editor
by email in first instance.

Coach

Email: editorial@coachmag.co.uk
Website: http://www.coachmag.co.uk

Publishes: Articles; News; Nonfiction;
Areas: Health; Leisure; Sport; *Markets:*
Adult

Free weekly health and fitness magazine.

Computeractive Magazine

800 Guillat Avenue
Kent Science Park
Sittingbourne
ME9 8GU
Tel: +44 (0) 1795 412882
Email: ca@servicehelpline.co.uk
Website: http://getcomputeractive.co.uk

Publishes: Articles; News; Nonfiction;
Reviews; *Areas:* How-to; Technology;
Markets: Adult

Magazine covering computers, smart phones,
tablets, and the internet, providing news,
reviews, and advice.

Cotswold Life

Archant House
Oriel Road
Cheltenham
Gloucestershire
GL50 1BB
Tel: +44 (0) 1242 216050
Email: mike.lowe@archant.co.uk
Website: http://www.cotswoldlife.co.uk

Publishes: Articles; Nonfiction; *Areas:*
Gardening; Leisure; Lifestyle; Nature;
Travel; *Markets:* Adult

Editors: Mike Lowe

Publishes articles relating to the Cotswolds.

Country Walking

Bauer Consumer Media Limited
Media House
Peterborough Business Park
Peterborough
PE2 6EA
Tel: +44 (0) 1733 468208
Email: guy.procter@lfto.com
Website: http://www.countrywalking.co.uk

Publishes: Articles; Features; News;
Nonfiction; Reviews; *Areas:* Hobbies;
Lifestyle; Nature; Travel; *Markets:* Adult

Editors: Guy Procter

Magazine on walking in the UK and Europe.
Publishes news, product tests and reviews,
features, and profiles of celebrity walkers.

Criminal Law & Justice Weekly (Incorporating Justice of the Peace)

Lexis House
30 Farringdon Street
London
EC4A 4HH
Tel: +44 (0) 20 7400 2828
Email: diana.rose@lexisnexis.co.uk
Website: http://www.
criminallawandjustice.co.uk

Publishes: Articles; Nonfiction; *Areas:*
Legal; *Markets:* Professional

Editors: Diana Rose

Weekly magazine covering key
developments in criminal law, plus practice
and procedure across the whole criminal
court system. Includes licensing and the
coroners' court. Send complete ms or précis
by email. See website for full details.

Critical Quarterly

Newbury
Crediton
Devon
EX17 5HA
Email: CQpoetry@gmail.com
Website: http://onlinelibrary.wiley.com/
journal/10.1111/(ISSN)1467-8705

Publishes: Essays; Fiction; Nonfiction;
Poetry; *Areas:* Criticism; Culture; Literature;
Short Stories; *Markets:* Adult; *Treatments:*
Literary

Editors: Colin MacCabe

Publishes literary criticism, cultural studies,
poetry and fiction. Send submissions by
email. See website for separate email address
for submissions of criticism.

Crystal Magazine

3 Bowness Avenue
Prenton
Birkenhead
CH43 0SD
Tel: +44 (0) 1516 089736
Email: christinecrystal@hotmail.com
Website: http://www.christinecrystal.
blogspot.com

Publishes: Articles; Fiction; Nonfiction;
Poetry; *Areas:* Adventure; Biography;
Fantasy; Horror; Humour; Literature;
Mystery; Nature; Romance; Sci-Fi; Short
Stories; Suspense; Thrillers; Travel;
Westerns; *Markets:* Adult; *Treatments:*
Light; Literary; Mainstream; Popular;
Positive; Traditional

Editors: Christine Carr

For subscribers only. Please don't send work
if you haven't subscribed.

Poems, stories, articles. A4, spiral-bound bimonthly. Forty pages with colour images.
Also includes the very popular
"Wordsmithing", a look into the lives of
writers and writing. The magazine usually
contains pages and pages in Readers' Letters.
Subscribers' News provides an opportunity
to share writing achievements.

There are PayPal buttons on the website for
subscription to Crystal and a sample copy.
There is also a button for £1 entry to
competitions for subscribers only.

Current Accounts

Apartment 2D
Beadshaw Hall
Hardcastle Gardens
Bolton
BL2 4NZ
Email: fjameshartnell@aol.com
Website: https://sites.google.com/site/
bankstreetwriters/current-accounts-magazine

Publishes: Essays; Fiction; Nonfiction;
Poetry; Scripts; *Areas:* Drama; Short Stories;
Translations; *Markets:* Adult; *Treatments:*
Literary

Editors: F. J. Hartnell

Web-based publication with one printed
collection per year. Submit up to four poems
or up to two stories, plays, or essays at a
time, by email or by post with SAE /IRCs.
Emailed submissions should be included in
the body of the email, not as an attachment.
Plays should be one act and no longer than 4
minutes when read aloud.

Custom Car
Kelsey Publishing Ltd
Cudham Tithe Barn
Berry's Hill
Cudham
Kent
TN16 3AG
Tel: +44 (0) 1959 543747
Email: cc.ed@kelseypb.co.uk
Website: http://www.customcarmag.co.uk

Publishes: Articles; Nonfiction; *Areas:*
Hobbies; *Markets:* Adult

Editors: Dave Biggadyke

Magazine covering the UK drag racing scene
and customised classics.

Custom PC
Dennis Publishing Ltd
PO Box 843
HAYWARDS HEATH
RH16 9NY
Tel: +44 (0) 330 333 9493
Email: subscriptions@custompc.co.uk
Website: http://www.custompc.co.uk

Publishes: Articles; Nonfiction; *Areas:*
Technology; *Markets:* Adult

Editors: Ben Hardwidge

PC modding and overclocking magazine for
people who are passionate about PC
technology and hardware.

The Dawntreader
24 Forest Houses
Halwill
Beaworthy
Devon
EX21 5UU
Email: dawnidp@gmail.com
Website: http://www.indigodreams.co.uk/
the-dawntreader

Publishes: Articles; Fiction; Nonfiction;
Poetry; *Areas:* Nature; Short Stories;
Spiritual; *Markets:* Adult; *Treatments:*
Literary

Editors: Ronnie Goodyer

A quarterly publication specialising in myth,
legend; in the landscape, nature; spirituality
and love; the mystic, the environment.

Descent
Wild Places Publishing
PO Box 100
Abergavenny
NP7 9WY
Tel: +44 (0) 1873 737707
Email: descent@wildplaces.co.uk
Website: https://www.wildplaces.co.uk

Publishes: Articles; Features; News;
Nonfiction; Reviews; *Areas:* Historical;
Hobbies; Technology; *Markets:* Adult

Editors: Chris Howes

Magazine publishing material for mine
enthusiasts and cavers, including news items,
equipment reviews, historical and modern
expeditions, etc.

Diabetes Balance
Diabetes UK Central Office
Macleod House
10 Parkway
London
NW1 7AA
Tel: +44 (0) 345 123 2399
Fax: +44 (0) 20 7424 1001
Email: info@diabetes.org.uk
Website: https://www.diabetes.org.uk

Publishes: Articles; Interviews; News;
Nonfiction; *Areas:* Health; Lifestyle;
Medicine; Science; *Markets:* Adult

Lifestyle magazine for people with diabetes,
publishing relevant news and research, as
well as celebrity interviews, recipes,
competitions, and regular free supplements.

Director
3-7 Herbal Hill
London
EC1R 5EJ
Email: director-ed@iod.com
Website: https://www.director.co.uk

Publishes: Articles; Features; News;
Nonfiction; *Areas:* Business; *Markets:*
Professional

Magazine for entrepreneurs and business leaders.

Diva

Millivres Prowler Ltd.
Unit M,Spectrum House
32-34 Gordon House Road
London
NW5 1LP
Tel: +44 (0) 20 7424 7400
Fax: +44 (0) 20 7424 7401
Email: edit@divamag.co.uk
Website: http://www.divamag.co.uk

Publishes: Articles; Features; Nonfiction; *Areas:* Culture; Lifestyle; Women's Interests; *Markets:* Adult

Editors: Jane Czyzselska

Monthly glossy newsstand magazine for lesbians and bisexual women. Send query or submissions by email.

The Dolls' House

The Guild of Master Craftsmen
166 High Street
Lewes
East Sussex
BN7 1XU
Tel: +44 (0) 1273 477374
Website: https://www.thegmcgroup.com

Publishes: Articles; Features; Nonfiction; Reviews; *Areas:* Crafts; Hobbies; How-to; *Markets:* Adult

Magazine publishing material related to dolls' houses.

Dream Catcher

Stairwell Books
161 Lowther Street
York
YO31 7LZ
Tel: +44 (0) 1904 733767
Email: rose@stairwellbooks.com
Website: http://www.
dreamcatchermagazine.co.uk

Publishes: Fiction; Interviews; Nonfiction; Poetry; Reviews; *Areas:* Short Stories; Translations; *Markets:* Adult; *Treatments:* Literary

Editors: John Gilham

Send submissions by post, following guidelines on website. No electronic submissions.

Eastern Art Report

EAPGROUP
PO Box 13666
London
SW14 8WF
Email: ear@eapgroup.com
Website: http://easternartreport.net

Publishes: Articles; News; Nonfiction; *Areas:* Arts; Culture; *Markets:* Adult

International magazine focused on the arts of Asia and Africa and the arts practiced by the people of Asian and African origin in North America, Europe and elsewhere. Increasingly, Australia, New Zealand the Pacific region are covered in articles and news. Send query by email or through online contact form.

Eat In Magazine

H Bauer Publishing
Academic House
24-28 Oval Road
London
NW1 7DT
Email: cookeryed@eatinmagazine.co.uk
Website: https://eatinmagazine.co.uk

Publishes: Articles; Nonfiction; *Areas:* Cookery; How-to; *Markets:* Adult

Editors: Margaret Nicholls

Cookery magazine.

The Engineer

Centaur Communications Ltd
Wells Point
79 Wells Street
London
W1T 3QN
Tel: +44 (0) 20 7970 4437
Email: jon.excell@centaurmedia.com
Website: https://www.theengineer.co.uk

Publishes: Articles; Features; News; Nonfiction; *Areas:* Technology; *Markets:* Adult; Professional

Editors: Jon Excell

Publishes news and features on the latest technology and engineering innovations.

Engineering In Miniature

Warners Group Publications
The Maltings
West Street, Bourne
LINCS
PE10 9PH
Website: https://www.world-of-railways.co.uk/engineering-in-miniature

Publishes: Articles; Nonfiction; *Areas:* Hobbies; Technology; *Markets:* Adult

Editors: Martin Evans

Magazine publishing technical articles on model engineering. Send query via website.

Envoi

Meirion House
Glan yr afon
Tanygrisiau
Blaenau Ffestiniog
LL41 3SU
Tel: +44 (0) 1766 832112
Email: envoi@cinnamonpress.com
Website: https://www.cinnamonpress.com/index.php/envoi

Publishes: Articles; Nonfiction; Poetry; Reviews; *Areas:* Literature; Translations; *Markets:* Adult; *Treatments:* Literary

Editors: Dr Jan Fortune-Wood

Magazine of poems, poetry sequences, reviews, and competitions, now more than 50 years old. Occasional poetry related articles and poetry in translation. Submit up to 6 poems up to 40 lines each or one or two longer poems by email only (in the body of the email; attachments will not be read). No submissions by post.

What others say:

"Probably the best poetry magazine currently available" – The Writers' College

"Without a grant and obviously well read, this poetry magazine excels itself." – Ore

"The policy of giving poets space to show their skills is the right one." – Haiku Quarterly

"Good quality, lots of bounce, poems, comps, reviews, reader comeback" – iota

"If you haven't tried it yet, do so, you'll get your money's worth." – New Hope International

Erotic Review

Email: editorial@ermagazine.org
Website: http://eroticreviewmagazine.com

Publishes: Articles; Features; Fiction; Nonfiction; Reviews; *Areas:* Erotic; Lifestyle; Short Stories; *Markets:* Adult

Editors: Jamie Maclean (Fiction)

Literary lifestyle publication about sex and sexuality aimed at sophisticated, intelligent and mature readers. Print version has been retired and is now online only. Publishes features, articles, short stories, and reviews. See website for full submission guidelines.

Essex Life

Portman House
120 Princes Street
Ipswich
IP1 1RS
Tel: +44 (0) 7834 101686
Email: julian.read@archant.co.uk
Website: http://www.essexlifemag.co.uk

Publishes: Articles; Nonfiction; *Areas:* Arts; Cookery; Culture; Design; Entertainment; Gardening; Leisure; Lifestyle; Nature; *Markets:* Adult

Magazine publishing material relating to Essex.

Everyday Practical Electronics

Wimborne Publishing Ltd
113 Lynwood Drive
Merley
Wimborne
Dorset
BH21 1UU
Tel: +44 (0) 1202 880299

Fax: +44 (0) 1202 843233
Email: editorial@wimborne.co.uk
Website: http://www.epemag.com

Publishes: Articles; Nonfiction; *Areas:* Hobbies; Technology; *Markets:* Academic; Adult

Editors: Matt Pulzer

Publishes articles on electronics for students and hobbyists.

Family Office Magazine
FOE Limited
27 Old Gloucester Street
London
WC1N 3AX
Tel: +44(0) 20 7193 8870
Email: contact@familyofficeelite.com
Website: http://www.familyofficemag.com

Publishes: Articles; *Areas:* Business; Finance; Leisure; *Markets:* Professional; *Treatments:* Mainstream

Editors: Ty Murphy

Caters for the ultra-wealthy Family Office sector. The publication is widely read by the world's leading experts from many of the World's leading institutions from the Family Office and the wealth sector. Many of these institutions are regular advertisers and sponsors while others are contributors who provide insightful interviews and contributions for the magazine.

Some of these institutions include Deloitte, Manulife Asset Management, Caplin & Drysdale, City Bank, BNY Mellon, PWC, Ernst & Young, BMO Private Bank, ING Private Bank, TSG Europe, Piraeus Bank, Global Family Offices, Trusted Family, Family Office Institute. Fuchs & AssociÃ©s Finance, Credit Suisse, Northwood Family Office, Lugen Family Office, Guernsey Finance, Family Office Association, FOSS Family Office Services Switzerland, Luxembourg For Family Office and many others. Family Office Elite also has publishing agreements in place with some these institutions including Deloitte which contribute expert articles in every issue.

Luxury brands include Heirloom, Tesla Cars,

Heathrow Airport VIP , Luxury Channel, Ghurka Luggage, British Polo Day, 1066 Pianos, Holland & Holland, Burgess Yachts, DOMOS Fine Art, Signature Golf Events, Global Fine Arts Awards, Concierge-Aviation, Timeless Art Gallery, Charterworld, Alpha-Centauri Hydroplanes, Zimbali Costal Resorts, Chivas Luggage, Caprice Products, Polo & Tweed, Blenheim Palace, and more. Non – Profit Adverts include the Universal Film & Festival Organisation and Amnesty.

The Fenland Reed
Email: thefenlandreed@gmail.com
Website: https://www.thefenlandreed.co.uk

Publishes: Fiction; Poetry; *Areas:* Short Stories; *Markets:* Adult; *Treatments:* Literary

Editors: Jonathan Totman and Mary Livingstone

East Anglian literary magazine published biannually, with one themed and one non-themed issue each year. Publishes poetry and short stories. See website for full guidelines and any current theme.

The Field
Time Inc. (UK) Ltd
Pinehurst II, Pinehurst Road
Farnborough Business Park, Farnborough
Hampshire
GU14 7BF
Tel: +44 (0) 1252 555220
Email: field.secretary@timeinc.com
Website: http://www.thefield.co.uk

Publishes: Articles; Features; Nonfiction; *Areas:* Nature; *Markets:* Adult

Editors: Jonathan Young

Publishes material relating to the countryside, including shooting, food and drink, fishing, country houses, gundogs, etc.

Flash: The International Short-Short Story Magazine
Department of English
University of Chester
Parkgate Road

Chester
CH1 4BJ
Email: flash.magazine@chester.ac.uk
Website: http://www.chester.ac.uk/flash.
magazine

Publishes: Fiction; *Areas:* Short Stories;
Markets: Adult; *Treatments:* Literary

Editors: Dr Peter Blair; Dr Ashley Chantler

**Closed to submissions as at December
2017. Check website for current status**

Publishes flash fiction up to 360 words,
including the title. Send up to four pieces per
issue. Attach submissions to a single email.
See website for full submission guidelines.

Flora International
Wimborne Publishing Ltd
113 Lynwood Drive
Merley
Wimborne
Dorset
BH21 1UU
Tel: +44 (0) 1202 880299
Fax: +44 (0) 1202 843233
Email: enquiries@flora-magazine.co.uk
Website: http://flora-magazine.co.uk

Publishes: Articles; Nonfiction; *Areas:*
Crafts; Hobbies; How-to; Nature; *Markets:*
Adult; Professional

Editors: Nina Tucknott

Magazine aimed at florists and flower
arrangers.

Fly Fishing & Fly Tying Magazine
Locus Centre
The Square
Aberfeldy
Perthshire
PH15 2DD
Tel: +44 (0) 1887 829868
Fax: +44 (0) 1887 829856
Email: MarkB.ffft@btinternet.com
Website: http://flyfishing-and-flytying.co.uk

Publishes: Articles; Nonfiction; Reviews;
Areas: Nature; Sport; *Markets:* Adult

Editors: Mark Bowler

Magazine publishing articles and reviews
relating to fly fishing and fly tying.

Forage
Email: foragepoetry@gmail.com
Website: https://foragepoetry.com

Publishes: Essays; Nonfiction; Poetry;
Reviews; *Markets:* Adult; *Treatments:*
Literary

Publishes poetry, essays / creative
nonfiction, reviews, art and photography.
Submit up to five poems per issue. See
website for upcoming issues and submit
appropriate work by email.

Frieze
1 Montclare Street
London
E2 7EU
Tel: +44 (0) 20 3372 6111
Email: editors@frieze.com
Website: https://frieze.com

Publishes: Articles; Essays; Nonfiction;
Reviews; *Areas:* Arts; Culture; *Markets:*
Adult; *Treatments:* Contemporary

Magazine of contemporary European arts
and culture.

Geographical
3.20 Q West
1100 Great West Road
Brentford
Middlesex
TW8 0GP
Tel: +44 (0) 20 8332 8445
Fax: +44 (0) 20 8332 8438
Email: magazine@geographical.co.uk
Website: http://geographical.co.uk

Publishes: Articles; Nonfiction; *Areas:*
Culture; Nature; Science; Travel; *Markets:*
Adult

Publishes authoritative and educational
material covering a wide range of subject
areas, including geography, culture, wildlife
and exploration.

Gold Dust

Email: sirat@davidgardiner.net
Website: http://www.
golddustmagazine.co.uk

Publishes: Fiction; Poetry; Reviews; Scripts;
Areas: Drama; Short Stories; *Markets:*
Adult; *Treatments:* Literary

Editors: David Gardiner (Prose); Adele C
Geraghty (Poetry)

Publishes short stories, flash fiction, and
plays up to 3,000 words, poetry up to 50
lines, and book reviews up to 2,000 words.
Submit up to 5 submissions at a time, by
email. Accepts submissions December to
February and June to August. No
simultaneous submissions. See website for
full guidelines.

Golf Monthly

Pinehurst 2
Pinehurst Road
Farnborough Business Park
Farnborough
Hampshire
GU14 7BF
Tel: +44 (0) 1252 555197
Email: golfmonthly@timeinc.com
Website: http://www.golf-monthly.co.uk

Publishes: Articles; Features; Nonfiction;
Areas: Sport; *Markets:* Adult

Editors: Michael Harris

Golfing magazine. Publishes profiles on
players, and general features and columns.
Welcomes unsolicited MSS but approach in
writing with ideas first. No instruction
material from external contributors.

Good Housekeeping

72 Broadwick Street
London
W1F 9EP
Tel: +44 (0) 20 7439 5000
Fax: +44 (0) 20 7437 6886
Email: goodh.mail@hearst.co.uk
Website: http://www.
goodhousekeeping.co.uk

Publishes: Features; Nonfiction; *Areas:*
Cookery; Health; Lifestyle; Women's
Interests; *Markets:* Adult

Editors: Lindsay Nicholson

Monthly glossy women's magazine
publishing material on health, lifestyle,
cookery, etc.

GQ Magazine

Vogue House
1 Hanover Square
London
W1S 1JU
Email: onlineworkexperience@
condenast.co.uk
Website: http://www.gq-magazine.co.uk

Publishes: Articles; News; Nonfiction;
Areas: Beauty and Fashion; Culture;
Lifestyle; Men's Interests; Technology;
Markets: Adult

Magazine for men, covering fashion, culture,
watches, grooming, lifestyle, and girls.

Granta

12 Addison Avenue
Holland Park
London
W11 4QR
Tel: +44 (0) 20 7605 1360
Fax: +44 (0) 20 7605 1361
Email: editorial@granta.com
Website: http://www.granta.com

Publishes: Fiction; Nonfiction; Poetry;
Areas: Short Stories; *Markets:* Adult;
Treatments: Contemporary; Literary

Editors: Sigrid Rausing

Submit one story or essay, or up to three
poems, via online submission system. £3
charge for prose submissions. No specific
length limits for prose, but most pieces are
between 3,000 and 6,000 words. Unlikely to
read anything over 10,000 words.

H&E Naturist

Hawk Editorial Ltd
PO Box 545
Hull
HU9 9JF

Tel: +44 (0) 1482 342000
Email: editor@henaturist.net
Website: http://www.henaturist.net

Publishes: Articles; Essays; Features; News; Nonfiction; *Areas:* Arts; Culture; Historical; Lifestyle; Politics; Sociology; *Markets:* Adult

Editors: Sam Hawcroft

Publishes articles, essays, features, and opinion on life from a naturist angle. Send submissions by email as a .doc or .txt file, or by post on a CD or DVD, along with any images being supplied. See website for full guidelines.

Harper's Bazaar

The National Magazine Company Ltd
72 Broadwick Street
London
W1F 9EP
Tel: +44 (0) 20 7439 5000
Email: Justine.picardie@hearst.co.uk
Website: http://www.harpersbazaar.co.uk

Publishes: Articles; Features; News; Nonfiction; *Areas:* Arts; Beauty and Fashion; Business; Film; Health; Lifestyle; Theatre; Travel; Women's Interests; *Markets:* Adult

Editors: Justine Picardie

Women's glossy magazine aimed at discerning, style-conscious, intelligent 30+ women who are cultured, well-travelled and independent.

History Today

2nd Floor, 9 Staple Inn
London
WC1V 7QH
Tel: +44 (0) 20 3219 7810
Email: p.lay@historytoday.com
Website: http://www.historytoday.com

Publishes: Articles; Features; Nonfiction; *Areas:* Historical; *Markets:* Adult

Historical magazine publishing short articles (600-1,000 words); mid-length articles (1,300-2,200 words) and feature articles (3,500 to 4,000 words). Send query by email with proposal and details of your career /

academic background. See website for full guidelines.

House & Garden

Email: houseandgarden@condenast.co.uk
Website: http://www.houseandgarden.co.uk

Publishes: Articles; Nonfiction; *Areas:* Architecture; Cookery; Design; Gardening; Lifestyle; Travel; *Markets:* Adult

Editors: Hatta Byng

Publishes articles on gardens, architecture, home decor, recipes, travel, and lifestyle.

The Huffington Post (United Kingdom)

Shropshire House
11-20 Capper Street
London
WC1E 6JA
Email: HuffPostUK@huffingtonpost.com
Website: http://www.huffingtonpost.co.uk

Publishes: Articles; News; Nonfiction; *Areas:* Business; Current Affairs; Entertainment; Politics; Sport; Technology; *Markets:* Adult

UK branch of international online magazine of news and commentary. Send query by email to suggest news items or pitch ideas for a blog post. See website for specific contact details.

Improve Your Coarse Fishing

Media House
Peterborough Business Park
Peterborough
PE2 6EA
Tel: +44 (0) 1733 395102
Email: ben.miles@bauermedia.co.uk
Website: https://www.anglingtimes.co.uk/magazines/improve-your-coarse-fishing/

Publishes: Articles; Features; News; *Areas:* Leisure; Sport; *Markets:* Adult

Editors: Ben Miles

Magazine on coarse fishing.

Ink Sweat and Tears

Email: inksweatandtearssubmissions@
gmail.com
Website: http://www.inksweatandtears.co.uk

Publishes: Poetry; Reviews; *Markets:* Adult;
Treatments: Literary

Editors: Helen Ivory

UK-based webzine publishing poetry, prose,
prose-poetry, word and image pieces, and
poetry reviews. Send 4-6 pieces by email
only. Accepts unsolicited reviews of poetry
and short story collections. See website for
full guidelines.

Inside Soap

Hearst Magazines UK
72 Broadwick Street
London
W1F 9EP
Email: editor@insidesoap.co.uk
Website: http://www.insidesoap.co.uk

Publishes: Articles; Interviews; News;
Nonfiction; *Areas:* Entertainment; Media;
Markets: Adult

Editors: Steven Murphy

Magazine about UK soap operas. Query by
email in first instance.

The Interpreter's House

37A Spencer Street
Holywood
County Down
Northern Ireland
BT18 9DN
Email: theinterpretershouse@aol.com
Website: http://www.
theinterpretershouse.com

Publishes: Fiction; Poetry; *Areas:* Short
Stories; *Markets:* Adult; *Treatments:*
Literary

Editors: Georgi Gill

Send up to five poems or up to two short
stories by email in a single Word attachment,
or by post with SAE. Accepts work in
October, February, and June.

Interzone

TTA Press
5 Martins Lane
Witcham
Ely
Cambs
CB6 2LB
Website: http://ttapress.com

Publishes: Fiction; *Areas:* Fantasy; Sci-Fi;
Short Stories; *Markets:* Adult

Editors: Andy Cox

Publishes science fiction and fantasy short
stories up to about 10,000 words. No
simultaneous submissions, multiple
submissions or reprints. See website for full
guidelines and online submission system.

Irish Pages

129 Ormeau Road
Belfast
BT7 1SH
Tel: +44 (0) 2890 434800
Email: editor@irishpages.org
Website: http://www.irishpages.org

Publishes: Essays; Fiction; Nonfiction;
Poetry; Reviews; *Areas:* Autobiography;
Historical; Nature; Science; Short Stories;
Translations; *Markets:* Adult; *Treatments:*
Literary

Editors: Chris Agee

Non-partisan and non-sectarian literary
journal publishing writing from the island of
Ireland and elsewhere in equal measure.
Publishes work in English, and in the Irish
Language or Ulster Scots with English
translations or glosses. Welcomes
submissions throughout the year by post only
with stamps, coupons or cash for return
postage (no self-addressed envelope is
needed). See website for more details.

Jewish Quarterly

28 St Albans Lane
London
NW11 7QE
Email: Community@JewishQuarterly.org
Website: http://www.jewishquarterly.org

Publishes: Essays; Fiction; News; Nonfiction; Poetry; *Areas:* Arts; Culture; Current Affairs; Film; Historical; Literature; Music; Philosophy; Politics; Religious; Short Stories; *Markets:* Adult; *Treatments:* Contemporary; Literary

Says of itself it "leads the field in Jewish writing, covering a wide spectrum of subjects including art, criticism, fiction, film, history, Judaism, literature, poetry, philosophy, politics, theatre, the Shoah, Zionism and much more".

Kitchen Garden

Mortons Media Group Ltd
Media Centre
Morton Way
Horncastle
LN9 6JR
Tel: +44 (0) 1507 523456
Email: sott@mortons.co.uk
Website: http://www.kitchengarden.co.uk

Publishes: Articles; Features; Nonfiction; *Areas:* Cookery; Gardening; Hobbies; How-to; *Markets:* Adult

Editors: Steve Ott

Magazine for people who grow their own fresh fruit and vegetables.

The Lawyer

Centaur Communications Ltd
Wells Point
79 Wells Street
London
W1T 3QN
Tel: +44 (0) 20 7970 4637
Email: editorial@thelawyer.com
Website: https://www.thelawyer.com

Publishes: Articles; Features; News; Nonfiction; *Areas:* Legal; *Markets:* Professional

Editors: Catrin Griffiths

Weekly magazine for the legal profession, publishing news, articles, and features.

Leisure Painter

The Artists' Publishing Company Ltd.
Caxton House

63-65 High Street
Tenterden
Kent TN30 6BD
Tel: +44 (0) 1580 763315
Website: http://www.painters-online.co.uk

Publishes: Articles; Features; Nonfiction; *Areas:* Arts; Hobbies; How-to; *Markets:* Adult

Editors: Ingrid Lyon

Magazine offering artistic inspiration, guidance, tuition and encouragement for beginners and amateur artists. Includes features and step-by-step painting and drawing demonstrations.

LGC (Local Government Chronicle)

EMAP Publishing Limited
Telephone House
69 – 77 Paul Street
London
EC2A 4NQ
Tel: +44 (0) 20 3953 2774
Email: lgcnews@emap.com
Website: https://www.lgcplus.com

Publishes: Articles; News; Nonfiction; *Areas:* Business; Politics; Sociology; *Markets:* Professional

Editors: Nick Golding

Magazine aimed at managers in local government.

Lighthouse

Email: submissions@lighthouse.gatehousepress.com
Website: http://www.gatehousepress.com/lighthouse/

Publishes: Fiction; Poetry; *Areas:* Short Stories; *Markets:* Adult; *Treatments:* Contemporary; Literary

Magazine of contemporary fiction and poetry, aimed at a UK audience. Submit up to six poems or up to one piece of fiction by email as attachments. No previously published material or simultaneous submissions. See website for full guidelines.

Litro Magazine
1-15 Cremer Street
Studio 213
E2 8HD
Tel: +44 (0) 20 3371 9971
Email: editor@litro.co.uk
Website: http://www.litro.co.uk

Publishes: Features; Fiction; Interviews;
Nonfiction; Poetry; Reviews; *Areas:* Arts;
Autobiography; Culture; Lifestyle;
Literature; Politics; Short Stories;
Translations; Travel; *Markets:* Adult;
Treatments: Literary

Free print publication and online platform
publishing short fiction, flash/micro fiction,
nonfiction (memoir, literary journalism,
travel narratives, etc), and original artwork in
the print magazine, and short fiction, essays,
reviews, and features on the online platform.
Publishes poetry and novel extracts in the
print magazine but does not accept
unsolicited submissions in these areas. Does
not publish poetry online. See website for
full guidelines and to submit.

The London Magazine
11 Queen's Gate
London
SW7 5EL
Tel: +44 (0) 20 7584 5977
Fax: +44 (0) 20 7225 3273
Email: info@thelondonmagazine.org
Website: http://thelondonmagazine.org

Publishes: Articles; Essays; Features;
Fiction; Nonfiction; Poetry; Reviews; *Areas:*
Arts; Autobiography; Criticism; Literature;
Short Stories; *Markets:* Adult; *Treatments:*
Literary

Send submissions by email, or through
online submission system. Does not
normally publish science fiction or fantasy
writing, or erotica. Will consider postal
submissions, but prefers submissions
electronically. See website for full
guidelines, specific submission email
addresses, and/or to access online
submission system.

London Review of Books
28 Little Russell Street
London
WC1A 2HN
Tel: +44 (0) 20 7209 1101
Fax: +44 (0) 20 7209 1151
Email: edit@lrb.co.uk
Website: http://www.lrb.co.uk

Publishes: Articles; Essays; Nonfiction;
Poetry; Reviews; *Areas:* Arts; Culture; Film;
Literature; Politics; Science; *Markets:* Adult;
Treatments: Literary

Editors: Mary-Kay Wilmers

Contact editor in writing in first instance,
including SAE. Publishes mainly reviews,
essays, and articles, but also publishes
poetry.

Lothian Life
4/8 Downfield Place
Edinburgh
EH11 2EW
Tel: +44 (0) 7905 614402
Email: anne@lothianlife.co.uk
Website: http://www.lothianlife.co.uk

Publishes: Articles; Features; News;
Nonfiction; *Areas:* Arts; Cookery; Design;
Gardening; Health; Travel; *Markets:* Adult

Editors: Anne Hamilton

Magazine relating to the Lothians. Publishes
regular articles, news stories, local walks,
and features relating to the area.

Magma
23 Pine Walk
Carshalton
SM5 4ES
Email: info@magmapoetry.com
Website: http://www.magmapoetry.com

Publishes: Nonfiction; Poetry; Reviews;
Areas: Literature; *Markets:* Adult;
Treatments: Literary

Editors: Laurie Smith

Prefers submissions through online
submission system. Postal submissions
accepted from the UK only, and must
include SAE. No submissions by email.

Accepts poems and artwork. Poems are considered for one issue only – they are not held over from one issue to the next. Seeks poems that give a direct sense of what it is to live today – honest about feelings, alert about world, sometimes funny, always well crafted. Also publishes reviews of books and pamphlets of poetry. See website for details.

marie claire

Time Inc. (UK) Ltd
Blue Fin Building
110 Southwark Street
London
SE1 0SU
Tel: +44 (0) 20 3148 5000
Email: marieclaire@timeinc.com
Website: http://www.timeincuk.com/brands/marie-claire-uk/

Publishes: Articles; Features; Nonfiction; *Areas:* Beauty and Fashion; Health; Lifestyle; Travel; Women's Interests; *Markets:* Adult; *Treatments:* Commercial

Editors: Trish Halpin

Glossy magazine for women.

Maritime Journal

Spinnaker House
Waterside Gardens
Fareham
Hampshire
PO16 8SD
Tel: +44 (0) 1329 825335
Fax: +44 (0) 1329 550192
Email: editor@maritimejournal.com
Website: http://www.maritimejournal.com

Publishes: Articles; News; Nonfiction; *Areas:* Business; Travel; *Markets:* Professional

Magazine providing insight for the European commercial marine business.

Modern Poetry in Translation

The Queens College
Oxford
OX1 4AW
Tel: +44 (0) 1865 244701
Email: submissions@mptmagazine.com

Website: http://modernpoetryintranslation.com

Publishes: Essays; Nonfiction; Poetry; *Areas:* Literature; Translations; *Markets:* Adult

Editors: Clare Pollard

Respected poetry series originally founded by prominent poets in the sixties. New Series continues their editorial policy: translation of good poets by translators who are often themselves poets, fluent in the foreign language, and sometimes working with the original poet. See website for submission guidelines.

Mojo

Bauer Media
Endeavour House
189 Shaftesbury Avenue
London
WC2H 8JG
Tel: +44 (0) 20 7208 3443
Email: MOJO@bauermedia.co.uk
Website: http://www.mojo4music.com

Publishes: Articles; Interviews; News; Nonfiction; Reviews; *Areas:* Music; *Markets:* Adult; *Treatments:* Serious

Rock music magazine publishing news, reviews, and interviews.

Moneywise

First Floor, Standon House
21 Mansell Street
London
E1 8AA
Email: editorial@moneywise.co.uk
Website: http://www.moneywise.co.uk

Publishes: Articles; News; Nonfiction; *Areas:* Business; Finance; *Markets:* Adult

Helps people learn how to make the most of their money, helping them to identify the right investment products, and avoid the unnecessary costs associated with some financial products.

Motorcycle News (MCN)

Media House
Lynch Wood

Peterborough
PE2 6EA
Tel: +44 (0) 1858 438884
Email: andy.calton@motorcyclenews.com
Website: https://www.motorcyclenews.com

Publishes: Articles; Features; Nonfiction;
Areas: Leisure; Technology; Travel;
Markets: Adult

Editors: Andy Calton

Magazine for motorbike enthusiasts.

The Motorship

Mercator Media Ltd
Spinnaker House
Waterside Gardens
Fareham
Hampshire
PO16 8SD
Tel: +44 (0) 1329 825335
Fax: +44 (0) 1329 550192
Email: editor@motorship.com
Website: http://www.motorship.com

Publishes: Articles; News; Nonfiction;
Areas: Business; Technology; Travel;
Markets: Professional

Magazine aimed at marine technology
professionals.

Mslexia

PO Box 656
Newcastle upon Tyne
NE99 1PZ
Tel: +44 (0) 1912 048860
Email: postbag@mslexia.co.uk
Website: http://www.mslexia.co.uk

Publishes: Articles; Essays; Features;
Fiction; Interviews; News; Nonfiction;
Poetry; Reference; Reviews; *Areas:*
Autobiography; Short Stories; Women's
Interests; *Markets:* Adult

By women, for women who write, who want
to write, who teach creative writing or who
have an interest in women's literature and
creativity. It is a mixture of original work,
features, news, views, advice and listings.
The UK's only magazine devoted to women
writers and their writing.

See website for themes of upcoming issues /

competitions.

Publishes features, columns, reviews, flash
fiction, and literature listings. Some themes
are open to subscribers only. Submit via
online submission system on website.

Music Week

NewBay Media Europe Ltd
Emerson Studios
4th Floor
4-8 Emerson Street
London
SE1 9DU
Tel: +44 (0) 20 7226 7246
Email: msutherland@nbmedia.com
Website: http://www.musicweek.com

Publishes: Articles; News; Nonfiction;
Areas: Business; Music; *Markets:* Adult;
Professional

Editors: Mark Sutherland

Weekly magazine covering the music
business, including production, marketing,
and retailing.

Nature

The Macmillan Building
4-6 Crinan Street
London
N1 9XW
Tel: +44 (0) 20 7833 4000
Fax: +44 (0) 20 7843 4596
Email: nature@nature.com
Website: http://www.nature.com

Publishes: Articles; News; Nonfiction;
Areas: Science; *Markets:* Academic; Adult;
Professional

Editors: Philip Campbell

Journal covering all aspects of science.
Scope for freelance writers with specialist
knowledge.

The New Accelerator

Email: editors@thenewaccelerator.com
Website: http://thenewaccelerator.com

Publishes: Fiction; *Areas:* Entertainment;
Fantasy; Horror; Religious; Science; Sci-Fi;
Short Stories; Spiritual; Technology;

Thrillers; *Markets:* Adult; *Treatments:* Commercial; Contemporary; Dark; Experimental; Literary; Positive; Progressive; Satirical; Serious; Traditional

Editors: Andy Coughlan and David Winstanley

A Science Fiction short story anthology. Published monthly through Apple's Newsstand app and Google Play, the anthology will be available to billions of iOS and Android users worldwide.

The aim of the anthology is to bring cutting-edge fiction to an eager and discerning global Science Fiction audience.

New Fairy Tales

Email: editor@newfairytales.co.uk
Website: http://www.newfairytales.co.uk

Publishes: Fiction; Poetry; *Areas:* Short Stories; *Markets:* Adult; Children's; Family; Youth

Editors: Claire Massey

Note: Closed to submissions as at January 2016

Publishes new original fairy tales, suitable for adults and children. Not looking for retellings or reimaginings of existing fairy tales. Send submissions and queries by email; see website for full guidelines.

New Scientist

110 High Holborn
London
WC1V 6EU
Email: richard.webb@newscientist.com
Website: http://www.newscientist.com

Publishes: Articles; Features; News; Nonfiction; Reviews; *Areas:* Science; Technology; *Markets:* Adult; Professional

Editors: Richard Webb

Weekly science magazine. No unsolicited MSS but accepts pitches by email. See website for more details and specific contact details and focus areas for the different editors. Reviews are commissioned.

New Statesman

John Carpenter House
7 Carmelite Street
Blackfriars
London
EC4Y 0BS
Tel: +44 (0) 20 7936 6400
Fax: +44 (0) 20 7305 7304
Email: editorial@newstatesman.co.uk
Website: http://www.newstatesman.com

Publishes: Articles; Features; News; Nonfiction; Poetry; Reviews; *Areas:* Arts; Current Affairs; Politics; *Markets:* Adult

Editors: Jason Cowley

Weekly political magazine. For nonfiction, send initial pitch by email to address provided on website. No fiction, but welcomes poems up to 30 lines, on any subject and in any style (do not need to be political). Send up to 4 poems by email in the body of the email or as a single Word attachment, to the specific poetry email address provided on the website.

New Welsh Reader

PO Box 170
Aberystwyth
SY23 1WZ
Tel: +44 (0) 1970 628410
Email: submissions@newwelshreview.com
Website: http://www.newwelshreview.com

Publishes: Features; Fiction; Nonfiction; Poetry; Reviews; *Areas:* Short Stories; *Markets:* Adult; *Treatments:* Literary

Editors: Gwen Davies

Focus is on Welsh writing in English, but has an outlook which is deliberately diverse, encompassing broader UK and international contexts. For feature articles, send 300-word query by email. Submit fiction or up to 6 poems by email only. Postal submissions will be returned unopened. Full details available on website.

Note: Not accepting fiction submissions as at May 2018 due to high volume of submissions. See website for current status.

Nine Muses Poetry

Email: ninemusespoetry@talktalk.net
Website: https://ninemusespoetry.com

Publishes: Poetry; *Markets:* Adult;
Treatments: Literary

Editors: Annest Gwilym

A webzine featuring all forms of poetry by
new, emerging and established poets,
showcasing the best of contemporary poetry.

The North

The Poetry Business
Campo House
54 Campo Lane
Sheffield
S1 2EG
Tel: +44 (0) 1144 384074
Email: office@poetrybusiness.co.uk
Website: http://www.poetrybusiness.co.uk

Publishes: Articles; Poetry; Reviews; *Areas:*
Autobiography; Criticism; Literature;
Markets: Adult; *Treatments:* Contemporary;
Literary

Editors: Peter Sansom; Ann Sansom

Send up to 6 poems with SASE / return
postage. We publish the best of
contemporary poetry. No "genre" or
derivative poetry. Submitters should be
aware of, should preferably have read, the
magazine before submitting. See our website
for notes on submitting poems. No
submissions by email.

Also publishes critical articles and reviews
of contemporary poetry. Submit
ideas/synopses only in first instance.

Nursing Times

EMAP Publishing Company
7th Floor, Vantage London
Great West Road
Brentford
TW8 9AG
Tel: +44 (0) 20 3953 2707
Fax: +44 (0) 20 7874 0505
Email: jenni.middleton@emap.com
Website: http://www.nursingtimes.net

Publishes: Articles; Nonfiction; *Areas:*
Health; Medicine; *Markets:* Professional;
Treatments: Contemporary

Editors: Jenni Middleton

Magazine aimed at nurses, covering all
aspects of health care and nursing.

The Oldie

65 Newman Street
London
W1T 3EG
Tel: +44 (0) 20 7436 8801
Email: editorial@theoldie.co.uk
Website: http://www.theoldie.co.uk

Publishes: Articles; Features; *Areas:*
Humour; *Markets:* Adult

Editors: Richard Ingrams

Prefers to receive completed articles by
email (see website for specific email
address). No commissions based on ideas.
Publishes cartoons, letters, articles, and
features on a range of topics, with a
humorous slant, aimed at the older reader.
No poetry.

Olive

Vineyard House
44 Brook Green
Hammersmith
London
W6 7BT
Tel: +44 (0) 020 7150 5000
Email: oliveweb@immediate.co.uk
Website: http://www.olivemagazine.com

Publishes: Articles; Features; Nonfiction;
Areas: Cookery; *Markets:* Adult

Monthly food magazine. Welcomes
unsolicited queries but responds only when
interested.

Orbis International Literary Journal

17 Greenhow Avenue
West Kirby
Wirral
CH48 5EL
Email: carolebaldock@hotmail.com
Website: http://www.orbisjournal.com

Publishes: Articles; Essays; Features; Fiction; News; Nonfiction; Poetry; Reviews; *Areas:* Arts; Humour; Short Stories; Women's Interests; *Markets:* Adult; *Treatments:* Literary

Editors: Carole Baldock

One of the longest running UK magazines; established 1969

And one of the most highly regarded; Peter Finch, Chief Executive of the Welsh Academi includes this magazine in his Top 10 publications (The Poetry Business).

Around one third of the poems in each issue are from Overseas (and around one fifth of subscribers):read, enjoy, inwardly digest; and improve your chances of being published abroad.

One of the few magazines which is also a useful resource. Includes news items, competition listings and magazine reviews.

One of the few magazines to provide contributors with proofs and editorial critique.

Readers' Award: £50 for the piece receiving the most votes, plus £50 between four runners-up.

Oxford Poetry
Magdalen College
Oxford
OX1 4AU
Email: editors@oxfordpoetry.co.uk
Website: http://www.oxfordpoetry.co.uk

Publishes: Essays; Interviews; Nonfiction; Poetry; Reviews; *Areas:* Translations; *Markets:* Adult; *Treatments:* Literary

Closed to submissions as at July 2018. Check website for current status.

Publishes poems, interviews, reviews, and essays. Accepts unpublished poems on any theme and of any length. Send up to four poems by email. See website for full details.

Park Home and Holiday Caravan
Kelsey Publishing
Cudham Tithe Barn
Berry's Hill
Cudham
Kent
TN16 3AG
Tel: +44 (0) 1959 541444
Email: phhc.ed@kelsey.co.uk
Website: https://www. parkhomemagazine.co.uk

Publishes: Articles; Features; News; Nonfiction; *Areas:* Hobbies; How-to; Lifestyle; Travel; *Markets:* Adult

Editors: Alex Melvin

Magazine for those owning holiday caravans or living in residential park homes.

People Management
Email: pmeditorial@haymarket.com
Website: http://www. peoplemanagement.co.uk

Publishes: Articles; Features; Nonfiction; *Areas:* Business; How-to; Legal; *Markets:* Professional

Editors: Robert Jeffery

Human resources magazine, publishing articles and features on all aspects of managing and developing people at work.

The People's Friend
80 Kingsway East
Dundee
DD4 8SL
Tel: +44 (0) 1382 462276
Fax: +44 (0) 1382 452491
Email: peoplesfriend@dcthomson.co.uk
Website: http://www.thepeoplesfriend.co.uk

Publishes: Articles; Features; Fiction; Nonfiction; Poetry; *Areas:* Adventure; Cookery; Crafts; Crime; Hobbies; Mystery; Nature; Romance; Short Stories; Thrillers; Travel; Women's Interests; *Markets:* Adult; Family; *Treatments:* Traditional

Publishes complete short stories (1,200-3,000 words (4,000 for specials)) and serials, focusing on character development rather than complex plots, plus 10,000-word crime thrillers. Also considers nonfiction from nature to nostalgia and from holidays to hobbies. Guidelines available on website.

People's Friend Pocket Novels

80 Kingsway East
Dundee
DD4 8SL
Tel: +44 (0) 1382 223131
Email: tsteel@dcthomson.co.uk
Website: http://www.thepeoplesfriend.co.uk

Publishes: Fiction; *Areas:* Romance; *Markets:* Adult; Family

Editors: Tracey Steel

Publishes romance and family fiction between 40,000 and 42,000 words, aimed at adults aged over 30. Send query by post or by email (preferred) with synopsis and first two chapters in first instance. See website for more information.

Picture Postcard Monthly

6 Carmarthen Avenue
Drayton
Portsmouth
Hampshire
PO6 2AQ
Tel: +44 (0) 2392 423527
Email: info@picturepostcardmagazine.co.uk
Website: http://www.picturepostcardmagazine.co.uk

Publishes: Articles; Features; News; Nonfiction; Reference; *Areas:* Arts; Hobbies; Photography; *Markets:* Adult

Editors: Mark Wingham

Magazine for postcard collectors, publishing news, views, stories and feature articles.

Planet

PO Box 44
Aberystwyth
Ceredigion
SY23 3ZZ
Tel: +44 (0) 1970 611255
Email: submissions@planetmagazine.org.uk
Website: http://www.planetmagazine.org.uk

Publishes: Articles; Features; Fiction; Nonfiction; Poetry; Reviews; *Areas:* Arts; Current Affairs; Literature; Music; Politics; Short Stories; Theatre; *Markets:* Adult; *Treatments:* Literary

Editors: Emily Trahair

Publishes mostly commissioned material, but will accept ideas for articles and reviews, and unsolicited submissions of fiction and poetry. Submit one piece of short fiction between 1,500 and 2,500 words, or 4-6 poems at a time. A range of styles and themes are accepted, but postal submissions will not be considered unless adequate return postage is provided. If you have an idea for a relevant article send a query with brief synopsis.

PN Review

4th Floor
Alliance House
Cross Street
Manchester
M2 7AP
Tel: +44 (0) 161 834 8730
Fax: +44 (0) 161 832 0084
Email: schmidt@carcanet.co.uk
Website: http://www.pnreview.co.uk

Publishes: Articles; Features; Interviews; News; Poetry; Reviews; *Areas:* Translations; *Markets:* Adult

Editors: Michael Schmidt

Send query with synopsis and sample pages, after having familiarised yourself with the magazine. Accepts prose up to 15 double-spaced pages or 4 poems / 5 pages of poetry.

Bimonthly magazine of poetry and poetry criticism. Includes editorial, letters, news, articles, interviews, features, poems, translations, and a substantial book review section. No short stories, children's prose / poetry, or non-poetry related work (academic, biography etc.). Accepts electronic submissions from individual subscribers only – otherwise only hard copy submissions are considered.

Poetry London

The Albany
Douglas Way
Deptford
London
SE8 4AG
Tel: +44 (0) 20 8691 7260
Email: admin@poetrylondon.co.uk
Website: http://www.poetrylondon.co.uk

Publishes: Features; Nonfiction; Poetry;
Reviews; *Areas:* Translations; *Markets:*
Adult; *Treatments:* Contemporary; Literary

Editors: Ahren Warner; Martha Kapos

Send up to six poems with SASE or adequate
return postage. Considers poems by both
new and established poets. Also publishes
book reviews. No submissions by email.

The Poetry Review

The Poetry Society
22 Betterton Street
London
WC2H 9BX
Tel: +44 (0) 20 7420 9880
Fax: +44 (0) 20 7240 4818
Email: poetryreview@poetrysociety.org.uk
Website: http://www.poetrysociety.org.uk

Publishes: Essays; Nonfiction; Poetry;
Reviews; *Areas:* Translations; *Markets:*
Adult; *Treatments:* Literary

Describes itself as "one of the liveliest and
most influential literary magazines in the
world", and has been associated with the rise
of the New Generation of British poets –
Carol Ann Duffy, Simon Armitage, Glyn
Maxwell, Don Paterson... though its scope
extends beyond the UK, with special issues
focusing on poetries from around the world.
Poets from the UK must submit by post;
those from elsewhere in the world may
submit using online system. See website for
details. Send up to 6 unpublished poems, or
literary translations of poems.

Poetry Wales

57 Nolton Street
Bridgend
CF31 3AE
Tel: +44 (0) 1656 663018

Email: info@poetrywales.co.uk
Website: http://poetrywales.co.uk

Publishes: Essays; Nonfiction; Poetry;
Reviews; *Markets:* Adult

Editors: Nia Davies

Publishes poetry, features, and reviews from
Wales and beyond. Send up to six poems in
one .doc file with your name, contact details,
and short bio up to 50 words, via online
submission system (see website).

The Police Journal

SAGE Publications Ltd
1 Oliver's Yard
55 City Road
London
EC1Y 1SP
Tel: +44 (0) 20 7324 8500
Fax: +44 (0) 20 7324 8600
Email: authorqueries@sagepub.co.uk
Website: https://uk.sagepub.com/en-gb/eur/
the-police-journal/journal202314

Publishes: Articles; Nonfiction; *Areas:*
Crime; Legal; *Markets:* Professional

Editors: Colin Rogers

Publishes articles aimed at police forces
around the world. Submit using online
submission manager only.

The Pool

Email: hello@thepoolltd.com
Website: https://www.the-pool.com

Publishes: Articles; News; Nonfiction;
Areas: Arts; Beauty and Fashion; Culture;
Health; Lifestyle; Women's Interests;
Markets: Adult

Online platform for news and comment
aimed at women. Send proposals by email.

The Practising Midwife

Medical Education Solutions Ltd
Monks Ridge
Burrows Lane
Gomshall
GU5 9QE
Tel: +44 (0) 20 8313 9617
Email: laurayeates@virginmedia.com

Website: http://www.
practisingmidwife.co.uk

Publishes: Articles; News; Nonfiction;
Areas: Health; Medicine; Women's
Interests; *Markets:* Professional

Editors: Laura Yeates

Publishes accessible, authoritative and
readable information for midwives, students
and other professionals in the maternity
services.

Press Gazette
40 Hatton Garden
London
EC1N 8EV
Tel: +44 (0) 20 7936 6433
Email: pged@pressgazette.co.uk
Website: http://www.pressgazette.co.uk

Publishes: Articles; Features; News;
Nonfiction; *Areas:* Current Affairs; Media;
Markets: Professional

Editors: Freddy Mayhew

Publishes news, features, and analysis related
to all areas of journalism: print,
broadcasting, online; national, regional,
magazines, etc. Pitch stories by phone or by
email.

Prole
Prolebooks
15 Maes-y-Dre
Abergele
Conwy
LL22 7HW
Email: submissionspoetry@
prolebooks.co.uk
Website: http://www.prolebooks.co.uk

Publishes: Fiction; Nonfiction; Poetry;
Areas: Short Stories; *Markets:* Adult;
Treatments: Literary

Publishes accessible literature of high
quality, including poetry, short fiction, and
creative nonfiction. Seeks to appeal to a wide
audience and avoid literary elitism (obscure
references and highly stylised structures and
forms are unlikely to find favour). No
previously published material or
simultaneous submissions. Submit one piece

of prose or up to five poems in the body of
an email, with your name, contact details,
word count and third person author bio up to
100 words. See website for appropriate email
addresses for prose and poetry submissions,
and full submission guidelines. No
attachments.

Psychologies
KELSEY Media Ltd
Cudham Tithe Barn
Berry's Hill
Cudham
Kent
TN16 3AG
Email: suzy.greaves@psychologies.co.uk
Website: https://www.psychologies.co.uk

Publishes: Articles; Nonfiction; *Areas:*
Beauty and Fashion; Cookery; Culture;
Health; Lifestyle; Travel; Women's
Interests; *Markets:* Adult

Editors: Suzy Greaves

Grown up women's lifestyle magazine,
seeking to enrich women's emotional lives.
Covers self, relationships, family, work,
beauty and wellbeing, culture, travel, food
and more.

Pulse
Cogora Limited
140 London Wall
London
EC2Y 5DN
Tel: +44 (0) 20 7214 0567
Email: jaimiekaffash@cogora.com
Website: http://www.pulsetoday.co.uk

Publishes: Articles; Nonfiction; *Areas:*
Medicine; *Markets:* Professional

Editors: Jaimie Kaffash

Magazine aimed at GPs.

Radio Times
Vineyard House
44 Brook Green
London
W6 7BT
Tel: +44 (0) 20 7150 5800
Fax: +44 (0) 20 8433 3160

Email: feedback@radiotimes.com
Website: http://www.radiotimes.com

Publishes: Articles; Interviews; News; Nonfiction; *Areas:* Entertainment; Radio; TV; *Markets:* Adult

Articles and interviews relating to UK TV and radio. All articles are commissioned. Willing to consider synopses and ideas, but no unsolicited mss.

The Railway Magazine
Mortons Media Group Ltd
Morton Way
Horncastle
Lincolnshire
LN9 6JR
Tel: +44 (0) 1507 529589
Email: cmilner@mortons.co.uk
Website: https://www.
railwaymagazine.co.uk

Publishes: Articles; News; Nonfiction; *Areas:* Historical; Technology; Travel; *Markets:* Adult

Editors: Chris Milner

Magazine for the railway community, covering all aspects from steam through to modern rail developments.

Reach
IDP
24 Forest Houses
Halwill
Beaworthy
Devon
EX21 5UU
Email: publishing@indigodreams.co.uk
Website: http://www.indigodreams.co.uk/
reach-poetry/4563791643

Publishes: Poetry; *Markets:* Adult; *Treatments:* Literary

Editors: Ronnie Goodyer

Publishes quality poetry from both experienced and new poets. Formal or free verse, haiku... everything is considered. Subscribers can comment on and vote for poetry from the previous issue, the winner receiving £50, plus regular in-house anthologies and competitions. Receives no external funding and depends entirely on subscriptions.

Record Collector Magazine
The Perfume Factory
Room 101, Diamond Publishing Ltd
140 Wales Farm Road
London
W3 6UG
Tel: +44 (0) 870 732 8080
Email: ian.mccann@metropolis.co.uk
Website: http://www.
recordcollectormag.com

Publishes: Articles; Features; Nonfiction; *Areas:* Hobbies; Music; *Markets:* Adult

Editors: Ian McCann

Magazine on record collecting. Most material is commissioned, but will consider unsolicited mss and welcomes ideas for articles and features.

Reform
86 Tavistock Place
London
WC1H 9RT
Tel: +44 (0) 20 7916 8630
Email: reform@urc.org.uk
Website: http://www.reform-magazine.co.uk

Publishes: Articles; Features; News; Nonfiction; *Areas:* Current Affairs; Religious; Sociology; Spiritual; *Markets:* Adult

Describes itself as a magazine for thinking people "who enjoy reading about Christian ideas from a range of viewpoints".

Report
Association of Teachers and Lecturers
7 Northumberland Street
London
WC2N 5RD
Tel: +44 (0) 20 7930 6441
Fax: +44 (0) 20 7930 1359
Website: http://www.atl.org.uk

Publishes: Articles; Nonfiction; *Markets:* Professional

Magazine for teachers and lecturers publishing articles of practical interest to the target audience.

Restaurant Magazine

William Reed Business Media Ltd
Broadfield Park
Crawley
RH11 9RT
Tel: +44 (0) 1293 610342
Email: Stefan.chomka@wrbm.com
Website: http://www.restaurantmagazine.co.uk

Publishes: Articles; Features; News; Nonfiction; *Areas:* Business; Cookery; *Markets:* Professional

Editors: Stefan Chomka

Magazine publishing articles, features, and news for the restaurant trade.

Retail Week

EMAP Publishing Limited
Telephone House
69 – 77 Paul Street
London
EC2A 4NQ
Email: chris.brook-carter@emap.com
Website: http://www.retail-week.com

Publishes: Articles; Features; News; Nonfiction; *Areas:* Business; *Markets:* Professional

Magazine for the retail industry.

The Rialto

PO Box 309
Aylsham
Norwich
NR11 6LN
Email: info@therialto.co.uk
Website: http://www.therialto.co.uk

Publishes: Articles; Nonfiction; Poetry; Reviews; *Markets:* Adult; *Treatments:* Literary

Editors: Michael Mackmin

Send up to six poems with SASE or adequate return postage, or submit through online submission system. No submissions by email. Reviews and articles commissioned.

Running

Kelsey Media
Cudham Tithe Barn
Berry's Hill
Cudham
Kent
TN16 3AG
Email: rf.ed@kelsey.co.uk
Website: https://www.runnersradar.com

Publishes: Articles; Nonfiction; *Areas:* Health; Hobbies; Leisure; Sport; *Markets:* Adult

Magazine for runners, including advice on health, fitness, and injury.

RUSI Journal

Royal United Services Institute
Whitehall
London
SW1A 2ET
Tel: +44 (0) 20 7747 2615
Email: publications@rusi.org
Website: https://rusi.org

Publishes: Articles; Nonfiction; Reviews; *Areas:* Historical; Military; Technology; *Markets:* Professional

Editors: Emma De Angelis

Journal publishing articles, book reviews, and letters to the editor, relating to defence, international security, military history, etc. See website for submission guidelines.

Sarasvati

24 Forest Houses
Halwill
Beaworthy
Devon
EX21 5UU
Email: dawnidp@gmail.com
Website: http://www.indigodreams.co.uk/sarasvati/4563791846

Publishes: Fiction; Poetry; *Areas:* Short Stories; *Markets:* Adult

Editors: Dawn Bauling

Showcases poetry and prose. Each contributor will have three to four A5 pages available to their work. Submit up to five poems, or prose up to 1,000 words.

The Savage Kick

Murder Slim Press
22 Bridge Meadow
Hemsby
Norfolk
NR29 4NE
Email: murderslimpress@gmail.com
Website: http://www.murderslim.com/
TheSavageKick.html

Publishes: Articles; Fiction; Interviews; Nonfiction; *Areas:* Crime; Literature; Military; Westerns; *Markets:* Adult; *Treatments:* Niche

Accepts only three or four stories per year. Publishes work dealing with any passionately held emotion and/or alternative viewpoints. Sleazy tales are encouraged. Prefers real-life stories. No genre fiction or poetry. See website for full submission guidelines. Also accepts articles and interviews relating to authors on the reading list provided on the website.

Scintilla

Email: subscriptions@ vaughanassociation.org
Website: http://www.vaughanassociation.org

Publishes: Articles; Essays; Fiction; Nonfiction; Poetry; *Areas:* Drama; Health; Nature; Science; Spiritual; *Markets:* Adult; *Treatments:* Literary

Editors: Joseph Sterrett; Damian Walford Davies; Dr. Kevin Mills; Erik Ankerberg

An international, peer-reviewed journal of literary criticism, prose, and new poetry in the metaphysical tradition. Submit using online submission form.

Scots Heritage Magazine

496 Ferry Road
Edinburgh
EH5 2DL
Tel: +44 (0) 1315 511000
Fax: +44 (0) 1315 517900

Email: editor@scotsheritagemagazine.com
Website: http://www.
scotsheritagemagazine.com

Publishes: Articles; Features; Nonfiction; *Areas:* Historical; *Markets:* Adult

Editors: Richard Bath

Magazine of Scottish history, aimed at people of Scottish descent all over the world.

SelfBuild & Design

151 Station Street
Burton on Trent
DE14 1BG
Tel: +44 (0) 1584 841417
Email: ross.stokes@sbdonline.co.uk
Website: http://www.selfbuildanddesign.com

Publishes: Articles; Nonfiction; *Areas:* Design; How-to; *Markets:* Adult

Editors: Ross Stokes

Magazine aimed at those intending to build or manage the build of their own home, or any major building project.

The Sewing Directory

11a Tedders Close
Hemyock
Cullompton
EX15 3XD
Tel: +44 (0) 1823 680588
Email: fiona@thesewingdirectory.net
Website: http://www.
thesewingdirectory.co.uk

Publishes: Articles; Features; Nonfiction; *Areas:* Crafts; Hobbies; *Markets:* Adult

Editors: Fiona Pullen

Online sewing directory, publishing articles on sewing and sewing projects.

SFX

Future Publishing Limited Quay House
The Ambury
Bath
BA1 1UA
Email: sfx@futurenet.com
Website: http://www.gamesradar.com/sfx/

Publishes: Articles; News; Nonfiction;
Areas: Fantasy; Film; Hobbies; Sci-Fi; TV;
Markets: Adult; Youth

Magazine covering science fiction and
fantasy TV, films, comics, and games.

Shooter Literary Magazine
Email: submissions.shooterlitmag@
gmail.com
Website: https://shooterlitmag.com

Publishes: Essays; Fiction; Nonfiction;
Poetry; *Markets:* Adult; *Treatments:* Literary

Publishes literary fiction, poetry, creative
nonfiction and narrative journalism relating
to specific themes for each issue. Send one
piece of prose between 2,000 and 7,500
words or up to three poems per issue, by
email. See website for current theme and full
submission guidelines.

ShortStorySunday.com
27 Old Gloucester Street
London
WC1N 3AX
Email: submissions@shortstorysunday.com
Website: http://www.shortstorysunday.com

Publishes: Fiction; *Areas:* Adventure;
Crime; Fantasy; Gothic; Historical; Horror;
Humour; Literature; Mystery; Nature; New
Age; Philosophy; Romance; Sci-Fi; Short
Stories; Suspense; Thrillers; Westerns;
Markets: Adult; Children's; Family; Youth;
Treatments: Commercial; Contemporary;
Dark; Experimental; Light; Literary;
Mainstream; Niche; Popular; Positive;
Progressive; Satirical; Traditional

**NOTE: On hiatus as at November 2016.
Check website for current status.**

A home for short stories and flash fiction
online.

Launched in November 2014, this is a new
'boutique' experience for readers, authors,
agents and publishers interested in reading
and contributing world-class short stories.
We wanted to create an experience for the
reader so that every Sunday they can take
half an hour and visit with a cup of tea and
read through that week's story on their

mobile, tablet or desktop either at home, at a
coffee shop or on their lunch break.

To ensure we have the best stories we put
together an editorial panel with an eye for a
good story to pick the most interesting and
original stories for our readers each Sunday.

Shout Magazine
2 Albert Square
Dundee
DD1 1DD
Tel: +44 (0) 1382 223131
Email: shout@dcthomson.co.uk
Website: https://www.shoutmag.co.uk

Publishes: Articles; Essays; Features;
Nonfiction; *Areas:* Beauty and Fashion;
Entertainment; Lifestyle; Music; Women's
Interests; *Markets:* Youth; *Treatments:*
Popular

Magazine for girls covering pop music,
soaps, hunks, beauty and fashion, etc.

Shropshire Magazine
Shropshire Newspapers Ltd
Ketley
Telford
TF1 5HU
Tel: +44 (0) 1952 241455
Email: neil.thomas@shropshirestar.co.uk
Website: http://www.
shropshiremagazine.com

Publishes: Articles; Features; News;
Nonfiction; Reviews; *Areas:* Beauty and
Fashion; Entertainment; Historical; Leisure;
Lifestyle; *Markets:* Adult

Glossy lifestyle magazine publishing
features, profiles, news and reviews relating
to the county.

Skald
2 Greenfield Terrace
Hill St
Menai Bridge
Anglesey
LL59 5AY
Email: submissions@skald.co.uk
Website: http://www.skald.co.uk

Fiction; Poetry; Short Stories

Editors: Zoe Skoulding

Predominantly a poetry magazine, though short prose is sometimes included. Work may be submitted in English or Welsh. Although based in Wales, this is an outward-looking magazine which publishes interesting writing from further afield. Visual poetry is welcome, as is any artwork which is easily reproducible in black and white. It need not be illustration to accompany text.

Sky at Night Magazine
Immediate Media Co.
Vineyard House
44 Brook Green
Hammersmith
London
W6 7BT
Tel: +44 (0) 20 7150 5000
Email: skyatnight@bbcmagazines.com
Website: http://www.skyatnightmagazine.com

Publishes: Articles; Features; News; Nonfiction; Reviews; *Areas:* How-to; Science; Technology; *Markets:* Adult

Magazine for those interested in space, publishing space science stories and tips and advice for astronomers.

Slimming World
Clover Nook Road
Alfreton
Derbyshire
DE55 4SW
Email: editorial@slimming-world.co.uk
Website: http://www.slimmingworld.co.uk/magazine/latest-issue.aspx

Publishes: Articles; Features; Nonfiction; *Areas:* Health; How-to; *Markets:* Adult

Magazine covering slimming, healthy eating, and fitness.

Slinglnk Magazine
The Old Lighthouse
83 High St
Belmont
Bolton
BL7 8AJ

Email: balloon@slingink.co.uk
Website: http://www.slingink.co.uk

Publishes: Articles; Fiction; *Areas:* Short Stories; *Markets:* Adult; *Treatments:* Literary

Editors: Rob Moss

Online community's regular fiction magazine, including articles on writing fiction and a myriad of different styles of short story written by the community members.

Snooker Scene
Hayley Green Court
130 Hagley Road
Halesowen
B63 1DY
Tel: +44 (0) 1215 859188
Fax: +44 (0) 01215 857117
Email: info@snookerscene.co.uk
Website: http://www.snookerscene.co.uk

Publishes: Articles; News; Nonfiction; *Areas:* Sport; *Markets:* Adult

Editors: Clive Everton

Magazine covering the sports of snooker and billiards.

South
PO Box 4228
Bracknell
RG42 9PX
Email: south@southpoetry.org
Website: http://www.southpoetry.org

Publishes: Poetry; *Markets:* Adult

Editors: Anne Peterson, Andrew Curtis, Peter Keeble, Patrick Osada, and Chrissie Williams

Submit up to three poems by post (two copies of each), along with submission form available on website. No previously published poems (including poems that have appeared on the internet). Submissions are not returned. See website for full details. No submissions by email.

Spear's Magazine
Tel: +44 (0) 20 7936 6445
Email: alec.marsh@spearswms.com
Website: http://www.spearswms.com

Publishes: Articles; News; Nonfiction;
Areas: Business; Finance; Lifestyle;
Markets: Adult

Editors: Alec Marsh

Wealth management and luxury lifestyle
magazine.

The Spectator
The Spectator (1828) Ltd
22 Old Queen Street
London
SW1H 9HP
Tel: +44 (0) 20 7961 0200
Email: editor@spectator.co.uk
Website: http://www.spectator.co.uk

Publishes: Articles; Features; *Areas:* Arts;
Current Affairs; Literature; Politics;
Markets: Adult

Editors: Fraser Nelson

Magazine of politics, literature, and arts.

The Stage
Stage House
47 Bermondsey Street
London
SE1 3XT
Tel: +44 (0) 20 7403 1818
Email: alistair@thestage.co.uk
Website: http://www.thestage.co.uk

Publishes: Articles; Features; News;
Nonfiction; *Areas:* Theatre; *Markets:*
Professional

Editors: Alistair Smith

Query with ideas in first instance. Publishes
material relating to the theatre: tabloid-style
articles up to 800 words, profiles up to 1,200
words, and news items up to 300 words.

Stand Magazine
School of English
Leeds University
Leeds

LS2 9JT
Tel: +44 (0) 113 233 4794
Fax: +44 (0) 113 233 2791
Email: stand@leeds.ac.uk
Website: http://standmagazine.org

Publishes: Fiction; Poetry; *Areas:* Short
Stories; Translations; *Markets:* Adult;
Treatments: Literary

A well established magazine of poetry and
literary fiction. Has previously published the
work of, among others, Samuel Beckett,
Angela Carter, Seamus Heaney, Geoffrey
Hill, and Andrew Motion. No electronic
submissions. See website for submission
guidelines and alternative US address for
American submissions.

Style at Home
Time Inc. (UK) Ltd
Blue Fin Building
110 Southwark Street
London
SE1 0SU
Tel: +44 (0) 20 3148 7112
Email: elizabeth.hudson@timeinc.com
Website: http://www.timeincuk.com/brands/
style-at-home/

Publishes: Articles; Nonfiction; *Areas:*
Design; How-to; Women's Interests;
Markets: Adult

Editors: Elizabeth Hudson

Magazine offering practical advice for
women taking a hands-on approach to
styling, decorating, and revamping their
homes on a budget.

Surrey Life
C/O Archant
28 Teville Road
Worthing
West Sussex
BN11 1UG
Tel: +44 (0) 1903 703730
Email: editor@surreylife.co.uk
Website: http://www.surreylife.co.uk

Publishes: Articles; Nonfiction; *Areas:* Arts;
Cookery; Gardening; Lifestyle; Travel;
Markets: Adult

Editors: Rebecca Younger

Magazine publishing articles on Surrey, covering such topics as home, gardens, popular destinations, history, food and drink, people, education, style, and motoring.

Television

Royal Television Society
3 Dorset Rise
London
EC4Y 8EN
Tel: +44 (0) 20 7822 2810
Email: info@rts.org.uk
Website: https://rts.org.uk

Publishes: Articles; Nonfiction; *Areas:* Technology; TV; *Markets:* Professional

Editors: Steve Clarke

Magazine covering the technical aspects of television and audio-visual equipment.

Tempo: A Quarterly Review of New Music

PO Box 171
Herne Bay
CT6 6WD
Email: tempoeditor@cambridge.org
Website: http://journals.cambridge.org/action/displayJournal?jid=TEM

Publishes: Articles; Nonfiction; Reviews; *Areas:* Music; *Markets:* Adult; *Treatments:* Contemporary

Editors: Christopher Fox; Juliet Fraser

Publishes articles and reviews on the new music scene. Emphasises musical developments of the 21st century, and developments of the late 20th century that have not yet received the deserved attention. Submit articles up to 5,000 words and reviews as Word format documents (no PDFs) with 100-word bio. See website for full guidelines.

TES (The Times Educational Supplement)

26 Red Lion Square
London
WC1R 4HQ
Tel: +44 (0) 20 3194 3000

Email: help@tesglobal.com
Website: https://www.tes.com

Publishes: Articles; Features; News; Nonfiction; Reviews; *Markets:* Academic; Adult

Weekly supplement of educational news and resources. Most material is commissioned, but accepts queries outlining ideas by email.

The Lady

39-40 Bedford Street
London
WC2E 9ER
Tel: +44 (0) 20 7379 4717
Email: editors@lady.co.uk
Website: http://www.lady.co.uk

Publishes: Articles; Features; Nonfiction; *Areas:* Arts; Beauty and Fashion; Cookery; Finance; Gardening; Health; Historical; Travel; Women's Interests; *Markets:* Adult

England's longest-running weekly magazine for women.

This England

The Lypiatts
Lansdown Road
Cheltenham
Gloucestershire
GL50 2JA
Tel: +44 (0) 1242 225780
Email: thisengland@dcthomson.co.uk
Website: https://www.thisengland.co.uk

Publishes: Articles; Features; Nonfiction; Poetry; *Areas:* Crafts; Culture; Historical; Nature; *Markets:* Adult

Magazine celebrating English culture, history, people, nature, traditions, customs, legends, etc. Generally rural. Publishes articles between 250 and 2,000 words and poems 12-24 lines.

Times Higher Education

TES Global Limited
26 Red Lion Square
London
WC1R 4HQ
Tel: +44 (0) 20 3194 3300
Email: john.gill@timeshighereducation.com

Website: https://www.
timeshighereducation.com

Publishes: Articles; Nonfiction; *Markets:*
Academic; Adult

Magazine publishing articles on higher
education.

The Times Literary Supplement (TLS)
1 London Bridge Street
London
SE1 9GF
Tel: +44 (0) 20 7782 5000
Email: letters@the-tls.co.uk
Website: http://www.the-tls.co.uk

Publishes: Articles; Features; News;
Nonfiction; Poetry; Reviews; *Areas:* Arts;
Film; Historical; Literature; Philosophy;
Science; Theatre; *Markets:* Adult

Editors: Stig Abell

Publishes coverage of the latest and most
important publications, as well as current
theatre, opera, exhibitions and film. Also
publishes letters to the editor and poetry.
Send books for review by post. For poetry,
submit up to six poems with SASE. Letters
to the Editor may be sent by post or by email
to the address provided on the website.

Top Sante
Bauer Media
Media House
Lynch Wood
Peterborough
PE2 6EA
Tel: +44 (0) 1733 468938
Email: nikki.dutton@bauermedia.co.uk
Website: http://www.topsante.co.uk

Publishes: Articles; Features; News;
Nonfiction; *Areas:* Beauty and Fashion;
Health; Women's Interests; *Markets:* Adult

Magazine publishing articles, features, and
news on health and beauty.

Trail
Bauer Consumer Media Limited
Media House
Peterborough Business Park

Peterborough
PE2 6EA
Email: simon.ingram@lfto.com
Website: http://www.livefortheoutdoors.com

Publishes: Articles; Features; Nonfiction;
Areas: Hobbies; Leisure; Travel; *Markets:*
Adult

Editors: Simon Ingram

Monthly walking magazine, covering
hillwalking, mountain climbing, gear,
historic walks, and gentle strolls in the
countryside.

Truck & Driver
Sixth Floor, Chancery House
St Nicholas Way
Sutton
SM1 1JB
Tel: +44 (0) 20 8912 2131
Email: pip.dunn@roadtransport.com
Website: http://truckanddriver.co.uk

Publishes: Articles; Features; News;
Nonfiction; *Areas:* Travel; *Markets:*
Professional

Editors: Pip Dunn

Magazine for truck drivers.

Vanity Fair
Conde Nast Publications
Vogue House
1-2 Hanover Square
London
W1S 1JU
Email: letters@vf.com
Website: http://www.vanityfair.com

Publishes: Articles; Nonfiction; *Areas:*
Beauty and Fashion; Culture; Current
Affairs; Entertainment; Media; Politics;
Markets: Adult; *Treatments:* Popular

Magazine of glamour, popular culture,
current affairs, fashion, and politics.

Vegan Life
Prime Impact Events & Media
Park House
The Business Centre
Earls Colne Business Park

Earls Colne
Colchester
CO6 2NS
Tel: +44 (0) 1787 224040
Email: info@veganlifemag.com
Website: http://www.veganlifemag.com

Publishes: Articles; Features; News;
Nonfiction; *Areas:* Cookery; Health;
Leisure; Lifestyle; Travel; *Markets:* Adult

Editors: Maria Chiorando

Vegan consumer magazine, aiming to bring
about a change in attitudes by encouraging
the adoption of a plant based diet.

Viz

30 Cleveland Street
London
W1T 4JD
Tel: +44 (0) 20 7907 6000
Fax: +44 (0) 20 7907 6020
Email: viz@viz.co.uk
Website: http://www.viz.co.uk

Publishes: Articles; Fiction; *Areas:* Humour;
Markets: Adult

Editors: Russell Blackman

Magazine of adult humour, including
cartoons, spoof articles, etc.

Wanderlust Magazine

PO Box 1832
Windsor
Berkshire
SL4 1YT
Tel: +44 (0) 1753 620426
Fax: +44 (0) 1753 620474
Email: submissions@wanderlust.co.uk
Website: http://www.wanderlust.co.uk

Publishes: Articles; Features; Nonfiction;
Areas: Travel; *Markets:* Adult

Magazine covering all aspects of
independent, semi-independent and special-
interest travel. Particularly interested in local
culture. No unsolicited mss. Send query by
email with one-paragraph proposal.

Wasafiri

1-11 Hawley Crescent
Camden Town
London
NW1 8NP
Tel: +44 (0) 20 7556 6110
Fax: +44 (0) 20 7556 6187
Email: wasafiri@open.ac.uk
Website: http://www.wasafiri.org

Publishes: Articles; Essays; Fiction;
Interviews; Nonfiction; Poetry; Reviews;
Areas: Criticism; Culture; Literature; Short
Stories; *Markets:* Adult; *Treatments:*
Literary

Editors: Susheila Nasta

The indispensable journal of contemporary
African, Asian Black British, Caribbean and
transnational literatures.

In over fifteen years of publishing, this
magazine has changed the face of
contemporary writing in Britain. As a literary
magazine primarily concerned with new and
postcolonial writers, it continues to stress the
diversity and range of black and diasporic
writers world-wide. It remains committed to
its original aims: to create a definitive forum
for the voices of new writers and to open up
lively spaces for serious critical discussion
not available elsewhere. It is Britain's only
international magazine for Black British,
African, Asian and Caribbean literatures. Get
the whole picture, get the magazine at the
core of contemporary international literature
today.

Weight Watchers Magazine

PO Box 326
Sittingbourne
Email: weightwatchers@
servicehelpline.co.uk
Website: https://www.weightwatchers.co.uk

Publishes: Articles; Features; News;
Nonfiction; *Areas:* Beauty and Fashion;
Cookery; Health; *Markets:* Adult

Magazine covering slimming, health, beauty,
etc.

What Car?

Teddington Studios
Teddington
Middlesex
TW11 9BE
Tel: +44 (0) 20 8267 5688
Fax: +44 (0) 20 8267 5750
Email: editorial@whatcar.com
Website: http://www.whatcar.com

Publishes: Articles; Features; News;
Nonfiction; Reviews; *Areas:* Technology;
Travel; *Markets:* Adult

Magazine providing new, reviews, articles
and features on cars.

Woman

Time Inc. UK
Blue Fin Building
110 Southwark Street
London
SE1 0SU
Tel: +44 (0) 20 3148 5000
Email: woman@timeinc.com
Website: http://www.womanmagazine.co.uk

Publishes: Articles; Features; News;
Nonfiction; *Areas:* Entertainment; Lifestyle;
Women's Interests; *Markets:* Adult

Magazine for women, publishing celebrity
and real-life features up to 1,000 words.

Woman's Own

Time Inc. (UK) Ltd
Blue Fin Building
110 Southwark Street
London
SE1 0SU
Tel: +44 (0) 20 3148 6530
Email: womansown@timeinc.com
Website: http://www.timeinc.com/brands/
womans-own/

Publishes: Articles; Features; Nonfiction;
Areas: Beauty and Fashion; Entertainment;
Lifestyle; Women's Interests; Markets

Editors: Karen Livermore

Magazine aimed at women aged 40 and
older.

Woman's Weekly

Time Inc (UK)
161 Marsh Wall
London
E14 9AP
Email: womansweeklypostbag@
timeinc.com
Website: http://www.womansweekly.com

Publishes: Features; Fiction; News;
Nonfiction; *Areas:* Beauty and Fashion;
Cookery; Crafts; Gardening; Health; Short
Stories; Travel; Women's Interests; *Markets:*
Adult; *Treatments:* Contemporary

Editors: Diane Kenwood; Sue Pilkington
(Features); Gaynor Davies (Fiction)

Publishes features of interest to women over
forty, plus fiction between 1,000 and 2,000
words and serials in three, four, or five parts
of 3,300 words each. Only uses experienced
journalists for nonfiction. No submissions by
email. Submit by post with SAE.

Woman's Weekly Fiction Special

Time Inc (UK)
161 Marsh Wall
London
E14 9AP
Email: womansweeklypostbag@
timeinc.com
Website: http://www.womansweekly.com

Publishes: Fiction; *Areas:* Short Stories;
Women's Interests; *Markets:* Adult

Editors: Gaynor Davies

Publishes short stories for women between
1,000 and 8,000 words. Send stories by post
with SAE – no correspondence by email.

Yachts & Yachting

Email: Georgie.Corlett-Pitt@
chelseamagazines.com
Website: http://www.yachtsandyachting.com

Publishes: Articles; Nonfiction; *Areas:*
Hobbies; How-to; Sport; Travel; *Markets:*
Adult

Editors: Georgie Corlett-Pitt

Magazine publishing articles on sailing techniques and lifestyle.

Yorkshire Life

PO Box 163
Ripon
HG4 9AG
Tel: +44 (0) 1928 240668
Email: esther.leach@yorkshirelife.co.uk
Website: http://www.yorkshirelife.co.uk

Publishes: Articles; Nonfiction; *Areas:* Arts; Entertainment; Historical; Lifestyle; Travel; *Markets:* Adult

Magazine covering the people, places, history, arts, food and events of Yorkshire.

Your Dog Magazine

BPG Stamford Ltd
1-6 Buckminster Yard
Main Street
Buckminster
Grantham
Lincs
NG33 5SA
Tel: +44 (0) 1476 859830
Email: editorial@yourdog.co.uk
Website: http://www.yourdog.co.uk

Publishes: Articles; Features; News; Nonfiction; *Areas:* Hobbies; How-to; Leisure; Lifestyle; *Markets:* Adult

Editors: Sarah Wright

Publishes news articles (up to 400 words) and feature articles (up to 2,500 words) aimed at dog owners, offering practical advice and some personal experience pieces. No fiction. Approach by phone in first instance.

Your Horse

Media House
Peterborough Business Park
Lynch Wood
Peterborough
PE2 6EA
Tel: +44 (0) 1733 395051
Email: getinvolved@yourhorse.co.uk
Website: http://www.yourhorse.co.uk

Publishes: Articles; Nonfiction; *Areas:* Hobbies; How-to; Nature; Travel; *Markets:* Adult

Magazine of horse ownership and riding. Most material produced in-house but willing to consider appropriate articles.

Canadian Magazines

For the most up-to-date listings of these and hundreds of other magazines, visit https://www.firstwriter.com/magazines

*To claim your **free** access to the site, please see the back of this book.*

Business London
PO Box 7400
London, ON
N5Y 4X3
Email: sajones@postmedia.com
Website: http://www.businesslondon.ca

Publishes: Articles; Nonfiction; *Areas:* Business; Health; Politics; Sport; Travel; *Markets:* Professional

Editors: Sarah Jones

Business magazine for southwestern Ontario.

Canadian Yachting
538 Elizabeth Street
Midland
Ontario
L4R 2A3
Email: elissacampbell@kerrwil.com
Website: http://www.kerrwil.com

Publishes: Articles; News; Nonfiction; *Areas:* Technology; Travel; *Markets:* Adult

Describes itself as the premier boating magazine in Canada.

The Capilano Review
281 Industrial Avenue
Vancouver, BC V6A 2P2
Email: contact@thecapilanoreview.ca
Website: https://www.thecapilanoreview.ca

Publishes: Fiction; Interviews; Nonfiction; Poetry; Reviews; *Markets:* Adult; *Treatments:* Experimental; Literary

Publishes experimental writing and art. Submit up to 8 pages of poetry; reviews up to 600 words; fiction up to 5,000 words; or interviews up to 4,000 words, through online submission system. No submissions by post or email.

The Claremont Review
Suite 101
1581-H Hillside Avenue
Victoria, BC V8T 2C1
Email: claremontreview@gmail.com
Website: http://www.theclaremontreview.ca

Publishes: Fiction; Poetry; Scripts; *Areas:* Drama; Short Stories; *Markets:* Children's; Youth

Publishes poetry, short stories, and short plays by young writers aged 13-19 from anywhere in the English-speaking world. Send submissions from September 1 to April 30 annually. See website for submission guidelines.

Event
PO Box 2503
New Westminster, BC
V3L 5B2
Tel: +1 (604) 527-5293

Email: event@douglascollege.ca
Website: http://event.douglas.bc.ca

Publishes: Fiction; Nonfiction; Poetry;
Reviews; *Markets:* Adult; *Treatments:*
Literary

Send one story or up to eight poems via
online submission system only. Occasional
unsolicited reviews published – query before
submitting.

Filling Station

filling Station Publications Society
Box 22135
Bankers Hall RPO
Calgary AB T2P 4J5
Email: mgmt@fillingstation.ca
Website: http://www.fillingstation.ca

Publishes: Articles; Fiction; Interviews;
Nonfiction; Poetry; Reviews; *Areas:* Arts;
Criticism; Literature; Short Stories; *Markets:*
Adult; *Treatments:* Literary

Publishes previously unpublished poetry,
fiction, creative nonfiction, and critical
nonfiction (about literature and occasionally
about visual art). Submit up to 10 pages of
fiction; up to 6 pages of poetry; or up to two
piece of nonfiction, via online submission
system. See website for full details.

The Grey Press

Email: editor@greypresspublishing.com
Website: https://greypresspublishing.com

Publishes: Fiction; Nonfiction; Poetry;
Areas: Short Stories; *Markets:* Adult;
Treatments: Literary

Online journal publishing short fiction up to
5,000 words, flash fiction up to 500 words,
micro-fiction up to 100 words, short
nonfiction up to 5,000 words, first chapters
of graphic novels up to 5,000 words, and
poetry (submit up to 5). Submissions must be
sent by email with the subject line
"Submission". See website for full details.

Quill & Quire

111 Queen Street East
Suite 320
Toronto, ON

M5C 1S2
Tel: +1 (416) 364-3333
Fax: +1 (416) 595-5415
Email: scflinn@quillandquire.com
Website: http://www.quillandquire.com

Publishes: Articles; News; Nonfiction;
Reviews; *Areas:* Business; Literature;
Markets: Professional

Editors: Sue Carter

Magazine of the Canadian book trade,
including news, author profiles, and reviews
of new titles.

The Starlit Path

1105 Mill hill
Laval, QC, H7W 1P7
Tel: N/A
Fax: N/A
Email: judie@stardragonpress.com
Website: http://starlitpathmagazine.com

Publishes: Articles; Essays; Features;
Fiction; Interviews; Nonfiction; Poetry;
Reference; Reviews; *Areas:* Entertainment;
Fantasy; Historical; How-to; New Age;
Religious; Sci-Fi; Short Stories; Spiritual;
Markets: Adult; Family; Professional;
Treatments: Contemporary; Experimental;
Positive; Traditional

Editors: Judie Troyansky

A new Online New Age magazine to become
a resource for people wanting to research a
variety of topics. I'm looking for articles and
artwork geared towards those looking for
information on all types of new age and
spiritual topics.

First edition March 20, 2018

Seeking articles, interviews, inspiration,
reviews, fiction, poetry, artwork and
photography centred around many New Age
topics: Spiritual practices, Tarot, gods and
goddesses, How-to, chakras, kabbalah, reiki,
healing, mindset work, guides, paganism,
wicca, mysticism, plants as medicine,
paranormal and psychic phenomenon, etc.
See our complete guidelines.

Toronto Life
111 Queen St. E., Suite 320
Toronto, Ont. M5C 1S2
Email: editorial@torontolife.com
Website: http://torontolife.com

Publishes: Articles; News; Nonfiction;
Areas: Lifestyle; *Markets:* Adult

Editors: Sarah Fulford

Local lifestyle magazine for Toronto. Send queries and unsolicited mss by email.

Windspeaker
13245 – 146 Street
Edmonton, Alberta, T5L 4S8

Tel: +1 (780) 455-2700
Fax: +1 (780) 455-7639
Email: dsteel@ammsa.com
Website: http://www.ammsa.com/
publications/windspeaker

Publishes: Articles; Features; News;
Nonfiction; Reviews; *Areas:* Arts; Culture;
Entertainment; Lifestyle; Politics; Sport;
Markets: Adult

Editors: Debora Steel

Publishes news, sports, arts, entertainment, reviews and features of interest to Aboriginal people. Accepts unsolicited mss, but prefers query by email in first instance. See website for full guidelines.

Irish Magazines

For the most up-to-date listings of these and hundreds of other magazines, visit https://www.firstwriter.com/magazines

*To claim your **free** access to the site, please see the back of this book.*

Crannóg Magazine

Email: editor@crannogmagazine.com
Website: http://www.crannogmagazine.com

Publishes: Fiction; Poetry; *Areas:* Literature; Short Stories; *Markets:* Adult; *Treatments:* Literary; Mainstream

Editors: Sandra Bunting, Tony O'Dwyer, Ger Burke, Jarlath Fahy

A literary magazine publishing fiction and poetry only. No reviews or nonfiction. Published thrice yearly in spring, summer and autumn. Authors intending to submit are advised to first to read back issues which are available as free downloads on the website.

Cyphers

3 Selskar Terrace
Ranelagh
Dublin 6
Email: letters@cyphers.ie
Website: http://www.cyphers.ie

Publishes: Fiction; Poetry; *Areas:* Short Stories; Translations; *Markets:* Adult; *Treatments:* Literary

Publishes poetry and fiction in English and Irish, from Ireland and around the world. Translations are welcome. No unsolicited critical articles. Submissions by post only. Attachments sent by email will be deleted. See website for full guidelines.

The Dublin Review

PO Box 7948
Dublin 1
Email: submissions@thedublinreview.com
Website: http://thedublinreview.com

Publishes: Essays; Fiction; Nonfiction; *Areas:* Criticism; Literature; Short Stories; *Markets:* Adult; *Treatments:* Literary

Publishes essays, criticism, reportage, and fiction for a general, intelligent readership. No poetry. No official length limit, but rarely publishes pieces in excess of 12,000 words. Accepts submissions by post with email address for response, but prefers submissions by email as Word or .rtf attachment. Physical material is not returned, so do not include return postage. No response without email address.

EarthLines Magazine

Teach Dhoire an Easa
Meenderry
Falcarragh
Co Donegal
F92 W732
Email: info@earthlinesmagazine.org
Website: http://www.earthlinesmagazine.org

Publishes: Articles; Essays; Features; Fiction; Interviews; Nonfiction; Poetry; Reviews; *Areas:* Autobiography; Nature; Short Stories; Travel; *Markets:* Adult

Editors: David Knowles

Magazine publishing features, essays, poetry, and perhaps a little short fiction, exploring nature, place and the environment. Send query/submissions by email. Accepts attachments as Word or RTF files.

Hot Press

13 Trinity Street
Dublin 2
Tel: +353 (1) 241 1500
Email: info@hotpress.ie
Website: http://www.hotpress.com

Publishes: Articles; Nonfiction; *Areas:* Culture; Entertainment; Film; Lifestyle; Media; Music; Politics; Sport; *Markets:* Adult; Youth

Magazine aimed at readers aged 16-39.

Into The Void Magazine

Email: intothevoidmag@gmail.com
Website: https://intothevoidmagazine.com

Publishes: Essays; Fiction; Nonfiction; Poetry; *Areas:* Adventure; Anthropology; Arts; Crime; Current Affairs; Drama; Fantasy; Film; Gothic; Historical; Horror; Humour; Literature; Mystery; Nature; Philosophy; Politics; Psychology; Romance; Science; Sci-Fi; Short Stories; Sociology; Suspense; Thrillers; Westerns; *Markets:* Adult; *Treatments:* Commercial; Contemporary; Cynical; Dark; Experimental; Light; Literary; Mainstream; Niche; Popular; Positive; Progressive; Satirical; Serious; Traditional

Editors: Philip Elliott, Gabriela McAdams

A non-profit print and digital literary magazine dedicated to providing a platform for fantastic fiction, nonfiction and poetry from all over the world. We accept writing of all genres and styles, striving to publish work that we feel is heartfelt, genuine and screaming to be read. We adore beautiful and unique styles of writing but clarity is most important. We are committed to giving writers of all experience levels an opportunity. Unpublished writers have just as good a chance of getting published as established ones – it's all about the writing.

Ireland's Own

Channing House
Rowe Street
Wexford
Tel: 053 9140140
Email: info@irelandsown.ie
Website: https://irelandsown.ie

Publishes: Articles; Features; Fiction; Nonfiction; *Areas:* Short Stories; *Markets:* Adult; Children's; Family; Youth; *Treatments:* Literary; Traditional

Editors: Sean Nolan

Magazine publishing stories and articles of Irish interest for the whole family, plus puzzles and games.

Irish Farmers Journal

Irish Farm Centre
Bluebell
Dublin 12
Tel: 01 419 9500
Email: jmccarthy@farmersjournal.ie
Website: http://www.farmersjournal.ie

Publishes: Articles; Nonfiction; *Areas:* Business; Nature; *Markets:* Professional

Editors: Justin McCarthy

Weekly magazine for Irish farmers.

Irish Journal of Medical Science

RAMI Office
Setanta House
2nd Floor
Setanta Place
Dublin 2
Tel: +353 1 633 4820
Email: helenmoore@rcpi.ie
Website: http://www.springer.com/medicine/internal/journal/11845

Publishes: Articles; News; Nonfiction; *Areas:* Medicine; *Markets:* Academic; Professional

Editors: William P. Tormey; Helen Moore

Quarterly medical science journal providing a forum for the exchange of scientific information, and promoting academic discussion.

Irish Medical Times
Tel: +353 (0) 1 817
Email: editor@imt.ie
Website: https://www.imt.ie

Publishes: Articles; News; Nonfiction;
Areas: Medicine; *Markets:* Professional

Editors: Lloyd Mudiwa

Newspaper for medical professionals.

The Moth
Ardan Grange
Milltown
Belturbet
Co. Cavan
Tel: 353 (0) 87 2657251
Email: editor@themothmagazine.com
Website: http://www.themothmagazine.com

Publishes: Fiction; Poetry; *Areas:* Short
Stories; *Markets:* Adult; *Treatments:*
Literary

Editors: Rebecca O'Connor

Submit up to six poems or up to two short
stories by post or by email. See website for
full submission guidelines.

Poetry Ireland Review
11 Parnell Square East
Dublin 1
D01 ND60
Tel: +353 (0)1 6789815
Fax: +353 (0)1 6789782
Email: info@poetryireland.ie
Website: http://www.poetryireland.ie

Publishes: Articles; Nonfiction; Poetry;
Reviews; *Areas:* Literature; *Markets:* Adult

Editors: Eavan Boland

Send up to 6 poems with SASE / IRCs or
email address for response. Poetry is
accepted from around the world, but must be
previously unpublished. No sexism or
racism. No submissions by email. Articles
and reviews are generally commissioned,
however proposals are welcome. No
unsolicited reviews or articles.

Woman's Way
Rosemount House
Dundrum Road
Dundrum
Dublin 14
Tel: +353 (0) 1 240 5318
Email: atoner@harmonia.ie
Website: http://womansway.ie

Publishes: Articles; Features; Interviews;
Nonfiction; *Areas:* Beauty and Fashion;
Entertainment; Lifestyle; Media; Women's
Interests; *Markets:* Adult

Magazine for women aged 35-65. Describes
itself as "Irelands best read and only Irish
Woman's Weekly" [sic].

Australasian Magazines

For the most up-to-date listings of these and hundreds of other magazines, visit https://www.firstwriter.com/magazines

*To claim your **free** access to the site, please see the back of this book.*

Idiom 23

PO Box 172
Central Queensland University
554-700 Yaamba Road
Rockhampton QLD 4702
Email: idiom@cqu.edu.au
Website: https://www.cqu.edu.au/about-us/
structure/schools/ea/idiom-23-literary-
magazine

Publishes: Essays; Fiction; Nonfiction;
Poetry; *Areas:* Short Stories; *Markets:* Adult;
Treatments: Literary

Editors: Dr Nicole Anae

Annual literary magazine publishing fiction
and nonfiction up to 3,000 words, and poems
up to one page. See website for full
submission guidelines and to submit via
online submission system.

Island

PO Box 4703
Hobart TAS 7000
Tel: +61 (0) 3 6234 1462
Email: admin@islandmag.com
Website: http://www.islandmag.com

Publishes: Articles; Essays; Fiction; Poetry;
Areas: Short Stories; *Markets:* Adult

**Closed to submissions as at January 2018.
Check website for current status.**

Welcomes submissions of nonfiction, fiction

and poetry during specific reading periods.
See website for details and to submit using
online submission system.

Landfall

Otago University Press
PO Box 56
Dunedin 9054
Tel: +64 (0) 3 479 4155
Email: landfall.press@otago.ac.nz
Website: http://www.otago.ac.nz/press/
landfall

Publishes: Essays; Fiction; Nonfiction;
Poetry; *Areas:* Arts; Biography; Criticism;
Markets: Adult; *Treatments:* Literary

Open to work by New Zealand and Pacific
writers or by writers whose work has a
connection to the region in subject matter or
location. Work from Australian writers is
occasionally included as a special feature.
Send up to 10 poems or up to three pieces of
prose per issue. Preferred length is 3,000
words, but longer pieces will be considered.

Online Quilt Magazine

Email: jody@onlinequiltmagazine.com
Website: http://www.
onlinequiltmagazine.com

Publishes: Articles; Features; Nonfiction;
Areas: Crafts; Hobbies; *Markets:* Adult

Editors: Jody Anderson

Online magazine covering quilt-making.

Vintage Made

ArtWear Publications Pty Ltd
PO Box 469
Ashburton VIC 3147
Tel: +61 (0) 3 9888 1853
Fax: +61 (0) 3 9807 0248
Email: thegirls@artwearpublications.com.au
Website: http://www.
artwearpublications.com.au

Publishes: Articles; Features; Nonfiction;
Areas: Beauty and Fashion; Crafts; Design;
Historical; Hobbies; How-to; *Markets:* Adult

Magazine on vintage style and design, with
tutorials and dress patterns, etc. See website
for full submission guidelines.

Yarn

ArtWear Publications Pty Ltd
PO Box 469
Ashburton, VIC, 3147
Tel: +61 (0) 3 9888 1853
Fax: +61 (0) 3 9807 0248
Email: thegirls@artwearpublications.com.au
Website: http://artwearpublications.com.au

Publishes: Articles; Nonfiction; *Areas:*
Crafts; Design; Hobbies; *Markets:* Adult

Publishes articles on knitting and patterns.
Send query by email with bio, details of any
previous writing credits, contact details, and
details of your proposal.

Magazines Subject Index

This section lists magazines by their subject matter, with directions to the section of the book where the full listing can be found.

You can create your own customised lists of magazines using different combinations of these subject areas, plus over a dozen other criteria, instantly online at https://www.firstwriter.com.

To claim your **free** access to the site, please see the back of this book.

Leisure Painter (*UK*)
Litro Magazine (*UK*)
Little Rose Magazine (*US*)
The London Magazine (*UK*)
London Review of Books (*UK*)
Lothian Life (*UK*)
The Mystic Blue Review (*US*)
New Statesman (*UK*)
Niche (*US*)
Nob Hill Gazette (*US*)
NY Literary Magazine (*US*)
Orbis International Literary Journal (*UK*)
Philly Weekly (*US*)
Picture Postcard Monthly (*UK*)
Planet (*UK*)
The Pool (*UK*)
Santa Barbara Magazine (*US*)
Sinister Wisdom (*US*)
The Spectator (*UK*)
StoryNews (*US*)
Sunshine Artist (*US*)
Surrey Life (*UK*)
Susquehanna Life (*US*)
The Lady (*UK*)
The Times Literary Supplement (TLS) (*UK*)
Windspeaker (*Can*)
Yorkshire Life (*UK*)
Autobiography
The Carolina Quarterly (*US*)
Cold Mountain Review (*US*)
Confrontation Magazine (*US*)
december Magazine (*US*)
Ducts (*US*)
EarthLines Magazine (*Ire*)
Guernica (*US*)
Hawai'i Review (*US*)
Hoot (*US*)
Infinite Rust (*US*)
Irish Pages (*UK*)
Litro Magazine (*UK*)
Little Rose Magazine (*US*)
The London Magazine (*UK*)
Mslexia (*UK*)
The North (*UK*)
Beauty and Fashion
Bust (*US*)
Cambridge Magazine (*UK*)
Charleston Style and Design Magazine (*US*)
Essence (*US*)
GQ Magazine (*UK*)
Harper's Bazaar (*UK*)
InJoy Magazine (*US*)
marie claire (*UK*)
Nob Hill Gazette (*US*)
Phoenix Magazine (*US*)
The Pool (*UK*)
Psychologies (*UK*)
Self (*US*)
Shout Magazine (*UK*)
Shropshire Magazine (*UK*)
Susquehanna Life (*US*)
The Lady (*UK*)
Top Sante (*UK*)

Vanity Fair (*UK*)
Vintage Made (*Aus*)
Weight Watchers Magazine (*UK*)
Woman's Own (*UK*)
Woman's Way (*Ire*)
Woman's Weekly (*UK*)
Biography
Crystal Magazine (*UK*)
december Magazine (*US*)
Landfall (Aus)
Business
Advisor Today (*US*)
America's Pharmacist (*US*)
American Quarter Horse Journal (*US*)
APICS Magazine (*US*)
The Author (*UK*)
Bartender (*US*)
BedTimes (*US*)
BizTimes Milwaukee (*US*)
BoxOffice Magazine (*US*)
Broadcast (*UK*)
Business London (*Can*)
The Caterer (*UK*)
Construction Equipment Guide (*US*)
Director (*UK*)
Family Office Magazine (*UK*)
Harper's Bazaar (*UK*)
The Huffington Post (United Kingdom) (*UK*)
Irish Farmers Journal (*Ire*)
LGC (Local Government Chronicle) (*UK*)
Maritime Journal (*UK*)
Moneywise (*UK*)
The Motorship (*UK*)
Music Week (*UK*)
Niche (*US*)
OfficePro (*US*)
People Management (*UK*)
Pizza Today (*US*)
Properties Magazine (*US*)
QSR (*US*)
Quill & Quire (*Can*)
Remodeling (*US*)
Restaurant Magazine (*UK*)
Retail Week (*UK*)
Rochester Business Journal (*US*)
SignCraft Publishing Co., Inc. (*US*)
Spear's Magazine (*UK*)
State Journal (*US*)
Stormwater (*US*)
Susquehanna Life (*US*)
Tallahassee Magazine (*US*)
TimberWest (*US*)
Tobacco International (*US*)
Underground Construction (*US*)
US Glass Magazine (*US*)
Water Well Journal (*US*)
Welding Design & Fabrication (*US*)
The Wholesaler (*US*)
Wire Rope News & Sling Technology (*US*)
Cookery
Bust (*US*)
Eat In Magazine (*UK*)
Essex Life (*UK*)

Good Housekeeping (*UK*)
House & Garden (*UK*)
Kitchen Garden (*UK*)
Lothian Life (*UK*)
Nob Hill Gazette (*US*)
Olive (*UK*)
The People's Friend (*UK*)
Phoenix Magazine (*US*)
Pizza Today (*US*)
Psychologies (*UK*)
QSR (*US*)
Real Simple (*US*)
Restaurant Magazine (*UK*)
Surrey Life (*UK*)
The Lady (*UK*)
Vegan Life (*UK*)
Weight Watchers Magazine (*UK*)
Woman's Weekly (*UK*)
Crafts
Bust (*US*)
Creative Knitting (*US*)
The Dolls' House (*UK*)
Flora International (*UK*)
Niche (*US*)
Online Quilt Magazine (*Aus*)
The People's Friend (*UK*)
Sew Simple (*US*)
The Sewing Directory (*UK*)
Spin Off (*US*)
The Stampers' Sampler (*US*)
Sunshine Artist (*US*)
This England (*UK*)
Vintage Made (*Aus*)
Vogue Patterns (*US*)
Willow and Sage (*US*)
Woman's Weekly (*UK*)
Yarn (*Aus*)
Crime
The Burnt Candle (*UK*)
Ellery Queen Mystery Magazine (*US*)
Into The Void Magazine (*Ire*)
The Mystic Blue Review (*US*)
The People's Friend (*UK*)
The Police Journal (*UK*)
The Savage Kick (*UK*)
ShortStorySunday.com (*UK*)
The Washington Pastime (*US*)
Criticism
Acumen (*UK*)
Adelaide Literary Magazine (*US*)
Agenda (*UK*)
ArtReview (*UK*)
Caveat Lector (*US*)
Chicago Review (*US*)
Critical Quarterly (*UK*)
The Dublin Review (*Ire*)
Empty Mirror (*US*)
Feminist Studies (*US*)
Filling Station (*Can*)
Landfall (*Aus*)
The London Magazine (*UK*)
The North (*UK*)
Wasafiri (*UK*)

Culture
Adelaide Literary Magazine (*US*)
Aesthetica: A Review of Contemporary Artists
(*UK*)
Alabama Heritage (*US*)
Bust (*US*)
Callaloo (*US*)
Cambridge Magazine (*UK*)
Central and Eastern European London Review
(*UK*)
Charleston Magazine (*US*)
The Christian Science Monitor (*US*)
Confrontation Magazine (*US*)
Critical Quarterly (*UK*)
december Magazine (*US*)
Diva (*UK*)
Eastern Art Report (*UK*)
Empty Mirror (*US*)
Essence (*US*)
Essex Life (*UK*)
Frieze (*UK*)
Geographical (*UK*)
GQ Magazine (*UK*)
H&E Naturist (*UK*)
Hot Press (*Ire*)
Infinite Rust (*US*)
InJoy Magazine (*US*)
Jewish Quarterly (*UK*)
Litro Magazine (*UK*)
Little Rose Magazine (*US*)
London Review of Books (*UK*)
The Pool (*UK*)
Psychologies (*UK*)
Rain Taxi (*US*)
Sinister Wisdom (*US*)
StoryNews (*US*)
This England (*UK*)
Vanity Fair (*UK*)
Wasafiri (*UK*)
Windspeaker (*Can*)
Current Affairs
Aesthetica: A Review of Contemporary Artists
(*UK*)
Charleston Magazine (*US*)
The Christian Science Monitor (*US*)
The Huffington Post (United Kingdom) (*UK*)
Infinite Rust (*US*)
Into The Void Magazine (*Ire*)
Jewish Quarterly (*UK*)
Little Rose Magazine (*US*)
New Statesman (*UK*)
Philly Weekly (*US*)
Planet (*UK*)
Press Gazette (*UK*)
Reform (*UK*)
The Spectator (*UK*)
StoryNews (*US*)
Vanity Fair (*UK*)
VFW (Veterans of Foreign Wars) Magazine
(*US*)
Yes! Magazine (*US*)
Design
Architectural Design (*UK*)

Architectural Record (*US*)
Boat International (*UK*)
Building Design (*UK*)
Charleston Style and Design Magazine (*US*)
Creative Knitting (*US*)
Essex Life (*UK*)
House & Garden (*UK*)
Lothian Life (*UK*)
Nob Hill Gazette (*US*)
Play & Playground Magazine (*US*)
Properties Magazine (*US*)
Remodeling (*US*)
SelfBuild & Design (*UK*)
Stone World (*US*)
Stormwater (*US*)
Style at Home (*UK*)
SuCasa (*US*)
This Old House (*US*)
Underground Construction (*US*)
Vintage Made (*Aus*)
Walls & Ceilings (*US*)
Window Fashion Vision (*US*)
Yarn (*Aus*)
Drama
Aesthetica: A Review of Contemporary Artists (*UK*)
Areté (*UK*)
The Burnt Candle (*UK*)
The Claremont Review (*Can*)
Connotation Press (*US*)
Current Accounts (*UK*)
The Evansville Review (*US*)
Flint Hills Review (*US*)
Gold Dust (*UK*)
The Helix (*US*)
Into The Void Magazine (*Ire*)
Scintilla (*UK*)
The Washington Pastime (*US*)
Entertainment
BoxOffice Magazine (*US*)
Broadcast (*UK*)
december Magazine (*US*)
Essence (*US*)
Essex Life (*UK*)
Hennen's Observer (*US*)
Hot Press (*Ire*)
The Huffington Post (United Kingdom) (*UK*)
InJoy Magazine (*US*)
Inside Soap (*UK*)
Little Rose Magazine (*US*)
The New Accelerator (*UK*)
Philly Weekly (*US*)
Radio Times (*UK*)
Shout Magazine (*UK*)
Shropshire Magazine (*UK*)
The Starlit Path (*Can*)
Susquehanna Life (*US*)
Tallahassee Magazine (*US*)
Vanity Fair (*UK*)
The Washington Pastime (*US*)
Windspeaker (*Can*)
Woman (*UK*)
Woman's Own (*UK*)

Woman's Way (*Ire*)
Yorkshire Life (*UK*)
Erotic
The Burnt Candle (*UK*)
Bust (*US*)
Erotic Review (*UK*)
Fantasy
Aphelion: The Webzine of Science Fiction and Fantasy (*US*)
Black Static (*UK*)
The Burnt Candle (*UK*)
Crystal Magazine (*UK*)
The Dark (*US*)
Enchanted Tales Literary Magazine (*US*)
The Fifth Di... (*US*)
Garbled Transmissions (*US*)
GUD Magazine (*US*)
Hawai'i Review (*US*)
Interzone (*UK*)
Into The Void Magazine (*Ire*)
The Mystic Blue Review (*US*)
The New Accelerator (*UK*)
Orson Scott Card's InterGalactic Medicine Show (*US*)
Seshat Literary Magazine (*US*)
SFX (*UK*)
ShortStorySunday.com (*UK*)
The Starlit Path (*Can*)
The Washington Pastime (*US*)
Fiction
The Account (*US*)
Adelaide Literary Magazine (*US*)
After Happy Hour Review (*US*)
Alebrijes (*US*)
Ambit (*UK*)
Amethyst Review (*UK*)
Aphelion: The Webzine of Science Fiction and Fantasy (*US*)
Areté (*UK*)
Banipal (*UK*)
Better Than Starbucks (*US*)
Big Fiction (*US*)
Black Static (*UK*)
Brittle Star (*UK*)
Bugle (*US*)
Bunbury Magazine (*UK*)
The Burnt Candle (*UK*)
Bust (*US*)
Cadaverous Magazine (*US*)
Cadet Quest (*US*)
The Cafe Irreal (*US*)
Cahoodaloodaling (*US*)
Callaloo (*US*)
Camas (*US*)
The Capilano Review (*Can*)
The Carolina Quarterly (*US*)
The Casket of Fictional Delights (*UK*)
Caveat Lector (*US*)
The Chaffin Journal (*US*)
The Chattahoochee Review (*US*)
Chicago Quarterly Review (*US*)
Chicago Review (*US*)
Cimarron Review (*US*)

The Claremont Review (*Can*)
Cloud Rodeo (*US*)
Cloudbank (*US*)
Coal City Review (*US*)
Cold Mountain Review (*US*)
The Collagist (*US*)
Colorado Review (*US*)
Columbia: A Journal of Literature and Art (*US*)
Compose (*US*)
Conduit (*US*)
Confrontation Magazine (*US*)
Connotation Press (*US*)
Cottonwood (*US*)
Crab Creek Review (*US*)
Crannóg Magazine (*Ire*)
Critical Quarterly (*UK*)
Crucible (*US*)
Crystal Magazine (*UK*)
The Cumberland River Review (*US*)
Current Accounts (*UK*)
Cyphers (*Ire*)
The Dark (*US*)
The Dawntreader (*UK*)
The Dead Mule School of Southern Literature (*US*)
december Magazine (*US*)
Denver Quarterly (*US*)
Devil's Lake (*US*)
Diagram (*US*)
The Dos Passos Review (*US*)
Down in the Dirt (*US*)
Dream Catcher (*UK*)
The Dublin Review (*Ire*)
Ducts (*US*)
Déraciné (*US*)
EarthLines Magazine (*Ire*)
Ellery Queen Mystery Magazine (*US*)
Emrys Journal (*US*)
Enchanted Tales Literary Magazine (*US*)
Erotic Review (*UK*)
The Evansville Review (*US*)
Event (*Can*)
failbetter.com (*US*)
Feminist Studies (*US*)
The Fenland Reed (*UK*)
The Fifth Di... (*US*)
Filling Station (*Can*)
Five:2:One (*US*)
Flash: The International Short-Short Story Magazine (*UK*)
Flint Hills Review (*US*)
Flyway: Journal of Writing & Environment (*US*)
Fogged Clarity (*US*)
Fourteen Hills (*US*)
Fugue (*US*)
Garbled Transmissions (*US*)
A Gathering of the Tribes (*US*)
Gertrude (*US*)
The Gettysburg Review (*US*)
Gold Dust (*UK*)
Granta (*UK*)
Grasslimb (*US*)
Green Hills Literary Lantern (*US*)

Green Mountains Review (GMR) (*US*)
The Grey Press (*Can*)
GUD Magazine (*US*)
Guernica (*US*)
Gulf Coast: A Journal of Literature and Fine Arts (*US*)
Gulf Stream Magazine (*US*)
Haight Ashbury Literary Journal (*US*)
Hanging Loose (*US*)
Hawai'i Pacific Review (*US*)
Hawai'i Review (*US*)
Hayden's Ferry Review (*US*)
The Helix (*US*)
HelloHorror (*US*)
Hennen's Observer (*US*)
Hoot (*US*)
Iconoclast (*US*)
Idaho Review (*US*)
Idiom 23 (*Aus*)
Indiana Review (*US*)
Infinite Rust (*US*)
InJoy Magazine (*US*)
The Interpreter's House (*UK*)
Interzone (*UK*)
Into The Void Magazine (*Ire*)
The Iowa Review (*US*)
Ireland's Own (*Ire*)
Irish Pages (*UK*)
Island (*Aus*)
Jewish Quarterly (*UK*)
Kaimana: Literary Arts Hawai'i (*US*)
Landfall (*Aus*)
Lighthouse (*UK*)
Litro Magazine (*UK*)
Little Rose Magazine (*US*)
The London Magazine (*UK*)
Long Life Magazine (*US*)
Longshot Island (*US*)
Louisiana Literature (*US*)
Midway Journal (*US*)
The Moth (*Ire*)
Mslexia (*UK*)
The Mystic Blue Review (*US*)
The New Accelerator (*UK*)
New Fairy Tales (*UK*)
New Welsh Reader (*UK*)
Old Red Kimono (*US*)
Orbis International Literary Journal (*UK*)
Orson Scott Card's InterGalactic Medicine Show (*US*)
Overtime (*US*)
The People's Friend (*UK*)
People's Friend Pocket Novels (*UK*)
Planet (*UK*)
Prole (*UK*)
Ripcord. (*US*)
Sarasvati (*UK*)
The Savage Kick (*UK*)
Scintilla (*UK*)
Seshat Literary Magazine (*US*)
Shooter Literary Magazine (*UK*)
ShortStorySunday.com (*UK*)
Sinister Wisdom (*US*)

Skald (*UK*)
SlingInk Magazine (*UK*)
St Anthony Messenger (*US*)
St Petersburg Review (*US*)
Stand Magazine (*UK*)
The Starlit Path (*Can*)
This Is Bill Gorton (*US*)
Viz (*UK*)
Wasafiri (*UK*)
The Washington Pastime (*US*)
Woman's Weekly (*UK*)
Woman's Weekly Fiction Special (*UK*)

Film
Aesthetica: A Review of Contemporary Artists
(*UK*)
BoxOffice Magazine (*US*)
Central and Eastern European London Review
(*UK*)
Columbia: A Journal of Literature and Art (*US*)
Garbled Transmissions (*US*)
Harper's Bazaar (*UK*)
Hot Press (*Ire*)
Into The Void Magazine (*Ire*)
Jewish Quarterly (*UK*)
London Review of Books (*UK*)
SFX (*UK*)
The Times Literary Supplement (TLS) (*UK*)

Finance
Advisor Today (*US*)
Africa Confidential (*UK*)
The Christian Science Monitor (*US*)
Family Office Magazine (*UK*)
Moneywise (*UK*)
Niche (*US*)
Nob Hill Gazette (*US*)
Phoenix Magazine (*US*)
Self (*US*)
Spear's Magazine (*UK*)
The Lady (*UK*)

Gardening
Amateur Gardening (*UK*)
Cambridge Magazine (*UK*)
Charleston Magazine (*US*)
Cotswold Life (*UK*)
Essex Life (*UK*)
House & Garden (*UK*)
Kitchen Garden (*UK*)
Lothian Life (*UK*)
Organic Life (*US*)
Santa Barbara Magazine (*US*)
Surrey Life (*UK*)
Susquehanna Life (*US*)
The Lady (*UK*)
Woman's Weekly (*UK*)

Gothic
Aphelion: The Webzine of Science Fiction and
Fantasy (*US*)
Déraciné (*US*)
Into The Void Magazine (*Ire*)
The Mystic Blue Review (*US*)
ShortStorySunday.com (*UK*)
The Washington Pastime (*US*)

Health

AARP Bulletin (*US*)
Alternative Therapies in Health and Medicine
(*US*)
America's Pharmacist (*US*)
American Baby (*US*)
Arthritis Today (*US*)
Athletic Business (*US*)
Business London (*Can*)
Bust (*US*)
Catster (*US*)
Charleston Style and Design Magazine (*US*)
Coach (*UK*)
Coping with Cancer Magazine (*US*)
Diabetes Balance (*UK*)
Essence (*US*)
Good Housekeeping (*UK*)
Harper's Bazaar (*UK*)
Lothian Life (*UK*)
marie claire (*UK*)
Nob Hill Gazette (*US*)
Nursing Times (*UK*)
Organic Life (*US*)
Phoenix Magazine (*US*)
PN (Paraplegia News) (*US*)
The Pool (*UK*)
The Practising Midwife (*UK*)
Psychologies (*UK*)
Running (*UK*)
Scintilla (*UK*)
Self (*US*)
Ski Patrol Magazine (*US*)
Slimming World (*UK*)
Susquehanna Life (*US*)
The Lady (*UK*)
Top Sante (*UK*)
Vegan Life (*UK*)
Weight Watchers Magazine (*UK*)
Woman's Weekly (*UK*)
Women's Health Magazine (*US*)

Historical
Aeroplane (*UK*)
Alabama Heritage (*US*)
American History (*US*)
Aviation History (*US*)
Bugle (*US*)
The Daily Tea (*US*)
Descent (*UK*)
GUD Magazine (*US*)
H&E Naturist (*UK*)
History Today (*UK*)
Infinite Rust (*US*)
Into The Void Magazine (*Ire*)
Irish Pages (*UK*)
Jewish Quarterly (*UK*)
Nob Hill Gazette (*US*)
Nostalgia Magazine (*US*)
Preservation in Print (*US*)
The Railway Magazine (*UK*)
RUSI Journal (*UK*)
Santa Barbara Magazine (*US*)
Scots Heritage Magazine (*UK*)
Seshat Literary Magazine (*US*)
ShortStorySunday.com (*UK*)

Shropshire Magazine (*UK*)
The Starlit Path (*Can*)
Tallahassee Magazine (*US*)
The Lady (*UK*)
This England (*UK*)
TimberWest (*US*)
The Times Literary Supplement (TLS) (*UK*)
VFW (Veterans of Foreign Wars) Magazine
(*US*)
Vintage Made (*Aus*)
World War II (*US*)
Yorkshire Life (*UK*)
Hobbies
American Snowmobiler (*US*)
Angler's Mail (*UK*)
Bugle (*US*)
Cadet Quest (*US*)
Climb Magazine (*UK*)
Country Walking (*UK*)
Creative Knitting (*US*)
Custom Car (*UK*)
Descent (*UK*)
The Dolls' House (*UK*)
Engineering In Miniature (*UK*)
Everyday Practical Electronics (*UK*)
Flora International (*UK*)
InJoy Magazine (*US*)
Kitchen Garden (*UK*)
Leisure Painter (*UK*)
Online Quilt Magazine (*Aus*)
Park Home and Holiday Caravan (*UK*)
The People's Friend (*UK*)
Picture Postcard Monthly (*UK*)
Record Collector Magazine (*UK*)
Running (*UK*)
Scouting (*US*)
Sew Simple (*US*)
The Sewing Directory (*UK*)
SFX (*UK*)
Southern Boating (*US*)
Spin Off (*US*)
The Stampers' Sampler (*US*)
Trail (*UK*)
Trailer Life Magazine (*US*)
Tropical Fish Hobbyist Magazine (*US*)
Vintage Made (*Aus*)
Vogue Patterns (*US*)
Western & Eastern Treasures (*US*)
Western Outdoor News (*US*)
Yachts & Yachting (*UK*)
Yarn (*Aus*)
Your Dog Magazine (*UK*)
Your Horse (*UK*)
Horror
Aphelion: The Webzine of Science Fiction and
Fantasy (*US*)
Black Static (*UK*)
Cadaverous Magazine (*US*)
Crystal Magazine (*UK*)
The Dark (*US*)
GUD Magazine (*US*)
HelloHorror (*US*)
Into The Void Magazine (*Ire*)

The Mystic Blue Review (*US*)
The New Accelerator (*UK*)
Scifaikuest (*US*)
ShortStorySunday.com (*UK*)
The Washington Pastime (*US*)
How-to
American Quarter Horse Journal (*US*)
American Snowmobiler (*US*)
Arizona Wildlife Views (*US*)
The Author (*UK*)
Catster (*US*)
Compose (*US*)
Computeractive Magazine (*UK*)
The Daily Tea (*US*)
The Dolls' House (*UK*)
Eat In Magazine (*UK*)
Flora International (*UK*)
InJoy Magazine (*US*)
Kitchen Garden (*UK*)
Leisure Painter (*UK*)
Park Home and Holiday Caravan (*UK*)
People Management (*UK*)
Play & Playground Magazine (*US*)
Police and Security News (*US*)
Remodeling (*US*)
Rider Magazine (*US*)
Runner's World (*US*)
SelfBuild & Design (*UK*)
Sew Simple (*US*)
Shutterbug (*US*)
SignCraft Publishing Co., Inc. (*US*)
Sky at Night Magazine (*UK*)
Slimming World (*UK*)
Southern Boating (*US*)
St Anthony Messenger (*US*)
The Starlit Path (*Can*)
Style at Home (*UK*)
This Old House (*US*)
Underground Construction (*US*)
Vintage Made (*Aus*)
Vogue Patterns (*US*)
Walls & Ceilings (*US*)
Water Well Journal (*US*)
Welding Design & Fabrication (*US*)
The Wholesaler (*US*)
Willow and Sage (*US*)
Window Fashion Vision (*US*)
Wisconsin Natural Resources Magazine (*US*)
Yachts & Yachting (*UK*)
Your Dog Magazine (*UK*)
Your Horse (*UK*)
Humour
Aesthetica: A Review of Contemporary Artists
(*UK*)
Aphelion: The Webzine of Science Fiction and
Fantasy (*US*)
Bugle (*US*)
Cadet Quest (*US*)
Crystal Magazine (*UK*)
The Daily Tea (*US*)
december Magazine (*US*)
Ducts (*US*)
GUD Magazine (*US*)

InJoy Magazine (*US*)
Into The Void Magazine (*Ire*)
The Mystic Blue Review (*US*)
The Oldie (*UK*)
Orbis International Literary Journal (*UK*)
ShortStorySunday.com (*UK*)
St Anthony Messenger (*US*)
Viz (*UK*)
The Washington Pastime (*US*)
Legal
The Author (*UK*)
Criminal Law & Justice Weekly (Incorporating Justice of the Peace) (*UK*)
The Lawyer (*UK*)
People Management (*UK*)
Police and Security News (*US*)
The Police Journal (*UK*)
Leisure
American Snowmobiler (*US*)
Arizona Wildlife Views (*US*)
Athletic Business (*US*)
Bartender (*US*)
Charleston Magazine (*US*)
Climb Magazine (*UK*)
Coach (*UK*)
Cotswold Life (*UK*)
Essex Life (*UK*)
Family Office Magazine (*UK*)
Improve Your Coarse Fishing (*UK*)
Motorcycle News (MCN) (*UK*)
Play & Playground Magazine (*US*)
PN (Paraplegia News) (*US*)
Runner's World (*US*)
Running (*UK*)
Scouting (*US*)
Shropshire Magazine (*UK*)
Southern Boating (*US*)
Trail (*UK*)
Trailer Life Magazine (*US*)
Vegan Life (*UK*)
Western & Eastern Treasures (*US*)
Western Outdoor News (*US*)
Wisconsin Natural Resources Magazine (*US*)
Your Dog Magazine (*UK*)
Lifestyle
AARP Bulletin (*US*)
American Quarter Horse Journal (*US*)
Boat International (*UK*)
Cambridge Magazine (*UK*)
Catster (*US*)
Charleston Magazine (*US*)
Charleston Style and Design Magazine (*US*)
Cotswold Life (*UK*)
Country Walking (*UK*)
Diabetes Balance (*UK*)
Diva (*UK*)
Erotic Review (*UK*)
Essence (*US*)
Essex Life (*UK*)
Good Housekeeping (*UK*)
GQ Magazine (*UK*)
H&E Naturist (*UK*)
Harper's Bazaar (*UK*)

Hot Press (*Ire*)
House & Garden (*UK*)
Litro Magazine (*UK*)
Little Rose Magazine (*US*)
marie claire (*UK*)
Nob Hill Gazette (*US*)
Organic Life (*US*)
Park Home and Holiday Caravan (*UK*)
Phoenix Magazine (*US*)
PN (Paraplegia News) (*US*)
The Pool (*UK*)
Psychologies (*UK*)
Real Simple (*US*)
San Diego Family Magazine (*US*)
Santa Barbara Magazine (*US*)
Self (*US*)
Shout Magazine (*UK*)
Shropshire Magazine (*UK*)
Southern Boating (*US*)
Spear's Magazine (*UK*)
St Anthony Messenger (*US*)
Surrey Life (*UK*)
Susquehanna Life (*US*)
Tallahassee Magazine (*US*)
Toronto Life (*Can*)
Vegan Life (*UK*)
Windspeaker (*Can*)
Woman (*UK*)
Woman's Own (*UK*)
Woman's Way (*Ire*)
Yorkshire Life (*UK*)
Your Dog Magazine (*UK*)
Literature
Acumen (*UK*)
Adelaide Literary Magazine (*US*)
Aesthetica: A Review of Contemporary Artists (*UK*)
Agenda (*UK*)
Aphelion: The Webzine of Science Fiction and Fantasy (*US*)
The Burnt Candle (*UK*)
Callaloo (*US*)
Caveat Lector (*US*)
Central and Eastern European London Review (*UK*)
Chicago Review (*US*)
The Christian Science Monitor (*US*)
The Collagist (*US*)
Compose (*US*)
Connotation Press (*US*)
Crannóg Magazine (*Ire*)
Critical Quarterly (*UK*)
Crystal Magazine (*UK*)
december Magazine (*US*)
The Dublin Review (*Ire*)
Déraciné (*US*)
Empty Mirror (*US*)
Envoi (*UK*)
Filling Station (*Can*)
Infinite Rust (*US*)
Into The Void Magazine (*Ire*)
Jewish Quarterly (*UK*)
Litro Magazine (*UK*)

Little Rose Magazine (*US*)
The London Magazine (*UK*)
London Review of Books (*UK*)
Magma (*UK*)
Modern Poetry in Translation (*UK*)
The North (*UK*)
Planet (*UK*)
Poetry Ireland Review (*Ire*)
Quill & Quire (*Can*)
Rain Taxi (*US*)
The Savage Kick (*UK*)
Seshat Literary Magazine (*US*)
ShortStorySunday.com (*UK*)
The Spectator (*UK*)
StoryNews (*US*)
The Times Literary Supplement (TLS) (*UK*)
Wasafiri (*UK*)
The Washington Pastime (*US*)
Media
Adelaide Literary Magazine (*US*)
BoxOffice Magazine (*US*)
British Journalism Review (*UK*)
Hot Press (*Ire*)
Infinite Rust (*US*)
Inside Soap (*UK*)
Press Gazette (*UK*)
StoryNews (*US*)
Vanity Fair (*UK*)
Woman's Way (*Ire*)
Medicine
Alternative Therapies in Health and Medicine (*US*)
American Baby (*US*)
Arthritis Today (*US*)
Coping with Cancer Magazine (*US*)
Diabetes Balance (*UK*)
Irish Journal of Medical Science (*Ire*)
Irish Medical Times (*Ire*)
Nurseweek (*US*)
Nursing Times (*UK*)
Pediatric Annals (*US*)
PracticeLink Magazine (*US*)
The Practising Midwife (*UK*)
Pulse (*UK*)
Men's Interests
GQ Magazine (*UK*)
Military
Air Force Times (*US*)
Aviation History (*US*)
RUSI Journal (*UK*)
The Savage Kick (*UK*)
VFW (Veterans of Foreign Wars) Magazine (*US*)
World War II (*US*)
Music
Aesthetica: A Review of Contemporary Artists (*UK*)
Bust (*US*)
Central and Eastern European London Review (*UK*)
Classical Singer (*US*)
Columbia: A Journal of Literature and Art (*US*)
Connotation Press (*US*)

Empty Mirror (*US*)
Hawai'i Review (*US*)
Hot Press (*Ire*)
Jewish Quarterly (*UK*)
Mojo (*UK*)
Music Week (*UK*)
Opera News (*US*)
Planet (*UK*)
Record Collector Magazine (*UK*)
Shout Magazine (*UK*)
Tempo: A Quarterly Review of New Music (*UK*)
Mystery
The Burnt Candle (*UK*)
Crystal Magazine (*UK*)
Ellery Queen Mystery Magazine (*US*)
GUD Magazine (*US*)
Into The Void Magazine (*Ire*)
The Mystic Blue Review (*US*)
The People's Friend (*UK*)
Seshat Literary Magazine (*US*)
ShortStorySunday.com (*UK*)
The Washington Pastime (*US*)
Nature
All Animals (*US*)
American Quarter Horse Journal (*US*)
Arizona Wildlife Views (*US*)
BBC Countryfile Magazine (*UK*)
BBC Wildlife Magazine (*UK*)
British Birds (*UK*)
Bugle (*US*)
Camas (*US*)
Catster (*US*)
The Christian Science Monitor (*US*)
Cotswold Life (*UK*)
Country Walking (*UK*)
Crystal Magazine (*UK*)
The Dawntreader (*UK*)
EarthLines Magazine (*Ire*)
Essex Life (*UK*)
The Field (*UK*)
Flora International (*UK*)
Fly Fishing & Fly Tying Magazine (*UK*)
Flyway: Journal of Writing & Environment (*US*)
Geographical (*UK*)
Into The Void Magazine (*Ire*)
Irish Farmers Journal (*Ire*)
Irish Pages (*UK*)
Organic Life (*US*)
The People's Friend (*UK*)
Pest Management Professional (*US*)
Scintilla (*UK*)
Scouting (*US*)
Seshat Literary Magazine (*US*)
ShortStorySunday.com (*UK*)
Susquehanna Life (*US*)
This England (*UK*)
Tropical Fish Hobbyist Magazine (*US*)
Vegetable Growers News Magazine (*US*)
Wisconsin Natural Resources Magazine (*US*)
Yes! Magazine (*US*)
Your Horse (*UK*)

New Age
ShortStorySunday.com (*UK*)
The Starlit Path (*Can*)
Nonfiction
AARP Bulletin (*US*)
The Account (*US*)
Acumen (*UK*)
Adelaide Literary Magazine (*US*)
Adornment (*US*)
Advisor Today (*US*)
Aeroplane (*UK*)
Aesthetica: A Review of Contemporary Artists (*UK*)
Africa Confidential (*UK*)
After Happy Hour Review (*US*)
Air Force Times (*US*)
Alabama Heritage (*US*)
Alebrijes (*US*)
All Animals (*US*)
All Out Cricket (*UK*)
Alternative Therapies in Health and Medicine (*US*)
Amateur Gardening (*UK*)
Amazing! Magazine (*UK*)
America's Pharmacist (*US*)
American Baby (*US*)
American History (*US*)
American Quarter Horse Journal (*US*)
American Snowmobiler (*US*)
Amethyst Review (*UK*)
Angler's Mail (*UK*)
AntiqueWeek (*US*)
Aphelion: The Webzine of Science Fiction and Fantasy (*US*)
APICS Magazine (*US*)
Architectural Design (*UK*)
Architectural Record (*US*)
Arizona Wildlife Views (*US*)
Art Quarterly (*UK*)
Arthritis Today (*US*)
ArtReview (*UK*)
Athletic Business (*US*)
The Author (*UK*)
Aviation History (*US*)
Bartender (*US*)
BBC Countryfile Magazine (*UK*)
BBC Wildlife Magazine (*UK*)
BedTimes (*US*)
Bella Grace New Generation (*US*)
BizTimes Milwaukee (*US*)
Boat International (*UK*)
BoxOffice Magazine (*US*)
British Birds (*UK*)
British Journalism Review (*UK*)
Broadcast (*UK*)
Bugle (*US*)
Building Design (*UK*)
Bunbury Magazine (*UK*)
Business London (*Can*)
Bust (*US*)
Cadet Quest (*US*)
Cahoodaloodaling (*US*)
Callaloo (*US*)

Camas (*US*)
Cambridge Magazine (*UK*)
Canadian Yachting (*Can*)
The Capilano Review (*Can*)
The Carolina Quarterly (*US*)
The Caterer (*UK*)
Catholic Pictorial (*UK*)
Catholic Universe (*UK*)
Catster (*US*)
Caveat Lector (*US*)
Central and Eastern European London Review (*UK*)
Charleston Magazine (*US*)
Charleston Style and Design Magazine (*US*)
The Chattahoochee Review (*US*)
Chicago Quarterly Review (*US*)
Chicago Review (*US*)
The Christian Science Monitor (*US*)
Classical Singer (*US*)
Climb Magazine (*UK*)
Climber (*UK*)
Cloud Rodeo (*US*)
Coach (*UK*)
Cold Mountain Review (*US*)
The Collagist (*US*)
Colorado Review (*US*)
Compose (*US*)
Computeractive Magazine (*UK*)
Confrontation Magazine (*US*)
Connotation Press (*US*)
Construction Equipment Guide (*US*)
Coping with Cancer Magazine (*US*)
Cotswold Life (*UK*)
Cottonwood (*US*)
Country Walking (*UK*)
Crab Creek Review (*US*)
Creative Knitting (*US*)
Criminal Law & Justice Weekly (Incorporating Justice of the Peace) (*UK*)
Critical Quarterly (*UK*)
Crystal Magazine (*UK*)
The Cumberland River Review (*US*)
Current Accounts (*UK*)
Custom Car (*UK*)
Custom PC (*UK*)
The Daily Tea (*US*)
The Dawntreader (*UK*)
The Dead Mule School of Southern Literature (*US*)
december Magazine (*US*)
Denver Quarterly (*US*)
Descent (*UK*)
Devil's Lake (*US*)
Diabetes Balance (*UK*)
Diagram (*US*)
Director (*UK*)
Diva (*UK*)
The Dolls' House (*UK*)
The Dos Passos Review (*US*)
Down in the Dirt (*US*)
Dream Catcher (*UK*)
The Dublin Review (*Ire*)
Ducts (*US*)

EarthLines Magazine (*Ire*)
Eastern Art Report (*UK*)
Eat In Magazine (*UK*)
Empty Mirror (*US*)
Emrys Journal (*US*)
The Engineer (*UK*)
Engineering In Miniature (*UK*)
Envoi (*UK*)
Erotic Review (*UK*)
Essence (*US*)
Essex Life (*UK*)
The Evansville Review (*US*)
Event (*Can*)
Everyday Practical Electronics (*UK*)
Feminist Studies (*US*)
The Field (*UK*)
Filling Station (*Can*)
Five:2:One (*US*)
Flint Hills Review (*US*)
Flora International (*UK*)
Fly Fishing & Fly Tying Magazine (*UK*)
Flyway: Journal of Writing & Environment (*US*)
Fogged Clarity (*US*)
Forage (*UK*)
Fourteen Hills (*US*)
Frieze (*UK*)
Fugue (*US*)
Garbled Transmissions (*US*)
A Gathering of the Tribes (*US*)
Geographical (*UK*)
Gertrude (*US*)
Golf Monthly (*UK*)
Good Housekeeping (*UK*)
GQ Magazine (*UK*)
Granta (*UK*)
Grasslimb (*US*)
Green Mountains Review (GMR) (*US*)
The Grey Press (*Can*)
GUD Magazine (*US*)
Guernica (*US*)
Gulf Coast: A Journal of Literature and Fine Arts (*US*)
Gulf Stream Magazine (*US*)
H&E Naturist (*UK*)
Harper's Bazaar (*UK*)
Hawai'i Pacific Review (*US*)
Hawai'i Review (*US*)
Hayden's Ferry Review (*US*)
The Helix (*US*)
HelloHorror (*US*)
Hennen's Observer (*US*)
History Today (*UK*)
Hoot (*US*)
Hot Press (*Ire*)
House & Garden (*UK*)
The Huffington Post (United Kingdom) (*UK*)
Idiom 23 (*Aus*)
Indiana Review (*US*)
Infinite Rust (*US*)
Inside Soap (*UK*)
Into The Void Magazine (*Ire*)
Ireland's Own (*Ire*)
Irish Farmers Journal (*Ire*)

Irish Journal of Medical Science (*Ire*)
Irish Medical Times (*Ire*)
Irish Pages (*UK*)
Jewish Quarterly (*UK*)
Kitchen Garden (*UK*)
Landfall (*Aus*)
The Lawyer (*UK*)
Leisure Painter (*UK*)
LGC (Local Government Chronicle) (*UK*)
Litro Magazine (*UK*)
Little Rose Magazine (*US*)
The London Magazine (*UK*)
London Review of Books (*UK*)
Long Life Magazine (*US*)
Lothian Life (*UK*)
Louisiana Literature (*US*)
Magma (*UK*)
marie claire (*UK*)
Maritime Journal (*UK*)
Midway Journal (*US*)
Modern Poetry in Translation (*UK*)
Mojo (*UK*)
Moneywise (*UK*)
Motorcycle News (MCN) (*UK*)
The Motorship (*UK*)
Mslexia (*UK*)
Music Week (*UK*)
The Mystic Blue Review (*US*)
Nature (*UK*)
New Scientist (*UK*)
New Statesman (*UK*)
New Welsh Reader (*UK*)
NFPA Journal (*US*)
Niche (*US*)
Nob Hill Gazette (*US*)
Nostalgia Magazine (*US*)
Nurseweek (*US*)
Nursing Times (*UK*)
OfficePro (*US*)
Olive (*UK*)
Online Quilt Magazine (*Aus*)
Opera News (*US*)
Orbis International Literary Journal (*UK*)
Organic Life (*US*)
Oxford Poetry (*UK*)
Park Home and Holiday Caravan (*UK*)
Pediatric Annals (*US*)
Pentecostal Evangel (*US*)
Pentecostal Messenger (*US*)
People Management (*UK*)
The People's Friend (*UK*)
Pest Management Professional (*US*)
Philly Weekly (*US*)
Phoenix Magazine (*US*)
Photonics & Imaging Technology (*US*)
Picture Postcard Monthly (*UK*)
Pizza Today (*US*)
Plain Truth Magazine (*US*)
Planet (*UK*)
Play & Playground Magazine (*US*)
PN (Paraplegia News) (*US*)
Poetry Ireland Review (*Ire*)
Poetry London (*UK*)

Woman (*UK*)
Woman's Own (*UK*)
Woman's Way (*Ire*)
Woman's Weekly (*UK*)
Women's Health Magazine (*US*)
WoodmenLife Magazine (*US*)
World War II (*US*)
Yachts & Yachting (*UK*)
Yarn (*Aus*)
Yes! Magazine (*US*)
Yorkshire Life (*UK*)
Your Dog Magazine (*UK*)
Your Horse (*UK*)
Zoning Practice (*US*)
Philosophy
Infinite Rust (*US*)
Into The Void Magazine (*Ire*)
Jewish Quarterly (*UK*)
ShortStorySunday.com (*UK*)
The Times Literary Supplement (TLS) (*UK*)
Photography
Infinite Rust (*US*)
Little Rose Magazine (*US*)
The Mystic Blue Review (*US*)
Picture Postcard Monthly (*UK*)
Shutterbug (*US*)
Poetry
Abramelin (*US*)
The Account (*US*)
Acumen (*UK*)
Adelaide Literary Magazine (*US*)
After Happy Hour Review (*US*)
Agenda (*UK*)
Alebrijes (*US*)
Ambit (*UK*)
Amethyst Review (*UK*)
Aphelion: The Webzine of Science Fiction and
Fantasy (*US*)
Areté (*UK*)
ARTEMISpoetry (*UK*)
Banipal (*UK*)
Better Than Starbucks (*US*)
Blithe Spirit (*UK*)
Brittle Star (*UK*)
Bugle (*US*)
Bunbury Magazine (*UK*)
The Burnt Candle (*UK*)
Cadaverous Magazine (*US*)
Cahoodaloodaling (*US*)
Callaloo (*US*)
Camas (*US*)
The Capilano Review (*Can*)
The Carolina Quarterly (*US*)
Caveat Lector (*US*)
The Chaffin Journal (*US*)
Chantarelle's Notebook (*US*)
The Chattahoochee Review (*US*)
Chicago Quarterly Review (*US*)
Chicago Review (*US*)
Cimarron Review (*US*)
The Claremont Review (*Can*)
Cloud Rodeo (*US*)
Cloudbank (*US*)

Coal City Review (*US*)
Cold Mountain Review (*US*)
The Collagist (*US*)
Colorado Review (*US*)
Columbia: A Journal of Literature and Art (*US*)
Compose (*US*)
Conduit (*US*)
Confrontation Magazine (*US*)
Connecticut River Review (*US*)
Connotation Press (*US*)
Contemporary Haibun Online (*US*)
Coping with Cancer Magazine (*US*)
Cottonwood (*US*)
Crab Creek Review (*US*)
Crannóg Magazine (*Ire*)
Critical Quarterly (*UK*)
Crucible (*US*)
Crystal Magazine (*UK*)
The Cumberland River Review (*US*)
Current Accounts (*UK*)
Cyphers (*Ire*)
Darkling (*US*)
The Dawntreader (*UK*)
The Dead Mule School of Southern Literature
(*US*)
december Magazine (*US*)
Denver Quarterly (*US*)
The Deronda Review (*US*)
Devil's Lake (*US*)
Diagram (*US*)
The Dos Passos Review (*US*)
Down in the Dirt (*US*)
Dream Catcher (*UK*)
Dressing Room Poetry Journal (*US*)
Ducts (*US*)
Déraciné (*US*)
EarthLines Magazine (*Ire*)
Earthshine (*US*)
Empty Mirror (*US*)
Emrys Journal (*US*)
Enchanted Tales Literary Magazine (*US*)
Envoi (*UK*)
The Evansville Review (*US*)
Event (*Can*)
failbetter.com (*US*)
Feminist Studies (*US*)
The Fenland Reed (*UK*)
Filling Station (*Can*)
Five:2:One (*US*)
Flint Hills Review (*US*)
Flyway: Journal of Writing & Environment (*US*)
Fogged Clarity (*US*)
Forage (*UK*)
Fourteen Hills (*US*)
Fugue (*US*)
A Gathering of the Tribes (*US*)
Gertrude (*US*)
The Gettysburg Review (*US*)
Gold Dust (*UK*)
Granta (*UK*)
Grasslimb (*US*)
Green Hills Literary Lantern (*US*)
Green Mountains Review (GMR) (*US*)

The Grey Press (*Can*)
GUD Magazine (*US*)
Guernica (*US*)
Gulf Coast: A Journal of Literature and Fine Arts (*US*)
Gulf Stream Magazine (*US*)
Haight Ashbury Literary Journal (*US*)
Hanging Loose (*US*)
Hawai'i Pacific Review (*US*)
Hawai'i Review (*US*)
Hayden's Ferry Review (*US*)
The Helix (*US*)
HelloHorror (*US*)
Hennen's Observer (*US*)
Hoot (*US*)
Iconoclast (*US*)
Idaho Review (*US*)
Idiom 23 (*Aus*)
Indefinite Space (*US*)
Infinite Rust (*US*)
InJoy Magazine (*US*)
Ink Sweat and Tears (*UK*)
The Interpreter's House (*UK*)
Into The Void Magazine (*Ire*)
The Iowa Review (*US*)
Irish Pages (*UK*)
Island (*Aus*)
Jewish Quarterly (*UK*)
Josephine Quarterly (*US*)
Kaimana: Literary Arts Hawai'i (*US*)
Landfall (*Aus*)
Lighthouse (*UK*)
Litro Magazine (*UK*)
Little Rose Magazine (*US*)
The London Magazine (*UK*)
London Review of Books (*UK*)
Long Life Magazine (*US*)
Louisiana Literature (*US*)
The Lyric (*US*)
Magma (*UK*)
Midway Journal (*US*)
Modern Poetry in Translation (*UK*)
The Moth (*Ire*)
Mslexia (*UK*)
The Mystic Blue Review (*US*)
New Fairy Tales (*UK*)
New Statesman (*UK*)
New Welsh Reader (*UK*)
Nine Muses Poetry (*UK*)
The North (*UK*)
NY Literary Magazine (*US*)
Old Red Kimono (*US*)
Orbis International Literary Journal (*UK*)
Oxford Poetry (*UK*)
The People's Friend (*UK*)
Pirene's Fountain (*US*)
Planet (*UK*)
PN Review (*UK*)
Poetica Magazine (*US*)
Poetry Ireland Review (*Ire*)
Poetry London (*UK*)
The Poetry Review (*UK*)
Poetry Wales (*UK*)

Prole (*UK*)
Reach (*UK*)
The Rialto (*UK*)
Ripcord. (*US*)
River Heron Review (*US*)
The Road Not Taken: The Journal of Formal Poetry (*US*)
Sarasvati (*UK*)
Scifaikuest (*US*)
Scintilla (*UK*)
Seshat Literary Magazine (*US*)
Shooter Literary Magazine (*UK*)
Sinister Wisdom (*US*)
Skald (*UK*)
South (*UK*)
St Anthony Messenger (*US*)
St Petersburg Review (*US*)
Stand Magazine (*UK*)
The Starlit Path (*Can*)
This England (*UK*)
The Times Literary Supplement (TLS) (*UK*)
Wasafiri (*UK*)
The Washington Pastime (*US*)
Politics
    AARP Bulletin (*US*)
    Africa Confidential (*UK*)
    Business London (*Can*)
    Confrontation Magazine (*US*)
    Essence (*US*)
    Guernica (*US*)
    H&E Naturist (*UK*)
    Hot Press (*Ire*)
    The Huffington Post (United Kingdom) (*UK*)
    Infinite Rust (*US*)
    Into The Void Magazine (*Ire*)
    Jewish Quarterly (*UK*)
    LGC (Local Government Chronicle) (*UK*)
    Litro Magazine (*UK*)
    Little Rose Magazine (*US*)
    London Review of Books (*UK*)
    New Statesman (*UK*)
    Planet (*UK*)
    The Spectator (*UK*)
    StoryNews (*US*)
    Vanity Fair (*UK*)
    Windspeaker (*Can*)
    Yes! Magazine (*US*)
    Zoning Practice (*US*)
Psychology
    HelloHorror (*US*)
    Into The Void Magazine (*Ire*)
    Little Rose Magazine (*US*)
Radio
    Radio Times (*UK*)
Reference
    Mslexia (*UK*)
    Picture Postcard Monthly (*UK*)
    The Starlit Path (*Can*)
Religious
    Amethyst Review (*UK*)
    Cadet Quest (*US*)
    Catholic Pictorial (*UK*)
    Catholic Universe (*UK*)

The Christian Science Monitor (*US*)
Jewish Quarterly (*UK*)
Little Rose Magazine (*US*)
The New Accelerator (*UK*)
Pentecostal Evangel (*US*)
Pentecostal Messenger (*US*)
Plain Truth Magazine (*US*)
Reform (*UK*)
St Anthony Messenger (*US*)
The Starlit Path (*Can*)

Romance
The Burnt Candle (*UK*)
Crystal Magazine (*UK*)
Enchanted Tales Literary Magazine (*US*)
GUD Magazine (*US*)
InJoy Magazine (*US*)
Into The Void Magazine (*Ire*)
The Mystic Blue Review (*US*)
The People's Friend (*UK*)
People's Friend Pocket Novels (*UK*)
Seshat Literary Magazine (*US*)
ShortStorySunday.com (*UK*)
The Washington Pastime (*US*)

Science
The Christian Science Monitor (*US*)
Diabetes Balance (*UK*)
Geographical (*UK*)
Hawai'i Review (*US*)
Infinite Rust (*US*)
Into The Void Magazine (*Ire*)
Irish Pages (*UK*)
London Review of Books (*UK*)
Long Life Magazine (*US*)
Nature (*UK*)
The New Accelerator (*UK*)
New Scientist (*UK*)
Photonics & Imaging Technology (*US*)
Popular Science (*US*)
Scintilla (*UK*)
Sky at Night Magazine (*UK*)
Tech Directions (*US*)
The Times Literary Supplement (TLS) (*UK*)

Sci-Fi
Aphelion: The Webzine of Science Fiction and
Fantasy (*US*)
Crystal Magazine (*UK*)
The Fifth Di... (*US*)
Garbled Transmissions (*US*)
GUD Magazine (*US*)
Hawai'i Review (*US*)
Interzone (*UK*)
Into The Void Magazine (*Ire*)
The Mystic Blue Review (*US*)
The New Accelerator (*UK*)
Orson Scott Card's InterGalactic Medicine Show
(*US*)
Scifaikuest (*US*)
Seshat Literary Magazine (*US*)
SFX (*UK*)
ShortStorySunday.com (*UK*)
The Starlit Path (*Can*)
The Washington Pastime (*US*)

Scripts
The Claremont Review (*Can*)
Connotation Press (*US*)
Current Accounts (*UK*)
The Evansville Review (*US*)
Flint Hills Review (*US*)
Gold Dust (*UK*)
Hawai'i Review (*US*)
The Helix (*US*)
St Petersburg Review (*US*)

Self-Help
Little Rose Magazine (*US*)

Short Stories
The Account (*US*)
Adelaide Literary Magazine (*US*)
Ambit (*UK*)
Amethyst Review (*UK*)
Aphelion: The Webzine of Science Fiction and
Fantasy (*US*)
Areté (*UK*)
Banipal (*UK*)
Better Than Starbucks (*US*)
Big Fiction (*US*)
Black Static (*UK*)
Brittle Star (*UK*)
Bunbury Magazine (*UK*)
The Burnt Candle (*UK*)
Cadet Quest (*US*)
The Cafe Irreal (*US*)
Callaloo (*US*)
The Carolina Quarterly (*US*)
The Casket of Fictional Delights (*UK*)
Caveat Lector (*US*)
The Chaffin Journal (*US*)
The Chattahoochee Review (*US*)
Chicago Quarterly Review (*US*)
Chicago Review (*US*)
Cimarron Review (*US*)
The Claremont Review (*Can*)
Cloudbank (*US*)
Coal City Review (*US*)
Cold Mountain Review (*US*)
The Collagist (*US*)
Colorado Review (*US*)
Columbia: A Journal of Literature and Art (*US*)
Compose (*US*)
Conduit (*US*)
Confrontation Magazine (*US*)
Connotation Press (*US*)
Cottonwood (*US*)
Crab Creek Review (*US*)
Crannóg Magazine (*Ire*)
Critical Quarterly (*UK*)
Crucible (*US*)
Crystal Magazine (*UK*)
The Cumberland River Review (*US*)
Current Accounts (*UK*)
Cyphers (*Ire*)
The Dawntreader (*UK*)
The Dead Mule School of Southern Literature
(*US*)
december Magazine (*US*)
Denver Quarterly (*US*)

Devil's Lake (*US*)
Diagram (*US*)
Down in the Dirt (*US*)
Dream Catcher (*UK*)
The Dublin Review (*Ire*)
Ducts (*US*)
EarthLines Magazine (*Ire*)
Ellery Queen Mystery Magazine (*US*)
Emrys Journal (*US*)
Enchanted Tales Literary Magazine (*US*)
Erotic Review (*UK*)
The Evansville Review (*US*)
failbetter.com (*US*)
Feminist Studies (*US*)
The Fenland Reed (*UK*)
The Fifth Di... (*US*)
Filling Station (*Can*)
Five:2:One (*US*)
Flash: The International Short-Short Story
Magazine (*UK*)
Flint Hills Review (*US*)
Flyway: Journal of Writing & Environment (*US*)
Fourteen Hills (*US*)
Fugue (*US*)
A Gathering of the Tribes (*US*)
The Gettysburg Review (*US*)
Gold Dust (*UK*)
Granta (*UK*)
Grasslimb (*US*)
Green Hills Literary Lantern (*US*)
Green Mountains Review (GMR) (*US*)
The Grey Press (*Can*)
GUD Magazine (*US*)
Guernica (*US*)
Haight Ashbury Literary Journal (*US*)
Hawai'i Review (*US*)
Hayden's Ferry Review (*US*)
The Helix (*US*)
HelloHorror (*US*)
Hennen's Observer (*US*)
Iconoclast (*US*)
Idaho Review (*US*)
Idiom 23 (*Aus*)
Indiana Review (*US*)
Infinite Rust (*US*)
InJoy Magazine (*US*)
The Interpreter's House (*UK*)
Interzone (*UK*)
Into The Void Magazine (*Ire*)
The Iowa Review (*US*)
Ireland's Own (*Ire*)
Irish Pages (*UK*)
Island (*Aus*)
Jewish Quarterly (*UK*)
Kaimana: Literary Arts Hawai'i (*US*)
Lighthouse (*UK*)
Litro Magazine (*UK*)
Little Rose Magazine (*US*)
The London Magazine (*UK*)
Long Life Magazine (*US*)
Louisiana Literature (*US*)
The Moth (*Ire*)
Mslexia (*UK*)

The Mystic Blue Review (*US*)
The New Accelerator (*UK*)
New Fairy Tales (*UK*)
New Welsh Reader (*UK*)
Old Red Kimono (*US*)
Orbis International Literary Journal (*UK*)
Orson Scott Card's InterGalactic Medicine Show
(*US*)
Overtime (*US*)
The People's Friend (*UK*)
Planet (*UK*)
Prole (*UK*)
Ripcord. (*US*)
Sarasvati (*UK*)
Seshat Literary Magazine (*US*)
ShortStorySunday.com (*UK*)
Sinister Wisdom (*US*)
Skald (*UK*)
SlingInk Magazine (*UK*)
St Anthony Messenger (*US*)
St Petersburg Review (*US*)
Stand Magazine (*UK*)
The Starlit Path (*Can*)
This Is Bill Gorton (*US*)
Wasafiri (*UK*)
The Washington Pastime (*US*)
Woman's Weekly (*UK*)
Woman's Weekly Fiction Special (*UK*)
Sociology
H&E Naturist (*UK*)
Infinite Rust (*US*)
Into The Void Magazine (*Ire*)
LGC (Local Government Chronicle) (*UK*)
Little Rose Magazine (*US*)
Reform (*UK*)
Spiritual
Amethyst Review (*UK*)
The Dawntreader (*UK*)
InJoy Magazine (*US*)
Little Rose Magazine (*US*)
The New Accelerator (*UK*)
Reform (*UK*)
Scintilla (*UK*)
The Starlit Path (*Can*)
Sport
All Out Cricket (*UK*)
Angler's Mail (*UK*)
Athletic Business (*US*)
Business London (*Can*)
Climb Magazine (*UK*)
Climber (*UK*)
Coach (*UK*)
Fly Fishing & Fly Tying Magazine (*UK*)
Golf Monthly (*UK*)
Hot Press (*Ire*)
The Huffington Post (United Kingdom) (*UK*)
Improve Your Coarse Fishing (*UK*)
PN (Paraplegia News) (*US*)
Referee (*US*)
Runner's World (*US*)
Running (*UK*)
Ski Patrol Magazine (*US*)
Snooker Scene (*UK*)

Southern Boating (*US*)
Tallahassee Magazine (*US*)
Western & Eastern Treasures (*US*)
Western Outdoor News (*US*)
Windspeaker (*Can*)
Yachts & Yachting (*UK*)
Suspense
Aphelion: The Webzine of Science Fiction and Fantasy (*US*)
The Burnt Candle (*UK*)
Crystal Magazine (*UK*)
GUD Magazine (*US*)
Into The Void Magazine (*Ire*)
The Mystic Blue Review (*US*)
ShortStorySunday.com (*UK*)
The Washington Pastime (*US*)
Technology
Aeroplane (*UK*)
American Snowmobiler (*US*)
Boat International (*UK*)
Broadcast (*UK*)
Cambridge Magazine (*UK*)
Canadian Yachting (*Can*)
Computeractive Magazine (*UK*)
Construction Equipment Guide (*US*)
Custom PC (*UK*)
Descent (*UK*)
The Engineer (*UK*)
Engineering In Miniature (*UK*)
Everyday Practical Electronics (*UK*)
GQ Magazine (*UK*)
The Huffington Post (United Kingdom) (*UK*)
Little Rose Magazine (*US*)
Long Life Magazine (*US*)
Motorcycle News (MCN) (*UK*)
The Motorship (*UK*)
The New Accelerator (*UK*)
New Scientist (*UK*)
Photonics & Imaging Technology (*US*)
Play & Playground Magazine (*US*)
Popular Science (*US*)
The Railway Magazine (*UK*)
Rider Magazine (*US*)
RUSI Journal (*UK*)
Screen Printing (*US*)
Shutterbug (*US*)
Sky at Night Magazine (*UK*)
SQL Server Pro (*US*)
Stone World (*US*)
Tech Directions (*US*)
Television (*UK*)
Texas Co-op Power (*US*)
Trailer Life Magazine (*US*)
Water Well Journal (*US*)
Welding Design & Fabrication (*US*)
What Car? (*UK*)
Wire Rope News & Sling Technology (*US*)
Theatre
Aesthetica: A Review of Contemporary Artists (*UK*)
Central and Eastern European London Review (*UK*)
Harper's Bazaar (*UK*)

Planet (*UK*)
St Petersburg Review (*US*)
The Stage (*UK*)
The Times Literary Supplement (TLS) (*UK*)
Thrillers
Aphelion: The Webzine of Science Fiction and Fantasy (*US*)
The Burnt Candle (*UK*)
Crystal Magazine (*UK*)
Into The Void Magazine (*Ire*)
The Mystic Blue Review (*US*)
The New Accelerator (*UK*)
The People's Friend (*UK*)
ShortStorySunday.com (*UK*)
The Washington Pastime (*US*)
Translations
Banipal (*UK*)
Better Than Starbucks (*US*)
The Chattahoochee Review (*US*)
Columbia: A Journal of Literature and Art (*US*)
Current Accounts (*UK*)
Cyphers (*Ire*)
Dream Catcher (*UK*)
Envoi (*UK*)
Guernica (*US*)
Hawai'i Review (*US*)
Indiana Review (*US*)
The Iowa Review (*US*)
Irish Pages (*UK*)
Litro Magazine (*UK*)
Modern Poetry in Translation (*UK*)
Oxford Poetry (*UK*)
PN Review (*UK*)
Poetry London (*UK*)
The Poetry Review (*UK*)
Stand Magazine (*UK*)
Travel
American Snowmobiler (*US*)
Aviation History (*US*)
Boat International (*UK*)
Business London (*Can*)
Bust (*US*)
Canadian Yachting (*Can*)
The Carolina Quarterly (*US*)
Central and Eastern European London Review (*UK*)
Charleston Magazine (*US*)
Charleston Style and Design Magazine (*US*)
Cotswold Life (*UK*)
Country Walking (*UK*)
Crystal Magazine (*UK*)
The Daily Tea (*US*)
EarthLines Magazine (*Ire*)
Geographical (*UK*)
Harper's Bazaar (*UK*)
House & Garden (*UK*)
Infinite Rust (*US*)
Litro Magazine (*UK*)
Lothian Life (*UK*)
marie claire (*UK*)
Maritime Journal (*UK*)
Motorcycle News (MCN) (*UK*)
The Motorship (*UK*)

Nob Hill Gazette (*US*)
Park Home and Holiday Caravan (*UK*)
The People's Friend (*UK*)
Phoenix Magazine (*US*)
Psychologies (*UK*)
The Railway Magazine (*UK*)
Recommend Magazine (*US*)
Rider Magazine (*US*)
School Bus Fleet (*US*)
Scouting (*US*)
Ski Patrol Magazine (*US*)
Southern Boating (*US*)
Surrey Life (*UK*)
Susquehanna Life (*US*)
Tallahassee Magazine (*US*)
The Lady (*UK*)
Trail (*UK*)
Trailer Life Magazine (*US*)
TravelWorld International Magazine (*US*)
Truck & Driver (*UK*)
Vegan Life (*UK*)
Wanderlust Magazine (*UK*)
What Car? (*UK*)
Woman's Weekly (*UK*)
Yachts & Yachting (*UK*)
Yorkshire Life (*UK*)
Your Horse (*UK*)
TV
Broadcast (*UK*)
Radio Times (*UK*)
SFX (*UK*)
Television (*UK*)
Westerns
Crystal Magazine (*UK*)
Into The Void Magazine (*Ire*)

The Savage Kick (*UK*)
ShortStorySunday.com (*UK*)
The Washington Pastime (*US*)
Women's Interests
Aesthetica: A Review of Contemporary Artists (*UK*)
Bella Grace New Generation (*US*)
Bust (*US*)
december Magazine (*US*)
Diva (*UK*)
Feminist Studies (*US*)
Good Housekeeping (*UK*)
Harper's Bazaar (*UK*)
InJoy Magazine (*US*)
marie claire (*UK*)
Mslexia (*UK*)
Orbis International Literary Journal (*UK*)
The People's Friend (*UK*)
The Pool (*UK*)
The Practising Midwife (*UK*)
Psychologies (*UK*)
Real Simple (*US*)
Self (*US*)
Shout Magazine (*UK*)
Sinister Wisdom (*US*)
Style at Home (*UK*)
The Lady (*UK*)
Top Sante (*UK*)
Woman (*UK*)
Woman's Own (*UK*)
Woman's Way (*Ire*)
Woman's Weekly (*UK*)
Woman's Weekly Fiction Special (*UK*)
Women's Health Magazine (*US*)

US Literary Agents

For the most up-to-date listings of these and hundreds of other literary agents, visit https://www.firstwriter.com/Agents

*To claim your **free** access to the site, please see the back of this book.*

A+B Works

Email: query@aplusbworks.com
Website: http://www.aplusbworks.com

Handles: Fiction; *Markets:* Children's; Youth

Specialises in young adult and middle grade fiction, women's fiction, and select narrative nonfiction. No thrillers, literary fiction, erotica, cook books, picture books, poetry, short fiction, or screenplays. Query by email only, or using form on website. Response not guaranteed. Accepts very few new clients.

Aaron M. Priest Literary Agency

200 West 41st Street, 21st Floor, New York, NY 10036
Tel: +1 (212) 818-0344
Fax: +1 (212) 573-9417
Email: querypriest@aaronpriest.com
Website: http://www.aaronpriest.com

Handles: Fiction; Nonfiction; *Areas:* Autobiography; Biography; Crime; Culture; Current Affairs; Fantasy; Gothic; Historical; How-to; Mystery; Politics; Science; Suspense; Thrillers; Translations; Women's Interests; *Markets:* Adult; Youth; *Treatments:* Commercial; Contemporary; Literary; Popular

Send one-page query by email, describing your work and your background. No attachments, but you may paste the first chapter into the body of the email. Query one agent only. See website for specific agent interests and email addresses. No poetry, screenplays, sci-fi, or horror.

Dominick Abel Literary Agency, Inc

146 W. 82nd Street, #1B, New York, NY 10024
Tel: +1 (212) 877-0710
Fax: +1 (212) 595-3133
Email: agency@dalainc.com
Website: http://dalainc.com

Handles: Fiction; Nonfiction; *Markets:* Adult

Handles adult fiction and nonfiction. Not accepting submissions as at September 2016.

Adams Literary

7845 Colony Road, C4 #215, Charlotte, NC 28226
Tel: +1 (704) 542-1440
Fax: +1 (704) 542-1450
Email: info@adamsliterary.com
Website: http://www.adamsliterary.com

Handles: Fiction; *Markets:* Children's; Youth

Handles books for children and young adults, from picture books to teen novels. No unsolicited MSS. Send query with complete ms via webform. See website for full submission guidelines.

Adler & Robin Books, Inc

3000 Connecticut Avenue, NW, Suite 317, Washington DC, 20008
Tel: +1 (202) 986-9275
Fax: +1 (202) 986-9485
Email: submissions@adlerrobin.com
Website: http://www.adlerrobin.com

Handles: Nonfiction; Reference; *Areas:* Autobiography; Biography; Culture; Historical; How-to; Humour; Lifestyle; Self-Help; *Markets:* Adult; Children's

Interested in biography/memoir, careers, gift books, how-to, humour, lifestyle, local history, pop culture, reference books, self-help, and children's books. Send queries by email only.

Agency for the Performing Arts (APA)

405 S. Beverly Dr, Beverly Hills, CA 90212
Tel: +1 (310) 888-4200
Fax: +1 (310) 888-4242
Website: http://www.apa-agency.com

Handles: Fiction; Nonfiction; Scripts; *Areas:* Film; Theatre; TV; *Markets:* Adult

Handles nonfiction, novels, scripts for film, theatre, and TV, as well as musicians and other performing artists.

The Ahearn Agency, Inc

2021 Pine Street, New Orleans, LA 70118
Tel: +1 (504) 861-8395
Fax: +1 (504) 866-6434
Email: pahearn@aol.com
Website: http://www.ahearnagency.com

Handles: Fiction; Nonfiction; *Areas:* Autobiography; Biography; Crime; Current Affairs; Health; Historical; Humour; Lifestyle; Mystery; Nature; Romance; Short Stories; Suspense; Thrillers; Women's Interests; *Markets:* Adult; *Treatments:* Literary

Send one page query with SASE, description, length, market info, and any writing credits. Accepts email queries

without attachments. Response in 2-3 months.

Specialises in women's fiction and suspense. No nonfiction, poetry, juvenile material or science fiction.

Aimee Entertainment Agency

15840 Ventura Blvd., Ste. 215, Encino, CA 91436
Tel: +1 (818) 783-3831
Fax: +1 (818) 783-4447
Email: info@onlinemediapublications.com
Website: http://www. aimeeentertainment.com

Handles: Fiction; Scripts; *Areas:* Film; *Markets:* Adult

Handles film scripts and book-length works.

Alive Literary Agency

7680 Goddard Street, Suite 200, Colorado Springs, CO 80920
Tel: +1 (719) 260-7080
Email: Submissions@aliveliterary.com
Website: http://aliveliterary.com

Handles: Fiction; Nonfiction; *Areas:* Adventure; Autobiography; Biography; Business; Crime; Historical; How-to; Humour; Lifestyle; Mystery; Religious; Self-Help; Short Stories; Spiritual; Sport; Suspense; Thrillers; Westerns; Women's Interests; *Markets:* Adult; Children's; *Treatments:* Commercial; Literary; Mainstream; Popular

Accepts queries from referred authors only. Works primarily with well-established, best-selling, and career authors. Referred authors may submit query by email with bio, name of the client referring you, synopsis, and first three chapters. See website for full details.

Ambassador Speakers Bureau & Literary Agency

PO Box 50358, Nashville, TN 37205
Tel: +1 (615) 370-4700
Email: info@ambassadorspeakers.com
Website: http://www. ambassadorspeakers.com

Handles: Fiction; Nonfiction; *Areas:* Adventure; Autobiography; Biography; Culture; Current Affairs; Finance; Health; Historical; How-to; Legal; Lifestyle; Medicine; Politics; Religious; Self-Help; Women's Interests; *Markets:* Adult; *Treatments:* Contemporary; Literary; Mainstream

Represents select authors and writers who are published by religious and general market publishers in the US and Europe. No short stories, children's books, screenplays, or poetry. Send query by email with short description. Submit work on invitation only.

Marcia Amsterdam Agency
41 W. 82nd St., New York, NY 10024-5613

Handles: Fiction; Scripts; *Areas:* Adventure; Crime; Film; Historical; Horror; Humour; Mystery; Romance; Science; Thrillers; TV; *Markets:* Adult; Youth; *Treatments:* Contemporary; Mainstream

Not taking on new clients as at June 2018.

Send query with SASE. No poetry, how-to, books for the 8-10 age-group, or unsolicited MSS. Response to queries usually in one month.

The Anderson Literary Agency
Tel: +1 (917) 363-6829
Email: giles@andersonliteraryagency.com
Website: http://andersonliteraryagency.com

Handles: Nonfiction; *Areas:* Autobiography; Biography; Crime; Religious; Science; *Markets:* Adult

Particularly interested in books that help us understand people, ideas and the possibility of change. Send query by email.

Andrea Brown Literary Agency, Inc.
1076 Eagle Drive, Salinas, CA 93905
Email: andrea@andreabrownlit.com
Website: http://www.andreabrownlit.com

Handles: Fiction; Nonfiction; *Areas:* Anthropology; Archaeology; Architecture;

Arts; Autobiography; Biography; Culture; Current Affairs; Design; Drama; Fantasy; Historical; How-to; Humour; Mystery; Nature; Photography; Romance; Science; Sci-Fi; Sociology; Sport; Technology; Thrillers; Women's Interests; *Markets:* Children's; Youth; *Treatments:* Commercial; Contemporary; Literary

Handles children's from picture books to young adult only. Send query by email only. Visit website and view individual agent profiles, then select one specific agent to send a query to at their own specific email address (given on website). Put the word "Query" in the subject line and include all material in the text of the email. No attachments.

For picture books, include full MS. For fiction send first ten pages. For nonfiction submit proposal and a sample chapter. For graphic novels, send summary and 2-3 sample page spreads in .jpg or .pdf format. Indicated which publishers, if any, the MS has been sent to. No queries by fax.

The Angela Rinaldi Literary Agency
PO Box 7875, Beverly Hills, CA 90212-7875
Tel: +1 (310) 287-0356
Fax: +1 (310) 837-8143
Email: info@rinaldiliterary.com
Website: http://www.rinaldiliterary.com

Handles: Fiction; Nonfiction; *Areas:* Autobiography; Biography; Business; Cookery; Culture; Current Affairs; Finance; Gothic; Health; Historical; Lifestyle; Medicine; Mystery; Psychology; Suspense; Thrillers; Women's Interests; *Markets:* Adult; *Treatments:* Commercial; Contemporary; Literary; Mainstream

Send query by email with the word "Query" in the subject line. For fiction, paste synopsis and first ten pages in the email. For nonfiction, include detailed cover letter and your credentials and platform, as well as any publishing history. See website for full guidelines. No humour, CIA espionage, drug thrillers, techno thrillers, category romances, science fiction, fantasy, horror / occult /

paranormal, poetry, film scripts, magazine articles or religion.

Ann Rittenberg Literary Agency

15 Maiden Lane, Suite 206, New York, NY 10038
Email: info@rittlit.com
Website: http://www.rittlit.com

Handles: Fiction; Nonfiction; *Areas:* Autobiography; Biography; Culture; Historical; Mystery; Sociology; Thrillers; Women's Interests; *Markets:* Adult; *Treatments:* Literary

Send three sample chapters with outline by email (pasted into the body of the email) or by post with SASE. Email queries receive a response only if interested. No Screenplays, Genre fiction, Poetry, or Self-help. No queries by fax.

Anonymous Content

155 Spring St, 3rd Floor, New York, NY 10012
Tel: +1 (212) 925-0055
Fax: +1 (212) 925-5030
Email: litmanagement@anonymouscontent.com
Website: http://www.anonymouscontent.com

Handles: Scripts; *Areas:* Film; TV; *Markets:* Adult

Works in the areas of film, TV, adverts, and music videos.

Aponte Literary

Email: agents@aponteliterary.com
Website: http://aponteliterary.com

Handles: Fiction; Nonfiction; *Areas:* Fantasy; Historical; Politics; Science; Sci-Fi; Women's Interests; *Markets:* Adult; *Treatments:* Commercial; Mainstream

Handles any genre of mainstream fiction and nonfiction, but particularly women's novels, historical novels, supernatural and paranormal fiction, fantasy novels, political and science thrillers. Closed to submissions as at June 2017. See website for current situation.

Arcadia

31 Lake Place North, Danbury, CT 06810
Email: arcadialit@gmail.com

Handles: Nonfiction; *Areas:* Biography; Culture; Current Affairs; Health; Historical; Medicine; Psychology; Science; *Markets:* Adult

Agency handling biography, current affairs, health, history, medicine, popular culture, psychology, and science. No fiction.

Audrey A. Wolf Literary Agency

2510 Virginia Avenue NW, #702N, Washington, DC 20037
Email: audreyrwolf@gmail.com

Handles: Nonfiction; *Areas:* Autobiography; Biography; Business; Current Affairs; Finance; Health; Historical; Lifestyle; Politics; Self-Help; Sport; *Markets:* Adult

Send query by post or email, including synopsis up to two pages long showing the full structure of the book: beginning, middle, and end. Also include chapter outline.

The Axelrod Agency

55 Main Street, P.O. Box 357, Chatham, NY 12037
Tel: +1 (518) 392-2100
Fax: +1 (518) 392-2944
Email: steve@axelrodagency.com
Website: http://axelrodagency.com

Handles: Fiction; *Areas:* Crime; Erotic; Mystery; Romance; Thrillers; Women's Interests; *Markets:* Adult

Send query by email only. No nonfiction, African-American, Christian, comedy, humour, comics, graphic novels, gay/lesbian, historical, horror, literary, poetry, puzzles, games, science fiction, fantasy, or westerns.

Ayesha Pande Literary

128 West 132 Street, New York, NY 10027
Tel: +1 (212) 283-5825
Email: queries@pandeliterary.com
Website: http://pandeliterary.com

Handles: Fiction; Nonfiction; *Areas:* Autobiography; Biography; Crime; Culture; Fantasy; Finance; Historical; Humour; Mystery; Romance; Sci-Fi; Thrillers; Women's Interests; *Markets:* Adult; Youth; *Treatments:* Commercial; Literary; Popular

A New York based boutique literary agency with a small and eclectic roster of clients. Submit queries via form on website. No poetry, business books, screenplays, illustrated children's books or middle grade fiction.

Azantian Literary Agency

Email: queries@azantianlitagency.com
Website: http://www.azantianlitagency.com

Handles: Fiction; *Areas:* Fantasy; Horror; Sci-Fi; *Markets:* Adult; Children's; Youth

Not accepting submissions (except through conferences, conventions, and contests) as at November 2017. Check website for current status.

Handles only subgenres of science fiction and fantasy plus smart, psychological horror for middle grade, young adult, and adult readers. Send query by email with 1-2 page synopsis and first 10-15 pages in the body of the email. No attachments.

B.J. Robbins Literary Agency

5130 Bellaire Avenue, North Hollywood, CA 91607
Tel: +1 (818) 760-6602
Fax: +1 (818) 760-6616
Email: Robbinsliterary@gmail.com

Handles: Fiction; Nonfiction; *Areas:* Autobiography; Biography; Culture; Health; Historical; Mystery; Science; Sport; Suspense; Thrillers; Travel; *Markets:* Adult

Send query with outline / proposal and first 50 pages (fiction) or three sample chapters (nonfiction) by post with SASE or by email (no attachments). No screenplays, plays, poetry, science fiction, horror, westerns, romance, techno-thrillers, religious tracts, dating books or anything with the word "unicorn" in the title.

Baldi Agency

233 West 99th Street, 19C, New York, NY 10025
Tel: +1 (212) 222-3213
Email: info@baldibooks.com
Website: http://www.baldibooks.com

Handles: Fiction; Nonfiction; Reference; *Areas:* Autobiography; Biography; Business; Cookery; Culture; Finance; Historical; How-to; Lifestyle; Literature; Science; Self-Help; Spiritual; Technology; Travel; *Markets:* Adult

Send one page query by email, or by post with SASE. See website for full guidelines.

Barbara Hogenson Agency

165 West End Ave., Suite 19-C, New York, NY 10023
Tel: +1 (212) 874-8084
Fax: +1 (212) 362-3011
Email: Bhogenson@aol.com

Handles: Fiction; Nonfiction; Scripts; *Areas:* Theatre; *Markets:* Adult

Represents fiction, nonfiction, and stage plays. Send query by email only. No unsolicited MSS.

Baror International, Inc.

P.O. Box 868, Armonk, NY 10504-0868
Email: Heather@Barorint.com
Website: http://www.barorint.com

Handles: Fiction; Nonfiction; *Areas:* Fantasy; Sci-Fi; *Markets:* Adult; Youth; *Treatments:* Commercial; Literary

Specialises in the international and domestic representation of literary works in both fiction and nonfiction, including commercial fiction, literary, science fiction, fantasy, young adult and more. Send query by post or by email with a few sample chapters. Taking on very few authors as at July 2017. Check website for current situation.

The Bent Agency

19 W. 21st St., #201, New York, NY 10010
Email: info@thebentagency.com
Website: http://www.thebentagency.com

Handles: Fiction; Nonfiction; *Areas:*
Adventure; Autobiography; Cookery; Crime;
Culture; Fantasy; Historical; Horror;
Humour; Lifestyle; Mystery; Romance;
Science; Sci-Fi; Sociology; Sport; Suspense;
Thrillers; Women's Interests; *Markets:*
Adult; Children's; Youth; *Treatments:*
Commercial; Literary; Popular

Accepts email queries only. See website for
agent bios and specific interests and email
addresses, then query one agent only. See
website for full submission guidelines.

Betsy Amster Literary Enterprises

607 Foothill Blvd #1061, La Canada
Flintridge, CA 91012
Email: b.amster.assistant@gmail.com
Website: http://amsterlit.com

Handles: Fiction; Nonfiction; *Areas:*
Autobiography; Biography; Cookery;
Culture; Gardening; Health; Historical;
Lifestyle; Medicine; Mystery; Psychology;
Self-Help; Sociology; Thrillers; Travel;
Women's Interests; *Markets:* Adult;
Treatments: Literary; Popular

Send query by email only. For fiction and
narrative nonfiction include the first three
pages in the body of your email; for
nonfiction include your proposal, again in
the body of the email. See website for
different email addresses for adult and
children's/YA submissions. No unsolicited
attachments or queries by phone or fax.

No romances, screenplays, adult poetry,
westerns, adult fantasy, horror, science
fiction, techno thrillers, spy capers,
apocalyptic scenarios, political or religious
arguments, or self-published books.

BiCoastal Talent

2600 West Olive Ave, Suite 500, Burbank,
CA 91505
Tel: +1 (818) 845-0150
Email: submissions@BiCoastaltalent.com
Website: http://www.bicoastaltalent.com

Handles: Scripts; *Areas:* Film; TV; *Markets:*
Adult

Accepts queries for completed screenplays
only. You must have a minimum of three
completed screenplays available for review.
Send query only, including list of completed
screenplays, title, genre, and one-paragraph
synopsis of four to eight lines. No authors of
self- or unpublished manuscripts, treatments,
concepts or TV pilots. Unsolicited materials
(scripts, manuscripts, graphics, DVDs, etc.)
will not be reviewed. Response only if
interested. Preference given to writers in LA.

firstwriter.com note: Website currently
contains potentially contradictory statements:

"Writers of feature-length screenplays may
submit queries at this time";

"NOT CURRENTLY ACCEPTING ANY
SUBMISSIONS"

Bidnick & Company
Email: bidnick@comcast.net

Handles: Nonfiction; *Areas:* Cookery;
Markets: Adult; *Treatments:* Commercial

Handles cookbooks and commercial
nonfiction. Send query by email only.

Vicky Bijur Literary Agency

27 West 20th Street, Suite 1003, New York,
NY 10011
Email: queries@vickybijuragency.com
Website: http://www.vickybijuragency.com

Handles: Fiction; Nonfiction; *Areas:*
Biography; Cookery; Health; Historical;
Politics; Psychology; Science; Self-Help;
Sociology; *Markets:* Adult

Send query by email or by post with SASE.
For fiction include synopsis and first chapter
(pasted into the body of the email if
submitting electronically). For nonfiction
include proposal. No attachments or queries
by phone or fax. No picture books, poetry,
self-help, science fiction, fantasy, horror, or
romance.

Bleecker Street Associates, Inc.

217 Thompson Street, #519, New York, NY
10012

Tel: +1 (212) 677-4492
Fax: +1 (212) 388-0001
Email: bleeckerst@hotmail.com

Handles: Fiction; Nonfiction; *Areas:*
Autobiography; Biography; Business;
Cookery; Crime; Culture; Current Affairs;
Entertainment; Erotic; Finance; Health;
Historical; Horror; How-to; Humour;
Lifestyle; Military; Mystery; Nature; New
Age; Politics; Psychology; Religious;
Romance; Science; Self-Help; Sociology;
Spiritual; Sport; Technology; Thrillers;
Women's Interests; *Markets:* Adult; Youth;
Treatments: Literary

Send query with SASE for response. No
poetry, plays, scripts, short stories, academic,
scholarly, professional, science fiction,
westerns, children's books, or phone calls,
faxes, or emails.

Bob Mecoy Creative Book Services

460 West 24th Street, Suite 3E, New York,
NY 10011
Tel: +1 (212) 296-1936
Fax: +1 (212) 226-1398
Email: bob.mecoy@gmail.com
Website: http://bobmecoy.com

Handles: Fiction; Nonfiction; *Areas:*
Adventure; Arts; Autobiography; Biography;
Business; Cookery; Crime; Current Affairs;
Fantasy; Finance; Historical; Literature;
Military; Mystery; Romance; Sci-Fi; Sport;
Technology; *Markets:* Adult; Children's;
Youth; *Treatments:* Literary; Mainstream

Send query with synopsis and sample
chapters.

Bond Literary Agency

4340 E Kentucky Avenue, Suite 471,
Denver, CO 80246
Tel: +1 (303) 781-9305
Email: queries@bondliteraryagency.com
Website: https://www.
bondliteraryagency.com

Handles: Fiction; Nonfiction; *Areas:*
Business; Crime; Fantasy; Historical;
Horror; Mystery; Science; Sci-Fi; Thrillers;
Markets: Adult; Youth; *Treatments:*
Commercial; Literary

Agency based in Colorado, representing
fiction and nonfiction for adults and young
adults. No romance, poetry, children's
picture books or screenplays. Send query by
email with first five pages of your novel (if
sending fiction) in the body of the email. For
nonfiction, a proposal must be available
before querying. No attachments. See
website for full guidelines.

Book Cents Literary Agency

Email: cw@bookcentsliteraryagency.com
Website: http://www.
bookcentsliteraryagency.com

Handles: Fiction; *Areas:* Fantasy; Humour;
Mystery; Romance; Suspense; Thrillers;
Women's Interests; *Markets:* Adult; Youth;
Treatments: Contemporary; Mainstream

**Closed to submissions (except by referral)
as at July 2017. Check website for current
status.**

No nonfiction, Third party submissions,
Previously published titles, Short Stories or
Novellas, Erotica, Inspirational, Historical,
Westerns, Sci-Fi/Fantasy (except young
adult fantasy), Horror/Pulp/slasher Thrillers,
Memoirs, Poetry, or Screenplays/Stageplays.

Books & Such Literary Management

52 Mission Circle, Suite 122, PMB 170,
Santa Rosa, CA 95409-5370
Email: representation@booksandsuch.com
Website: http://www.booksandsuch.biz

Handles: Fiction; Nonfiction; *Areas:*
Historical; Humour; Lifestyle; Religious;
Romance; Women's Interests; *Markets:*
Adult; Children's; Youth

Send query by email only. No attachments.
Query should be up to one page detailing
your book, your market, your experience,
etc. No queries by post or phone. See
website for full details.

BookStop Literary Agency, LLC

67 Meadow View Road, Orinda, CA 94563
Tel: +1 (925) 254-2664

Fax: +1 (925) 254-2668
Email: info@bookstopliterary.com
Website: http://www.bookstopliterary.com

Handles: Fiction; Nonfiction; *Areas:*
Adventure; Fantasy; Gothic; Historical;
Mystery; Science; Thrillers; *Markets:*
Children's; Youth; *Treatments:* Literary

Handles fiction and nonfiction for children
and young adults. See website for full
submission guidelines.

Brandt & Hochman Literary Agents, Inc.

1501 Broadway, Suite 2310, New York, NY
10036
Tel: +1 (212) 840-5760
Fax: +1 (212) 840-5776
Email: ghochman@bromasite.com
Website: http://brandthochman.com

Handles: Fiction; Nonfiction; *Areas:* Arts;
Autobiography; Culture; Current Affairs;
Health; Historical; Lifestyle; Mystery;
Science; Thrillers; *Markets:* Adult;
Children's; Youth; *Treatments:* Commercial;
Literary; Popular

Send query by post with SASE or by email
with query letter up to two pages long,
including overview and author details and
writing credits. See website for full
submission guidelines and for details of
individual agents' interests and direct contact
details, then approach one agent specifically.
No screenplays or textbooks. Response to
email queries not guaranteed.

The Brattle Agency LLC

PO Box 380537, Cambridge, MA 02238
Tel: +1 (617) 721-5375
Email: submissions@thebrattleagency.com
Website: https://thebrattleagency.com

Handles: Fiction; Nonfiction; *Areas:* Arts;
Culture; Historical; Politics; Sport; *Markets:*
Academic; Adult; *Treatments:* Literary

Send query by email with cover letter, brief
synopsis, and (if submitting an academic
manuscript) an author CV. Responds to
queries within 72 hours. Unsolicited mss will
not be read or replied to, whether sent by
post or email.

Not accepting fiction submissions as at
September 2017. Check website for current
status.

Bresnick Weil Literary Agency, LLC

115 West 29th Street, 3rd Floor, New York,
NY 10001
Tel: +1 (212) 239-3166
Fax: +1 (212) 239-3165
Email: query@bresnickagency.com
Website: http://bresnickagency.com

Handles: Fiction; Nonfiction; *Areas:*
Autobiography; Biography; Crime; Culture;
Health; Historical; Humour; Lifestyle;
Music; Politics; Psychology; Science; Sport;
Travel; Women's Interests; *Markets:* Adult;
Treatments: Commercial; Literary; Popular

Send query by email only, with two sample
chapters (fiction) or proposal (nonfiction).

Browne & Miller Literary Associates

52 Village Place, Hinsdale, IL 60521
Tel: +1 (312) 922-3063
Email: mail@browneandmiller.com
Website: http://www.browneandmiller.com

Handles: Fiction; Nonfiction; *Markets:*
Adult; *Treatments:* Commercial

Handles books for the adult commercial
book markets. No young adult fiction, adult
memoir, children's books, academic, short
stories, poetry, original screenplays, or
articles. Send query only by email. No
attachments.

Don Buchwald and Associates

5900 Wilshire Boulevard, 31st floor, Los
Angeles, CA 90036
Tel: +1 (323) 655-7400
Email: info@buchwald.com
Website: https://www.buchwald.com

Handles: Scripts; *Areas:* Film; Theatre; TV;
Markets: Adult

Send query by post with SASE or by fax. No
unsolicited MSS. Finds most new clients by
combing the NY and LA theatre scenes, and

by attending film festivals, entertainment symposiums and other industry gatherings.

Capital Talent Agency
419 South Washington Street, Alexandria, VA 22314
Tel: +1 (703) 349-1649
Email: literary.submissions@ capitaltalentagency.com
Website: http://capitaltalentagency.com

Handles: Fiction; Nonfiction; *Markets:* Adult

Represents authors in all genres of fiction and nonfiction. Send query by email only. Response in 6 weeks, if interested. See website for full guidelines.

Carol Mann Agency
55 Fifth Avenue, New York, NY 10003
Tel: +1 (212) 206-5635
Fax: +1 (212) 674-4809
Email: submissions@carolmannagency.com
Website: http://www.carolmannagency.com

Handles: Fiction; Nonfiction; *Areas:* Anthropology; Archaeology; Architecture; Arts; Autobiography; Biography; Business; Culture; Current Affairs; Design; Finance; Health; Historical; Humour; Legal; Lifestyle; Medicine; Music; Nature; Politics; Psychology; Religious; Self-Help; Sociology; Spiritual; Sport; Women's Interests; *Markets:* Adult; Youth; *Treatments:* Commercial; Literary

Send query by email only, including synopsis, brief bio, and first 25 pages, all pasted into the body of your email. No attachments. No submissions by post, or phone calls. Allow 3-4 weeks for response.

Carolyn Jenks Agency
30 Cambridge Park Drive, Cambridge, MA 02140
Tel: +1 (617) 354-5099
Email: queries@carolynjenksagency.com
Website: http://www. carolynjenksagency.com

Handles: Fiction; Nonfiction; Scripts; *Areas:* Adventure; Autobiography; Biography; Crime; Historical; Literature; Mystery;

Romance; Sci-Fi; Suspense; Theatre; Thrillers; Women's Interests; *Markets:* Adult; Youth; *Treatments:* Contemporary; Experimental; Literary; Mainstream

Send one-page query using form on website. No reading fees or expenses charged.

Chase Literary Agency
11 Broadway, Suite 1010, New York, NY 10004
Tel: +1 (212) 477-5100
Email: farley@chaseliterary.com
Website: http://chaseliterary.com

Handles: Fiction; Nonfiction; *Areas:* Autobiography; Culture; Historical; Humour; Military; Mystery; Nature; Science; Sport; *Markets:* Adult; *Treatments:* Commercial; Contemporary; Literary

New York agency, representing narrative nonfiction and fiction. No science fiction, romance, supernatural or young adult. Send query by email, specifically addressing an agent by name. For fiction, include the first few pages. See website for full guidelines.

Elyse Cheney Literary Associates, LLC
78 Fifth Avenue, 3rd Floor, New York, NY 10011
Tel: +1 (212) 277-8007
Fax: +1 (212) 614-0728
Email: submissions@cheneyliterary.com
Website: http://www.cheneyliterary.com

Handles: Fiction; Nonfiction; *Areas:* Autobiography; Biography; Business; Culture; Current Affairs; Finance; Historical; Horror; Literature; Politics; Romance; Science; Sport; Suspense; Thrillers; Women's Interests; *Markets:* Adult; *Treatments:* Commercial; Contemporary; Literary

Send query with up to three chapters of sample material by post with SASE, or by email (no attachments). Response not guaranteed.

Cherry Weiner Literary Agency
925 Oak Bluff Ct, Dacula, GA 30019-6660
Tel: +1 (732) 446-2096
Fax: +1 (732) 792-0506
Email: Cherry8486@aol.com

Handles: Fiction; Nonfiction; *Areas:*
Adventure; Crime; Fantasy; Historical;
Lifestyle; Mystery; Romance; Sci-Fi; Self-
Help; Suspense; Thrillers; Westerns;
Markets: Adult; *Treatments:* Mainstream

Only considers submissions by referral or
personal contact at writers' conferences.

The Chudney Agency
72 North State Road, Suite 501, Briarcliff
Manor, NY 10510
Tel: +1 (914) 465-5560
Fax: +1 (914) 465-5560
Email: steven@thechudneyagency.com
Website: http://www.thechudneyagency.com

Handles: Fiction; *Areas:* Historical;
Humour; Mystery; *Markets:* Adult;
Children's; Youth; *Treatments:* Commercial;
Literary; Mainstream

Specialises in children's and young adult
books, but will also consider adult fiction.
Send query only in first instance. Happy to
accept queries by email. Submit material
upon invitation only. No fantasy, science
fiction, early readers, or scripts. See website
for full guidelines.

Cine/Lit Representation
PO Box 802918, Santa Clarita, CA 91380-
2918
Tel: +1 (661) 513-0268
Fax: +1 (661) 513-0915
Email: cinelit@att.net
Website: http://www.
cinelitrepresentation.com

Handles: Fiction; Nonfiction; *Areas:*
Adventure; Biography; Culture; Horror;
Mystery; Nature; Thrillers; Travel; *Markets:*
Adult; *Treatments:* Mainstream; Popular

Handles nonfiction and novels. Send query
with SASE or by email. No romance,
westerns, or science fiction.

Compass Talent
6 E 32nd St, New York, NY 10016
Tel: +1 (646) 376-7718
Email: query@compasstalent.com
Website: http://www.compasstalent.com

Handles: Fiction; *Areas:* Autobiography;
Cookery; Historical; Science; *Markets:*
Adult; Children's; *Treatments:* Commercial;
Literary

Full service literary agency representing
literary and commercial fiction, children's
books, and a range of up-market nonfiction,
including memoir, journalism, history,
science and cookbooks. No unsolicited
queries.

Corvisiero Literary Agency
275 Madison Avenue, at 40th, 14th Floor,
New York, NY 10016
Tel: +1 (646) 992-1647
Fax: +1 (646) 217-3758
Email: info@corvisieroagency.com
Website: http://www.corvisieroagency.com

Handles: Fiction; Nonfiction; *Areas:*
Adventure; Antiques; Architecture; Arts;
Fantasy; Horror; Humour; Mystery;
Romance; Sci-Fi; Thrillers; *Markets:* Adult;
Children's; Youth; *Treatments:*
Contemporary

Accepts queries from both established and
emerging authors. See agent profiles on
website and select specific agent to query.
Send queries via online submission system
only (see website for details).

The Cowles-Ryan Literary Agency
Email: katherine@cowlesryan.com
Website: http://www.cowlesryan.com

Handles: Fiction; Nonfiction; *Areas:* Arts;
Autobiography; Biography; Cookery;
Culture; Current Affairs; Historical;
Literature; Mystery; Nature; Psychology;
Science; Self-Help; Spiritual; *Markets:*
Adult; Children's; *Treatments:* Commercial;
Contemporary; Literary; Mainstream;
Popular; Satirical

We specialise in quality fiction and
nonfiction. Our primary areas of interest

include literary and selected commercial fiction, history, journalism, culture, biography, memoir, science, natural history, spirituality, cooking, gardening, building and design, and young adult and children's books. We also work with institutions and organisations to develop books and book programs. We do not represent authors in a number of categories, e.g. romance and westerns, and we do not represent screenplays. See website for full submission guidelines.

Creative Trust, Inc.

210 Jamestown Park Drive, Suite 200, Brentwood, TN 37027
Tel: +1 (615) 297-5010
Fax: +1 (615) 297-5020
Email: info@creativetrust.com
Website: http://www.creativetrust.com

Handles: Fiction; Nonfiction; Scripts; *Areas:* Autobiography; Film; *Markets:* Adult

Literary division founded in 2001 to handle authors with particular potential in cross-media development, including movie scripts, graphic novels, etc. Accepts queries by email from previously published authors only. No attachments.

Creative Media Agency

Email: paige@cmalit.com
Website: http://cmalit.com

Handles: Fiction; Nonfiction; *Areas:* Business; Historical; Lifestyle; Mystery; Psychology; Religious; Romance; Thrillers; Women's Interests; *Markets:* Adult; *Treatments:* Commercial; Contemporary

Handles fiction and nonfiction, but no children's, science fiction, or fantasy, and no academic nonfiction. Send query by email only. No submissions by post. See website for full submission guidelines.

The Culinary Entertainment Agency (CEA)

53 W 36, #706, New York, NY 10018
Tel: +1 (212) 380-1264
Email: info@the-cea.com
Website: http://www.the-cea.com

Handles: Nonfiction; *Areas:* Cookery; Lifestyle; *Markets:* Adult

Literary agency focused on the cooking and lifestyle markets.

Richard Curtis Associates, Inc.

200 East 72nd Street, Suite 28J, New York, NY 10021
Email: info@curtisagency.com
Website: http://www.curtisagency.com

Handles: Fiction; Nonfiction; *Areas:* Autobiography; Biography; Business; Fantasy; Finance; Health; Historical; Medicine; Mystery; Romance; Science; Sci-Fi; Technology; Thrillers; Westerns; *Markets:* Adult; Children's; Youth

Send query with sample chapter via online submission form on website. No screenplays, stage scripts, playwrights, or screenwriters.

Curtis Brown Ltd

10 Astor Place, New York, NY 10003
Tel: +1 (212) 473-5400
Fax: +1 (212) 598-0917
Email: info@cbltd.com
Website: http://www.curtisbrown.com

Handles: Fiction; Nonfiction; *Markets:* Adult; Children's; Youth

Handles material for adults and children in all genres. See website for individual agent interests and submission policies. No unsolicited MSS. No scripts.

Cynthia Cannell Literary Agency

54 West 40th Street, New York, NY 10018
Tel: +1 (212) 396-9595
Email: info@cannellagency.com
Website: http://cannellagency.com

Handles: Fiction; Nonfiction; *Areas:* Autobiography; Biography; Current Affairs; Health; Religious; Self-Help; Spiritual; *Markets:* Adult; *Treatments:* Contemporary; Literary

Full-service literary agency based in New York. Represents fiction, memoir, biography, self-improvement, spirituality, and nonfiction on contemporary issues. No screenplays, children's books, illustrated books, cookbooks, romance, category mystery, or science fiction. Send query by post with SASE or by email, including brief description of the project, relevant biographical information, and any publishing credits. No attachments. Response not guaranteed.

D4EO Literary Agency

7 Indian Valley Road, Weston, CT 06883
Tel: +1 (203) 544-7180
Fax: +1 (203) 544-7160
Email: bob@d4eo.com
Website: http://www.d4eoliteraryagency.com

Handles: Fiction; Nonfiction; Reference; *Areas:* Adventure; Architecture; Arts; Biography; Business; Cookery; Crime; Current Affairs; Design; Erotic; Fantasy; Finance; Health; Historical; Horror; How-to; Humour; Lifestyle; Military; Mystery; Psychology; Romance; Science; Sci-Fi; Self-Help; Spiritual; Sport; Technology; Thrillers; Westerns; Women's Interests; *Markets:* Adult; Children's; Youth; *Treatments:* Commercial; Contemporary; Literary; Mainstream

See website for individual agent preferences and submission guidelines, then submit directly to one agent only.

Daniel Literary Group

601 Old Hickory Boulevard, #56, Brentwood, TN 37027
Tel: +1 (615) 730-8207
Email: submissions@ danielliterarygroup.com
Website: http://www.danielliterarygroup.com

Handles: Nonfiction; *Markets:* Adult; *Treatments:* Popular

Specialises in nonfiction and is closed to submissions of fiction. Query by email only, including brief synopsis, key selling points, author biography, and publishing history, all pasted into the body of the email. No attachments, or queries by post or telephone. Response not guaranteed if guidelines are not adhered to.

David Black Literary Agency

335 Adams Street, Suite 2707, Brooklyn, NY 11201
Tel: +1 (718) 852-5500
Fax: +1 (718) 852-5539
Email: dblack@dblackagency.com
Website: http://www.davidblackagency.com

Handles: Fiction; Nonfiction; *Areas:* Arts; Autobiography; Biography; Business; Cookery; Crafts; Culture; Current Affairs; Entertainment; Finance; Health; Historical; How-to; Humour; Lifestyle; Music; Nature; Philosophy; Politics; Psychology; Science; Sociology; Sport; Thrillers; Travel; Women's Interests; *Markets:* Adult; Children's; Youth; *Treatments:* Commercial; Literary

See website for details of different agents, and specific interests and submission guidelines of each. Otherwise, query the agency generally by post only and allow 8 weeks for a response. See website for full details.

DeFiore and Company

47 East 19th Street, 3rd Floor, New York, NY 10003
Tel: +1 (212) 925-7744
Fax: +1 (212) 925-9803
Email: submissions@defioreandco.com
Website: http://www.defioreandco.com

Handles: Fiction; Nonfiction; *Areas:* Arts; Biography; Culture; Current Affairs; Historical; Lifestyle; Literature; Medicine; Military; Music; Nature; Philosophy; Politics; Psychology; Romance; Science; Short Stories; Sociology; Technology; Thrillers; *Markets:* Adult; Children's; Youth; *Treatments:* Commercial; Literary; Mainstream

Always looking for exciting, fresh, new talent, and currently accepting queries for both fiction and nonfiction. Send query with summary, description of why you're writing the book, any specific credentials, and (for fiction) first five pages. Send by email (with all material in the body of the text; no attachments; and the word "Query" in the subject line) or post with SASE. See website for specific agent interests and methods of approach. No scripts for film, TV, or theatre.

The Doe Coover Agency

PO Box 668, Winchester, MA 01890
Tel: +1 (781) 721-6000
Fax: +1 (781) 721-6727
Email: info@doecooveragency.com
Website: http://doecooveragency.com

Handles: Fiction; Nonfiction; Reference;
Areas: Autobiography; Biography; Business;
Cookery; Current Affairs; Finance;
Gardening; Health; Historical; Humour;
Music; Politics; Psychology; Science;
Sociology; Sport; Technology; *Markets:*
Adult; *Treatments:* Commercial; Literary;
Popular

Handles nonfiction, popular reference,
literary fiction and narrative nonfiction.

Don Congdon Associates, Inc.

110 William St. Suite 2202, New York, NY
10038
Tel: +1 (212) 645-1229
Fax: +1 (212) 727-2688
Email: dca@doncongdon.com
Website: http://doncongdon.com

Handles: Fiction; Nonfiction; *Areas:*
Adventure; Anthropology; Archaeology;
Arts; Autobiography; Biography; Cookery;
Crime; Criticism; Culture; Current Affairs;
Fantasy; Film; Health; Historical; Humour;
Legal; Lifestyle; Literature; Medicine;
Military; Music; Mystery; Nature; Politics;
Psychology; Science; Sport; Suspense;
Technology; Theatre; Thrillers; Travel;
Women's Interests; *Markets:* Adult;
Children's; Youth; *Treatments:* Commercial;
Literary; Mainstream

Send query by email (no attachments) or by
post with SASE. Include one-page synopsis,
relevant background info, and first chapter,
all within the body of the email if submitting
by email. Include the word "Query" in the
subject line. See website for full guidelines.
No unsolicited MSS.

Donaghy Literary Group

Email: stacey@donaghyliterary.com
Website: http://www.donaghyliterary.com

Handles: Fiction; *Areas:* Fantasy; Historical;
Mystery; Romance; Sci-Fi; Suspense;

Thrillers; Women's Interests; *Markets:*
Adult; Children's; Youth

See website for individual agent interests,
and submit using online submission system.

Jim Donovan Literary

5635 SMU Boulevard, Suite 201, Dallas, TX
75206
Email: jdliterary@sbcglobal.net

Handles: Fiction; Nonfiction; Reference;
Areas: Adventure; Autobiography;
Biography; Business; Crime; Culture;
Current Affairs; Finance; Health; Historical;
How-to; Legal; Lifestyle; Medicine;
Military; Music; Mystery; Nature; Politics;
Science; Sport; Suspense; Thrillers;
Westerns; Women's Interests; *Markets:*
Adult; *Treatments:* Commercial;
Contemporary; Literary; Mainstream;
Popular

Send query with SASE or by email. For
fiction, include first 30-50 pages and a 2-5
page outline. Handles mainly nonfiction, and
specialises in commercial fiction and
nonfiction. No poetry, children's, science
fiction, fantasy short stories, autobiography,
or inspirational.

Doug Grad Literary Agency

156 Prospect Park West, #3L, Brooklyn, NY
11215
Tel: +1 (718) 788-6067
Email: query@dgliterary.com
Website: http://www.dgliterary.com

Handles: Nonfiction; *Areas:* Autobiography;
Business; Cookery; Entertainment;
Historical; Military; Music; Mystery;
Romance; Science; Self-Help; Sport;
Theatre; Thrillers; *Markets:* Adult

Handles narrative nonfiction, military,
sports, celebrity memoir, thrillers, mysteries,
historical fiction, romance, music, style,
business, home improvement, cookbooks,
self-help, science and theatre. Send query by
email with "query" in the subject line, and
synopsis and biography explaining what the
book is and who you are. Do not include
sample material.

The Dravis Agency, Inc.

4370 Tujunga AVE, Suite 145, Studio City, CA 91604
Tel: +1 (818) 501-1177
Fax: +1 (818) 501-1194
Email: monrose@monteiro-rose.com
Website: http://www.monteiro-rose.com

Handles: Scripts; *Areas:* Adventure; Crime; Drama; Film; Historical; Humour; Mystery; Romance; Sci-Fi; Suspense; Thrillers; TV; *Markets:* Adult; Children's; Family; Youth; *Treatments:* Contemporary; Mainstream

Handles for TV, film, and animation. No unsolicited mss. Accepts new clients by referral only.

Dunham Literary, Inc.

110 William Street, Suite 2202, New York, NY 10038
Tel: +1 (212) 929-0994
Fax: +1 (212) 929-0904
Email: query@dunhamlit.com
Website: http://www.dunhamlit.com

Handles: Fiction; Nonfiction; *Areas:* Autobiography; Biography; Culture; Current Affairs; Fantasy; Historical; Lifestyle; Music; Mystery; Nature; Politics; Science; Sci-Fi; Spiritual; Technology; Thrillers; Travel; Women's Interests; *Markets:* Adult; Children's; Youth; *Treatments:* Literary

Handles quality fiction and nonfiction for adults and children. Send query by email or by post with SASE. See website for full guidelines. No genre romance, Christian, erotica, Westerns, poetry, cookery, proeffesional, reference, textbooks, plays, or approaches by phone or fax. No email attachments.

Dystel, Goderich & Bourret LLC

One Union Square West, Suite 904, New York, NY 10003
Tel: +1 (212) 627-9100
Fax: +1 (212) 627-9313
Email: miriam@dystel.com
Website: http://www.dystel.com

Handles: Fiction; Nonfiction; *Areas:* Adventure; Anthropology; Archaeology; Autobiography; Biography; Business; Cookery; Crime; Culture; Current Affairs; Fantasy; Finance; Health; Historical; Humour; Lifestyle; Military; Mystery; New Age; Politics; Psychology; Religious; Romance; Science; Sci-Fi; Spiritual; Suspense; Technology; Thrillers; Women's Interests; *Markets:* Adult; Children's; Youth; *Treatments:* Commercial; Contemporary; Literary; Mainstream; Popular

See website for individual agent interests and contact details and approach one agent only. Send query by email with brief synopsis and sample chapter in the body of the email. Attachments to blank emails will not be opened. Queries should be brief, devoid of gimmicks, and professionally presented, including author details and any writing credits. See website for more details.

E. J. McCarthy Agency

Mill Valley, CA
Tel: +1 (415) 383-6639
Email: ejmagency@gmail.com
Website: https://twitter.com/ejmccarthy

Handles: Nonfiction; *Areas:* Autobiography; Biography; Historical; Media; Military; Politics; Sport; *Markets:* Adult

Literary agency from former executive editor with experience at some of the world's largest publishing houses, specialising in military history, politics, history, biography, memoir, media, public policy, and sports.

Anne Edelstein Literary Agency

800 Riverside Drive #5E, New York, NY 10032
Tel: +1 (212) 414-4923
Fax: +1 (212) 414-2930
Email: info@aeliterary.com
Website: http://www.aeliterary.com

Handles: Fiction; Nonfiction; *Areas:* Autobiography; Historical; Psychology; Religious; *Markets:* Adult; *Treatments:* Commercial; Literary

Note: Note accepting approaches as at September 2017

Send query letter with SASE and for fiction

a summary of your novel plus the first 25 pages, or for nonfiction an outline of your book and one or two sample chapters. No queries by email.

Elaine Markson Literary Agency

450 Seventh Ave, Suite 1408, New York, NY 10123
Tel: +1 (212) 243-8480
Fax: +1 (212) 691-9014
Email: gary@marksonagency.com
Website: http://www.marksonagency.com

Handles: Fiction; Nonfiction; *Markets:* Adult; *Treatments:* Literary

New York literary agency working with co-agents in the UK, Germany, France, and Italy.

Emerald City Literary Agency

718 Griffin Avenue, #195, Enumclaw, WA 98022
Email: Mandy@EmeraldCityLiterary.com
Website: https://emeraldcityliterary.com

Handles: Fiction; Nonfiction; *Areas:* Fantasy; Horror; Romance; Sci-Fi; *Markets:* Adult; Children's; Youth; *Treatments:* Contemporary

See website for individual agent interests, contact details, and submission guidelines. Welcomes submissions about LGBTQ themes and diverse characters and by traditionally underrepresented authors. All queries must be sent by email – no snail mail submissions. No screenplays, poetry, short stories, adult nonfiction, or fiction for adults that does not fall into romance or SFF genres.

Empire Literary, LLC

115 West 29th Street, 3rd Floor, New York, NY 10001
Tel: +1 (917) 213-7082
Email: Queries@empireliterary.com
Website: http://www.empireliterary.com

Handles: Fiction; Nonfiction; *Areas:* Autobiography; Culture; Health; Lifestyle; Women's Interests; *Markets:* Adult;

Children's; Youth; *Treatments:* Literary; Popular

See website for specific agent guidelines and contact details, and query one agent at a time. Response not guaranteed unless interested.

Energy Entertainment

729 Seward Street, 2nd Floor, Los Angeles, CA 90038
Tel: +1 (323) 785-5370
Email: info@energyentertainment.net
Website: http://www.energyentertainment.net

Handles: Scripts; *Areas:* Film; TV; *Markets:* Adult

Agency specialising in discovering new and edgy screenwriters. No unsolicited MSS or calls; send query only.

Ethan Ellenberg Literary Agency

155 Suffolk Street, #2R, New York, NY 10002
Tel: +1 (212) 431-4554
Fax: +1 (212) 941-4652
Email: agent@ethanellenberg.com
Website: http://www.ethanellenberg.com

Handles: Fiction; Nonfiction; *Areas:* Adventure; Autobiography; Biography; Cookery; Crime; Culture; Current Affairs; Fantasy; Health; Historical; Mystery; New Age; Psychology; Romance; Science; Sci-Fi; Spiritual; Thrillers; Women's Interests; *Markets:* Adult; Children's; *Treatments:* Commercial; Literary

Send query by email (no attachments; paste material into the body of the email) or by post with SASE. For fiction send synopsis and first 50 pages. For nonfiction send proposal, author bio, and sample chapters. For picture books send complete MS. No poetry, short stories, scripts, or queries by fax.

We have been in business for over 17 years. We are a member of the AAR. We accept unsolicited submissions and, of course, do not charge reading fees.

Mary Evans, Inc.

242 East Fifth Street, New York, NY 10003
Tel: +1 (212) 979-0880
Fax: +1 (212) 979-5344
Email: info@maryevansinc.com
Website: http://www.maryevansinc.com

Handles: Fiction; Nonfiction; *Areas:*
Culture; Historical; Medicine; Politics;
Science; Sociology; Technology; *Markets:*
Adult; Children's; Youth; *Treatments:*
Commercial; Literary

Send query by email or by with SASE. Does
not represent scriptwriters, unless they also
write books. See website for full submission
guidelines.

FinePrint Literary Management

207 West 106th Street, Suite 1D, New York,
NY 10025
Tel: +1 (212) 279-1282
Email: peter@fineprintlit.com
Website: http://www.fineprintlit.com

Handles: Fiction; Nonfiction; Reference;
Areas: Autobiography; Beauty and Fashion;
Biography; Business; Cookery; Crime;
Culture; Entertainment; Fantasy; Health;
Historical; Horror; How-to; Humour;
Lifestyle; Military; Music; Mystery; Nature;
Religious; Romance; Science; Sci-Fi; Self-
Help; Spiritual; Suspense; Technology;
Thrillers; Travel; Women's Interests;
Markets: Adult; Children's; Youth;
Treatments: Contemporary; Dark; Literary;
Serious

Consult agent profiles on website for
individual interests and approach appropriate
agent for your work.

Flannery Literary

1140 Wickfield Court, Naperville, IL 60563-
3300
Tel: +1 (630) 428-2682
Fax: +1 (630) 428-2683
Email: jennifer@flanneryliterary.com
Website: http://flanneryliterary.com

Handles: Fiction; Nonfiction; *Markets:*
Children's; Youth

Send query by email, with the word "Query"
in the subject line. Deals exclusively in
children's and young adults' fiction and
nonfiction, including picture books. See
website for full guidelines.

Fletcher & Company

78 Fifth Avenue, Third Floor, New York,
NY 10011
Tel: +1 (212) 614-0778
Fax: +1 (212) 614-0728
Email: info@fletcherandco.com
Website: http://www.fletcherandco.com

Handles: Fiction; Nonfiction; *Areas:*
Autobiography; Biography; Business; Crime;
Culture; Current Affairs; Health; Historical;
Humour; Lifestyle; Politics; Science; Self-
Help; Sport; Travel; Women's Interests;
Markets: Adult; Youth; *Treatments:*
Commercial; Literary

Full-service literary agency representing
writers of nonfiction and commercial and
literary fiction. Send query by email only
with brief synopsis and first 5-10 pages of
your manuscript / proposal pasted into the
body of the email. No attachments. Query
only one agent at a time (see website for list
of individual agent interests). Response
normally in 4-6 weeks. No queries by post.

Folio Literary Management, LLC

630 9th Avenue, Suite 1101, New York, NY
10036
Tel: +1 (212) 400-1494
Fax: +1 (212) 967-0977
Email: jeff@foliolit.com
Website: http://www.foliolit.com

Handles: Fiction; Nonfiction; Reference;
Areas: Autobiography; Business; Cookery;
Crime; Culture; Entertainment; Fantasy;
Health; Historical; Horror; How-to; Humour;
Lifestyle; Media; Military; Music; Mystery;
Politics; Psychology; Religious; Romance;
Science; Sci-Fi; Self-Help; Spiritual; Sport;
Suspense; Technology; Thrillers; Women's
Interests; *Markets:* Adult; Children's; Youth;
Treatments: Commercial; Contemporary;
Dark; Literary; Popular; Serious

Read agent bios on website and decide which agent to approach. Do not submit to multiple agents simultaneously. Each agent has different submission requirements: consult website for details. No unsolicited MSS or multiple submissions.

Foundry Literary + Media

33 West 17th Street, PH, New York, NY 10011
Tel: +1 (212) 929-5064
Fax: +1 (212) 929-5471
Email: info@foundrymedia.com
Website: http://www.foundrymedia.com

Handles: Fiction; Nonfiction; *Areas:* Adventure; Autobiography; Biography; Business; Cookery; Culture; Current Affairs; Health; Historical; How-to; Humour; Lifestyle; Music; Psychology; Religious; Science; Sci-Fi; Spiritual; Sport; Thrillers; Travel; Women's Interests; *Markets:* Adult; Children's; Youth; *Treatments:* Commercial; Literary; Niche; Popular

Queries should be addressed to a specific agent (see website) and sent by email or by post with SASE, according to requirements of individual agent (see website). For fiction queries, send letter with synopsis, First Three Chapters of Manuscript, and Author Bio. For nonfiction approaches send letter with Sample Chapters, Table of Contents, and Author Bio.

Fox Literary

110 W 40th St, Suite 2305, New York, NY 10018
Tel: +1 (212) 710-5907
Email: submissions@foxliterary.com
Website: http://www.foxliterary.com

Handles: Fiction; Nonfiction; *Areas:* Autobiography; Biography; Culture; Fantasy; Historical; Romance; Sci-Fi; Thrillers; *Markets:* Adult; Youth; *Treatments:* Commercial; Literary

A boutique agency which represents commercial fiction, along with select works of literary fiction and nonfiction that have broad commercial appeal.

I am actively seeking the following: young adult fiction (all genres), science

fiction/fantasy, romance, historical fiction, thrillers, and graphic novels. I'm always interested in books that cross genres and reinvent popular concepts with an engaging new twist (especially when there's a historical and/or speculative element involved).

On the nonfiction side I'm interested in memoirs, biography, and smart narrative nonfiction; I particularly enjoy memoirs and other nonfiction about sex work, addiction and recovery, and pop culture.

Email a query letter and the first 5 pages of your novel IN THE BODY OF THE EMAIL.

Email will receive a faster reply than snail mail, but query letters can be sent. If you do choose to send me a hard copy submission, you must include your email address in your letter as I will respond to queries exclusively via email from now on. Do NOT include a SASE, as I will no longer be sending out paper rejections.

Please do not send unsolicited email attachments or manuscripts, as I cannot open the former or return the latter.

Note: does not represent screenplays, poetry, category Westerns, horror, Christian/inspirational, or children's picture books.

Frances Collin Literary Agent

PO Box 33, Wayne, PA 19087-0033
Tel: +1 (610) 254-0555
Fax: +1 (610) 254-5029
Email: queries@francescollin.com
Website: http://www.francescollin.com

Handles: Fiction; Nonfiction; *Areas:* Autobiography; Biography; Culture; Fantasy; Historical; Nature; Sci-Fi; Travel; Women's Interests; *Markets:* Adult; *Treatments:* Literary

Send query by email (no attachments) or by post with SASE, or IRCs if outside the US. No queries by phone or fax.

Fraser-Bub Literary, LLC
401 Park Avenue South, 10th Floor, New York, NY 10016
Tel: +1 (917) 524-6982
Email: submissions@fraserbubliterary.com
Website: http://www.fraserbubliterary.com

Handles: Fiction; Nonfiction; *Areas:* Beauty and Fashion; Cookery; Crime; Design; Health; Historical; Lifestyle; Mystery; Psychology; Romance; Self-Help; Thrillers; Women's Interests; *Markets:* Adult; Youth; *Treatments:* Popular

Closed to submissions, with the exception of referrals and conference requests. Check website for current status.

Send query by email only, with first chapter (fiction) or first ten pages (nonfiction) in the body of the email. Attachments will not be opened. No queries by phone.

Fuse Literary
Email: querylaurie@fuseliterary.com
Website: http://www.fuseliterary.com

Handles: Fiction; Nonfiction; *Markets:* Adult; Children's

A full-service, hybrid literary agency based in the Silicon Valley with offices in New York, Chicago, Dallas, North Dakota, and Vancouver. See website for individual agent interests and submission guidelines.

The G Agency, LLC
PO Box 374, Bronx, NY 10471
Tel: +1 (718) 664-4505
Email: gagencyquery@gmail.com

Handles: Fiction; Nonfiction; *Areas:* Biography; Business; Culture; Finance; Historical; Military; Mystery; Sport; Technology; *Markets:* Adult; *Treatments:* Commercial; Literary; Mainstream; Serious

Send queries by email only with sample chapters or proposal. Write "QUERY" in the subject line. No screenplays, sci-fi, or romance. Response not guaranteed.

Gallt & Zacker Literary Agency
273 Charlton Avenue, South Orange , NJ 07079
Tel: +1 (973) 761-6358
Email: nancy@galltzacker.com
Website: http://www.galltzacker.com

Handles: Fiction; Nonfiction; *Areas:* Horror; Romance; Women's Interests; *Markets:* Children's; Youth; *Treatments:* Literary

Handles fiction and nonfiction for children, young adults, and adults. See website for submission guidelines and specific agent interests / contact details and approach relevant agent by email.

Gelfman Schneider / ICM Partners
850 Seventh Avenue, Suite 903, New York, NY 10019
Tel: +1 (212) 245-1993
Email: mail@gelfmanschneider.com
Website: http://www.gelfmanschneider.com

Handles: Fiction; Nonfiction; *Areas:* Autobiography; Culture; Current Affairs; Historical; Mystery; Politics; Science; Suspense; Thrillers; Women's Interests; *Markets:* Adult; Youth; *Treatments:* Commercial; Literary; Mainstream; Popular

Different agents within the agency have different submission guidelines. See website for full details. No screenplays, or poetry.

Georges Borchardt, Inc.
136 East 57th Street, New York, NY 10022
Tel: +1 (212) 753-5785
Email: anne@gbagency.com
Website: http://www.gbagency.com

Handles: Fiction; Nonfiction; *Areas:* Arts; Biography; Current Affairs; Historical; Literature; Philosophy; Politics; Religious; Science; Short Stories; *Markets:* Adult; Youth; *Treatments:* Commercial; Literary

New York based literary agency founded in 1967. No unsolicited MSS or screenplays.

The Gernert Company

136 East 57th Street, New York, NY 10022
Tel: +1 (212) 838-7777
Fax: +1 (212) 838-6020
Email: info@thegernertco.com
Website: http://www.thegernertco.com

Handles: Fiction; Nonfiction; *Areas:*
Adventure; Arts; Autobiography; Biography;
Crafts; Crime; Current Affairs; Fantasy;
Historical; Politics; Science; Sci-Fi;
Sociology; Sport; Thrillers; Women's
Interests; *Markets:* Academic; Adult;
Children's; Youth; *Treatments:* Commercial;
Literary; Popular

Send query describing work by post with
SASE or email with author info and sample
chapter. If querying by email, send to generic
email and indicate which agent you would
like to query. No queries by fax. Response
only if interested.

Gina Maccoby Agency

PO Box 60, Chappaqua, NY 10514
Tel: +1 (914) 238-5630
Email: query@maccobylit.com

Handles: Fiction; Nonfiction; *Areas:*
Autobiography; Biography; Culture; Current
Affairs; Entertainment; Health; Historical;
Lifestyle; Mystery; Nature; Politics; Self-
Help; Suspense; Thrillers; Women's
Interests; *Markets:* Adult; Children's; Youth;
Treatments: Literary; Mainstream

Send query by email only. Response not
guaranteed.

Glass Literary Management LLC

138 West 25th Street, 10th Floor, New York,
NY 10001
Tel: +1 (646) 237-4881
Email: alex@glassliterary.com
Website: http://www.glassliterary.com

Handles: Fiction; Nonfiction; *Areas:*
Autobiography; Biography; Business;
Culture; Entertainment; Health; Historical;
Media; Sport; *Markets:* Adult; Children's;
Treatments: Literary; Mainstream; Popular

Send query by email only, directly to one of
the two agents -- see website for both email

addresses. No attachments, picture books for
children, or approaches by post. No response
to queries not directly addressed to either one
of the agents. Send query letter in the body
of your email. Response not guaranteed
unless interested.

Global Lion Intellectual Property Management, Inc.

PO BOX 669238, Pompano Beach, FL
33066
Tel: +1 (754) 222-6948
Email: queriesgloballionmgt@gmail.com
Website: http://www.
globallionmanagement.com

Handles: Fiction; Nonfiction; *Areas:*
Spiritual; *Markets:* Adult

Specialises in nonfiction, spirituality, and
generally anything that "improvement" for
the world and human race. Looks for cutting-
edge authors of both fiction and nonfiction
with global marketing and motion
picture/television production potential.
Authors must not only have a great book and
future, but also a specific game-plan of how
to use social media to grow their fan base.
Send query by email only with synopsis, up
to 20 pages if available (otherwise, chapter
synopsis), author bio, and any social media
outlets. See website for full details.

Grace Freedson's Publishing Network

7600 Jericho Turnpike, Suite 300,
Woodbury, NY 11797
Tel: +1 (516) 931-7757
Fax: +1 (516) 931-7759
Email: gfreedson@gmail.com

Handles: Nonfiction; *Areas:* Autobiography;
Business; Cookery; Crafts; Crime; Culture;
Current Affairs; Design; Finance;
Gardening; Health; Historical; Hobbies;
How-to; Humour; Legal; Leisure; Lifestyle;
Medicine; Military; Nature; Philosophy;
Psychology; Religious; Science; Self-Help;
Sport; Technology; Women's Interests;
Markets: Adult; Children's; Youth

Literary agency and book packager. Handles
nonfiction from qualified authors with

credentials and platforms only. No fiction. Send query with synopsis and SASE.

The Greenhouse Literary Agency

Tel: +1 (571) 758-5615
Email: submissions@ greenhouseliterary.com
Website: http://www.greenhouseliterary.com

Handles: Fiction; *Markets:* Children's; Youth

Closed to submissions until July 30, 2018.

Handles fiction for children and young adults only. No nonfiction, poetry, picturebooks, or illustrators. Send query by email only including plot outline up to three paragraphs, a paragraph about you and any other information relevant to you or your work, and in the case of a novel the first five pages, pasted into the body of the email.

Blanche C. Gregory Inc.

2 Tudor City Place, New York, NY 10017
Tel: +1 (212) 697-0828
Email: info@bcgliteraryagency.com
Website: http://www.bcgliteraryagency.com

Handles: Fiction; Nonfiction; *Markets:* Adult; Children's

Specialises in adult fiction and nonfiction, but will also consider children's literature. Send query describing your background with SASE and synopsis. No stage, film or TV scripts, or queries by fax or email.

Greyhaus Literary Agency

3021 20th St. Pl. SW, Puyallup, WA 98373
Email: submissions@greyhausagency.com
Website: http://www.greyhausagency.com

Handles: Fiction; *Areas:* Romance; Women's Interests; *Markets:* Adult; *Treatments:* Contemporary; Traditional

Small agency focussing only on romance and women's fiction. To query, send query by email (no attachments); complete online form on website; or send query by post with 3-5 page synopsis, first three pages, and SASE.

Hannigan Salky Getzler (HSG) Agency

37 West 28th St, 8th floor, New York, NY 10001
Tel: +1 (646) 442-5770
Email: channigan@hsgagency.com
Website: http://hsgagency.com

Handles: Fiction; Nonfiction; *Areas:* Adventure; Autobiography; Business; Cookery; Crafts; Culture; Current Affairs; Design; Finance; Gardening; Health; Historical; Humour; Lifestyle; Mystery; Photography; Politics; Psychology; Science; Sociology; Suspense; Thrillers; Travel; Women's Interests; *Markets:* Adult; Children's; Youth; *Treatments:* Commercial; Literary; Popular

Send query by email only with first five pages pasted into the body of the email (no attachments), or the full ms for picture books. See website for agent interests and individual email addresses, and contact one agent only. No screenplays, romance fiction, science fiction, or religious fiction.

Harold Ober Associates, Inc.

425 Madison Avenue, New York, NY 10017
Tel: +1 (212) 759-8600
Fax: +1 (212) 759-9428
Email: phyllis@haroldober.com
Website: http://www.haroldober.com

Handles: Fiction; Nonfiction; *Markets:* Adult; Children's

Send query addressed to a specific agent by post only, including first five pages and SASE for reply. No plays, screenplays, or queries by fax.

Joy Harris Literary Agency, Inc.

1501 Broadway, Suite 2310, New York, NY 10036
Tel: +1 (212) 924-6269
Fax: +1 (212) 840-5776
Email: submissions@joyharrisliterary.com
Website: http://www.joyharrisliterary.com

Handles: Fiction; Nonfiction; *Areas:* Autobiography; Biography; Culture; Historical; Humour; Media; Mystery; Short

Stories; Spiritual; Suspense; Translations; Women's Interests; *Markets:* Adult; Youth; *Treatments:* Experimental; Literary; Mainstream; Satirical

Send query by email, including sample chapter or outline. No poetry, screenplays, genre fiction, self-help, or unsolicited mss. See website for full guidelines.

The Helen Brann Agency, Inc.
94 Curtis Road, Bridgewater, CT 06752
Fax: +1 (860) 355-2572
Email: helenbrannagency@earthlink.net

Handles: Fiction; Nonfiction; *Markets:* Adult

Works mostly with established writers and referrals.

Herman Agency Inc.
350 Central Park West, New York, NY 10025
Tel: +1 (212) 749-4907
Email: ronnie@hermanagencyinc.com
Website: https://www.hermanagencyinc.com

Handles: Fiction; Nonfiction; *Markets:* Children's; Youth

Represents fiction and nonfiction for children and young adults, including picture books and middle grade books, educational books and supplementary materials, children's toys, magazines, cartoons, licensed characters, stationery, advertising, and editorial illustrations. Not taking on any new clients.

Hill Nadell Literary Agency
6442 Santa Monica Blvd, Suite 201, Los Angeles, CA 90038
Tel: +1 (310) 860-9605
Fax: +1 (323) 380-5206
Email: queries@hillnadell.com
Website: http://www.hillnadell.com

Handles: Fiction; Nonfiction; *Areas:* Autobiography; Biography; Cookery; Culture; Current Affairs; Health; Historical; Legal; Nature; Politics; Science; Thrillers; Women's Interests; *Markets:* Adult; Youth; *Treatments:* Literary; Mainstream

Handles current affairs, food, memoirs and other narrative nonfiction, fiction, thrillers, upmarket women's fiction, literary fiction, genre fiction, graphic novels, and occasional young adult novels. No scripts or screenplays. Accepts queries both by post and by email. See website for full submission guidelines.

Holloway Literary
Raleigh, NC
Email: submissions@ hollowayliteraryagency.com
Website: https://hollowayliteraryagency.com

Handles: Fiction; Nonfiction; *Areas:* Autobiography; Crime; Historical; Humour; Lifestyle; Military; Mystery; Nature; Politics; Romance; Sci-Fi; Self-Help; Short Stories; Suspense; Thrillers; Travel; Women's Interests; *Markets:* Adult; Youth; *Treatments:* Commercial; Contemporary; Literary; Satirical

See website for individual agent preferences and select one to submit to. Send query by email with first 15 pages pasted into the body of your email. Approach only one agent at a time.

Hornfischer Literary Management, L.P.
Austin, Texas
Email: queries@hornfischerlit.com
Website: http://www.hornfischerlit.com

Handles: Nonfiction; *Areas:* Anthropology; Archaeology; Autobiography; Biography; Business; Crime; Culture; Current Affairs; Finance; Health; Historical; How-to; Humour; Legal; Lifestyle; Medicine; Military; Nature; Politics; Psychology; Religious; Science; Self-Help; Sociology; Sport; Technology; *Markets:* Adult; *Treatments:* Commercial; Satirical; Serious

Send query by email. Response only if interested.

Hudson Agency
3 Travis Lane, Montrose, NY 10548
Tel: +1 (914) 737-1475
Fax: +1 (914) 736-3064

Email: Sue@hudsonagency.net
Website: http://www.hudsonagency.net

Handles: Scripts; *Areas:* Crime; Drama;
Fantasy; Film; Humour; Mystery; Romance;
TV; Westerns; *Markets:* Adult; Children's;
Family; Youth; *Treatments:* Contemporary

Send query with SASE. Most new clients
taken on by recommendation from industry
professionals.

Andrea Hurst Literary Management

PO Box 1467, Coupeville, WA 98239
Email: info@andreahurst.com
Website: http://www.andreahurst.com

Handles: Fiction; Nonfiction; *Areas:*
Adventure; Autobiography; Business;
Cookery; Crime; Current Affairs; Fantasy;
Historical; How-to; Humour; Politics;
Psychology; Religious; Romance; Science;
Sci-Fi; Self-Help; Thrillers; Westerns;
Women's Interests; *Markets:* Adult; Youth;
Treatments: Commercial; Contemporary

Agent has semi-retired from the agent
division of her business and is now accepting
queries by referral through an existing client,
agent, or publisher only.

Inklings Literary Agency, LLC

3419 Virginia Beach Blvd #183, Virginia
Beach, VA 23452
Tel: +1 (757) 802-0996
Fax: +1 (904) 758-5440
Email: query@inklingsliterary.com
Website: http://www.inklingsliterary.com

Handles: Fiction; Nonfiction; *Areas:*
Archaeology; Arts; Fantasy; Historical;
Horror; Mystery; Romance; Sci-Fi;
Sociology; Suspense; Thrillers; Women's
Interests; *Markets:* Adult; Children's; Youth;
Treatments: Commercial; Contemporary

Generally accepts submissions by email
only, with brief synopsis, brief author bio,
and first 10 pages – however closed to
submission as of July 1, 2017. Check website
for current status.

J de S Associates Inc.

9 Shagbark Road, Wilson Point, South
Norwalk, CT 06854
Tel: +1 (203) 838-7571
Fax: +1 (203) 866-2713
Email: jdespoel@aol.com
Website: http://www.jdesassociates.com

Handles: Fiction; *Areas:* Autobiography;
Biography; Business; Crime; Culture;
Current Affairs; Finance; Health; Historical;
How-to; Legal; Lifestyle; Medicine;
Military; Mystery; New Age; Politics; Self-
Help; Sociology; Sport; Suspense; Thrillers;
Translations; Westerns; *Markets:* Adult;
Children's; Youth; *Treatments:* Commercial;
Literary; Mainstream

Welcomes brief queries by post and by
email, but no samples or other material
unless requested.

Jane Rotrosen Agency

85 Broad Street, 28th Floor, New York, NY
10004
Tel: +1 (212) 593-4330
Fax: +1 (212) 935-6985
Email: acirillo@janerotrosen.com
Website: http://www.janerotrosen.com

Handles: Fiction; Nonfiction; *Areas:*
Autobiography; Historical; Mystery;
Romance; Suspense; Thrillers; Women's
Interests; *Markets:* Adult; Youth;
Treatments: Commercial; Mainstream

Send query by email to one of the agent
email addresses provided on the agency bios
page of the website, or by post with SASE,
describing your work and giving relevant
biographical details and publishing history,
along with synopsis and the first three
chapters in the case of fiction, or proposal in
the case of nonfiction. Submissions without
an SASE will be recycled without response.
Attachments to a blank email will not be
opened. See website for full guidelines and
individual agent details.

Janklow & Nesbit Associates

285 Madison Ave, 21st Floor, New York,
NY 10017
Tel: +1 (212) 421-1700
Fax: +1 (212) 355-1403

Email: submissions@janklow.com
Website: http://www.janklowandnesbit.com

Handles: Fiction; Nonfiction; *Markets:* Adult; *Treatments:* Literary

Commercial as well as literary fiction. See website for full list of agents and address your query to a specific agent. Send query with first 10 pages by post or by email. See website for full guidelines.

Jeanne Fredericks Literary Agency, Inc.

221 Benedict Hill Road, New Canaan, CT 06840
Tel: +1 (203) 972-3011
Fax: +1 (203) 972-3011
Email: jeanne.fredericks@gmail.com
Website: http://jeannefredericks.com

Handles: Nonfiction; Reference; *Areas:* Antiques; Arts; Biography; Business; Cookery; Crafts; Design; Finance; Gardening; Health; Historical; How-to; Legal; Leisure; Lifestyle; Medicine; Nature; Photography; Psychology; Science; Self-Help; Sport; Travel; Women's Interests; *Markets:* Adult; *Treatments:* Popular

Send query by email (no attachments) or post with SASE. Specialises in adult nonfiction by authorities in their fields. No fiction, true crime, juvenile, textbooks, poetry, essays, screenplays, short stories, science fiction, pop culture, guides to computers and software, politics, horror, pornography, books on overly depressing or violent topics, romance, teacher's manuals, or memoirs. See website for full guidelines.

Jill Grinberg Literary Management LLC

392 Vanderbilt Avenue, Brooklyn, NY 11238
Tel: +1 (212) 620-5883
Email: info@jillgrinbergliterary.com
Website: http://www.jillgrinbergliterary.com

Handles: Fiction; Nonfiction; *Areas:* Autobiography; Biography; Business; Culture; Current Affairs; Entertainment; Fantasy; Finance; Health; Historical; Humour; Legal; Lifestyle; Medicine; Nature;

Politics; Psychology; Romance; Science; Sci-Fi; Spiritual; Sport; Technology; Travel; Women's Interests; *Markets:* Adult; Children's; Youth; *Treatments:* Commercial; Literary

Send query with synopsis and first 50 pages for fiction, or proposal and author bio for nonfiction.

Jill Corcoran Literary Agency

2150 Park Place, Suite 100, El Segundo, CA 90245
Tel: +1 (310) 773-3699
Email: Jill@
JillCorcoranLiteraryAgency.com
Website: https://
jillcorcoranliteraryagency.com

Handles: Fiction; Nonfiction; *Areas:* Crime; Culture; Fantasy; Humour; Mystery; Psychology; Romance; Sci-Fi; Thrillers; *Markets:* Adult; Children's; Youth; *Treatments:* Contemporary; Literary; Popular

See website for individual agent interests and submission methods, and query one agent only, using online submission system.

Jill Grosjean Literary Agency

1390 Millstone Road, Sag Harbor, NY 11963-2214
Tel: +1 (631) 725-7419
Email: JillLit310@aol.com

Handles: Fiction; *Areas:* Crime; Gardening; Historical; Humour; Mystery; Nature; Romance; Suspense; Thrillers; Travel; Women's Interests; *Markets:* Adult; *Treatments:* Literary; Mainstream

Prefers email queries. No attachments. Particularly interested in literary novels and mysteries.

Joanna Pulcini Literary Management

Email: info@jplm.com
Website: http://www.jplm.com

Handles: Fiction; Nonfiction; *Markets:* Adult

Closed to submissions as at December 2017. See website for current status.

John Hawkins & Associates, Inc.

80 Maiden Lane, STE 1503, New York, NY 10038
Tel: +1 (212) 807-7040
Fax: +1 (212) 807-9555
Email: jha@jhalit.com
Website: http://www.jhalit.com

Handles: Fiction; Nonfiction; *Areas:* Autobiography; Biography; Business; Crime; Current Affairs; Fantasy; Gardening; Health; Historical; Lifestyle; Mystery; Nature; Politics; Psychology; Science; Sci-Fi; Short Stories; Technology; Thrillers; Travel; Women's Interests; *Markets:* Adult

Send query by email with details about you and your writing, and for fiction the first three chapters as a single Word attachment, or for nonfiction include proposal as a single attachment. Include the word "Query" in the subject line. See website for full guidelines.

Joëlle Delbourgo Associates, Inc.

101 Park St., Montclair, Montclair, NJ 07042
Tel: +1 (973) 773-0836
Email: joelle@delbourgo.com
Website: http://www.delbourgo.com

Handles: Fiction; Nonfiction; *Areas:* Autobiography; Cookery; Current Affairs; Historical; Humour; Lifestyle; Politics; Psychology; Science; *Markets:* Adult; *Treatments:* Popular

We are a highly selective agency, broad in our interests. No category romance, Westerns, early readers, or picture books. Send query by email to specific agent (see website for interests and email addresses). Submissions must include the word "QUERY" in the subject line. See website for full guidelines.

JYLA (Jason Yarn Literary Agency)

3544 Broadway #68, New York, NY 10031
Email: jason@jasonyarnliteraryagency.com

Website: http://www. jasonyarnliteraryagency.com

Handles: Fiction; Nonfiction; *Areas:* Adventure; Current Affairs; Fantasy; Historical; Science; Sci-Fi; Suspense; Thrillers; *Markets:* Adult; Children's; Youth; *Treatments:* Commercial; Literary

Accepts electronic submissions only. Send email with the word "Query" in the subject line, and the first ten pages of your manuscript or proposal in the body of the email. No attachments, or queries for film, TV, or stage scripts.

Kathi J. Paton Literary Agency

PO Box 2236, Radio City Station, New York, NY 10101-2236
Tel: +1 (212) 265-6586
Email: kjplitbiz@optonline.net
Website: http://www.PatonLiterary.com

Handles: Fiction; Nonfiction; *Areas:* Biography; Business; Culture; Current Affairs; Finance; Health; Historical; Humour; Lifestyle; Politics; Religious; Science; Sport; Technology; *Markets:* Adult; *Treatments:* Literary; Mainstream; Popular

Send query with brief description by email only. No attachments or referrals to websites. Specialises in adult nonfiction. No science fiction, fantasy, horror, category romance, juvenile, young adult or self-published books. Response only if interested. Also offers editorial services.

Ken Sherman & Associates

1275 N. Hayworth, Suite 103, Los Angeles, CA 90046
Tel: +1 (310) 273-8840
Fax: +1 (310) 271-2875
Email: ken@kenshermanassociates.com
Website: http://www. kenshermanassociates.com

Handles: Fiction; Nonfiction; Scripts; *Areas:* Film; TV; *Markets:* Adult

Handles fiction, nonfiction, and writers for film and TV. Query by referral only.

Kimberley Cameron & Associates

1550 Tiburon Blvd #704, Tiberon, CA 94920
Tel: +1 (415) 789-9191
Email: info@kimberleycameron.com
Website: http://www.kimberleycameron.com

Handles: Fiction; Nonfiction; *Areas:* Autobiography; Biography; Cookery; Culture; Current Affairs; Fantasy; Health; Historical; Horror; Lifestyle; Mystery; Politics; Religious; Science; Sci-Fi; Self-Help; Spiritual; Technology; Thrillers; Travel; Women's Interests; *Markets:* Adult; Family; Youth; *Treatments:* Contemporary; Literary; Mainstream

See website for specific agent interests and submit to most suitable agent through their online submission system.

The Knight Agency

Email: submissions@knightagency.net
Website: http://www.knightagency.net

Handles: Fiction; *Areas:* Autobiography; Beauty and Fashion; Business; Cookery; Crime; Culture; Entertainment; Fantasy; Finance; Health; Historical; How-to; Lifestyle; Media; Mystery; Psychology; Religious; Romance; Sci-Fi; Self-Help; Suspense; Thrillers; Women's Interests; *Markets:* Adult; Children's; Youth; *Treatments:* Commercial; Contemporary; Literary; Popular

Send one-page query by email, with the first five pages of your manuscript in the body of the email. No attachments or paper or phone queries. Paper queries will not be returned.

Not accepting Screen Plays, Short Story Collections, Poetry Collections, Essay Collections, Photography, Film Treatments, Picture Books (excluding graphic novels), Children's Books (excluding young adult and middle grade), Biographies, Nonfiction Historical Treatments.

Linda Konner Literary Agency

10 West 15 Street, Suite 1918, New York, NY 10011
Email: ldkonner@cs.com

Website: http://www. lindakonnerliteraryagency.com

Handles: Nonfiction; Reference; *Areas:* Biography; Business; Cookery; Culture; Entertainment; Finance; Health; How-to; Lifestyle; Psychology; Science; Self-Help; Women's Interests; *Markets:* Adult; *Treatments:* Popular

Send one to two page query by email or by post with SASE, synopsis, and author bio. Attachments from unknown senders will be deleted unread. Nonfiction only. Books must be written by or with established experts in their field. No Fiction, Memoir, Religion, Spiritual/Christian, Children's/young adult, Games/puzzles, Humour, History, Politics, or unsolicited MSS. See website for full guidelines.

Barbara S. Kouts, Literary Agent

PO Box 560, Bellport, NY 11713
Tel: +1 (631) 286-1278
Fax: +1 (631) 286-1538
Email: bkouts@aol.com

Handles: Fiction; *Areas:* Autobiography; Biography; Crime; Current Affairs; Health; Historical; Lifestyle; Mystery; Nature; Psychology; Suspense; Thrillers; Women's Interests; *Markets:* Adult; Children's; *Treatments:* Literary

Note: Not accepting submissions as at January 2017.

Send query with SASE. Postal queries only. Particularly interested in adult fiction and nonfiction and children's books.

KT Literary

9249 S. Broadway #200-543, Highlands Ranch, CO 80129
Tel: +1 (720) 344-4728
Fax: +1 (720) 344-4728
Email: contact@ktliterary.com
Website: http://ktliterary.com

Handles: Fiction; *Areas:* Erotic; Fantasy; Romance; Sci-Fi; *Markets:* Adult; Children's; Youth; *Treatments:* Contemporary; Dark

Actively seeking new clients for middle grade, young adult, and adult categories. See website for individual agent interests and contact details and query one agent at a time. See website for full details.

L. Perkins Associates

5800 Arlington Ave, Riverdale, NY 10471
Tel: +1 (718) 543-5344
Fax: +1 (718) 543-5354
Email: submissions@lperkinsagency.com
Website: http://lperkinsagency.com

Handles: Fiction; Nonfiction; *Areas:* Arts; Autobiography; Biography; Cookery; Crime; Culture; Erotic; Fantasy; Film; Historical; Horror; How-to; Humour; Music; Mystery; Psychology; Romance; Science; Sci-Fi; Theatre; Thrillers; Westerns; *Markets:* Adult; Children's; Youth; *Treatments:* Commercial; Dark; Literary; Popular

Send query by email with synopsis, bio, and first five pages of your novel / proposal in the body of the email. No email attachments and no queries by post or any other means apart from email. Pitch only one book at a time, and to only one agent. Specific agent email addresses are available at website, or use general address provided below. No screenplays, short story collections, or poetry.

Larsen Pomada Literary Agents

1029 Jones Street, San Francisco, CA 94109-5023
Tel: +1 (415) 673-0939
Fax: +1 (415) 673-0367
Email: larsenpoma@aol.com
Website: http://www.larsenpomada.com

Handles: Fiction; Nonfiction; *Areas:* Anthropology; Architecture; Arts; Autobiography; Biography; Business; Cookery; Crime; Culture; Current Affairs; Design; Fantasy; Film; Finance; Health; Historical; How-to; Humour; Legal; Lifestyle; Medicine; Music; Mystery; Nature; New Age; Politics; Psychology; Religious; Romance; Science; Self-Help; Sociology; Sport; Suspense; Thrillers; Travel; Women's Interests; *Markets:* Adult;

Children's; *Treatments:* Commercial; Literary; Mainstream; Satirical

Not accepting new clients as at August 2016. Check website for current status.

Laura Dail Literary Agency

121 West 27th Street, Suite 1201, New York, NY 10001
Tel: +1 (212) 239-7477
Fax: +1 (212) 947-0460
Email: queries@ldlainc.com
Website: http://www.ldlainc.com

Handles: Fiction; Nonfiction; *Areas:* Autobiography; Biography; Cookery; Crime; Culture; Current Affairs; Fantasy; Historical; Humour; Mystery; Romance; Science; Sci-Fi; Technology; Thrillers; Women's Interests; *Markets:* Adult; Children's; Youth; *Treatments:* Commercial; Light; Literary; Serious

Send query by email only with synopsis and first 5 to 10 pages. No screenplays, poetry, illustrated adult books or queries or manuscripts in Spanish.

Lawrence Jordan Literary Agency

231 Lenox Avenue, Suite One, New York, NY 10027
Tel: +1 (212) 662-7871
Fax: +1 (212) 865-7171
Email: ljlagency@aol.com

Handles: Fiction; Nonfiction; *Areas:* Autobiography; Biography; Mystery; Religious; Spiritual; Suspense; Thrillers; *Markets:* Adult

Send query by email only. Particularly interested in spiritual / religion; biographies, autobiographies and celebrity books; mysteries, suspense, and thrillers. No poetry, movie or stage scripts, juvenile, fantasy, or science fiction.

Sarah Lazin Books

19 West 21st Street, Suite 501, New York, NY 10001
Tel: +1 (212) 989-5757
Fax: +1 (212) 989-1393

Email: slazin@lazinbooks.com
Website: http://lazinbooks.com

Handles: Fiction; Nonfiction; *Areas:*
Autobiography; Biography; Culture; Current
Affairs; Historical; Music; Politics; *Markets:*
Adult

Accepting queries via referral only. No
queries by email.

Leigh Feldman Literary

Email: query@lfliterary.com
Website: http://www.lfliterary.com

Handles: Fiction; Nonfiction; *Areas:*
Autobiography; Historical; *Markets:* Adult;
Youth; *Treatments:* Contemporary

Particularly interested in historical fiction,
contemporary YA, literary fiction, memoir,
and narrative nonfiction. No adult and YA
paranormal, fantasy, science fiction,
romance, thrillers, mysteries, or picture
books. Send query by email with first ten
pages. Only makes personal response if
interested.

The Leshne Agency

590 West End Avenue, Suite 11D, New
York, NY 10024
Email: Submissions@LeshneAgency.com
Website: http://leshneagency.com

Handles: Fiction; Nonfiction; *Areas:* Arts;
Autobiography; Business; Cookery; Crafts;
Culture; Film; Gardening; Health; Historical;
Hobbies; Humour; Photography; Science;
Self-Help; Spiritual; Sport; Technology;
Travel; Women's Interests; *Markets:* Adult;
Children's; Youth; *Treatments:* Commercial;
Literary

Seeking new and existing authors across all
genres. Particularly interested in narrative,
memoir, prescriptive nonfiction (including
sports, health, wellness, business, political
and parenting topics), commercial fiction,
young adult and middle grade books. No
screenplays, scripts, poetry, or picture books.
Submit online through online submissions
system or by email. See website for full
details.

Levine Greenberg Rostan Literary Agency

307 Seventh Ave., Suite 2407, New York,
NY 10001
Tel: +1 (212) 337-0934
Fax: +1 (212) 337-0948
Email: submit@lgrliterary.com
Website: http://lgrliterary.com

Handles: Fiction; Nonfiction; *Areas:* Arts;
Autobiography; Beauty and Fashion;
Biography; Business; Cookery; Crafts;
Crime; Culture; Finance; Gardening; Health;
Historical; Hobbies; Humour; Leisure;
Lifestyle; Mystery; Nature; New Age;
Politics; Psychology; Religious; Romance;
Science; Self-Help; Sociology; Spiritual;
Sport; Suspense; Technology; Thrillers;
Travel; Women's Interests; *Markets:* Adult;
Children's; Youth; *Treatments:* Commercial;
Literary; Mainstream; Popular

No queries by post. Send query using online
form at website, or send email attaching no
more than 50 pages. See website for detailed
submission guidelines. No response to
submissions by post.

Linda Chester & Associates

630 Fifth Avenue, Suite 2000, Rockefeller
Center, New York, NY 10111
Tel: +1 (212) 218-3350
Email: submissions@lindachester.com
Website: http://www.lindachester.com

Handles: Fiction; Nonfiction; *Markets:*
Adult; *Treatments:* Commercial; Literary

Send query by email only with short bio and
first five pages pasted directly into the body
of the email. Response within 4 weeks if
interested only. No submissions by post.

Linda Roghaar Literary Agency, Inc.

133 High Point Drive, Amherst, MA 01002
Email: contact@lindaroghaar.com
Website: http://www.LindaRoghaar.com

Handles: Fiction; Nonfiction; *Areas:*
Anthropology; Autobiography; Biography;
Business; Crafts; Culture; Gardening;
Health; Historical; Hobbies; How-to;
Lifestyle; Music; Nature; Religious; Self-

Help; Spiritual; Women's Interests; *Markets:* Adult

Send query by email (mentioning "query" in the subject line) or by post with SASE. For fiction, include the first five pages. Specialises in nonfiction. No romance, science fiction, fantasy, westerns, children's, young adult, or horror. Scripts handled through sub-agents.

Linn Prentis, Literary Agent

c/o Trodayne Northern, Acquisitions Director, for: Amy Hayden, Acquisitions, Linn Prentis Literary, 3 Inverness Drive, New Hartford, NY 13413
Tel: +1 (315) 790-5174
Email: ahayden@linnprentis.com
Website: http://www.linnprentis.com

Handles: Fiction; Nonfiction; *Areas:* Autobiography; Fantasy; Mystery; Sci-Fi; Women's Interests; *Markets:* Adult; Children's; Youth; *Treatments:* Contemporary; Literary; Mainstream

Not accepting submissions as at January 2017, but expects to resume shortly. See website for current status.

Send query by email or by post with SASE, including synopsis and first ten pages. No books for small children, or queries by fax or phone.

The Lisa Ekus Group, LLC

57 North Street, Hatfield, MA 01038
Tel: +1 (413) 247-9325
Email: info@lisaekus.com
Website: http://www.lisaekus.com

Handles: Nonfiction; *Areas:* Cookery; *Markets:* Adult

Handles cookery books only. Submit proposal through submission system on website.

Literary & Creative Artists Inc.

3543 Albemarle Street NW, Washington, DC 20008-4213
Tel: +1 (202) 362-4688
Fax: +1 (202) 362-8875

Email: lca9643@lcadc.com
Website: http://www.lcadc.com

Handles: Fiction; Nonfiction; *Areas:* Arts; Autobiography; Biography; Business; Cookery; Crime; Current Affairs; Drama; Health; Historical; How-to; Legal; Lifestyle; Medicine; Nature; Philosophy; Politics; Religious; Spiritual; *Markets:* Adult

Send query by post with SASE, or by email without attachments. No poetry, academic / educational textbooks, or unsolicited MSS. Currently only accepts projects from established authors.

The Literary Group International

1357 Broadway, Suite 316, New York, NY 10018
Tel: +1 (212) 400-1494
Email: fweimann@theliterarygroup.com
Website: http://www.theliterarygroup.com

Handles: Fiction; Nonfiction; *Areas:* Adventure; Anthropology; Autobiography; Biography; Business; Crime; Culture; Fantasy; Historical; How-to; Humour; Lifestyle; Military; Music; Mystery; Psychology; Religious; Romance; Science; Self-Help; Sociology; Sport; Thrillers; Travel; Women's Interests; *Markets:* Adult; Youth; *Treatments:* Contemporary; Experimental; Literary

Send query by email only, with writing credentials, 2 page synopsis, and 50-page writing sample. Response only if interested. Asks for a 30-day exclusivity period, beginning from the date the material is received.

The LKG Agency

60 Riverside Blvd, #1101, New York, NY 10069
Email: query@LKGAgency.com
Website: http://lkgagency.com

Handles: Fiction; Nonfiction; *Areas:* Autobiography; Beauty and Fashion; Design; Entertainment; Health; Lifestyle; Psychology; Women's Interests; *Markets:* Adult; Children's; Youth

Specialises in nonfiction, but will also consider middle grade and young adult fiction. No history, spirituality, biography, screenplays, true crime, poetry, religion, picture books, or any other fiction besides middle grade and young adult. See website for full submission guidelines.

MacGregor Literary

PO Box 1316, Manzanita, OR 97130
Tel: +1 (503) 389-4803
Email: chip@macgregorliterary.com
Website: http://www.macgregorliterary.com

Handles: Fiction; Nonfiction; *Areas:* Autobiography; Biography; Business; Crime; Culture; Current Affairs; Finance; Historical; How-to; Humour; Lifestyle; Mystery; Religious; Romance; Self-Help; Short Stories; Sport; Suspense; Thrillers; Women's Interests; *Markets:* Academic; Adult; *Treatments:* Contemporary; Mainstream

Handles work in a variety of genres, but all from a Christian perspective. Not accepting unpublished authors, except through conferences and referrals from current clients. Unsolicited MSS will not be returned, even if an SASE is provided.

Manus & Associates Literary Agency, Inc.

425 Sherman Avenue, Suite 200, Palo Alto, CA 94306
Tel: +1 (650) 470-5151
Fax: +1 (650) 470-5159
Email: ManusLit@ManusLit.com
Website: http://www.ManusLit.com

Handles: Fiction; Nonfiction; *Areas:* Autobiography; Biography; Business; Culture; Current Affairs; Finance; Health; How-to; Lifestyle; Mystery; Nature; Psychology; Romance; Science; Self-Help; Suspense; Thrillers; Women's Interests; *Markets:* Adult; *Treatments:* Literary; Mainstream

Send query letter describing your project and giving pertinent biographical info only by fax or email, or send query letter by post with SASE and include complete proposal (nonfiction), or first 30 pages (fiction). When querying by email use one of the direct

personal emails of a specific agent as given on the website, not the generic inbox shown on this page. Approach only one agent. No screenplays, academic, romance, science fiction, fantasy, western, young adult, children's, poetry, cookbooks, or magazine articles. See website for full guidelines.

Maria Carvainis Agency, Inc.

1270 Avenue of the Americas, Suite 2915, New York, NY 10020
Tel: +1 (212) 245-6365
Fax: +1 (212) 245-7196
Email: mca@mariacarvainisagency.com
Website: http://mariacarvainisagency.com

Handles: Fiction; Nonfiction; *Areas:* Adventure; Autobiography; Biography; Business; Crime; Culture; Finance; Historical; Horror; Humour; Mystery; Psychology; Romance; Science; Suspense; Technology; Thrillers; Women's Interests; *Markets:* Adult; Children's; Youth; *Treatments:* Commercial; Contemporary; Literary; Mainstream; Popular

Send query with synopsis, two sample chapters, and details of any previous writing credits, by post or by email. If sending by post and return of the material is required, include SASE; otherwise include email address for response, usually within 5-10 days. If submitting by email, all documents must be Word or PDF. No screenplays, children's picture books, science fiction, or poetry.

Marsal Lyon Literary Agency LLC

PMB 121, 665 San Rodolfo Dr. 124, Solana Beach, CA 92075
Email: Kevan@ MarsalLyonLiteraryAgency.com
Website: http://www. marsallyonliteraryagency.com

Handles: Fiction; Nonfiction; *Areas:* Autobiography; Biography; Business; Cookery; Culture; Current Affairs; Finance; Health; Historical; Lifestyle; Music; Mystery; Politics; Psychology; Romance; Self-Help; Sport; Suspense; Thrillers; Women's Interests; *Markets:* Adult;

Children's; Youth; *Treatments:* Commercial; Mainstream

Send query by email only to one agent only. See website for individual agent interests and email addresses. No submissions by post.

The Martell Agency

1350 Avenue of the Americas, Suite 1205, New York, NY 10019
Tel: +1 (212) 317-2672
Email: submissions@themartellagency.com
Website: http://www.themartellagency.com

Handles: Fiction; Nonfiction; *Areas:* Autobiography; Business; Finance; Health; Historical; Medicine; Mystery; Psychology; Self-Help; Suspense; Thrillers; Women's Interests; *Markets:* Adult; *Treatments:* Commercial

Send query by post or by email, including summary, short bio, any information, if appropriate, as to why you are qualified to write on the subject of your book, any publishing credits, the year of publication and the publisher. No original screenplays or poetry.

Martin Literary Management

Email: Sharlene@
martinliterarymanagement.com
Website: http://www.
martinliterarymanagement.com

Handles: Fiction; Nonfiction; *Areas:* Autobiography; Biography; Business; Crime; Culture; Current Affairs; Entertainment; Health; How-to; Lifestyle; Media; Religious; Self-Help; Women's Interests; *Markets:* Adult; Children's; Youth; *Treatments:* Commercial; Literary; Mainstream; Popular; Positive; Traditional

This agency has strong ties to film/TV. Interested in nonfiction that is highly commercial and that can be adapted to film. Please review our website carefully to make sure we're a good match for your work. How to contact: Completely electronic: emails and MS Word only. No attachments on queries. Place letter in body of email. See submission requirements on website. Do not send materials unless requested. We give very

serious consideration to the material requested.

No adult fiction. Principal agent handles adult nonfiction only. See website for submission guidelines and separate email address for submissions of picture books, middle grade, and young adult fiction and nonfiction.

Massie & McQuilkin

27 West 20th Street, Suite 305, New York, NY 10011
Tel: +1 (212) 352-2055
Fax: +1 (212) 352-2059
Email: info@lmqlit.com
Website: http://www.mmqlit.com

Handles: Fiction; Nonfiction; *Areas:* Autobiography; Biography; Crime; Culture; Current Affairs; Fantasy; Health; Historical; Humour; Politics; Psychology; Science; Sociology; Sport; Suspense; Thrillers; Women's Interests; *Markets:* Adult; Children's; Youth; *Treatments:* Commercial; Literary

See website for specific agent interests and contact details. Query only one agent at a time.

Max Gartenburg Literary Agency

912 North Pennsylvania Avenue, Yardley, PA 19067
Tel: +1 (215) 295-9230
Fax: +1 (215) 295-9240
Email: agdevlin@aol.com
Website: http://www.maxgartenberg.com

Handles: Fiction; Nonfiction; *Areas:* Biography; Culture; Current Affairs; Health; Lifestyle; Nature; Politics; Science; Sport; Women's Interests; *Markets:* Adult

Send query by email to a specific member of staff. See website for specific interests and contact details.

Margret McBride Literary Agency

PO Box 9128, La Jolla, CA 92037
Tel: +1 (858) 454-1550

Email: staff@mcbridelit.com
Website: http://www.mcbrideliterary.com

Handles: Fiction; Nonfiction; *Areas:*
Autobiography; Biography; Business;
Culture; Health; Historical; Humour; Legal;
Medicine; Music; Sci-Fi; Self-Help;
Suspense; Thrillers; Travel; Westerns;
Women's Interests; *Markets:* Adult; Youth;
Treatments: Commercial; Dark

Accepts submissions by email only. See
website for full submission guidelines.

McCormick Literary
37 West 20th Street, New York, NY 10011
Email: queries@mccormicklit.com
Website: http://mccormicklit.com

Handles: Fiction; Nonfiction; *Areas:* Arts;
Autobiography; Biography; Cookery;
Culture; Historical; Humour; Lifestyle;
Politics; Science; Self-Help; Sport; Women's
Interests; *Markets:* Adult; Youth;
Treatments: Commercial; Literary

Send queries by email with short bio and ten
sample pages, indicating in the subject line
which agent you are querying (see website
for individual agent interests). No
attachments. Will also consider submissions
by post, but these will not be returned.
Response only if interested.

McIntosh & Otis, Inc
353 Lexington Avenue, New York, NY
10016
Tel: +1 (212) 687-7400
Fax: +1 (212) 687-6894
Email: info@mcintoshandotis.com
Website: http://www.mcintoshandotis.com

Handles: Fiction; Nonfiction; *Areas:*
Adventure; Culture; Current Affairs;
Fantasy; Historical; Horror; Humour; Music;
Mystery; Nature; Psychology; Romance;
Sci-Fi; Self-Help; Spiritual; Sport; Suspense;
Thrillers; Travel; Women's Interests;
Markets: Adult; Children's; Youth;
Treatments: Commercial; Contemporary;
Literary; Mainstream; Popular

Submissions by email only. See website for
specific agent interests and email addresses,
and query appropriate agent. No longer

accepts submissions by post. See website for
full details.

Meredith Bernstein Literary Agency, Inc.
2095 Broadway, Suite 505, New York, NY
10023
Tel: +1 (212) 799-1007
Fax: +1 (212) 799-1145
Email: mgoodbern@aol.com
Website: http://www.
meredithbernsteinliteraryagency.com

Handles: Fiction; Nonfiction; *Areas:*
Mystery; Romance; Thrillers; *Markets:*
Adult; Youth; *Treatments:* Literary

An eclectic agency which does not specialise
in any one particular area. Accepts queries
by post with SASE, or via form on website.
No poetry or screenplays. See website for
full guidelines.

Patricia Moosbrugger Literary Agency
Email: pm@pmagency.net
Website: http://www.pmagency.net

Handles: Fiction; Nonfiction; *Areas:*
Literature; *Markets:* Adult; Youth

Accepts submissions of adult fiction and
nonfiction and young adult literature. No
science fiction, fantasy or category romance.
Send query by email with brief synopsis.

Howard Morhaim Literary Agency
30 Pierrepont Street, Brooklyn, NY 11201
Tel: +1 (718) 222-8400
Fax: +1 (718) 222-5056
Email: kmckean@morhaimliterary.com
Website: http://morhaimliterary.com

Handles: Fiction; Nonfiction; *Areas:*
Autobiography; Biography; Business;
Cookery; Crafts; Culture; Design; Fantasy;
Finance; Health; Historical; Horror;
Humour; Romance; Sci-Fi; Sport; Thrillers;
Women's Interests; *Markets:* Adult;
Children's; Youth; *Treatments:*
Contemporary; Literary

Enthusiastically accept unsolicited submissions. Send query by email only with outline / proposal for nonfiction, or three sample chapters for fiction. Attachments are accepted. See website for specific agent interests and contact details.

Nappaland Literary Agency

PO Box 1674, Loveland, CO 80539-1674
Fax: +1 (970) 635-9869
Email: Literary@nappaland.com
Website: http://www.nappaland.com/literary

Handles: Fiction; Nonfiction; *Areas:* Culture; Historical; Humour; Lifestyle; Religious; Suspense; Women's Interests; *Markets:* Adult; Youth; *Treatments:* Literary; Popular

Deliberately small boutique-sized agency. Send query letter only by email during specific submission windows (see website). No children's books, memoirs, screenplays, poetry, or anything about cats.

New Leaf Literary & Media, Inc.

110 West 40th Street, Suite 410, New York, NY 10018
Tel: +1 (646) 248-7989
Fax: +1 (646) 861-4654
Email: query@newleafliterary.com
Website: http://www.newleafliterary.com

Handles: Fiction; Nonfiction; *Areas:* Culture; Entertainment; Erotic; Fantasy; Historical; Romance; Sci-Fi; Technology; Thrillers; Women's Interests; *Markets:* Adult; Children's; Youth; *Treatments:* Mainstream

Send query by email only, with the word "Query" along with the specific agent's name in the subject line. Do not query more than one agent. Include up to five double-spaced sample pages in the body of the email -- no attachments. Response only if interested.

Niad Management

15021 Ventura Blvd. #860, Sherman Oaks, CA 91403
Tel: +1 (818) 774-0051
Fax: +1 (818) 774-1740

Email: queries@niadmanagement.com
Website: http://www.niadmanagement.com

Handles: Fiction; Nonfiction; Scripts; *Areas:* Adventure; Autobiography; Biography; Crime; Culture; Drama; Film; Humour; Mystery; Romance; Sport; Suspense; Theatre; Thrillers; TV; *Markets:* Adult; Youth; *Treatments:* Contemporary; Literary; Mainstream

Manages mainly Hollywood writers, actors, and directors, although does also handle a very small number of books. Send query by email or by post with SASE. Responds only if interested.

Northern Lights Literary Services

762 State Road 458, Bedford, IN 47421
Email: queries@northernlightsls.com
Website: http://www.northernlightsls.com

Handles: Fiction; Nonfiction; *Areas:* Biography; Business; Health; Historical; How-to; Lifestyle; Medicine; Mystery; New Age; Psychology; Romance; Self-Help; Suspense; Women's Interests; *Markets:* Adult

Our goal is to provide personalized service to clients and create a bond that will endure throughout your career. We seriously consider each query we receive and will accept hardworking new authors who are willing to develop their talents and skills.

Encourages email queries but responds only if interested (within 5 working days). No horror or books for children.

One Track Literary Agency, Inc.

Tel: +1 (401) 595-1949
Email: tara@onetrackliterary.com
Website: http://www.onetrackliterary.com

Handles: Fiction; *Areas:* Mystery; Romance; Thrillers; Women's Interests; *Markets:* Adult; *Treatments:* Commercial; Contemporary; Light; Mainstream; Niche; Popular; Progressive; Satirical; Serious; Traditional

A full-service boutique agency providing hands-on guidance throughout each and every part of the publishing pursuit. OTLA is single-minded and fully dedicated to getting you on the right track to launch your career or progress to the next level. From honing manuscripts to be their very best, to identifying the right market for placement, through contract advisement and negotiation, to crafting promotional campaigns to help grow your audience, the prime objective is to help you achieve your goals. Currently seeking completed works with vibrant, fresh voices in these genres: romance, women's fiction, mysteries, and young adult.

Paradigm Talent and Literary Agency

360 Park Avenue South, 16th Floor, New York, NY 10010
Tel: +1 (212) 897-6400
Fax: +1 (212) 764-8941
Email: books@paradigmagency.com
Website: http://www.paradigmagency.com

Handles: Scripts; *Areas:* Film; Theatre; TV; *Markets:* Adult

Talent agency with offices in Los Angeles, New York City, Monterey, California and Nashville, Tennessee, representing actors, musical artists, directors, writers and producers. No unsolicited approaches unless by referral or through meeting an agent at an event.

The Park Literary Group LLC

270 Lafayette Street, Suite 1504, New York, NY 10012
Tel: +1 (212) 691-3500
Fax: +1 (212) 691-3540
Email: queries@parkliterary.com
Website: http://www.parkliterary.com

Handles: Fiction; Nonfiction; *Areas:* Adventure; Arts; Autobiography; Culture; Current Affairs; Historical; Politics; Science; Women's Interests; *Markets:* Adult; *Treatments:* Commercial; Literary

Send query by email only, with all materials in the body of the email (no attachments). See website for individual agent details and query one specific agent with their first and last name in the subject line of your email. See website for full guidelines. No poetry or screenplays.

Pavilion Literary Management

660 Massachusetts Avenue, Suite 4, Boston, MA 02118
Tel: +1 (617) 792-5218
Email: jeff@pavilionliterary.com
Website: http://www.pavilionliterary.com

Handles: Fiction; Nonfiction; *Areas:* Adventure; Autobiography; Fantasy; Historical; Mystery; Science; Thrillers; *Markets:* Adult; Children's; Youth; *Treatments:* Popular

Only accepting approaches for fiction work by previously published authors or client referral. Send query by email specifying fiction or nonfiction and title of work in the subject line. No attachments. See website for full details.

Pippin Properties, Inc

110 West 40th Street, Suite 1704, New York, NY 10016
Tel: +1 (212) 338-9310
Fax: +1 (212) 338-9579
Email: info@pippinproperties.com
Website: http://www.pippinproperties.com

Handles: Fiction; *Markets:* Adult; Children's; Youth

Devoted primarily to picture books, middle-grade, and young adult novels, but also represents adult projects on occasion. Send query by email with synopsis, first chapter, or entire picture book manuscript in the body of your email. No attachments. See website for full guidelines.

Publication Riot Group, Inc.

Email: db@priotgroup.com
Website: http://priotgroup.com

Handles: Fiction; Nonfiction; *Areas:* Autobiography; Culture; Historical; Politics; Science; Sociology; Thrillers; Women's Interests; *Markets:* Adult; *Treatments:* Literary; Mainstream

Closed to submissions as at December 2017. Check website for current status.

The Purcell Agency, LLC

Email: TPAqueries@gmail.com
Website: http://thepurcellagency.com

Handles: Fiction; Nonfiction; *Areas:* Culture; Romance; Sport; Women's Interests; *Markets:* Adult; Children's; Youth

Closed to submissions as at May 2018. Check website for current status.

Handles middle grade, young adult, women's fiction, and some new adult. No science fiction or fantasy, or picture book manuscripts. See website for full submission guidelines.

Queen Literary Agency, Inc.

30 East 60th Street, Suite 1004, New York, NY 10024
Tel: +1 (212) 974-8333
Fax: +1 (212) 974-8347
Email: submissions@queenliterary.com
Website: http://www.queenliterary.com

Handles: Fiction; Nonfiction; *Areas:* Business; Cookery; Historical; Mystery; Psychology; Science; Sport; Thrillers; *Markets:* Adult; *Treatments:* Commercial; Literary

Founded by a former publishing executive, most recently head of IMG WORLDWIDE'S literary division. Handles a wide range of nonfiction titles, with a particular interest in business books, food writing, science and popular psychology, as well as books by well-known chefs, radio and television personalities and sports figures. Also handles commercial and literary fiction, including historical fiction, mysteries, and thrillers.

Lynne Rabinoff Agency

72-11 Austin Street, No. 201, Forest Hills, NY 11375
Tel: +1 (718) 459-6894
Email: lynne@lynnerabinoff.com

Handles: Nonfiction; *Areas:* Anthropology; Archaeology; Autobiography; Biography;

Business; Culture; Current Affairs; Finance; Historical; Legal; Military; Politics; Psychology; Religious; Science; Technology; Women's Interests; *Markets:* Adult

Particularly interested in politics, history, current affairs, and religion. Send query by email or by post with SASE, including proposal, sample chapter, and author bio. No queries by fax.

Raines & Raines

103 Kenyon Road, Medusa, NY 12120
Tel: +1 (518) 239-8311
Fax: +1 (518) 239-6029

Handles: Fiction; Nonfiction; *Areas:* Adventure; Autobiography; Biography; Crime; Fantasy; Finance; Historical; Military; Mystery; Psychology; Sci-Fi; Suspense; Thrillers; Westerns; *Markets:* Adult

Handles nonfiction in all areas, and fiction in the areas specified above. Send query with SASE.

Regal Hoffmann & Associates LLC

143 West 29th Street, Suite 901, New York, NY 10001
Tel: +1 (212) 684-7900
Fax: +1 (212) 684-7906
Email: submissions@rhaliterary.com
Website: http://www.rhaliterary.com

Handles: Fiction; Nonfiction; *Areas:* Autobiography; Biography; Historical; Science; Short Stories; Thrillers; *Markets:* Adult; Children's; Youth; *Treatments:* Literary

Send one-page query by email or by post with SASE, outline, and author bio/qualifications. For fiction, include first ten pages or one story from a collection. No response unless interested.

The Amy Rennert Agency, Inc.

1550 Tiburon Boulevard #302, Tiburon, CA 94920
Email: queries@amyrennert.com
Website: http://www.amyrennert.com

Handles: Fiction; Nonfiction; *Areas:* Autobiography; Biography; Business; Finance; Health; Historical; Lifestyle; Literature; Mystery; Spiritual; Sport; *Markets:* Adult; *Treatments:* Literary

Not accepting unsolicited mss, but referrals still welcome. Send query by email, with cover letter in body of email and a Word file attachment containing proposal and first chapter (nonfiction) or first 10-20 pages (fiction). For picture books, send cover letter in the body of the email and attach file with the text. Include phone number. Response only if interested.

Richard Henshaw Group LLC

145 W. 28th Street, 12th Floor, New York, NY 10001
Tel: +1 (212) 414-1172
Email: submissions@henshaw.com
Website: https://richardhenshawgroup.com

Handles: Fiction; Nonfiction; Reference; *Areas:* Biography; Business; Culture; Current Affairs; Fantasy; Film; Health; Historical; Horror; How-to; Literature; Mystery; Psychology; Romance; Science; Sci-Fi; Sport; Thrillers; *Markets:* Adult; Youth; *Treatments:* Popular

Only considers works between 65,000 and 150,000 words. No children's books, screenplays, short fiction, poetry, textbooks, scholarly works, or coffee-table books. Send query up to 250 words by email only. No postal submissions.

Rita Rosenkranz Literary Agency

440 West End Ave, Suite 15D, New York, NY 10024
Tel: +1 (212) 873-6333
Email: rrosenkranz@mindspring.com
Website: http://www. ritarosenkranzliteraryagency.com

Handles: Nonfiction; Reference; *Areas:* Cookery; Health; Historical; How-to; Humour; Lifestyle; Music; Science; Spiritual; *Markets:* Adult; *Treatments:* Commercial; Niche; Popular

Send query only by post or email. Submit proposal on request only. Deals specifically

in adult nonfiction. No screenplays, poetry, fiction, children's or YA books. Response within two weeks.

Riverside Literary Agency

41 Simon Keets Road, Leyden, MA 01337
Tel: +1 (413) 772-0067
Fax: +1 (413) 772-0969
Email: rivlit@sover.net

Handles: Fiction; Nonfiction; *Markets:* Adult

Send query with outline by email. Usually obtains new clients by referral.

RLR Associates

Literary Department, 7 West 51st Street, New York, NY 10019
Tel: +1 (212) 541-8641
Email: website.info@rlrassociates.net
Website: http://www.rlrliterary.net

Handles: Fiction; Nonfiction; *Areas:* Biography; Culture; Historical; Humour; Romance; Sport; Women's Interests; *Markets:* Adult; Children's; Youth; *Treatments:* Commercial; Literary; Mainstream; Popular

Represents literary and commercial fiction, genre fiction, and narrative nonfiction. Particularly interested in history, pop culture, humour, food and beverage, biography, and sports. Also represents all types of children's literature. Send query or proposal by post or by email. For fiction, include writing sample (normally the first few chapters). If no response after three months, assume rejection.

The Robbins Office, Inc.

405 Park Avenue, New York, NY 10022
Tel: +1 (212) 223-0720
Fax: +1 (212) 223-2535
Email: translation@robbinsoffice.com
Website: http://robbinsoffice.com

Handles: Fiction; Nonfiction; *Markets:* Adult; *Treatments:* Commercial; Literary; Serious

Literary agency based in New York. Does not accept submissions of unsolicited material.

Robin Straus Agency, Inc.

229 East 79th Street, Suite 5A, New York, NY 10075
Tel: +1 (212) 472-3282
Fax: +1 (212) 472-3833
Email: info@robinstrausagency.com
Website: http://www.robinstrausagency.com

Handles: Fiction; Nonfiction; *Areas:* Autobiography; Biography; Cookery; Culture; Current Affairs; Historical; Lifestyle; Nature; Psychology; Science; Women's Interests; *Markets:* Adult; *Treatments:* Commercial; Literary

Prefers submissions by email. Send query with bio, synopsis or outline, submission history, and market information. You may also include the opening chapter. All material must be in the body of the email. No attachments. Approaches by post are accepted, but no response without SASE. No juvenile, young adult, science fiction/fantasy, horror, romance, westerns, poetry or screenplays. No metered postage. If no response after 6 weeks, assume rejection.

Rodeen Literary Management

3501 N. Southport #497, Chicago, IL 60657
Email: submissions@rodeenliterary.com
Website: http://www.rodeenliterary.com

Handles: Fiction; Nonfiction; *Markets:* Children's; Youth

Independent literary agency providing career management for experienced and aspiring authors and illustrators of children's literature. Actively seeking talented writers and illustrators of all genres of children's literature including picture books, early readers, middle-grade fiction and nonfiction, graphic novels and comic books as well as young adult fiction and nonfiction. See website for full submission guidelines.

Andy Ross Agency

767 Santa Ray Avenue, Oakland, CA 94610
Tel: +1 (510) 238-8965

Email: andyrossagency@hotmail.com
Website: http://www.andyrossagency.com

Handles: Fiction; Nonfiction; *Areas:* Culture; Current Affairs; Historical; Religious; Science; *Markets:* Adult; Children's; Youth; *Treatments:* Commercial; Contemporary; Literary

We encourage queries for material in our fields of interest. No poetry, short stories, adult romance, science fiction and fantasy, adult and teen paranormal, or film scripts.

The agent has worked in the book business for 36 years, all of his working life. He was owner and general manager of Cody's Books in Berkeley, California from 1977-2006. Cody's has been recognised as one of America's great independent book stores.

During this period, the agent was the primary trade book buyer. This experience has given him a unique understanding of the retail book market, of publishing trends and, most importantly and uniquely, the hand selling of books to book buyers.

The agent is past president of the Northern California Booksellers Association, a board member and officer of the American Booksellers Association and a national spokesperson for issues concerning independent businesses. He has had significant profiles in the Wall Street Journal, Time Magazine, and the San Francisco Chronicle.

Queries by email only. See website for full guidelines.

Ross Yoon Agency

1666 Connecticut Avenue, NW, Suite 500, Washington, DC 20009
Tel: +1 (202) 328-3282
Email: submissions@rossyoon.com
Website: http://www.rossyoon.com

Handles: Nonfiction; *Areas:* Autobiography; Biography; Business; Culture; Current Affairs; Historical; Psychology; Science; *Markets:* Adult; *Treatments:* Commercial; Popular; Serious

Handles adult nonfiction only. Send query or complete book proposal by email only with proposal in body of email or as .doc or .docx attachment. No unsolicited MSS or approaches by post or phone. See website for full guidelines.

The Rudy Agency

825 Wildlife Lane, Estes Park, CO 80517
Tel: +1 (970) 577-8500
Fax: +1 (970) 577-8600
Email: mak@rudyagency.com
Website: http://www.rudyagency.com

Handles: Fiction; Nonfiction; *Areas:* Autobiography; Biography; Business; Culture; Current Affairs; Health; Historical; Lifestyle; Medicine; Military; Politics; Science; Technology; Thrillers; *Markets:* Adult; Children's

Concentrates on adult nonfiction in the areas listed above. In fiction, accepts only historical fiction and thrillers. See website for full guidelines, and appropriate email addresses for different types of submissions.

Marly Rusoff & Associates, Inc.

PO Box 524, Bronxville, NY 10708
Tel: +1 (914) 961-7939
Email: mra_queries3@rusoffagency.com
Website: http://www.rusoffagency.com

Handles: Fiction; Nonfiction; *Areas:* Architecture; Arts; Autobiography; Biography; Business; Culture; Design; Finance; Health; Historical; Medicine; Psychology; *Markets:* Adult; *Treatments:* Commercial; Literary

Note: Not accepting new clients as at January 2016. See website for current status

Send 1-2 page query by post or email, including synopsis and relevant author info and page or word count. Queries sent by email should include the word "query" in the subject line. Changes email address regularly to avoid spam, so check website before querying and notify firstwriter.com via the "Report an Error" button if address has changed from that displayed. May not

respond if not interested. No PDFs, CDs, or directions to view material on websites.

The Sagalyn Literary Agency

2 Wisconsin Circle, Suite 650, Chevy Chase, MD 20815
Email: query@sagalyn.com
Website: http://www.sagalyn.com

Handles: Fiction; Nonfiction; *Areas:* Biography; Business; Culture; Finance; Historical; Science; Technology; *Markets:* Adult; *Treatments:* Mainstream

Specialises in quality nonfiction and mainstream fiction. No romance, westerns, science fiction, poetry, children's books, or screenplays. Query by email only, but no attachments. Visit website for details on submissions.

Salkind Literary Agency

62 Nassau Drive, Great Neck, NY 11021
Tel: +1 (785) 371-0101
Fax: +1 (516) 706-2369
Email: neil@studiob.com
Website: http://www.salkindagency.com

Handles: Fiction; Nonfiction; *Areas:* Adventure; Arts; Autobiography; Biography; Business; Cookery; Crafts; Crime; Culture; Current Affairs; Design; Fantasy; Finance; Health; Historical; How-to; Humour; Lifestyle; Mystery; Photography; Politics; Psychology; Religious; Science; Sci-Fi; Self-Help; Spiritual; Suspense; Technology; Thrillers; Travel; Women's Interests; *Markets:* Academic; Adult; *Treatments:* Commercial

Handles general nonfiction trade, fiction, and textbook authors. Query by email or telephone.

Sandra Dijkstra Literary Agency

PMB 515, 1155 Camino Del Mar, Del Mar, CA 92014
Tel: +1 (858) 755-3115
Fax: +1 (858) 794-2822
Email: queries@dijkstraagency.com
Website: http://www.dijkstraagency.com

Handles: Fiction; Nonfiction; *Areas:* Autobiography; Biography; Business; Cookery; Culture; Current Affairs; Design; Fantasy; Health; Historical; Humour; Lifestyle; Music; Mystery; Nature; Philosophy; Politics; Religious; Romance; Science; Sci-Fi; Self-Help; Short Stories; Sociology; Sport; Suspense; Thrillers; Travel; Women's Interests; *Markets:* Adult; Children's; Youth; *Treatments:* Commercial; Contemporary; Literary

Check author bios on website and submit query by email to one agent only. For fiction, include a one-page synopsis, brief bio, and first 10-15 pages. For nonfiction, include overview, chapter outline, brief bio, and first 10-15 pages. All material must be in the body of the email. No attachments. See website for full submission guidelines.

Sanford J. Greenburger Associates, Inc.

15th Floor, 55 Fifth Avenue, New York, NY 10003
Tel: +1 (212) 206-5600
Fax: +1 (212) 463-8718
Email: queryHL@sjga.com
Website: http://www.greenburger.com

Handles: Fiction; Nonfiction; Reference; *Areas:* Arts; Autobiography; Biography; Business; Entertainment; Fantasy; Health; Historical; Humour; Lifestyle; Music; Mystery; Nature; Politics; Psychology; Romance; Science; Sci-Fi; Self-Help; Sociology; Sport; Thrillers; Women's Interests; *Markets:* Adult; Children's; Youth; *Treatments:* Commercial; Literary; Popular

Check website for specific agent interests, guidelines, and contact details. Most will not accept submissions by post. Aims to respond to queries within 6-8 weeks.

Scott Treimel NY

434 Lafayette Street, New York, NY 10003
Tel: +1 (212) 505-8353
Email: general@scotttreimelny.com
Website: http://www.scotttreimelny.com

Handles: Fiction; Nonfiction; *Markets:* Children's; Youth

Children's books only – from concept / board books to teen fiction. Accepts submissions only from published authors, or by referral from contacts, or from attendees at conferences.

Scovil Galen Ghosh Literary Agency, Inc.

276 Fifth Avenue, Suite 708, New York, NY 10001
Tel: +1 (212) 679-8686
Fax: +1 (212) 679-6710
Email: russellgalen@sgglit.com
Website: http://www.sgglit.com

Handles: Fiction; Nonfiction; *Areas:* Adventure; Arts; Autobiography; Biography; Business; Cookery; Culture; Health; Historical; Nature; Politics; Psychology; Religious; Science; Sociology; Sport; Women's Interests; *Markets:* Adult; Children's; Youth; *Treatments:* Commercial; Contemporary; Literary

Send query letter only in first instance. Prefers contact by email, but no attachments. If contacting by post include letter only, with email address for response rather than an SASE.

Scribe Agency LLC

5508 Joylynne Drive, Madison, WI 53716
Tel: +1 (608) 259-0491
Email: submissions@scribeagency.com
Website: http://www.scribeagency.com

Handles: Fiction; *Areas:* Fantasy; Literature; Sci-Fi; Short Stories; *Markets:* Adult; *Treatments:* Commercial; Literary; Mainstream

Handles science fiction, fantasy, and literary fiction. No nonfiction, humour, cozy mysteries, faith-based fiction, screenplays, poetry, or works based on another's ideas. Send query in body of email, with synopsis and first three chapters as Word docs, RTFs, or PDFs. No hard copy approaches. If unable to submit material electronically, send email query in first instance.

Secret Agent Man

PO Box 1078, Lake Forest, CA 92609-1078
Tel: +1 (949) 698-6987

Email: query@secretagentman.net
Website: http://www.secretagentman.net

Handles: Fiction; Nonfiction; *Areas:* Crime;
Mystery; Religious; Suspense; Thrillers;
Westerns; *Markets:* Adult

Send query by email only (no postal
submissions) with the word "Query" in the
subject line, sample consecutive chapter(s),
synopsis and/or outline. No first contact by
phone. Not interested in vampire; sci-fi;
fantasy; horror; cold war, military or political
thrillers; children's or young adult; short
stories; screenplays; poetry collections;
romance; or historical. Christian nonfiction
should be based on Biblical theology, not
speculative. No self-published works.

Lynn Seligman, Literary Agent

400 Highland Avenue, Upper Montclair, NJ
07043
Tel: +1 (973) 783-3631

Handles: Fiction; Nonfiction; *Areas:*
Anthropology; Arts; Biography; Business;
Cookery; Crime; Culture; Current Affairs;
Design; Fantasy; Film; Finance; Health;
Historical; Horror; How-to; Humour;
Lifestyle; Music; Mystery; Nature;
Photography; Politics; Psychology;
Romance; Science; Sci-Fi; Self-Help;
Sociology; Women's Interests; *Markets:*
Adult; *Treatments:* Contemporary; Literary;
Mainstream

Send query with SASE.

Sheree Bykofsky Associates, Inc.

4326 Harbor Beach Boulevard, PO Box 706,
Brigantine, NJ 08203
Email: submitbee@aol.com
Website: http://www.shereebee.com

Handles: Fiction; Nonfiction; Reference;
Areas: Biography; Business; Cookery;
Culture; Current Affairs; Film; Hobbies;
Humour; Lifestyle; Mystery; Psychology;
Self-Help; Spiritual; Women's Interests;
Markets: Adult; *Treatments:* Commercial;
Literary

Send query by email only. Include one page
query, and for fiction a one page synopsis,
and first page of manuscript, all in the body
of the email. No attachments. Always
looking for a bestseller in any category, but
generally not interested in poetry, thrillers,
westerns, romances, occult, science fiction,
fantasy, children's or young adult.

Signature Literary Agency

4200 Wisconsin Ave, NW #106-233,
Washington, DC 20016
Email: gary@signaturelit.com
Website: http://www.signaturelit.com

Handles: Fiction; Nonfiction; Reference;
Areas: Autobiography; Biography;
Criticism; Culture; Fantasy; Health;
Historical; Mystery; Politics; Psychology;
Religious; Romance; Science; Sci-Fi;
Spiritual; Technology; *Markets:* Adult;
Treatments: Commercial; Literary

Agency established in Washington DC. The
principal agent formerly worked at the
Graybill and English Literary Agency. She
has a law degree from George Washington
University and extensive editorial
experience.

Send query by email to specific agent (see
website for individual contact details and
"wishlists").

Offices in both New York and Washington
DC.

SLW Literary Agency

4100 Ridgeland Avenue, Northbrook, IL
60062
Tel: +1 (847) 207-2075
Email: shariwenk@swenkagency.com

Handles: Nonfiction; *Areas:* Sport; *Markets:*
Adult

Handles sports celebrities and sports writers
only.

Solow Literary Enterprises, Inc.

769 Center Blvd., #148, Fairfax, CA 94930
Email: info@solowliterary.com
Website: http://www.solowliterary.com

*Claim your free access to **www.firstwriter.com**: See p.389*

Handles: Nonfiction; *Areas:* Autobiography; Business; Culture; Finance; Health; Historical; Nature; Psychology; Science; *Markets:* Adult

Handles nonfiction in the stated areas only. Send single-page query by email or by post with SASE, providing information on what your book is about; why you think it has to be written; and why you are the best person to write it. Response only if interested.

Spectrum Literary Agency

320 Central Park West, Suite 1-D, New York, NY 10025
Tel: +1 (212) 362-4323
Fax: +1 (212) 362-4562
Email: ruddigore1@aol.com
Website: http://www.spectrumliteraryagency.com

Handles: Fiction; Nonfiction; *Areas:* Fantasy; Historical; Mystery; Romance; Sci-Fi; Suspense; *Markets:* Adult; *Treatments:* Contemporary; Mainstream

Send query with SASE describing your book and providing background information, publishing credits, and relevant qualifications. The first 10 pages of the work may also be included. Response within three months. No unsolicited MSS or queries by fax, email, or phone.

Speilburg Literary Agency

Email: speilburgliterary@gmail.com
Website: https://speilburgliterary.com

Handles: Fiction; Nonfiction; *Areas:* Culture; Fantasy; Historical; Horror; Mystery; Romance; Science; Suspense; *Markets:* Adult; Youth; *Treatments:* Mainstream; Popular

Closed to submissions between July 4 and September 3, 2018.

Send query by email with first three chapters (fiction), or proposal, including table of contents and sample chapter (nonfiction). No picture books, poetry, or screenplays. See website for full guidelines and individual agent interests.

Spencerhill Associates

8131 Lakewood Main Street, #205, Lakewood Ranch, FL 34202
Tel: +1 (941) 907-3700
Email: submission@spencerhillassociates.com
Website: http://spencerhillassociates.com

Handles: Fiction; Nonfiction; *Areas:* Erotic; Fantasy; Historical; Mystery; Romance; Thrillers; *Markets:* Adult; Youth; *Treatments:* Commercial; Literary

Handles commercial, general-interest fiction, romance including historical romance, paranormal romance, urban fantasy, erotic fiction, category romance, literary fiction, thrillers and mysteries, young adult, and nonfiction. No children's. Send query by email with synopsis and first three chapters attached in .doc / .rtf / .txt format. See website for full details.

The Spieler Agency

27 West 20th Street, Suite 305, New York, NY 10011
Tel: +1 (212) 757-4439, ext.1
Fax: +1 (212) 333-2019
Email: joe@TheSpielerAgency.com
Website: http://thespieleragency.com

Handles: Fiction; Nonfiction; Poetry; *Areas:* Architecture; Autobiography; Biography; Business; Cookery; Crime; Culture; Current Affairs; Film; Finance; Gardening; Health; Historical; Humour; Legal; Lifestyle; Music; Mystery; Nature; Photography; Politics; Science; Sociology; Spiritual; Theatre; Thrillers; Travel; Women's Interests; *Markets:* Adult; Children's; Youth; *Treatments:* Literary; Popular

Consult website for details of specific agents' interests and contact details. Send query by email or by post with SASE. Response not guaranteed if not interested. No response to postal submissions without SASE.

Philip G. Spitzer Literary Agency, Inc.

50 Talmage Farm Lane, East Hampton, NY 11937
Tel: +1 (631) 329-3650

Fax: +1 (631) 329-3651
Email: kim.lombardini@spitzeragency.com
Website: http://spitzeragency.com

Handles: Fiction; Nonfiction; *Areas:*
Biography; Current Affairs; Fantasy;
Historical; Mystery; Politics; Sci-Fi; Short
Stories; Sport; Suspense; Thrillers; Travel;
Markets: Adult; Children's; *Treatments:*
Literary

Full client list, but will consider queries by
email with proposal and first chapter. No
telephone calls.

Stephanie Tade Literary Agency

Email: submissions@
stephanietadeagency.com
Website: http://www.
stephanietadeagency.com

Handles: Nonfiction; *Areas:* Autobiography;
Culture; Health; Philosophy; Politics;
Psychology; Spiritual; *Markets:* Adult

Send single-page query by email with
information about your proposed book, your
publishing history, and any media or online
platform you have developed. Response only
if interested.

Sterling Lord Literistic, Inc.

115 Broadway, New York, NY 10006
Tel: +1 (212) 780-6050
Fax: +1 (212) 780-6095
Email: info@sll.com
Website: http://www.sll.com

Handles: Fiction; Nonfiction; *Areas:*
Autobiography; Beauty and Fashion;
Biography; Business; Cookery; Culture;
Current Affairs; Health; Historical; Lifestyle;
Nature; Politics; Science; Self-Help;
Technology; Travel; Women's Interests;
Markets: Adult; Children's; Youth;
Treatments: Commercial; Literary; Popular

Send query with SASE, synopsis, brief
author bio, and first three chapters. Literary
value considered above all else. No response
to unsolicited email queries.

Stone Manners Salners Agency

6100 Wilshire Boulevard, Suite 1400, Los
Angeles, CA 90048
Tel: +1 (323) 655-1313 / +1 (212) 505-1400
Email: info@smsagency.com
Website: http://www.smsagency.com

Handles: Scripts; *Areas:* Film; TV; *Markets:*
Adult

Handles movie and TV scripts. Send query
by email or post with SASE. No queries by
fax.

The Stringer Literary Agency LLC

PO Box 111255, Naples, FL 34108
Email: mstringer@stringerlit.com
Website: http://www.stringerlit.com

Handles: Fiction; *Areas:* Fantasy; Historical;
Horror; Mystery; Romance; Sci-Fi; Thrillers;
Women's Interests; *Markets:* Adult;
Children's; Youth

Welcomes queries from both published and
unpublished writers. Particularly interested
in upmarket women's fiction, fantasy,
romance, and thrillers. No christian, comedy,
humour, comics, graphic novels, erotica,
poetry, puzzles, games, picture books, early
readers, middle grade, new adult, stage
plays, or screenplays. Submit query via form
on website.

Stuart Krichevsky Literary Agency, Inc.

6 East 39th Street, Suite 500, New York, NY
10016
Tel: +1 (212) 725-5288
Fax: +1 (212) 725-5275
Email: query@skagency.com
Website: http://www.skagency.com

Handles: Fiction; Nonfiction; *Areas:*
Adventure; Autobiography; Biography;
Business; Culture; Current Affairs; Fantasy;
Historical; Nature; Politics; Science; Sci-Fi;
Technology; *Markets:* Adult; Youth;
Treatments: Commercial; Literary

Send query by email with first few pages of
your manuscript (up to 10) pasted into body

of the email (no attachments). See website for complete submission guidelines and appropriate submission addresses for each agent.

The Stuart Agency

260 West 52 Street, Suite #25C, New York, NY 10019
Tel: +1 (212) 586-2711
Email: andrew@stuartagency.com
Website: http://www.stuartagency.com

Handles: Fiction; Nonfiction; *Areas:* Arts; Autobiography; Business; Culture; Current Affairs; Design; Health; Historical; Horror; Humour; Lifestyle; Music; Psychology; Religious; Science; Sport; Thrillers; *Markets:* Adult; *Treatments:* Commercial; Literary

Send query using submission form on website.

Susan Rabiner, Literary Agent, Inc.

315 West 39th Street, Suite 1501, New York, NY 10018
Email: susan@rabiner.net
Website: http://www.rabinerlit.com

Handles: Fiction; Nonfiction; *Areas:* Arts; Autobiography; Entertainment; Finance; Historical; Humour; Politics; Science; Sport; *Markets:* Adult

Send query by email only. Response within two weeks if interested. See website for details and email addresses of individual agents.

Talcott Notch Literary

31 Cherry Street, Suite 104, Milford, CT 06460
Fax: +1 (203) 876-9517
Email: editorial@talcottnotch.net
Website: http://www.talcottnotch.net

Handles: Fiction; Nonfiction; *Areas:* Autobiography; Business; Cookery; Crafts; Crime; Fantasy; Gardening; Historical; Horror; Lifestyle; Mystery; Nature; Science; Sci-Fi; Suspense; Technology; Thrillers; Women's Interests; *Markets:* Adult;

Children's; Family; Youth; *Treatments:* Mainstream

Currently closed to unsolicited queries and submissions. Will continue to consider works requested as a result of meeting writers through conferences, pitch slams, writing workshops, bootcamps, and client referrals.

Tessler Literary Agency

27 West 20th Street, Suite 1003, New York, NY 10011
Tel: +1 (212) 242-0466
Fax: +1 (212) 242-2366
Website: http://www.tessleragency.com

Handles: Fiction; Nonfiction; *Areas:* Autobiography; Biography; Business; Cookery; Culture; Health; Historical; Psychology; Science; Travel; Women's Interests; *Markets:* Adult; *Treatments:* Commercial; Literary; Popular

Welcomes appropriate queries. Handles quality nonfiction and literary and commercial fiction. No genre fiction or children's fiction. Send query via form on website only.

Tracy Brown Literary Agency

PO Box 772, Nyack, NY 10960
Tel: +1 (914) 400-4147
Fax: +1 (914) 931-1746
Email: tracy@brownlit.com

Handles: Fiction; Nonfiction; *Areas:* Biography; Current Affairs; Health; Historical; Psychology; Travel; Women's Interests; *Markets:* Adult; *Treatments:* Literary; Popular; Serious

Particularly interested in serious nonfiction and fiction. Send query with author bio, outline/proposal, and synopsis. Queries accepted by email but not by fax. No Young Adult, Science Fiction, or Romance.

TriadaUS Literary Agency, Inc.

P.O.Box 561, Sewickley, PA 15143
Tel: +1 (412) 401-3376
Email: uwe@triadaus.com
Website: http://www.triadaus.com

Handles: Fiction; Nonfiction; *Areas:* Adventure; Autobiography; Biography; Business; Cookery; Crafts; Crime; Culture; Current Affairs; Fantasy; Finance; Gardening; Health; Historical; How-to; Humour; Lifestyle; Music; Mystery; Politics; Psychology; Romance; Science; Sci-Fi; Self-Help; Sport; Suspense; Thrillers; Travel; Women's Interests; *Markets:* Adult; Children's; Youth; *Treatments:* Commercial; Literary; Mainstream

Prefers email queries. No attachments, unless requested. Accepts submissions by post, but no response without SASE. No response to queries that do not follow the guidelines.

Trident Media Group, LLC

41 Madison Avenue, 36th Fl., New York, NY 10010
Tel: +1 (212) 333-1511
Email: info@tridentmediagroup.com
Website: http://www.tridentmediagroup.com

Handles: Fiction; Nonfiction; *Areas:* Adventure; Autobiography; Biography; Business; Crime; Criticism; Culture; Current Affairs; Fantasy; Film; Health; Historical; Humour; Lifestyle; Music; Mystery; Politics; Religious; Romance; Science; Sci-Fi; Sport; Suspense; Technology; Thrillers; Women's Interests; *Markets:* Adult; Children's; Youth; *Treatments:* Commercial; Literary; Popular

Send query using form on website. Check website for details and interests of specific agents and approach one agent only. Do not approach more than one agent at a time. No unsolicited MSS.

2M Literary Agency Ltd

19 West 21 Street Suite 501, New York, NY 10010
Tel: +1 (212) 741-1509
Fax: +1 (212) 691-4460
Email: morel@2mcommunications.com
Website: http://www. 2mcommunications.com

Handles: Nonfiction; *Areas:* Autobiography; Beauty and Fashion; Business; Cookery; Crime; Culture; Film; Health; Lifestyle; Medicine; Music; Politics; Psychology; Science; Sport; *Markets:* Adult; Family;

Treatments: Contemporary; Mainstream; Niche; Popular; Progressive; Traditional

Only accepts queries from established ghostwriters, collaborators, and editors with experience in the fields of business; film, music and television; health and fitness; medicine and psychology; parenting; politics; science; sport; true crime; or the world of food.

Union Literary

30 Vandam Street, Suite 5A, New York, NY 10013
Tel: +1 (212) 255-2112
Email: queries@threeseaslit.com
Website: https://www.unionliterary.com

Handles: Fiction; Nonfiction; *Areas:* Autobiography; Business; Cookery; Historical; Science; Sociology; *Markets:* Adult; *Treatments:* Literary; Popular

Prefers queries by email. Include a proposal and sample chapter for nonfiction, or a synopsis and sample pages for fiction. See website for specific agent interests and contact details, and approach one agent only. No romance or science fiction. Response only if interested.

United Talent Agency

142 West 57th Street, Sixth Floor, New York, NY 10019
Tel: +1 (212) 581-3100
Fax: +1 (212) 581-0015
Email: Sasha.Raskin@Unitedtalent.com
Website: http://www.theagencygroup.com

Handles: Fiction; Nonfiction; *Areas:* Business; Historical; Science; Sci-Fi; *Markets:* Adult; *Treatments:* Literary

Multimedia agency representing recording artists, celebrities, and with a literary agency operating out of the New York and London offices. Send query letter with synopsis and first 100 pages.

The Unter Agency

23 West 73rd Street, Suite 100, New York, NY 10023
Tel: +1 (212) 401-4068

Email: Jennifer@theunteragency.com
Website: http://www.theunteragency.com

Handles: Fiction; Nonfiction; *Areas:*
Adventure; Autobiography; Biography;
Cookery; Crime; Culture; Health; Nature;
Politics; Travel; *Markets:* Adult; Children's;
Youth

Interested in quality fiction and general
nonfiction, particularly memoir,
food/cooking, nature/environment,
biography, pop culture, travel/adventure, true
crime, politics and health/fitness. Also all
types of children's literature (picture books,
middle grade, and young adult). Send query
letter by email or via online form on website.
If no response within three months, assume
rejection.

Upstart Crow Literary

244 Fifth Avenue, 11th Floor, New York,
NY 10001
Email: danielle.submission@gmail.com
Website: http://www.upstartcrowliterary.com

Handles: Fiction; Nonfiction; *Areas:*
Autobiography; Cookery; Current Affairs;
Fantasy; Historical; Humour; Lifestyle;
Mystery; Sci-Fi; *Markets:* Adult; Children's;
Youth; *Treatments:* Commercial;
Contemporary

Send query by email with 20 pages of your
ms, in the body of an email. No attachments
or hard copy submissions. See website for
more details, and specific agent interests and
contact details.

Veritas Literary Agency

601 Van Ness Avenue, Opera Plaza Suite E,
San Francisco, CA 94102
Tel: +1 (415) 647-6964
Fax: +1 (415) 647-6965
Email: submissions@veritasliterary.com
Website: http://www.veritasliterary.com

Handles: Fiction; Nonfiction; *Areas:*
Autobiography; Business; Crime; Culture;
Erotic; Fantasy; Health; Historical; Lifestyle;
Mystery; Nature; Science; Sci-Fi; Self-Help;
Thrillers; Women's Interests; *Markets:*
Adult; Children's; Youth; *Treatments:*
Commercial; Literary; Popular

Send query or proposal by email only.
Submit further information on request only.
For fiction, include cover letter listing
previously published work, one-page
summary and first two chapters. For
nonfiction, include author bio, overview,
chapter-by-chapter summary, and analysis of
competing titles.

Victoria Sanders & Associates LLC

440 Buck Road, Stone Ridge, NY 12484
Tel: +1 (212) 633-8811
Email: queriesvsa@gmail.com
Website: http://www.victoriasanders.com

Handles: Fiction; Nonfiction; *Areas:*
Adventure; Arts; Autobiography; Biography;
Crime; Culture; Current Affairs; Fantasy;
Film; Historical; Humour; Legal; Literature;
Music; Mystery; Politics; Psychology;
Sociology; Suspense; Theatre; Thrillers;
Translations; Women's Interests; *Markets:*
Adult; Children's; Youth; *Treatments:*
Commercial; Contemporary; Light; Literary;
Mainstream; Satirical

Send one-page query describing the work
and the author by email only, with the first
25 pages pasted into the body of the email.
No attachments or submissions by post.
Response usually between 1 and 4 weeks.

Watkins / Loomis Agency, Inc.

PO Box 20925, New York, NY 10025
Tel: +1 (212) 532-0080
Fax: +1 (646) 383-2449
Email: assistant@watkinsloomis.com
Website: http://www.watkinsloomis.com

Handles: Fiction; Nonfiction; *Areas:*
Autobiography; Biography; Culture; Current
Affairs; Historical; Nature; Politics; Short
Stories; Technology; Travel; *Markets:* Adult;
Youth; *Treatments:* Contemporary; Literary;
Popular

Specialises in literary fiction, memoir,
biography, essay, travel, and political
journalism. No unsolicited MSS and does
not guarantee a response to queries.

Waxman Leavell Literary Agency

443 Park Ave South, #1004, New York, NY 10016
Tel: +1 (212) 675-5556
Fax: +1 (212) 675-1381
Email: scottsubmit@waxmanleavell.com
Website: http://www.waxmanleavell.com

Handles: Fiction; Nonfiction; *Areas:* Adventure; Autobiography; Biography; Business; Cookery; Fantasy; Health; Historical; Humour; Mystery; Romance; Science; Self-Help; Sport; Suspense; Women's Interests; *Markets:* Adult; Children's; Youth; *Treatments:* Commercial; Contemporary; Literary

Send query by email to one of the agent-specific addresses on the website. Do not query more than one agent at a time. For details of what each agent is looking for, see details on website. No attachments, but for fiction include 5-10 pages in the body of the email.

The Weingel-Fidel Agency

310 East 46th Street, Suite 21-E, New York, NY 10017
Tel: +1 (212) 599-2959

Handles: Fiction; Nonfiction; *Areas:* Arts; Autobiography; Biography; Music; Psychology; Science; Sociology; Technology; Women's Interests; *Markets:* Adult; *Treatments:* Commercial; Literary; Mainstream

Accepts new clients by referral only – approach only via an existing client or industry contact. Specialises in commercial and literary fiction and nonfiction. Particularly interested in investigative journalism. No children's books, science fiction, fantasy, or self-help.

Wells Arms Literary

Email: victoria@wellsarms.com
Website: https://www.wellsarms.com

Handles: Fiction; *Markets:* Children's; Youth

Represents authors and illustrators of books for children of all ages, including picture books, middle grade, early readers, and young adult. Closed to submissions as at February 2018. Check website for current status.

Wendy Schmalz Agency

402 Union St. #831, Hudson, NY 12534
Email: wendy@schmalzagency.com
Website: http://www.schmalzagency.com

Handles: Fiction; Nonfiction; *Markets:* Children's; Youth

Handles books for middle grade and young adults. No science fiction, fantasy, or picture books. Send query by email. No unsolicited mss or sample chapters. If no response after two weeks, assume no interest.

Wendy Sherman Associates, Inc.

138 West 25th Street, Suite 1018, New York, NY 10001
Tel: +1 (212) 279-9027
Email: submissions@wsherman.com
Website: http://www.wsherman.com

Handles: Fiction; Nonfiction; *Areas:* Autobiography; Biography; Cookery; Culture; Entertainment; Health; Historical; Lifestyle; Nature; Psychology; Self-Help; Spiritual; Sport; Suspense; Women's Interests; *Markets:* Adult; Youth; *Treatments:* Literary

Send queries by email only, including query letter and (for fiction) first ten pages pasted into the body of the email, or (for nonfiction) author bio. No unsolicited attachments. Do not send emails to personal agent addresses (these are deleted unread). Response only if interested. Does not handle poetry, screenplays, cozy mysteries, genre romance, westerns, science fiction, horror, fantasy, or children's picture books

William Morris Endeavor Entertainment

11 Madison Avenue, New York, NY 10010
Tel: +1 (212) 586-5100
Fax: +1 (212) 246-3583
Email: jrw@wmeentertainment.com
Website: http://www.wma.com

Handles: Fiction; Nonfiction; Scripts; *Areas:* Film; TV; *Markets:* Adult

Accepts unsolicited submissions through conferences or by referral only.

Wm Clark Associates

Tel: +1 (212) 675-2784
Email: general@wmclark.com
Website: http://www.wmclark.com

Handles: Fiction; Nonfiction; *Areas:* Architecture; Arts; Autobiography; Biography; Culture; Current Affairs; Design; Film; Historical; Music; Philosophy; Religious; Science; Sociology; Technology; Theatre; Translations; *Markets:* Adult; *Treatments:* Contemporary; Literary; Mainstream

Query through online form on website only. No simultaneous submissions or screenplays.

Writers' Representatives, LLC

116 W. 14th St., 11th Fl., New York, NY 10011-7305
Tel: +1 (212) 620-0023
Fax: +1 (212) 620-0023
Email: transom@writersreps.com
Website: http://www.writersreps.com

Handles: Fiction; Nonfiction; Poetry; Reference; *Areas:* Autobiography; Biography; Business; Cookery; Criticism; Current Affairs; Finance; Historical; Humour; Legal; Literature; Mystery; Philosophy; Politics; Science; Self-Help; Thrillers; *Markets:* Adult; *Treatments:* Literary; Serious

Send email describing your project and yourself, or send proposal, outline, CV, and sample chapters, or complete unsolicited MS, with SASE. See website for submission requirements in FAQ section. Specialises in serious and literary fiction and nonfiction. No screenplays. No science fiction or children's or young adult fiction unless it aspires to serious literature.

Writers House, LLC

21 West 26th Street, New York, NY 10010
Tel: +1 (212) 685-2400
Fax: +1 (212) 685-1781

Email: Azuckerman@writershouse.com
Website: http://writershouse.com

Handles: Fiction; Nonfiction; *Areas:* Autobiography; Biography; Business; Cookery; Fantasy; Finance; Historical; How-to; Lifestyle; Psychology; Science; Sci-Fi; Self-Help; Women's Interests; *Markets:* Adult; Children's; Youth; *Treatments:* Commercial; Literary

Handles adult and juvenile fiction and nonfiction, commercial and literary, including picture books. Policies of individual agents vary, but most prefer email queries. Postal submissions with an SASE are still accepted, however. Do not query more than one agent at a time. See website for full details.

The Wylie Agency

250 West 57th Street, Suite 2114, New York, NY 10107
Email: mail@wylieagency.com
Website: http://www.wylieagency.com

Handles: Fiction; *Markets:* Adult

Agency with offices in New York and London. Not accepting submissions as at February 2018.

Yates & Yates

1551 North Tustin Avenue, Suite 710, Santa Ana, CA 92705
Tel: +1 (714) 480-4000
Email: email@yates2.com
Website: http://www.yates2.com

Handles: Fiction; Nonfiction; *Areas:* Autobiography; Biography; Business; Current Affairs; Legal; Politics; Religious; Sport; Thrillers; Women's Interests; *Markets:* Adult; *Treatments:* Literary

Literary agency based in California, representing "gifted Christian communicators". Takes a holistic approach, combining agency representation, expert legal advice, marketing guidance, career coaching, creative counseling, and business management consulting.

The Zack Company, Inc

PMB 525, 4653 Carmel Mountain Rd, Ste
308, San Diego, CA 92130-6650
Website: http://www.zackcompany.com

Handles: Fiction; Nonfiction; Reference;
Areas: Adventure; Autobiography;
Biography; Cookery; Crime; Culture;
Current Affairs; Erotic; Fantasy; Film;
Finance; Gardening; Health; Historical;
Horror; How-to; Humour; Medicine;
Military; Music; Mystery; Nature; Politics;
Religious; Romance; Science; Sci-Fi; Self-
Help; Spiritual; Sport; Suspense;
Technology; Thrillers; TV; Women's
Interests; *Markets:* Adult; *Treatments:*
Popular

Requirements change frequently, so check
the agency website before approaching.
Please note that approaches are not accepted
to the former submissions email address
(submissions@zackcompany.com).
Electronic approaches must be made via the
form on the website. Also accepts
approaches by post.

Zoë Pagnamenta Agency, LLC

20 West 22nd Street, Suite 1603, New York,
NY 10010
Tel: +1 (212) 253-1074
Fax: +1 (212) 253-1075
Email: mail@zpagency.com
Website: http://www.zpagency.com

Handles: Fiction; Nonfiction; *Areas:*
Autobiography; Biography; Business;
Historical; Science; Short Stories; *Markets:*
Adult; *Treatments:* Commercial; Literary;
Popular

No screenplays, poetry, self-help, or genre
fiction, including mystery, romance or
science fiction. Send queries by post only,
with SASE (or return email address) and up
to 25 pages of sample material.

UK Literary Agents

For the most up-to-date listings of these and hundreds of other literary agents, visit https://www.firstwriter.com/Agents

*To claim your **free** access to the site, please see the back of this book.*

A for Authors

73 Hurlingham Road, Bexleyheath, Kent DA7 5PE
Email: enquiries@aforauthors.co.uk
Website: http://aforauthors.co.uk

Handles: Fiction; *Markets:* Adult; *Treatments:* Commercial; Literary

Query by email only. Include synopsis and first three chapters (or up to 50 pages) and short author bio. All attachments must be Word format documents. No nonfiction, scripts, poetry, fantasy, SF, horror, short stories, adult illustrated books on art, architecture, design, visual culture, or submissions by post, hand delivery, or on discs, memory sticks, or other electronic devices. No longer accepting young adult or children's or nonfiction. See website for full details.

A & B Personal Management Ltd

PO Box 64671, London, NW3 9LH
Tel: +44 (0) 20 7794 3255
Email: b.ellmain@aandb.co.uk

Handles: Fiction; Nonfiction; Scripts; *Areas:* Film; Theatre; TV; *Markets:* Adult

Handles full-length mss and scripts for film, TV, and theatre. No unsolicited mss. Query by email or by phone in first instance.

A.M. Heath & Company Limited, Author's Agents

6 Warwick Court, Holborn, London, WC1R 5DJ
Tel: +44 (0) 20 7242 2811
Email: enquiries@amheath.com
Website: http://www.amheath.com

Handles: Fiction; Nonfiction; *Areas:* Biography; Cookery; Crime; Health; Historical; Nature; Psychology; Sport; Suspense; Thrillers; Travel; Women's Interests; *Markets:* Adult; Children's; Youth; *Treatments:* Commercial; Contemporary; Literary

Handles general commercial and literary fiction and nonfiction. Submit work with cover letter and synopsis via online submission system only. No paper submissions. Aims to respond within six weeks.

Abner Stein

10 Roland Gardens, London, SW7 3PH
Tel: +44 (0) 20 7373 0456
Email: caspian@abnerstein.co.uk
Website: http://www.abnerstein.co.uk

Handles: Fiction; Nonfiction; *Markets:* Adult; Children's

Agency based in London. Handles fiction, general nonfiction, and children's.

The Agency (London) Ltd
24 Pottery Lane, Holland Park, London,
W11 4LZ
Tel: +44 (0) 20 7727 1346
Email: hd-office@theagency.co.uk
Website: http://www.theagency.co.uk

Handles: Fiction; Nonfiction; Scripts; *Areas:*
Film; Humour; Radio; Theatre; TV;
Markets: Adult; Children's; Youth

**Closed to submissions of children's books
as at January 2018. Check website for
current status.**

Represents writers and authors for film,
television, radio and the theatre. Also
represents directors, producers, composers,
and film and television rights in books, as
well as authors of children's books from
picture books to teen fiction. **Handles adult
fiction and nonfiction for existing clients
only.** Does not consider adult fiction or
nonfiction from writers who are not already
clients. For script writers, only considers
unsolicited material if it has been
recommended by a producer, development
executive or course tutor. If this is the case
send CV, covering letter and details of your
referee to the relevant agent, or to the email
address below. Do not email more than one
agent at a time. For directors, send CV,
showreel and cover letter by email. For
children's authors, send query by email with
synopsis and first three chapters (middle
grade, teen, or Young Adult) or complete ms
(picture books) to address given on website.

AHA Talent Ltd
74 Clerkenwell Road, London, EC1M 5QA
Tel: +44 (0) 20 7250 1760
Email: mail@ahacreatives.co.uk
Website: http://www.ahatalent.co.uk

Handles: Nonfiction; Scripts; *Areas:*
Autobiography; How-to; Humour; *Markets:*
Adult; *Treatments:* Popular

Handles actors, writers, creatives, and voice-
over artists. Send query with return postage,
CV/bio, and 10-page writing sample. No
poetry.

Aitken Alexander Associates
291 Gray's Inn Road, Kings Cross, London,
WC1X 8QJ
Tel: +44 (0) 20 7373 8672
Fax: +44 (0) 20 7373 6002
Email: submissions@aitkenalexander.co.uk
Website: http://www.aitkenalexander.co.uk

Handles: Fiction; Nonfiction; *Markets:*
Adult

Send query by email, with short synopsis,
and first 30 pages as a Word document. See
website for list of agents and their interests
and indicate in the subject line which agent
you would like to query. No illustrated
children's books, or poetry. No submissions
or queries by post.

Alan Brodie Representation Ltd
Paddock Suite, The Courtyard, 55
Charterhouse Street, London, EC1M 6HA
Tel: +44 (0) 20 7253 6226
Fax: +44 (0) 20 7183 7999
Email: ABR@alanbrodie.com
Website: http://www.alanbrodie.com

Handles: Scripts; *Areas:* Film; Radio;
Theatre; TV; *Markets:* Adult

Handles scripts only. No books. Approach
with preliminary letter, recommendation
from industry professional, and CV. Do not
send a sample of work unless requested. No
fiction, nonfiction, or poetry.

The Ampersand Agency Ltd
Ryman's Cottages, Little Tew, Chipping
Norton, Oxfordshire OX7 4JJ
Tel: +44 (0) 1608 683677 / 683898
Fax: +44 (0) 1608 683449
Email: submissions@
theampersandagency.co.uk
Website: http://www.
theampersandagency.co.uk

Handles: Fiction; Nonfiction; *Areas:*
Autobiography; Biography; Crime; Current
Affairs; Fantasy; Historical; Horror; Science;
Sci-Fi; Sport; Thrillers; Women's Interests;
Markets: Adult; Youth; *Treatments:*
Commercial; Contemporary; Literary

We handle literary and commercial fiction and nonfiction, including contemporary and historical novels, crime, thrillers, biography, women's fiction, history, current affairs, and memoirs. Send query by post or email with brief bio, outline, and first two chapters. If emailing material, send as attachments rather than pasted into the body of the email. Also accepts science fiction, fantasy, horror, and Young Adult material to separate email address listed on website. No scripts except those by existing clients, no poetry, self-help or illustrated children's books. No unpublished American writers, because in our experience British and European publishers aren't interested unless there is an American publisher on board. And we'd like to make it clear that American stamps are no use outside America!

Darley Anderson Children's

Estelle House, 11 Eustace Road, London, SW6 1JB
Tel: +44 (0) 20 7386 2674
Fax: +44 (0) 20 7386 5571
Email: childrens@darleyanderson.com
Website: http://www.darleyandersonchildrens.com

Handles: Fiction; Nonfiction; *Markets:* Children's

Handles fiction and nonfiction for children. Send query by email with short synopsis, and first three consecutive chapters. For picture books, send complete text or picture book. Prefers to read material exclusively, but will accept simultaneous submissions if notice given on cover letter. No submissions by post or by fax.

Andlyn

Tel: +44 (0) 20 3290 5638
Email: submissions@andlyn.co.uk
Website: http://www.andlyn.co.uk

Handles: Fiction; Nonfiction; *Markets:* Children's; Youth

Specialises in children's/teen fiction and content. Handles picture books, middle-grade, young adult, and cross-over. Send query by email with one-page synopsis and first three chapters (fiction) or proposal and market analysis (nonfiction). Not accepting

picture book submissions as at February 2017. Check website for current status.

Andrew Lownie Literary Agency Ltd

36 Great Smith Street, London, SW1P 3BU
Tel: +44 (0) 20 7222 7574
Fax: +44 (0) 20 7222 7576
Email: mail@andrewlownie.co.uk
Website: http://www.andrewlownie.co.uk

Handles: Fiction; Nonfiction; *Areas:* Autobiography; Biography; Crime; Culture; Current Affairs; Fantasy; Finance; Health; Historical; Horror; How-to; Lifestyle; Literature; Media; Medicine; Men's Interests; Military; Music; Mystery; Politics; Psychology; Romance; Science; Sci-Fi; Self-Help; Sport; Suspense; Technology; Thrillers; Translations; Westerns; *Markets:* Academic; Adult; Family; Professional; *Treatments:* Commercial; Mainstream; Popular; Serious; Traditional

This agency, founded in 1988, is now one of the UK's leading boutique literary agencies with some two hundred nonfiction and fiction authors and is actively building its fiction list (see website for specific contact address for fiction submissions). It prides itself on its personal attention to its clients and specialises both in launching new writers and taking established writers to a new level of recognition.

Andrew Mann Ltd

6 Quernmore Road, London, N4 4QU
Tel: +44 (0) 20 7609 6218
Email: tina@andrewmann.co.uk
Website: http://www.andrewmann.co.uk

Handles: Fiction; *Areas:* Crime; Historical; Thrillers; *Markets:* Adult; *Treatments:* Commercial; Literary

Closed to submissions as at March 2018. Check website for current status.

Interested in literary and commercial fiction, historical, and crime/thriller. Send query by email, or by post if absolutely necessary with SAE, with brief synopsis and first three chapters or 30 pages. See website for specific email address for crime/thriller submissions. No children's, screenplays or theatre, misery memoirs, new age philosophy, nonfiction, fantasy, science fiction, poetry, short stories, vampires, or dystopian fiction. See website for full submission guidelines.

Andrew Nurnberg Associates, Ltd

20-23 Greville Street, London, EC1N 8SS
Tel: +44 (0) 20 3327 0400
Fax: +44 (0) 20 7430 0801
Email: submissions@nurnberg.co.uk
Website: http://www.andrewnurnberg.com

Handles: Fiction; Nonfiction; *Markets:* Adult; Children's

Handles adult fiction and nonfiction, and children's fiction. No poetry, children's picture books, or scripts for film, TV, radio or theatre. Send query by email with one-page synopsis and first three chapters as attachments. Prefers email approaches but will also accept submissions of the same material by post with SAE.

Anne Clark Literary Agency

PO Box 1221, Harlton, Cambridge, CB23 1WW
Tel: +44 (0) 1223 262160
Email: submissions@
anneclarkliteraryagency.co.uk
Website: http://www.
anneclarkliteraryagency.co.uk

Handles: Fiction; *Markets:* Children's; Youth

Handles fiction and picture books for children and young adults. Send query by email only with the following pasted into the body of the email (not as an attachment): for fiction, include brief synopsis and first 3,000 words; for picture books, send complete ms; for nonfiction, send short proposal and the text of three sample pages. No submissions by post. See website for full guidelines.

Anthony Sheil in Association with Aitken Alexander Associates

291 Gray's Inn Road, Kings Cross, London, WC1X 8QJ
Tel: +44 (0) 20 7373 8672
Fax: +44 (0) 20 7373 6002
Website: http://www.aitkenalexander.co.uk/agents/anthony-sheil/

Handles: Fiction; Nonfiction; *Markets:* Adult

Handles fiction and nonfiction. No scripts, poetry, short stories, or children's fiction. Send query by post with SAE, synopsis up to half a page, and first 30 pages.

Antony Harwood Limited

103 Walton Street, Oxford, OX2 6EB
Tel: +44 (0) 1865 559615
Fax: +44 (0) 1865 310660
Email: mail@antonyharwood.com
Website: http://www.antonyharwood.com

Handles: Fiction; Nonfiction; *Areas:* Adventure; Anthropology; Antiques; Archaeology; Architecture; Arts; Autobiography; Beauty and Fashion; Biography; Business; Cookery; Crafts; Crime; Criticism; Culture; Current Affairs; Design; Drama; Entertainment; Erotic; Fantasy; Film; Finance; Gardening; Gothic; Health; Historical; Hobbies; Horror; How-to; Humour; Legal; Leisure; Lifestyle; Literature; Media; Medicine; Men's Interests; Military; Music; Mystery; Nature; New Age; Philosophy; Photography; Politics; Psychology; Radio; Religious; Romance; Science; Sci-Fi; Self-Help; Short Stories; Sociology; Spiritual; Sport; Suspense; Technology; Theatre; Thrillers; Translations; Travel; TV; Westerns; Women's Interests; *Markets:* Adult; Children's; Youth

Handles fiction and nonfiction in every genre and category, except for screenwriting and poetry. Send brief outline and first 50 pages by email, or by post with SASE.

Artellus Limited

30 Dorset House, Gloucester Place, London, NW1 5AD

Tel: +44 (0) 20 7935 6972
Fax: +44 (0) 20 8609 0347
Email: artellussubmissions@gmail.com
Website: http://www.artellusltd.co.uk

Handles: Fiction; Nonfiction; *Areas:* Arts;
Beauty and Fashion; Biography; Crime;
Culture; Current Affairs; Entertainment;
Fantasy; Historical; Military; Science; Sci-
Fi; *Markets:* Adult; Youth; *Treatments:*
Contemporary; Literary

Welcomes submissions from new fiction and
nonfiction writers. Send first three chapters
and synopsis in first instance, or send query
by email. No film or TV scripts. If you
would prefer to submit electronically send
query by email in advance.

The Authors Care Service ltd

50 Cecil Road, Croydon, Surrey CR0 3BG
Tel: +44 (0) 7984 316734
Email: vanessa@theauthorscare.co.uk
Website: http://www.theauthorscare.co.uk

Handles: Fiction; Nonfiction; *Areas:*
Autobiography; Business; Religious; Self-
Help; *Markets:* Adult; Children's; Youth;
Treatments: Positive

This is a Christian based agency. In
nonfiction, handles bible studies and
Christian based testimonial memoirs. You
must be established and have a strong
platform to submit a memoir. Occasionally
also represents nonfiction that is not
Christian based such as motivational,
business books, educational, or children's
books. In fiction, handles Christian-themed
allegory type manuscripts, and edgy
Christian fiction. No obscene language,
exotic or dark paranormal. Also represents
children's and young adult fiction which has
positive messages.Currently open only to
approaches from established authors – no
new authors. We are looking for authors who
either already have a vast platform, or strong
marketing skills. We also require authors to
have strong writing skills. It is advised for
authors to get their work checked by a
professional editor before they submit. As
we want to submit high quality work to
publishers.

Barbara Levy Literary Agency

64 Greenhill, Hampstead High Street,
London, NW3 5TZ
Tel: +44 (0) 20 7435 9046
Email: blevysubmissions@gmail.com
Website: http://barbaralevyagency.com

Handles: Fiction; Nonfiction; *Markets:*
Adult

Send query with synopsis and first three
chapters (approximately 50 pages) by email
or by post with SAE. No poetry, plays,
original screenplays, scripts or picture books
for children.

Bath Literary Agency

5 Gloucester Road, Bath, BA1 7BH
Email: submissions@
bathliteraryagency.com
Website: http://bathliteraryagency.com

Handles: Fiction; Nonfiction; *Markets:*
Children's; Youth

Handles fiction and nonfiction for children,
from picture books to Young Adult. Send
query by email or by post with SAE for reply
and return of materials if required, along
with the first three chapters (fiction) or the
full manuscript (picture books). See website
for full details.

Bell Lomax Moreton Agency

Suite C, 131 Queensway, Petts Wood, Kent
BR5 1DG
Tel: +44 (0) 20 7930 4447
Fax: +44 (0) 1689 820061
Email: agency@bell-lomax.co.uk
Website: http://www.
belllomaxmoreton.co.uk

Handles: Fiction; Nonfiction; *Areas:*
Biography; Business; Sport; *Markets:* Adult;
Children's

Considers most fiction, nonfiction, and
children's book proposals. No poetry, short
stories, novellas, textbooks, film scripts,
stage plays, or science fiction. Send query by
email with details of any previous work,
short synopsis, and first three chapters (up to
50 pages). For children's picture books send
complete ms. Also accepts postal
submissions. See website for full guidelines.

Berlin Associates

7 Tyers Gate, London, SE1 3HX
Tel: +44 (0) 20 7836 1112
Fax: +44 (0) 20 7632 5296
Email: submissions@berlinassociates.com
Website: http://www.berlinassociates.com

Handles: Scripts; *Areas:* Film; Radio;
Theatre; TV; *Markets:* Adult

Most clients through recommendation or
invitation, but accepts queries by email with
CV, experience, and outline of work you
would like to submit.

The Blair Partnership

PO Box, 7828, London, W1A 4GE
Tel: +44 (0) 20 7504 2520
Email: submissions@
theblairpartnership.com
Website: http://www.theblairpartnership.com

Handles: Fiction; Nonfiction; *Markets:*
Adult; Children's; Family; Youth

Open to all genres of fiction and nonfiction.
Send query by email with one-page synopsis
and first three chapters, including some
detail about yourself.

Blake Friedmann Literary Agency Ltd

First Floor, Selous House, 5-12 Mandela
Street, London, NW1 0DU
Tel: +44 (0) 20 7387 0842
Email: info@blakefriedmann.co.uk
Website: http://www.blakefriedmann.co.uk

Handles: Fiction; Nonfiction; Scripts; *Areas:*
Autobiography; Biography; Cookery; Crime;
Culture; Current Affairs; Film; Finance;
Historical; Military; Mystery; Politics;
Psychology; Radio; Science; Sociology;
Suspense; Technology; Thrillers; Travel;
TV; Women's Interests; *Markets:* Adult;
Children's; Youth; *Treatments:* Commercial;
Contemporary; Literary; Popular

Send query by email to a specific agent best
suited to your work. See website for full
submission guidelines, details of agents, and
individual agent contact details.

No poetry or plays. Short stories and
journalism for existing clients only.

Media department currently only accepting
submissions from writers with produced
credits.

Reply not guaranteed. If no response within
8 weeks, assume rejection.

Bookseeker Agency

PO Box 7535, Perth, PH2 1AF
Tel: +44 (0) 1738 620688
Email: bookseeker@blueyonder.co.uk
Website: http://bookseekeragency.com

Handles: Fiction; Poetry; *Markets:* Adult

Handles fiction and (under some
circumstances) poetry. No nonfiction. Send
query by post or email outlining what you
have written and your current projects, along
with synopsis and sample chapter (novels).

The Bright Literary Academy

Studio 102, 250 York Road, London, SW11
1RJ
Tel: +44 (0) 20 7326 9140
Email: literarysubmissions@
brightgroupinternational.com
Website: http://brightliteraryagency.com

Handles: Fiction; *Areas:* Autobiography;
Entertainment; Literature; Mystery; Sci-Fi;
Self-Help; Short Stories; Thrillers; TV;
Women's Interests; *Markets:* Children's;
Youth; *Treatments:* Commercial;
Contemporary; Mainstream; Positive

A boutique literary agency representing the
most fabulous new talent to grace the
publishing industry in recent years. Born out
of the success of a leading illustration agency
with an outstanding global client list this
agency aims to produce sensational material
across all genres of children's publishing,
including novelty, picture books, fiction and
adult autobiographies, in order to become a
one-stop-shop for publishers looking for
something extra special to fit into their lists.

Prides itself on nurturing the creativity of its
authors and illustrators so that they can
concentrate on their craft rather than
negotiate their contracts. As a creative
agency we develop seeds of ideas into
something extraordinary, before searching
for the right publisher with which to develop

them further to create incredible and unforgettable books.

We are fortunate enough to have a never-ending source of remarkable material at our fingertips and a stable of exceptional creators who are all united by one common goal – a deep passion and dedication to children's books and literature in all its shapes and forms.

Send query by email only, with synopsis and first three chapters, or whole text for picture books.

Brotherstone Creative Management

Mortimer House, 37-41 Mortimer Street, London, W1T 3JH
Tel: +44 (0) 7908 542866
Email: submissions@bcm-agency.com
Website: http://bcm-agency.com

Handles: Fiction; Nonfiction; *Markets:* Adult; *Treatments:* Commercial; Literary

Always on the search for talented new writers. Send query by email. For fiction, include the first three chapters or 50 pages and 2-page synopsis. For nonfiction, include detailed outline and sample chapter. No scripts.

Caroline Davidson Literary Agency

5 Queen Anne's Gardens, London, W4 1TU
Tel: +44 (0) 20 8995 5768
Email: enquiries@cdla.co.uk
Website: http://www.cdla.co.uk

Handles: Fiction; Nonfiction; Reference; *Areas:* Archaeology; Architecture; Arts; Biography; Cookery; Culture; Design; Gardening; Health; Historical; Lifestyle; Medicine; Nature; Politics; Psychology; Science; *Markets:* Adult

Send query with CV, SAE, outline and history of work, and (for fiction) the first 50 pages and last 10 pages of novel. For nonfiction, include table of contents, detailed chapter-by-chapter synopsis, description of sources and / or research for the book, market and competition analysis, and (if

possible) one or two sample chapters.

Submissions without adequate return postage are neither returned or considered. No Chick lit, romance, erotica, Crime and thrillers, Science fiction, fantasy, Poetry, Individual short stories, Children's, Young Adult, Misery memoirs or fictionalised autobiography. Completed and polished first novels positively welcomed. See website for more details. No submissions by fax and only in exceptional circumstances accepts submissions by email.

See website for full details.

Caroline Sheldon Literary Agency

71 Hillgate Place, London, W8 7SS
Tel: +44 (0) 20 7727 9102
Email: carolinesheldon@ carolinesheldon.co.uk
Website: http://www.carolinesheldon.co.uk

Handles: Fiction; Nonfiction; *Areas:* Autobiography; Fantasy; Historical; Humour; Suspense; Women's Interests; *Markets:* Adult; Children's; Youth; *Treatments:* Commercial; Contemporary; Literary

Send query by email only. Do not query both agents. See website for both email addresses and appropriate subject line to include. Handles fiction and human-interest nonfiction for adults, and fiction for children, including full-length and picture books.

The Catchpole Agency

53 Cranham Street, Oxford, OX2 6DD
Tel: +44 (0) 7789 588070
Email: submissions@ thecatchpoleagency.co.uk
Website: http://www. thecatchpoleagency.co.uk

Handles: Fiction; *Markets:* Children's

Closed to submissions as at July 2018. Check website for current status.

Works on children's books with both artists and writers. Send query by email with sample pasted directly into the body of the email (the whole text of a picture book or a couple of chapters of a novel). No attachments. See website for full guidelines.

Catherine Pellegrino & Associates

148 Russell Court, Woburn Place, London, WC1H 0LR
Email: catherine@catherinepellegrino.co.uk
Website: http://catherinepellegrino.co.uk

Handles: Fiction; *Markets:* Children's; Youth; *Treatments:* Commercial; Literary

Handles children's books, from picture books to young adult. Send query by email with some background on you and the book, plus synopsis and first three chapters or approximately 50 pages, up to a natural break. See website for full details.

Cecily Ware Literary Agents

19C John Spencer Square, London, N1 2LZ
Tel: +44 (0) 20 7359 3787
Email: info@cecilyware.com
Website: http://www.cecilyware.com

Handles: Scripts; *Areas:* Drama; Film; Humour; TV; *Markets:* Adult; Children's

Handles film and TV scripts only. No books or theatre scripts. Submit complete script with covering letter, CV, and SAE. No email submissions or return of material without SAE and correct postage.

Chartwell

14 Gray's Inn Road, London, WC1X 8HN
Tel: +44 (0) 20 7293 0864
Email: hello@chartwellspeakers.com
Website: http://www.chartwellspeakers.com

Handles: Fiction; Nonfiction; *Areas:* Autobiography; Biography; Cookery; Crime; Health; Historical; Lifestyle; Mystery; Psychology; Science; Suspense; Technology; Thrillers; Women's Interests; *Markets:* Adult; Children's; Youth

Agency handling speakers and authors. Will consider all fiction and nonfiction, but particularly interested in General fiction, Mystery/suspense/thriller/crime, Women's fiction, Children's and YA (fiction); and

Biography/memoir, Technology, Science, History, Personal development, Health (including popular psychology), Cookery and lifestyle (nonfiction). Send query by email only. See website for full guidelines.

Mic Cheetham Literary Agency

50 Albemarle Street, London, W1S 4BD
Tel: +44 (0) 20 7495 2002
Fax: +44 (0) 20 7399 2801
Email: simon@miccheetham.com
Website: http://www.miccheetham.com

Handles: Fiction; Nonfiction; *Areas:* Crime; Fantasy; Historical; Sci-Fi; Thrillers; *Markets:* Adult; *Treatments:* Commercial; Literary; Mainstream

Send query with SAE, first three chapters, and publishing history. Focuses on fiction, and is not elitist about genre or literary fiction, providing it combines good writing, great storytelling, intelligence, imagination, and (as a bonus) anarchic wit. Film and TV scripts handled for existing clients only. No poetry, children's, illustrated books, or unsolicited MSS. Do not send manuscripts by email. Approach in writing in the first instance (no email scripts accepted).

Christine Green Authors' Agent

PO Box 70098, London, SE15 5AU
Tel: +44 (0) 7507 764632
Email: info@christinegreen.co.uk
Website: http://www.christinegreen.co.uk

Handles: Fiction; Nonfiction; *Markets:* Adult; Youth; *Treatments:* Commercial; Literary

Focusses on fiction for adult and young adult, and also considers narrative nonfiction. No children's books, genre science-fiction/fantasy, poetry or scripts. Send query by email (preferred) or by post with SAE. No submissions by fax or CD. See website for full submission guidelines.

The Christopher Little Literary Agency

48 Walham Grove, London, SW6 1QR
Tel: +44 (0) 20 7736 4455
Fax: +44 (0) 20 7736 4490
Email: submissions@christopherlittle.net
Website: http://www.christopherlittle.net

Handles: Fiction; Nonfiction; *Markets:*
Adult; *Treatments:* Commercial; Literary

Closed to submissions as at February 2018

Handles commercial and literary full-length
fiction and nonfiction. Film scripts handled
for existing clients only (no submissions of
film scripts). Send query by email (preferred)
or by post with SAE or IRCs. Attach one-
page synopsis and three consecutive chapters
(fiction) or proposal (nonfiction). No poetry,
plays, textbooks, short stories, illustrated
children's books, science fiction, fantasy, or
submissions by email.

Clare Hulton Literary Agency

Tel: +44 (0) 7929 407589
Email: info@clarehulton.co.uk
Website: http://www.clarehulton.com

Handles: Fiction; Nonfiction; *Areas:*
Autobiography; Cookery; Culture;
Historical; Humour; Lifestyle; Music;
Philosophy; Self-Help; TV; *Markets:* Adult;
Children's; *Treatments:* Commercial;
Popular

Specialises in nonfiction, but also has a small
commercial fiction and children's list. Finds
most authors through recommendation, but
open to brief queries by email, explaining
what your book is about. No attachments. If
no response within two weeks, assume
rejection.

Conville & Walsh Ltd

5th Floor, Haymarket House, 28-29
Haymarket, London, SW1Y 4SP
Tel: +44 (0) 20 7393 4200
Email: sue@cwagency.co.uk
Website: http://cwagency.co.uk

Handles: Fiction; Nonfiction; *Areas:*
Autobiography; Biography; Crime; Current
Affairs; Fantasy; Historical; Humour;

Leisure; Lifestyle; Men's Interests; Military;
Mystery; Psychology; Science; Sci-Fi; Sport;
Suspense; Thrillers; Travel; Women's
Interests; *Markets:* Adult; Children's; Youth;
Treatments: Commercial; Literary

See website for agent profiles and submit to
one particular agent only. Send submissions
by email as Word .doc files only. No postal
submissions. For fiction, please submit the
first three sample chapters of the completed
manuscript (or about 50 pages) with a one to
two page synopsis. For nonfiction, send 30-
page proposal. No poetry or scripts, or
picture books. See website for full
guidelines.

Coombs Moylett & Maclean Literary Agency

120 New Kings Road, London, SW6 4LZ
Tel: +44 (0) 20 8740 0454
Email: info@cmm.agency
Website: http://cmm.agency

Handles: Fiction; Nonfiction; *Areas:*
Biography; Cookery; Crime; Current Affairs;
Historical; Mystery; Suspense; Thrillers;
Women's Interests; *Markets:* Adult;
Children's; Youth; *Treatments:* Commercial;
Contemporary; Literary

Handles historical fiction, crime/
mystery/suspense and thrillers, women's
fiction from chick-lit to sagas to
contemporary and literary fiction. Also
looking to build a children's list
concentrating on Young Adult fiction. In
nonfiction, considers history, biography,
current affairs and cookery.

Send query with synopsis and first three
chapters via online form. No submissions by
fax or by post. No poetry, plays or scripts for
film and TV. Whole books and postal
submissions will not be read.

Creative Authors Ltd

11A Woodlawn Street, Whitstable, Kent
CT5 1HQ
Tel: +44 (0) 01227 770947
Email: write@creativeauthors.co.uk
Website: http://www.creativeauthors.co.uk

Handles: Fiction; Nonfiction; *Areas:* Arts; Autobiography; Biography; Business; Cookery; Crafts; Crime; Culture; Health; Historical; Humour; Nature; Women's Interests; *Markets:* Adult; Children's; *Treatments:* Commercial; Literary

As at June 2017, not accepting new fiction clients. See website for current situation.

We are a dynamic literary agency – established to provide an attentive and unique platform for writers and scriptwriters and representing a growing list of clients. We're on the lookout for fresh talent and books with strong commercial potential. No unsolicited MSS, but considers queries by email. No paper submissions. Do not telephone regarding submissions.

Curtis Brown Group Ltd

Haymarket House, 28/29 Haymarket, London, SW1Y 4SP
Tel: +44 (0) 20 7393 4400
Fax: +44 (0) 20 7393 4401
Email: info@curtisbrown.co.uk
Website: http://www.curtisbrowncreative.co.uk

Handles: Fiction; Nonfiction; Scripts; *Areas:* Biography; Crime; Fantasy; Film; Historical; Radio; Science; Suspense; Theatre; Thrillers; TV; *Markets:* Adult; Children's; Youth; *Treatments:* Literary; Mainstream; Popular

Renowned and long established London agency. Handles general fiction and nonfiction, and scripts. Also represents directors, designers, and presenters. No longer accepts submissions by post or email – all submissions must be made using online submissions manager. Also offers services such as writing courses for which authors are charged.

The Darley Anderson Agency

Estelle House, 11 Eustace Road, London, SW6 1JB
Tel: +44 (0) 20 7386 2674
Email: camilla@darleyanderson.com
Website: http://www.darleyanderson.com

Handles: Fiction; *Areas:* Crime; Romance; Suspense; Thrillers; Women's Interests;

Markets: Adult; Children's; Youth; *Treatments:* Commercial; Literary

Accepts submissions by email and by post. See website for individual agent requirements, submission guidelines, and contact details. No poets or short story writers.

David Luxton Associates

23 Hillcourt Avenue, London, N12 8EY
Tel: +44 (0) 20 8922 3942
Email: nick@davidluxtonassociates.co.uk
Website: http://www.davidluxtonassociates.co.uk

Handles: Nonfiction; Reference; *Areas:* Autobiography; Biography; Culture; Historical; Politics; Sport; Travel; *Markets:* Adult; *Treatments:* Popular

Specialises in nonfiction, including sports, memoir, history, popular reference and politics. No scripts or screenplays. Most clients by recommendation, but will consider email queries. See website for correct email addresses for different subjects. No submissions by post.

David Godwin Associates

55 Monmouth Street, London, WC2H 9DG
Tel: +44 (0) 20 7240 9992
Email: sebastiangodwin@davidgodwinassociates.co.uk
Website: http://www.davidgodwinassociates.com

Handles: Fiction; Nonfiction; *Markets:* Adult; *Treatments:* Literary

Handles a range of nonfiction and fiction. Send query by email with synopsis and first 30 pages. No poetry. No picture books, except for existing clients.

David Higham Associates Ltd

6th Floor, Waverley House, 7–12 Noel Street, London, W1F 8GQ
Tel: +44 (0) 20 7434 5900
Fax: +44 (0) 20 7437 1072
Email: submissions@davidhigham.co.uk
Website: http://www.davidhigham.co.uk

Handles: Fiction; Nonfiction; Scripts; *Areas:* Autobiography; Biography; Cookery; Crime; Current Affairs; Drama; Film; Historical; Humour; Nature; Theatre; Thrillers; TV; *Markets:* Adult; Children's; Youth; *Treatments:* Commercial; Literary; Serious

For adult fiction and nonfiction contact "Adult Submissions Department" by post only with SASE, covering letter, CV, and synopsis (fiction)/proposal (nonfiction) and first two or three chapters. For children's / YA fiction submit by email to the specific children's submission address given on the website, with covering letter, synopsis, CV, and first two or three chapters (or complete MS if a picture book). See website for complete guidelines. Scripts by referral only.

DHH Literary Agency Ltd

23-27 Cecil Court, London, WC2N 4EZ
Tel: +44 (0) 20 7836 7376
Email: enquiries@dhhliteraryagency.com
Website: http://www.dhhliteraryagency.com

Handles: Fiction; Nonfiction; Scripts; *Areas:* Adventure; Archaeology; Autobiography; Biography; Crime; Fantasy; Film; Historical; Sci-Fi; Theatre; Thrillers; TV; Women's Interests; *Markets:* Adult; Children's; Youth; *Treatments:* Literary

Accepts submissions by email only. No postal submissions. See website for specific agent interests and email addresses and approach one agent only. Do not send submissions to generic "enquiries" email address.

Diamond Kahn and Woods (DKW) Literary Agency Ltd

Top Floor, 66 Onslow Gardens, London, N10 3JX
Tel: +44 (0) 20 3514 6544
Email: info@dkwlitagency.co.uk
Website: http://dkwlitagency.co.uk

Handles: Fiction; Nonfiction; *Areas:* Adventure; Archaeology; Biography; Crime; Culture; Fantasy; Gothic; Historical; Humour; Politics; Sci-Fi; Sociology; Suspense; Thrillers; *Markets:* Adult; Children's; Youth; *Treatments:* Commercial; Contemporary; Literary

Send submissions by email. See website for specific agent interests and contact details. Do not send submissions to general agency email address.

Dinah Wiener Ltd

12 Cornwall Grove, Chiswick, London, W4 2LB
Tel: +44 (0) 20 8994 6011
Email: dinah@dwla.co.uk

Handles: Fiction; Nonfiction; *Areas:* Autobiography; Biography; Cookery; Science; *Markets:* Adult

Note: Not taking on new clients as at January 2017.

Send preliminary query letter with SAE. No poetry, scripts, or children's books.

Toby Eady Associates Ltd

Third Floor, 9 Orme Court, London, W2 4RL
Tel: +44 (0) 20 7792 0092
Fax: +44 (0) 20 7792 0879
Email: submissions@ tobyeadyassociates.co.uk
Website: http://www. tobyeadyassociates.co.uk

Handles: Fiction; Nonfiction; *Markets:* Adult

Send first 50 pages of your fiction or nonfiction work by email, with a synopsis, and a letter including biographical information. If submitting by post, include SAE for return of material, if required. No film / TV scripts or poetry. Particular interest in China, Middle East, India, and Africa.

Eddison Pearson Ltd

West Hill House, 6 Swains Lane, London, N6 6QS
Tel: +44 (0) 20 7700 7763
Email: enquiries@eddisonpearson.com
Website: http://www.eddisonpearson.com

Handles: Fiction; Nonfiction; Poetry; *Markets:* Children's; Youth; *Treatments:* Literary

Send query by email only (or even blank email) for auto-response containing up-to-date submission guidelines and email address for submissions. No unsolicited MSS. No longer accepts submissions or enquiries by post. Send query with one to three chapters by email only to address provided in auto-response. Response in 6-10 weeks. If no response after 10 weeks, follow up by email.

Edwards Fuglewicz

49 Great Ormond Street, London, WC1N 3HZ
Tel: +44 (0) 20 7405 6725
Fax: +44 (0) 20 7405 6726

Handles: Fiction; Nonfiction; *Areas:* Biography; Crime; Culture; Historical; Humour; Mystery; Romance; Thrillers; *Markets:* Adult; *Treatments:* Commercial; Literary

Handles literary and commercial fiction, and nonfiction. No children's, science fiction, horror, or email submissions.

Elaine Steel

49 Greek Street, London, W1D 4EG
Tel: +44 (0) 1273 739022
Email: info@elainesteel.com
Website: http://www.elainesteel.com

Handles: Fiction; Nonfiction; Scripts; *Areas:* Film; Radio; TV; *Markets:* Adult

Send query by email with CV and outline, along with details of experience. No unsolicited mss.

Elise Dillsworth Agency (EDA)

9 Grosvenor Road, London, N10 2DR
Email: submissions@
elisedillsworthagency.com
Website: http://elisedillsworthagency.com

Handles: Fiction; Nonfiction; *Areas:* Autobiography; Biography; Cookery; Travel; *Markets:* Adult; *Treatments:* Commercial; Literary

Represents writers from around the world. Looking for literary and commercial fiction, and nonfiction (especially memoir, autobiography, biography, cookery and

travel writing). No science fiction, fantasy, poetry, film scripts, or plays. No young adult, or children's, except for existing authors. Send query by email only (postal submissions no longer accepted). For fiction, include synopsis up to two pages and first three chapters, up to about 50 pages, as Word or PDF attachments. For nonfiction, send details of expertise / credentials, proposal, chapter outline, and writing sample of around 30 pages as a Word file attachment. See website for full guidelines. Response in 6-8 weeks.

Elizabeth Roy Literary Agency

White Cottage, Greatford, Stamford, Linconshire PE9 4PR
Tel: +44 (0) 1778 560672
Website: http://www.elizabethroy.co.uk

Handles: Fiction; Nonfiction; *Areas:* Humour; Romance; *Markets:* Children's

Handles fiction and nonfiction for children. Particularly interested in funny fiction, gentle romance for young teens, picture book texts for pre-school children, and books with international market appeal. Send query by post with return postage, synopsis, and sample chapters. No science fiction, poetry, plays or adult books.

Emily Sweet Associates

Website: http://www.
emilysweetassociates.com

Handles: Fiction; Nonfiction; *Areas:* Biography; Cookery; Current Affairs; Historical; *Markets:* Adult; *Treatments:* Commercial; Literary

No Young Adult or children's. Query through form on website in first instance.

Eve White: Literary Agent

54 Gloucester Street, London, SW1V 4EG
Tel: +44 (0) 20 7630 1155
Email: eve@evewhite.co.uk
Website: http://www.evewhite.co.uk

Handles: Fiction; Nonfiction; *Markets:* Adult; Children's; Youth; *Treatments:* Commercial; Literary

Important! Check and follow website submission guidelines before contacting!

DO NOT send submissions to email address listed on this page – see website for specific submission email addresses for different areas.

QUERIES ONLY to the email address on this page.

This agency requests that you go to their website for up-to-date submission procedure.

Commercial and literary fiction, nonfiction, children's fiction and picture books ages 7+ (home 15%, overseas 20%). No reading fee. No poetry, short stories, novellas, screenplays, or science fiction/fantasy for adults. Does not consider approaches from US writers. See website for detailed submission guidelines. Submission by email only.

Faith Evans Associates

27 Park Avenue North, London, N8 7RU
Tel: +44 (0) 20 8340 9920
Email: faith@faith-evans.co.uk
Website: https://www.faith-evans.co.uk

Handles: Fiction; Nonfiction; *Markets:* Adult

Small agency with full list. Not accepting new clients as at July 2017. No phone calls, or unsolicited MSS.

The Feldstein Agency

54 Abbey Street, Bangor, Northern Ireland BT20 4JB
Tel: +44 (0) 2891 472823
Email: submissions@thefeldsteinagency.co.uk
Website: http://www.thefeldsteinagency.co.uk

Handles: Fiction; Nonfiction; *Areas:* Adventure; Autobiography; Biography; Business; Cookery; Crime; Criticism; Current Affairs; Historical; Humour; Leisure; Lifestyle; Media; Military; Music; Mystery; Philosophy; Politics; Sociology; Sport; Thrillers; Travel; Women's Interests;

Markets: Adult; *Treatments:* Commercial; Literary

Handles adult fiction and nonfiction only. No children's, young adult, romance, science fiction, fantasy, poetry, scripts, or short stories. Send query by email with 1-2 pages synopsis. No reading fees or evaluation fees. The only instance in which an author would be charged a fee is for ghost-writing.

Felicity Bryan Associates

2a North Parade Avenue, Banbury Road, Oxford, OX2 6LX
Tel: +44 (0) 1865 513816
Fax: +44 (0) 1865 310055
Email: agency@felicitybryan.com
Website: http://www.felicitybryan.com

Handles: Fiction; Nonfiction; *Areas:* Biography; Current Affairs; Historical; Science; *Markets:* Adult; Children's; Youth; *Treatments:* Commercial; Literary

Particularly interested in commercial and literary fiction and nonfiction for the adult market, children's fiction for 8+, and Young Adult. Send query by post with sufficient postage, or via submission form on website. See website for detailed submission guidelines. No science fiction, horror, adult fantasy, light romance, self-help, gardening, film and TV scripts, plays, poetry or picture/illustrated books.

Felix de Wolfe

20 Old Compton Street, London, W1D 4TW
Tel: +44 (0) 20 7242 5066
Fax: +44 (0) 20 7242 8119
Email: info@felixdewolfe.com
Website: http://www.felixdewolfe.com

Handles: Fiction; Scripts; *Areas:* Film; Radio; Theatre; TV; *Markets:* Adult

Send query letter with SAE, short synopsis, and CV by post only, unless alternative arrangements have been made with the agency in advance. Quality fiction and scripts only. No nonfiction, children's books, or unsolicited MSS.

Film Rights Ltd in association with Laurence Fitch Ltd

11 Pandora Road, London, NW6 1TS
Tel: +44 (0) 20 8001 3040
Fax: +44 (0) 20 8711 3171
Email: information@filmrights.ltd.uk
Website: http://filmrights.ltd.uk

Handles: Fiction; Scripts; *Areas:* Film;
Horror; Radio; Theatre; TV; *Markets:* Adult;
Children's

Represents films, plays, and novels, for
adults and children.

Fox & Howard Literary Agency

39 Eland Road, London, SW11 5JX
Tel: +44 (0) 20 7223 9452
Email: enquiries@foxandhoward.co.uk
Website: http://www.foxandhoward.co.uk

Handles: Nonfiction; Reference; *Areas:*
Biography; Business; Culture; Health;
Historical; Lifestyle; Psychology; Self-Help;
Spiritual; *Markets:* Adult

**Closed to submissions as at July 2017.
Please check website for current status.**

Send query with synopsis and SAE for
response. Small agency specialising in
nonfiction that works closely with its
authors. No unsolicited MSS.

Frances Kelly Agency

111 Clifton Road, Kingston upon Thames,
Surrey KT2 6PL
Tel: +44 (0) 20 8549 7830

Handles: Nonfiction; Reference; *Areas:*
Arts; Biography; Business; Cookery;
Finance; Health; Historical; Lifestyle;
Medicine; Self-Help; *Markets:* Academic;
Adult; Professional

Send query with SAE, CV, and synopsis or
brief description of work. Scripts handled for
existing clients only. No unsolicited MSS.

Fraser Ross Associates

6/2 Wellington Place, Edinburgh, Scotland
EH6 7EQ
Tel: +44 (0) 01315 532759

Email: fraserrossassociates@gmail.com
Website: http://www.fraserross.co.uk

Handles: Fiction; Nonfiction; *Markets:*
Adult; Children's; *Treatments:* Commercial;
Literary; Mainstream

Send query by email or by post (with SAE if
return of ms required (not available to
overseas writers)), including CV, the first
three chapters and synopsis for fiction, or a
one page proposal and the opening and a
further two chapters for nonfiction. For
picture books, send complete MS, without
illustrations. No poetry, playscripts or short
stories.

Furniss Lawton

James Grant Group Ltd, 4th Floor, 180 Great
Portland Street, London, W1W 5QZ
Tel: +44 (0) 20 8742 4950
Email: info@furnisslawton.co.uk
Website: http://www.jamesgrant.com/
furniss-lawton/

Handles: Fiction; Nonfiction; *Areas:*
Autobiography; Biography; Business;
Cookery; Crime; Historical; Humour;
Politics; Science; Sociology; Sport; Thrillers;
Markets: Adult; *Treatments:* Contemporary;
Popular

Send query with synopsis and first 10,000
words / three chapters as a Word or PDF
document by email. Include the word
"Submission" in the subject line, and your
name and the title of the work in any
attachments. No submissions by post. Does
not handle screenwriters for film or TV. See
website for full details.

Noel Gay

19 Denmark Street, London, WC2H 8NA
Tel: +44 (0) 20 7836 3941
Email: info@noelgay.com
Website: http://www.noelgay.com

Handles: Scripts; *Markets:* Adult

Agency representing writers, directors,
performers, presenters, comedians, etc. Send
query with SASE.

Georgina Capel Associates Ltd

29 Wardour Street, London, W1D 6PS
Tel: +44 (0) 20 7734 2414
Email: georgina@georginacapel.com
Website: http://www.georginacapel.com

Handles: Fiction; Nonfiction; *Areas:* Biography; Film; Historical; Radio; TV; *Markets:* Adult; *Treatments:* Commercial; Literary

Handles general fiction and nonfiction. Send query outlining writing history (for nonfiction, what qualifies you to write your book), with synopsis around 500 words and first three chapters, plus SAE or email address for reply. Submissions are not returned. Mark envelope for the attention of the Submissions Department. Accepts submissions by email, but prefers them by post. Response only if interested, normally within 6 weeks. Film and TV scripts handled for established clients only.

Eric Glass Ltd

25 Ladbroke Crescent, London, W11 1PS
Tel: +44 (0) 20 7229 9500
Fax: +44 (0) 20 7229 6220
Email: eglassltd@aol.com

Handles: Fiction; Nonfiction; Scripts; *Areas:* Film; Theatre; TV; *Markets:* Adult

Handles full-length mss and scripts for film, TV, and theatre. Send query with SAE. No children's books, short stories, poetry, or unsolicited MSS.

The Good Literary Agency

Email: info@thegoodliteraryagency.org
Website: https://www.thegoodliteraryagency.org

Handles: Fiction; Nonfiction; *Markets:* Adult; Children's; Family; Youth

Focused on discovering, developing and launching the careers of writers of colour, disability, working class, LGBTQ+ and anyone who feels their story is not being told in the mainstream. Writers must be born or resident in Britain. No poetry, plays, or screenplays. See website for full guidelines and to submit via online form.

Graham Maw Christie Literary Agency

37 Highbury Place, London, N5 1QP
Tel: +44 (0) 7971 268342
Email: submissions@grahammawchristie.com
Website: http://www.grahammawchristie.com

Handles: Nonfiction; Reference; *Areas:* Autobiography; Business; Cookery; Crafts; Gardening; Health; Historical; Humour; Lifestyle; Philosophy; Science; Self-Help; *Markets:* Adult; Children's

No fiction, poetry, or scripts. Send query with one-page summary, a paragraph on the contents of each chapter, your qualifications for writing it, details of your online presence, market analysis, what you could do to help promote your book, and a sample chapter. Prefers approaches by email.

Greene & Heaton Ltd

37 Goldhawk Road, London, W12 8QQ
Tel: +44 (0) 20 8749 0315
Email: submissions@greeneheaton.co.uk
Website: http://www.greeneheaton.co.uk

Handles: Fiction; Nonfiction; *Areas:* Autobiography; Biography; Cookery; Crime; Current Affairs; Fantasy; Gardening; Health; Historical; Humour; Science; Sci-Fi; Thrillers; Travel; Women's Interests; *Markets:* Adult; Youth; *Treatments:* Contemporary; Literary

Send query by email or by post with SAE, including synopsis and three chapters or approximately 50 pages. No response to unsolicited MSS with no SAE or inadequate means of return postage provided. No response to email submissions unless interested. Handles all types of fiction and nonfiction, but no scripts or children's picture books.

The Greenhouse Literary Agency

Tel: +44 (0) 20 7841 3959
Email: submissions@greenhouseliterary.com
Website: http://www.greenhouseliterary.com

Handles: Fiction; *Markets:* Children's; Youth

Closed to submissions until July 30, 2018.

Transatlantic agency with offices in the US and London. Handles children's and young adult fiction only. For novels, send query by email with first five pages pasted into the body of the email. For picture books (maximum 1,000 words) paste full text into the box of the email. No picture book submissions from authors who are not also illustrators. No attachments or hard copy submissions. See website for full guidelines.

Gregory & Company, Authors' Agents

6th Floor, Waverley House, 7–12 Noel Street, London, W1F 8GQ
Tel: +44 (0) 20 7610 4676
Email: maryjones@davidhigham.co.uk
Website: http://www.gregoryandcompany.co.uk

Handles: Fiction; *Areas:* Crime; Historical; Thrillers; *Markets:* Adult; *Treatments:* Commercial

Particularly interested in Crime, Family Sagas, Historical Fiction, Thrillers and Upmarket Commercial Fiction. Send query with CV, one-page synopsis, future writing plans, and first ten pages, by post with SAE, or by email. No unsolicited MSS, Business Books, Children's, Young Adult Fiction, Nonfiction, Plays, Screenplays, Poetry, Science Fiction, Future Fiction, Fantasy, Self Help, Lifestyle books, Short Stories, Spiritual, New Age, Philosophy, Supernatural, Paranormal, Horror, Travel, or True Crime.

David Grossman Literary Agency Ltd

118b Holland Park Avenue, London, W11 4UA
Tel: +44 (0) 20 7221 2770
Email: david@dglal.co.uk

Handles: Fiction; Nonfiction; *Markets:* Adult

Send preliminary letter before making a submission. No approaches or submissions by fax or email. Usually works with published fiction writers, but well-written and original work from beginners considered. No poetry, scripts, technical books for students, or unsolicited MSS.

Gunn Media Associates

50 Albemarle Street, London, W1S 4BD
Tel: +44 (0) 20 7529 3745
Website: http://www.gunnmedia.co.uk

Handles: Fiction; Nonfiction; *Areas:* Autobiography; Entertainment; Thrillers; *Markets:* Adult; *Treatments:* Commercial; Literary

Handles commercial fiction and nonfiction, including literary, thrillers, and celebrity autobiographies.

Hardman & Swainson

S86, New Wing, Somerset House, Strand, London, WC2R 1LA
Tel: +44 (0) 20 3701 7449
Email: submissions@hardmanswainson.com
Website: http://www.hardmanswainson.com

Handles: Fiction; Nonfiction; *Areas:* Autobiography; Crime; Health; Historical; Horror; Humour; Medicine; Philosophy; Psychology; Science; Suspense; Thrillers; Women's Interests; *Markets:* Adult; Children's; Youth; *Treatments:* Commercial; Contemporary; Literary; Popular

Agency launched June 2012 by former colleagues at an established agency. Welcomes submissions of fiction and nonfiction, but no submissions by post. See website for full submission guidelines.

hhb agency ltd

62 Grafton Way, London, W1T 5DW
Tel: +44 (0) 20 7405 5525
Email: heather@hhbagency.com
Website: http://www.hhbagency.com

Handles: Fiction; Nonfiction; *Areas:* Adventure; Autobiography; Biography; Business; Cookery; Crime; Culture; Entertainment; Historical; Humour; Politics; Travel; TV; Women's Interests; *Markets:*

Adult; *Treatments:* Commercial; Contemporary; Literary; Popular

Represents nonfiction writers, particularly in the areas of journalism, history and politics, travel and adventure, contemporary autobiography and biography, books about words and numbers, popular culture and quirky humour, entertainment and television, business, family memoir, food and cookery. Also handles commercial fiction. Not accepting unsolicited submissions as at October 2017.

Holroyde Cartey

Email: claire@holroydecartey.com
Website: http://www.holroydecartey.com

Handles: Fiction; Nonfiction; *Markets:* Children's

Handles fiction and nonfiction for children of all ages, including picture books. Also represents illustrators. Welcomes submissions from debut and established authors and illustrators. Send query by email only, with cover letter, synopsis, and full ms as separate Word file attachments. See website for individual agent details and interests and approach one agent only. Aims to respond to every submission, within six weeks.

Vanessa Holt Ltd

59 Crescent Road, Leigh-on-Sea, Essex SS9 2PF
Tel: +44 (0) 1702 473787
Email: v.holt791@btinternet.com

Handles: Fiction; Nonfiction; *Markets:* Adult

General fiction and nonfiction. No unsolicited mss or overseas approaches.

Independent Talent Group Ltd

40 Whitfield Street, London, W1T 2RH
Tel: +44 (0) 20 7636 6565
Website: http://www.independenttalent.com

Handles: Scripts; *Areas:* Film; Radio; Theatre; TV; *Markets:* Adult

Specialises in scripts and works in association with agencies in Los Angeles and New York. No unsolicited MSS. Materials submitted will not be returned.

Intercontinental Literary Agency

5 New Concordia Wharf, Mill Street, London, SE1 2BB
Tel: +44 (0) 20 7379 6611
Fax: +44 (0) 20 7240 4724
Email: ila@ila-agency.co.uk
Website: http://www.ila-agency.co.uk

Handles: Fiction; Nonfiction; *Areas:* Translations; *Markets:* Adult; Children's

Handles translation rights only for, among others, the authors of LAW Ltd, London; Harold Matson Co. Inc., New York; PFD, London. Submissions accepted via client agencies and publishers only – no submissions from writers seeking agents.

Isabel White Literary Agent

Tel: +44 (0) 20 3070 1602
Email: query.isabelwhite@googlemail.com
Website: http://www.isabelwhite.co.uk

Handles: Fiction; Nonfiction; *Markets:* Adult

Selective one-woman agency, not taking on new clients as at January 2017.

Jane Conway-Gordon Ltd

38 Cromwell Grove, London, W6 7RG
Tel: +44 (0) 20 7371 6939
Email: jane@conway-gordon.co.uk
Website: http://www.janeconwaygordon.com

Handles: Fiction; Nonfiction; *Markets:* Adult

Handles fiction and general nonfiction. Prefers to receive queries by post with SASE, synopsis, and first 3 chapters or 40 pages; but will also accept short email describing the book (no attachments). No poetry, children's or science fiction.

Jane Judd Literary Agency

18 Belitha Villas, London, N1 1PD
Tel: +44 (0) 20 7607 0273

Email: info@janejudd.com
Website: http://www.janejudd.com

Handles: Fiction; Nonfiction; *Areas:* Biography; Cookery; Film; Health; Historical; Self-Help; Sport; *Markets:* Adult; *Treatments:* Commercial; Literary

For fiction, send query with synopsis, first two or three chapters, and SAE. For nonfiction send first and/or other sample chapter, synopsis, market info, chapter breakdown, and any supporting evidence or articles. You may telephone in advance to save time for both parties. Also option of submitting online using contact form on website. Particularly interested in self-help, health, biography, popular history and narrative nonfiction, general and historical fiction and literary fiction.

Jane Turnbull

Barn Cottage, Veryan, Truro TR2 5QA
Tel: +44 (0) 20 7727 9409 / +44 (0) 1872 501317
Email: jane@janeturnbull.co.uk
Website: http://www.janeturnbull.co.uk

Handles: Fiction; Nonfiction; *Areas:* Biography; Current Affairs; Entertainment; Gardening; Historical; Humour; Lifestyle; Nature; TV; *Markets:* Adult; Youth; *Treatments:* Commercial; Literary; Mainstream

Agency with offices in London and Cornwall. New clients always welcome and a few taken on every year. Will occasionally take on fiction for older children, but no science fiction, fantasy, or "misery memoirs". Send query by post to Cornwall office with short description of your book or idea. No unsolicited MSS.

Janet Fillingham Associates

52 Lowther Road, London, SW13 9NU
Tel: +44 (0) 20 8748 5594
Email: info@janetfillingham.com
Website: http://www.janetfillingham.com

Handles: Scripts; *Areas:* Film; Theatre; TV; *Markets:* Adult; Children's; Youth

Represents writers and directors for stage, film and TV, as well as librettists, lyricists

and composers in musical theatre. Does not represent books. Prospective clients may register via website.

Jenny Brown Associates

31 Marchmont Road, Edinburgh, Scotland EH9 1HU
Tel: +44 (0) 1312 295334
Email: submissions@jennybrownassociates.com
Website: http://www.jennybrownassociates.com

Handles: Fiction; Nonfiction; *Areas:* Autobiography; Biography; Crime; Culture; Finance; Historical; Humour; Music; Romance; Science; Sport; Thrillers; Women's Interests; *Markets:* Adult; Children's; *Treatments:* Commercial; Literary; Popular

Strongly prefers queries by email. Approach by post only if not possible to do so by email. Send query with market information, bio, synopsis and first 50 pages in one document (fiction) or sample chapter and info on market and your background (nonfiction). No academic, poetry, short stories, science fiction, or fantasy. Responds only if interested. If no response in 8 weeks assume rejection. Different agents are open to queries at different times. See website for individual agent interests, submission status, and email addresses.

Jill Foster Ltd (JFL)

48 Charlotte Street, London, W1T 2NS
Tel: +44 (0) 20 3137 8182
Email: agents@jflagency.com
Website: http://www.jflagency.com

Handles: Scripts; *Areas:* Drama; Film; Humour; Radio; Theatre; TV; *Markets:* Adult

Handles scripts only (for television, film, theatre and radio). Considers approaches from established writers with broadcast experience, but only accepts submissions from new writers during specific periods – consult website for details.

Jo Unwin Literary Agency

West Wing, Somerset House, London,
WC2R 1LA
Tel: +44 (0) 20 7257 9599
Email: info@jounwin.co.uk
Website: http://www.jounwin.co.uk

Handles: Fiction; Nonfiction; *Areas:*
Humour; Translations; Women's Interests;
Markets: Adult; Children's; Youth;
Treatments: Commercial; Literary

Handles literary fiction, commercial
women's fiction, comic writing, narrative
nonfiction, Young Adult fiction and fiction
for children aged 9+. No poetry, picture
books, or screenplays, except for existing
clients. Accepts submissions by email.
Mainly represents authors from the UK and
Ireland, and sometimes Australia and New
Zealand. Only represents US authors in very
exceptional circumstances. See website for
full guidelines.

Johnson & Alcock

Bloomsbury House, 74-77 Great Russell
Street, London, WC1B 3DA
Tel: +44 (0) 20 7251 0125
Email: michael@johnsonandalcock.co.uk
Website: http://www.
johnsonandalcock.co.uk

Handles: Fiction; Nonfiction; *Areas:* Arts;
Autobiography; Biography; Crime; Culture;
Current Affairs; Design; Fantasy; Film;
Health; Historical; Lifestyle; Music; Nature;
Psychology; Science; Sci-Fi; Self-Help;
Sport; Suspense; Thrillers; Women's
Interests; *Markets:* Adult; Children's; Youth;
Treatments: Commercial; Literary; Popular

Send query by email (response only if
interested), or by post with SASE. Include
synopsis and first three chapters
(approximately 50 pages). Email
submissions should go to specific agents. See
website for list of agents and full submission
guidelines. No poetry, screenplays,
children's books 0-7, or board or picture
books.

Jonathan Clowes Ltd

10 Iron Bridge House, Bridge Approach,
London, NW1 8BD

Tel: +44 (0) 20 7722 7674
Fax: +44 (0) 20 7722 7677
Email: cara@jonathanclowes.co.uk
Website: http://www.jonathanclowes.co.uk

Handles: Fiction; Nonfiction; Scripts; *Areas:*
Film; Radio; Theatre; TV; *Markets:* Adult;
Treatments: Commercial; Literary

Send query with synopsis and three chapters
(or equivalent sample) by email. No science
fiction, poetry, short stories, academic. Only
considers film/TV clients with previous
success in TV/film/theatre. If no response
within six weeks, assume rejection.

Jonathan Pegg Literary Agency

67 Wingate Square, London, SW4 OAF
Tel: +44 (0) 20 7603 6830
Email: submissions@jonathanpegg.com
Website: http://www.jonathanpegg.com

Handles: Fiction; Nonfiction; *Areas:* Arts;
Autobiography; Biography; Culture; Current
Affairs; Historical; Lifestyle; Nature;
Psychology; Science; Thrillers; *Markets:*
Adult; *Treatments:* Commercial; Literary;
Popular

Established by the agent after twelve years at
Curtis Brown. The agency's main areas of
interest are:

Fiction: literary fiction, thrillers and quality
commercial in general
Non-Fiction: current affairs, memoir and
biography, history, popular science, nature,
arts and culture, lifestyle, popular
psychology

Rights:
Aside from the UK market, the agency will
work in association with translation, US, TV
& film agents according to each client's best
interests.

If you're looking for an agent:
I accept submissions by email. See website
for full submission guidelines.

Judith Murdoch Literary Agency

19 Chalcot Square, London, NW1 8YA
Tel: +44 (0) 20 7722 4197
Email: jmlitag@btinternet.com
Website: http://www.judithmurdoch.co.uk

Handles: Fiction; *Areas:* Crime; Women's Interests; *Markets:* Adult; *Treatments:* Commercial; Literary; Popular

Send query by post with SAE or email address for response, brief synopsis, and and first three chapters. Provides editorial advice. No science fiction, fantasy, children's stories, email submissions, or unsolicited MSS.

Juliet Burton Literary Agency

2 Clifton Avenue, London, W12 9DR
Tel: +44 (0) 20 8762 0148
Email: juliet.burton@btinternet.com

Handles: Fiction; Nonfiction; *Areas:* Crime; Women's Interests; *Markets:* Adult

Particularly interested in crime and women's fiction. Send query with SAE, synopsis, and two sample chapters. No poetry, plays, film scripts, children's, articles, academic material, science fiction, fantasy, unsolicited MSS, or email submissions.

Michelle Kass Associates

85 Charing Cross Road, London, WC2H 0AA
Tel: +44 (0) 20 7439 1624
Email: office@michellekass.co.uk
Website: http://www.michellekass.co.uk

Handles: Fiction; Scripts; *Areas:* Film; Literature; TV; *Markets:* Adult; *Treatments:* Literary

No email submissions. Approach by telephone in first instance.

Kate Hordern Literary Agency

Tel: +44 (0) 117 923 9368
Email: katehordern@blueyonder.co.uk
Website: http://www.katehordern.co.uk

Handles: Fiction; Nonfiction; Reference; *Areas:* Autobiography; Business; Crime;

Culture; Current Affairs; Historical; Nature; Sociology; Thrillers; Women's Interests; *Markets:* Adult; Children's; Youth; *Treatments:* Commercial; Contemporary; Literary; Popular

Send query by email only with pitch, outline or synopsis, and first three chapters. No submissions by post, or from authors not resident in the UK. If no response within six weeks, assume rejection.

Kate Nash Literary Agency

1 Swift Way, Brackley, Northants NN13 6PY
Tel: +44 (0) 844 415 7844
Email: submissions.kn@gmail.com
Website: http://www.katenashliterary.co.uk

Handles: Fiction; Nonfiction; *Markets:* Adult; *Treatments:* Popular

Open to approaches from both new and established authors. Represents general and genre fiction and popular nonfiction. No poetry, drama, or genre SFF. Send query by email with synopsis and first chapter / 10 pages pasted into the body of the email (no attachments).

Keane Kataria Literary Agency

Email: info@keanekataria.co.uk
Website: http://www.keanekataria.co.uk

Handles: Fiction; Nonfiction; *Areas:* Crime; Women's Interests; *Markets:* Adult; *Treatments:* Commercial

Currently accepting submissions in the crime, domestic noir and women's fiction genres. No science fiction, fantasy or children's books. Send query by email only with synopsis and first three chapters. Attachments in PDF format only.

Ki Agency Ltd

Studio 315, Screenworks, 22 Highbury Grove, London, N5 2ER
Tel: +44 (0) 20 3214 8287
Email: meg@ki-agency.co.uk
Website: http://www.ki-agency.co.uk

Handles: Fiction; Nonfiction; Scripts; *Areas:* Culture; Film; Historical; Politics; Science;

Self-Help; Sport; Theatre; TV; *Markets:* Adult; *Treatments:* Popular

Represents novelists and scriptwriters in all media. No children's or YA novels, humorous science fiction or commercial women's fiction. Send synopsis and first three chapters by email. See website for individual agent interests.

Kingsford Campbell Literary & Marketing Agents
Email: info@kingsfordcampbell.com
Website: http://kingsfordcampbell.com

Handles: Fiction; Nonfiction; *Markets:* Adult

Actively seeking submissions from new and established writers. Very broad tastes and interests in both fiction and nonfiction across genres, subjects and ages, but no poetry, screenplays, or children's books. See website for full submission guidelines and online submission form.

Knight Hall Agency
Lower Ground Floor, 7 Mallow Street, London, EC1Y 8RQ
Tel: +44 (0) 20 3397 2901
Fax: +44 (0) 871 918 6068
Email: office@knighthallagency.com
Website: http://www.knighthallagency.com

Handles: Scripts; *Areas:* Drama; Film; Theatre; TV; *Markets:* Adult

Note: Closed to submissions as at January 2018. Check website for current status.

Send query by post or email (no attachments). Only send sample if requested. Represents playwrights, screenwriters and writer-directors. Handles adaptation rights for novels, but does not handle books directly.

Knight Features
Trident Business Centre, 89 Bickersteth Road, London, SW17 9SH
Tel: +44 (0) 20 7622 1467
Email: sam@knightfeatures.co.uk
Website: http://www.knightfeatures.com

Handles: Fiction; Nonfiction; *Areas:* Autobiography; Biography; Business; Health; Historical; Humour; Spiritual; Sport; *Markets:* Adult; Children's

Send query by email or by post with SAE, including CV, synopsis, and three sample chapters. Main areas of interest are: Motorsports; Business; History; Biography; Autobiography. No poetry, cookery, or science fiction. Initial contact may be made by phone or email. See website for full submission guidelines.

LAW (Lucas Alexander Whitley)
2nd Floor, 16–17 Wardour Mews, London, W1F 8AT
Tel: +44 (0) 20 7471 7900
Fax: +44 (0) 20 7471 7910
Email: lawagencysubmissions@gmail.com
Website: http://www.lawagency.co.uk

Handles: Fiction; Nonfiction; Reference; Scripts; *Areas:* Autobiography; Beauty and Fashion; Biography; Business; Cookery; Crime; Culture; Current Affairs; Fantasy; Health; Historical; Horror; Military; Music; Nature; Philosophy; Politics; Science; Sci-Fi; Sport; Technology; Thrillers; Women's Interests; *Markets:* Adult; Children's; Youth; *Treatments:* Commercial; Literary

Send query by email only. Include short synopsis and the first three chapters or up to 30 pages (whichever is greatest). For children's picture books, submit complete ms. See website for separate email address for children's submissions. No plays, poetry, or textbooks. Film and TV scripts handled for existing clients only. Unlikely to accept submissions from overseas.

LBA Books Ltd
91 Great Russell Street, London, WC1B 3PS
Tel: +44 (0) 20 7637 1234
Fax: +44 (0) 20 7637 2111
Email: info@lbabooks.com
Website: http://www.lbabooks.com

Handles: Fiction; Nonfiction; *Areas:* Adventure; Cookery; Crime; Fantasy; Health; Historical; Lifestyle; Romance; Science; Sci-Fi; Thrillers; TV; Women's

Interests; *Markets:* Adult; Children's; Youth; *Treatments:* Commercial; Literary

Send query with synopsis and first three chapters by post with SAE (if return of material required) or by email to specific agent. See website for specific agents' interests and email addresses. No scripts, short stories, or poetry.

Limelight Management

10 Filmer Mews, 75 Filmer Road, London, SW6 7JF
Tel: +44 (0) 20 7384 9950
Fax: +44 (0) 20 7384 9955
Email: mail@limelightmanagement.com
Website: http://www.limelightmanagement.com

Handles: Fiction; Nonfiction; *Areas:* Arts; Autobiography; Biography; Business; Cookery; Crafts; Crime; Health; Historical; Lifestyle; Mystery; Nature; Science; Sport; Suspense; Thrillers; Travel; Women's Interests; *Markets:* Adult; *Treatments:* Commercial; Literary

Always looking for exciting new authors. Send query by email with the word "Submission" in the subject line and synopsis and first three chapters as Word or Open Document attachments. Also include market info, and details of your professional life and writing ambitions. Film and TV scripts for existing clients only. See website for full guidelines.

Linda Seifert Management

Screenworks, Room 315, 22 Highbury Grove, Islington, London, N5 2ER
Tel: +44 (0) 20 3214 8293
Email: contact@lindaseifert.com
Website: http://www.lindaseifert.com

Handles: Scripts; *Areas:* Film; TV; *Markets:* Adult; Children's

A London-based management company representing screenwriters and directors for film and television. Our outstanding client list ranges from the highly established to the new and exciting emerging talent of tomorrow. Represents UK-based writers and directors only. Not currently accepting unsolicited submissions as at October 2016.

Lindsay Literary Agency

East Worldham House, East Worldham, Alton GU34 3AT
Tel: +44 (0) 0142 083143
Email: info@lindsayliteraryagency.co.uk
Website: http://www.lindsayliteraryagency.co.uk

Handles: Fiction; Nonfiction; *Markets:* Adult; Children's; *Treatments:* Literary; Serious

Send query by email only, including single-page synopsis and first three chapters. For picture books send complete ms. No submissions by post.

London Independent Books

26 Chalcot Crescent, London, NW1 8YD
Tel: +44 (0) 20 7722 7160

Handles: Fiction; Nonfiction; *Areas:* Fantasy; *Markets:* Adult; Youth; *Treatments:* Commercial

Send query with synopsis, SASE, and first two chapters. All fiction and nonfiction subjects considered if treatment is strong and saleable, but no computer books, young children's, or unsolicited MSS. Particularly interested in commercial fiction, fantasy, and teen fiction. Scripts handled for existing clients only.

Lorella Belli Literary Agency (LBLA)

54 Hartford House, 35 Tavistock Crescent, Notting Hill, London, W11 1AY
Tel: +44 (0) 20 7727 8547
Fax: +44 (0) 870 787 4194
Email: info@lorellabelliagency.com
Website: http://www.lorellabelliagency.com

Handles: Fiction; Nonfiction; *Markets:* Adult; *Treatments:* Literary

Send query by post or by email in first instance. No attachments. Particularly interested in multicultural / international writing, and books relating to Italy, or written in Italian; first novelists, and journalists; successful sel-published authors. Welcomes queries from new authors and will suggest revisions where appropriate. No poetry, children's, original scripts, academic, SF, or fantasy.

Louise Greenberg Books Ltd

The End House, Church Crescent, London, N3 1BG
Tel: +44 (0) 20 8349 1179
Email: louisegreenberg@btinternet.com
Website: http://louisegreenbergbooks.co.uk

Handles: Fiction; Nonfiction; *Markets:* Adult; *Treatments:* Literary; Serious

Not accepting new writers as at August 2017. Check website for current status.

Handles full-length literary fiction and serious nonfiction only. Only considers new writers by recommendation.

Lutyens and Rubinstein

21 Kensington Park Road, London, W11 2EU
Tel: +44 (0) 20 7792 4855
Email: submissions@lutyensrubinstein.co.uk
Website: http://www.lutyensrubinstein.co.uk

Handles: Fiction; Nonfiction; *Areas:* Cookery; *Markets:* Adult; Children's; Youth; *Treatments:* Commercial; Literary

Send up to 5,000 words or first three chapters by email with covering letter and short synopsis. No film or TV scripts, or unsolicited submissions by hand or by post.

Madeleine Milburn Literary, TV & Film Agency

10 Shepherd Market, Mayfair, London, W1J 7QF
Tel: +44 (0) 20 7499 7550
Email: submissions@madeleinemilburn.com
Website: http://madeleinemilburn.co.uk

Handles: Fiction; Nonfiction; Scripts; *Areas:* Autobiography; Crime; Fantasy; Film; Historical; Horror; Humour; Lifestyle; Mystery; Nature; Psychology; Romance; Science; Sci-Fi; Self-Help; Sport; Suspense; Thrillers; Translations; TV; Women's Interests; *Markets:* Adult; Children's; Youth; *Treatments:* Commercial; Literary

Send query by email only, with one-page synopsis and first three chapters for fiction, or proposal and 30-page writing sample for nonfiction. See website for full submission guidelines. Film and TV scripts for established clients only.

Maggie Pearlstine Associates Ltd

31 Ashley Gardens, Ambrosden Avenue, London, SW1P 1QE
Tel: +44 (0) 20 7828 4212
Fax: +44 (0) 20 7834 5546
Email: maggie@pearlstine.co.uk

Handles: Fiction; Nonfiction; *Areas:* Biography; Current Affairs; Health; Historical; *Markets:* Adult

Small, selective agency, not currently taking on new clients.

The Marsh Agency

50 Albemarle Street, London, W1S 4BD
Tel: +44 (0) 20 7493 4361
Fax: +44 (0) 20 7495 8961
Email: english.language@marsh-agency.co.uk
Website: http://www.marsh-agency.co.uk

Handles: Fiction; Nonfiction; *Markets:* Adult; Youth; *Treatments:* Literary

Not currently accepting unsolicited mss as at March 2018. Most new clients come through recommendations.

Martin Leonardis Ltd

71-75 Shelton Street, London, WC2H 9JQ
Email: submissions@martinleonardis.com
Website: http://martinleonardis.com

Handles: Fiction; Nonfiction; *Areas:* Cookery; Lifestyle; Self-Help; *Markets:* Adult; *Treatments:* Commercial

For fiction, send complete ms by email with 250-word pitch. For nonfiction, send pitch with proposal and details of your platform. No fantasy, space-operas, horror or gothic fiction, historical nonfiction, YA or children's fiction, or poetry or short stories. See website for full details.

Mary Clemmey Literary Agency

6 Dunollie Road, London, NW5 2XP
Tel: +44 (0) 20 7267 1290
Fax: +44 (0) 20 7813 9757
Email: mcwords@googlemail.com

Handles: Fiction; Nonfiction; Scripts; *Areas:* Film; Radio; Theatre; TV; *Markets:* Adult

Send query with SAE and description of work only. Handles high-quality work with an international market. No children's books, science fiction, fantasy, or unsolicited MSS or submissions by email. Scripts handled for existing clients only. Do not submit a script or idea for a script unless you are already a client.

MBA Literary Agents Ltd

62 Grafton Way, London, W1T 5DW
Tel: +44 (0) 20 7387 2076
Email: submissions@mbalit.co.uk
Website: http://www.mbalit.co.uk

Handles: Fiction; Nonfiction; Scripts; *Areas:* Arts; Biography; Crafts; Film; Health; Historical; Lifestyle; Radio; Self-Help; Theatre; TV; *Markets:* Adult; Children's; Youth; *Treatments:* Commercial; Literary

For books, send query with CV, synopsis and first three chapters. Not currently accepting unsolicited film and television submissions. Submissions by email only, in Word, PDF or Final Draft format. No submissions by post. See website for full submission guidelines. Works in conjunction with agents in most countries.

Duncan McAra

3 Viewfield Avenue, Bishopbriggs, Glasgow, Scotland G64 2AG
Tel: +44 (0) 1417 721067
Email: duncanmcara@mac.com

Handles: Fiction; Nonfiction; *Areas:* Archaeology; Architecture; Arts; Biography; Historical; Military; Travel; *Markets:* Adult; *Treatments:* Literary

Also interested in books of Scottish interest. Send query letter with SAE in first instance.

Bill McLean Personal Management Ltd

23B Deodar Road, London, SW15 2NP
Tel: +44 (0) 20 8789 8191

Handles: Scripts; *Areas:* Film; Radio; Theatre; TV; *Markets:* Adult

Theatrical agent handling scripts for all media. No books.

The Michael Greer Literary Agency

51 Aragon Court, 8 Hotspur Street, Kennington, London SE11 6BX
Tel: +44 (0) 777 592 0885
Email: mmichaelgreer@yahoo.co.uk
Website: http://www.wix.com/mmichaelgreer/mgla

Handles: Fiction; Nonfiction; Scripts; *Areas:* Business; Lifestyle; Psychology; Sport; *Markets:* Adult; Children's; Professional; Youth; *Treatments:* Commercial; Contemporary; Literary; Mainstream; Popular; Positive

Currently, represents writing mainly in the Sports genre – be that covering certain players, or covering certain games and the philosophy of sports.

We also accept manuscripts in the Young Adult / Teen Fiction category, and in the Literary Fiction category – the latter with an emphasis on work set in a City environment.

Mulcahy Associates (Part of MMB Creative)

The Old Truman Brewery, 91 Brick Lane, London, E1 6QL
Tel: +44 (0) 20 3582 9370
Fax: +44 (0) 20 3582 9377
Email: talent@mmbcreative.com
Website: https://mmbcreative.com

Handles: Fiction; Nonfiction; *Areas:* Biography; Crime; Finance; Historical; Lifestyle; Sport; Thrillers; Women's Interests; *Markets:* Adult; Children's; Youth; *Treatments:* Commercial; Literary

See books pages of website to get an idea of the kind of material represented, and submit via online form.

MNLA (Maggie Noach Literary Agency)
Hop Hill Cottage, Harmston Road, Aubourn, Lincoln, LN5 9DZ
Tel: +44 (0) 1522 788110
Email: info@mnla.co.uk
Website: http://www.mnla.co.uk

Handles: Fiction; Nonfiction; *Areas:* Biography; Historical; Travel; *Markets:* Adult; Children's

Note: As at June 2013 not accepting submissions. Check website for current situation.

Deals with UK residents only. Send query with SAE, outline, and two or three sample chapters. No email attachments or fax queries. Very few new clients taken on. Deals in general adult nonfiction and non-illustrated children's books for ages 8 and upwards. No poetry, scripts, short stories, cookery, gardening, mind, body, and spirit, scientific, academic, specialist nonfiction, or unsolicited MSS.

Northbank Talent Management
Email: info@northbanktalent.com
Website: http://www.northbanktalent.com

Handles: Fiction; Nonfiction; *Areas:* Autobiography; Business; Crime; Current Affairs; Drama; Fantasy; Health; Historical; Lifestyle; Politics; Psychology; Science; Sci-Fi; Self-Help; Suspense; Thrillers; Women's Interests; *Markets:* Adult; Children's; Youth; *Treatments:* Commercial

Literary and talent agency based in central London. Actively seeking new clients. Send query by email with synopsis and first three chapters as Word or Open Document attachments. See website for specific email addresses to use for different types of material.

Deborah Owen Ltd
78 Narrow Street, Limehouse, London, E14 8BP
Tel: +44 (0) 20 7987 5119 / 5441

Handles: Fiction; Nonfiction

Represents only two authors worldwide. Not accepting any new authors.

Peters Fraser + Dunlop
55 New Oxford Street, London, WC1A 1BS
Tel: +44 (0) 20 7344 1000
Fax: +44 (0) 20 7836 9539
Email: info@pfd.co.uk
Website: http://www.pfd.co.uk

Handles: Fiction; Nonfiction; Scripts; *Areas:* Autobiography; Cookery; Crime; Culture; Film; Finance; Gothic; Historical; Horror; Humour; Nature; Psychology; Radio; Science; Sport; Suspense; Theatre; Thrillers; TV; Women's Interests; *Markets:* Adult; Children's; Youth; *Treatments:* Commercial; Dark; Literary; Popular

See website for individual agent interests and submission guidelines.

PEW Literary
46 Lexington Street, London, W1F 0LP
Tel: +44 (0) 20 7734 4464
Email: submissions@pewliterary.com
Website: http://www.pewliterary.com

Handles: Fiction; Nonfiction; *Areas:* Crime; Thrillers; *Markets:* Adult; *Treatments:* Literary

Send query by post or by email, with synopsis and first three chapters (or fifty pages) (fiction); or proposal (nonfiction). If submitting by email, send material in Word or PDF attachment. If submitting by post, do not include SAE as material will be recycled once read. Include email address for response. Aims to respond within six weeks.

Shelley Power Literary Agency Ltd
33 Dumbrells Court, North End, Ditchling, East Sussex BN6 8TG
Tel: +44 (0) 1273 844467
Email: sp@shelleypower.co.uk

Handles: Fiction; Nonfiction; *Markets:* Adult

Send query by email or by post with return postage. No attachments. No poetry, scripts, science fiction, fantasy, young adult, or children's books.

Puttick Literary Agency
Email: editorial@puttick.com
Website: http://www.puttick.com

Handles: Nonfiction; *Areas:* Biography; Culture; Current Affairs; Health; Historical; Philosophy; Science; Self-Help; *Markets:* Adult

Closed to submissions as at May 2017. See website for current situation.

Send query with short two or three page synopsis and CV by email (by preference), or by post with SAE. No fiction, poetry, drama, screenplays, children's books, or submissions by email (enquiries only). Enquiries only should be clearly marked in the subject line to avoid being deleted as spam. Make sure it is made clear if the material is under consideration elsewhere at the same time. Owing to the large volume of submissions we receive, we are only able to reply to those we wish to take further.

Redhammer
Website: http://redhammer.info

Handles: Fiction; Nonfiction; *Areas:* Autobiography; Crime; Entertainment; Mystery; Thrillers; *Markets:* Adult

Generally too busy to consider approaches from writers, unless they already have some experience of the publishing industry. However does offer occasional pop-up submission opportunities. Check website for details.

Richford Becklow Literary Agency
Tel: +44 (0) 20 3737 1068 / + 44 (0) 7510 023823
Email: enquiries@richfordbecklow.co.uk
Website: http://www.richfordbecklow.com

Handles: Fiction; Nonfiction; *Areas:* Arts; Autobiography; Biography; Cookery; Crime; Fantasy; Gardening; Gothic; Historical; Horror; Lifestyle; Literature; Romance; Sci-Fi; Self-Help; Women's Interests; *Markets:* Adult; Youth; *Treatments:* Commercial; Contemporary; Literary; Satirical; Serious

Closed to submissions as at May 2018. Check website for current status.

Company founded in 2012 by an experienced agent, previously at the longest established literary agency in the world. Interested in fiction and nonfiction. Email submissions only. Does not accept postal submissions and cannot currently offer to represent American or Australian authors. No picture book texts for babies and toddlers, or erotica. No submissions in April or October. See website for full submission guidelines.

Robert Dudley Agency
135A Bridge Street, Ashford, Kent TN25 5DP
Email: info@robertdudleyagency.co.uk
Website: http://www.robertdudleyagency.co.uk

Handles: Nonfiction; *Areas:* Adventure; Biography; Business; Current Affairs; Historical; Medicine; Military; Self-Help; Sport; Technology; Travel; *Markets:* Adult; *Treatments:* Popular

Specialises in nonfiction. No fiction submissions. Send submissions by email, preferably in Word format, as opposed to PDF.

Robin Jones Literary Agency
66 High Street, Dorchester on Thames, OX10 7HN
Tel: +44 (0) 1865 341486
Email: robijones@gmail.com
Website: https://twitter.com/AgentRobinJones

Handles: Fiction; Nonfiction; *Markets:* Adult; *Treatments:* Commercial; Literary

Literary agency founded in 2007 by an agent who has previously worked at four other agencies, and was the UK scout for international publishers in 11 countries. Handles commercial and literary fiction and nonfiction for adults. Welcomes Russian language fiction and nonfiction. No children's, poetry, young adult, or original scripts. Send query with synopsis and 50-page sample.

Rochelle Stevens & Co.
2 Terretts Place, Upper Street, London, N1 1QZ
Tel: +44 (0) 20 7359 3900
Email: info@rochellestevens.com
Website: http://www.rochellestevens.com

Handles: Scripts; *Areas:* Film; Radio; Theatre; TV; *Markets:* Adult

Handles script writers for film, television, theatre, and radio. No longer handles writers of fiction, nonfiction, or children's books. Submit by post only. See website for full submission guidelines.

Rocking Chair Books
2 Rudgwick Terrace, St Stephens Close, London, NW8 6BR
Tel: +44 (0) 7809 461342
Email: representme@rockingchairbooks.com
Website: http://www.rockingchairbooks.com

Handles: Fiction; Nonfiction; *Areas:* Adventure; Arts; Crime; Culture; Current Affairs; Entertainment; Historical; Horror; Lifestyle; Literature; Mystery; Nature; Romance; Thrillers; Translations; Travel; Women's Interests; *Markets:* Adult; *Treatments:* Commercial; Contemporary; Cynical; Dark; Experimental; In-depth; Light; Literary; Mainstream; Popular; Positive; Progressive; Satirical; Serious; Traditional

Founded in 2011 after the founder worked for five years as a Director at an established London literary agency. Send complete ms or a few chapters by email only. No Children's, YA or Science Fiction / Fantasy.

Rosica Colin Ltd
1 Clareville Grove Mews, London, SW7 5AH
Tel: +44 (0) 20 7370 1080

Handles: Fiction; Nonfiction; Scripts; *Areas:* Autobiography; Beauty and Fashion; Biography; Cookery; Crime; Current Affairs; Erotic; Fantasy; Film; Gardening; Health; Historical; Horror; Humour; Leisure; Lifestyle; Men's Interests; Military; Mystery; Nature; Psychology; Radio; Religious; Romance; Science; Sport; Suspense; Theatre; Thrillers; TV; Women's Interests; *Markets:* Academic; Adult; Children's; *Treatments:* Literary

Send query with SAE, CV, synopsis, and list of other agents and publishers where MS has already been sent. Considers any full-length mss (except science fiction and poetry), but send synopsis only in initial query.

Rupert Heath Literary Agency
50 Albemarle Street, London, W1S 4BD
Tel: +44 (0) 20 7060 3385
Email: emailagency@rupertheath.com
Website: http://www.rupertheath.com

Handles: Fiction; Nonfiction; *Areas:* Arts; Autobiography; Biography; Crime; Culture; Current Affairs; Historical; Humour; Nature; Politics; Science; Sci-Fi; Thrillers; *Markets:* Adult; *Treatments:* Commercial; Literary; Popular

Send query giving some information about yourself and the work you would like to submit. Prefers queries by email. Response only if interested.

The Ruppin Agency
London,
Email: submissions@ruppinagency.com
Website: http://www.ruppinagency.com

Handles: Fiction; Nonfiction; *Areas:* Adventure; Anthropology; Antiques; Archaeology; Architecture; Arts; Autobiography; Biography; Crime; Culture; Current Affairs; Design; Entertainment; Film; Gothic; Historical; Hobbies; Literature; Men's Interests; Military; Music; Mystery; Nature; Philosophy; Politics; Science; Short Stories; Sociology; Sport; Thrillers; Translations; Travel; TV; Women's Interests; *Markets:* Adult; *Treatments:* Commercial; Contemporary; Experimental; In-depth; Literary;

Mainstream; Niche; Popular; Progressive; Serious

Literary agency set up by a former bookseller, offering writers a new perspective on finding the right publisher for their work. Keen to find writers with something to say about society today and particularly looking for storylines that showcase voices and communities that have tended to be overlooked by the publishing world, although that should deter no-one from sending their writing. No poetry, children's, young adult, graphic novels, plays and film scripts, self-help, illustrated, academic or professional titles.

Sarah Such Literary Agency
81 Arabella Drive, London, SW15 5LL
Tel: +44 (0) 20 8876 4228
Email: info@sarah-such.com
Website: http://www.sarahsuch.com

Handles: Fiction; Nonfiction; *Areas:* Autobiography; Biography; Culture; Historical; Humour; *Markets:* Adult; Children's; Youth; *Treatments:* Commercial; Literary; Popular

Handles literary and commercial nonfiction and fiction for adults, young adults and children. Particularly interested in debut novels, biography, memoir, history, popular culture and humour. Works mainly by recommendation, but does also accept unsolicited approaches, by email only. Send synopsis, author bio, and sample chapter as Word attachment. No unsolicited mss or queries by phone. Handles TV and film scripts for existing clients, but no radio or theatre scripts. No poetry, fantasy, self-help or short stories.

The Sayle Literary Agency
1 Petersfield, Cambridge, CB1 1BB
Tel: +44 (0) 1223 303035
Email: info@sayleliteraryagency.com
Website: http://www. sayleliteraryagency.com

Handles: Fiction; Nonfiction; *Areas:* Biography; Crime; Current Affairs; Historical; Music; Science; Travel; *Markets:* Adult; *Treatments:* Literary

Note: Not accepting new manuscripts as at July 2018. See website for current status.

Send query with CV, synopsis, and three sample chapters. No text books, technical, legal, medical, children's, plays, poetry, unsolicited MSS, or approaches by email. Do not include SAE as all material submitted is recycled. If no response after three months assume rejection.

Sayle Screen Ltd
11 Jubilee Place, London, SW3 3TD
Tel: +44 (0) 20 7823 3883
Email: info@saylescreen.com
Website: http://www.saylescreen.com

Handles: Scripts; *Areas:* Film; Radio; Theatre; TV; *Markets:* Adult

Only considers material which has been recommended by a producer, development executive or course tutor. In this case send query by email with cover letter and details of your referee to the relevant agent. Query only one agent at a time.

Sheil Land Associates Ltd
52 Doughty Street, London, WC1N 2LS
Tel: +44 (0) 20 7405 9351
Fax: +44 (0) 20 7831 2127
Email: info@sheilland.co.uk
Website: http://www.sheilland.co.uk

Handles: Fiction; Nonfiction; Scripts; *Areas:* Autobiography; Biography; Cookery; Crime; Drama; Fantasy; Film; Gardening; Historical; Humour; Lifestyle; Military; Mystery; Politics; Psychology; Radio; Romance; Science; Sci-Fi; Self-Help; Theatre; Thrillers; Travel; TV; Women's Interests; *Markets:* Adult; Children's; Youth; *Treatments:* Commercial; Contemporary; Literary

Send query with synopsis, CV, and first three chapters (or around 50 pages), by post addressed to "The Submissions Dept", or by email. If posting mss, do not send only copy as submissions are recycled and responses sent by email. If you require response by post, include SAE.

Sheila Ableman Literary Agency

36 Duncan House, Fellows Road, London, NW3 3LZ
Tel: +44 (0) 20 7586 2339
Email: sheila@sheilaableman.co.uk
Website: http://www.sheilaableman.com

Handles: Nonfiction; *Areas:* Autobiography; Biography; Historical; Science; TV; *Markets:* Adult; *Treatments:* Commercial; Popular

Not taking on new clients as at February 2017

Send query with SAE, brief bio, one-page synopsis, and two sample chapters. Specialises in popular history, science, biography, autobiography, general narrative and 'quirky' nonfiction with strong commercial appeal, TV tie-ins and celebrity ghost writing. No poetry, children's books, gardening, or sport.

Sophie Hicks Agency

60 Gray's Inn Road, London, WC1X 8AQ
Tel: +44 (0) 20 3735 8870
Email: submissions@sophiehicksagency.com
Website: http://www.sophiehicksagency.com

Handles: Fiction; Nonfiction; *Markets:* Adult; Children's; Youth

Welcomes submissions. Send query by email only with sample pages attached as Word or PDF documents. See website for full guidelines. No poetry or scripts for theatre, film or television, and not currently accepting illustrated books for children.

Standen Literary Agency

12 Tetherdown, London, N10 1NB
Tel: +44 (0) 20 8245 2606
Fax: +44 (0) 20 8245 2606
Email: yasmin@standenliteraryagency.com
Website: http://www.standenliteraryagency.com

Handles: Fiction; Nonfiction; *Markets:* Adult; Children's; Youth; *Treatments:* Commercial; Literary

Based in London. For fiction, send synopsis and first three chapters by email only. No picture books. Responds if interested only. If no response in 6 weeks assume rejection. For nonfiction, query in first instance.

Susanna Lea Associates (UK)

55 Monmouth Street, London, WC2H 9DG
Tel: +44 (0) 20 7287 7757
Fax: +44 (0) 20 7287 7775
Email: london@susannalea.com
Website: http://www.susannalea.com

Handles: Fiction; Nonfiction; *Markets:* Adult

Literary agency with offices in Paris, London, and New York. Always on the lookout for exciting new talent. No poetry, plays, screen plays, science fiction, educational text books, short stories or illustrated works. No queries by fax or post. Accepts queries by email only. Include cover letter, synopsis, and first three chapters or proposal. Response not guaranteed.

The Susijn Agency

820 Harrow Road, London, NW10 5JU
Tel: +44 (0) 20 8968 7435
Email: submissions@thesusijnagency.com
Website: http://www.thesusijnagency.com

Handles: Fiction; Nonfiction; *Markets:* Adult; *Treatments:* Literary

Send query with synopsis and three sample chapters only by post or by email. Include SASE if return of material required. Response in 8-10 weeks. Specialises in selling rights worldwide and also represents non-English language authors and publishers for US, UK, and translation rights worldwide. No self-help, science-fiction, fantasy, romance, children's, illustrated, business, screenplays, or theatre plays.

SYLA – Susan Yearwood Literary Agency

2 Knebworth House, Londesborough Road, Stoke Newington, London N16 8RL
Tel: +44 (0) 20 7503 0954
Email: submissions@susanyearwood.com
Website: http://www.susanyearwood.com

Handles: Fiction; Nonfiction; *Areas:* Autobiography; Biography; Business; Crime; Lifestyle; Psychology; Thrillers; Women's Interests; *Markets:* Adult; Children's; Youth; *Treatments:* Commercial; Literary; Popular

Send query by email, including synopsis and sample thirty pages (fiction) or ten pages (nonfiction) in one Word file attachment. No poetry or screenwriting, or submissions by post.

The Tennyson Agency

109 Tennyson Avenue, New Malden, Surrey KT3 6NA
Tel: +44 (0) 20 8543 5939
Email: agency@tenagy.co.uk
Website: http://www.tenagy.co.uk

Handles: Scripts; *Areas:* Drama; Film; Radio; Theatre; TV; *Markets:* Adult

Mainly deals in scripts for film, TV, theatre, and radio, along with related material on an ad-hoc basis. Handles writers in the European Union only. Send query with CV and outline of work. Prefers queries by email. No nonfiction, poetry, short stories, science fiction and fantasy or children's writing, or unsolicited MSS.

Teresa Chris Literary Agency Ltd

43 Musard Road, London, W6 8NR
Tel: +44 (0) 20 7386 0633
Email: teresachris@litagency.co.uk
Website: http://www.
teresachrisliteraryagency.co.uk

Handles: Fiction; Nonfiction; *Areas:* Biography; Cookery; Crafts; Crime; Gardening; Historical; Lifestyle; Women's Interests; *Markets:* Adult; *Treatments:* Commercial; Literary

Welcomes submissions. Overseas authors may approach by email, otherwise hard copy submissions preferred. For fiction, send query with SAE, first three chapters, and one-page synopsis. For nonfiction, send overview with two sample chapters. Specialises in crime fiction and commercial women's fiction. No poetry, short stories, fantasy, science fiction, horror, children's fiction or young adult.

Tibor Jones & Associates

PO Box 74604, London, SW2 9NH
Email: enquiries@tiborjones.com
Website: http://www.tiborjones.com

Handles: Fiction; Nonfiction; *Areas:* Autobiography; Biography; Culture; Literature; Music; *Markets:* Adult; *Treatments:* Commercial; Literary

Welcomes fiction and nonfiction proposals from writers who are looking to publish something different. Send query by email giving details about you and your writing background, with one-page synopsis and first five pages of the novel/proposal.

Toby Mundy Associates Ltd

38 Berkeley Square, London, W1J 5AE
Tel: +44 (0) 20 3713 0067
Email: submissions@tma-agency.com
Website: http://tma-agency.com

Handles: Fiction; Nonfiction; *Areas:* Autobiography; Biography; Crime; Current Affairs; Historical; Politics; Science; Thrillers; *Markets:* Adult; *Treatments:* Literary

Send query by email with brief synopsis, first chapter, and a note about yourself, all pasted into the body of the email. No poetry, plays, short stories, science fiction, horror, attachments or hard copy submissions.

Lavinia Trevor Agency

29 Addison Place, London, W11 4RJ
Tel: +44 (0) 20 7603 0895
Email: info@laviniatrevor.co.uk
Website: http://www.laviniatrevor.co.uk

Handles: Fiction; Nonfiction; *Areas:* Science; *Markets:* Adult; *Treatments:* Commercial; Literary

Does not handle poetry, children's, technical, academic, fantasy, science fiction, or scripts. No unsolicited material.

Uli Rushby-Smith Literary Agency

72 Plimsoll Road, London, N4 2EE
Tel: +44 (0) 20 7354 2718
Email: uli.rushby-smith@btconnect.com

Handles: Fiction; Nonfiction; *Markets:* Adult; *Treatments:* Commercial; Literary

Send query with SAE, outline, and two or three sample chapters. Film and TV rights handled in conjunction with a sub-agent. No disks, poetry, picture books, films, or plays.

United Agents

12–26 Lexington Street, London, W1F 0LE
Tel: +44 (0) 20 3214 0800
Fax: +44 (0) 20 3214 0801
Email: info@unitedagents.co.uk
Website: http://unitedagents.co.uk

Handles: Fiction; Nonfiction; Scripts; *Areas:* Biography; Film; Radio; Theatre; TV; *Markets:* Adult; Children's; Youth

Do not approach the book department generally. Consult website and view details of each agent before selecting a specific agent to approach personally. Accepts submissions by email only. Submissions by post will not be returned or responded to.

Valerie Hoskins Associates

20 Charlotte Street, London, W1T 2NA
Tel: +44 (0) 20 7637 4490
Email: info@vhassociates.co.uk
Website: http://www.vhassociates.co.uk

Handles: Scripts; *Areas:* Film; Radio; TV; *Markets:* Adult

Always on the lookout for screenwriters with an original voice and creatives with big ideas. Query by email or by phone. Allow up to eight weeks for response to submissions.

The Viney Shaw Agency

23 Erlanger Road, Telegraph Hill, London, SE14 5TF
Tel: +44 (0) 20 7732 3331
Email: charlie@thevineyagency.com
Website: http://www. thevineyshawagency.com

Handles: Fiction; Nonfiction; *Markets:* Adult; Children's

Handles high quality nonfiction, and adult and children's fiction. See website for examples of the kinds of books represented. Send query by first or second class post to

one of the postal addresses shown on the website.

Wade & Co Literary Agency

33 Cormorant Lodge, Thomas More Street, London, E1W 1AU
Tel: +44 (0) 20 7488 4171
Fax: +44 (0) 20 7488 4172
Email: rw@rwla.com
Website: http://www.rwla.com

Handles: Fiction; Nonfiction; *Markets:* Adult; Youth

New full-length proposals for adult and young adult fiction and nonfiction always welcome. Send query with detailed 1–6 page synopsis, brief biography, and first 10,000 words via email as Word documents (.doc) or PDF; or by post with SAE if return required. We much prefer to correspond by email. Actively seeking new writers across the literary spectrum. No poetry, children's, short stories, scripts or plays.

Watson, Little Ltd

Suite 315, ScreenWorks, 22 Highbury Grove, London, N5 2ER
Tel: +44 (0) 20 7388 7529
Email: submissions@watsonlittle.com
Website: http://www.watsonlittle.com

Handles: Fiction; Nonfiction; *Areas:* Business; Crime; Film; Historical; Humour; Leisure; Music; Psychology; Science; Self-Help; Sport; Technology; Women's Interests; *Markets:* Adult; Children's; Youth; *Treatments:* Commercial; Literary; Popular

Send query by email only with synopsis and sample material, addressed to a specific agent. See website for full guidelines and details of specific agents. No scripts, poetry, or unsolicited MSS.

Whispering Buffalo Literary Agency Ltd

97 Chesson Road, London, W14 9QS
Tel: +44 (0) 20 7565 4737
Email: info@whisperingbuffalo.com
Website: http://www.whisperingbuffalo.com

Handles: Fiction; Nonfiction; *Areas:* Adventure; Anthropology; Arts;

Autobiography; Beauty and Fashion; Design; Entertainment; Film; Health; Humour; Lifestyle; Music; Nature; Politics; Romance; Sci-Fi; Self-Help; Thrillers; *Markets:* Adult; Children's; Youth; *Treatments:* Commercial; Literary

Handles commercial/literary fiction/nonfiction and children's/YA fiction with special interest in book to film adaptations. No TV, film, radio or theatre scripts, or poetry or academic. Accepts submissions by email only. For fiction, send query with CV, synopsis, and first three chapters. For nonfiction, send proposal and sample chapter. Response only if interested. Aims to respond within 6-8 weeks.

William Morris Endeavor (WME) London

100 New Oxford Street, London, WC1A 1HB
Tel: +44 (0) 20 7534 6800
Fax: +44 (0) 20 7534 6900
Email: ldnsubmissions@
wmeentertainment.com
Website: http://www.wmeentertainment.com

Handles: Fiction; Nonfiction; *Areas:* Autobiography; Biography; Crime; Culture; Historical; Thrillers; *Markets:* Adult; Youth; *Treatments:* Commercial; Literary

London office of a worldwide theatrical and literary agency, with offices in New York, Beverly Hills, Nashville, Miami, and Shanghai, as well as associates in Sydney. Always on the lookout for exciting new work and welcomes submissions across all genres. Send query by email, using link on website. See website for full guidelines.

The Writers' Practice

6 Denmark Street, London, WC2H 8LX
Tel: +44 (0) 845 680 6578
Email: jemima@thewriterspractice.com
Website: http://www.thewriterspractice.com

Handles: Fiction; Nonfiction; *Markets:* Adult; *Treatments:* Commercial; Literary

Send query by email with for fiction a synopsis, brief bio, and first three chapters;

and for nonfiction a pitch, brief bio, chapter outline, and at least one sample chapter. Also offers consultancy services to writers.

The Wylie Agency (UK) Ltd

17 Bedford Square, London, WC2B 3JA
Tel: +44 (0) 20 7908 5900
Fax: +44 (0) 20 7908 5901
Email: mail@wylieagency.co.uk
Website: http://www.wylieagency.co.uk

Handles: Fiction; Nonfiction; *Markets:* Adult

Note: Not accepting unsolicited mss as at January 2017

Send query by post or email before submitting. All submissions must include adequate return postage. No scripts, children's books, or unsolicited MSS.

Zeno Agency Ltd

Primrose Hill Business Centre, 110 Gloucester Avenue, London, NW1 3LH
Tel: +44 (0) 20 7096 0927
Email: info@zenoagency.com
Website: http://zenoagency.com

Handles: Fiction; *Areas:* Crime; Fantasy; Historical; Horror; Sci-Fi; Thrillers; Women's Interests; *Markets:* Adult; Children's; Youth; *Treatments:* Commercial

Note: Closed to submissions as at September 2017. Check website for current status.

London-based literary agency specialising in Science Fiction, Fantasy, and Horror, but expanding into other areas such as crime, thrillers, women's fiction, and young adult fiction. Adult fiction must be at least 75,000 words and children's fiction should be at least 50,000 words. Send query by email with synopsis up to two pages, and first three chapters (or approximately 50 double-spaced pages) as attachments in .docx or .pdf format. No submissions by post.

Canadian Literary Agents

For the most up-to-date listings of these and hundreds of other literary agents, visit https://www.firstwriter.com/Agents

*To claim your **free** access to the site, please see the back of this book.*

K2 Literary

Toronto, Ontario
Tel: +1 (416) 910-1661
Website: https://k2literary.com

Handles: Fiction; Nonfiction; *Markets:* Adult; Children's

As at January 2018, considering submissions by referral only. See website for current status.

P.S. Literary Agency

20033-520 Kerr Street, Oakville, Ontario
L6K 3C7
Tel: +1 (416) 907-8325
Email: query@psliterary.com
Website: http://www.PSLiterary.com

Handles: Fiction; Nonfiction; *Areas:* Autobiography; Business; Cookery; Current Affairs; Design; Fantasy; Health; Historical; Humour; Lifestyle; Literature; Mystery; Nature; Photography; Politics; Psychology; Romance; Science; Sci-Fi; Sport; Suspense; Thrillers; Women's Interests; *Markets:* Adult; Children's; Youth; *Treatments:* Commercial; Contemporary; Literary; Mainstream; Popular

A literary agency representing both fiction and nonfiction for adults, young adults, and children. Does not handle poetry or screenplays. Send one-page query by email only. No attachments. See website for full submission guidelines and address query to the agent best matched to your work.

The Rights Factory

PO Box 499, Station C, Toronto, Ontario
M6J 3P6
Website: http://therightsfactory.com

Handles: Fiction; Nonfiction; *Areas:* Adventure; Autobiography; Biography; Business; Cookery; Crime; Culture; Fantasy; Health; Historical; Lifestyle; Mystery; Politics; Romance; Science; Sci-Fi; Spiritual; Sport; Thrillers; Travel; Women's Interests; *Markets:* Adult; Children's; Youth; *Treatments:* Commercial; Contemporary; Literary; Popular

Send first three chapters (fiction), proposal (nonfiction), or complete ms (picture books) via online submission form on website.

Westwood Creative Artists

94 Harbord Street, Toronto, Ontario M5S
1G6
Tel: +1 (416) 964-3302
Fax: +1 (416) 975-9209
Email: wca_office@wcaltd.com
Website: http://www.wcaltd.com

Handles: Fiction; Nonfiction; *Areas:* Autobiography; Biography; Current Affairs;

Historical; Mystery; Science; Thrillers;
Markets: Adult; Children's; Youth;
Treatments: Commercial; Literary

Send query by email with your credentials, a
synopsis, and short sample up to ten pages in
the body of the email. No attachments.

Irish Literary Agents

For the most up-to-date listings of these and hundreds of other literary agents, visit https://www.firstwriter.com/Agents

*To claim your **free** access to the site, please see the back of this book.*

Author Rights Agency

20 Victoria Road, Dublin, D06 DR02
Tel: +353 1 4922112
Email: submissions@
authorrightsagency.com
Website: http://www.authorrightsagency.com

Handles: Fiction; Nonfiction; *Areas:* Crime; Historical; *Markets:* Adult; Children's; Youth; *Treatments:* Contemporary; Literary

Currently concentrating on literary fiction and genre fiction of literary quality (particularly crime and Noir). Welcomes submissions in English, particularly from Ireland, UK, and the US. Send query by email only with synopsis, ideally one page long, and writing sample up to 10 pages or about 3,000 words, as a Word or RTF attachment. Do not include in the body of the email, or send full manuscripts. See website for full guidelines. No phone calls.

The Book Bureau Literary Agency

7 Duncairn Avenue, Bray, Co. Wicklow
Tel: +353 (0) 1276 4996
Fax: +353 (0) 1276 4834
Email: thebookbureau@oceanfree.net

Handles: Fiction; Nonfiction; *Areas:* Crime; Thrillers; Women's Interests; *Markets:* Adult; *Treatments:* Commercial; Literary

Handles mainly general and literary fiction, plus some nonfiction. Particularly interested in women's, crime, Irish novels, and thrillers. Send query by email (preferred) or by post with SAE, synopsis, and first three chapters. Prefers single line spacing. No poetry, children's, horror, or science fiction. Strong editorial support provided before submission to publishers.

Frank Fahy

5 Barna Village Centre, Seapoint, Galway
H91 DF24
Tel: +353 (0) 86 226 9330
Email: submissions@frank-fahy.com
Website: http://www.frank-fahy.com

Handles: Fiction; *Markets:* Adult; Youth

Handles adult and young adult fiction. No picture books, poetry, or nonfiction. Send query by email with author profile, synopsis, and first three chapters by email. No hard copy submissions.

Marianne Gunn O'Connor Literary Agency

Morrison Chambers, Suite 17, 32 Nassau Street, Dublin, D02 XW77
Tel: 353 1 677 9100
Fax: 353 1 677 9101
Email: mgoclitagency@eircom.net

Handles: Fiction; Nonfiction; *Areas:* Biography; Health; *Markets:* Adult; Children's; *Treatments:* Commercial; Literary

Send query with half-page synopsis by email.

The Lisa Richards Agency

108 Upper Leeson Street, Dublin, 4
Tel: +353 1 637 5000
Fax: +353 1 667 1256
Email: info@lisarichards.ie
Website: http://www.lisarichards.ie

Handles: Fiction; Nonfiction; Scripts; *Areas:* Autobiography; Biography; Culture; Historical; Humour; Lifestyle; Self-Help; Sport; Theatre; *Markets:* Adult; Children's; *Treatments:* Commercial; Literary; Popular

Send query by email or by post with SASE, including three or four sample chapters in the case of fiction, or proposal and sample chapter for nonfiction. No horror, science fiction, screenplays, or children's picture books.

The Rights Bureau

The Old Post Office, Kilmacanogue, Co Wicklow
Email: dominic@therightsbureau.ie
Website: http://www.therightsbureau.ie

Handles: Fiction; Nonfiction; *Areas:* Autobiography; Cookery; Historical; How-to; Self-Help; *Markets:* Children's; Youth

Specialises in nonfiction, though also represents some children's and young adult fiction. Accepts proposals for nonfiction projects only. These should be sent hard copy by post. See website for full guidelines. Sister company provides chargeable services to writers.

Literary Agents Subject Index

This section lists literary agents by their subject matter, with directions to the section of the book where the full listing can be found.

You can create your own customised lists of literary agents using different combinations of these subject areas, plus over a dozen other criteria, instantly online at https://www.firstwriter.com.

*To claim your **free** access to the site, please see the back of this book.*

Adventure

Alive Literary Agency (*US*)
Ambassador Speakers Bureau & Literary Agency (*US*)
Marcia Amsterdam Agency (*US*)
Antony Harwood Limited (*UK*)
The Bent Agency (*US*)
Bob Mecoy Creative Book Services (*US*)
BookStop Literary Agency, LLC (*US*)
Carolyn Jenks Agency (*US*)
Cherry Weiner Literary Agency (*US*)
Cine/Lit Representation (*US*)
Corvisiero Literary Agency (*US*)
D4EO Literary Agency (*US*)
DHH Literary Agency Ltd (*UK*)
Diamond Kahn and Woods (DKW) Literary Agency Ltd (*UK*)
Don Congdon Associates, Inc. (*US*)
Jim Donovan Literary (*US*)
The Dravis Agency, Inc. (*US*)
Dystel, Goderich & Bourret LLC (*US*)
Ethan Ellenberg Literary Agency (*US*)
The Feldstein Agency (*UK*)
Foundry Literary + Media (*US*)
The Gernert Company (*US*)
Hannigan Salky Getzler (HSG) Agency (*US*)
hhb agency ltd (*UK*)
Andrea Hurst Literary Management (*US*)
JYLA (Jason Yarn Literary Agency) (*US*)
LBA Books Ltd (*UK*)
The Literary Group International (*US*)
Maria Carvainis Agency, Inc. (*US*)
McIntosh & Otis, Inc (*US*)
Niad Management (*US*)
The Park Literary Group LLC (*US*)
Pavilion Literary Management (*US*)
Raines & Raines (*US*)
The Rights Factory (*Can*)
Robert Dudley Agency (*UK*)
Rocking Chair Books (*UK*)
The Ruppin Agency (*UK*)
Salkind Literary Agency (*US*)
Scovil Galen Ghosh Literary Agency, Inc. (*US*)
Stuart Krichevsky Literary Agency, Inc. (*US*)
TriadaUS Literary Agency, Inc. (*US*)
Trident Media Group, LLC (*US*)
The Unter Agency (*US*)
Victoria Sanders & Associates LLC (*US*)
Waxman Leavell Literary Agency (*US*)
Whispering Buffalo Literary Agency Ltd (*UK*)
The Zack Company, Inc (*US*)

Anthropology

Andrea Brown Literary Agency, Inc. (*US*)
Antony Harwood Limited (*UK*)
Carol Mann Agency (*US*)
Don Congdon Associates, Inc. (*US*)
Dystel, Goderich & Bourret LLC (*US*)
Hornfischer Literary Management, L.P. (*US*)
Larsen Pomada Literary Agents (*US*)
Linda Roghaar Literary Agency, Inc. (*US*)
The Literary Group International (*US*)
Lynne Rabinoff Agency (*US*)
The Ruppin Agency (*UK*)
Lynn Seligman, Literary Agent (*US*)
Whispering Buffalo Literary Agency Ltd (*UK*)

Antiques

Antony Harwood Limited (*UK*)
Corvisiero Literary Agency (*US*)

Jeanne Fredericks Literary Agency, Inc. (*US*)
The Ruppin Agency (*UK*)

Archaeology

Andrea Brown Literary Agency, Inc. (*US*)
Antony Harwood Limited (*UK*)
Carol Mann Agency (*US*)
Caroline Davidson Literary Agency (*UK*)
DHH Literary Agency Ltd (*UK*)
Diamond Kahn and Woods (DKW) Literary Agency Ltd (*UK*)
Don Congdon Associates, Inc. (*US*)
Dystel, Goderich & Bourret LLC (*US*)
Hornfischer Literary Management, L.P. (*US*)
Inklings Literary Agency, LLC (*US*)
Duncan McAra (*UK*)
Lynne Rabinoff Agency (*US*)
The Ruppin Agency (*UK*)

Architecture

Andrea Brown Literary Agency, Inc. (*US*)
Antony Harwood Limited (*UK*)
Carol Mann Agency (*US*)
Caroline Davidson Literary Agency (*UK*)
Corvisiero Literary Agency (*US*)
D4EO Literary Agency (*US*)
Larsen Pomada Literary Agents (*US*)
Duncan McAra (*UK*)
The Ruppin Agency (*UK*)
Marly Rusoff & Associates, Inc. (*US*)
The Spieler Agency (*US*)
Wm Clark Associates (*US*)

Arts

Andrea Brown Literary Agency, Inc. (*US*)
Antony Harwood Limited (*UK*)
Artellus Limited (*UK*)
Bob Mecoy Creative Book Services (*US*)
Brandt & Hochman Literary Agents, Inc. (*US*)
The Brattle Agency LLC (*US*)
Carol Mann Agency (*US*)
Caroline Davidson Literary Agency (*UK*)
Corvisiero Literary Agency (*US*)
The Cowles-Ryan Literary Agency (*US*)
Creative Authors Ltd (*UK*)
D4EO Literary Agency (*US*)
David Black Literary Agency (*US*)
DeFiore and Company (*US*)
Don Congdon Associates, Inc. (*US*)
Frances Kelly Agency (*UK*)
Georges Borchardt, Inc. (*US*)
The Gernert Company (*US*)
Inklings Literary Agency, LLC (*US*)
Jeanne Fredericks Literary Agency, Inc. (*US*)
Johnson & Alcock (*UK*)
Jonathan Pegg Literary Agency (*UK*)
L. Perkins Associates (*US*)
Larsen Pomada Literary Agents (*US*)
The Leshne Agency (*US*)
Levine Greenberg Rostan Literary Agency (*US*)
Limelight Management (*UK*)
Literary & Creative Artists Inc. (*US*)
MBA Literary Agents Ltd (*UK*)
Duncan McAra (*UK*)
McCormick Literary (*US*)
The Park Literary Group LLC (*US*)

Richford Becklow Literary Agency (*UK*)
Rocking Chair Books (*UK*)
Rupert Heath Literary Agency (*UK*)
The Ruppin Agency (*UK*)
Marly Rusoff & Associates, Inc. (*US*)
Salkind Literary Agency (*US*)
Sanford J. Greenburger Associates, Inc. (*US*)
Scovil Galen Ghosh Literary Agency, Inc. (*US*)
Lynn Seligman, Literary Agent (*US*)
The Stuart Agency (*US*)
Susan Rabiner, Literary Agent, Inc. (*US*)
Victoria Sanders & Associates LLC (*US*)
The Weingel-Fidel Agency (*US*)
Whispering Buffalo Literary Agency Ltd (*UK*)
Wm Clark Associates (*US*)

Autobiography

Aaron M. Priest Literary Agency (*US*)
Adler & Robin Books, Inc (*US*)
AHA Talent Ltd (*UK*)
The Ahearn Agency, Inc (*US*)
Alive Literary Agency (*US*)
Ambassador Speakers Bureau & Literary Agency (*US*)
The Ampersand Agency Ltd (*UK*)
The Anderson Literary Agency (*US*)
Andrea Brown Literary Agency, Inc. (*US*)
Andrew Lownie Literary Agency Ltd (*UK*)
The Angela Rinaldi Literary Agency (*US*)
Ann Rittenberg Literary Agency (*US*)
Antony Harwood Limited (*UK*)
Audrey A. Wolf Literary Agency (*US*)
The Authors Care Service ltd (*UK*)
Ayesha Pande Literary (*US*)
B.J. Robbins Literary Agency (*US*)
Baldi Agency (*US*)
The Bent Agency (*US*)
Betsy Amster Literary Enterprises (*US*)
Blake Friedmann Literary Agency Ltd (*UK*)
Bleecker Street Associates, Inc. (*US*)
Bob Mecoy Creative Book Services (*US*)
Brandt & Hochman Literary Agents, Inc. (*US*)
Bresnick Weil Literary Agency, LLC (*US*)
The Bright Literary Academy (*UK*)
Carol Mann Agency (*US*)
Caroline Sheldon Literary Agency (*UK*)
Carolyn Jenks Agency (*US*)
Chartwell (*UK*)
Chase Literary Agency (*US*)
Elyse Cheney Literary Associates, LLC (*US*)
Clare Hulton Literary Agency (*UK*)
Compass Talent (*US*)
Conville & Walsh Ltd (*UK*)
The Cowles-Ryan Literary Agency (*US*)
Creative Trust, Inc. (*US*)
Creative Authors Ltd (*UK*)
Richard Curtis Associates, Inc. (*US*)
Cynthia Cannell Literary Agency (*US*)
David Luxton Associates (*UK*)
David Black Literary Agency (*US*)
David Higham Associates Ltd (*UK*)
DHH Literary Agency Ltd (*UK*)
Dinah Wiener Ltd (*UK*)
The Doe Coover Agency (*US*)

Waxman Leavell Literary Agency (*US*)
The Weingel-Fidel Agency (*US*)
Wendy Sherman Associates, Inc. (*US*)
Westwood Creative Artists (*Can*)
Whispering Buffalo Literary Agency Ltd (*UK*)
William Morris Endeavor (WME) London (*UK*)
Wm Clark Associates (*US*)
Writers' Representatives, LLC (*US*)
Writers House, LLC (*US*)
Yates & Yates (*US*)
The Zack Company, Inc (*US*)
Zoë Pagnamenta Agency, LLC (*US*)
Beauty and Fashion
Antony Harwood Limited (*UK*)
Artellus Limited (*UK*)
FinePrint Literary Management (*US*)
Fraser-Bub Literary, LLC (*US*)
The Knight Agency (*US*)
LAW (Lucas Alexander Whitley) (*UK*)
Levine Greenberg Rostan Literary Agency (*US*)
The LKG Agency (*US*)
Rosica Colin Ltd (*UK*)
Sterling Lord Literistic, Inc. (*US*)
2M Literary Agency Ltd (*US*)
Whispering Buffalo Literary Agency Ltd (*UK*)
Biography
A.M. Heath & Company Limited, Author's Agents (*UK*)
Aaron M. Priest Literary Agency (*US*)
Adler & Robin Books, Inc (*US*)
The Ahearn Agency, Inc (*US*)
Alive Literary Agency (*US*)
Ambassador Speakers Bureau & Literary Agency (*US*)
The Ampersand Agency Ltd (*UK*)
The Anderson Literary Agency (*US*)
Andrea Brown Literary Agency, Inc. (*US*)
Andrew Lownie Literary Agency Ltd (*UK*)
The Angela Rinaldi Literary Agency (*US*)
Ann Rittenberg Literary Agency (*US*)
Antony Harwood Limited (*UK*)
Arcadia (*US*)
Artellus Limited (*UK*)
Audrey A. Wolf Literary Agency (*US*)
Ayesha Pande Literary (*US*)
B.J. Robbins Literary Agency (*US*)
Baldi Agency (*US*)
Bell Lomax Moreton Agency (*UK*)
Betsy Amster Literary Enterprises (*US*)
Vicky Bijur Literary Agency (*US*)
Blake Friedmann Literary Agency Ltd (*UK*)
Bleecker Street Associates, Inc. (*US*)
Bob Mecoy Creative Book Services (*US*)
Bresnick Weil Literary Agency, LLC (*US*)
Carol Mann Agency (*US*)
Caroline Davidson Literary Agency (*UK*)
Carolyn Jenks Agency (*US*)
Chartwell (*UK*)
Elyse Cheney Literary Associates, LLC (*US*)
Cine/Lit Representation (*US*)
Conville & Walsh Ltd (*UK*)
Coombs Moylett & Maclean Literary Agency (*UK*)

The Cowles-Ryan Literary Agency (*US*)
Creative Authors Ltd (*UK*)
Curtis Brown Group Ltd (*UK*)
Richard Curtis Associates, Inc. (*US*)
Cynthia Cannell Literary Agency (*US*)
D4EO Literary Agency (*US*)
David Luxton Associates (*UK*)
David Black Literary Agency (*US*)
David Higham Associates Ltd (*UK*)
DeFiore and Company (*US*)
DHH Literary Agency Ltd (*UK*)
Diamond Kahn and Woods (DKW) Literary Agency Ltd (*UK*)
Dinah Wiener Ltd (*UK*)
The Doe Coover Agency (*US*)
Don Congdon Associates, Inc. (*US*)
Jim Donovan Literary (*US*)
Dunham Literary, Inc. (*US*)
Dystel, Goderich & Bourret LLC (*US*)
E. J. McCarthy Agency (*US*)
Edwards Fuglewicz (*UK*)
Elise Dillsworth Agency (EDA) (*UK*)
Emily Sweet Associates (*UK*)
Ethan Ellenberg Literary Agency (*US*)
The Feldstein Agency (*UK*)
Felicity Bryan Associates (*UK*)
FinePrint Literary Management (*US*)
Fletcher & Company (*US*)
Foundry Literary + Media (*US*)
Fox Literary (*US*)
Fox & Howard Literary Agency (*UK*)
Frances Collin Literary Agent (*US*)
Frances Kelly Agency (*UK*)
Furniss Lawton (*UK*)
The G Agency, LLC (*US*)
Georges Borchardt, Inc. (*US*)
Georgina Capel Associates Ltd (*UK*)
The Gernert Company (*US*)
Gina Maccoby Agency (*US*)
Glass Literary Management LLC (*US*)
Greene & Heaton Ltd (*UK*)
Marianne Gunn O'Connor Literary Agency (*Ire*)
Joy Harris Literary Agency, Inc. (*US*)
hhb agency ltd (*UK*)
Hill Nadell Literary Agency (*US*)
Hornfischer Literary Management, L.P. (*US*)
J de S Associates Inc. (*US*)
Jane Judd Literary Agency (*UK*)
Jane Turnbull (*UK*)
Jeanne Fredericks Literary Agency, Inc. (*US*)
Jenny Brown Associates (*UK*)
Jill Grinberg Literary Management LLC (*US*)
John Hawkins & Associates, Inc. (*US*)
Johnson & Alcock (*UK*)
Jonathan Pegg Literary Agency (*UK*)
Kathi J. Paton Literary Agency (*US*)
Kimberley Cameron & Associates (*US*)
Knight Features (*UK*)
Linda Konner Literary Agency (*US*)
Barbara S. Kouts, Literary Agent (*US*)
L. Perkins Associates (*US*)
Larsen Pomada Literary Agents (*US*)
Laura Dail Literary Agency (*US*)

LAW (Lucas Alexander Whitley) (*UK*)
Lawrence Jordan Literary Agency (*US*)
Sarah Lazin Books (*US*)
Levine Greenberg Rostan Literary Agency (*US*)
Limelight Management (*UK*)
Linda Roghaar Literary Agency, Inc. (*US*)
The Lisa Richards Agency (*Ire*)
Literary & Creative Artists Inc. (*US*)
The Literary Group International (*US*)
MacGregor Literary (*US*)
Maggie Pearlstine Associates Ltd (*UK*)
Manus & Associates Literary Agency, Inc. (*US*)
Maria Carvainis Agency, Inc. (*US*)
Marsal Lyon Literary Agency LLC (*US*)
Martin Literary Management (*US*)
Massie & McQuilkin (*US*)
Max Gartenburg Literary Agency (*US*)
MBA Literary Agents Ltd (*UK*)
Duncan McAra (*UK*)
Margret McBride Literary Agency (*US*)
McCormick Literary (*US*)
Howard Morhaim Literary Agency (*US*)
Mulcahy Associates (Part of MMB Creative) (*UK*)
Niad Management (*US*)
MNLA (Maggie Noach Literary Agency) (*UK*)
Northern Lights Literary Services (*US*)
Puttick Literary Agency (*UK*)
Lynne Rabinoff Agency (*US*)
Raines & Raines (*US*)
Regal Hoffmann & Associates LLC (*US*)
The Amy Rennert Agency, Inc. (*US*)
Richard Henshaw Group LLC (*US*)
Richford Becklow Literary Agency (*UK*)
The Rights Factory (*Can*)
RLR Associates (*US*)
Robert Dudley Agency (*UK*)
Robin Straus Agency, Inc. (*US*)
Rosica Colin Ltd (*UK*)
Ross Yoon Agency (*US*)
The Rudy Agency (*US*)
Rupert Heath Literary Agency (*UK*)
The Ruppin Agency (*UK*)
Marly Rusoff & Associates, Inc. (*US*)
The Sagalyn Literary Agency (*US*)
Salkind Literary Agency (*US*)
Sandra Dijkstra Literary Agency (*US*)
Sanford J. Greenburger Associates, Inc. (*US*)
Sarah Such Literary Agency (*UK*)
The Sayle Literary Agency (*UK*)
Scovil Galen Ghosh Literary Agency, Inc. (*US*)
Lynn Seligman, Literary Agent (*US*)
Sheil Land Associates Ltd (*UK*)
Sheila Ableman Literary Agency (*UK*)
Sheree Bykofsky Associates, Inc. (*US*)
Signature Literary Agency (*US*)
The Spieler Agency (*US*)
Philip G. Spitzer Literary Agency, Inc. (*US*)
Sterling Lord Literistic, Inc. (*US*)
Stuart Krichevsky Literary Agency, Inc. (*US*)
SYLA – Susan Yearwood Literary Agency (*UK*)
Teresa Chris Literary Agency Ltd (*UK*)
Tessler Literary Agency (*US*)

Tibor Jones & Associates (*UK*)
Toby Mundy Associates Ltd (*UK*)
Tracy Brown Literary Agency (*US*)
TriadaUS Literary Agency, Inc. (*US*)
Trident Media Group, LLC (*US*)
United Agents (*UK*)
The Unter Agency (*US*)
Victoria Sanders & Associates LLC (*US*)
Watkins / Loomis Agency, Inc. (*US*)
Waxman Leavell Literary Agency (*US*)
The Weingel-Fidel Agency (*US*)
Wendy Sherman Associates, Inc. (*US*)
Westwood Creative Artists (*Can*)
William Morris Endeavor (WME) London (*UK*)
Wm Clark Associates (*US*)
Writers' Representatives, LLC (*US*)
Writers House, LLC (*US*)
Yates & Yates (*US*)
The Zack Company, Inc (*US*)
Zoë Pagnamenta Agency, LLC (*US*)
Business
Alive Literary Agency (*US*)
The Angela Rinaldi Literary Agency (*US*)
Antony Harwood Limited (*UK*)
Audrey A. Wolf Literary Agency (*US*)
The Authors Care Service ltd (*UK*)
Baldi Agency (*US*)
Bell Lomax Moreton Agency (*UK*)
Bleecker Street Associates, Inc. (*US*)
Bob Mecoy Creative Book Services (*US*)
Bond Literary Agency (*US*)
Carol Mann Agency (*US*)
Elyse Cheney Literary Associates, LLC (*US*)
Creative Authors Ltd (*UK*)
Creative Media Agency (*US*)
Richard Curtis Associates, Inc. (*US*)
D4EO Literary Agency (*US*)
David Black Literary Agency (*US*)
The Doe Coover Agency (*US*)
Jim Donovan Literary (*US*)
Doug Grad Literary Agency (*US*)
Dystel, Goderich & Bourret LLC (*US*)
The Feldstein Agency (*UK*)
FinePrint Literary Management (*US*)
Fletcher & Company (*US*)
Folio Literary Management, LLC (*US*)
Foundry Literary + Media (*US*)
Fox & Howard Literary Agency (*UK*)
Frances Kelly Agency (*UK*)
Furniss Lawton (*UK*)
The G Agency, LLC (*US*)
Glass Literary Management LLC (*US*)
Grace Freedson's Publishing Network (*US*)
Graham Maw Christie Literary Agency (*UK*)
Hannigan Salky Getzler (HSG) Agency (*US*)
hhb agency ltd (*UK*)
Hornfischer Literary Management, L.P. (*US*)
Andrea Hurst Literary Management (*US*)
J de S Associates Inc. (*US*)
Jeanne Fredericks Literary Agency, Inc. (*US*)
Jill Grinberg Literary Management LLC (*US*)
John Hawkins & Associates, Inc. (*US*)
Kate Hordern Literary Agency (*UK*)

McCormick Literary (*US*)
Howard Morhaim Literary Agency (*US*)
P.S. Literary Agency (*Can*)
Peters Fraser + Dunlop (*UK*)
Queen Literary Agency, Inc. (*US*)
Richford Becklow Literary Agency (*UK*)
The Rights Bureau (*Ire*)
The Rights Factory (*Can*)
Rita Rosenkranz Literary Agency (*US*)
Robin Straus Agency, Inc. (*US*)
Rosica Colin Ltd (*UK*)
Salkind Literary Agency (*US*)
Sandra Dijkstra Literary Agency (*US*)
Scovil Galen Ghosh Literary Agency, Inc. (*US*)
Lynn Seligman, Literary Agent (*US*)
Sheil Land Associates Ltd (*UK*)
Sheree Bykofsky Associates, Inc. (*US*)
The Spieler Agency (*US*)
Sterling Lord Literistic, Inc. (*US*)
Talcott Notch Literary (*US*)
Teresa Chris Literary Agency Ltd (*UK*)
Tessler Literary Agency (*US*)
TriadaUS Literary Agency, Inc. (*US*)
2M Literary Agency Ltd (*US*)
Union Literary (*US*)
The Unter Agency (*US*)
Upstart Crow Literary (*US*)
Waxman Leavell Literary Agency (*US*)
Wendy Sherman Associates, Inc. (*US*)
Writers' Representatives, LLC (*US*)
Writers House, LLC (*US*)
The Zack Company, Inc (*US*)

Crafts
Antony Harwood Limited (*UK*)
Creative Authors Ltd (*UK*)
David Black Literary Agency (*US*)
The Gernert Company (*US*)
Grace Freedson's Publishing Network (*US*)
Graham Maw Christie Literary Agency (*UK*)
Hannigan Salky Getzler (HSG) Agency (*US*)
Jeanne Fredericks Literary Agency, Inc. (*US*)
The Leshne Agency (*US*)
Levine Greenberg Rostan Literary Agency (*US*)
Limelight Management (*UK*)
Linda Roghaar Literary Agency, Inc. (*US*)
MBA Literary Agents Ltd (*UK*)
Howard Morhaim Literary Agency (*US*)
Salkind Literary Agency (*US*)
Talcott Notch Literary (*US*)
Teresa Chris Literary Agency Ltd (*UK*)
TriadaUS Literary Agency, Inc. (*US*)

Crime
A.M. Heath & Company Limited, Author's
Agents (*UK*)
Aaron M. Priest Literary Agency (*US*)
The Ahearn Agency, Inc (*US*)
Alive Literary Agency (*US*)
The Ampersand Agency Ltd (*UK*)
Marcia Amsterdam Agency (*US*)
The Anderson Literary Agency (*US*)
Andrew Lownie Literary Agency Ltd (*UK*)
Andrew Mann Ltd (*UK*)
Antony Harwood Limited (*UK*)

Artellus Limited (*UK*)
Author Rights Agency (*Ire*)
The Axelrod Agency (*US*)
Ayesha Pande Literary (*US*)
The Bent Agency (*US*)
Blake Friedmann Literary Agency Ltd (*UK*)
Bleecker Street Associates, Inc. (*US*)
Bob Mecoy Creative Book Services (*US*)
Bond Literary Agency (*US*)
The Book Bureau Literary Agency (*Ire*)
Bresnick Weil Literary Agency, LLC (*US*)
Carolyn Jenks Agency (*US*)
Chartwell (*UK*)
Mic Cheetham Literary Agency (*UK*)
Cherry Weiner Literary Agency (*US*)
Conville & Walsh Ltd (*UK*)
Coombs Moylett & Maclean Literary Agency
(*UK*)
Creative Authors Ltd (*UK*)
Curtis Brown Group Ltd (*UK*)
D4EO Literary Agency (*US*)
The Darley Anderson Agency (*UK*)
David Higham Associates Ltd (*UK*)
DHH Literary Agency Ltd (*UK*)
Diamond Kahn and Woods (DKW) Literary
Agency Ltd (*UK*)
Don Congdon Associates, Inc. (*US*)
Jim Donovan Literary (*US*)
The Dravis Agency, Inc. (*US*)
Dystel, Goderich & Bourret LLC (*US*)
Edwards Fuglewicz (*UK*)
Ethan Ellenberg Literary Agency (*US*)
The Feldstein Agency (*UK*)
FinePrint Literary Management (*US*)
Fletcher & Company (*US*)
Folio Literary Management, LLC (*US*)
Fraser-Bub Literary, LLC (*US*)
Furniss Lawton (*UK*)
The Gernert Company (*US*)
Grace Freedson's Publishing Network (*US*)
Greene & Heaton Ltd (*UK*)
Gregory & Company, Authors' Agents (*UK*)
Hardman & Swainson (*UK*)
hhb agency ltd (*UK*)
Holloway Literary (*US*)
Hornfischer Literary Management, L.P. (*US*)
Hudson Agency (*US*)
Andrea Hurst Literary Management (*US*)
J de S Associates Inc. (*US*)
Jenny Brown Associates (*UK*)
Jill Corcoran Literary Agency (*US*)
Jill Grosjean Literary Agency (*US*)
John Hawkins & Associates, Inc. (*US*)
Johnson & Alcock (*UK*)
Judith Murdoch Literary Agency (*UK*)
Juliet Burton Literary Agency (*UK*)
Kate Hordern Literary Agency (*UK*)
Keane Kataria Literary Agency (*UK*)
The Knight Agency (*US*)
Barbara S. Kouts, Literary Agent (*US*)
L. Perkins Associates (*US*)
Larsen Pomada Literary Agents (*US*)
Laura Dail Literary Agency (*US*)

Larsen Pomada Literary Agents (*US*)
Laura Dail Literary Agency (*US*)
LAW (Lucas Alexander Whitley) (*UK*)
Sarah Lazin Books (*US*)
The Leshne Agency (*US*)
Levine Greenberg Rostan Literary Agency (*US*)
Linda Roghaar Literary Agency, Inc. (*US*)
The Lisa Richards Agency (*Ire*)
The Literary Group International (*US*)
MacGregor Literary (*US*)
Manus & Associates Literary Agency, Inc. (*US*)
Maria Carvainis Agency, Inc. (*US*)
Marsal Lyon Literary Agency LLC (*US*)
Martin Literary Management (*US*)
Massie & McQuilkin (*US*)
Max Gartenburg Literary Agency (*US*)
Margret McBride Literary Agency (*US*)
McCormick Literary (*US*)
McIntosh & Otis, Inc (*US*)
Howard Morhaim Literary Agency (*US*)
Nappaland Literary Agency (*US*)
New Leaf Literary & Media, Inc. (*US*)
Niad Management (*US*)
The Park Literary Group LLC (*US*)
Peters Fraser + Dunlop (*UK*)
Publication Riot Group, Inc. (*US*)
The Purcell Agency, LLC (*US*)
Puttick Literary Agency (*UK*)
Lynne Rabinoff Agency (*US*)
Richard Henshaw Group LLC (*US*)
The Rights Factory (*Can*)
RLR Associates (*US*)
Robin Straus Agency, Inc. (*US*)
Rocking Chair Books (*UK*)
Andy Ross Agency (*US*)
Ross Yoon Agency (*US*)
The Rudy Agency (*US*)
Rupert Heath Literary Agency (*UK*)
The Ruppin Agency (*UK*)
Marly Rusoff & Associates, Inc. (*US*)
The Sagalyn Literary Agency (*US*)
Salkind Literary Agency (*US*)
Sandra Dijkstra Literary Agency (*US*)
Sarah Such Literary Agency (*UK*)
Scovil Galen Ghosh Literary Agency, Inc. (*US*)
Lynn Seligman, Literary Agent (*US*)
Sheree Bykofsky Associates, Inc. (*US*)
Signature Literary Agency (*US*)
Solow Literary Enterprises, Inc. (*US*)
Speilburg Literary Agency (*US*)
The Spieler Agency (*US*)
Stephanie Tade Literary Agency (*US*)
Sterling Lord Literistic, Inc. (*US*)
Stuart Krichevsky Literary Agency, Inc. (*US*)
The Stuart Agency (*US*)
Tessler Literary Agency (*US*)
Tibor Jones & Associates (*UK*)
TriadaUS Literary Agency, Inc. (*US*)
Trident Media Group, LLC (*US*)
2M Literary Agency Ltd (*US*)
The Unter Agency (*US*)
Veritas Literary Agency (*US*)
Victoria Sanders & Associates LLC (*US*)

Watkins / Loomis Agency, Inc. (*US*)
Wendy Sherman Associates, Inc. (*US*)
William Morris Endeavor (WME) London (*UK*)
Wm Clark Associates (*US*)
The Zack Company, Inc (*US*)
Current Affairs
Aaron M. Priest Literary Agency (*US*)
The Ahearn Agency, Inc (*US*)
Ambassador Speakers Bureau & Literary
Agency (*US*)
The Ampersand Agency Ltd (*UK*)
Andrea Brown Literary Agency, Inc. (*US*)
Andrew Lownie Literary Agency Ltd (*UK*)
The Angela Rinaldi Literary Agency (*US*)
Antony Harwood Limited (*UK*)
Arcadia (*US*)
Artellus Limited (*UK*)
Audrey A. Wolf Literary Agency (*US*)
Blake Friedmann Literary Agency Ltd (*UK*)
Bleecker Street Associates, Inc. (*US*)
Bob Mecoy Creative Book Services (*US*)
Brandt & Hochman Literary Agents, Inc. (*US*)
Carol Mann Agency (*US*)
Elyse Cheney Literary Associates, LLC (*US*)
Conville & Walsh Ltd (*UK*)
Coombs Moylett & Maclean Literary Agency
(*UK*)
The Cowles-Ryan Literary Agency (*US*)
Cynthia Cannell Literary Agency (*US*)
D4EO Literary Agency (*US*)
David Black Literary Agency (*US*)
David Higham Associates Ltd (*UK*)
DeFiore and Company (*US*)
The Doe Coover Agency (*US*)
Don Congdon Associates, Inc. (*US*)
Jim Donovan Literary (*US*)
Dunham Literary, Inc. (*US*)
Dystel, Goderich & Bourret LLC (*US*)
Emily Sweet Associates (*UK*)
Ethan Ellenberg Literary Agency (*US*)
The Feldstein Agency (*UK*)
Felicity Bryan Associates (*UK*)
Fletcher & Company (*US*)
Foundry Literary + Media (*US*)
Gelfman Schneider / ICM Partners (*US*)
Georges Borchardt, Inc. (*US*)
The Gernert Company (*US*)
Gina Maccoby Agency (*US*)
Grace Freedson's Publishing Network (*US*)
Greene & Heaton Ltd (*UK*)
Hannigan Salky Getzler (HSG) Agency (*US*)
Hill Nadell Literary Agency (*US*)
Hornfischer Literary Management, L.P. (*US*)
Andrea Hurst Literary Management (*US*)
J de S Associates Inc. (*US*)
Jane Turnbull (*UK*)
Jill Grinberg Literary Management LLC (*US*)
John Hawkins & Associates, Inc. (*US*)
Johnson & Alcock (*UK*)
Jonathan Pegg Literary Agency (*UK*)
Joëlle Delbourgo Associates, Inc. (*US*)
JYLA (Jason Yarn Literary Agency) (*US*)
Kate Hordern Literary Agency (*UK*)

Kathi J. Paton Literary Agency (*US*)
Kimberley Cameron & Associates (*US*)
Barbara S. Kouts, Literary Agent (*US*)
Larsen Pomada Literary Agents (*US*)
Laura Dail Literary Agency (*US*)
LAW (Lucas Alexander Whitley) (*UK*)
Sarah Lazin Books (*US*)
Literary & Creative Artists Inc. (*US*)
MacGregor Literary (*US*)
Maggie Pearlstine Associates Ltd (*UK*)
Manus & Associates Literary Agency, Inc. (*US*)
Marsal Lyon Literary Agency LLC (*US*)
Martin Literary Management (*US*)
Massie & McQuilkin (*US*)
Max Gartenburg Literary Agency (*US*)
McIntosh & Otis, Inc (*US*)
Northbank Talent Management (*UK*)
P.S. Literary Agency (*Can*)
The Park Literary Group LLC (*US*)
Puttick Literary Agency (*UK*)
Lynne Rabinoff Agency (*US*)
Richard Henshaw Group LLC (*US*)
Robert Dudley Agency (*UK*)
Robin Straus Agency, Inc. (*US*)
Rocking Chair Books (*UK*)
Rosica Colin Ltd (*UK*)
Andy Ross Agency (*US*)
Ross Yoon Agency (*US*)
The Rudy Agency (*US*)
Rupert Heath Literary Agency (*UK*)
The Ruppin Agency (*UK*)
Salkind Literary Agency (*US*)
Sandra Dijkstra Literary Agency (*US*)
The Sayle Literary Agency (*UK*)
Lynn Seligman, Literary Agent (*US*)
Sheree Bykofsky Associates, Inc. (*US*)
The Spieler Agency (*US*)
Philip G. Spitzer Literary Agency, Inc. (*US*)
Sterling Lord Literistic, Inc. (*US*)
Stuart Krichevsky Literary Agency, Inc. (*US*)
The Stuart Agency (*US*)
Toby Mundy Associates Ltd (*UK*)
Tracy Brown Literary Agency (*US*)
TriadaUS Literary Agency, Inc. (*US*)
Trident Media Group, LLC (*US*)
Upstart Crow Literary (*US*)
Victoria Sanders & Associates LLC (*US*)
Watkins / Loomis Agency, Inc. (*US*)
Westwood Creative Artists (*Can*)
Wm Clark Associates (*US*)
Writers' Representatives, LLC (*US*)
Yates & Yates (*US*)
The Zack Company, Inc (*US*)

Design

Andrea Brown Literary Agency, Inc. (*US*)
Antony Harwood Limited (*UK*)
Carol Mann Agency (*US*)
Caroline Davidson Literary Agency (*UK*)
D4EO Literary Agency (*US*)
Fraser-Bub Literary, LLC (*US*)
Grace Freedson's Publishing Network (*US*)
Hannigan Salky Getzler (HSG) Agency (*US*)
Jeanne Fredericks Literary Agency, Inc. (*US*)

Johnson & Alcock (*UK*)
Larsen Pomada Literary Agents (*US*)
The LKG Agency (*US*)
Howard Morhaim Literary Agency (*US*)
P.S. Literary Agency (*Can*)
The Ruppin Agency (*UK*)
Marly Rusoff & Associates, Inc. (*US*)
Salkind Literary Agency (*US*)
Sandra Dijkstra Literary Agency (*US*)
Lynn Seligman, Literary Agent (*US*)
The Stuart Agency (*US*)
Whispering Buffalo Literary Agency Ltd (*UK*)
Wm Clark Associates (*US*)

Drama

Andrea Brown Literary Agency, Inc. (*US*)
Antony Harwood Limited (*UK*)
Cecily Ware Literary Agents (*UK*)
David Higham Associates Ltd (*UK*)
The Dravis Agency, Inc. (*US*)
Hudson Agency (*US*)
Jill Foster Ltd (JFL) (*UK*)
Knight Hall Agency (*UK*)
Literary & Creative Artists Inc. (*US*)
Niad Management (*US*)
Northbank Talent Management (*UK*)
Sheil Land Associates Ltd (*UK*)
The Tennyson Agency (*UK*)

Entertainment

Antony Harwood Limited (*UK*)
Artellus Limited (*UK*)
Bleecker Street Associates, Inc. (*US*)
The Bright Literary Academy (*UK*)
David Black Literary Agency (*US*)
Doug Grad Literary Agency (*US*)
FinePrint Literary Management (*US*)
Folio Literary Management, LLC (*US*)
Gina Maccoby Agency (*US*)
Glass Literary Management LLC (*US*)
Gunn Media Associates (*UK*)
hhb agency ltd (*UK*)
Jane Turnbull (*UK*)
Jill Grinberg Literary Management LLC (*US*)
The Knight Agency (*US*)
Linda Konner Literary Agency (*US*)
The LKG Agency (*US*)
Martin Literary Management (*US*)
New Leaf Literary & Media, Inc. (*US*)
Redhammer (*UK*)
Rocking Chair Books (*UK*)
The Ruppin Agency (*UK*)
Sanford J. Greenburger Associates, Inc. (*US*)
Susan Rabiner, Literary Agent, Inc. (*US*)
Wendy Sherman Associates, Inc. (*US*)
Whispering Buffalo Literary Agency Ltd (*UK*)

Erotic

Antony Harwood Limited (*UK*)
The Axelrod Agency (*US*)
Bleecker Street Associates, Inc. (*US*)
D4EO Literary Agency (*US*)
KT Literary (*US*)
L. Perkins Associates (*US*)
New Leaf Literary & Media, Inc. (*US*)
Rosica Colin Ltd (*UK*)

Spencerhill Associates (*US*)
Veritas Literary Agency (*US*)
The Zack Company, Inc (*US*)
Fantasy
Aaron M. Priest Literary Agency (*US*)
The Ampersand Agency Ltd (*UK*)
Andrea Brown Literary Agency, Inc. (*US*)
Andrew Lownie Literary Agency Ltd (*UK*)
Antony Harwood Limited (*UK*)
Aponte Literary (*US*)
Artellus Limited (*UK*)
Ayesha Pande Literary (*US*)
Azantian Literary Agency (*US*)
Baror International, Inc. (*US*)
The Bent Agency (*US*)
Bob Mecoy Creative Book Services (*US*)
Bond Literary Agency (*US*)
Book Cents Literary Agency (*US*)
BookStop Literary Agency, LLC (*US*)
Caroline Sheldon Literary Agency (*UK*)
Mic Cheetham Literary Agency (*UK*)
Cherry Weiner Literary Agency (*US*)
Conville & Walsh Ltd (*UK*)
Corvisiero Literary Agency (*US*)
Curtis Brown Group Ltd (*UK*)
Richard Curtis Associates, Inc. (*US*)
D4EO Literary Agency (*US*)
DHH Literary Agency Ltd (*UK*)
Diamond Kahn and Woods (DKW) Literary
Agency Ltd (*UK*)
Don Congdon Associates, Inc. (*US*)
Donaghy Literary Group (*US*)
Dunham Literary, Inc. (*US*)
Dystel, Goderich & Bourret LLC (*US*)
Emerald City Literary Agency (*US*)
Ethan Ellenberg Literary Agency (*US*)
FinePrint Literary Management (*US*)
Folio Literary Management, LLC (*US*)
Fox Literary (*US*)
Frances Collin Literary Agent (*US*)
The Gernert Company (*US*)
Greene & Heaton Ltd (*UK*)
Hudson Agency (*US*)
Andrea Hurst Literary Management (*US*)
Inklings Literary Agency, LLC (*US*)
Jill Grinberg Literary Management LLC (*US*)
Jill Corcoran Literary Agency (*US*)
John Hawkins & Associates, Inc. (*US*)
Johnson & Alcock (*UK*)
JYLA (Jason Yarn Literary Agency) (*US*)
Kimberley Cameron & Associates (*US*)
The Knight Agency (*US*)
KT Literary (*US*)
L. Perkins Associates (*US*)
Larsen Pomada Literary Agents (*US*)
Laura Dail Literary Agency (*US*)
LAW (Lucas Alexander Whitley) (*UK*)
LBA Books Ltd (*UK*)
Linn Prentis, Literary Agent (*US*)
The Literary Group International (*US*)
London Independent Books (*UK*)
Madeleine Milburn Literary, TV & Film Agency
(*UK*)

Massie & McQuilkin (*US*)
McIntosh & Otis, Inc (*US*)
Howard Morhaim Literary Agency (*US*)
New Leaf Literary & Media, Inc. (*US*)
Northbank Talent Management (*UK*)
P.S. Literary Agency (*Can*)
Pavilion Literary Management (*US*)
Raines & Raines (*US*)
Richard Henshaw Group LLC (*US*)
Richford Becklow Literary Agency (*UK*)
The Rights Factory (*Can*)
Rosica Colin Ltd (*UK*)
Salkind Literary Agency (*US*)
Sandra Dijkstra Literary Agency (*US*)
Sanford J. Greenburger Associates, Inc. (*US*)
Scribe Agency LLC (*US*)
Lynn Seligman, Literary Agent (*US*)
Sheil Land Associates Ltd (*UK*)
Signature Literary Agency (*US*)
Spectrum Literary Agency (*US*)
Speilburg Literary Agency (*US*)
Spencerhill Associates (*US*)
Philip G. Spitzer Literary Agency, Inc. (*US*)
The Stringer Literary Agency LLC (*US*)
Stuart Krichevsky Literary Agency, Inc. (*US*)
Talcott Notch Literary (*US*)
TriadaUS Literary Agency, Inc. (*US*)
Trident Media Group, LLC (*US*)
Upstart Crow Literary (*US*)
Veritas Literary Agency (*US*)
Victoria Sanders & Associates LLC (*US*)
Waxman Leavell Literary Agency (*US*)
Writers House, LLC (*US*)
The Zack Company, Inc (*US*)
Zeno Agency Ltd (*UK*)
Fiction
A for Authors (*UK*)
A & B Personal Management Ltd (*UK*)
A+B Works (*US*)
A.M. Heath & Company Limited, Author's
Agents (*UK*)
Aaron M. Priest Literary Agency (*US*)
Dominick Abel Literary Agency, Inc (*US*)
Abner Stein (*UK*)
Adams Literary (*US*)
Agency for the Performing Arts (APA) (*US*)
The Agency (London) Ltd (*UK*)
The Ahearn Agency, Inc (*US*)
Aimee Entertainment Agency (*US*)
Aitken Alexander Associates (*UK*)
Alive Literary Agency (*US*)
Ambassador Speakers Bureau & Literary
Agency (*US*)
The Ampersand Agency Ltd (*UK*)
Marcia Amsterdam Agency (*US*)
Darley Anderson Children's (*UK*)
Andlyn (*UK*)
Andrea Brown Literary Agency, Inc. (*US*)
Andrew Lownie Literary Agency Ltd (*UK*)
Andrew Mann Ltd (*UK*)
Andrew Nurnberg Associates, Ltd (*UK*)
The Angela Rinaldi Literary Agency (*US*)
Ann Rittenberg Literary Agency (*US*)

Claim your free access to www.firstwriter.com: See p.389

Anne Clark Literary Agency (*UK*)
Anthony Sheil in Association with Aitken
Alexander Associates (*UK*)
Antony Harwood Limited (*UK*)
Aponte Literary (*US*)
Artellus Limited (*UK*)
Author Rights Agency (*Ire*)
The Authors Care Service ltd (*UK*)
The Axelrod Agency (*US*)
Ayesha Pande Literary (*US*)
Azantian Literary Agency (*US*)
B.J. Robbins Literary Agency (*US*)
Baldi Agency (*US*)
Barbara Hogenson Agency (*US*)
Barbara Levy Literary Agency (*UK*)
Baror International, Inc. (*US*)
Bath Literary Agency (*UK*)
Bell Lomax Moreton Agency (*UK*)
The Bent Agency (*US*)
Betsy Amster Literary Enterprises (*US*)
Vicky Bijur Literary Agency (*US*)
The Blair Partnership (*UK*)
Blake Friedmann Literary Agency Ltd (*UK*)
Bleecker Street Associates, Inc. (*US*)
Bob Mecoy Creative Book Services (*US*)
Bond Literary Agency (*US*)
The Book Bureau Literary Agency (*Ire*)
Book Cents Literary Agency (*US*)
Books & Such Literary Management (*US*)
Bookseeker Agency (*UK*)
BookStop Literary Agency, LLC (*US*)
Brandt & Hochman Literary Agents, Inc. (*US*)
The Brattle Agency LLC (*US*)
Bresnick Weil Literary Agency, LLC (*US*)
The Bright Literary Academy (*UK*)
Brotherstone Creative Management (*UK*)
Browne & Miller Literary Associates (*US*)
Capital Talent Agency (*US*)
Carol Mann Agency (*US*)
Caroline Davidson Literary Agency (*UK*)
Caroline Sheldon Literary Agency (*UK*)
Carolyn Jenks Agency (*US*)
The Catchpole Agency (*UK*)
Catherine Pellegrino & Associates (*UK*)
Chartwell (*UK*)
Chase Literary Agency (*US*)
Mic Cheetham Literary Agency (*UK*)
Elyse Cheney Literary Associates, LLC (*US*)
Cherry Weiner Literary Agency (*US*)
Christine Green Authors' Agent (*UK*)
The Christopher Little Literary Agency (*UK*)
The Chudney Agency (*US*)
Cine/Lit Representation (*US*)
Clare Hulton Literary Agency (*UK*)
Compass Talent (*US*)
Conville & Walsh Ltd (*UK*)
Coombs Moylett & Maclean Literary Agency (*UK*)
Corvisiero Literary Agency (*US*)
The Cowles-Ryan Literary Agency (*US*)
Creative Trust, Inc. (*US*)
Creative Authors Ltd (*UK*)
Creative Media Agency (*US*)

Curtis Brown Group Ltd (*UK*)
Richard Curtis Associates, Inc. (*US*)
Curtis Brown Ltd (*US*)
Cynthia Cannell Literary Agency (*US*)
D4EO Literary Agency (*US*)
The Darley Anderson Agency (*UK*)
David Black Literary Agency (*US*)
David Godwin Associates (*UK*)
David Higham Associates Ltd (*UK*)
DeFiore and Company (*US*)
DHH Literary Agency Ltd (*UK*)
Diamond Kahn and Woods (DKW) Literary Agency Ltd (*UK*)
Dinah Wiener Ltd (*UK*)
The Doe Coover Agency (*US*)
Don Congdon Associates, Inc. (*US*)
Donaghy Literary Group (*US*)
Jim Donovan Literary (*US*)
Dunham Literary, Inc. (*US*)
Dystel, Goderich & Bourret LLC (*US*)
Toby Eady Associates Ltd (*UK*)
Eddison Pearson Ltd (*UK*)
Anne Edelstein Literary Agency (*US*)
Edwards Fuglewicz (*UK*)
Elaine Markson Literary Agency (*US*)
Elaine Steel (*UK*)
Elise Dillsworth Agency (EDA) (*UK*)
Elizabeth Roy Literary Agency (*UK*)
Emerald City Literary Agency (*US*)
Emily Sweet Associates (*UK*)
Empire Literary, LLC (*US*)
Ethan Ellenberg Literary Agency (*US*)
Mary Evans, Inc. (*US*)
Eve White: Literary Agent (*UK*)
Faith Evans Associates (*UK*)
The Feldstein Agency (*UK*)
Felicity Bryan Associates (*UK*)
Felix de Wolfe (*UK*)
Film Rights Ltd in association with Laurence Fitch Ltd (*UK*)
FinePrint Literary Management (*US*)
Flannery Literary (*US*)
Fletcher & Company (*US*)
Folio Literary Management, LLC (*US*)
Foundry Literary + Media (*US*)
Fox Literary (*US*)
Frances Collin Literary Agent (*US*)
Frank Fahy (*Ire*)
Fraser Ross Associates (*UK*)
Fraser-Bub Literary, LLC (*US*)
Furniss Lawton (*UK*)
Fuse Literary (*US*)
The G Agency, LLC (*US*)
Gallt & Zacker Literary Agency (*US*)
Gelfman Schneider / ICM Partners (*US*)
Georges Borchardt, Inc. (*US*)
Georgina Capel Associates Ltd (*UK*)
The Gernert Company (*US*)
Gina Maccoby Agency (*US*)
Eric Glass Ltd (*UK*)
Glass Literary Management LLC (*US*)
Global Lion Intellectual Property Management, Inc. (*US*)

The Good Literary Agency (*UK*)
Greene & Heaton Ltd (*UK*)
The Greenhouse Literary Agency (*US*)
The Greenhouse Literary Agency (*UK*)
Blanche C. Gregory Inc. (*US*)
Gregory & Company, Authors' Agents (*UK*)
Greyhaus Literary Agency (*US*)
David Grossman Literary Agency Ltd (*UK*)
Marianne Gunn O'Connor Literary Agency (*Ire*)
Gunn Media Associates (*UK*)
Hannigan Salky Getzler (HSG) Agency (*US*)
Hardman & Swainson (*UK*)
Harold Ober Associates, Inc. (*US*)
Joy Harris Literary Agency, Inc. (*US*)
The Helen Brann Agency, Inc. (*US*)
Herman Agency Inc. (*US*)
hhb agency ltd (*UK*)
Hill Nadell Literary Agency (*US*)
Holloway Literary (*US*)
Holroyde Cartey (*UK*)
Vanessa Holt Ltd (*UK*)
Andrea Hurst Literary Management (*US*)
Inklings Literary Agency, LLC (*US*)
Intercontinental Literary Agency (*UK*)
Isabel White Literary Agent (*UK*)
J de S Associates Inc. (*US*)
Jane Conway-Gordon Ltd (*UK*)
Jane Judd Literary Agency (*UK*)
Jane Rotrosen Agency (*US*)
Jane Turnbull (*UK*)
Janklow & Nesbit Associates (*US*)
Jenny Brown Associates (*UK*)
Jill Grinberg Literary Management LLC (*US*)
Jill Corcoran Literary Agency (*US*)
Jill Grosjean Literary Agency (*US*)
Jo Unwin Literary Agency (*UK*)
Joanna Pulcini Literary Management (*US*)
John Hawkins & Associates, Inc. (*US*)
Johnson & Alcock (*UK*)
Jonathan Clowes Ltd (*UK*)
Jonathan Pegg Literary Agency (*UK*)
Joëlle Delbourgo Associates, Inc. (*US*)
Judith Murdoch Literary Agency (*UK*)
Juliet Burton Literary Agency (*UK*)
JYLA (Jason Yarn Literary Agency) (*US*)
K2 Literary (*Can*)
Michelle Kass Associates (*UK*)
Kate Hordern Literary Agency (*UK*)
Kate Nash Literary Agency (*UK*)
Kathi J. Paton Literary Agency (*US*)
Keane Kataria Literary Agency (*UK*)
Ken Sherman & Associates (*US*)
Ki Agency Ltd (*UK*)
Kimberley Cameron & Associates (*US*)
Kingsford Campbell Literary & Marketing Agents (*UK*)
The Knight Agency (*US*)
Knight Features (*UK*)
Barbara S. Kouts, Literary Agent (*US*)
KT Literary (*US*)
L. Perkins Associates (*US*)
Larsen Pomada Literary Agents (*US*)
Laura Dail Literary Agency (*US*)

LAW (Lucas Alexander Whitley) (*UK*)
Lawrence Jordan Literary Agency (*US*)
Sarah Lazin Books (*US*)
LBA Books Ltd (*UK*)
Leigh Feldman Literary (*US*)
The Leshne Agency (*US*)
Levine Greenberg Rostan Literary Agency (*US*)
Limelight Management (*UK*)
Linda Chester & Associates (*US*)
Linda Roghaar Literary Agency, Inc. (*US*)
Lindsay Literary Agency (*UK*)
Linn Prentis, Literary Agent (*US*)
The Lisa Richards Agency (*Ire*)
Literary & Creative Artists Inc. (*US*)
The Literary Group International (*US*)
The LKG Agency (*US*)
London Independent Books (*UK*)
Lorella Belli Literary Agency (LBLA) (*UK*)
Louise Greenberg Books Ltd (*UK*)
Lutyens and Rubinstein (*UK*)
MacGregor Literary (*US*)
Madeleine Milburn Literary, TV & Film Agency (*UK*)
Maggie Pearlstine Associates Ltd (*UK*)
Manus & Associates Literary Agency, Inc. (*US*)
Maria Carvainis Agency, Inc. (*US*)
Marsal Lyon Literary Agency LLC (*US*)
The Marsh Agency (*UK*)
The Martell Agency (*US*)
Martin Leonardis Ltd (*UK*)
Martin Literary Management (*US*)
Mary Clemmey Literary Agency (*UK*)
Massie & McQuilkin (*US*)
Max Gartenburg Literary Agency (*US*)
MBA Literary Agents Ltd (*UK*)
Duncan McAra (*UK*)
Margret McBride Literary Agency (*US*)
McCormick Literary (*US*)
McIntosh & Otis, Inc (*US*)
Meredith Bernstein Literary Agency, Inc. (*US*)
The Michael Greer Literary Agency (*UK*)
Patricia Moosbrugger Literary Agency (*US*)
Howard Morhaim Literary Agency (*US*)
Mulcahy Associates (Part of MMB Creative) (*UK*)
Nappaland Literary Agency (*US*)
New Leaf Literary & Media, Inc. (*US*)
Niad Management (*US*)
MNLA (Maggie Noach Literary Agency) (*UK*)
Northbank Talent Management (*UK*)
Northern Lights Literary Services (*US*)
One Track Literary Agency, Inc. (*US*)
Deborah Owen Ltd (*UK*)
P.S. Literary Agency (*Can*)
The Park Literary Group LLC (*US*)
Pavilion Literary Management (*US*)
Peters Fraser + Dunlop (*UK*)
PEW Literary (*UK*)
Pippin Properties, Inc (*US*)
Shelley Power Literary Agency Ltd (*UK*)
Publication Riot Group, Inc. (*US*)
The Purcell Agency, LLC (*US*)
Queen Literary Agency, Inc. (*US*)

Ki Agency Ltd (*UK*)
Knight Hall Agency (*UK*)
L. Perkins Associates (*US*)
Larsen Pomada Literary Agents (*US*)
The Leshne Agency (*US*)
Linda Seifert Management (*UK*)
Madeleine Milburn Literary, TV & Film Agency (*UK*)
Mary Clemmey Literary Agency (*UK*)
MBA Literary Agents Ltd (*UK*)
Bill McLean Personal Management Ltd (*UK*)
Niad Management (*US*)
Paradigm Talent and Literary Agency (*US*)
Peters Fraser + Dunlop (*UK*)
Richard Henshaw Group LLC (*US*)
Rochelle Stevens & Co. (*UK*)
Rosica Colin Ltd (*UK*)
The Ruppin Agency (*UK*)
Sayle Screen Ltd (*UK*)
Lynn Seligman, Literary Agent (*US*)
Sheil Land Associates Ltd (*UK*)
Sheree Bykofsky Associates, Inc. (*US*)
The Spieler Agency (*US*)
Stone Manners Salners Agency (*US*)
The Tennyson Agency (*UK*)
Trident Media Group, LLC (*US*)
2M Literary Agency Ltd (*US*)
United Agents (*UK*)
Valerie Hoskins Associates (*UK*)
Victoria Sanders & Associates LLC (*US*)
Watson, Little Ltd (*UK*)
Whispering Buffalo Literary Agency Ltd (*UK*)
William Morris Endeavor Entertainment (*US*)
Wm Clark Associates (*US*)
The Zack Company, Inc (*US*)

Finance

Ambassador Speakers Bureau & Literary Agency (*US*)
Andrew Lownie Literary Agency Ltd (*UK*)
The Angela Rinaldi Literary Agency (*US*)
Antony Harwood Limited (*UK*)
Audrey A. Wolf Literary Agency (*US*)
Ayesha Pande Literary (*US*)
Baldi Agency (*US*)
Blake Friedmann Literary Agency Ltd (*UK*)
Bleecker Street Associates, Inc. (*US*)
Bob Mecoy Creative Book Services (*US*)
Carol Mann Agency (*US*)
Elyse Cheney Literary Associates, LLC (*US*)
Richard Curtis Associates, Inc. (*US*)
D4EO Literary Agency (*US*)
David Black Literary Agency (*US*)
The Doe Coover Agency (*US*)
Jim Donovan Literary (*US*)
Dystel, Goderich & Bourret LLC (*US*)
Frances Kelly Agency (*UK*)
The G Agency, LLC (*US*)
Grace Freedson's Publishing Network (*US*)
Hannigan Salky Getzler (HSG) Agency (*US*)
Hornfischer Literary Management, L.P. (*US*)
J de S Associates Inc. (*US*)
Jeanne Fredericks Literary Agency, Inc. (*US*)
Jenny Brown Associates (*UK*)

Jill Grinberg Literary Management LLC (*US*)
Kathi J. Paton Literary Agency (*US*)
The Knight Agency (*US*)
Linda Konner Literary Agency (*US*)
Larsen Pomada Literary Agents (*US*)
Levine Greenberg Rostan Literary Agency (*US*)
MacGregor Literary (*US*)
Manus & Associates Literary Agency, Inc. (*US*)
Maria Carvainis Agency, Inc. (*US*)
Marsal Lyon Literary Agency LLC (*US*)
The Martell Agency (*US*)
Howard Morhaim Literary Agency (*US*)
Mulcahy Associates (Part of MMB Creative) (*UK*)
Peters Fraser + Dunlop (*UK*)
Lynne Rabinoff Agency (*US*)
Raines & Raines (*US*)
The Amy Rennert Agency, Inc. (*US*)
Marly Rusoff & Associates, Inc. (*US*)
The Sagalyn Literary Agency (*US*)
Salkind Literary Agency (*US*)
Lynn Seligman, Literary Agent (*US*)
Solow Literary Enterprises, Inc. (*US*)
The Spieler Agency (*US*)
Susan Rabiner, Literary Agent, Inc. (*US*)
TriadaUS Literary Agency, Inc. (*US*)
Writers' Representatives, LLC (*US*)
Writers House, LLC (*US*)
The Zack Company, Inc (*US*)

Gardening

Antony Harwood Limited (*UK*)
Betsy Amster Literary Enterprises (*US*)
Caroline Davidson Literary Agency (*UK*)
The Doe Coover Agency (*US*)
Grace Freedson's Publishing Network (*US*)
Graham Maw Christie Literary Agency (*UK*)
Greene & Heaton Ltd (*UK*)
Hannigan Salky Getzler (HSG) Agency (*US*)
Jane Turnbull (*UK*)
Jeanne Fredericks Literary Agency, Inc. (*US*)
Jill Grosjean Literary Agency (*US*)
John Hawkins & Associates, Inc. (*US*)
The Leshne Agency (*US*)
Levine Greenberg Rostan Literary Agency (*US*)
Linda Roghaar Literary Agency, Inc. (*US*)
Richford Becklow Literary Agency (*UK*)
Rosica Colin Ltd (*UK*)
Sheil Land Associates Ltd (*UK*)
The Spieler Agency (*US*)
Talcott Notch Literary (*US*)
Teresa Chris Literary Agency Ltd (*UK*)
TriadaUS Literary Agency, Inc. (*US*)
The Zack Company, Inc (*US*)

Gothic

Aaron M. Priest Literary Agency (*US*)
The Angela Rinaldi Literary Agency (*US*)
Antony Harwood Limited (*UK*)
BookStop Literary Agency, LLC (*US*)
Diamond Kahn and Woods (DKW) Literary Agency Ltd (*UK*)
Peters Fraser + Dunlop (*UK*)
Richford Becklow Literary Agency (*UK*)
The Ruppin Agency (*UK*)

Health

A.M. Heath & Company Limited, Author's Agents (*UK*)
The Ahearn Agency, Inc (*US*)
Ambassador Speakers Bureau & Literary Agency (*US*)
Andrew Lownie Literary Agency Ltd (*UK*)
The Angela Rinaldi Literary Agency (*US*)
Antony Harwood Limited (*UK*)
Arcadia (*US*)
Audrey A. Wolf Literary Agency (*US*)
B.J. Robbins Literary Agency (*US*)
Betsy Amster Literary Enterprises (*US*)
Vicky Bijur Literary Agency (*US*)
Bleecker Street Associates, Inc. (*US*)
Brandt & Hochman Literary Agents, Inc. (*US*)
Bresnick Weil Literary Agency, LLC (*US*)
Carol Mann Agency (*US*)
Caroline Davidson Literary Agency (*UK*)
Chartwell (*UK*)
Creative Authors Ltd (*UK*)
Richard Curtis Associates, Inc. (*US*)
Cynthia Cannell Literary Agency (*US*)
D4EO Literary Agency (*US*)
David Black Literary Agency (*US*)
The Doe Coover Agency (*US*)
Don Congdon Associates, Inc. (*US*)
Jim Donovan Literary (*US*)
Dystel, Goderich & Bourret LLC (*US*)
Empire Literary, LLC (*US*)
Ethan Ellenberg Literary Agency (*US*)
FinePrint Literary Management (*US*)
Fletcher & Company (*US*)
Folio Literary Management, LLC (*US*)
Foundry Literary + Media (*US*)
Fox & Howard Literary Agency (*UK*)
Frances Kelly Agency (*UK*)
Fraser-Bub Literary, LLC (*US*)
Gina Maccoby Agency (*US*)
Glass Literary Management LLC (*US*)
Grace Freedson's Publishing Network (*US*)
Graham Maw Christie Literary Agency (*UK*)
Greene & Heaton Ltd (*UK*)
Marianne Gunn O'Connor Literary Agency (*Ire*)
Hannigan Salky Getzler (HSG) Agency (*US*)
Hardman & Swainson (*UK*)
Hill Nadell Literary Agency (*US*)
Hornfischer Literary Management, L.P. (*US*)
J de S Associates Inc. (*US*)
Jane Judd Literary Agency (*UK*)
Jeanne Fredericks Literary Agency, Inc. (*US*)
Jill Grinberg Literary Management LLC (*US*)
John Hawkins & Associates, Inc. (*US*)
Johnson & Alcock (*UK*)
Kathi J. Paton Literary Agency (*US*)
Kimberley Cameron & Associates (*US*)
The Knight Agency (*US*)
Knight Features (*UK*)
Linda Konner Literary Agency (*US*)
Barbara S. Kouts, Literary Agent (*US*)
Larsen Pomada Literary Agents (*US*)
LAW (Lucas Alexander Whitley) (*UK*)
LBA Books Ltd (*UK*)

The Leshne Agency (*US*)
Levine Greenberg Rostan Literary Agency (*US*)
Limelight Management (*UK*)
Linda Roghaar Literary Agency, Inc. (*US*)
Literary & Creative Artists Inc. (*US*)
The LKG Agency (*US*)
Maggie Pearlstine Associates Ltd (*UK*)
Manus & Associates Literary Agency, Inc. (*US*)
Marsal Lyon Literary Agency LLC (*US*)
The Martell Agency (*US*)
Martin Literary Management (*US*)
Massie & McQuilkin (*US*)
Max Gartenberg Literary Agency (*US*)
MBA Literary Agents Ltd (*UK*)
Margret McBride Literary Agency (*US*)
Howard Morhaim Literary Agency (*US*)
Northbank Talent Management (*UK*)
Northern Lights Literary Services (*US*)
P.S. Literary Agency (*Can*)
Puttick Literary Agency (*UK*)
The Amy Rennert Agency, Inc. (*US*)
Richard Henshaw Group LLC (*US*)
The Rights Factory (*Can*)
Rita Rosenkranz Literary Agency (*US*)
Rosica Colin Ltd (*UK*)
The Rudy Agency (*US*)
Marly Rusoff & Associates, Inc. (*US*)
Salkind Literary Agency (*US*)
Sandra Dijkstra Literary Agency (*US*)
Sanford J. Greenburger Associates, Inc. (*US*)
Scovil Galen Ghosh Literary Agency, Inc. (*US*)
Lynn Seligman, Literary Agent (*US*)
Signature Literary Agency (*US*)
Solow Literary Enterprises, Inc. (*US*)
The Spieler Agency (*US*)
Stephanie Tade Literary Agency (*US*)
Sterling Lord Literistic, Inc. (*US*)
The Stuart Agency (*US*)
Tessler Literary Agency (*US*)
Tracy Brown Literary Agency (*US*)
TriadaUS Literary Agency, Inc. (*US*)
Trident Media Group, LLC (*US*)
2M Literary Agency Ltd (*US*)
The Unter Agency (*US*)
Veritas Literary Agency (*US*)
Waxman Leavell Literary Agency (*US*)
Wendy Sherman Associates, Inc. (*US*)
Whispering Buffalo Literary Agency Ltd (*UK*)
The Zack Company, Inc (*US*)

Historical

A.M. Heath & Company Limited, Author's Agents (*UK*)
Aaron M. Priest Literary Agency (*US*)
Adler & Robin Books, Inc (*US*)
The Ahearn Agency, Inc (*US*)
Alive Literary Agency (*US*)
Ambassador Speakers Bureau & Literary Agency (*US*)
The Ampersand Agency Ltd (*UK*)
Marcia Amsterdam Agency (*US*)
Andrea Brown Literary Agency, Inc. (*US*)
Andrew Lownie Literary Agency Ltd (*UK*)
Andrew Mann Ltd (*UK*)

The Angela Rinaldi Literary Agency (*US*)
Ann Rittenberg Literary Agency (*US*)
Antony Harwood Limited (*UK*)
Aponte Literary (*US*)
Arcadia (*US*)
Artellus Limited (*UK*)
Audrey A. Wolf Literary Agency (*US*)
Author Rights Agency (*Ire*)
Ayesha Pande Literary (*US*)
B.J. Robbins Literary Agency (*US*)
Baldi Agency (*US*)
The Bent Agency (*US*)
Betsy Amster Literary Enterprises (*US*)
Vicky Bijur Literary Agency (*US*)
Blake Friedmann Literary Agency Ltd (*UK*)
Bleecker Street Associates, Inc. (*US*)
Bob Mecoy Creative Book Services (*US*)
Bond Literary Agency (*US*)
Books & Such Literary Management (*US*)
BookStop Literary Agency, LLC (*US*)
Brandt & Hochman Literary Agents, Inc. (*US*)
The Brattle Agency LLC (*US*)
Bresnick Weil Literary Agency, LLC (*US*)
Carol Mann Agency (*US*)
Caroline Davidson Literary Agency (*UK*)
Caroline Sheldon Literary Agency (*UK*)
Carolyn Jenks Agency (*US*)
Chartwell (*UK*)
Chase Literary Agency (*US*)
Mic Cheetham Literary Agency (*UK*)
Elyse Cheney Literary Associates, LLC (*US*)
Cherry Weiner Literary Agency (*US*)
The Chudney Agency (*US*)
Clare Hulton Literary Agency (*UK*)
Compass Talent (*US*)
Conville & Walsh Ltd (*UK*)
Coombs Moylett & Maclean Literary Agency
(*UK*)
The Cowles-Ryan Literary Agency (*US*)
Creative Authors Ltd (*UK*)
Creative Media Agency (*US*)
Curtis Brown Group Ltd (*UK*)
Richard Curtis Associates, Inc. (*US*)
D4EO Literary Agency (*US*)
David Luxton Associates (*UK*)
David Black Literary Agency (*US*)
David Higham Associates Ltd (*UK*)
DeFiore and Company (*US*)
DHH Literary Agency Ltd (*UK*)
Diamond Kahn and Woods (DKW) Literary
Agency Ltd (*UK*)
The Doe Coover Agency (*US*)
Don Congdon Associates, Inc. (*US*)
Donaghy Literary Group (*US*)
Jim Donovan Literary (*US*)
Doug Grad Literary Agency (*US*)
The Dravis Agency, Inc. (*US*)
Dunham Literary, Inc. (*US*)
Dystel, Goderich & Bourret LLC (*US*)
E. J. McCarthy Agency (*US*)
Anne Edelstein Literary Agency (*US*)
Edwards Fuglewicz (*UK*)
Emily Sweet Associates (*UK*)

Ethan Ellenberg Literary Agency (*US*)
Mary Evans, Inc. (*US*)
The Feldstein Agency (*UK*)
Felicity Bryan Associates (*UK*)
FinePrint Literary Management (*US*)
Fletcher & Company (*US*)
Folio Literary Management, LLC (*US*)
Foundry Literary + Media (*US*)
Fox Literary (*US*)
Fox & Howard Literary Agency (*UK*)
Frances Collin Literary Agent (*US*)
Frances Kelly Agency (*UK*)
Fraser-Bub Literary, LLC (*US*)
Furniss Lawton (*UK*)
The G Agency, LLC (*US*)
Gelfman Schneider / ICM Partners (*US*)
Georges Borchardt, Inc. (*US*)
Georgina Capel Associates Ltd (*UK*)
The Gernert Company (*US*)
Gina Maccoby Agency (*US*)
Glass Literary Management LLC (*US*)
Grace Freedson's Publishing Network (*US*)
Graham Maw Christie Literary Agency (*UK*)
Greene & Heaton Ltd (*UK*)
Gregory & Company, Authors' Agents (*UK*)
Hannigan Salky Getzler (HSG) Agency (*US*)
Hardman & Swainson (*UK*)
Joy Harris Literary Agency, Inc. (*US*)
hhb agency ltd (*UK*)
Hill Nadell Literary Agency (*US*)
Holloway Literary (*US*)
Hornfischer Literary Management, L.P. (*US*)
Andrea Hurst Literary Management (*US*)
Inklings Literary Agency, LLC (*US*)
J de S Associates Inc. (*US*)
Jane Judd Literary Agency (*UK*)
Jane Rotrosen Agency (*US*)
Jane Turnbull (*UK*)
Jeanne Fredericks Literary Agency, Inc. (*US*)
Jenny Brown Associates (*UK*)
Jill Grinberg Literary Management LLC (*US*)
Jill Grosjean Literary Agency (*US*)
John Hawkins & Associates, Inc. (*US*)
Johnson & Alcock (*UK*)
Jonathan Pegg Literary Agency (*UK*)
Joëlle Delbourgo Associates, Inc. (*US*)
JYLA (Jason Yarn Literary Agency) (*US*)
Kate Hordern Literary Agency (*UK*)
Kathi J. Paton Literary Agency (*US*)
Ki Agency Ltd (*UK*)
Kimberley Cameron & Associates (*US*)
The Knight Agency (*US*)
Knight Features (*UK*)
Barbara S. Kouts, Literary Agent (*US*)
L. Perkins Associates (*US*)
Larsen Pomada Literary Agents (*US*)
Laura Dail Literary Agency (*US*)
LAW (Lucas Alexander Whitley) (*UK*)
Sarah Lazin Books (*US*)
LBA Books Ltd (*UK*)
Leigh Feldman Literary (*US*)
The Leshne Agency (*US*)
Levine Greenberg Rostan Literary Agency (*US*)

*Claim your free access to **www.firstwriter.com**: See p.389*

Limelight Management (*UK*)
Linda Roghaar Literary Agency, Inc. (*US*)
The Lisa Richards Agency (*Ire*)
Literary & Creative Artists Inc. (*US*)
The Literary Group International (*US*)
MacGregor Literary (*US*)
Madeleine Milburn Literary, TV & Film Agency (*UK*)
Maggie Pearlstine Associates Ltd (*UK*)
Maria Carvainis Agency, Inc. (*US*)
Marsal Lyon Literary Agency LLC (*US*)
The Martell Agency (*US*)
Massie & McQuilkin (*US*)
MBA Literary Agents Ltd (*UK*)
Duncan McAra (*UK*)
Margret McBride Literary Agency (*US*)
McCormick Literary (*US*)
McIntosh & Otis, Inc (*US*)
Howard Morhaim Literary Agency (*US*)
Mulcahy Associates (Part of MMB Creative) (*UK*)
Nappaland Literary Agency (*US*)
New Leaf Literary & Media, Inc. (*US*)
MNLA (Maggie Noach Literary Agency) (*UK*)
Northbank Talent Management (*UK*)
Northern Lights Literary Services (*US*)
P.S. Literary Agency (*Can*)
The Park Literary Group LLC (*US*)
Pavilion Literary Management (*US*)
Peters Fraser + Dunlop (*UK*)
Publication Riot Group, Inc. (*US*)
Puttick Literary Agency (*UK*)
Queen Literary Agency, Inc. (*US*)
Lynne Rabinoff Agency (*US*)
Raines & Raines (*US*)
Regal Hoffmann & Associates LLC (*US*)
The Amy Rennert Agency, Inc. (*US*)
Richard Henshaw Group LLC (*US*)
Richford Becklow Literary Agency (*UK*)
The Rights Bureau (*Ire*)
The Rights Factory (*Can*)
Rita Rosenkranz Literary Agency (*US*)
RLR Associates (*US*)
Robert Dudley Agency (*UK*)
Robin Straus Agency, Inc. (*US*)
Rocking Chair Books (*UK*)
Rosica Colin Ltd (*UK*)
Andy Ross Agency (*US*)
Ross Yoon Agency (*US*)
The Rudy Agency (*US*)
Rupert Heath Literary Agency (*UK*)
The Ruppin Agency (*UK*)
Marly Rusoff & Associates, Inc. (*US*)
The Sagalyn Literary Agency (*US*)
Salkind Literary Agency (*US*)
Sandra Dijkstra Literary Agency (*US*)
Sanford J. Greenburger Associates, Inc. (*US*)
Sarah Such Literary Agency (*UK*)
The Sayle Literary Agency (*UK*)
Scovil Galen Ghosh Literary Agency, Inc. (*US*)
Lynn Seligman, Literary Agent (*US*)
Sheil Land Associates Ltd (*UK*)
Sheila Ableman Literary Agency (*UK*)

Signature Literary Agency (*US*)
Solow Literary Enterprises, Inc. (*US*)
Spectrum Literary Agency (*US*)
Speilburg Literary Agency (*US*)
Spencerhill Associates (*US*)
The Spieler Agency (*US*)
Philip G. Spitzer Literary Agency, Inc. (*US*)
Sterling Lord Literistic, Inc. (*US*)
The Stringer Literary Agency LLC (*US*)
Stuart Krichevsky Literary Agency, Inc. (*US*)
The Stuart Agency (*US*)
Susan Rabiner, Literary Agent, Inc. (*US*)
Talcott Notch Literary (*US*)
Teresa Chris Literary Agency Ltd (*UK*)
Tessler Literary Agency (*US*)
Toby Mundy Associates Ltd (*UK*)
Tracy Brown Literary Agency (*US*)
TriadaUS Literary Agency, Inc. (*US*)
Trident Media Group, LLC (*US*)
Union Literary (*US*)
United Talent Agency (*US*)
Upstart Crow Literary (*US*)
Veritas Literary Agency (*US*)
Victoria Sanders & Associates LLC (*US*)
Watkins / Loomis Agency, Inc. (*US*)
Watson, Little Ltd (*UK*)
Waxman Leavell Literary Agency (*US*)
Wendy Sherman Associates, Inc. (*US*)
Westwood Creative Artists (*Can*)
William Morris Endeavor (WME) London (*UK*)
Wm Clark Associates (*US*)
Writers' Representatives, LLC (*US*)
Writers House, LLC (*US*)
The Zack Company, Inc (*US*)
Zeno Agency Ltd (*UK*)
Zoë Pagnamenta Agency, LLC (*US*)

Hobbies
Antony Harwood Limited (*UK*)
Grace Freedson's Publishing Network (*US*)
The Leshne Agency (*US*)
Levine Greenberg Rostan Literary Agency (*US*)
Linda Roghaar Literary Agency, Inc. (*US*)
The Ruppin Agency (*UK*)
Sheree Bykofsky Associates, Inc. (*US*)

Horror
The Ampersand Agency Ltd (*UK*)
Marcia Amsterdam Agency (*US*)
Andrew Lownie Literary Agency Ltd (*UK*)
Antony Harwood Limited (*UK*)
Azantian Literary Agency (*US*)
The Bent Agency (*US*)
Bleecker Street Associates, Inc. (*US*)
Bond Literary Agency (*US*)
Elyse Cheney Literary Associates, LLC (*US*)
Cine/Lit Representation (*US*)
Corvisiero Literary Agency (*US*)
D4EO Literary Agency (*US*)
Emerald City Literary Agency (*US*)
Film Rights Ltd in association with Laurence Fitch Ltd (*UK*)
FinePrint Literary Management (*US*)
Folio Literary Management, LLC (*US*)
Gallt & Zacker Literary Agency (*US*)

Hardman & Swainson (*UK*)
Inklings Literary Agency, LLC (*US*)
Kimberley Cameron & Associates (*US*)
L. Perkins Associates (*US*)
LAW (Lucas Alexander Whitley) (*UK*)
Madeleine Milburn Literary, TV & Film Agency (*UK*)
Maria Carvainis Agency, Inc. (*US*)
McIntosh & Otis, Inc (*US*)
Howard Morhaim Literary Agency (*US*)
Peters Fraser + Dunlop (*UK*)
Richard Henshaw Group LLC (*US*)
Richford Becklow Literary Agency (*UK*)
Rocking Chair Books (*UK*)
Rosica Colin Ltd (*UK*)
Lynn Seligman, Literary Agent (*US*)
Speilburg Literary Agency (*US*)
The Stringer Literary Agency LLC (*US*)
The Stuart Agency (*US*)
Talcott Notch Literary (*US*)
The Zack Company, Inc (*US*)
Zeno Agency Ltd (*UK*)

How-to
Aaron M. Priest Literary Agency (*US*)
Adler & Robin Books, Inc (*US*)
AHA Talent Ltd (*UK*)
Alive Literary Agency (*US*)
Ambassador Speakers Bureau & Literary Agency (*US*)
Andrea Brown Literary Agency, Inc. (*US*)
Andrew Lownie Literary Agency Ltd (*UK*)
Antony Harwood Limited (*UK*)
Baldi Agency (*US*)
Bleecker Street Associates, Inc. (*US*)
D4EO Literary Agency (*US*)
David Black Literary Agency (*US*)
Jim Donovan Literary (*US*)
FinePrint Literary Management (*US*)
Folio Literary Management, LLC (*US*)
Foundry Literary + Media (*US*)
Grace Freedson's Publishing Network (*US*)
Hornfischer Literary Management, L.P. (*US*)
Andrea Hurst Literary Management (*US*)
J de S Associates Inc. (*US*)
Jeanne Fredericks Literary Agency, Inc. (*US*)
The Knight Agency (*US*)
Linda Konner Literary Agency (*US*)
L. Perkins Associates (*US*)
Larsen Pomada Literary Agents (*US*)
Linda Roghaar Literary Agency, Inc. (*US*)
Literary & Creative Artists Inc. (*US*)
The Literary Group International (*US*)
MacGregor Literary (*US*)
Manus & Associates Literary Agency, Inc. (*US*)
Martin Literary Management (*US*)
Northern Lights Literary Services (*US*)
Richard Henshaw Group LLC (*US*)
The Rights Bureau (*Ire*)
Rita Rosenkranz Literary Agency (*US*)
Salkind Literary Agency (*US*)
Lynn Seligman, Literary Agent (*US*)
TriadaUS Literary Agency, Inc. (*US*)
Writers House, LLC (*US*)

The Zack Company, Inc (*US*)
Humour
Adler & Robin Books, Inc (*US*)
The Agency (London) Ltd (*UK*)
AHA Talent Ltd (*UK*)
The Ahearn Agency, Inc (*US*)
Alive Literary Agency (*US*)
Marcia Amsterdam Agency (*US*)
Andrea Brown Literary Agency, Inc. (*US*)
Antony Harwood Limited (*UK*)
Ayesha Pande Literary (*US*)
The Bent Agency (*US*)
Bleecker Street Associates, Inc. (*US*)
Book Cents Literary Agency (*US*)
Books & Such Literary Management (*US*)
Bresnick Weil Literary Agency, LLC (*US*)
Carol Mann Agency (*US*)
Caroline Sheldon Literary Agency (*UK*)
Cecily Ware Literary Agents (*UK*)
Chase Literary Agency (*US*)
The Chudney Agency (*US*)
Clare Hulton Literary Agency (*UK*)
Conville & Walsh Ltd (*UK*)
Corvisiero Literary Agency (*US*)
Creative Authors Ltd (*UK*)
D4EO Literary Agency (*US*)
David Black Literary Agency (*US*)
David Higham Associates Ltd (*UK*)
Diamond Kahn and Woods (DKW) Literary Agency Ltd (*UK*)
The Doe Coover Agency (*US*)
Don Congdon Associates, Inc. (*US*)
The Dravis Agency, Inc. (*US*)
Dystel, Goderich & Bourret LLC (*US*)
Edwards Fuglewicz (*UK*)
Elizabeth Roy Literary Agency (*UK*)
The Feldstein Agency (*UK*)
FinePrint Literary Management (*US*)
Fletcher & Company (*US*)
Folio Literary Management, LLC (*US*)
Foundry Literary + Media (*US*)
Furniss Lawton (*UK*)
Grace Freedson's Publishing Network (*US*)
Graham Maw Christie Literary Agency (*UK*)
Greene & Heaton Ltd (*UK*)
Hannigan Salky Getzler (HSG) Agency (*US*)
Hardman & Swainson (*UK*)
Joy Harris Literary Agency, Inc. (*US*)
hhb agency ltd (*UK*)
Holloway Literary (*US*)
Hornfischer Literary Management, L.P. (*US*)
Hudson Agency (*US*)
Andrea Hurst Literary Management (*US*)
Jane Turnbull (*UK*)
Jenny Brown Associates (*UK*)
Jill Grinberg Literary Management LLC (*US*)
Jill Corcoran Literary Agency (*US*)
Jill Foster Ltd (JFL) (*UK*)
Jill Grosjean Literary Agency (*US*)
Jo Unwin Literary Agency (*UK*)
Joëlle Delbourgo Associates, Inc. (*US*)
Kathi J. Paton Literary Agency (*US*)
Knight Features (*UK*)

L. Perkins Associates (*US*)
Larsen Pomada Literary Agents (*US*)
Laura Dail Literary Agency (*US*)
The Leshne Agency (*US*)
Levine Greenberg Rostan Literary Agency (*US*)
The Lisa Richards Agency (*Ire*)
The Literary Group International (*US*)
MacGregor Literary (*US*)
Madeleine Milburn Literary, TV & Film Agency (*UK*)
Maria Carvainis Agency, Inc. (*US*)
Massie & McQuilkin (*US*)
Margret McBride Literary Agency (*US*)
McCormick Literary (*US*)
McIntosh & Otis, Inc (*US*)
Howard Morhaim Literary Agency (*US*)
Nappaland Literary Agency (*US*)
Niad Management (*US*)
P.S. Literary Agency (*Can*)
Peters Fraser + Dunlop (*UK*)
Rita Rosenkranz Literary Agency (*US*)
RLR Associates (*US*)
Rosica Colin Ltd (*UK*)
Rupert Heath Literary Agency (*UK*)
Salkind Literary Agency (*US*)
Sandra Dijkstra Literary Agency (*US*)
Sanford J. Greenburger Associates, Inc. (*US*)
Sarah Such Literary Agency (*UK*)
Lynn Seligman, Literary Agent (*US*)
Sheil Land Associates Ltd (*UK*)
Sheree Bykofsky Associates, Inc. (*US*)
The Spieler Agency (*US*)
The Stuart Agency (*US*)
Susan Rabiner, Literary Agent, Inc. (*US*)
TriadaUS Literary Agency, Inc. (*US*)
Trident Media Group, LLC (*US*)
Upstart Crow Literary (*US*)
Victoria Sanders & Associates LLC (*US*)
Watson, Little Ltd (*UK*)
Waxman Leavell Literary Agency (*US*)
Whispering Buffalo Literary Agency Ltd (*UK*)
Writers' Representatives, LLC (*US*)
The Zack Company, Inc (*US*)

Legal
Ambassador Speakers Bureau & Literary Agency (*US*)
Antony Harwood Limited (*UK*)
Carol Mann Agency (*US*)
Don Congdon Associates, Inc. (*US*)
Jim Donovan Literary (*US*)
Grace Freedson's Publishing Network (*US*)
Hill Nadell Literary Agency (*US*)
Hornfischer Literary Management, L.P. (*US*)
J de S Associates Inc. (*US*)
Jeanne Fredericks Literary Agency, Inc. (*US*)
Jill Grinberg Literary Management LLC (*US*)
Larsen Pomada Literary Agents (*US*)
Literary & Creative Artists Inc. (*US*)
Margret McBride Literary Agency (*US*)
Lynne Rabinoff Agency (*US*)
The Spieler Agency (*US*)
Victoria Sanders & Associates LLC (*US*)
Writers' Representatives, LLC (*US*)

Yates & Yates (*US*)
Leisure
Antony Harwood Limited (*UK*)
Conville & Walsh Ltd (*UK*)
The Feldstein Agency (*UK*)
Grace Freedson's Publishing Network (*US*)
Jeanne Fredericks Literary Agency, Inc. (*US*)
Levine Greenberg Rostan Literary Agency (*US*)
Rosica Colin Ltd (*UK*)
Watson, Little Ltd (*UK*)
Lifestyle
Adler & Robin Books, Inc (*US*)
The Ahearn Agency, Inc (*US*)
Alive Literary Agency (*US*)
Ambassador Speakers Bureau & Literary Agency (*US*)
Andrew Lownie Literary Agency Ltd (*UK*)
The Angela Rinaldi Literary Agency (*US*)
Antony Harwood Limited (*UK*)
Audrey A. Wolf Literary Agency (*US*)
Baldi Agency (*US*)
The Bent Agency (*US*)
Betsy Amster Literary Enterprises (*US*)
Bleecker Street Associates, Inc. (*US*)
Books & Such Literary Management (*US*)
Brandt & Hochman Literary Agents, Inc. (*US*)
Bresnick Weil Literary Agency, LLC (*US*)
Carol Mann Agency (*US*)
Caroline Davidson Literary Agency (*UK*)
Chartwell (*UK*)
Cherry Weiner Literary Agency (*US*)
Clare Hulton Literary Agency (*UK*)
Conville & Walsh Ltd (*UK*)
Creative Media Agency (*US*)
The Culinary Entertainment Agency (CEA) (*US*)
D4EO Literary Agency (*US*)
David Black Literary Agency (*US*)
DeFiore and Company (*US*)
Don Congdon Associates, Inc. (*US*)
Jim Donovan Literary (*US*)
Dunham Literary, Inc. (*US*)
Dystel, Goderich & Bourret LLC (*US*)
Empire Literary, LLC (*US*)
The Feldstein Agency (*UK*)
FinePrint Literary Management (*US*)
Fletcher & Company (*US*)
Folio Literary Management, LLC (*US*)
Foundry Literary + Media (*US*)
Fox & Howard Literary Agency (*UK*)
Frances Kelly Agency (*UK*)
Fraser-Bub Literary, LLC (*US*)
Gina Maccoby Agency (*US*)
Grace Freedson's Publishing Network (*US*)
Graham Maw Christie Literary Agency (*UK*)
Hannigan Salky Getzler (HSG) Agency (*US*)
Holloway Literary (*US*)
Hornfischer Literary Management, L.P. (*US*)
J de S Associates Inc. (*US*)
Jane Turnbull (*UK*)
Jeanne Fredericks Literary Agency, Inc. (*US*)
Jill Grinberg Literary Management LLC (*US*)
John Hawkins & Associates, Inc. (*US*)
Johnson & Alcock (*UK*)

Jonathan Pegg Literary Agency (*UK*)
Joëlle Delbourgo Associates, Inc. (*US*)
Kathi J. Paton Literary Agency (*US*)
Kimberley Cameron & Associates (*US*)
The Knight Agency (*US*)
Linda Konner Literary Agency (*US*)
Barbara S. Kouts, Literary Agent (*US*)
Larsen Pomada Literary Agents (*US*)
LBA Books Ltd (*UK*)
Levine Greenberg Rostan Literary Agency (*US*)
Limelight Management (*UK*)
Linda Roghaar Literary Agency, Inc. (*US*)
The Lisa Richards Agency (*Ire*)
Literary & Creative Artists Inc. (*US*)
The Literary Group International (*US*)
The LKG Agency (*US*)
MacGregor Literary (*US*)
Madeleine Milburn Literary, TV & Film Agency (*UK*)
Manus & Associates Literary Agency, Inc. (*US*)
Marsal Lyon Literary Agency LLC (*US*)
Martin Leonardis Ltd (*UK*)
Martin Literary Management (*US*)
Max Gartenburg Literary Agency (*US*)
MBA Literary Agents Ltd (*UK*)
McCormick Literary (*US*)
The Michael Greer Literary Agency (*UK*)
Mulcahy Associates (Part of MMB Creative) (*UK*)
Nappaland Literary Agency (*US*)
Northbank Talent Management (*UK*)
Northern Lights Literary Services (*US*)
P.S. Literary Agency (*Can*)
The Amy Rennert Agency, Inc. (*US*)
Richford Becklow Literary Agency (*UK*)
The Rights Factory (*Can*)
Rita Rosenkranz Literary Agency (*US*)
Robin Straus Agency, Inc. (*US*)
Rocking Chair Books (*UK*)
Rosica Colin Ltd (*UK*)
The Rudy Agency (*US*)
Salkind Literary Agency (*US*)
Sandra Dijkstra Literary Agency (*US*)
Sanford J. Greenburger Associates, Inc. (*US*)
Lynn Seligman, Literary Agent (*US*)
Sheil Land Associates Ltd (*UK*)
Sheree Bykofsky Associates, Inc. (*US*)
The Spieler Agency (*US*)
Sterling Lord Literistic, Inc. (*US*)
The Stuart Agency (*US*)
SYLA – Susan Yearwood Literary Agency (*UK*)
Talcott Notch Literary (*US*)
Teresa Chris Literary Agency Ltd (*UK*)
TriadaUS Literary Agency, Inc. (*US*)
Trident Media Group, LLC (*US*)
2M Literary Agency Ltd (*US*)
Upstart Crow Literary (*US*)
Veritas Literary Agency (*US*)
Wendy Sherman Associates, Inc. (*US*)
Whispering Buffalo Literary Agency Ltd (*UK*)
Writers House, LLC (*US*)
Literature
Andrew Lownie Literary Agency Ltd (*UK*)

Antony Harwood Limited (*UK*)
Baldi Agency (*US*)
Bob Mecoy Creative Book Services (*US*)
The Bright Literary Academy (*UK*)
Carolyn Jenks Agency (*US*)
Elyse Cheney Literary Associates, LLC (*US*)
The Cowles-Ryan Literary Agency (*US*)
DeFiore and Company (*US*)
Don Congdon Associates, Inc. (*US*)
Georges Borchardt, Inc. (*US*)
Michelle Kass Associates (*UK*)
Patricia Moosbrugger Literary Agency (*US*)
P.S. Literary Agency (*Can*)
The Amy Rennert Agency, Inc. (*US*)
Richard Henshaw Group LLC (*US*)
Richford Becklow Literary Agency (*UK*)
Rocking Chair Books (*UK*)
The Ruppin Agency (*UK*)
Scribe Agency LLC (*US*)
Tibor Jones & Associates (*UK*)
Victoria Sanders & Associates LLC (*US*)
Writers' Representatives, LLC (*US*)
Media
Andrew Lownie Literary Agency Ltd (*UK*)
Antony Harwood Limited (*UK*)
E. J. McCarthy Agency (*US*)
The Feldstein Agency (*UK*)
Folio Literary Management, LLC (*US*)
Glass Literary Management LLC (*US*)
Joy Harris Literary Agency, Inc. (*US*)
The Knight Agency (*US*)
Martin Literary Management (*US*)
Medicine
Ambassador Speakers Bureau & Literary Agency (*US*)
Andrew Lownie Literary Agency Ltd (*UK*)
The Angela Rinaldi Literary Agency (*US*)
Antony Harwood Limited (*UK*)
Arcadia (*US*)
Betsy Amster Literary Enterprises (*US*)
Carol Mann Agency (*US*)
Caroline Davidson Literary Agency (*UK*)
Richard Curtis Associates, Inc. (*US*)
DeFiore and Company (*US*)
Don Congdon Associates, Inc. (*US*)
Jim Donovan Literary (*US*)
Mary Evans, Inc. (*US*)
Frances Kelly Agency (*UK*)
Grace Freedson's Publishing Network (*US*)
Hardman & Swainson (*UK*)
Hornfischer Literary Management, L.P. (*US*)
J de S Associates Inc. (*US*)
Jeanne Fredericks Literary Agency, Inc. (*US*)
Jill Grinberg Literary Management LLC (*US*)
Larsen Pomada Literary Agents (*US*)
Literary & Creative Artists Inc. (*US*)
The Martell Agency (*US*)
Margret McBride Literary Agency (*US*)
Northern Lights Literary Services (*US*)
Robert Dudley Agency (*UK*)
The Rudy Agency (*US*)
Marly Rusoff & Associates, Inc. (*US*)
2M Literary Agency Ltd (*US*)

The Zack Company, Inc (*US*)

Men's Interests
Andrew Lownie Literary Agency Ltd (*UK*)
Antony Harwood Limited (*UK*)
Conville & Walsh Ltd (*UK*)
Rosica Colin Ltd (*UK*)
The Ruppin Agency (*UK*)

Military
Andrew Lownie Literary Agency Ltd (*UK*)
Antony Harwood Limited (*UK*)
Artellus Limited (*UK*)
Blake Friedmann Literary Agency Ltd (*UK*)
Bleecker Street Associates, Inc. (*US*)
Bob Mecoy Creative Book Services (*US*)
Chase Literary Agency (*US*)
Conville & Walsh Ltd (*UK*)
D4EO Literary Agency (*US*)
DeFiore and Company (*US*)
Don Congdon Associates, Inc. (*US*)
Jim Donovan Literary (*US*)
Doug Grad Literary Agency (*US*)
Dystel, Goderich & Bourret LLC (*US*)
E. J. McCarthy Agency (*US*)
The Feldstein Agency (*UK*)
FinePrint Literary Management (*US*)
Folio Literary Management, LLC (*US*)
The G Agency, LLC (*US*)
Grace Freedson's Publishing Network (*US*)
Holloway Literary (*US*)
Hornfischer Literary Management, L.P. (*US*)
J de S Associates Inc. (*US*)
LAW (Lucas Alexander Whitley) (*UK*)
The Literary Group International (*US*)
Duncan McAra (*UK*)
Lynne Rabinoff Agency (*US*)
Raines & Raines (*US*)
Robert Dudley Agency (*UK*)
Rosica Colin Ltd (*UK*)
The Rudy Agency (*US*)
The Ruppin Agency (*UK*)
Sheil Land Associates Ltd (*UK*)
The Zack Company, Inc (*US*)

Music
Andrew Lownie Literary Agency Ltd (*UK*)
Antony Harwood Limited (*UK*)
Bresnick Weil Literary Agency, LLC (*US*)
Carol Mann Agency (*US*)
Clare Hulton Literary Agency (*UK*)
David Black Literary Agency (*US*)
DeFiore and Company (*US*)
The Doe Coover Agency (*US*)
Don Congdon Associates, Inc. (*US*)
Jim Donovan Literary (*US*)
Doug Grad Literary Agency (*US*)
Dunham Literary, Inc. (*US*)
The Feldstein Agency (*UK*)
FinePrint Literary Management (*US*)
Folio Literary Management, LLC (*US*)
Foundry Literary + Media (*US*)
Jenny Brown Associates (*UK*)
Johnson & Alcock (*UK*)
L. Perkins Associates (*US*)
Larsen Pomada Literary Agents (*US*)

LAW (Lucas Alexander Whitley) (*UK*)
Sarah Lazin Books (*US*)
Linda Roghaar Literary Agency, Inc. (*US*)
The Literary Group International (*US*)
Marsal Lyon Literary Agency LLC (*US*)
Margret McBride Literary Agency (*US*)
McIntosh & Otis, Inc (*US*)
Rita Rosenkranz Literary Agency (*US*)
The Ruppin Agency (*UK*)
Sandra Dijkstra Literary Agency (*US*)
Sanford J. Greenburger Associates, Inc. (*US*)
The Sayle Literary Agency (*UK*)
Lynn Seligman, Literary Agent (*US*)
The Spieler Agency (*US*)
The Stuart Agency (*US*)
Tibor Jones & Associates (*UK*)
TriadaUS Literary Agency, Inc. (*US*)
Trident Media Group, LLC (*US*)
2M Literary Agency Ltd (*US*)
Victoria Sanders & Associates LLC (*US*)
Watson, Little Ltd (*UK*)
The Weingel-Fidel Agency (*US*)
Whispering Buffalo Literary Agency Ltd (*UK*)
Wm Clark Associates (*US*)
The Zack Company, Inc (*US*)

Mystery
Aaron M. Priest Literary Agency (*US*)
The Ahearn Agency, Inc (*US*)
Alive Literary Agency (*US*)
Marcia Amsterdam Agency (*US*)
Andrea Brown Literary Agency, Inc. (*US*)
Andrew Lownie Literary Agency Ltd (*UK*)
The Angela Rinaldi Literary Agency (*US*)
Ann Rittenberg Literary Agency (*US*)
Antony Harwood Limited (*UK*)
The Axelrod Agency (*US*)
Ayesha Pande Literary (*US*)
B.J. Robbins Literary Agency (*US*)
The Bent Agency (*US*)
Betsy Amster Literary Enterprises (*US*)
Blake Friedmann Literary Agency Ltd (*UK*)
Bleecker Street Associates, Inc. (*US*)
Bob Mecoy Creative Book Services (*US*)
Bond Literary Agency (*US*)
Book Cents Literary Agency (*US*)
BookStop Literary Agency, LLC (*US*)
Brandt & Hochman Literary Agents, Inc. (*US*)
The Bright Literary Academy (*UK*)
Carolyn Jenks Agency (*US*)
Chartwell (*UK*)
Chase Literary Agency (*US*)
Cherry Weiner Literary Agency (*US*)
The Chudney Agency (*US*)
Cine/Lit Representation (*US*)
Conville & Walsh Ltd (*UK*)
Coombs Moylett & Maclean Literary Agency (*UK*)
Corvisiero Literary Agency (*US*)
The Cowles-Ryan Literary Agency (*US*)
Creative Media Agency (*US*)
Richard Curtis Associates, Inc. (*US*)
D4EO Literary Agency (*US*)
Don Congdon Associates, Inc. (*US*)

Manus & Associates Literary Agency, Inc. (US)
Max Gartenburg Literary Agency (US)
McIntosh & Otis, Inc (US)
P.S. Literary Agency (Can)
Peters Fraser + Dunlop (UK)
Robin Straus Agency, Inc. (US)
Rocking Chair Books (UK)
Rosica Colin Ltd (UK)
Rupert Heath Literary Agency (UK)
The Ruppin Agency (UK)
Sandra Dijkstra Literary Agency (US)
Sanford J. Greenburger Associates, Inc. (US)
Scovil Galen Ghosh Literary Agency, Inc. (US)
Lynn Seligman, Literary Agent (US)
Solow Literary Enterprises, Inc. (US)
The Spieler Agency (US)
Sterling Lord Literistic, Inc. (US)
Stuart Krichevsky Literary Agency, Inc. (US)
Talcott Notch Literary (US)
The Unter Agency (US)
Veritas Literary Agency (US)
Watkins / Loomis Agency, Inc. (US)
Wendy Sherman Associates, Inc. (US)
Whispering Buffalo Literary Agency Ltd (UK)
The Zack Company, Inc (US)

New Age
Antony Harwood Limited (UK)
Bleecker Street Associates, Inc. (US)
Dystel, Goderich & Bourret LLC (US)
Ethan Ellenberg Literary Agency (US)
J de S Associates Inc. (US)
Larsen Pomada Literary Agents (US)
Levine Greenberg Rostan Literary Agency (US)
Northern Lights Literary Services (US)

Nonfiction
A & B Personal Management Ltd (UK)
A.M. Heath & Company Limited, Author's
Agents (UK)
Aaron M. Priest Literary Agency (US)
Dominick Abel Literary Agency, Inc (US)
Abner Stein (UK)
Adler & Robin Books, Inc (US)
Agency for the Performing Arts (APA) (US)
The Agency (London) Ltd (UK)
AHA Talent Ltd (UK)
The Ahearn Agency, Inc (US)
Aitken Alexander Associates (UK)
Alive Literary Agency (US)
Ambassador Speakers Bureau & Literary
Agency (US)
The Ampersand Agency Ltd (UK)
Darley Anderson Children's (UK)
The Anderson Literary Agency (US)
Andlyn (UK)
Andrea Brown Literary Agency, Inc. (US)
Andrew Lownie Literary Agency Ltd (UK)
Andrew Nurnberg Associates, Ltd (UK)
The Angela Rinaldi Literary Agency (US)
Ann Rittenberg Literary Agency (US)
Anthony Sheil in Association with Aitken
Alexander Associates (UK)
Antony Harwood Limited (UK)
Aponte Literary (US)

Arcadia (US)
Artellus Limited (UK)
Audrey A. Wolf Literary Agency (US)
Author Rights Agency (Ire)
The Authors Care Service ltd (UK)
Ayesha Pande Literary (US)
B.J. Robbins Literary Agency (US)
Baldi Agency (US)
Barbara Hogenson Agency (US)
Barbara Levy Literary Agency (UK)
Baror International, Inc. (US)
Bath Literary Agency (UK)
Bell Lomax Moreton Agency (UK)
The Bent Agency (US)
Betsy Amster Literary Enterprises (US)
Bidnick & Company (US)
Vicky Bijur Literary Agency (US)
The Blair Partnership (UK)
Blake Friedmann Literary Agency Ltd (UK)
Bleecker Street Associates, Inc. (US)
Bob Mecoy Creative Book Services (US)
Bond Literary Agency (US)
The Book Bureau Literary Agency (Ire)
Books & Such Literary Management (US)
BookStop Literary Agency, LLC (US)
Brandt & Hochman Literary Agents, Inc. (US)
The Brattle Agency LLC (US)
Bresnick Weil Literary Agency, LLC (US)
Brotherstone Creative Management (UK)
Browne & Miller Literary Associates (US)
Capital Talent Agency (US)
Carol Mann Agency (US)
Caroline Davidson Literary Agency (UK)
Caroline Sheldon Literary Agency (UK)
Carolyn Jenks Agency (US)
Chartwell (UK)
Chase Literary Agency (US)
Mic Cheetham Literary Agency (UK)
Elyse Cheney Literary Associates, LLC (US)
Cherry Weiner Literary Agency (US)
Christine Green Authors' Agent (UK)
The Christopher Little Literary Agency (UK)
Cine/Lit Representation (US)
Clare Hulton Literary Agency (UK)
Conville & Walsh Ltd (UK)
Coombs Moylett & Maclean Literary Agency
(UK)
Corvisiero Literary Agency (US)
The Cowles-Ryan Literary Agency (US)
Creative Trust, Inc. (US)
Creative Authors Ltd (UK)
Creative Media Agency (US)
The Culinary Entertainment Agency (CEA) (US)
Curtis Brown Group Ltd (UK)
Richard Curtis Associates, Inc. (US)
Curtis Brown Ltd (US)
Cynthia Cannell Literary Agency (US)
D4EO Literary Agency (US)
Daniel Literary Group (US)
David Luxton Associates (UK)
David Black Literary Agency (US)
David Godwin Associates (UK)
David Higham Associates Ltd (UK)

DeFiore and Company (*US*)
DHH Literary Agency Ltd (*UK*)
Diamond Kahn and Woods (DKW) Literary Agency Ltd (*UK*)
Dinah Wiener Ltd (*UK*)
The Doe Coover Agency (*US*)
Don Congdon Associates, Inc. (*US*)
Jim Donovan Literary (*US*)
Doug Grad Literary Agency (*US*)
Dunham Literary, Inc. (*US*)
Dystel, Goderich & Bourret LLC (*US*)
E. J. McCarthy Agency (*US*)
Toby Eady Associates Ltd (*UK*)
Eddison Pearson Ltd (*UK*)
Anne Edelstein Literary Agency (*US*)
Edwards Fuglewicz (*UK*)
Elaine Markson Literary Agency (*US*)
Elaine Steel (*UK*)
Elise Dillsworth Agency (EDA) (*UK*)
Elizabeth Roy Literary Agency (*UK*)
Emerald City Literary Agency (*US*)
Emily Sweet Associates (*UK*)
Empire Literary, LLC (*US*)
Ethan Ellenberg Literary Agency (*US*)
Mary Evans, Inc. (*US*)
Eve White: Literary Agent (*UK*)
Faith Evans Associates (*UK*)
The Feldstein Agency (*UK*)
Felicity Bryan Associates (*UK*)
FinePrint Literary Management (*US*)
Flannery Literary (*US*)
Fletcher & Company (*US*)
Folio Literary Management, LLC (*US*)
Foundry Literary + Media (*US*)
Fox Literary (*US*)
Fox & Howard Literary Agency (*UK*)
Frances Collin Literary Agent (*US*)
Frances Kelly Agency (*UK*)
Fraser Ross Associates (*UK*)
Fraser-Bub Literary, LLC (*US*)
Furniss Lawton (*UK*)
Fuse Literary (*US*)
The G Agency, LLC (*US*)
Gallt & Zacker Literary Agency (*US*)
Gelfman Schneider / ICM Partners (*US*)
Georges Borchardt, Inc. (*US*)
Georgina Capel Associates Ltd (*UK*)
The Gernert Company (*US*)
Gina Maccoby Agency (*US*)
Eric Glass Ltd (*UK*)
Glass Literary Management LLC (*US*)
Global Lion Intellectual Property Management, Inc. (*US*)
The Good Literary Agency (*UK*)
Grace Freedson's Publishing Network (*US*)
Graham Maw Christie Literary Agency (*UK*)
Greene & Heaton Ltd (*UK*)
Blanche C. Gregory Inc. (*US*)
David Grossman Literary Agency Ltd (*UK*)
Marianne Gunn O'Connor Literary Agency (*Ire*)
Gunn Media Associates (*UK*)
Hannigan Salky Getzler (HSG) Agency (*US*)
Hardman & Swainson (*UK*)

Harold Ober Associates, Inc. (*US*)
Joy Harris Literary Agency, Inc. (*US*)
The Helen Brann Agency, Inc. (*US*)
Herman Agency Inc. (*US*)
hhb agency ltd (*UK*)
Hill Nadell Literary Agency (*US*)
Holloway Literary (*US*)
Holroyde Cartey (*UK*)
Vanessa Holt Ltd (*UK*)
Hornfischer Literary Management, L.P. (*US*)
Andrea Hurst Literary Management (*US*)
Inklings Literary Agency, LLC (*US*)
Intercontinental Literary Agency (*UK*)
Isabel White Literary Agent (*UK*)
Jane Conway-Gordon Ltd (*UK*)
Jane Judd Literary Agency (*UK*)
Jane Rotrosen Agency (*US*)
Jane Turnbull (*UK*)
Janklow & Nesbit Associates (*US*)
Jeanne Fredericks Literary Agency, Inc. (*US*)
Jenny Brown Associates (*UK*)
Jill Grinberg Literary Management LLC (*US*)
Jill Corcoran Literary Agency (*US*)
Jo Unwin Literary Agency (*UK*)
Joanna Pulcini Literary Management (*US*)
John Hawkins & Associates, Inc. (*US*)
Johnson & Alcock (*UK*)
Jonathan Clowes Ltd (*UK*)
Jonathan Pegg Literary Agency (*UK*)
Joëlle Delbourgo Associates, Inc. (*US*)
Juliet Burton Literary Agency (*UK*)
JYLA (Jason Yarn Literary Agency) (*US*)
K2 Literary (*Can*)
Kate Hordern Literary Agency (*UK*)
Kate Nash Literary Agency (*UK*)
Kathi J. Paton Literary Agency (*US*)
Keane Kataria Literary Agency (*UK*)
Ken Sherman & Associates (*US*)
Ki Agency Ltd (*UK*)
Kimberley Cameron & Associates (*US*)
Kingsford Campbell Literary & Marketing Agents (*UK*)
Knight Features (*UK*)
Linda Konner Literary Agency (*US*)
L. Perkins Associates (*US*)
Larsen Pomada Literary Agents (*US*)
Laura Dail Literary Agency (*US*)
LAW (Lucas Alexander Whitley) (*UK*)
Lawrence Jordan Literary Agency (*US*)
Sarah Lazin Books (*US*)
LBA Books Ltd (*UK*)
Leigh Feldman Literary (*US*)
The Leshne Agency (*US*)
Levine Greenberg Rostan Literary Agency (*US*)
Limelight Management (*UK*)
Linda Chester & Associates (*US*)
Linda Roghaar Literary Agency, Inc. (*US*)
Lindsay Literary Agency (*UK*)
Linn Prentis, Literary Agent (*US*)
The Lisa Ekus Group, LLC (*US*)
The Lisa Richards Agency (*Ire*)
Literary & Creative Artists Inc. (*US*)
The Literary Group International (*US*)

The LKG Agency (*US*)
London Independent Books (*UK*)
Lorella Belli Literary Agency (LBLA) (*UK*)
Louise Greenberg Books Ltd (*UK*)
Lutyens and Rubinstein (*UK*)
MacGregor Literary (*US*)
Madeleine Milburn Literary, TV & Film Agency (*UK*)
Maggie Pearlstine Associates Ltd (*UK*)
Manus & Associates Literary Agency, Inc. (*US*)
Maria Carvainis Agency, Inc. (*US*)
Marsal Lyon Literary Agency LLC (*US*)
The Marsh Agency (*UK*)
The Martell Agency (*US*)
Martin Leonardis Ltd (*UK*)
Martin Literary Management (*US*)
Mary Clemmey Literary Agency (*UK*)
Massie & McQuilkin (*US*)
Max Gartenburg Literary Agency (*US*)
MBA Literary Agents Ltd (*UK*)
Duncan McAra (*UK*)
Margret McBride Literary Agency (*US*)
McCormick Literary (*US*)
McIntosh & Otis, Inc (*US*)
Meredith Bernstein Literary Agency, Inc. (*US*)
The Michael Greer Literary Agency (*UK*)
Patricia Moosbrugger Literary Agency (*US*)
Howard Morhaim Literary Agency (*US*)
Mulcahy Associates (Part of MMB Creative) (*UK*)
Nappaland Literary Agency (*US*)
New Leaf Literary & Media, Inc. (*US*)
Niad Management (*US*)
MNLA (Maggie Noach Literary Agency) (*UK*)
Northbank Talent Management (*UK*)
Northern Lights Literary Services (*US*)
Deborah Owen Ltd (*UK*)
P.S. Literary Agency (*Can*)
The Park Literary Group LLC (*US*)
Pavilion Literary Management (*US*)
Peters Fraser + Dunlop (*UK*)
PEW Literary (*UK*)
Shelley Power Literary Agency Ltd (*UK*)
Publication Riot Group, Inc. (*US*)
The Purcell Agency, LLC (*US*)
Puttick Literary Agency (*UK*)
Queen Literary Agency, Inc. (*US*)
Lynne Rabinoff Agency (*US*)
Raines & Raines (*US*)
Redhammer (*UK*)
Regal Hoffmann & Associates LLC (*US*)
The Amy Rennert Agency, Inc. (*US*)
Richard Henshaw Group LLC (*US*)
Richford Becklow Literary Agency (*UK*)
The Rights Bureau (*Ire*)
The Rights Factory (*Can*)
Rita Rosenkranz Literary Agency (*US*)
Riverside Literary Agency (*US*)
RLR Associates (*US*)
The Robbins Office, Inc. (*US*)
Robert Dudley Agency (*UK*)
Robin Jones Literary Agency (*UK*)
Robin Straus Agency, Inc. (*US*)

Rocking Chair Books (*UK*)
Rodeen Literary Management (*US*)
Rosica Colin Ltd (*UK*)
Andy Ross Agency (*US*)
Ross Yoon Agency (*US*)
The Rudy Agency (*US*)
Rupert Heath Literary Agency (*UK*)
The Ruppin Agency (*UK*)
Marly Rusoff & Associates, Inc. (*US*)
The Sagalyn Literary Agency (*US*)
Salkind Literary Agency (*US*)
Sandra Dijkstra Literary Agency (*US*)
Sanford J. Greenburger Associates, Inc. (*US*)
Sarah Such Literary Agency (*UK*)
The Sayle Literary Agency (*UK*)
Scott Treimel NY (*US*)
Scovil Galen Ghosh Literary Agency, Inc. (*US*)
Secret Agent Man (*US*)
Lynn Seligman, Literary Agent (*US*)
Sheil Land Associates Ltd (*UK*)
Sheila Ableman Literary Agency (*UK*)
Sheree Bykofsky Associates, Inc. (*US*)
Signature Literary Agency (*US*)
SLW Literary Agency (*US*)
Solow Literary Enterprises, Inc. (*US*)
Sophie Hicks Agency (*UK*)
Spectrum Literary Agency (*US*)
Speilburg Literary Agency (*US*)
Spencerhill Associates (*US*)
The Spieler Agency (*US*)
Philip G. Spitzer Literary Agency, Inc. (*US*)
Standen Literary Agency (*UK*)
Stephanie Tade Literary Agency (*US*)
Sterling Lord Literistic, Inc. (*US*)
Stuart Krichevsky Literary Agency, Inc. (*US*)
The Stuart Agency (*US*)
Susan Rabiner, Literary Agent, Inc. (*US*)
Susanna Lea Associates (UK) (*UK*)
The Susijn Agency (*UK*)
SYLA – Susan Yearwood Literary Agency (*UK*)
Talcott Notch Literary (*US*)
Teresa Chris Literary Agency Ltd (*UK*)
Tessler Literary Agency (*US*)
Tibor Jones & Associates (*UK*)
Toby Mundy Associates Ltd (*UK*)
Tracy Brown Literary Agency (*US*)
Lavinia Trevor Agency (*UK*)
TriadaUS Literary Agency, Inc. (*US*)
Trident Media Group, LLC (*US*)
2M Literary Agency Ltd (*US*)
Uli Rushby-Smith Literary Agency (*UK*)
Union Literary (*US*)
United Talent Agency (*US*)
United Agents (*UK*)
The Unter Agency (*US*)
Upstart Crow Literary (*US*)
Veritas Literary Agency (*US*)
Victoria Sanders & Associates LLC (*US*)
The Viney Shaw Agency (*UK*)
Wade & Co Literary Agency (*UK*)
Watkins / Loomis Agency, Inc. (*US*)
Watson, Little Ltd (*UK*)
Waxman Leavell Literary Agency (*US*)

The Weingel-Fidel Agency (*US*)
Wendy Schmalz Agency (*US*)
Wendy Sherman Associates, Inc. (*US*)
Westwood Creative Artists (*Can*)
Whispering Buffalo Literary Agency Ltd (*UK*)
William Morris Endeavor (WME) London (*UK*)
William Morris Endeavor Entertainment (*US*)
Wm Clark Associates (*US*)
The Writers' Practice (*UK*)
Writers' Representatives, LLC (*US*)
Writers House, LLC (*US*)
The Wylie Agency (UK) Ltd (*UK*)
Yates & Yates (*US*)
The Zack Company, Inc (*US*)
Zoë Pagnamenta Agency, LLC (*US*)

Philosophy
Antony Harwood Limited (*UK*)
Clare Hulton Literary Agency (*UK*)
David Black Literary Agency (*US*)
DeFiore and Company (*US*)
The Feldstein Agency (*UK*)
Georges Borchardt, Inc. (*US*)
Grace Freedson's Publishing Network (*US*)
Graham Maw Christie Literary Agency (*UK*)
Hardman & Swainson (*UK*)
LAW (Lucas Alexander Whitley) (*UK*)
Literary & Creative Artists Inc. (*US*)
Puttick Literary Agency (*UK*)
The Ruppin Agency (*UK*)
Sandra Dijkstra Literary Agency (*US*)
Stephanie Tade Literary Agency (*US*)
Wm Clark Associates (*US*)
Writers' Representatives, LLC (*US*)

Photography
Andrea Brown Literary Agency, Inc. (*US*)
Antony Harwood Limited (*UK*)
Hannigan Salky Getzler (HSG) Agency (*US*)
Jeanne Fredericks Literary Agency, Inc. (*US*)
The Leshne Agency (*US*)
P.S. Literary Agency (*Can*)
Salkind Literary Agency (*US*)
Lynn Seligman, Literary Agent (*US*)
The Spieler Agency (*US*)

Poetry
Bookseeker Agency (*UK*)
Eddison Pearson Ltd (*UK*)
The Spieler Agency (*US*)
Writers' Representatives, LLC (*US*)

Politics
Aaron M. Priest Literary Agency (*US*)
Ambassador Speakers Bureau & Literary Agency (*US*)
Andrew Lownie Literary Agency Ltd (*UK*)
Antony Harwood Limited (*UK*)
Aponte Literary (*US*)
Audrey A. Wolf Literary Agency (*US*)
Vicky Bijur Literary Agency (*US*)
Blake Friedmann Literary Agency Ltd (*UK*)
Bleecker Street Associates, Inc. (*US*)
The Brattle Agency LLC (*US*)
Bresnick Weil Literary Agency, LLC (*US*)
Carol Mann Agency (*US*)
Caroline Davidson Literary Agency (*UK*)

Elyse Cheney Literary Associates, LLC (*US*)
David Luxton Associates (*UK*)
David Black Literary Agency (*US*)
DeFiore and Company (*US*)
Diamond Kahn and Woods (DKW) Literary Agency Ltd (*UK*)
The Doe Coover Agency (*US*)
Don Congdon Associates, Inc. (*US*)
Jim Donovan Literary (*US*)
Dunham Literary, Inc. (*US*)
Dystel, Goderich & Bourret LLC (*US*)
E. J. McCarthy Agency (*US*)
Mary Evans, Inc. (*US*)
The Feldstein Agency (*UK*)
Fletcher & Company (*US*)
Folio Literary Management, LLC (*US*)
Furniss Lawton (*UK*)
Gelfman Schneider / ICM Partners (*US*)
Georges Borchardt, Inc. (*US*)
The Gernert Company (*US*)
Gina Maccoby Agency (*US*)
Hannigan Salky Getzler (HSG) Agency (*US*)
hhb agency ltd (*UK*)
Hill Nadell Literary Agency (*US*)
Holloway Literary (*US*)
Hornfischer Literary Management, L.P. (*US*)
Andrea Hurst Literary Management (*US*)
J de S Associates Inc. (*US*)
Jill Grinberg Literary Management LLC (*US*)
John Hawkins & Associates, Inc. (*US*)
Joëlle Delbourgo Associates, Inc. (*US*)
Kathi J. Paton Literary Agency (*US*)
Ki Agency Ltd (*UK*)
Kimberley Cameron & Associates (*US*)
Larsen Pomada Literary Agents (*US*)
LAW (Lucas Alexander Whitley) (*UK*)
Sarah Lazin Books (*US*)
Levine Greenberg Rostan Literary Agency (*US*)
Literary & Creative Artists Inc. (*US*)
Marsal Lyon Literary Agency LLC (*US*)
Massie & McQuilkin (*US*)
Max Gartenburg Literary Agency (*US*)
McCormick Literary (*US*)
Northbank Talent Management (*UK*)
P.S. Literary Agency (*Can*)
The Park Literary Group LLC (*US*)
Publication Riot Group, Inc. (*US*)
Lynne Rabinoff Agency (*US*)
The Rights Factory (*Can*)
The Rudy Agency (*US*)
Rupert Heath Literary Agency (*UK*)
The Ruppin Agency (*UK*)
Salkind Literary Agency (*US*)
Sandra Dijkstra Literary Agency (*US*)
Sanford J. Greenburger Associates, Inc. (*US*)
Scovil Galen Ghosh Literary Agency, Inc. (*US*)
Lynn Seligman, Literary Agent (*US*)
Sheil Land Associates Ltd (*UK*)
Signature Literary Agency (*US*)
The Spieler Agency (*US*)
Philip G. Spitzer Literary Agency, Inc. (*US*)
Stephanie Tade Literary Agency (*US*)
Sterling Lord Literistic, Inc. (*US*)

Stuart Krichevsky Literary Agency, Inc. (*US*)
Susan Rabiner, Literary Agent, Inc. (*US*)
Toby Mundy Associates Ltd (*UK*)
TriadaUS Literary Agency, Inc. (*US*)
Trident Media Group, LLC (*US*)
2M Literary Agency Ltd (*US*)
The Unter Agency (*US*)
Victoria Sanders & Associates LLC (*US*)
Watkins / Loomis Agency, Inc. (*US*)
Whispering Buffalo Literary Agency Ltd (*UK*)
Writers' Representatives, LLC (*US*)
Yates & Yates (*US*)
The Zack Company, Inc (*US*)
Psychology
A.M. Heath & Company Limited, Author's
Agents (*UK*)
Andrew Lownie Literary Agency Ltd (*UK*)
The Angela Rinaldi Literary Agency (*US*)
Antony Harwood Limited (*UK*)
Arcadia (*US*)
Betsy Amster Literary Enterprises (*US*)
Vicky Bijur Literary Agency (*US*)
Blake Friedmann Literary Agency Ltd (*UK*)
Bleecker Street Associates, Inc. (*US*)
Bresnick Weil Literary Agency, LLC (*US*)
Carol Mann Agency (*US*)
Caroline Davidson Literary Agency (*UK*)
Chartwell (*UK*)
Conville & Walsh Ltd (*UK*)
The Cowles-Ryan Literary Agency (*US*)
Creative Media Agency (*US*)
D4EO Literary Agency (*US*)
David Black Literary Agency (*US*)
DeFiore and Company (*US*)
The Doe Coover Agency (*US*)
Don Congdon Associates, Inc. (*US*)
Dystel, Goderich & Bourret LLC (*US*)
Anne Edelstein Literary Agency (*US*)
Ethan Ellenberg Literary Agency (*US*)
Folio Literary Management, LLC (*US*)
Foundry Literary + Media (*US*)
Fox & Howard Literary Agency (*UK*)
Fraser-Bub Literary, LLC (*US*)
Grace Freedson's Publishing Network (*US*)
Hannigan Salky Getzler (HSG) Agency (*US*)
Hardman & Swainson (*UK*)
Hornfischer Literary Management, L.P. (*US*)
Andrea Hurst Literary Management (*US*)
Jeanne Fredericks Literary Agency, Inc. (*US*)
Jill Grinberg Literary Management LLC (*US*)
Jill Corcoran Literary Agency (*US*)
John Hawkins & Associates, Inc. (*US*)
Johnson & Alcock (*UK*)
Jonathan Pegg Literary Agency (*UK*)
Joëlle Delbourgo Associates, Inc. (*US*)
The Knight Agency (*US*)
Linda Konner Literary Agency (*US*)
Barbara S. Kouts, Literary Agent (*US*)
L. Perkins Associates (*US*)
Larsen Pomada Literary Agents (*US*)
Levine Greenberg Rostan Literary Agency (*US*)
The Literary Group International (*US*)
The LKG Agency (*US*)

Madeleine Milburn Literary, TV & Film Agency
(*UK*)
Manus & Associates Literary Agency, Inc. (*US*)
Maria Carvainis Agency, Inc. (*US*)
Marsal Lyon Literary Agency LLC (*US*)
The Martell Agency (*US*)
Massie & McQuilkin (*US*)
McIntosh & Otis, Inc (*US*)
The Michael Greer Literary Agency (*UK*)
Northbank Talent Management (*UK*)
Northern Lights Literary Services (*US*)
P.S. Literary Agency (*Can*)
Peters Fraser + Dunlop (*UK*)
Queen Literary Agency, Inc. (*US*)
Lynne Rabinoff Agency (*US*)
Raines & Raines (*US*)
Richard Henshaw Group LLC (*US*)
Robin Straus Agency, Inc. (*US*)
Rosica Colin Ltd (*UK*)
Ross Yoon Agency (*US*)
Marly Rusoff & Associates, Inc. (*US*)
Salkind Literary Agency (*US*)
Sanford J. Greenburger Associates, Inc. (*US*)
Scovil Galen Ghosh Literary Agency, Inc. (*US*)
Lynn Seligman, Literary Agent (*US*)
Sheil Land Associates Ltd (*UK*)
Sheree Bykofsky Associates, Inc. (*US*)
Signature Literary Agency (*US*)
Solow Literary Enterprises, Inc. (*US*)
Stephanie Tade Literary Agency (*US*)
The Stuart Agency (*US*)
SYLA – Susan Yearwood Literary Agency (*UK*)
Tessler Literary Agency (*US*)
Tracy Brown Literary Agency (*US*)
TriadaUS Literary Agency, Inc. (*US*)
2M Literary Agency Ltd (*US*)
Victoria Sanders & Associates LLC (*US*)
Watson, Little Ltd (*UK*)
The Weingel-Fidel Agency (*US*)
Wendy Sherman Associates, Inc. (*US*)
Writers House, LLC (*US*)
Radio
The Agency (London) Ltd (*UK*)
Alan Brodie Representation Ltd (*UK*)
Antony Harwood Limited (*UK*)
Berlin Associates (*UK*)
Blake Friedmann Literary Agency Ltd (*UK*)
Curtis Brown Group Ltd (*UK*)
Elaine Steel (*UK*)
Felix de Wolfe (*UK*)
Film Rights Ltd in association with Laurence
Fitch Ltd (*UK*)
Georgina Capel Associates Ltd (*UK*)
Independent Talent Group Ltd (*UK*)
Jill Foster Ltd (JFL) (*UK*)
Jonathan Clowes Ltd (*UK*)
Mary Clemmey Literary Agency (*UK*)
MBA Literary Agents Ltd (*UK*)
Bill McLean Personal Management Ltd (*UK*)
Peters Fraser + Dunlop (*UK*)
Rochelle Stevens & Co. (*UK*)
Rosica Colin Ltd (*UK*)
Sayle Screen Ltd (*UK*)

Sheil Land Associates Ltd (*UK*)
The Tennyson Agency (*UK*)
United Agents (*UK*)
Valerie Hoskins Associates (*UK*)
Reference
Adler & Robin Books, Inc (*US*)
Baldi Agency (*US*)
Caroline Davidson Literary Agency (*UK*)
D4EO Literary Agency (*US*)
David Luxton Associates (*UK*)
The Doe Coover Agency (*US*)
Jim Donovan Literary (*US*)
FinePrint Literary Management (*US*)
Folio Literary Management, LLC (*US*)
Fox & Howard Literary Agency (*UK*)
Frances Kelly Agency (*UK*)
Graham Maw Christie Literary Agency (*UK*)
Jeanne Fredericks Literary Agency, Inc. (*US*)
Kate Hordern Literary Agency (*UK*)
Linda Konner Literary Agency (*US*)
LAW (Lucas Alexander Whitley) (*UK*)
Richard Henshaw Group LLC (*US*)
Rita Rosenkranz Literary Agency (*US*)
Sanford J. Greenburger Associates, Inc. (*US*)
Sheree Bykofsky Associates, Inc. (*US*)
Signature Literary Agency (*US*)
Writers' Representatives, LLC (*US*)
The Zack Company, Inc (*US*)
Religious
Alive Literary Agency (*US*)
Ambassador Speakers Bureau & Literary
Agency (*US*)
The Anderson Literary Agency (*US*)
Antony Harwood Limited (*UK*)
The Authors Care Service ltd (*UK*)
Bleecker Street Associates, Inc. (*US*)
Books & Such Literary Management (*US*)
Carol Mann Agency (*US*)
Creative Media Agency (*US*)
Cynthia Cannell Literary Agency (*US*)
Dystel, Goderich & Bourret LLC (*US*)
Anne Edelstein Literary Agency (*US*)
FinePrint Literary Management (*US*)
Folio Literary Management, LLC (*US*)
Foundry Literary + Media (*US*)
Georges Borchardt, Inc. (*US*)
Grace Freedson's Publishing Network (*US*)
Hornfischer Literary Management, L.P. (*US*)
Andrea Hurst Literary Management (*US*)
Kathi J. Paton Literary Agency (*US*)
Kimberley Cameron & Associates (*US*)
The Knight Agency (*US*)
Larsen Pomada Literary Agents (*US*)
Lawrence Jordan Literary Agency (*US*)
Levine Greenberg Rostan Literary Agency (*US*)
Linda Roghaar Literary Agency, Inc. (*US*)
Literary & Creative Artists Inc. (*US*)
The Literary Group International (*US*)
MacGregor Literary (*US*)
Martin Literary Management (*US*)
Nappaland Literary Agency (*US*)
Lynne Rabinoff Agency (*US*)
Rosica Colin Ltd (*UK*)

Andy Ross Agency (*US*)
Salkind Literary Agency (*US*)
Sandra Dijkstra Literary Agency (*US*)
Scovil Galen Ghosh Literary Agency, Inc. (*US*)
Secret Agent Man (*US*)
Signature Literary Agency (*US*)
The Stuart Agency (*US*)
Trident Media Group, LLC (*US*)
Wm Clark Associates (*US*)
Yates & Yates (*US*)
The Zack Company, Inc (*US*)
Romance
The Ahearn Agency, Inc (*US*)
Marcia Amsterdam Agency (*US*)
Andrea Brown Literary Agency, Inc. (*US*)
Andrew Lownie Literary Agency Ltd (*UK*)
Antony Harwood Limited (*UK*)
The Axelrod Agency (*US*)
Ayesha Pande Literary (*US*)
The Bent Agency (*US*)
Bleecker Street Associates, Inc. (*US*)
Bob Mecoy Creative Book Services (*US*)
Book Cents Literary Agency (*US*)
Books & Such Literary Management (*US*)
Carolyn Jenks Agency (*US*)
Elyse Cheney Literary Associates, LLC (*US*)
Cherry Weiner Literary Agency (*US*)
Corvisiero Literary Agency (*US*)
Creative Media Agency (*US*)
Richard Curtis Associates, Inc. (*US*)
D4EO Literary Agency (*US*)
The Darley Anderson Agency (*UK*)
DeFiore and Company (*US*)
Donaghy Literary Group (*US*)
Doug Grad Literary Agency (*US*)
The Dravis Agency, Inc. (*US*)
Dystel, Goderich & Bourret LLC (*US*)
Edwards Fuglewicz (*UK*)
Elizabeth Roy Literary Agency (*UK*)
Emerald City Literary Agency (*US*)
Ethan Ellenberg Literary Agency (*US*)
FinePrint Literary Management (*US*)
Folio Literary Management, LLC (*US*)
Fox Literary (*US*)
Fraser-Bub Literary, LLC (*US*)
Gallt & Zacker Literary Agency (*US*)
Greyhaus Literary Agency (*US*)
Holloway Literary (*US*)
Hudson Agency (*US*)
Andrea Hurst Literary Management (*US*)
Inklings Literary Agency, LLC (*US*)
Jane Rotrosen Agency (*US*)
Jenny Brown Associates (*UK*)
Jill Grinberg Literary Management LLC (*US*)
Jill Corcoran Literary Agency (*US*)
Jill Grosjean Literary Agency (*US*)
The Knight Agency (*US*)
KT Literary (*US*)
L. Perkins Associates (*US*)
Larsen Pomada Literary Agents (*US*)
Laura Dail Literary Agency (*US*)
LBA Books Ltd (*UK*)
Levine Greenberg Rostan Literary Agency (*US*)

The Literary Group International (*US*)
MacGregor Literary (*US*)
Madeleine Milburn Literary, TV & Film Agency (*UK*)
Manus & Associates Literary Agency, Inc. (*US*)
Maria Carvainis Agency, Inc. (*US*)
Marsal Lyon Literary Agency LLC (*US*)
McIntosh & Otis, Inc (*US*)
Meredith Bernstein Literary Agency, Inc. (*US*)
Howard Morhaim Literary Agency (*US*)
New Leaf Literary & Media, Inc. (*US*)
Niad Management (*US*)
Northern Lights Literary Services (*US*)
One Track Literary Agency, Inc. (*US*)
P.S. Literary Agency (*Can*)
The Purcell Agency, LLC (*US*)
Richard Henshaw Group LLC (*US*)
Richford Becklow Literary Agency (*UK*)
The Rights Factory (*Can*)
RLR Associates (*US*)
Rocking Chair Books (*UK*)
Rosica Colin Ltd (*UK*)
Sandra Dijkstra Literary Agency (*US*)
Sanford J. Greenburger Associates, Inc. (*US*)
Lynn Seligman, Literary Agent (*US*)
Sheil Land Associates Ltd (*UK*)
Signature Literary Agency (*US*)
Spectrum Literary Agency (*US*)
Speilburg Literary Agency (*US*)
Spencerhill Associates (*US*)
The Stringer Literary Agency LLC (*US*)
TriadaUS Literary Agency, Inc. (*US*)
Trident Media Group, LLC (*US*)
Waxman Leavell Literary Agency (*US*)
Whispering Buffalo Literary Agency Ltd (*UK*)
The Zack Company, Inc (*US*)

Science

Aaron M. Priest Literary Agency (*US*)
The Ampersand Agency Ltd (*UK*)
Marcia Amsterdam Agency (*US*)
The Anderson Literary Agency (*US*)
Andrea Brown Literary Agency, Inc. (*US*)
Andrew Lownie Literary Agency Ltd (*UK*)
Antony Harwood Limited (*UK*)
Aponte Literary (*US*)
Arcadia (*US*)
Artellus Limited (*US*)
B.J. Robbins Literary Agency (*US*)
Baldi Agency (*US*)
The Bent Agency (*US*)
Vicky Bijur Literary Agency (*US*)
Blake Friedmann Literary Agency Ltd (*UK*)
Bleecker Street Associates, Inc. (*US*)
Bond Literary Agency (*US*)
BookStop Literary Agency, LLC (*US*)
Brandt & Hochman Literary Agents, Inc. (*US*)
Bresnick Weil Literary Agency, LLC (*US*)
Caroline Davidson Literary Agency (*UK*)
Chartwell (*UK*)
Chase Literary Agency (*US*)
Elyse Cheney Literary Associates, LLC (*US*)
Compass Talent (*US*)
Conville & Walsh Ltd (*UK*)

The Cowles-Ryan Literary Agency (*US*)
Curtis Brown Group Ltd (*UK*)
Richard Curtis Associates, Inc. (*US*)
D4EO Literary Agency (*US*)
David Black Literary Agency (*US*)
DeFiore and Company (*US*)
Dinah Wiener Ltd (*UK*)
The Doe Coover Agency (*US*)
Don Congdon Associates, Inc. (*US*)
Jim Donovan Literary (*US*)
Doug Grad Literary Agency (*US*)
Dunham Literary, Inc. (*US*)
Dystel, Goderich & Bourret LLC (*US*)
Ethan Ellenberg Literary Agency (*US*)
Mary Evans, Inc. (*US*)
Felicity Bryan Associates (*UK*)
FinePrint Literary Management (*US*)
Fletcher & Company (*US*)
Folio Literary Management, LLC (*US*)
Foundry Literary + Media (*US*)
Furniss Lawton (*UK*)
Gelfman Schneider / ICM Partners (*US*)
Georges Borchardt, Inc. (*US*)
The Gernert Company (*US*)
Grace Freedson's Publishing Network (*US*)
Graham Maw Christie Literary Agency (*UK*)
Greene & Heaton Ltd (*UK*)
Hannigan Salky Getzler (HSG) Agency (*US*)
Hardman & Swainson (*UK*)
Hill Nadell Literary Agency (*US*)
Hornfischer Literary Management, L.P. (*US*)
Andrea Hurst Literary Management (*US*)
Jeanne Fredericks Literary Agency, Inc. (*US*)
Jenny Brown Associates (*UK*)
Jill Grinberg Literary Management LLC (*US*)
John Hawkins & Associates, Inc. (*US*)
Johnson & Alcock (*UK*)
Jonathan Pegg Literary Agency (*UK*)
Joëlle Delbourgo Associates, Inc. (*US*)
JYLA (Jason Yarn Literary Agency) (*US*)
Kathi J. Paton Literary Agency (*US*)
Ki Agency Ltd (*UK*)
Kimberley Cameron & Associates (*US*)
Linda Konner Literary Agency (*US*)
L. Perkins Associates (*US*)
Larsen Pomada Literary Agents (*US*)
Laura Dail Literary Agency (*US*)
LAW (Lucas Alexander Whitley) (*UK*)
LBA Books Ltd (*UK*)
The Leshne Agency (*US*)
Levine Greenberg Rostan Literary Agency (*US*)
Limelight Management (*UK*)
The Literary Group International (*US*)
Madeleine Milburn Literary, TV & Film Agency (*UK*)
Manus & Associates Literary Agency, Inc. (*US*)
Maria Carvainis Agency, Inc. (*US*)
Massie & McQuilkin (*US*)
Max Gartenburg Literary Agency (*US*)
McCormick Literary (*US*)
Northbank Talent Management (*UK*)
P.S. Literary Agency (*Can*)
The Park Literary Group LLC (*US*)

Pavilion Literary Management (*US*)
Peters Fraser + Dunlop (*UK*)
Publication Riot Group, Inc. (*US*)
Puttick Literary Agency (*UK*)
Queen Literary Agency, Inc. (*US*)
Lynne Rabinoff Agency (*US*)
Regal Hoffmann & Associates LLC (*US*)
Richard Henshaw Group LLC (*US*)
The Rights Factory (*Can*)
Rita Rosenkranz Literary Agency (*US*)
Robin Straus Agency, Inc. (*US*)
Rosica Colin Ltd (*UK*)
Andy Ross Agency (*US*)
Ross Yoon Agency (*US*)
The Rudy Agency (*US*)
Rupert Heath Literary Agency (*UK*)
The Ruppin Agency (*UK*)
The Sagalyn Literary Agency (*US*)
Salkind Literary Agency (*US*)
Sandra Dijkstra Literary Agency (*US*)
Sanford J. Greenburger Associates, Inc. (*US*)
The Sayle Literary Agency (*UK*)
Scovil Galen Ghosh Literary Agency, Inc. (*US*)
Lynn Seligman, Literary Agent (*US*)
Sheil Land Associates Ltd (*UK*)
Sheila Ableman Literary Agency (*UK*)
Signature Literary Agency (*US*)
Solow Literary Enterprises, Inc. (*US*)
Speilburg Literary Agency (*US*)
The Spieler Agency (*US*)
Sterling Lord Literistic, Inc. (*US*)
Stuart Krichevsky Literary Agency, Inc. (*US*)
The Stuart Agency (*US*)
Susan Rabiner, Literary Agent, Inc. (*US*)
Talcott Notch Literary (*US*)
Tessler Literary Agency (*US*)
Toby Mundy Associates Ltd (*UK*)
Lavinia Trevor Agency (*UK*)
TriadaUS Literary Agency, Inc. (*US*)
Trident Media Group, LLC (*US*)
2M Literary Agency Ltd (*US*)
Union Literary (*US*)
United Talent Agency (*US*)
Veritas Literary Agency (*US*)
Watson, Little Ltd (*UK*)
Waxman Leavell Literary Agency (*US*)
The Weingel-Fidel Agency (*US*)
Westwood Creative Artists (*Can*)
Wm Clark Associates (*US*)
Writers' Representatives, LLC (*US*)
Writers House, LLC (*US*)
The Zack Company, Inc (*US*)
Zoë Pagnamenta Agency, LLC (*US*)
Sci-Fi
The Ampersand Agency Ltd (*UK*)
Andrea Brown Literary Agency, Inc. (*US*)
Andrew Lownie Literary Agency Ltd (*UK*)
Antony Harwood Limited (*UK*)
Aponte Literary (*US*)
Artellus Limited (*UK*)
Ayesha Pande Literary (*US*)
Azantian Literary Agency (*US*)
Baror International, Inc. (*US*)

The Bent Agency (*US*)
Bob Mecoy Creative Book Services (*US*)
Bond Literary Agency (*US*)
The Bright Literary Academy (*UK*)
Carolyn Jenks Agency (*US*)
Mic Cheetham Literary Agency (*UK*)
Cherry Weiner Literary Agency (*US*)
Conville & Walsh Ltd (*UK*)
Corvisiero Literary Agency (*US*)
Richard Curtis Associates, Inc. (*US*)
D4EO Literary Agency (*US*)
DHH Literary Agency Ltd (*UK*)
Diamond Kahn and Woods (DKW) Literary
Agency Ltd (*UK*)
Donaghy Literary Group (*US*)
The Dravis Agency, Inc. (*US*)
Dunham Literary, Inc. (*US*)
Dystel, Goderich & Bourret LLC (*US*)
Emerald City Literary Agency (*US*)
Ethan Ellenberg Literary Agency (*US*)
FinePrint Literary Management (*US*)
Folio Literary Management, LLC (*US*)
Foundry Literary + Media (*US*)
Fox Literary (*US*)
Frances Collin Literary Agent (*US*)
The Gernert Company (*US*)
Greene & Heaton Ltd (*UK*)
Holloway Literary (*US*)
Andrea Hurst Literary Management (*US*)
Inklings Literary Agency, LLC (*US*)
Jill Grinberg Literary Management LLC (*US*)
Jill Corcoran Literary Agency (*US*)
John Hawkins & Associates, Inc. (*US*)
Johnson & Alcock (*UK*)
JYLA (Jason Yarn Literary Agency) (*US*)
Kimberley Cameron & Associates (*US*)
The Knight Agency (*US*)
KT Literary (*US*)
L. Perkins Associates (*US*)
Laura Dail Literary Agency (*US*)
LAW (Lucas Alexander Whitley) (*UK*)
LBA Books Ltd (*UK*)
Linn Prentis, Literary Agent (*US*)
Madeleine Milburn Literary, TV & Film Agency
(*UK*)
Margret McBride Literary Agency (*US*)
McIntosh & Otis, Inc (*US*)
Howard Morhaim Literary Agency (*US*)
New Leaf Literary & Media, Inc. (*US*)
Northbank Talent Management (*UK*)
P.S. Literary Agency (*Can*)
Raines & Raines (*US*)
Richard Henshaw Group LLC (*US*)
Richford Becklow Literary Agency (*UK*)
The Rights Factory (*Can*)
Rupert Heath Literary Agency (*UK*)
Salkind Literary Agency (*US*)
Sandra Dijkstra Literary Agency (*US*)
Sanford J. Greenburger Associates, Inc. (*US*)
Scribe Agency LLC (*US*)
Lynn Seligman, Literary Agent (*US*)
Sheil Land Associates Ltd (*UK*)
Signature Literary Agency (*US*)

Spectrum Literary Agency (*US*)
Philip G. Spitzer Literary Agency, Inc. (*US*)
The Stringer Literary Agency LLC (*US*)
Stuart Krichevsky Literary Agency, Inc. (*US*)
Talcott Notch Literary (*US*)
TriadaUS Literary Agency, Inc. (*US*)
Trident Media Group, LLC (*US*)
United Talent Agency (*US*)
Upstart Crow Literary (*US*)
Veritas Literary Agency (*US*)
Whispering Buffalo Literary Agency Ltd (*UK*)
Writers House, LLC (*US*)
The Zack Company, Inc (*US*)
Zeno Agency Ltd (*UK*)

Scripts

A & B Personal Management Ltd (*UK*)
Agency for the Performing Arts (APA) (*US*)
The Agency (London) Ltd (*UK*)
AHA Talent Ltd (*UK*)
Aimee Entertainment Agency (*US*)
Alan Brodie Representation Ltd (*UK*)
Marcia Amsterdam Agency (*US*)
Anonymous Content (*US*)
Barbara Hogenson Agency (*US*)
Berlin Associates (*UK*)
BiCoastal Talent (*US*)
Blake Friedmann Literary Agency Ltd (*UK*)
Don Buchwald and Associates (*US*)
Carolyn Jenks Agency (*US*)
Cecily Ware Literary Agents (*UK*)
Creative Trust, Inc. (*US*)
Curtis Brown Group Ltd (*UK*)
David Higham Associates Ltd (*UK*)
DHH Literary Agency Ltd (*UK*)
The Dravis Agency, Inc. (*US*)
Elaine Steel (*UK*)
Energy Entertainment (*US*)
Felix de Wolfe (*UK*)
Film Rights Ltd in association with Laurence
Fitch Ltd (*UK*)
Noel Gay (*UK*)
Eric Glass Ltd (*UK*)
Hudson Agency (*US*)
Independent Talent Group Ltd (*UK*)
Janet Fillingham Associates (*UK*)
Jill Foster Ltd (JFL) (*UK*)
Jonathan Clowes Ltd (*UK*)
Michelle Kass Associates (*UK*)
Ken Sherman & Associates (*US*)
Ki Agency Ltd (*UK*)
Knight Hall Agency (*UK*)
LAW (Lucas Alexander Whitley) (*UK*)
Linda Seifert Management (*UK*)
The Lisa Richards Agency (*Ire*)
Madeleine Milburn Literary, TV & Film Agency
(*UK*)
Mary Clemmey Literary Agency (*UK*)
MBA Literary Agents Ltd (*UK*)
Bill McLean Personal Management Ltd (*UK*)
The Michael Greer Literary Agency (*UK*)
Niad Management (*US*)
Paradigm Talent and Literary Agency (*US*)
Peters Fraser + Dunlop (*UK*)

Rochelle Stevens & Co. (*UK*)
Rosica Colin Ltd (*UK*)
Sayle Screen Ltd (*UK*)
Sheil Land Associates Ltd (*UK*)
Stone Manners Salners Agency (*US*)
The Tennyson Agency (*UK*)
United Agents (*UK*)
Valerie Hoskins Associates (*UK*)
William Morris Endeavor Entertainment (*US*)

Self-Help

Adler & Robin Books, Inc (*US*)
Alive Literary Agency (*US*)
Ambassador Speakers Bureau & Literary
Agency (*US*)
Andrew Lownie Literary Agency Ltd (*UK*)
Antony Harwood Limited (*UK*)
Audrey A. Wolf Literary Agency (*US*)
The Authors Care Service ltd (*UK*)
Baldi Agency (*US*)
Betsy Amster Literary Enterprises (*US*)
Vicky Bijur Literary Agency (*US*)
Bleecker Street Associates, Inc. (*US*)
The Bright Literary Academy (*UK*)
Carol Mann Agency (*US*)
Cherry Weiner Literary Agency (*US*)
Clare Hulton Literary Agency (*UK*)
The Cowles-Ryan Literary Agency (*US*)
Cynthia Cannell Literary Agency (*US*)
D4EO Literary Agency (*US*)
Doug Grad Literary Agency (*US*)
FinePrint Literary Management (*US*)
Fletcher & Company (*US*)
Folio Literary Management, LLC (*US*)
Fox & Howard Literary Agency (*UK*)
Frances Kelly Agency (*UK*)
Fraser-Bub Literary, LLC (*US*)
Gina Maccoby Agency (*US*)
Grace Freedson's Publishing Network (*US*)
Graham Maw Christie Literary Agency (*UK*)
Holloway Literary (*US*)
Hornfischer Literary Management, L.P. (*US*)
Andrea Hurst Literary Management (*US*)
J de S Associates Inc. (*US*)
Jane Judd Literary Agency (*UK*)
Jeanne Fredericks Literary Agency, Inc. (*US*)
Johnson & Alcock (*UK*)
Ki Agency Ltd (*UK*)
Kimberley Cameron & Associates (*US*)
The Knight Agency (*US*)
Linda Konner Literary Agency (*US*)
Larsen Pomada Literary Agents (*US*)
The Leshne Agency (*US*)
Levine Greenberg Rostan Literary Agency (*US*)
Linda Roghaar Literary Agency, Inc. (*US*)
The Lisa Richards Agency (*Ire*)
The Literary Group International (*US*)
MacGregor Literary (*US*)
Madeleine Milburn Literary, TV & Film Agency
(*UK*)
Manus & Associates Literary Agency, Inc. (*US*)
Marsal Lyon Literary Agency LLC (*US*)
The Martell Agency (*US*)
Martin Leonardis Ltd (*UK*)

Martin Literary Management (*US*)
MBA Literary Agents Ltd (*UK*)
Margret McBride Literary Agency (*US*)
McCormick Literary (*US*)
McIntosh & Otis, Inc (*US*)
Northbank Talent Management (*UK*)
Northern Lights Literary Services (*US*)
Puttick Literary Agency (*UK*)
Richford Becklow Literary Agency (*UK*)
The Rights Bureau (*Ire*)
Robert Dudley Agency (*UK*)
Salkind Literary Agency (*US*)
Sandra Dijkstra Literary Agency (*US*)
Sanford J. Greenburger Associates, Inc. (*US*)
Lynn Seligman, Literary Agent (*US*)
Sheil Land Associates Ltd (*UK*)
Sheree Bykofsky Associates, Inc. (*US*)
Sterling Lord Literistic, Inc. (*US*)
TriadaUS Literary Agency, Inc. (*US*)
Veritas Literary Agency (*US*)
Watson, Little Ltd (*UK*)
Waxman Leavell Literary Agency (*US*)
Wendy Sherman Associates, Inc. (*US*)
Whispering Buffalo Literary Agency Ltd (*UK*)
Writers' Representatives, LLC (*US*)
Writers House, LLC (*US*)
The Zack Company, Inc (*US*)
Short Stories
The Ahearn Agency, Inc (*US*)
Alive Literary Agency (*US*)
Antony Harwood Limited (*UK*)
The Bright Literary Academy (*UK*)
DeFiore and Company (*US*)
Georges Borchardt, Inc. (*US*)
Joy Harris Literary Agency, Inc. (*US*)
Holloway Literary (*US*)
John Hawkins & Associates, Inc. (*US*)
MacGregor Literary (*US*)
Regal Hoffmann & Associates LLC (*US*)
The Ruppin Agency (*UK*)
Sandra Dijkstra Literary Agency (*US*)
Scribe Agency LLC (*US*)
Philip G. Spitzer Literary Agency, Inc. (*US*)
Watkins / Loomis Agency, Inc. (*US*)
Zoë Pagnamenta Agency, LLC (*US*)
Sociology
Andrea Brown Literary Agency, Inc. (*US*)
Ann Rittenberg Literary Agency (*US*)
Antony Harwood Limited (*UK*)
The Bent Agency (*US*)
Betsy Amster Literary Enterprises (*US*)
Vicky Bijur Literary Agency (*US*)
Blake Friedmann Literary Agency Ltd (*UK*)
Bleecker Street Associates, Inc. (*US*)
Carol Mann Agency (*US*)
David Black Literary Agency (*US*)
DeFiore and Company (*US*)
Diamond Kahn and Woods (DKW) Literary
Agency Ltd (*UK*)
The Doe Coover Agency (*US*)
Mary Evans, Inc. (*US*)
The Feldstein Agency (*UK*)
Furniss Lawton (*UK*)

The Gernert Company (*US*)
Hannigan Salky Getzler (HSG) Agency (*US*)
Hornfischer Literary Management, L.P. (*US*)
Inklings Literary Agency, LLC (*US*)
J de S Associates Inc. (*US*)
Kate Hordern Literary Agency (*UK*)
Larsen Pomada Literary Agents (*US*)
Levine Greenberg Rostan Literary Agency (*US*)
The Literary Group International (*US*)
Massie & McQuilkin (*US*)
Publication Riot Group, Inc. (*US*)
The Ruppin Agency (*UK*)
Sandra Dijkstra Literary Agency (*US*)
Sanford J. Greenburger Associates, Inc. (*US*)
Scovil Galen Ghosh Literary Agency, Inc. (*US*)
Lynn Seligman, Literary Agent (*US*)
The Spieler Agency (*US*)
Union Literary (*US*)
Victoria Sanders & Associates LLC (*US*)
The Weingel-Fidel Agency (*US*)
Wm Clark Associates (*US*)
Spiritual
Alive Literary Agency (*US*)
Antony Harwood Limited (*UK*)
Baldi Agency (*US*)
Bleecker Street Associates, Inc. (*US*)
Carol Mann Agency (*US*)
The Cowles-Ryan Literary Agency (*US*)
Cynthia Cannell Literary Agency (*US*)
D4EO Literary Agency (*US*)
Dunham Literary, Inc. (*US*)
Dystel, Goderich & Bourret LLC (*US*)
Ethan Ellenberg Literary Agency (*US*)
FinePrint Literary Management (*US*)
Folio Literary Management, LLC (*US*)
Foundry Literary + Media (*US*)
Fox & Howard Literary Agency (*UK*)
Global Lion Intellectual Property Management,
Inc. (*US*)
Joy Harris Literary Agency, Inc. (*US*)
Jill Grinberg Literary Management LLC (*US*)
Kimberley Cameron & Associates (*US*)
Knight Features (*UK*)
Lawrence Jordan Literary Agency (*US*)
The Leshne Agency (*US*)
Levine Greenberg Rostan Literary Agency (*US*)
Linda Roghaar Literary Agency, Inc. (*US*)
Literary & Creative Artists Inc. (*US*)
McIntosh & Otis, Inc (*US*)
The Amy Rennert Agency, Inc. (*US*)
The Rights Factory (*Can*)
Rita Rosenkranz Literary Agency (*US*)
Salkind Literary Agency (*US*)
Sheree Bykofsky Associates, Inc. (*US*)
Signature Literary Agency (*US*)
The Spieler Agency (*US*)
Stephanie Tade Literary Agency (*US*)
Wendy Sherman Associates, Inc. (*US*)
The Zack Company, Inc (*US*)
Sport
A.M. Heath & Company Limited, Author's
Agents (*UK*)
Alive Literary Agency (*US*)

The Ampersand Agency Ltd (*UK*)
Andrea Brown Literary Agency, Inc. (*US*)
Andrew Lownie Literary Agency Ltd (*UK*)
Antony Harwood Limited (*UK*)
Audrey A. Wolf Literary Agency (*US*)
B.J. Robbins Literary Agency (*US*)
Bell Lomax Moreton Agency (*UK*)
The Bent Agency (*US*)
Bleecker Street Associates, Inc. (*US*)
Bob Mecoy Creative Book Services (*US*)
The Brattle Agency LLC (*US*)
Bresnick Weil Literary Agency, LLC (*US*)
Carol Mann Agency (*US*)
Chase Literary Agency (*US*)
Elyse Cheney Literary Associates, LLC (*US*)
Conville & Walsh Ltd (*UK*)
D4EO Literary Agency (*US*)
David Luxton Associates (*UK*)
David Black Literary Agency (*US*)
The Doe Coover Agency (*US*)
Don Congdon Associates, Inc. (*US*)
Jim Donovan Literary (*US*)
Doug Grad Literary Agency (*US*)
E. J. McCarthy Agency (*US*)
The Feldstein Agency (*UK*)
Fletcher & Company (*US*)
Folio Literary Management, LLC (*US*)
Foundry Literary + Media (*US*)
Furniss Lawton (*UK*)
The G Agency, LLC (*US*)
The Gernert Company (*US*)
Glass Literary Management LLC (*US*)
Grace Freedson's Publishing Network (*US*)
Hornfischer Literary Management, L.P. (*US*)
J de S Associates Inc. (*US*)
Jane Judd Literary Agency (*UK*)
Jeanne Fredericks Literary Agency, Inc. (*US*)
Jenny Brown Associates (*UK*)
Jill Grinberg Literary Management LLC (*US*)
Johnson & Alcock (*UK*)
Kathi J. Paton Literary Agency (*US*)
Ki Agency Ltd (*UK*)
Knight Features (*UK*)
Larsen Pomada Literary Agents (*US*)
LAW (Lucas Alexander Whitley) (*UK*)
The Leshne Agency (*US*)
Levine Greenberg Rostan Literary Agency (*US*)
Limelight Management (*UK*)
The Lisa Richards Agency (*Ire*)
The Literary Group International (*US*)
MacGregor Literary (*US*)
Madeleine Milburn Literary, TV & Film Agency (*UK*)
Marsal Lyon Literary Agency LLC (*US*)
Massie & McQuilkin (*US*)
Max Gartenburg Literary Agency (*US*)
McCormick Literary (*US*)
McIntosh & Otis, Inc (*US*)
The Michael Greer Literary Agency (*UK*)
Howard Morhaim Literary Agency (*US*)
Mulcahy Associates (Part of MMB Creative) (*UK*)
Niad Management (*US*)

P.S. Literary Agency (*Can*)
Peters Fraser + Dunlop (*UK*)
The Purcell Agency, LLC (*US*)
Queen Literary Agency, Inc. (*US*)
The Amy Rennert Agency, Inc. (*US*)
Richard Henshaw Group LLC (*US*)
The Rights Factory (*Can*)
RLR Associates (*US*)
Robert Dudley Agency (*UK*)
Rosica Colin Ltd (*UK*)
The Ruppin Agency (*UK*)
Sandra Dijkstra Literary Agency (*US*)
Sanford J. Greenburger Associates, Inc. (*US*)
Scovil Galen Ghosh Literary Agency, Inc. (*US*)
SLW Literary Agency (*US*)
Philip G. Spitzer Literary Agency, Inc. (*US*)
The Stuart Agency (*US*)
Susan Rabiner, Literary Agent, Inc. (*US*)
TriadaUS Literary Agency, Inc. (*US*)
Trident Media Group, LLC (*US*)
2M Literary Agency Ltd (*US*)
Watson, Little Ltd (*UK*)
Waxman Leavell Literary Agency (*US*)
Wendy Sherman Associates, Inc. (*US*)
Yates & Yates (*US*)
The Zack Company, Inc (*US*)

Suspense
A.M. Heath & Company Limited, Author's Agents (*UK*)
Aaron M. Priest Literary Agency (*US*)
The Ahearn Agency, Inc (*US*)
Alive Literary Agency (*US*)
Andrew Lownie Literary Agency Ltd (*UK*)
The Angela Rinaldi Literary Agency (*US*)
Antony Harwood Limited (*UK*)
B.J. Robbins Literary Agency (*US*)
The Bent Agency (*US*)
Blake Friedmann Literary Agency Ltd (*UK*)
Book Cents Literary Agency (*US*)
Caroline Sheldon Literary Agency (*UK*)
Carolyn Jenks Agency (*US*)
Chartwell (*UK*)
Elyse Cheney Literary Associates, LLC (*US*)
Cherry Weiner Literary Agency (*US*)
Conville & Walsh Ltd (*UK*)
Coombs Moylett & Maclean Literary Agency (*UK*)
Curtis Brown Group Ltd (*UK*)
The Darley Anderson Agency (*UK*)
Diamond Kahn and Woods (DKW) Literary Agency Ltd (*UK*)
Don Congdon Associates, Inc. (*US*)
Donaghy Literary Group (*US*)
Jim Donovan Literary (*US*)
The Dravis Agency, Inc. (*US*)
Dystel, Goderich & Bourret LLC (*US*)
FinePrint Literary Management (*US*)
Folio Literary Management, LLC (*US*)
Gelfman Schneider / ICM Partners (*US*)
Gina Maccoby Agency (*US*)
Hannigan Salky Getzler (HSG) Agency (*US*)
Hardman & Swainson (*UK*)
Joy Harris Literary Agency, Inc. (*US*)

Holloway Literary (*US*)
Inklings Literary Agency, LLC (*US*)
J de S Associates Inc. (*US*)
Jane Rotrosen Agency (*US*)
Jill Grosjean Literary Agency (*US*)
Johnson & Alcock (*UK*)
JYLA (Jason Yarn Literary Agency) (*US*)
The Knight Agency (*US*)
Barbara S. Kouts, Literary Agent (*US*)
Larsen Pomada Literary Agents (*US*)
Lawrence Jordan Literary Agency (*US*)
Levine Greenberg Rostan Literary Agency (*US*)
Limelight Management (*UK*)
MacGregor Literary (*US*)
Madeleine Milburn Literary, TV & Film Agency (*UK*)
Manus & Associates Literary Agency, Inc. (*US*)
Maria Carvainis Agency, Inc. (*US*)
Marsal Lyon Literary Agency LLC (*US*)
The Martell Agency (*US*)
Massie & McQuilkin (*US*)
Margret McBride Literary Agency (*US*)
McIntosh & Otis, Inc (*US*)
Nappaland Literary Agency (*US*)
Niad Management (*US*)
Northbank Talent Management (*UK*)
Northern Lights Literary Services (*US*)
P.S. Literary Agency (*Can*)
Peters Fraser + Dunlop (*UK*)
Raines & Raines (*US*)
Rosica Colin Ltd (*UK*)
Salkind Literary Agency (*US*)
Sandra Dijkstra Literary Agency (*US*)
Secret Agent Man (*US*)
Spectrum Literary Agency (*US*)
Speilburg Literary Agency (*US*)
Philip G. Spitzer Literary Agency, Inc. (*US*)
Talcott Notch Literary (*US*)
TriadaUS Literary Agency, Inc. (*US*)
Trident Media Group, LLC (*US*)
Victoria Sanders & Associates LLC (*US*)
Waxman Leavell Literary Agency (*US*)
Wendy Sherman Associates, Inc. (*US*)
The Zack Company, Inc (*US*)
Technology
Andrea Brown Literary Agency, Inc. (*US*)
Andrew Lownie Literary Agency Ltd (*UK*)
Antony Harwood Limited (*UK*)
Baldi Agency (*US*)
Blake Friedmann Literary Agency Ltd (*UK*)
Bleecker Street Associates, Inc. (*US*)
Bob Mecoy Creative Book Services (*US*)
Chartwell (*UK*)
Richard Curtis Associates, Inc. (*US*)
D4EO Literary Agency (*US*)
DeFiore and Company (*US*)
The Doe Coover Agency (*US*)
Don Congdon Associates, Inc. (*US*)
Dunham Literary, Inc. (*US*)
Dystel, Goderich & Bourret LLC (*US*)
Mary Evans, Inc. (*US*)
FinePrint Literary Management (*US*)
Folio Literary Management, LLC (*US*)

The G Agency, LLC (*US*)
Grace Freedson's Publishing Network (*US*)
Hornfischer Literary Management, L.P. (*US*)
Jill Grinberg Literary Management LLC (*US*)
John Hawkins & Associates, Inc. (*US*)
Kathi J. Paton Literary Agency (*US*)
Kimberley Cameron & Associates (*US*)
Laura Dail Literary Agency (*US*)
LAW (Lucas Alexander Whitley) (*UK*)
The Leshne Agency (*US*)
Levine Greenberg Rostan Literary Agency (*US*)
Maria Carvainis Agency, Inc. (*US*)
New Leaf Literary & Media, Inc. (*US*)
Lynne Rabinoff Agency (*US*)
Robert Dudley Agency (*UK*)
The Rudy Agency (*US*)
The Sagalyn Literary Agency (*US*)
Salkind Literary Agency (*US*)
Signature Literary Agency (*US*)
Sterling Lord Literistic, Inc. (*US*)
Stuart Krichevsky Literary Agency, Inc. (*US*)
Talcott Notch Literary (*US*)
Trident Media Group, LLC (*US*)
Watkins / Loomis Agency, Inc. (*US*)
Watson, Little Ltd (*UK*)
The Weingel-Fidel Agency (*US*)
Wm Clark Associates (*US*)
The Zack Company, Inc (*US*)
Theatre
A & B Personal Management Ltd (*UK*)
Agency for the Performing Arts (APA) (*US*)
The Agency (London) Ltd (*UK*)
Alan Brodie Representation Ltd (*UK*)
Antony Harwood Limited (*UK*)
Barbara Hogenson Agency (*US*)
Berlin Associates (*UK*)
Don Buchwald and Associates (*US*)
Carolyn Jenks Agency (*US*)
Curtis Brown Group Ltd (*UK*)
David Higham Associates Ltd (*UK*)
DHH Literary Agency Ltd (*UK*)
Don Congdon Associates, Inc. (*US*)
Doug Grad Literary Agency (*US*)
Felix de Wolfe (*UK*)
Film Rights Ltd in association with Laurence Fitch Ltd (*UK*)
Eric Glass Ltd (*UK*)
Independent Talent Group Ltd (*UK*)
Janet Fillingham Associates (*UK*)
Jill Foster Ltd (JFL) (*UK*)
Jonathan Clowes Ltd (*UK*)
Ki Agency Ltd (*UK*)
Knight Hall Agency (*UK*)
L. Perkins Associates (*US*)
The Lisa Richards Agency (*Ire*)
Mary Clemmey Literary Agency (*UK*)
MBA Literary Agents Ltd (*UK*)
Bill McLean Personal Management Ltd (*UK*)
Niad Management (*US*)
Paradigm Talent and Literary Agency (*US*)
Peters Fraser + Dunlop (*UK*)
Rochelle Stevens & Co. (*UK*)
Rosica Colin Ltd (*UK*)

Claim your free access to **www.firstwriter.com**: *See p.389*

Sayle Screen Ltd (*UK*)
Sheil Land Associates Ltd (*UK*)
The Spieler Agency (*US*)
The Tennyson Agency (*UK*)
United Agents (*UK*)
Victoria Sanders & Associates LLC (*US*)
Wm Clark Associates (*US*)
Thrillers
A.M. Heath & Company Limited, Author's
Agents (*UK*)
Aaron M. Priest Literary Agency (*US*)
The Ahearn Agency, Inc (*US*)
Alive Literary Agency (*US*)
The Ampersand Agency Ltd (*UK*)
Marcia Amsterdam Agency (*US*)
Andrea Brown Literary Agency, Inc. (*US*)
Andrew Lownie Literary Agency Ltd (*UK*)
Andrew Mann Ltd (*UK*)
The Angela Rinaldi Literary Agency (*US*)
Ann Rittenberg Literary Agency (*US*)
Antony Harwood Limited (*UK*)
The Axelrod Agency (*US*)
Ayesha Pande Literary (*US*)
B.J. Robbins Literary Agency (*US*)
The Bent Agency (*US*)
Betsy Amster Literary Enterprises (*US*)
Blake Friedmann Literary Agency Ltd (*UK*)
Bleecker Street Associates, Inc. (*US*)
Bond Literary Agency (*US*)
The Book Bureau Literary Agency (*Ire*)
Book Cents Literary Agency (*US*)
BookStop Literary Agency, LLC (*US*)
Brandt & Hochman Literary Agents, Inc. (*US*)
The Bright Literary Academy (*UK*)
Carolyn Jenks Agency (*US*)
Chartwell (*UK*)
Mic Cheetham Literary Agency (*UK*)
Elyse Cheney Literary Associates, LLC (*US*)
Cherry Weiner Literary Agency (*US*)
Cine/Lit Representation (*US*)
Conville & Walsh Ltd (*UK*)
Coombs Moylett & Maclean Literary Agency
(*UK*)
Corvisiero Literary Agency (*US*)
Creative Media Agency (*US*)
Curtis Brown Group Ltd (*UK*)
Richard Curtis Associates, Inc. (*US*)
D4EO Literary Agency (*US*)
The Darley Anderson Agency (*UK*)
David Black Literary Agency (*US*)
David Higham Associates Ltd (*UK*)
DeFiore and Company (*US*)
DHH Literary Agency Ltd (*UK*)
Diamond Kahn and Woods (DKW) Literary
Agency Ltd (*UK*)
Don Congdon Associates, Inc. (*US*)
Donaghy Literary Group (*US*)
Jim Donovan Literary (*US*)
Doug Grad Literary Agency (*US*)
The Dravis Agency, Inc. (*US*)
Dunham Literary, Inc. (*US*)
Dystel, Goderich & Bourret LLC (*US*)
Edwards Fuglewicz (*UK*)

Ethan Ellenberg Literary Agency (*US*)
The Feldstein Agency (*UK*)
FinePrint Literary Management (*US*)
Folio Literary Management, LLC (*US*)
Foundry Literary + Media (*US*)
Fox Literary (*US*)
Fraser-Bub Literary, LLC (*US*)
Furniss Lawton (*UK*)
Gelfman Schneider / ICM Partners (*US*)
The Gernert Company (*US*)
Gina Maccoby Agency (*US*)
Greene & Heaton Ltd (*UK*)
Gregory & Company, Authors' Agents (*UK*)
Gunn Media Associates (*UK*)
Hannigan Salky Getzler (HSG) Agency (*US*)
Hardman & Swainson (*UK*)
Hill Nadell Literary Agency (*US*)
Holloway Literary (*US*)
Andrea Hurst Literary Management (*US*)
Inklings Literary Agency, LLC (*US*)
J de S Associates Inc. (*US*)
Jane Rotrosen Agency (*US*)
Jenny Brown Associates (*UK*)
Jill Corcoran Literary Agency (*US*)
Jill Grosjean Literary Agency (*US*)
John Hawkins & Associates, Inc. (*US*)
Johnson & Alcock (*UK*)
Jonathan Pegg Literary Agency (*UK*)
JYLA (Jason Yarn Literary Agency) (*US*)
Kate Hordern Literary Agency (*UK*)
Kimberley Cameron & Associates (*US*)
The Knight Agency (*US*)
Barbara S. Kouts, Literary Agent (*US*)
L. Perkins Associates (*US*)
Larsen Pomada Literary Agents (*US*)
Laura Dail Literary Agency (*US*)
LAW (Lucas Alexander Whitley) (*UK*)
Lawrence Jordan Literary Agency (*US*)
LBA Books Ltd (*UK*)
Levine Greenberg Rostan Literary Agency (*US*)
Limelight Management (*UK*)
The Literary Group International (*US*)
MacGregor Literary (*US*)
Madeleine Milburn Literary, TV & Film Agency
(*UK*)
Manus & Associates Literary Agency, Inc. (*US*)
Maria Carvainis Agency, Inc. (*US*)
Marsal Lyon Literary Agency LLC (*US*)
The Martell Agency (*US*)
Massie & McQuilkin (*US*)
Margret McBride Literary Agency (*US*)
McIntosh & Otis, Inc (*US*)
Meredith Bernstein Literary Agency, Inc. (*US*)
Howard Morhaim Literary Agency (*US*)
Mulcahy Associates (Part of MMB Creative)
(*UK*)
New Leaf Literary & Media, Inc. (*US*)
Niad Management (*US*)
Northbank Talent Management (*UK*)
One Track Literary Agency, Inc. (*US*)
P.S. Literary Agency (*Can*)
Pavilion Literary Management (*US*)
Peters Fraser + Dunlop (*UK*)

Jill Grinberg Literary Management LLC (*US*)
Jill Grosjean Literary Agency (*US*)
Jo Unwin Literary Agency (*UK*)
John Hawkins & Associates, Inc. (*US*)
Johnson & Alcock (*UK*)
Judith Murdoch Literary Agency (*UK*)
Juliet Burton Literary Agency (*UK*)
Kate Hordern Literary Agency (*UK*)
Keane Kataria Literary Agency (*UK*)
Kimberley Cameron & Associates (*US*)
The Knight Agency (*US*)
Linda Konner Literary Agency (*US*)
Barbara S. Kouts, Literary Agent (*US*)
Larsen Pomada Literary Agents (*US*)
Laura Dail Literary Agency (*US*)
LAW (Lucas Alexander Whitley) (*UK*)
LBA Books Ltd (*UK*)
The Leshne Agency (*US*)
Levine Greenberg Rostan Literary Agency (*US*)
Limelight Management (*UK*)
Linda Roghaar Literary Agency, Inc. (*US*)
Linn Prentis, Literary Agent (*US*)
The Literary Group International (*US*)
The LKG Agency (*US*)
MacGregor Literary (*US*)
Madeleine Milburn Literary, TV & Film Agency (*UK*)
Manus & Associates Literary Agency, Inc. (*US*)
Maria Carvainis Agency, Inc. (*US*)
Marsal Lyon Literary Agency LLC (*US*)
The Martell Agency (*US*)
Martin Literary Management (*US*)
Massie & McQuilkin (*US*)
Max Gartenburg Literary Agency (*US*)
Margret McBride Literary Agency (*US*)
McCormick Literary (*US*)
McIntosh & Otis, Inc (*US*)
Howard Morhaim Literary Agency (*US*)
Mulcahy Associates (Part of MMB Creative) (*UK*)
Nappaland Literary Agency (*US*)
New Leaf Literary & Media, Inc. (*US*)
Northbank Talent Management (*UK*)

Northern Lights Literary Services (*US*)
One Track Literary Agency, Inc. (*US*)
P.S. Literary Agency (*Can*)
The Park Literary Group LLC (*US*)
Peters Fraser + Dunlop (*UK*)
Publication Riot Group, Inc. (*US*)
The Purcell Agency, LLC (*US*)
Lynne Rabinoff Agency (*US*)
Richford Becklow Literary Agency (*UK*)
The Rights Factory (*Can*)
RLR Associates (*US*)
Robin Straus Agency, Inc. (*US*)
Rocking Chair Books (*UK*)
Rosica Colin Ltd (*UK*)
The Ruppin Agency (*UK*)
Salkind Literary Agency (*US*)
Sandra Dijkstra Literary Agency (*US*)
Sanford J. Greenburger Associates, Inc. (*US*)
Scovil Galen Ghosh Literary Agency, Inc. (*US*)
Lynn Seligman, Literary Agent (*US*)
Sheil Land Associates Ltd (*UK*)
Sheree Bykofsky Associates, Inc. (*US*)
The Spieler Agency (*US*)
Sterling Lord Literistic, Inc. (*US*)
The Stringer Literary Agency LLC (*US*)
SYLA – Susan Yearwood Literary Agency (*UK*)
Talcott Notch Literary (*US*)
Teresa Chris Literary Agency Ltd (*UK*)
Tessler Literary Agency (*US*)
Tracy Brown Literary Agency (*US*)
TriadaUS Literary Agency, Inc. (*US*)
Trident Media Group, LLC (*US*)
Veritas Literary Agency (*US*)
Victoria Sanders & Associates LLC (*US*)
Watson, Little Ltd (*UK*)
Waxman Leavell Literary Agency (*US*)
The Weingel-Fidel Agency (*US*)
Wendy Sherman Associates, Inc. (*US*)
Writers House, LLC (*US*)
Yates & Yates (*US*)
The Zack Company, Inc (*US*)
Zeno Agency Ltd (*UK*)

US Publishers

For the most up-to-date listings of these and hundreds of other publishers, visit https://www.firstwriter.com/publishers

*To claim your **free** access to the site, please see the back of this book.*

Abdo Publishing Co

8000 W. 78th St.
Suite 310
Edina
MN 55439
Tel: +1 (800) 800-1312
Fax: +1 (952) 831-1632
Email: fiction@abdobooks.com
Website: http://abdopublishing.com

Publishes: Fiction; Nonfiction; *Areas:* Anthropology; Arts; Biography; Cookery; Crafts; Culture; Current Affairs; Design; Entertainment; Historical; Hobbies; Medicine; Military; Politics; Religious; Science; Sociology; Sport; Technology; Travel; *Markets:* Children's

Contact: Paul Abdo

Publishes nonfiction, educational material for children up to the 12th grade, plus fiction series for children. Not accepting nonfiction submissions as at May 2017 (see website for current situation). Writers with a concept for a fiction series should send samples of manuscripts by email.

Academy Chicago

814 North Franklin Street
Chicago, Illinois 60610
Tel: +1 (312) 337-0747
Fax: +1 (312) 337-5110
Email: csherry@chicagoreviewpress.com

Website: http://www.chicagoreviewpress.com

Publishes: Fiction; Nonfiction; *Areas:* Autobiography; Mystery; *Markets:* Adult; *Treatments:* Contemporary; Mainstream

Contact: Cynthia Sherry

Send query by email with one-sentence description of your novel, a brief synopsis (a couple of paragraphs), word count, author bio, market info, and a few sample chapters. No mind/body/spirit, religion, diet/fitness/nutrition, family memoir, self-help, business, poetry, or photography.

ACTA Publications

4848 N. Clark Street
Chicago, IL 60640
Tel: +1 (800) 397-2282
Fax: +1 (800) 397-0079
Email: acta@actapublications.com
Website: http://www.actapublications.com

Publishes: Nonfiction; *Areas:* Religious; Self-Help; Spiritual; *Markets:* Adult

Send query with SASE, outline, table of contents, and one sample chapter. Publishes religious books, particularly Catholic, for a mainstream nonacademic audience. Do not submit unless you have read catalog or one of the books published by this company.

Albert Whitman & Company

250 South Northwest Highway, Suite 320
Park Ridge, Illinois 60068
Tel: +1 (800) 255-7675
Fax: +1 (847) 581-0039
Email: submissions@albertwhitman.com
Website: http://www.albertwhitman.com

Publishes: Fiction; Nonfiction; *Markets:*
Children's; Youth

Contact: Kathleen Tucker, Editor-in-Chief

Publishes picture books, middle-grade
fiction, and young adult novels. Will
consider fiction and nonfiction manuscripts
for picture books for children ages 1 to 8, up
to 1,000 words; fiction queries and sample
pages for middle-grade novels up to 35,000
words for children up to the age of 12; and
fiction queries and sample pages for young
adult novels up to 70,000 words for ages 12-
18. See website for full submission
guidelines.

Algora Publishing

1732 1st Ave #20330
New York, NY 10128
Tel: +1 (212) 678-0232
Fax: +1 (212) 202-5488
Website: http://www.algora.com

Publishes: Nonfiction; *Areas:* Anthropology;
Archaeology; Finance; Historical; Literature;
Military; Music; Nature; Philosophy;
Politics; Psychology; Religious; Science;
Sociology; Translations; Women's Interests;
Markets: Academic; Adult

Describes itself as an "academic-type press,
publishing general nonfiction for the
educated reader". Accepts proposal packages
by post. An email query may optionally be
sent prior to the proposal package. See
website for full guidelines.

Alice James Books

114 Prescott Street
Farmington, ME 04938
Tel: +1 (207) 778-7071
Fax: +1 (207) 778-7766
Email: info@alicejamesbooks.org
Website: http://alicejamesbooks.org

Publishes: Poetry; *Markets:* Adult

Poetry press accepting submissions through
its various competitions only. Competitions
include large cash prizes and reasonable
entry fees.

Allyn and Bacon / Merrill Education

445 Hutchinson Avenue
Columbus, OH 43235
Email: education.service@pearson.com
Website: http://www.allynbaconmerrill.com

Publishes: Nonfiction; *Markets:* Academic;
Professional

Publishes books focused on the professional
development of teachers, that effectively
blend academic research and practical
application for today's K-12 educators.

Alpine Publications, Inc.

38262 Linman Road
Crawford, CO 81415
Email: editorialdept@alpinepub.com
Website: http://www.alpinepub.com

Publishes: Nonfiction; *Areas:* Biography;
Hobbies; Nature; *Markets:* Adult

Publishes books on dogs and horses.
Welcomes submissions. Send query by post
or by email with synopsis, chapter outline,
author bio, market analysis, and 1-3 sample
chapters.

American Counseling Association

6101 Stevenson Avenue
Alexandria, VA 22304
Tel: +1 (703) 823-9800
Fax: +1 (703) 823-0252
Email: cbaker@counseling.org
Website: https://www.counseling.org

Publishes: Nonfiction; *Areas:* Health;
Markets: Academic; Professional

Publishes books on mental health for the
professional and academic markets.

American Psychiatric Association Publishing

1000 Wilson Boulevard, Suite 1825
Arlington, VA 22209
Tel: +1 (703) 907-7871
Email: hkoch@psych.org
Website: https://www.appi.org

Publishes: Nonfiction; *Areas:* Health;
Psychology; Science; *Markets:* Academic;
Adult; Professional

Contact: Heidi Koch (Editorial Support
Services Manager)

Publishes books, journals, and multimedia on
psychiatry, mental health and behavioral
science, geared toward psychiatrists, other
mental health professionals, psychiatric
residents, medical students and the general
public.

American Quilter's Society

5801 Kentucky Dam Road
Paducah, KY 42003-9323
Tel: +1 (270) 898-7903
Fax: +1 (270) 898-1173
Email: editor@aqsquilt.com
Website: http://www.americanquilter.com

Publishes: Fiction; Nonfiction; *Areas:*
Crafts; Hobbies; How-to; Humour; Mystery;
Romance; *Markets:* Adult

Publishes nonfiction and fiction related to
quilts. Send proposal by post. See website
for complete guidelines.

Andrews McMeel Publishing

attn: Book Submissions
1130 Walnut Street
Kansas City, MO 64106
Tel: +1 (816) 581-8921
Email: booksubmissions@amuniversal.com
Website: http://www.andrewsmcmeel.com

Publishes: Fiction; Nonfiction; Poetry;
Areas: Cookery; Humour; Lifestyle;
Markets: Adult; Children's

Publishes humour, inspiration, poetry,
middle grade children's books, and
calendars. Will consider submissions via a
literary agent or direct from authors, if

submission guidelines on website are
adhered to.

Appalachian Mountain Club Books

5 Joy Street
Boston, MA 02108
Tel: +1 (617) 523-0636
Fax: +1 (617) 523-0722
Email: amcbooks@outdoors.org
Website: http://www.outdoors.org

Publishes: Nonfiction; *Areas:* Leisure;
Nature; Travel; *Markets:* Adult

Publishes books for people interested in
outdoor recreation, conservation, nature, and
the outdoor world of the American north east
in general.

Arbordale Publishing

612 Johnnie Dodds., Suite A2
Mount Pleasant, SC 29464
Email: katie@arbordalepublishing.com
Website: http://www.
arbordalepublishing.com

Publishes: Fiction; Nonfiction; *Areas:*
Science; *Markets:* Children's

Contact: Katie Hall, Associate Editor

Publishes picture books that aim to get
children excited about science and maths.
Publishes mainly fiction with nonfiction
facts woven into the story, but will also
consider nonfiction stories. Submit by email
only. See website for full submission
guidelines.

Arthur A. Levine Books

557 Broadway
New York, NY 10012
Email: arthuralevinebooks@scholastic.com
Website: http://www.arthuralevinebooks.com

Publishes: Fiction; Nonfiction; *Markets:*
Children's; Youth

Publishes books for children and young
adults. Send query with full text (picture
books), first two chapters and synopsis
(novels), or ten sample pages (nonfiction),
via online submission system. Monthly
submission quota, so if submission system is

---

not accepting submissions check back next month.

Asabi Publishing

Email: apsubmit@asabipublishing.com
Website: http://www.asabipublishing.com

Publishes: Fiction; Nonfiction; *Areas:*
Autobiography; Biography; Crime; Culture;
Erotic; Historical; Horror; Mystery;
Thrillers; *Markets:* Adult; Children's; Youth

Check website for submission windows.
Submit query by email or through form on
website, with table of contents and three
sample chapters. No religious or spiritual
books of any kind.

ASCE Press

1801 Alexander Bell Drive
Reston, VA 20191
Tel: +1 (703) 295-6300
Email: ascepress@asce.org
Website: http://www.asce.org

Publishes: Nonfiction; *Areas:* Architecture;
Design; Science; Technology; *Markets:*
Professional

Publishes books for professional civil
engineers. Send proposal by email or by
post. See website for full submission
guidelines.

Association for Supervision and Curriculum Development (ASCD)

1703 North Beauregard Street
Alexandria, VA 22311
Tel: +1 (703) 578-9600
Email: acquisitions@ascd.org
Website: http://www.ascd.org

Publishes: Nonfiction; *Markets:* Professional

Publishes books for educators. Continually
searching for writers with new ideas, fresh
voices, and diverse backgrounds. Submit via
online submission system on website.

Astragal Press

5995 149th Street West, Suite 105
Apple Valley, MN 55124

Tel: +1 (866) 543-3045
Fax: +1 (800) 330-6232
Email: info@finneyco.com
Website: http://www.astragalpress.com

Publishes: Nonfiction; *Areas:* Antiques;
Crafts; Historical; Science; Technology;
Markets: Adult; *Treatments:* Niche

Send query with SASE, one-page overview,
table of contents, introduction, at least three
chapters, market info, and details of your
background and qualifications. Publishes
books for a niche market on subjects such as
antique tools, early sciences, the history of
the railroad, etc. See website for more
details.

Augsburg Fortress

PO Box 1209
Minneapolis, MN 55440-1209
Tel: +1 (800) 328-4648
Fax: +1 (800) 722-7766
Website: https://www.augsburgfortress.org

Publishes: Fiction; Nonfiction; *Areas:*
Culture; Historical; Lifestyle; Religious;
Markets: Adult; Children's

Publishes bibles, adult nonfiction, and
children's fiction for a Lutheran audience.

Avatar Press

515 N. Century Blvd,
Rantoul, IL 61866
Fax: +1 (217) 893-9671
Email: submissions@avatarpress.net
Website: http://www.avatarpress.com

Publishes: Fiction; *Markets:* Adult; Youth

Comic book publisher. Accepts submissions
from artists, but no script-only submissions
at this time. See website for current status
and full submission guidelines.

Baen Books

PO Box 1188
Wake Forest, NC 27588
Email: info@baen.com
Website: http://www.baen.com

Publishes: Fiction; *Areas:* Fantasy; Sci-Fi;
Markets: Adult; *Treatments:* Contemporary

Publishes only science fiction and fantasy. Interested in science fiction with powerful plots and solid scientific and philosophical underpinnings. For fantasy, any magical system must be both rigorously coherent and integral to the plot. Work must at least strive for originality. Prefers manuscripts between 100,000 and 130,000 words. No submissions via mail or email. Full manuscripts can be submitted online, in rtf format, via an electronic submission system.

Baker Publishing Group

6030 East Fulton Road
Ada, MI 49301
Tel: +1 (616) 676-9185
Fax: +1 (616) 676-9573
Email: submissions@bakeracademic.com
Website: http://bakerpublishinggroup.com

Publishes: Nonfiction; *Areas:* Religious; *Markets:* Academic; Adult; Professional

Publishes Christian books. No unsolicited mss. Accepts approaches only through literary agent, writers' conferences, or third part manuscript submission services (see website for details).

Ball Publishing

622 Town Road
PO Box 1660
West Chicago, IL 60186
Tel: +1 (630) 231-3675
Fax: +1 (630) 231-5254
Email: cbeytes@ballpublishing.com
Website: http://www.ballpublishing.com

Publishes: Nonfiction; *Areas:* Gardening; *Markets:* Adult; Professional

Contact: Chris Beytes (Editor)

Send query describing book and its "hook" with SASE. Include your qualifications to write the book (possibly in the form of a CV), market overview (including details of competing books, and how your book is different and superior), details of contents (table of contents, word count, illustrations), estimated completion time, and two or three sample chapters. See website for full guidelines. Publishes books on gardening and horticulture for both professionals and home gardeners.

Bancroft Press

PO Box 65360
Baltimore, MD 21209-9945
Tel: +1 (410) 358-0658
Fax: +1 (410) 764-1967
Email: bruceb@bancroftpress.com
Website: https://bancroftpress.com

Publishes: Fiction; Nonfiction; *Areas:* Autobiography; Biography; Finance; Health; Historical; Humour; Lifestyle; Mystery; Sport; Thrillers; *Markets:* Adult; Youth; *Treatments:* Commercial; Literary

Contact: Bruce Bortz

Will consider any genre, but unlikely to ever publish children's fiction or poetry. Mark envelopes fiction or nonfiction and include email address for confirmation of receipt on outside of envelope. Do not use any priority mail service. Include query letter giving information on audience/marketing, plus CV and either complete MS or as many chapters as you have written (minimum 5 for nonfiction).

Beacon Hill Press of Kansas City

PO Box 419527
Kansas City, MO 64141
Tel: +1 (816) 931-1900
Fax: +1 (816) 753-4071
Email: customerservice@
beaconhillbooks.com
Website: http://beaconhillbooks.com

Publishes: Nonfiction; *Areas:* Religious; *Markets:* Adult

Publishes Wesleyan Christian books, Bible studies, and Bible commentaries. Send query by email.

Beacon Press

24 Farnsworth Street
Boston, MA 02210
Tel: +1 (617) 742-2110
Fax: +1 (617) 723-3097
Email: editorial@beacon.org
Website: http://www.beacon.org

Publishes: Nonfiction; *Areas:* Arts; Autobiography; Biography; Current Affairs; Historical; Lifestyle; Literature; Medicine;

Nature; Politics; Religious; Science; Sociology; Women's Interests; *Markets:* Adult

Contact: Editorial Department

Publishes general trade nonfiction, in particular religion, history, current affairs, political science, gay/lesbian/gender studies, education, African-American studies, women's studies, child and family issues and nature and the environment. No poetry, fiction, or self-help books. Send query by email with 250-word description of your proposal. If interested, a full proposal will be requested within three weeks. Response not guaranteed.

Beacon Publishing Group
New York, NY
Tel: +1 (800) 817-8480
Email: submissions@ beaconpublishinggroup.com
Website: https://www. beaconpublishinggroup.com

Publishes: Fiction; Nonfiction; *Markets:* Adult

A traditional publisher that specialises in fiction and nonfiction work.

Bear Star Press
185 Hollow Oak Drive
Cohasset, CA 95973
Website: http://www.bearstarpress.com

Publishes: Poetry; *Markets:* Adult

Publishes poets living west of the central time zone. Gives priority to work submitted via annual poetry contest ($25 reading fee), but will accept submissions not made through this competition.

BearManor Media
PO Box 71426
Albany, GA 31708
Tel: +1 (580) 252-3547
Fax: +1 (800) 332-8092
Email: books@benohmart.com
Website: http://www.bearmanormedia.com

Publishes: Fiction; Nonfiction; *Areas:* Autobiography; Biography; Film; Humour; Radio; TV; *Markets:* Adult

Contact: Ben Ohmart

Publisher of books on the past of TV, film, and radio. Particularly interested in books on voice actors and supporting actors. Also expanding ebook-only range to include such areas as fiction, humour, etc. Send query by email.

Belle Lutte Press
PO Box 49858
Austin, TX 78765
Email: Inquiries@BelleLutte.com
Website: http://bellelutte.com

Publishes: Fiction; *Markets:* Adult; *Treatments:* Literary

Publishes fiction. Send cover letter and up to 30 pages or three chapters of your work via online submission system.

BenBella Books
10300 North Central Expy, Suite 530 Dallas, TX 75231
Tel: +1 (214) 750-3600
Email: glenn@benbellabooks.com
Website: http://www.benbellabooks.com

Publishes: Nonfiction; *Areas:* Autobiography; Biography; Business; Cookery; Culture; Health; Lifestyle; Politics; Science; Self-Help; Sociology; Sport; *Markets:* Adult; *Treatments:* Popular

Contact: Glenn Yeffeth

Marketing-focussed publishing house, publishing 30-40 titles a year. Actively acquiring strong nonfiction manuscripts. Send pitch of no more than a few pages describing your book, how it differs from others, your qualifications to write it, and explaining why you think the book will sell.

Beyond Words Publishing
20827 NW Cornell Road, Suite 500
Hillsboro, OR 97124
Tel: +1 (503) 531-8700
Fax: +1 (503) 531-8773

Email: info@beyondword.com
Website: http://www.beyondword.com

Publishes: Fiction; Nonfiction; *Areas:*
Health; Lifestyle; Spiritual; Women's
Interests; *Markets:* Adult; Children's; Youth

Publishes books on mind, body, and spirit;
holistic living; spiritual parenting; spiritual
lifestyles; native wisdom; and spiritual
needs. Also publishes fiction for children and
young adults. No children's picture books
(including poetry/rhyme); adult fiction, short
stories, memoirs, or poetry; cookbooks,
textbooks, or other reference books; or
illustrated coffee table or photography
books. Accepts approaches through agents
only.

BkMk Press
University of Missouri-Kansas City
5101 Rockhill Road
Kansas City, MO 64110-2499
Tel: +1 (816) 235-2558
Fax: +1 (816) 235-2611
Email: bkmk@umkc.edu
Website: http://www.newletters.org

Publishes: Fiction; Nonfiction; Poetry;
Areas: Short Stories; *Markets:* Adult;
Treatments: Literary

Send query with SASE and sample (around
ten pages for poetry; around 50 pages for
prose). Publishes collections of poetry, short
stories, and creative nonfiction essays. No
novels, mystery, western, or romance.
Novellas considered very occasionally. No
submissions by email, or in any other way
online. Accepts submissions between Feb 1
and June 30.

Black Dome Press
649 Delaware Avenue
Delmar, NY 12054
Tel: +1 (518) 439-6512
Email: blackdomep@aol.com
Website: http://www.blackdomepress.com

Publishes: Nonfiction; *Areas:* Architecture;
Arts; Biography; Culture; Historical;
Lifestyle; Nature; Science; *Markets:* Adult;
Children's

Publishes nonfiction on New York State, in
particular the Hudson River Valley and
Catskill Mountains regions.

Black Rose Writing
PO Box 1540
Castroville, TX 78009
Email: creator@blackrosewriting.com
Website: http://www.blackrosewriting.com

Publishes: Fiction; Nonfiction; *Markets:*
Adult; Children's

Accepts all fiction and nonfiction for adults.
Accepts children's books with full
illustrations only. No poetry or short story
collections. Submit via online submission
system.

Bloomberg Press
Professional Development
111 River Street
Hoboken, NJ 07030
Tel: +1 (201) 748-6000
Fax: +1 (201) 748-6088
Email: info@wiley.com
Website: http://www.wiley.com

Publishes: Nonfiction; Reference; *Areas:*
Current Affairs; Finance; How-to; *Markets:*
Professional

Publishes books on finance and public affairs
for professionals. No management, strategy,
leadership, professional development,
entrepreneurship, personal finance, or
general consumer books.

Blue Mountain Arts, Inc.
PO Box 4549
Boulder, CO 80306
Email: editorial@sps.com
Website: http://www.sps.com

Publishes: Nonfiction; Poetry; *Areas:*
Lifestyle; Self-Help; *Markets:* Adult;
Treatments: Commercial

Publishes nonfiction on personal growth,
families and relationships, etc. and poetry
appropriate for gift books and greetings
cards. No literary poetry.

Blue River Press

2402 N. Shadeland Ave., Ste. A
Indianapolis, IN 46219
Tel: +1 (317) 352-8200
Fax: +1 (317) 352-8200
Email: proposals@brpressbooks.com
Website: http://www.brpressbooks.com

Publishes: Nonfiction; *Areas:* Culture;
Health; Sport; Travel; *Markets:* Adult;
Treatments: Popular

Publishes nonfiction for a general or
specialised audience. Interested in both
series products and stand-alone books. Seeks
knowledgeable authors with a passion for
their subject and a willingness to promote
their ideas and books. Send proposals by
email.

BLVNP Incorporated

Email: info@blvnp.com
Website: http://www.blvnp.com

Publishes: Fiction; *Areas:* Fantasy; Humour;
Literature; Mystery; Romance; Sci-Fi; Self-
Help; Short Stories; *Markets:* Adult; Family;
Youth; *Treatments:* Contemporary; Light;
Positive

So here's what we do:

When a book is getting published it is read
by our team of Grammar Nazis/Ninjas
(they're both) who will literally cut out any
misspelled words and grammar errors (it was
really hard on laptop screens until we got
them touch screens and padded swords).

Once the author approves the edits, our team
of Graphic Ninjas meditate and visualize
deep into the cosmic group mind and create
eye-catching covers, ready to blind an
innocent book reader.

Our Marketing Ninjas step in to make sure
that the book would be seen by the people
who want your book for and make sure they
buy it!

Of course being ninjas we have grown
quickly with thousands of books and now
magazines.

Honestly, we love this. It is so much more

fun than killing people in their sleep. Of
course killing monsters (especially gorgons)
is still pretty fun. Look behind the scenes in
some of the team photos, and you will see a
bit of gorgon blood.

Plus, we all love being with one another.
We're all fun, crazy, and we patch ourselves
up whenever someone hits someone else
with their sword accidentally.

Brewers Publications

1327 Spruce Street
Boulder, CO 80302
Tel: +1 (888) 822-6273
Email: Kristi@BrewersAssociation.org
Website: https://www.
brewerspublications.com

Publishes: Nonfiction; *Markets:* Adult;
Professional

Contact: Kristi Switzer

Publishes books on brewing beer for
professional and amateur brewers. Send
query with proposal and sample chapter. See
website for full guidelines.

Bucknell University Press

Bucknell University, One Dent Drive,
Lewisburg, PA 17837
Tel: +1 (570) 577-3674
Email: clingham@bucknell.edu
Website: http://www.bucknell.edu/
universitypress

Publishes: Nonfiction; *Areas:* Anthropology;
Architecture; Arts; Criticism; Culture;
Historical; Legal; Literature; Medicine;
Philosophy; Politics; Psychology; Religious;
Science; Sociology; *Markets:* Academic

Contact: Greg Clingham

Publishes scholarship in the humanities and
social sciences, particularly literary criticism,
Modern Languages, Classics, theory, cultural
studies, historiography (including the history
of law, of medicine, and of science),
philosophy, psychology and psychoanalysis,
religion, political science, cultural and
political geography, and interdisciplinary
combinations of the above. Send proposal by
post or by email.

Bull Publishing Company

PO Box 1377
Boulder, CO 80306
Tel: +1 (800) 676-2855
Fax: +1 (303) 545-6354
Email: jim@bullpub.com
Website: http://www.bullpub.com

Publishes: Nonfiction; *Areas:* Cookery;
Health; How-to; Medicine; Psychology;
Self-Help; Sport; Women's Interests;
Markets: Adult

Contact: Jim Bull

Send query with content outline or table of
contents; a discussion of why you are writing
the book; an overview of competing books
and a concise description of what sets your
book apart from the rest of the pack; and a
sample chapter or two, ideally from different
parts of the manuscript. Focuses on books on
health, diet, nutrition, etc.

Butte Publications, Inc.

PO Box 1328
Hillsboro, OR 97123-1328
Tel: +1 (503) 648-9791
Email: service@buttepublications.com
Website: http://www.buttepublications.com

Publishes: Nonfiction; *Markets:* Academic;
Professional

Publishes special educational resources. All
titles must be useful to Deaf and Hard of
Hearing, Speech and Hearing, Special
Education, English as a Second Language, or
Early Intervention and Early Childhood. See
website for submission guidelines.

C&T Publishing

1651 Challenge Drive
Concord, CA 94520-5206
Tel: +1 (925) 677-0377
Fax: +1 (925) 677-0373
Email: support@ctpub.com
Website: http://www.ctpub.com

Publishes: Nonfiction; *Areas:* Crafts;
Hobbies; *Markets:* Adult

Publishes books on sewing and related crafts.

Capstone Professional

Capstone Nonfiction
1710 Roe Crest Drive
North Mankato, MN 56003
Tel: +1 (312) 324-5200
Fax: +1 (312) 324-5201
Email: info@maupinhouse.com
Website: http://www.capstonepub.com/
classroom/professional-development/

Publishes: Nonfiction; *Markets:* Academic;
Professional

Publishes books for teaching professionals,
written by classroom practitioners with vast
experiences. Send query by US mail only,
with cover letter, CV, and up to three writing
samples.

Career Press

65 Parker Street, Suite 7
Newburyport, MA 01950
Tel: +1 (978) 465-0504
Fax: +1 (978) 465-0243
Email: mpye@rwwbooks.com
Website: http://www.careerpress.com

Publishes: Nonfiction; Reference; *Areas:*
Business; Finance; How-to; Leisure;
Lifestyle; Self-Help; Spiritual; *Markets:*
Adult

Contact: Michael Pye, Senior Acquisitions
Editor

If available, send completed MS with SASE.
Otherwise, submit outline, author bio,
marketing plan, and one or two sample
chapters with SASE. Publishes books of
practical information and self improvement
for adults, covering such topics as education,
health, money matters, spiritual matters,
business philosophy, etc. Author should
familiarise themselves with the catalogue
before submitting. No children's books,
fiction, cookbooks, humour books, picture
books, photography books, memoirs,
gambling titles, or coffee-table publications.

Carson-Dellosa Publishing Company, Inc.

PO Box 35665
Greensboro, NC 27425-5665
Tel: +1 (336) 632-0084

Fax: +1 (336) 632-0087
Email: webhelp@carsondellosa.com
Website: http://www.carsondellosa.com

Publishes: Nonfiction; *Markets:* Academic; Children's

Contact: Donna Walkush

Publishes teacher resource books, activity books, student workbooks, and education books for grades PK–8. Not accepting ideas or proposals as at September 2017.

CATO Institute

1000 Massachusetts Ave, NW
Washington, DC 20001-5403
Tel: +1 (202) 842 0200
Website: http://www.cato.org

Publishes: Nonfiction; *Areas:* Philosophy; Politics; Sociology; *Markets:* Adult

Public policy think tank promoting individual liberty, limited government, free markets and peace. Send query by post with SASE.

Cave Hollow Press

PO Drawer J
Warrensburg, MO 64093
Email: gbcrump@cavehollowpress.com
Website: http://www.cavehollowpress.com

Publishes: Fiction; *Markets:* Adult; *Treatments:* Mainstream

Contact: Georgia R. Nagel; R.M. Kinder

Note: Not accepting new material as at April 2016

Actively seeking mainstream novels between 60,000 and 80,000 words by authors from Missouri, the Midwest, and surrounding regions. Send query with SASE, 1-3 page synopsis, and first three chapters or 30-40 pages of the completed MS.

Cedar Fort

2373 W. 700
S. Springville, UT 84663
Tel: +1 (801) 489-4084
Website: http://www.cedarfort.com

Publishes: Fiction; Nonfiction; *Areas:* Historical; Religious; Self-Help; Short Stories; Spiritual; *Markets:* Adult; Children's; Youth; *Treatments:* Positive

Publishes books with strong moral or religious values that inspire readers to be better people. No poetry. Rarely publishes biographies, autobiographies, or memoirs, and is very selective about children's books. See website for full submission guidelines, and to submit using online submission system.

Charlesbridge Publishing

85 Main Street
Watertown, MA 02472
Tel: +1 (617) 926-0329
Fax: +1 (800) 926-5775
Email: tradeeditorial@charlesbridge.com
Website: http://www.charlesbridge.com

Publishes: Fiction; Nonfiction; *Areas:* Culture; Historical; Nature; Science; *Markets:* Academic; Children's; Youth

Publishes research-based instructional materials for teachers and students, and award-winning picture books for children of all ages. Produces books with a strategic approach to reading, writing, maths, and science. Also publishes full-length fiction for middle grade and young adults. Send complete ms by post. Do not include SASE, as response is only given if interested. All other materials are recycled. YA novels may also be sent by email (see website for details).

Chelsea Green Publishing, Inc.

85 North Main Street, Suite 120
White River Junction, VT 05001
Tel: +1 (802) 295-6300
Fax: +1 (802) 295-6444
Email: web@chelseagreen.com
Website: http://www.chelseagreen.com

Publishes: Nonfiction; *Areas:* Cookery; Finance; Gardening; How-to; Lifestyle; Nature; New Age; Politics; Science; Spiritual; *Markets:* Academic; Adult; Professional

Publishes books on organic gardening and market farming, from home to professional scale, and related topics, including renewable energy, food politics, and alternative economic models. Will only occasionally publish academic, new age, or spiritual, and does not publish fiction, poetry, or books for children. See website for submission guidelines.

Chicago Review Press

814 North Franklin Street
Chicago, Illinois 60610
Tel: +1 (312) 337-0747
Fax: +1 (312) 337-5110
Email: frontdesk@chicagoreviewpress.com
Website: http://www.
chicagoreviewpress.com

Publishes: Fiction; Nonfiction; *Areas:* Autobiography; Biography; Crafts; Culture; Film; Gardening; Historical; Lifestyle; Music; Politics; Science; Sport; Travel; Women's Interests; *Markets:* Adult; Children's; Youth

Closed to fiction proposals as at January 2018. Check website for current status.

Publishes nonfiction through all imprints, and fiction through specific imprint listed above. Also publishes children's and young adult titles, but no picture books. See website for full submission guidelines.

Chronicle Books LLC

680 Second Street
San Francisco, California 94107
Tel: +1 (415) 537 4200
Email: submissions@chroniclebooks.com
Website: http://www.chroniclebooks.com

Publishes: Fiction; Nonfiction; *Areas:* Architecture; Arts; Beauty and Fashion; Cookery; Crafts; Design; Film; Health; Humour; Lifestyle; Music; Photography; Travel; TV; *Markets:* Children's; *Treatments:* Literary

Publishes nonfiction for adults, and fiction and nonfiction for children. Children submissions must be sent by post; adult submission can be sent by post or email, but email is preferred. See website for full guidelines.

Clarity Press, Inc.

2625 Piedmont Road NE, Suite 56
Atlanta, GA 30324
Tel: +1 (877) 613-1495
Fax: +1 (877) 613-7868
Email: claritypress@usa.net
Website: http://www.claritypress.com

Publishes: Nonfiction; *Areas:* Current Affairs; Finance; Historical; Legal; Military; Politics; Sociology; *Markets:* Adult

Contact: Diana G. Collier, Editorial Director

Send query letter first, with CV, table of contents and synopsis by email. No submissions by post. Publishes books on human rights issues and social justice. Visit website before querying.

Clarkson Potter

1745 Broadway
New York, NY 10019
Tel: +1 (212) 782-9000
Website: http://crownpublishing.com/
archives/imprint/clarkson-potter

Publishes: Nonfiction; *Areas:* Arts; Cookery; Design; Lifestyle; *Markets:* Adult; *Treatments:* Commercial; Literary

Imprint dedicated to lifestyle, publishing books by chefs, cooks, designers, artists, and writers. Accepts approaches via literary agents only.

College Press Publishing

2111 N. Main Street, Suite C
Joplin, MO 64801
PO Box 1132
Joplin, MO 64802
Tel: +1 (800) 289-3300
Fax: +1 (417) 623-1929
Email: collpressjoplin@gmail.com
Website: http://collegepress.com

Publishes: Nonfiction; *Areas:* Biography; Historical; Religious; *Markets:* Adult

Publishes Bible studies, topical studies (biblically based), apologetic studies, historical biographies of Christians, Sunday/Bible School curriculum (adult electives). No poetry, game or puzzle books, books on prophecy from a premillennial or dispensational viewpoint, or any books that do not contain a Christian message. Send query by email or by post with SASE. See website for required contents.

Concordia Publishing House

3558 S. Jefferson
St. Louis, MO 63118-3968
Tel: +1 (314) 268-1000
Fax: +1 (800) 490 9889
Email: ideas@cph.org
Website: http://www.cph.org

Publishes: Nonfiction; *Areas:* Culture; Lifestyle; Religious; Spiritual; *Markets:* Adult; Children's; Family; Youth

No Christian fiction, autobiographies, poetry, or children's picture books. Send query by email.

CQ Press

2455 Teller Road
Thousand Oaks, CA 91320
Tel: +1 (800) 818-7243
Fax: +1 (800) 583-2665
Email: michael.kerns@sagepub.com
Website: http://www.cqpress.com

Publishes: Nonfiction; Reference; *Areas:* Historical; Politics; *Markets:* Academic; Adult; Professional

Contact: Michael Kerns

Publishes books on American and international politics and people, including academic text books on political science, directories on governments, elections, etc. See website for full submission guidelines and individual Acquisition Editor contact details.

Crabtree Publishing

PMB 59051
350 Fifth Avenue, 59th Floor
New York, NY 10118
Tel: +1 (212) 496-5040
Fax: +1 (800) 355-7166
Website: http://www.crabtreebooks.com

Publishes: Nonfiction; *Areas:* Historical; Science; Sociology; *Markets:* Academic; Children's

Publishes educational books for children. No unsolicited mss -- all material is generated in-house.

The Crossroad Publishing Company

831 Chestnut Ridge Road
Chestnut Ridge, NY 10977
Tel: +1 (845) 517-0180
Email: submissions@ crossroadpublishing.com
Website: http://www. crossroadpublishing.com

Publishes: Nonfiction; *Areas:* Philosophy; Religious; Spiritual; Women's Interests; *Markets:* Adult

Send proposal by email, with your name, address, credentials, any endorsements supporting your work, an outline, table of contents, and at least one full chapter. For more information, see full guidelines on website.

The Crown Publishing Group

1745 Broadway
New York, NY 10019
Tel: +1 (212) 782-9000
Website: http://crownpublishing.com

Publishes: Fiction; Nonfiction; *Areas:* Arts; Autobiography; Biography; Business; Cookery; Historical; Humour; Politics; *Markets:* Adult

Division of large international publisher, accepting submissions via literary agent only.

CSLI Publications

Cordura Hall
Stanford University
Stanford, CA 94305
Tel: +1 (650) 723-1839
Email: pubs@csli.stanford.edu
Website: https://cslipublications.stanford.edu

Publishes: Nonfiction; *Markets:* Academic

Publishes books, lecture notes, and monographs on the study of language, information, logic, and computation. No unsolicited mss.

Cuil Press
509 Gypsy Hill Gardens
Lehighton, PA 18235
Email: admin@cuilpress.com
Website: http://www.cuilpress.com

Publishes: Fiction; *Areas:* Fantasy;
Romance; Sci-Fi; *Markets:* Adult;
Treatments: Experimental; Niche;
Progressive

Contact: Jessica Burde

Publisher launched in 2017, specialising in
inclusive speculative fiction and romance.

We plan to release our first book in late 2017
and are accepting manuscripts.

Cynren Press
101 Lindenwood Drive, Suite 225
Malvern, PA 19355
Tel: +1 (484) 875-3113
Email: press@cynren.com
Website: http://www.cynren.com

Publishes: Nonfiction; *Areas:* Adventure;
Autobiography; Biography; Crime; Culture;
Historical; Humour; Leisure; Lifestyle;
Men's Interests; Mystery; Philosophy;
Spiritual; Travel; Women's Interests;
Markets: Adult; Family

Contact: Holly Monteith

We publish memoir and historical nonfiction
with the aim of publishing insightful and
unique perspectives on the human story.

David R. Godine, Publisher
Fifteen Court Square, Suite 320
Boston, MA 02108-2536
Tel: +1 (617) 451-9600
Fax: +1 (617) 350-0250
Email: info@godine.com
Website: http://www.godine.com

Publishes: Fiction; Nonfiction; Poetry;
Areas: Architecture; Arts; Biography;
Criticism; Gardening; Historical; Humour;
Literature; Nature; Photography;
Translations; *Markets:* Adult; *Treatments:*
Literary

Recommends writers make approaches via
agents. Any unsolicited material received
without return postage will be disposed of.
No telephone calls or email submissions.

Dawn Publications
12402 Bitney Springs Road
Nevada City, CA 95959
Tel: +1 (530) 274-7775
Fax: +1 (530) 274-7778
Email: submission@dawnpub.com
Website: http://www.dawnpub.com

Publishes: Nonfiction; *Areas:* Nature;
Markets: Adult; Children's

Contact: Carol Malnor

Publisher of nature awareness titles for
adults and children. Send complete MS by
email or by post with SASE, with description
of your work, including: audience age;
previous publications (if any); your
motivation; relevant background. No
response to postal submissions without
SASE.

Divertir Publishing LLC
PO Box 232
North Salem, NH 03073
Email: query@divertirpublishing.com
Website: http://divertirpublishing.com

Publishes: Fiction; Nonfiction; Poetry;
Areas: Crafts; Current Affairs; Fantasy;
Historical; Hobbies; Humour; Mystery;
Politics; Religious; Romance; Sci-Fi; Self-
Help; Short Stories; Spiritual; Suspense;
Markets: Adult; Youth; *Treatments:*
Contemporary; Satirical

Publishes full-length fiction, short fiction,
poetry, and nonfiction. No erotica or material
which is disrespectful to the opinions of
others. Accepts queries and submissions by
email only. See website for full guidelines.

Down The Shore Publishing
Attn: Acquisitions Editor
PO Box 100
West Creek, NJ 08092
Tel: +1 (609) 812-5076
Fax: +1 (609) 812-5098
Email: info@down-the-shore.com
Website: http://www.down-the-shore.com

Publishes: Fiction; Nonfiction; Poetry;
Areas: Historical; Nature; Short Stories;
Markets: Adult

Closed to submissions as at November 2017.
Check website for current status.

Small regional publisher focusing on New
Jersey, the Jersey Shore, the mid-Atlantic,
and seashore and coastal subjects.
Specialises in regional histories; pictorial,
coffee table books; literary anthologies; and
natural history titles appropriate to the
market. Rarely publishes fiction, and does
not generally publish poetry unless as part of
an anthology. Willing to consider any
exceptional work appropriate to the market,
however. See website for more details.

Dream of Things

PO Box 872
Downers Grove, IL. 60515
Tel: +1 (847) 321-1390
Website: http://www.dreamofthings.com

Publishes: Nonfiction; *Areas:*
Autobiography; *Markets:* Adult

Publishes memoirs, essays, and anthologies.
Accepts submissions during specific
submission windows only. See website
and/or subscribe to newsletter for details.

Dreamriver Press

19 Grace Court, Apt.2D
Brooklyn, NY 11201
Tel: +1 (215) 253-4621
Email: info@dreamriverpress.com
Website: http://www.dreamriverpress.com

Publishes: Fiction; Nonfiction; *Areas:*
Adventure; Anthropology; Arts;
Autobiography; Biography; Cookery; Crafts;
Culture; Current Affairs; Drama; Gardening;
Health; Historical; How-to; Lifestyle;
Literature; Medicine; Nature; New Age;
Philosophy; Politics; Psychology; Religious;
Science; Self-Help; Sociology; Spiritual;
Technology; *Markets:* Adult; Family; Youth;
Treatments: Light; Literary; Positive;
Progressive

Contact: Theodore Poulis

**Closed to submissions as at September
2016. Check website for current situation.**

An independent publishing house that aims
to print books in the fields of mind-body-
spirit and spirituality, holistic health,
environment and sustainable living, as well
as inspirational fables for all age groups.

We prefer to receive submission inquiries by
email. Queries can include a synopsis of the
work, the first three chapters as well as a
short bio of the writer.

Please visit our web site for further
information.

Duquesne University Press

600 Forbes Avenue
Pittsburgh, PA 15282
Tel: +1 (800) 666-2211
Email: wadsworth@duq.edu
Website: http://www.dupress.duq.edu

Publishes: Nonfiction; *Areas:* Literature;
Philosophy; Psychology; Religious;
Sociology; Spiritual; *Markets:* Academic

Contact: Susan Wadsworth-Booth, Director

Publishes monographs and collections in the
humanities and social sciences, particularly
literature studies (Medieval and
Renaissance), philosophy, psychology,
religious studies and theology, plus
spirituality. No fiction, poetry, children's
books, technical or "hard" science works, or
unrevised theses or dissertations. Send query
with outline, table of contents, sample
chapter or introduction, author CV, and
details of any previous publications. Submit
by post (with SASE if return of material
required) or by email (in the body of the
email only – no attachments).

Eagle's View Publishing

6756 North Fork Road
Liberty, UT 84310
Tel: +1 (801) 393-4555
Email: sales@eaglefeathertrading.com
Website: http://www.eaglesviewpub.com

Publishes: Nonfiction; *Areas:* Anthropology;
Archaeology; Crafts; Culture; Historical;
Hobbies; How-to; *Markets:* Adult

Contact: Denise Knight

Publishes books on Native American crafts, history, and culture. Send outline with one or two sample chapters.

Eastland Press
PO Box 99749
Seattle, WA 98139
Tel: +1 (206) 931-6957
Fax: +1 (206) 283-7084
Email: info@eastlandpress.com
Website: http://www.eastlandpress.com

Publishes: Nonfiction; *Areas:* Health; Medicine; *Markets:* Professional

Publishes textbooks for practitioners of Chinese medicine, osteopathy, and other forms of bodywork.

Edward Elgar Publishing Inc.
The William Pratt House
9 Dewey Court
Northampton, MA 01060-3815
Tel: +1 (413) 584-5551
Fax: +1 (413) 584-9933
Email: elgarinfo@e-elgar.com
Website: http://www.e-elgar.com

Publishes: Nonfiction; *Areas:* Business; Finance; Legal; Sociology; Travel; *Markets:* Academic; Professional

Contact: Alan Sturmer; Stephen Gutierrez

International academic and professional publisher with a strong focus on the social sciences and legal fields. Actively commissioning new titles and happy to consider and advise on ideas for monograph books, textbooks, professional law books and academic journals at any stage. See website for more details and proposal forms.

Ellysian Press
Email: submissions@ellysianpress.com
Website: http://www.ellysianpress.com

Publishes: Fiction; *Areas:* Fantasy; Horror; Romance; Sci-Fi; *Markets:* Adult; Youth

Publishes novels between 60,000 and 120,000 words. Send query by email with synopsis and first ten pages in the body of the email. See website for full guidelines.

Elm Books
Laramie, WY
Email: Leila.ElmBooks@gmail.com
Website: http://www.elm-books.com

Publishes: Fiction; Nonfiction; Poetry; *Areas:* Anthropology; Culture; Historical; Mystery; Romance; Sci-Fi; Short Stories; *Markets:* Academic; Adult; Children's

Small, independent publisher and distributor based in Laramie, Wyoming. Publishes mysteries, romance, science fiction, disability literature, short story anthologies, scholarly publications in history and anthropology, and multicultural children's books. No picture books. See website for current open calls.

Encante Press, LLC
1572 Blue Lupine Lane
Victor, MT 59875
Email: Books@EncantePress.com
Website: http://encantepress.com

Publishes: Nonfiction; *Areas:* Nature; Politics; Science; Travel; *Markets:* Adult

Eco-friendly publishing company, publishing books on animals, the environment, nature, politics, science, travel, and wildlife. Closed to submissions as of June 2016. See website for current status.

Entangled Teen
Website: http://www.entangledteen.com

Publishes: Fiction; *Areas:* Fantasy; Historical; Romance; Sci-Fi; Thrillers; *Markets:* Youth; *Treatments:* Contemporary

Publishes young adult romances between 50,000 and 100,000 words, aimed at ages 16-19. Submit via website using online submission system.

FalconGuides
246 Goose Lane
Guilford, CT 06357
Tel: +1 (203) 458-4500

Email: info@rowman.com
Website: http://www.falcon.com

Publishes: Nonfiction; *Areas:* Adventure;
Nature; Travel; *Markets:* Adult

Publishes outdoor guidebooks covering
hiking, climbing, paddling, and outdoor
adventure.

Familius
1254 Commerce Way
Sanger, CA 93657
Tel: +1 (559) 876-2170
Fax: +1 (559) 876-2180
Email: bookideas@familius.com
Website: http://familius.com

Publishes: Fiction; Nonfiction; *Areas:*
Autobiography; Cookery; Finance; Health;
Hobbies; Humour; Lifestyle; Medicine; Self-
Help; *Markets:* Adult; Children's; Youth

Publishes fiction and nonfiction for adults,
young adults, and children, focussed on
family as the fundamental unit of society.
Submit by post or using online submission
system. See website for full details.

Fantagraphics
7563 Lake City Way NE
Seattle, WA 98115
Tel: +1 (206) 524-1967
Fax: +1 (206) 524-2104
Email: FBIComix@fantagraphics.com
Website: http://www.fantagraphics.com

Publishes: Fiction; *Areas:* Arts;
Autobiography; Culture; Humour; *Markets:*
Adult; *Treatments:* Literary

Publishes comics for thinking readers.
Previous work has covered autobiographical
journalism, surrealism, arts, culture, etc. No
mainstream comic genres or material aimed
at children. Submit by post only. No
response unless interested. See website for
full guidelines.

Farrar, Straus and Giroux Books for Younger Readers
175 Fifth Avenue
New York, NY 10010
Email: childrens.editorial@fsgbooks.com

Website: http://us.macmillan.com/publishers/
farrar-straus-giroux#FYR

Publishes: Fiction; Nonfiction; *Markets:*
Children's; Youth

Publishes fiction, nonfiction, and picture
books for children and teenagers. Send query
by post only with first 50 pages.

Fence Books
Science Library 320
University at Albany
1400 Washington Avenue
Albany, NY 12222
Tel: +1 (518) 591-8162
Email: jessp.fence@gmail.com
Website: http://www.fenceportal.org

Publishes: Fiction; Nonfiction; Poetry;
Areas: Criticism; Literature; Short Stories;
Markets: Adult

Contact: Jess Puglisi

Publishes poetry and fiction often received
through its book contests. Has occasional
open reading periods. See website for details.

Ferguson Publishing
132 West 31st Street, 17th Floor
New York, NY 10001
Tel: +1 (800) 322-8755
Fax: +1 (800) 678-3633
Email: editorial@factsonfile.com
Website: http://ferguson.
infobasepublishing.com

Publishes: Nonfiction; Reference; *Areas:*
How-to; Lifestyle; Self-Help; *Markets:*
Academic; Adult; Children's; Professional;
Youth

Publishes career education books aimed at
the middle school, high school, and public
library markets. Send query or outline with
one sample chapter. See website for full
submission guidelines.

Finney Company
5995 149th Street West, Suite 105
Apple Valley, MN 55124
Tel: +1 (952) 469-6699
Fax: +1 (952) 469-1968

Email: info@finneyco.com
Website: http://www.finneyco.com

Publishes: Nonfiction; *Areas:* Arts; Crafts; Culture; Gardening; Historical; Leisure; Nature; Science; Sport; Technology; Travel; *Markets:* Adult; Children's

Independent publisher, distributor, and manufacturer of educational materials. No mysteries, romances, science fiction, poems, collections of short stories, religious material, or recipe/cookbooks. Send query outlining your MS and background with SASE, one-page outline, table of contents, at least the first three chapters, and market info. No submissions by email. See website for full guidelines.

First Second
175 5th Avenue
New York, NY 10010
Email: mail@firstsecondbooks.com
Website: http://firstsecondbooks.com

Publishes: Fiction; *Markets:* Children's

Contact: Mark Siegel

Publishes graphic novels for children. Not accepting submissions as at December 2017. Check website for current status.

Floating Bridge Press
909 NE 43rd Street, #205
Seattle, WA 98105
Email: floatingbridgepress@yahoo.com
Website: http://www.floatingbridgepress.org

Publishes: Poetry; *Markets:* Adult

Publishes books of poetry by Washington State poets. All submissions must be made through the annual competition, entry fee: $12. Submit online.

Folded Word LLC
Attn: Barbara Flaherty, Submissions Editor
79 Tracy Way
Meredith, NH 03253
Website: https://folded.wordpress.com

Publishes: Fiction; Nonfiction; Poetry; *Areas:* Humour; Literature; Nature;

Translations; Travel; *Markets:* Adult; *Treatments:* Literary

Publishes fiction, poetry, literary essays, travel narratives, translation, and novels in verse / flash. Only accepting queries for chapbook-length manuscripts as at March 2016. Check website for current status. Send query by post only, with cover letter, three sample pages, and SASE (writers outside the US may omit the stamp). See website for full guidelines.

Fonthill Media LLC
60 Thoreau Street #204
Concord, MA 01742

UK OFFICE:
Millview House
Toadsmoor Road
Stroud
Gloucestershire
GL5 2TB
Email: submissions@fonthillmedia.com
Website: http://fonthillmedia.com

Publishes: Nonfiction; *Areas:* Archaeology; Biography; Historical; Military; Sociology; Sport; Travel; *Markets:* Adult

Independent publisher with offices in the UK and US. Publishes nonfiction only. Send query through website submissions form or by email, providing your project's title, description up to 200 words, description of yourself up to 100 words, proposed word count, and nature and number of illustrations.

Fordham University Press
2546 Belmont Avenue
University Box L
Bronx, NY 10458
Tel: +1 (718) 817-4795
Fax: +1 (718) 817-4785
Email: tlay@fordham.edu
Website: http://fordhampress.com

Publishes: Nonfiction; *Areas:* Anthropology; Architecture; Arts; Biography; Business; Culture; Finance; Historical; Legal; Literature; Media; Medicine; Music; Philosophy; Photography; Politics; Religious; Science; Sociology; Women's Interests; *Markets:* Academic; Adult

Contact: Tom Lay, Acquisitions Editor

Publishes scholarly books in the humanities and social sciences, as well as trade books of interest to the general public. Particularly interested in philosophy, religion, theology, literature, history, media studies, and books of both scholarly and general appeal about New York City and the Hudson Valley. Send proposal by post only (see website for list of appropriate contacts for different subjects). No fiction, or submissions by email.

Forward Movement Publications

412 Sycamore Street
Cincinnati, OH 45202-4110
Tel: +1 (513) 721-6659
Email: editorial@forwardmovement.org
Website: http://www.forwardmovement.org

Publishes: Nonfiction; *Areas:* Biography; Religious; Spiritual; *Markets:* Adult; Children's

Publishes resources that strengthen and support discipleship and evangelism. Generally does not publish fiction or poetry, and only rarely books for children. See website for submission guidelines.

Four Way Books

PO Box 535, Village Station
New York, NY 10014
Tel: +1 (212) 334-5430
Email: editors@fourwaybooks.com
Website: http://www.fourwaybooks.com

Publishes: Fiction; Poetry; *Areas:* Short Stories; *Markets:* Adult

Not-for-profit literary press publishing poetry and short fiction by both established and emerging writers. Submit to contests operated by the press, or during specific reading periods (see website for full details). $30 processing fee.

4RV Publishing

2912 Rankin Terrace
Edmond, OK 73013
Tel: +1 (405) 225-6851
Email: President@4rvpublishingllc.com
Website: http://4rvpublishing.com

Publishes: Fiction; Nonfiction; *Areas:* Adventure; Fantasy; Humour; Mystery; Religious; Romance; Sci-Fi; Suspense; Thrillers; *Markets:* Adult; Children's; Youth; *Treatments:* Mainstream

Accepts most genres of fiction and nonfiction books for all ages, including nonfiction, mystery, romance, mainstream, western, Christian, and science-fiction, as well as children's books, middle grade and young adult novels. No poetry or graphic sex or violence. Language should not be overly profane or vulgar. Accepts submissions by email from the US, UK, and Australia. Not accepting children's books as at January 2018. See website for current status and full guidelines.

Franciscan Media Books

28 West Liberty Street
Cincinnati, OH 45202
Tel: +1 (513) 241-5615
Email: info@franciscanmedia.org
Website: https://www.franciscanmedia.org

Publishes: Nonfiction; *Areas:* Religious; *Markets:* Adult

Catholic publisher based in Ohio. Not accepting submissions as at November 2017. Check website for current status.

FutureCycle Press

Email: dkistner@gmail.com
Website: http://www.futurecycle.org

Publishes: Poetry; *Markets:* Adult

Publishes contemporary English language poetry books and chapbooks. Submit via website through online submission system. $15 reading fee.

Gallaudet University Press

800 Florida Avenue, NE
Washington, DC 20002
Email: ivey.wallace@gallaudet.edu
Website: http://gupress.gallaudet.edu

Publishes: Nonfiction; *Areas:* Biography; Culture; Historical; Literature; Psychology; Sociology; *Markets:* Academic; Adult

Contact: Ivey Pittle Wallace

Publishes books about deaf and hard of hearing people, their languages, their communities, their history, and their education. Publishes scholarly and trade books in fields such as biography by and about deaf adults, culture, deaf studies, disability studies, education, history, interpretation, linguistics, literary works by deaf authors, psychology, sign language, and sociology. See website for full guidelines.

Genealogical Publishing Company
3600 Clipper Mill Road, Suite 260
Baltimore, Maryland 21211
Tel: +1 (410) 837-8271
Fax: +1 (410) 752-8492
Email: info@genealogical.com
Website: http://www.genealogical.com

Publishes: Nonfiction; *Areas:* Historical; Hobbies; How-to; *Markets:* Adult

Publishes books for amateur genealogists.

George Braziller, Inc.
277 Broadway, Suite 708
New York, NY 10007
Tel: +1 (212) 260-9256
Fax: +1 (212) 267-3165
Website: http://www.georgebraziller.com

Publishes: Fiction; Nonfiction; Poetry; *Areas:* Architecture; Arts; Biography; Literature; Short Stories; Translations; Travel; *Markets:* Adult; *Treatments:* Contemporary

Closed to submissions as at June 2018. Check website for current status.

Prefers online approaches, but will accept paper submissions by post. Include SASE if return of material is required. Does not respond to email queries unless interested.

Gibbs Smith, Publisher
PO Box 667
Layton, UT 84041
Tel: +1 (801) 544-9800
Fax: +1 (801) 544-5582
Email: debbie.uribe@gibbs-smith.com
Website: http://www.gibbs-smith.com

Publishes: Nonfiction; *Areas:* Architecture; Arts; Cookery; Crafts; Design; Humour; *Markets:* Adult; Children's

Send query by email only. Main emphasis is on interior design, architecture, children's activities, and cookbooks. Will also accept submissions of: Arts & Crafts, western humour with general appeal, general humour, gift books, and children's activity books and board books. See website for full submission guidelines. At this time not accepting fiction or poetry books.

Golden West Books
PO Box 80250
San Marino, CA 91118-8250
Tel: +1 (626) 458-8148
Fax: +1 (626) 458-8148
Website: http://www.goldenwestbooks.com

Publishes: Nonfiction; *Areas:* Historical; Travel; *Markets:* Adult

Publishes books on railroad history. Send query via online form on website in first instance.

Goosebottom Books LLC
543 Trinidad Lane
Foster City, CA 94404
Tel: +1 (800) 788-3123
Fax: +1 (888) 407-5286
Email: submissions@
goosebottombooks.com
Website: http://goosebottombooks.com

Publishes: Fiction; Nonfiction; *Areas:* Adventure; Historical; *Markets:* Children's; Youth

Publishes books for children and young adults, including fiction and nonfiction, particularly historical. All work is commissioned. Send writing samples if you would like to be considered as a writer for future projects.

Great Potential Press, Inc.
1650 North Kolb Road, #200
Tucson, AZ 85715
Tel: +1 (520) 777-6161
Fax: +1 (520) 777-6217

Email: info@greatpotentialpress.com
Website: http://www.greatpotentialpress.com

Publishes: Nonfiction; *Markets:* Academic;
Adult; Children's

Publishes books that support the academic,
social, or emotional needs of gifted children
and adults. No fiction, poetry, or K-12
classroom materials. Approach via proposal
submission form on website.

Greenhaven Publishing
Attn: Publisher Â– Greenhaven Press
27500 Drake Rd.
Farmington Hills, MI 48331
Tel: +1 (800) 877-4253
Website: http://www.gale.cengage.com/
greenhaven

Publishes: Nonfiction; Reference; *Areas:*
Arts; Current Affairs; Health; Historical;
Literature; Medicine; Music; Nature;
Politics; Science; Sociology; *Markets:*
Academic

Publishes young adult academic reference
titles. No submissions of mss, but will hire
writers to produce material. Send query by
email with CV and list of published works
by email.

Gryphon House, Inc.
PO Box 10
Lewisville, NC 27023
Tel: +1 (800) 638-0928
Fax: +1 (877) 638-7576
Email: info@ghbooks.com
Website: http://www.gryphonhouse.com

Publishes: Nonfiction; *Areas:* How-to;
Markets: Adult; Children's; Professional

Publishes books intended to help teachers
and parents enrich the lives of children from
birth to age eight. See website for proposal
submission guidelines.

Hachai Publishing
527 Empire Boulevard
Brooklyn, NY 11225
Tel: +1 (718) 633-0100
Fax: +1 (718) 633-0103

Email: editor@hachai.com
Website: http://hachai.com

Publishes: Fiction; Nonfiction; *Areas:*
Historical; Religious; *Markets:* Children's

Publishes children's fiction and nonfiction
relating to the Jewish experience. No animal
stories, romance, violence, preachy
sermonising, or elements that violate Jewish
Law. See website for full submission
guidelines.

Hal Leonard Performing Arts Publishing Group
33 Plymouth Street, Suite 302
Montclair, NJ 07042
Email: submissions@halleonardbooks.com
Website: https://www.halleonardbooks.com

Publishes: Nonfiction; *Areas:* Arts; Music;
Markets: Adult

Welcomes submissions pertaining to music
and the performing arts.Send proposal by
email as a Word or PDF attachment. See
website for full guidelines.

Hanser Publications
6915 Valley Avenue
Cincinnati, OH 45244-3029
Tel: +1 (800) 950-8977
Fax: +1 (513) 527-8801
Email: info@hanserpublications.com
Website: http://www.hanserpublications.com

Publishes: Nonfiction; Reference; *Areas:*
Business; Science; Technology; *Markets:*
Academic; Professional

Publisher of plastics technology and
metalworking titles for manufacturers and
educators. Send query with proposal, CV,
and brief writing sample.

Harken Media
Seattle, WA
Email: hmeditors@gmail.com
Website: http://www.harkenmedia.com

Publishes: Fiction; *Areas:* Fantasy;
Historical; Humour; Mystery; Sci-Fi;
Markets: Adult; Youth; *Treatments:* Literary

Publishes books with unique insights or compelling themes for young adult, new adult, and adult audiences. Send query by email only. See website for full guidelines.

Harlequin American Romance

PO Box 5190
Buffalo, NY 14240-5190
Email: submisssions@harlequin.com
Website: http://www.harlequin.com

Publishes: Fiction; *Areas:* Romance; Westerns; *Markets: Treatments:* Contemporary

Contact: Kathleen Scheibling

Publishes heart-warming contemporary romances featuring small town America and cowboys, up to 55,000 words. See website for more details and to submit.

Harmony Ink Press

5032 Capital Circle SW, Ste 2 PMB 279
Tallahassee, FL 32305-7886
Tel: +1 (800) 970-3759
Fax: +1 (888) 308-3739
Email: submissions@harmonyinkpress.com
Website: https://www.harmonyinkpress.com

Publishes: Fiction; *Areas:* Fantasy; Mystery; Romance; Sci-Fi; *Markets:* Youth

Publishes Teen and New Adult fiction featuring significant personal growth of unforgettable characters across the LGBTQ+ spectrum. Closed to general submissions as at May 2016.

Harper Business

195 Broadway
New York, NY 10007
Tel: +1 (212) 207-7000
Website: http://www.harperbusiness.com

Publishes: Nonfiction; *Areas:* Business; *Markets:* Adult; Professional

Publishes books on business. Agented submissions only.

HarperCollins

195 Broadway
New York, NY 10007

Tel: +1 (212) 207-7000
Website: https://www.harpercollins.com

Publishes: Fiction; Nonfiction; Reference; *Areas:* Adventure; Autobiography; Biography; Business; Cookery; Fantasy; Finance; Gothic; Historical; Mystery; Religious; Romance; Sci-Fi; Self-Help; Suspense; Travel; Westerns; *Markets:* Adult; Children's; Family; Youth; *Treatments:* Commercial; Contemporary; Literary

One of the world's largest publishers, almost all imprints are open to agented submissions only. Of the two imprints that accept approaches direct from authors the first seeks romance, and the second seeks visionary and transformational fiction for digital first format. See submission section of website for further details.

Hartman Publishing, Inc.

1313 Iron Ave SW
Albuquerque, NM 87102
Tel: +1 (800) 999-9534
Fax: +1 (800) 474-6106
Email: info@hartmanonline.com
Website: http://www.hartmanonline.com

Publishes: Nonfiction; *Areas:* Health; *Markets:* Professional

Contact: Susan Alvare

Provides in-service education materials for health professionals delivering long-term care, plus textbooks for training nursing assistants and home health aides. See website for more details, and online query form or PDF query form to return by post.

The Harvard Common Press

100 Cummings Center, Suite 253C
Beverly, MA 01915
Tel: +1 (978) 282-9590
Fax: +1 (978) 282-7765
Email: dan.rosenberg@quarto.com
Website: http://www.
harvardcommonpress.com

Publishes: Nonfiction; *Areas:* Cookery; Lifestyle; *Markets:* Adult

Contact: Dan Rosenberg, Editorial Director

Publishes books on cookery and parenting. See website for full guidelines.

Health Communications, Inc.
3201 S.W. 15th Street
Deerfield Beach, Florida 33442
Tel: +1 (954) 360-0909
Fax: +1 (954) 360-0034
Email: Editorial@hcibooks.com
Website: http://www.hcibooks.com

Publishes: Nonfiction; *Areas:* Autobiography; Biography; Cookery; Health; How-to; Lifestyle; Medicine; Men's Interests; Psychology; Religious; Self-Help; Spiritual; Women's Interests; *Markets:* Adult; Youth; *Treatments:* Contemporary; Popular; Positive

Contact: Editorial Committee

Life issues publisher, publishing books on self improvement, personal health and development, recovery, etc. Authors should be experts in the field or write from experience. Books should be affirming, readable, and offer positive long-term life-changing solutions. See website for full requirements and proposal guidelines.

Health Professions Press
Acquisitions Department
Health Professions Press
P.O. Box 10624
Baltimore , MD 21285-0624
Tel: +1 (410) 337-9585
Fax: +1 (410) 337-8539
Email: mmagnus@healthpropress.com
Website: http://www.healthpropress.com

Publishes: Nonfiction; Reference; *Areas:* Health; How-to; Medicine; Psychology; Self-Help; *Markets:* Academic; Adult; Professional

Publishes health books aimed primarily at professionals, students, and educated consumers interested in topics related to ageing and eldercare. See website for submission guidelines and to download Publication Questionnaire.

Helicon Nine Editions
PO Box 22412
Kansas City, MO 64113
Tel: +1 (816) 753-1095
Fax: +1 (816) 753-1016
Email: helicon9@aol.com
Website: http://www.heliconnine.com

Publishes: Fiction; Poetry; *Areas:* Short Stories; *Markets:* Adult; *Treatments:* Literary

Independent small, literary publisher, publishing books, chapbooks, and magazines of poetry and fiction.

Hendrick-Long Publishing Co.
10635 Tower Oaks, Suite D
Houston, Texas 77070
Tel: +1 (281) 635-0583
Email: hendrick-long@att.net
Website: http://hendricklongpublishing.com

Publishes: Fiction; Nonfiction; *Areas:* Arts; Biography; Cookery; Culture; Historical; Military; Science; Westerns; *Markets:* Children's; Youth

Contact: Michael Long; Vilma Long; Joann Taylor Long; Caroline Ingrid Long

Publishes Texas-related fiction and nonfiction for children and young adults. Send query with SASE, outline, synopsis, and two sample chapters.

Hendrickson Publishers
PO Box 3473
Peabody, MA 01961-3473
Tel: +1 (978) 532-6546
Fax: +1 (978) 573-8111
Email: editorial@hendrickson.com
Website: http://www.hendrickson.com

Publishes: Nonfiction; Reference; *Areas:* Religious; *Markets:* Academic; Adult

Christian publisher. Publishes bibles and academic, trade, and reference books. Accepts approaches only from literary agents or through conferences.

Henry Holt and Company

175 Fifth Avenue
New York, NY 10010
Website: http://www.henryholt.com

Publishes: Fiction; Nonfiction; *Markets:*
Adult

No submissions. Any material submitted will
be recycled or discarded unread.

Heyday Books

PO Box 9145
Berkeley, CA 94709
Tel: +1 (510) 549-3564
Fax: +1 (510) 549-1889
Email: heyday@heydaybooks.com
Website: http://www.heydaybooks.com

Publishes: Fiction; Nonfiction; Poetry;
Areas: Arts; Culture; Historical; Literature;
Nature; *Markets:* Adult; Children's;
Treatments: Literary

Small publisher of natural and cultural
history, literature, and arts, concentrating on
California and the West. Consult website to
see if your book is appropriate, then send
query by post with author details, outline,
table of contents and list of illustrations,
market details, sample chapter, and SASE.
Submissions for children's books may be
sent by email. See website for full details.

Hipso Media

8151 East 29th Avenue
Denver, CO 80238
Email: rob@hipsomedia.com
Website: http://www.hipsomedia.com

Publishes: Fiction; Nonfiction; *Areas:*
Cookery; Culture; Erotic; Health; How-to;
Humour; Lifestyle; Medicine; Mystery; Self-
Help; Short Stories; Travel; *Markets:* Adult;
Youth

Contact: Rob Simon, Publisher

Digital-first publisher. Particularly keen on
work that lends itself to media enhancements
such as illustrations, videos, music, sound
effects, animations, hyperlinks, etc. Send
query by email with synopsis and author bio.
See website for full guidelines.

Hohm Press

PO Box 4410
Chino Valley, AZ 86323
Tel: +1 (800) 381-2700
Fax: +1 (928) 636-7519
Email: publisher@hohmpress.com
Website: http://www.hohmpress.com

Publishes: Nonfiction; *Areas:* Arts; Health;
Lifestyle; Literature; Nature; Religious;
Women's Interests; *Markets:* Adult

Publishes books that provide readers with
alternatives to the materialistic values of the
current culture and promote self-awareness,
the recognition of interdependence and
compassion. Send query by post with small
sample.

Holiday House, Inc.

425 Madison Ave
New York, NY 10017
Tel: +1 (212) 688-0085
Fax: +1 (212) 421-6134
Email: info@holidayhouse.com
Website: http://www.holidayhouse.com

Publishes: Fiction; Nonfiction; *Markets:*
Children's; Youth

Contact: Editorial Department

Independent publisher of children's books,
from picture books to young adult fiction and
nonfiction. Send complete ms by post only.
No need to include SASE. No submissions
by fax or email.

Human Kinetics

1607 N Market Street
PO Box 5076
Champaign, Illinois 61825-5076
Tel: +1 (800) 747-4457
Fax: +1 (217) 351-1549
Email: info@hkusa.com
Website: http://www.humankinetics.com

Publishes: Nonfiction; *Areas:* Health;
Leisure; Medicine; Psychology; Science;
Sport; *Markets:* Academic; Adult;
Professional

Publishes books on health, fitness, and sport,
aimed at the academic market, professionals

in the field, and the general public. Send query with outline and sample chapters.

Humanix Books

Tel: +1 (855) 371-7810
Email: sherries@humanixbooks.com
Website: http://www.humanixbooks.com

Publishes: Nonfiction; *Areas:* Autobiography; Business; Finance; Health; Historical; Politics; Science; *Markets:* Adult

Contact: Sherrie Slopianka

Publishes books for independent thinkers from acclaimed experts in health and wellness, finance and investing, and politics and history.

ICS Publications

ICS Editorial
11041 Broken Woods Drive
Miamisburg, OH 45342
Email: editor@icspublications.org
Website: http://www.icspublications.org

Publishes: Nonfiction; *Areas:* Historical; Religious; Spiritual; Translations; *Markets:* Adult

Publishes books in the field of Carmelite spirituality, particularly Carmelite saints and related topics.

IDW Publishing

2765 Truxtun Road
San Diego, CA 92106
Email: letters@idwpublishing.com
Website: http://www.idwpublishing.com

Publishes: Fiction; *Areas:* Adventure; Sci-Fi; *Markets:* Adult; Children's; Youth

Publisher of comic books and graphic novels based on well known intellectual properties, for both children and adults.

Illusio & Baqer

Email: submissions@zharmae.com
Website: https://illusiobaqer.com

Publishes: Fiction; *Markets:* Children's; Youth

Contact: T Denise Clary; Emily Stanford; Cynthia Kumancik

Publishes Young Adult, New Adult, and Middle Grade. Always on the lookout for new, dynamic, and fresh voices. Send query by email with word count, brief author bio (100-200 words), one-page synopsis, and first 3-5 chapters. See website for full guidelines.

Image Comics

Submissions
c/o Image Comics
2001 Center Street, Sixth Floor
Berkeley, CA 94704
Email: submissions@imagecomics.com
Website: http://www.imagecomics.com

Publishes: Fiction; *Markets:* Adult; Youth

Third largest comic book publisher in the United States. Publishes comics and graphic novels. Only interested in creator-owned comics. Does not acquire any rights. Looking for comics that are well written and well drawn, by people who are dedicated and can meet deadlines, not any specific genre or type of comic book. See website for full submission guidelines.

Incentive Publications

2400 Crestmoor Road
Nashville, TN 37215
Tel: +1 (800) 967-5325
Email: incentive@worldbook.com
Website: http://incentivepublications.com

Publishes: Nonfiction; *Markets:* Academic; Children's; Professional

Publishes supplemental resources for student use and instruction and classroom management improvement materials for teachers. Always looking for talented authors and illustrators with a love of entertaining and educating children. Send manuscripts by email.

Indiana Historical Society Press

450 West Ohio Street
Indianapolis, IN 46202
Tel: +1 (317) 232-1882

Email: ihspress@indianahistory.org
Website: https://indianahistory.org

Publishes: Nonfiction; *Areas:* Historical;
Markets: Adult; Children's; Family

Publishes books on the history of Indiana.
Send query with SASE.

Information Today, Inc.

143 Old Marlton Pike
Medford, NJ 08055-8750

Tel: +1 (609) 654-6266
Fax: +1 (609) 654-4309
Email: custserv@infotoday.com
Website: http://www.infotoday.com

Publishes: Nonfiction; *Areas:* Technology;
Markets: Adult

Publishes books and magazines on
information technology.

Interlink Publishing Group, Inc.

46 Crosby Street
Northampton, MA 01060
Tel: +1 (413) 582 7054
Fax: +1 (413) 582 7057
Email: info@interlinkbooks.com
Website: http://www.interlinkbooks.com

Publishes: Fiction; Nonfiction; Reference;
Areas: Arts; Cookery; Film; Historical;
Leisure; Literature; Music; Photography;
Politics; Sport; Translations; Travel;
Markets: Adult; Children's

Research the types of books published by
reading examples first. If you think your
work is suitable, send query by email. In
fiction, only publishes work by authors born
outside the US, bringing it to the American
audience. All children's books are aimed at
ages between three and eight, and are
illustrated. Manuscripts that do not have
illustrations already included are not
considered.

Publishes fiction, travel, Children's, politics,
cookbooks, and specialises in Middle East
titles and ethnicity. No poetry, plays,

unsolicited MSS, or queries by fax or email.
See website for full guidelines.

International Wealth Success (IWS) Inc.

24 Canterbury Road
Rockville Centre, NY 11570
Tel: +1 (516) 766-5850
Fax: +1 (516) 766-5919
Email: admin@iwsmoney.com
Website: http://www.iwsmoney.com

Publishes: Nonfiction; *Areas:* Business;
Finance; How-to; Self-Help; *Markets:* Adult

Publishes books that help people become
more independent and wealthy through real
estate and small businesses.

Interweave Press

4868 Innovation Dr
Ft. Collins, CO 80525-5576
Tel: +1 (866) 949-1646
Email: kerry.bogert@fwcommunity.com
Website: https://www.interweave.com

Publishes: Nonfiction; *Areas:* Crafts;
Hobbies; *Markets:* Adult

Contact: Kerry Bogert

Publishes books, magazines, DVDs etc. on
crafts such as knitting, crocheting, spinning,
weaving, needlework and jewelry.

Italica Press

99 Wall Street, Suite 650
New York, NY 10005
Tel: +1 (917) 371-0563
Email: inquiries@ItalicaPress.com
Website: http://www.italicapress.com

Publishes: Fiction; Nonfiction; Poetry;
Scripts; *Areas:* Arts; Drama; Historical;
Translations; Travel; *Markets:* Adult

Publishes English translations of medieval,
Renaissance and early-modern texts,
historical travel, English translations of
modern Italian fiction, dual-language poetry,
drama, and a series of studies in art and
history.

Jolly Fish Press
PO Box 1773
Provo, UT 84603-1773
Email: submit@jollyfishpress.com
Website: http://www.jollyfishpress.com

Publishes: Fiction; *Areas:* Autobiography;
Biography; Fantasy; Historical; Horror;
Humour; Mystery; Sci-Fi; Self-Help;
Suspense; Thrillers; *Markets:* Adult;
Children's; Youth; *Treatments:* Commercial;
Literary

Accepts submissions by email only. For
fiction, send one-page query, one-page
synopsis, and first three chapters, in the body
of your email. For nonfiction, send one-page
query and book proposal. No attachments.
No children's picture books, novellas, gift
books, poetry, or religious books. See
website for full details.

JourneyForth
1430 Hampton Boulevard
Greenville, SC 29609-5046
Tel: +1 (800) 845-5731
Email: journeyforth@bjupress.com
Website: http://www.bjupress.com

Publishes: Fiction; Nonfiction; *Areas:*
Adventure; Biography; Historical; Mystery;
Nature; Religious; Sport; Westerns; *Markets:*
Adult; Children's; Youth

Contact: Nancy Lohr

Publishes adult nonfiction and children's and
youth fiction, all from a conservative
Christian worldview.

Judaica Press
Tel: +1 (718) 972-6200
Email: submissions@judaicapress.com
Website: https://www.judaicapress.com

Publishes: Fiction; Nonfiction; *Areas:*
Biography; Historical; Religious; Self-Help;
Short Stories; *Markets:* Adult; Children's;
Family; Youth

Publishes books for a varied audience, that
conform to Torah-observant Jewish values.
Send complete ms by email as Word,
DavkaWriter, RTF, or PDF files, with cover

letter and author contact details. See website
for full details.

Judson Press
PO Box 851
Valley Forge, PA 19482-0851
Tel: +1 (800) 458-3766
Fax: +1 (610) 768-2107
Email: acquisitions@judsonpress.com
Website: https://www.judsonpress.com

Publishes: Nonfiction; *Areas:* Religious;
Markets: Adult

Publishes adult nonfiction for Christians.

Kaeden Books
PO Box 16190
Rocky River, OH 44116
Email: sales@kaeden.com
Website: http://www.kaeden.com

Publishes: Fiction; Nonfiction; *Areas:*
Science; *Markets:* Academic; Children's

Publishes reading materials for primary
teachers to use with children in their first
years of the reading experience.

Kansas City Star Quilts
C&T Publishing
1651 Challenge Drive
Concord, CA 94520
Email: roxanec@ctpub.com
Website: http://www.
kansascitystarquilts.com

Publishes: Nonfiction; *Areas:* Crafts;
Hobbies; *Markets:* Adult

Contact: Roxane Cerda

Publishes quilt books.

Kar-Ben Publishing
1251 Washington Ave N
Minneapolis, MN 55401
Tel: +1 (800) 452-7236
Email: editorial@karben.com
Website: http://www.karben.com

Publishes: Fiction; Nonfiction; *Areas:*
Religious; *Markets:* Children's; Family

Publishes fiction and nonfiction on Jewish themes for children and families. No adult, young adult, games, textbooks, or books in Hebrew. Send submissions by email and allow 6-8 weeks for reply.

Kathy Dawson Books

Penguin Group
375 Hudson Street
New York, NY 10014
Website: http://kathydawsonbooks.
tumblr.com

Publishes: Fiction; *Markets:* Children's; Youth

Publishes middle grade and young adult fiction. Submit query by post only, with first 10 pages and details of any relevant publishing history. Do not include SASE – all submissions are recycled. Response only if interested.

Kaya Press

c/o USC ASE
3620 S. Vermont Ave KAP 462
Los Angeles, CA 90089
Email: acquisitions@kaya.com
Website: http://www.kaya.com

Publishes: Fiction; Nonfiction; Poetry; *Areas:* Arts; Criticism; Culture; Literature; *Markets:* Adult

Independent not-for-profit publisher of Asian and Pacific Islander diasporic literature, publishing fiction, poetry, critical essays, art, and culture. Send complete MS by email as Word or PDF attachment, with contact info, description of project, why you feel this publisher is appropriate, and list of any previous publications / awards. See website for full details.

Kent State University Press

1118 Library
PO Box 5190
Kent, OH 44242
Tel: +1 (330) 672-7913
Fax: +1 (330) 672-3104
Email: ksupress@kent.edu
Website: http://www.
kentstateuniversitypress.com

Publishes: Nonfiction; *Areas:* Arts; Biography; Criticism; Historical; Literature; *Markets:* Academic

Contact: Will Underwood, Acquiring Editor

Publishes general nonfiction, but particularly scholarly works in the fields of American studies, biography, history, and literary studies.

Kirkbride Bible Company

1102 Deloss Street
Indianapolis, IN 46203
Tel: +1 (800) 428-4385
Fax: +1 (317) 633-1444
Email: info@kirkbride.com
Website: http://www.kirkbride.com

Publishes: Nonfiction; Reference; *Areas:* Religious; *Markets:* Adult

Publisher of bible reference titles.

Krause Publications

700 East State Street
Iola, WI 54990-0001
Tel: +1 (715) 445-2214
Fax: +1 (715) 445-4087
Email: info@krause.com
Website: http://www.krause.com

Publishes: Nonfiction; Reference; *Areas:* Antiques; Hobbies; How-to; Sport; *Markets:* Adult

Largest publisher of material on hobbies and collectibles in the world. Send query with outline, sample chapter, and description of how your book will make a unique contribution.

Lawrence Hill Books

Chicago Review Press
814 North Franklin Street
Chicago, Illinois 60610
Tel: +1 (312) 337-0747
Email: ytaylor@chicagoreviewpress.com
Website: http://www.
chicagoreviewpress.com

Publishes: Nonfiction; *Areas:* Politics; Women's Interests; *Markets:* Adult

Contact: Yuval Taylor

Publishes nonfiction on progressive politics, civil and human rights, feminism, and topics of interest to African Americans and other underrepresented groups. Send query by email.

Leapfrog Press

PO Box 505
Fredonia, NY 14063
Email: acquisitions@leapfrogpress.com
Website: http://www.leapfrogpress.com

Publishes: Fiction; Nonfiction; Poetry; *Areas:* Short Stories; *Markets:* Adult; Children's; Youth; *Treatments:* Literary

Publisher with an eclectic list of fiction, poetry, and nonfiction, including paperback originals of adult and middle-grade fiction and nonfiction. Closed to general submissions between January 15 and around June 15 each year, but accepts adult, young adult (YA) and middle grade (MG) novels, novellas, and short story collections through its annual fiction contest until May 1. Submit online through online submission system.

Lee & Low Books

95 Madison Avenue, suite 1205
New York, NY 10016
Tel: +1 (212) 779-4400
Fax: +1 (212) 532-6035
Email: general@leeandlow.com
Website: http://www.leeandlow.com

Publishes: Fiction; Nonfiction; *Areas:* Culture; *Markets:* Children's; *Treatments:* Positive

Contact: Submissions Editor

Publisher of multicultural books featuring people of colour, aimed at ages 5 to 12. For picture books submit complete MS, but do not include artwork unless you are a professional illustrator. Fiction picture books should be no more than 1,500 words, while nonfiction picture books should be no more than 3,000 words. For middlegrade MSS more than 10,000 words send query with short synopsis and chapter outline (do not send complete MS). All submissions must include SASE. No folklore or animal stories.

Lillenas Drama Resources

PO Box 419527
Kansas City, MO 64141
Tel: +1 (800) 877-0700
Fax: +1 (816) 412-8390
Email: drama@lillenas.com
Website: http://www.lillenas.com

Publishes: Scripts; *Areas:* Religious; *Markets:* Adult; Children's; Family; Youth

Publishes sketches and plays. Not accepting unsolicited submissions as at April 2018. Check website for current status.

Little Pickle Press, Inc.

3701 Sacramento Street #494
San Francisco, CA 94118
Tel: +1 (800) 788-3123
Email: info@littlepicklepress.com
Website: http://www.littlepicklepress.com

Publishes: Fiction; Nonfiction; *Markets:* Children's; Youth

Publishes books that foster kindness in young people. Submit via website through online submission system.

Livingston Press

University of West Alabama
100 North Washington Street, Station 22
University of West Alabama
Livingston, AL 35470
Email: jwt@uwa.edu
Website: http://www.livingstonpress.uwa.edu

Publishes: Fiction; *Areas:* Short Stories; *Markets:* Adult; *Treatments:* Contemporary; Literary; Progressive

Publishes off-beat (as opposed to mainstream) and southern literature; both novels and short story collections (but strong preference given to novels, as short story collections are generally published through annual short story contest). Send query by post with SASE and about 30 pages of work in June only.

Lost Horse Press

105 Lost Horse Lane
Sandpoint, ID 83864

Tel: +1 (208) 255-4410
Email: losthorsepress@mindspring.com
Website: http://www.losthorsepress.org

Publishes: Fiction; Poetry; *Areas:* Short Stories; *Markets:* Adult; *Treatments:* Literary

Publishes collections of poetry and short stories, submitted through their annual competitions (reading fee applies). No general submissions.

Loyola Press
3441 North Ashland Avenue
Chicago, IL 60657
Tel: +1 (773) 281-1818
Fax: +1 (773) 281-0152
Email: durepos@loyolapress.com
Website: http://www.loyolapress.org

Publishes: Nonfiction; *Areas:* Religious; Spiritual; *Markets:* Adult

Contact: Joseph Durepos, Executive Editor/Trade Acquisitions

Catholic publisher of books on Catholic tradition, prayer, and spirituality. Send one-page query email or by post. See website for full guidelines.

LSU Press
338 Johnston Hall
Louisiana State University
Baton Rouge, LA 70803
Tel: +1 (225) 578-6294
Email: mkc@lsu.edu
Website: http://lsupress.org

Publishes: Fiction; Nonfiction; Poetry; *Areas:* Archaeology; Culture; Historical; Literature; Media; Military; Music; Nature; *Markets:* Academic; Adult; *Treatments:* Literary

Academic publisher publishing scholarly monographs and general interest books about Louisiana and the South. Approach by post only. Send query with CV and proposal for nonfiction; one-page summary and brief sample for fiction; and 4-5 sample pages for poetry. See website for full details.

Luna Bisonte Prods
137 Leland Avenue
Columbus OH 43214-7505
Email: bennettjohnm@gmail.com
Website: http://www.johnmbennett.net

Publishes: Poetry; *Markets:* Adult; *Treatments:* Experimental

Publisher of poetry chapbooks. Avant-garde and experimental work only. Send query with brief bio, publishing history, and a few sample poems.

Mage Publishers
1780 Crossroads Drive
Odenton, MD 21113
Tel: +1 (202) 342-1642
Fax: +1 (202) 342-9269
Email: as@mage.com
Website: http://www.mage.com

Publishes: Fiction; Nonfiction; Poetry; *Areas:* Anthropology; Archaeology; Architecture; Arts; Autobiography; Biography; Cookery; Culture; Historical; Literature; Music; Short Stories; Translations; *Markets:* Adult; Children's; *Treatments:* Contemporary; Literary; Mainstream

Contact: Amin Sepehri

Publishes English language books about Persian culture, including nonfiction, cookbooks, translations of literature, history, children's tales, biography and autobiography, architectural studies, and books on music and poetry. Send query by email with brief biographical statement.

Martin Sisters Publishing
Email: submissions@
martinsisterspublishing.com
Website: http://www.
martinsisterspublishing.com

Publishes: Fiction; Nonfiction; *Areas:* Fantasy; Religious; Sci-Fi; Self-Help; Short Stories; *Markets:* Adult; Children's; Family; Youth

Accepts queries for all genres of fiction, including science fiction and fantasy, and nonfiction, including self-help. Submissions may include Christian fiction, inspirational, collections of stories. No poetry, torrid or any books containing extreme violence. Send query by email with marketing plan and (for fiction) 5-10 pages in the body of the email. No attachments. See website for full guidelines.

Maven House Press

4 Snead Court
Palmyra, VA 22963
Tel: +1 (610) 883-7988
Email: jim@mavenhousepress.com
Website: http://mavenhousepress.com

Publishes: Nonfiction; *Areas:* Business; *Markets:* Professional

Publishes business books for executives and managers to help them lead their organisations to greatness. Download proposal form from website and submit proposal by email. See website for full submission guidelines.

MC Press

3695 W. Quail Heights Court
Boise, ID 83703-3861
Tel: +1 (208) 629-7275 Ext. 502
Email: agrubb@mcpressonline.com
Website: http://www.mcpressonline.com

Publishes: Nonfiction; *Areas:* How-to; Technology; *Markets:* Professional

Contact: Anne Grub

Publisher of computer books (IBM technologies) aimed at midrange IT professionals. Send proposals by email.

McGraw-Hill Education

PO Box 182605
Columbus, OH 43218
Tel: +1 (800) 338-3987
Fax: +1 (800) 953-8691
Website: https://www.mheducation.com

Publishes: Nonfiction; *Areas:* Arts; Business; Film; Health; Historical; Legal; Music; Politics; Psychology; Science; Sociology; Technology; Theatre; *Markets:* Academic

Publishes a wide range of nonfiction educational books.

McSweeney's Publishing

849 Valencia St.
San Francisco, CA 94110
Tel: +1 (415) 642-5609
Email: custservice@mcsweeneys.net
Website: https://www.mcsweeneys.net

Publishes: Fiction; Nonfiction; Poetry; *Areas:* Arts; Cookery; Humour; *Markets:* Adult; Children's

Accepts electronic submissions of complete manuscripts only (except in the case of cookbooks, which may be submitted as complete mss or proposals). Not currently accepting poetry submissions. See website for full details.

Melange Books, LLC

Email: submissions-nancy@melange-books.com
Website: http://www.melange-books.com

Publishes: Fiction; *Areas:* Erotic; Romance; Short Stories; *Markets:* Adult; Youth; *Treatments:* Mainstream

Contact: Nancy Schumacher

Publishes mainstream general fiction, romance, and erotica. Send first three chapters or complete short story if under 15,000 words, as RFT file by email. See website for full guidelines.

Messianic Jewish Publishers

6120 Day Long Lane
Clarksville, MD 21029
Tel: +1 (410) 531-6644
Email: editor@messianicjewish.net
Website: http://www.messianicjewish.net

Publishes: Fiction; Nonfiction; *Areas:* Religious; *Markets:* Adult

Publishes books which address Jewish evangelism; the Jewish roots of Christianity; Messianic Judaism; Israel; the Jewish People. Publishes mainly nonfiction, but some fiction. See website for full submission guidelines.

Mountaineers Books

1001 SW Klickitat Way, Suite 201
Seattle, WA 98134
Tel: +1 (206) 223-6303
Fax: +1 (206) 223-6306
Email: submissions@mountaineersbooks.org
Website: https://www.mountaineers.org

Publishes: Nonfiction; *Areas:* Adventure;
Leisure; Nature; Travel; *Markets:* Adult

Publishes books on adventure travel, biking,
camping, climbing, conservation,
environment/nature, hiking, mountaineering,
mountaineering literature, natural history,
outdoor adventure, paddle sports (canoeing,
kayaking, SUP), safety/first aid, skiing
(alpine, Nordic, boarding), snowshoeing,
surfing, walking, and wilderness skills.
Imprint publishes books on sustainable
foods, urban and wilderness foraging,
organic/sustainable gardening, wildlife
gardening, urban farming, general wildlife,
natural living, and general outdoor-related
gift topics. No fiction, children's books,
general tourist/travel guides, or guides
dealing with hunting, fishing, snowmobiling,
horseback riding, or organised spectator
sports. Send proposal or complete ms by
email. See website for full guidelines.

NBM Publishing

160 Broadway, Suite 700 East Wing
New York, NY 10038
Email: tnantier@nbmpub.com
Website: http://nbmpub.com

Publishes: Fiction; *Areas:* Erotic; Fantasy;
Horror; Humour; Mystery; Sci-Fi; *Markets:*
Adult; Youth; *Treatments:* Satirical

Contact: Terry Nantier

Publisher of graphic novels, interested in
general fiction, humour, satire of fantasy and
horror, erotica, and mystery. No superheroes.
Accepting approaches from previously
published authors only (including those with
proven success in online comics). No
submissions from authors outside North
America, except for adult. See website for
full submission guidelines.

New Directions Publishing

80 Eighth Avenue
New York, NY 10011
Email: editorial@ndbooks.com
Website: http://www.ndbooks.com

Publishes: Fiction; Poetry; *Areas:* Historical;
Humour; Short Stories; Suspense;
Translations; *Markets:* Adult; *Treatments:*
Experimental; Literary

Literary publisher of poetry and fiction.
Unable to accept unsolicited mss, but will
make an effort to answer all brief queries.

Nightboat Books

PO Box 10
Callicoon, NY 12723
Email: info@nightboat.org
Website: http://nightboat.org

Publishes: Fiction; Nonfiction; Poetry;
Areas: Translations; *Markets:* Adult;
Treatments: Literary

Publishes poetry, fiction, essay, intergenre,
and translations. Currently only accepting
submissions for poetry, and then only
through its annual poetry competition (closes
in November; $28 entry fee), open to poetry
manuscripts between 60 and 90 pages. For
status on prose and translation submissions
check website after start of 2017.

No Starch Press, Inc.

245 8th Street
San Francisco, CA 94103
Tel: +1 (415) 863-9900
Fax: +1 (415) 863-9950
Email: editors@nostarch.com
Website: https://nostarch.com

Publishes: Nonfiction; *Areas:* Technology;
Markets: Adult; Children's; Youth

Publishes unique books on technology, with
a focus on open source, security, hacking,
programming, alternative operating systems,
LEGO®, science, and maths. See website for
full guidelines.

Nomad Press

2456 Christian Street
White River Junction, VT 05001

Email: info@nomadpress.net
Website: http://nomadpress.net

Publishes: Nonfiction; *Areas:* Historical;
Science; Sociology; *Markets:* Academic;
Children's

Publishes educational activity books for
children exploring the science and history
behind a wide variety of topics, using hands-
on projects to provide experiential education.
Send query by post or by email. No
unsolicited mss.

NorthSouth Books

600 Third Avenue, 2nd Floor
NY, NY 10016
Tel: +1 (917) 210-5868
Email: submissionsnsb@gmail.com
Website: https://northsouth.com

Publishes: Fiction; *Markets:* Children's

Publishes picture books for children up to
1,000 words. Seeks fresh, original fiction on
universal themes that would appeal to
children aged 3-8. Generally does not
acquire rhyming texts, as must also be
translated into German. Send submissions by
email as Word document or pasted directly
into the body of the email. Authors do not
need to include illustrations, but if the author
is also an illustrator sample sketches can be
included in PDF or JPEG form.

Oak Knoll Press

310 Delaware Street
New Castle, DE 19720
Tel: +1 (302) 328-7232
Email: publishing@oakknoll.com
Website: http://www.oakknoll.com

Publishes: Nonfiction; *Areas:* Antiques;
Historical; Literature; *Markets:* Academic

Contact: Robert Fleck

Publishes academic titles about printed
books: book selling; book collecting;
typography; antique books; book binding;
etc.

Oceanview Publishing

CEO Center at Mediterranean Plaza
595 Bay Isles Road, Suite 120-G

Longboat Key, FL 34228
Tel: +1 (941) 387-8500
Email: submissions@oceanviewpub.com
Website: http://oceanviewpub.com

Publishes: Fiction; *Areas:* Mystery;
Thrillers; *Markets:* Adult

Publishes adult fiction, with a primary
interest in the mystery/thriller genre. No
children's or young adult literature, poetry,
memoirs, cookbooks, technical manuals, or
short stories. Accepts submissions only from
authors who either have a literary agent;
have been previously published by a
traditional publishing house; or have been
specifically invited to submit by a
representative or author of the publishing
house. See website for more details.

Oregon State University Press

Oregon State University Press
121 The Valley Library, Room 3733
Corvallis, OR 97331-4501
Tel: +1 (541) 737-3873
Fax: +1 (541) 737-3170
Email: mary.braun@oregonstate.edu
Website: http://osupress.oregonstate.edu

Publishes: Nonfiction; *Areas:* Biography;
Culture; Historical; Literature; Nature;
Science; *Markets:* Academic

Published academic books of importance to
the Pacific Northwest, particularly those
dealing with the history, natural history,
cultures, and literature of the region. Send
query by post. No unsolicited mss or queries
by phone or email. See website for full
guidelines.

O'Reilly Media

1005 Gravenstein Hwy N
Sebastopol, CA 95472
Tel: +1 (707) 827-7019
Fax: +1 (707) 824-8268
Email: workwithus@oreilly.com
Website: http://www.oreilly.com

Publishes: Nonfiction; *Areas:* Business;
Design; Health; Photography; Science; Self-
Help; Technology; *Markets:* Adult

Publishes informative books written by smart
people, for smart people, on topics such as

technology, programming, business, health, etc. Send query or proposal by email.

Page Street Publishing Co.

27 Congress Street, Suite 103
Salem, MA 01970
Tel: +1 (978) 594-8758
Email: submissions@
pagestreetpublishing.com
Website: http://www.
pagestreetpublishing.com

Publishes: Fiction; Nonfiction; *Areas:*
Cookery; Crafts; Design; Fantasy; Historical;
Lifestyle; Mystery; Nature; Science; Sport;
Markets: Adult; Youth; *Treatments:* Literary

Publishes nonfiction and young adult fiction.
Send query by email, stating "YA" or
"NONFICTION" in the subject line, and
"AGENTED" if being submitted by a
literary agent. For fiction, include 1-2 page
query with synopsis and bio. Fiction should
be 60-90,000 words with a protagonist aged
15-18. For nonfiction, send one-page
synopsis with writing sample and details of
any media exposure. See website for full
guidelines.

Paladin Press

5540 Central Avenue, Suite 200
Boulder, CO 80301
Tel: +1 (303) 443-7250
Fax: +1 (303) 442-8741
Email: editorial@paladin-press.com
Website: http://www.paladin-press.com

Publishes: Nonfiction; *Areas:* Historical;
How-to; Military; Politics; Technology;
Markets: Adult

Publishes books and videos on personal
freedom, survival and preparedness, firearms
and shooting, martial arts and self-defense,
military and police tactics, knives and knife
fighting, etc. Send outline with one or two
sample chapters or complete MS.

PassKey Publications

5348 Vegas Drive PMB 1670
Las Vegas, NV 89108
Tel: +1 (702) 418-3326
Fax: +1 (702) 418-3326
Email: support@

passkeylearningsystems.com
Website: https://www.
passkeypublications.com

Publishes: Nonfiction; *Areas:* Business;
Finance; *Markets:* Adult

Publishes taxation and accountancy
textbooks.

Paulist Press

997 Macarthur Boulevard
Mahwah, NJ 07430
Tel: +1 (201) 825-7300
Fax: +1 (201) 825-8345
Email: submissions@paulistpress.com
Website: http://www.paulistpress.com

Publishes: Fiction; Nonfiction; *Areas:*
Culture; Philosophy; Religious; Self-Help;
Markets: Adult; Children's

Contact: Rev. Lawrence Boadt, CSP (Adult);
Susan O'Keefe (Children's)

Catholic publishing house, publishing
mainly religious and spiritual nonfiction for
adults, as well as a small but growing
number of religious fiction books for
children. Send proposal by email or by post
the SASE. See website for full guidelines.

Pelican Publishing Company

1000 Burmaster Street
Gretna, Louisiana 70053-2246
Tel: +1 (800) 843-1724
Fax: +1 (504) 368-1195
Email: editorial@pelicanpub.com
Website: http://www.pelicanpub.com

Publishes: Fiction; Nonfiction; Poetry;
Areas: Antiques; Architecture; Arts;
Autobiography; Biography; Business;
Cookery; Crafts; Crime; Criticism;
Gardening; Health; Historical; Hobbies;
Humour; Legal; Leisure; Lifestyle;
Literature; Medicine; Music; Nature;
Photography; Politics; Psychology;
Religious; Science; Self-Help; Sociology;
Sport; Travel; *Markets:* Adult; Children's

Publishes nonfiction for all ages and fiction
for children only. No adult fiction. Send
query briefly describing the project with
SASE, author bio and CV, and optionally a
synopsis and one or two sample chapters.

Query should outline the length of the book, its intended market, the author's writing and professional background, etc. See website for full guidelines. No queries or submissions by email.

Penguin Group (USA) Inc.

375 Hudson Street
New York, NY 10014
Tel: +1 (212) 366-2000
Fax: +1 (212) 366-2666
Email: online@us.penguingroup.com
Website: http://www.penguin.com

Publishes: Fiction; Nonfiction; *Markets:* Adult; Children's

Generally closed to submissions except through an agent, however some specific imprints may be accepting unsolicited material. See website for information and submission guidelines in these cases.

Penguin Random House

1745 Broadway
New York, NY 10019
Tel: +1 (212) 366-2000
Website: https://www.
penguinrandomhouse.com

Publishes: Fiction; Nonfiction; Poetry; Reference; *Areas:* Arts; Autobiography; Biography; Cookery; Entertainment; Fantasy; Historical; Humour; Mystery; Politics; Romance; Science; Sci-Fi; Suspense; Travel; *Markets:* Adult; Children's; Youth

One of the world's largest publishing houses. Accepts approaches via literary agents only.

Philosophy Documentation Center

PO Box 7147
Charlottesville, VA 22906-7147
Tel: +1 (434) 220-3300
Email: leaman@pdcnet.org
Website: https://www.pdcnet.org

Publishes: Nonfiction; Reference; *Areas:* Philosophy; *Markets:* Academic

Contact: George Leaman, Director

Publishes books, journals, and reference materials on philosophy and related fields.

Pinata Books

Arte Publico Press
University of Houston
4902 Gulf Fwy, Bldg 19, Rm100
Houston, TX 77204-2004
Tel: +1 (713) 743-2843
Fax: +1 (713) 743-2847
Email: submapp@uh.edu
Website: https://artepublicopress.com/contact/

Publishes: Fiction; *Areas:* Culture; *Markets:* Children's; Youth

Publishes children's and young adult literature that authentically and realistically portrays themes, characters, and customs unique to US Hispanic culture. Submit via form on website.

Pocol Press

3911 Prosperity Avenue
Fairfax, VA 22031
Tel: +1 (703) 870-9611
Website: http://www.pocolpress.com

Publishes: Fiction; Nonfiction; *Areas:* Horror; Short Stories; *Markets:* Adult; *Treatments:* Contemporary; Literary; Mainstream

Send query with SASE, author bio, publishing credits, audience details, and synopsis. No unsolicited MSS, queries by email, or self-published books.

Polis Books

Email: submissions@polisbooks.com
Website: http://polisbooks.com

Publishes: Fiction; *Areas:* Crime; Erotic; Fantasy; Horror; Humour; Mystery; Romance; Sci-Fi; Suspense; Thrillers; Women's Interests; *Markets:* Adult; Youth; *Treatments:* Commercial; Literary

Send query by email with author bio and three sample chapters. No children's picture books, graphic novels, short stories, stand-alone novellas, or religious-based titles.

Princeton Architectural Press

202 Warren Street
Hudson, NY 12534
Tel: +1 (518) 671-6100
Email: submissions@papress.com
Website: http://www.papress.com

Publishes: Nonfiction; *Areas:* Architecture;
Design; *Markets:* Adult

Download submission guidelines from
website and submit by post.

Quirk Books

215 Church Street
Philadelphia, PA 19106
Email: jason@quirkbooks.com
Website: http://www.quirkbooks.com

Publishes: Fiction; Nonfiction; *Areas:*
Culture; Historical; Humour; Mystery;
Science; Sci-Fi; Women's Interests;
Markets: Adult; Children's; Youth;
Treatments: Experimental; Literary; Popular

Publishes unconventional books across a
broad range of categories. Query one editor
directly (see website for list of interests and
specific contact details) by post with SASE
or by email. Limit query to one page and
include sample chapters if available.

Red Empress Publishing

Email: submissions@
redempresspublishing.com
Website: http://redempresspublishing.com

Publishes: Fiction; *Areas:* Adventure;
Culture; Fantasy; Gothic; Historical;
Mystery; Romance; Translations; Women's
Interests; *Markets:* Adult; *Treatments:*
Commercial; Light; Literary; Mainstream;
Niche; Popular; Positive; Progressive;
Traditional

A full-service publisher offering traditional
and new services for our authors to help
them succeed and stand out in an ever-
changing market. Here are some of the
benefits our authors enjoy.

Professional preparation – editing, cover
design, layout, etc.
Digital book distribution through all major
outlets – Amazon, Barns and Noble, iBooks,

Kobo and more.
Physical book distribution at higher returns
than CreateSpace or any other POD
publisher because we invest in large print
runs of our authors' books.
Audiobook creation and distribution.
Negotiate foreign rights with our partner
publishers around the world.
Book launch tours with hundreds of book
bloggers to get your book in front of as many
readers as possible.

Red Moon Press

P.0. Box 2461
Winchester, VA 22604-1661
Tel: +1 (540) 722-2156
Email: jim.kacian@redmoonpress.com
Website: http://www.redmoonpress.com

Publishes: Fiction; Nonfiction; Poetry;
Areas: Biography; Criticism; Literature;
Translations; *Markets:* Adult

Publishes anthologies of haiku, Haibun, and
related forms, plus relevant works of fiction,
collections of essays, translations, criticism,
etc. Send query in first instance.

Red Wheel

65 Parker Street, Suite 7
Newburyport, MA 01950
Tel: +1 (978) 465-0504
Fax: +1 (978) 465-0243
Email: submissions@rwwbooks.com
Website: http://www.redwheelweiser.com

Publishes: Nonfiction; *Areas:* Arts;
Business; Cookery; Culture; Design; Health;
Historical; Humour; Lifestyle; Nature; New
Age; Philosophy; Psychology; Religious;
Self-Help; Spiritual; Women's Interests;
Markets: Adult; Children's; Youth

Publishes "Spunky Self-Help", Self-
Help/Inspiration, Spirituality/Self-Help,
Magic, Wicca, Tarot, Astrology, Qabalah,
Spirituality, Personal Growth, Parenting, and
Social Issues. Send query by email only. See
website for full guidelines.

Robert D. Reed Publishers

POB 1992
Bandon, OR 97411
Tel: +1 (541) 347-9882

Fax: +1 (541) 347-9883
Email: bob@rdrpublishers.com
Website: http://www.rdrpublishers.com

Publishes: Nonfiction; *Areas:*
Autobiography; Business; Finance; Health;
Historical; Humour; Lifestyle; Psychology;
Self-Help; Spiritual; *Markets:* Adult;
Children's

Publishes nonfiction by authors with a
platform to sell their books. Manuscripts
must have been professionally edited. Send
query through contact form on website. No
longer publishes fiction.

SAE International
400 Commonwealth Drive
Warrendale, PA 15096-0001
Tel: +1 (724) 776-4970
Fax: +1 (724) 776-0790
Email: writeabook@sae.org
Website: https://www.sae.org

Publishes: Nonfiction; *Areas:* Technology;
Markets: Professional

Seeks authors who can write books for
automotive, aerospace and commercial
vehicle engineers. See website for
guidelines.

Saguaro Books, LLC
16201 E. Keymar Drive
Fountain Hills, AZ 85268
Tel: +1 (602) 309-7670
Fax: +1 (480) 284-4855
Email: mjnickum@saguarobooks.com
Website: http://www.saguarobooks.com

Publishes: Fiction; *Markets:* Children's;
Youth

Contact: Mary Nickum

Publishes books for children and young
adults aged 10-18, but first-time authors over
the age of 18. Send query by email
describing your submission in first instance.
Exclusive submissions only.

Salvo Press
101 Hudson Street, 37th Floor, Suite 3705
Jersey City, NJ 07302
Tel: +1 (212) 431-5455

Email: info@salvopress.com
Website: http://salvopress.com

Publishes: Fiction; *Areas:* Mystery;
Thrillers; *Markets:* Adult; *Treatments:*
Literary

Publishes quality mysteries, thrillers, and
literary books in eBook and audiobook
formats.

Santa Monica Press
P.O. Box 850
Solana Beach, CA 92075
Tel: +1 (800) 784-9553
Email: acquisitions@santamonicapress.com
Website: http://www.santamonicapress.com

Publishes: Nonfiction; Reference; *Areas:*
Architecture; Arts; Biography; Culture;
Entertainment; Film; Historical; Humour;
Literature; Photography; Sport; Travel;
Markets: Adult

Accepts proposals from agents and directly
from authors, but post or by email. See
website for full submission guidelines.

Scholastic Library Publishing
PO Box 3765
Jefferson City, MO 65102-3765
Tel: +1 (800) 621-1115
Fax: +1 (866) 783-4361
Email: slpservice@scholastic.com
Website: http://scholasticlibrary.digital.
scholastic.com

Publishes: Fiction; Nonfiction; Reference;
Markets: Children's

Publishes children's fiction, nonfiction, and
reference.

Scribner
1230 Avenue of the Americas, 12th Floor
New York, NY 10020
Tel: +1 (212) 698-7000
Email: info@simonsays.com
Website: http://www.
simonandschusterpublishing.com/scribner/

Publishes: Fiction; Nonfiction; *Areas:*
Historical; Mystery; Philosophy;
Psychology; Religious; Science; Suspense;
Markets: Adult; *Treatments:* Literary

Accepts submissions via literary agents only.

Seaworthy Publications

6300 N Wickham Road, Unit #130-416
Melbourne, FL 32940
Tel: +1 (321) 610-3634
Fax: +1 (321) 259-6872
Email: queries@seaworthy.com
Website: http://www.seaworthy.com

Publishes: Nonfiction; *Areas:* Hobbies;
Leisure; Travel; *Markets:* Adult

Nautical book publisher specialising in
recreational boating. Send query by email
outlining your work and attaching sample
table of contents and two or three sample
chapters. See website for full submission
guidelines.

Seven Stories Press

140 Watts Street
New York, NY 10013
Tel: +1 (212) 226-8760
Fax: +1 (212) 226-1411
Email: info@sevenstories.com
Website: http://www.sevenstories.com

Publishes: Fiction; Nonfiction; *Areas:*
Autobiography; Current Affairs; Health;
Historical; Politics; Translations;
Treatments: Literary

Publishes works of the imagination and
political titles by voices of conscience. Send
query by post with two sample chapters and
46 cent SASE or postcard for reply. If you
require submission materials returned to you,
include adequate return postage. No
unsolicited mss and no email submissions.

Sibling Rivalry Press, LLC

PO Box 26147
Little Rock, AR 72221
Tel: +1 (870) 723-6008
Email: info@siblingrivalrypress.com
Website: https://siblingrivalrypress.com

Publishes: Poetry; *Markets:* Adult;
Treatments: Literary

Contact: Bryan Borland, Publisher; Seth
Pennington, Editor

Publishes poetry that disturbs and enraptures.
Has had award-winning success publishing
LGBTIQ authors, but is an inclusive
publishing house welcoming all authors,
regardless of sexual orientation or identity.
Open to submissions from march 1 to June 1
annually.

Silver Lake Publishing, LLC

PO Box 173
Aberdeen, WA 98520
Tel: +1 (360) 532-5758
Fax: +1 (360) 532-5728
Email: publisher@silverlakepub.com
Website: http://www.silverlakepub.com

Publishes: Nonfiction; Reference; *Areas:*
Business; Finance; How-to; Legal; Lifestyle;
Medicine; Politics; *Markets:* Adult

Publishes books that give readers tools for
making smart, aggressive decisions about
risk, security and financial matters. Send
query with synopsis, two sample chapters,
and author CV. No fiction or poetry, or
submissions by email.

Sky Pony Press

307 West 36th Street, 11th Floor
New York, NY 10018
Tel: +1 (212) 643-6816
Fax: +1 (212) 643-6819
Email: skyponysubmissions@
skyhorsepublishing.com
Website: http://skyponypress.com

Publishes: Fiction; Nonfiction; *Markets:*
Children's; Youth

Publishes picture books, chapter books,
middle grade, and YA fiction and nonfiction,
in any genre or style. Send proposal or
complete ms by email as a Word attachment.
Do not send hard copy unless requested.

Southern Illinois University Press

1915 University Press Drive
Carbondale, IL 62901-4323
Tel: +1 (618) 453-2281
Fax: +1 (618) 453-1221
Email: kageff@siu.edu
Website: http://www.siupress.com

Publishes: Fiction; Nonfiction; Poetry; *Areas:* Arts; Biography; Crime; Film; Health; Historical; Legal; Philosophy; Photography; Politics; Theatre; Women's Interests; *Markets:* Academic

Contact: Karl Kageff

Publishes nonfiction books for academic and general audiences. No fiction, conference proceedings, edited primary sources, unrevised dissertations, or festschriften. See website for full guidelines.

St Pauls

2187 Victory Boulevard
Staten Island, NY 10314
Tel: +1 (718) 698-2759
Fax: +1 (718) 698-8390
Email: sales@stpauls.us
Website: http://www.stpaulsusa.com

Publishes: Nonfiction; *Areas:* Biography; Religious; Self-Help; Spiritual; *Markets:* Adult

Publishes books for a Roman Catholic readership.

Star Bright Books

13 Landsdowne Street
Cambridge, MA 02139
Tel: +1 (617) 354-1300
Fax: +1 (617) 354-1399
Email: info@starbrightbooks.com
Website: https://starbrightbooks.org

Publishes: Fiction; Nonfiction; *Markets:* Children's

Publishes books that are entertaining, meaningful and sensitive to the needs of all children. Welcomes submissions for picture books and longer works, both fiction and nonfiction. See website for full submission guidelines.

Sterling Publishing Co. Inc.

1166 Avenue of the Americas, Floor 17
New York, NY 10036
Tel: +1 (212) 532-7160
Fax: +1 (212) 213-2495
Email: editorial@sterlingpublishing.com
Website: https://www.sterlingpublishing.com

Publishes: Fiction; Nonfiction; Reference; *Areas:* Arts; Crafts; Crime; Finance; Gardening; Health; Hobbies; How-to; Humour; Lifestyle; Literature; Music; Mystery; Nature; New Age; Photography; Science; Spiritual; Sport; Travel; *Markets:* Adult; Children's; Youth

Publishes mainly adult nonfiction, reference, and how-to, plus fiction for children. No adult fiction. Send query with SASE, outline of idea, sample chapter, sample illustrations (where appropriate), and details about yourself, including any publishing history. No submissions by email.

Sunstone Press

Box 2321
Santa Fe, NM 87504-2321
Tel: +1 (800) 243-5644
Fax: +1 (505) 988-1025
Website: http://www.sunstonepress.com

Publishes: Fiction; Nonfiction; Poetry; Reference; *Areas:* Adventure; Archaeology; Architecture; Arts; Autobiography; Biography; Business; Cookery; Crafts; Crime; Fantasy; Gardening; Health; Historical; How-to; Humour; Legal; Military; Music; Mystery; Nature; Photography; Politics; Religious; Romance; Sci-Fi; Short Stories; Spiritual; Sport; Theatre; Travel; Westerns; Women's Interests; *Markets:* Adult; Children's; Family

Began in the 1970s with a focus on nonfiction about the American Southwest, but has since expanded its focus to include mainstream themes and categories in both fiction and nonfiction. Send query by post only with short summary, author bio, one sample chapter, table of contents, marketing plan, and statement on why this is the right publisher for your book.

Syracuse University Press

Syracuse University Press
621 Skytop Road, Suite 110
Syracuse, NY 13244-5290
Tel: +1 (315) 443-5534
Fax: +1 (315) 443-5545
Email: supress@syr.edu
Website: http://www.
syracuseuniversitypress.syr.edu

Publishes: Nonfiction; *Areas:* Anthropology; Biography; Culture; Current Affairs; Entertainment; Historical; Literature; Politics; Religious; Sociology; Sport; Translations; TV; Women's Interests; *Markets:* Academic

Publishes scholarly books on international affairs, the Middle East, women and religion, politics, Irish studies, medieval history, television, translations of Middle Eastern literature, etc. Complete book proposal form (available on website) and submit by email with CV and preliminary table of contents. No unsolicited mss.

Temple University Press
1852 North 10th Street
Philadelphia, PA 19122
Tel: +1 (215) 204-8787
Email: tempress@temple.edu
Website: http://www.temple.edu/tempress/

Publishes: Nonfiction; *Areas:* Anthropology; Arts; Biography; Business; Crime; Culture; Drama; Film; Finance; Health; Historical; Legal; Leisure; Lifestyle; Literature; Media; Nature; Photography; Politics; Psychology; Religious; Science; Sociology; Sport; Technology; Women's Interests; *Markets:* Academic

Send query with brief outline, including email address for response. Publishes scholarly books, usually authored by academics. Best known for publishing in the areas of the social sciences and humanities.

Thomas Dunne Books
St. Martin's Press
175 5th Avenue
New York, NY 10010
Email: thomasdunnebooks@stmartins.com
Website: us.macmillan.com/thomasdunne

Publishes: Fiction; Nonfiction; *Areas:* Historical; Mystery; Politics; Sport; Suspense; Thrillers; Women's Interests; *Markets:* Adult; *Treatments:* Popular

Publishes popular trade fiction and nonfiction. Accepts approaches via literary agents only.

ThunderStone Books
Email: info@thunderstonebooks.com
Website: http://thunderstonebooks.com

Publishes: Fiction; Nonfiction; *Markets:* Children's

Publish children's fiction and nonfiction that has an educational aspect. Send query by email with up to first 50 pages as Word attachment.

Torah Aura Productions
2710 Supply Avenue
Los Angeles CA, 90040
Tel: +1 (800) 238-6724
Fax: +1 (323) 585-0327
Email: misrad@torahaura.com
Website: http://www.torahaura.com

Publishes: Nonfiction; *Areas:* Historical; Lifestyle; Religious; *Markets:* Academic; Children's; Youth

Contact: Jane Golub, Acquisitions

Publisher of educational materials for Jewish classrooms. No picture books.

Triangle Square
140 Watts Street
New York, NY 10013
Tel: +1 (212) 226-8760
Fax: +1 (212) 226-1411
Email: info@sevenstories.com
Website: https://www.sevenstories.com/imprints/triangle-square

Publishes: Fiction; Nonfiction; *Areas:* Autobiography; Biography; Health; Historical; Music; Nature; Philosophy; Politics; Religious; *Markets:* Children's; Youth

Publishes fiction and nonfiction for children and young adults, on such subjects as environmentalism, human rights, gender and feminism, etc.

Truman State University Press
100 East Normal Avenue
Kirksville, MO 63501-4221
Tel: +1 (660) 785-7336
Fax: +1 (660) 785-4480

Email: tsup@truman.edu
Website: http://tsup.truman.edu

Publishes: Nonfiction; *Areas:* Anthropology;
Archaeology; Architecture; Arts;
Autobiography; Biography; Criticism;
Historical; Literature; Nature; Religious;
Translations; Travel; *Markets:* Academic;
Adult

Publishes peer-reviewed research and
literature for the scholarly community and
the reading public. See website for full
submission guidelines.

Tumblehome Learning, Inc.
Boston, MA
Tel: +1 (781) 924-5036
Email: submissions@
tumblehomelearning.com
Website: http://tumblehomelearning.com

Publishes: Fiction; *Areas:* Adventure;
Science; *Markets:* Children's

Publishes books that allow kids to
experience science through adventure and
discovery. Submit complete ms by email.

University of Alaska Press
Editorial Department
University of Alaska Press
PO Box 756240
104 Eielson Building
Fairbanks, AK 99775-6240
Tel: +1 (907) 474-5831
Fax: +1 (907) 474-5502
Email: UA-acquisitions@alaska.edu
Website: http://www.alaska.edu/uapress/

Publishes: Fiction; Nonfiction; Poetry;
Areas: Autobiography; Biography; Culture;
Historical; Nature; Politics; Science; Sport;
Translations; *Markets:* Academic; Adult

Publisher based in Alaska, publishing
academic and general trade books on an
expanding range of subject areas, including
politics and history, Native languages and
cultures, science and natural history,
biography and memoir, poetry, fiction and
anthologies, and original translations. Send
proposals by post. No unsolicited mss.

The University of Michigan Press
839 Greene Street
Ann Arbor, MI 48104-3209
Tel: +1 (734) 764-4388
Fax: +1 (734) 615-1540
Email: scottom@umich.edu
Website: http://www.press.umich.edu

Publishes: Fiction; Nonfiction; Reference;
Areas: Anthropology; Archaeology; Arts;
Autobiography; Biography; Business;
Cookery; Culture; Finance; Historical;
Legal; Literature; Media; Music; Nature;
Philosophy; Politics; Psychology; Religious;
Sociology; Sport; Theatre; Travel; Women's
Interests; *Markets:* Academic

Send query with table of contents, outline of
chapters, overview, and CV. Queries should
include statements on the rationale of your
book, similar and competing books in the
field, your target audience, why you think it
is right for this list, the length of MS, number
of illustrations, and what your anticipated
date of completion is. Send queries and
proposals by email to specific editor
(guidelines on website). See website for
particular guidelines realting to fiction and
certain series published by the press.

University of Pittsburgh Press
7500 Thomas Boulevard
Pittsburgh, PA 15260
Tel: +1 (412) 383-2456
Fax: +1 (412) 383-2466
Email: scrooms@upress.pitt.edu
Website: http://www.upress.pitt.edu

Publishes: Nonfiction; Poetry; *Areas:*
Architecture; Historical; Philosophy;
Science; *Markets:* Academic

Publishes books on Latin American studies,
Russian and East European studies,
international relations, poetry, Pittsburgh and
Western Pennsylvania regional studies,
environmental studies, architecture and
landscape history, urban studies,
composition and literacy, the history of
science, and the philosophy of science. No
hard sciences, memoirs, or fiction. Only
considers poetry manuscripts from poets who
have already published full-length
collections of at least 48 pages. Poets who

have not may submit to the first-book competition run by the press. See website for full guidelines.

University of Washington Press
4333 Brooklyn Avenue NE
Seattle, WA 98105
Tel: +1 (206) 543-4050
Fax: +1 (206) 543-3932
Email: uwapress@uw.edu
Website: http://www.washington.edu/uwpress/

Publishes: Nonfiction; *Areas:* Anthropology; Arts; Biography; Culture; Historical; Nature; *Markets:* Academic

Publishes scholarly books and distinguished works of regional nonfiction in the Pacific Northwest. Particularly known for Asian studies, Middle East studies, anthropology, Western history and biography, environmental studies, and natural history.

Venture Publishing, Inc.
1807 N. Federal Drive
Urbana, IL 61801
Tel: +1 (217) 359-5940
Fax: +1 (217) 359-5975
Email: books@sagamorepub.com
Website: http://www.sagamorepub.com

Publishes: Nonfiction; *Areas:* Leisure; Nature; Sociology; *Markets:* Adult; Professional

Publishes educational material for the park and recreation industry.

Walch Education
40 Walch Drive
PO Box 658
Portland, ME 04104-0658
Tel: +1 (207) 772-2846
Fax: +1 (207) 772-3105
Email: customerservice@walch.com
Website: http://www.walch.com

Publishes: Nonfiction; *Areas:* Arts; Science; Sociology; *Markets:* Academic

Publishes high school math curriculum and resources aligned to the Common Core and selected state and district standards.

WaterBrook & Multnomah
10807 New Allegiance Drive Suite 500
Colorado Springs, CO 80921
Tel: +1 (719) 590-4999
Fax: +1 (719) 590-8977
Email: info@waterbrookpress.com
Website: http://waterbrookmultnomah.com

Publishes: Fiction; Nonfiction; *Areas:* Adventure; Historical; Mystery; Religious; Romance; Sci-Fi; Spiritual; Suspense; *Markets:* Adult; Children's

Publishes fiction and nonfiction with a Christian perspective. Agented submissions only.

Wave Books
1938 Fairview Avenue East, Suite 201
Seattle, WA 98102
Tel: +1 (206) 676-5337
Email: info@wavepoetry.com
Website: https://www.wavepoetry.com

Publishes: Poetry; *Markets:* Adult; *Treatments:* Contemporary

Contact: Charlie Wright, Publisher

Independent poetry press based in Seattle. Accepts submissions only in response to specific calls for submissions posted on the website (see the submissions page).

Wesleyan University Press
215 Long Lane
Middletown, CT 06459
Tel: +1 (860) 685-7730
Fax: +1 (860) 685-7712
Email: stamminen@wesleyan.edu
Website: http://www.wesleyan.edu/wespress

Publishes: Nonfiction; *Areas:* Culture; Film; Historical; Literature; Music; *Markets:* Academic

Publishes nonfiction in the areas of dance, music/culture, poetry, literature and literary studies. See website for submission guidelines.

WhiteFire Publishing

13607 Bedford Rd NE
Cumberland, MD 21502
Tel: +1 (443) 321-3663
Fax: +1 (443) 321-3675
Email: publishing@whitefireprinting.com
Website: http://www.whitefireprinting.com/publishing

Publishes: Fiction; Poetry; *Areas:* Arts; Crime; Culture; Current Affairs; Drama; Entertainment; Fantasy; Historical; Horror; Humour; Leisure; Literature; Mystery; Philosophy; Photography; Psychology; Religious; Romance; Sci-Fi; Short Stories; Suspense; Thrillers; *Markets:* Adult; Family; Youth; *Treatments:* Contemporary; Literary; Mainstream; Traditional

A small Christian publisher devoted to putting out the best books possible without impinging on the author's own vision. Mainly soliciting novel-length work that can be marketed to a Christian audience. Authors are therefore expected to actively participate in the promotion and sales of their own books. See website for full submission guidelines.

Willow Creek Press, Inc.

PO Box 147
Minocqua, WI 54548
Tel: +1 (800) 850-9453
Fax: +1 (715) 358-2807
Email: andread@willowcreekpress.com
Website: http://www.willowcreekpress.com

Publishes: Nonfiction; Reference; *Areas:* Cookery; Gardening; How-to; Leisure; Nature; Sport; *Markets:* Adult

Send query with SASE, outline / table of contents, one or two sample chapters, author bio, and indication as to whether the proposal is simultaneously under consideration elsewhere. See website for full details. May consider but will generally not accept personal memoirs, children's books, or MSS dealing with limited regional subject matter.

World Weaver Press

Email: publisher@worldweaverpress.com
Website: http://www.worldweaverpress.com

Publishes: Fiction; *Areas:* Fantasy; Romance; Sci-Fi; Short Stories; *Markets:* Adult

Publishes speculative romance, including Paranormal Romance, Epic Fantasy, Urban Fantasy, Fairy Tale, Hard Science Fiction, Soft Science Fiction, Space Opera, Solarpunk, Steampunk, Dieselpunk, Decopunk, Fantasy Romance, Science Fiction Romance, Paranormal Mystery, and Time Travel Romance. No horror, grimdark, or dystopia. Accepts submissions in specific submission windows only (see website for details). Also publishes anthologies of short stories. See website for current opportunities.

WorthyKids / Ideals

6100 Tower Circle, Suite 210
Franklin, TN 37067
Tel: +1 (615) 932-7600
Email: idealsinfo@worthy-ideals.com
Website: https://www.idealsbooks.com

Publishes: Fiction; Nonfiction; *Areas:* Lifestyle; Religious; *Markets:* Children's

Publishes fiction and nonfiction board books, novelty books, and picture books for children aged 0-8. Subjects include inspiration/faith, patriotism, and holidays, particularly Easter and Christmas; relationships and values; and general fiction. Board book manuscripts should be no longer than 250 words. Picture book manuscripts should be no longer than 800 words. Submit complete ms by post only – no queries or proposals or submissions by email. See website for full submission guidelines.

YMAA Publication Center, Inc.

PO Box 480
Wolfeboro, NH 03894
Tel: +1 (603) 569-7988
Fax: +1 (603) 569-1889
Website: https://ymaa.com

Publishes: Nonfiction; *Areas:* Health; Medicine; Philosophy; Spiritual; Sport; *Markets:* Adult

Publishes books on martial arts, Eastern philosophy, Chinese medicine, etc.

Zumaya Publications

3209 S. Interstate 35 #1086
Austin, TX 78741
Email: acquisitions@
zumayapublications.com
Website: http://www.
zumayapublications.com

Publishes: Fiction; Nonfiction; *Areas:*
Autobiography; Crime; Fantasy; Gothic;
Historical; Horror; Mystery; Romance; Sci-
Fi; Short Stories; Thrillers; Westerns;
Markets: Adult; Children's; Youth;
Treatments: Mainstream; Niche

Contact: Adrienne Rose

Publishes adult fiction of at least 50,000
words, and juvenile fiction of at least 40,000
words. Send queries by email only, with
sample as an attachment, with a brief
synopsis up to 1,000 words at its start. See
website for full submission guidelines.

UK Publishers

For the most up-to-date listings of these and hundreds of other publishers, visit https://www.firstwriter.com/publishers

*To claim your **free** access to the site, please see the back of this book.*

ACC Art Books Ltd

Sandy Lane
Old Martlesham
Woodbridge
Suffolk
IP12 4SD
Tel: +44 (0) 1394 389950
Fax: +44 (0) 1394 389999
Email: submissions@antique-acc.com
Website: http://www.
antiquecollectorsclub.com

Publishes: Nonfiction; *Areas:* Antiques; Architecture; Arts; Beauty and Fashion; Business; Crafts; Design; Gardening; Historical; Photography; Travel; *Markets:* Adult; Children's

Publishes books on antiques and decorative arts. Send queries or submit manuscripts by post or by email.

Allison & Busby Ltd

12 Fitzroy Mews
London
W1T 6DW
Tel: +44 (0) 20 7580 1080
Fax: +44 (0) 20 7580 1180
Email: susie@allisonandbusby.com
Website: http://www.allisonandbusby.com

Publishes: Fiction; Nonfiction; *Areas:* Autobiography; Biography; Crime; Culture; Fantasy; Historical; Military; Mystery; Sci-Fi; Self-Help; Short Stories; Thrillers; Travel; Women's Interests; *Markets:* Adult; Youth; *Treatments:* Contemporary; Literary

Contact: Susie Dunlop, Publishing Director

Accepts approaches via a literary agent only. No unsolicited MSS or queries from authors. In field of nonfiction publishes guides for writers. No horror, romance, spirituality, short stories, self-help, poetry or plays.

Alma Books Ltd

3 Castle Yard
Richmond
TW10 6TF
Tel: +44 (0) 20 8940 6917
Fax: +44 (0) 20 8948 5599
Email: info@almabooks.com
Website: http://www.almabooks.com

Publishes: Fiction; Nonfiction; *Areas:* Historical; Literature; *Markets:* Adult; *Treatments:* Contemporary; Literary

Publishes literary fiction and a small number of nonfiction titles with a strong literary or historical connotation. No novellas, short stories, children's books, poetry, academic works, science fiction, horror, or fantasy. Accepts unsolicited MSS by post with synopsis, two sample chapters, and SAE if return of material required. No submissions by email, or submissions from outside the UK. Submissions received from outside the UK will not receive a response.

Alma Classics

3 Castle Yard
Richmond
TW10 6TF
Tel: +44 (0) 20 8940 6917
Fax: +44 (0) 20 8948 5599
Email: info@almabooks.com
Website: http://www.almaclassics.com

Publishes: Fiction; Poetry; Scripts; *Areas:*
Arts; Autobiography; Biography; Literature;
Sociology; Translations; *Markets:* Adult;
Treatments: Literary

Publishes classic European literature.
Welcomes suggestions and ideas for the list,
as well as proposals from translators. Send
proposals by email.

Amberley Publishing

The Hill
Merrywalks
Stroud
GL5 4EP
Tel: +44 (0) 1453 847800
Fax: +44 (0) 1453 847820
Email: submissions@amberley-books.com
Website: http://www.amberleybooks.com

Publishes: Nonfiction; *Areas:* Archaeology;
Biography; Historical; Military; Sport;
Travel; *Markets:* Adult

Publishes local interest and niche history.
Send query by email, with one-page proposal
describing the book; reason for writing the
book; proposed word count; proposed
number of images; and any other relevant
information.

Andersen Press Ltd

20 Vauxhall Bridge Road
London
SW1V 2SA
Tel: +44 (0) 20 7840 8701
Email: anderseneditorial@
penguinrandomhouse.co.uk
Website: http://www.andersenpress.co.uk

Publishes: Fiction; *Markets:* Children's

Publishes picture books and longer
children's fiction up to 75,000 words.
Publishes rhyming stories, but no poetry,
adult fiction, nonfiction, or short story

collections. Send query with complete ms for
picture books, or synopsis and first three
chapters by post only, with SAE if return of
work required. See website for full
guidelines.

Appletree Press Ltd

Roycroft House
164 Malone Road
Belfast
BT9 5LL
Tel: +44 (0) 28 90 243074
Fax: +44 (0) 28 90 246756
Email: editorial@appletree.ie
Website: http://www.appletree.ie

Publishes: Nonfiction; *Markets:* Adult

Send query with synopsis, descriptive
chapter list, and two or three chapters by
email. Publishes small-format gift books and
general nonfiction books of Irish and
Scottish interest. No unsolicited MSS.

Arc Publications

Nanholme Mill
Shaw Wood Road
Todmorden
Lancs
OL14 6DA
Tel: +44 (0) 1706 812338
Email: info@arcpublications.co.uk
Website: http://www.arcpublications.co.uk/
submissions

Publishes: Poetry; *Areas:* Music;
Translations; *Markets:* Adult; *Treatments:*
Contemporary

Send 16-24 poems by email as a Word / PDF
attachment, maximum one poem per page,
during December or June only. Submissions
from outside the UK and Ireland should be
sent to specific address for international
submissions, available on website. Cover
letter should include short bio and details of
the contemporary poets you read. See
website for full guidelines.

Arrowhead Press

70 Clifton Road
Darlington
Co. Durham
DL1 5DX

Email: editor@arrowheadpress.co.uk
Website: http://www.arrowheadpress.co.uk

Publishes: Poetry; *Markets:* Adult

Contact: Joanna Boulter, Poetry Editor

Publishes poetry books and pamphlets. Not accepting unsolicited submissions as at February 2016.

Ashgate Publishing Limited
Taylor & Francis Group Ltd
2 Park Square
Milton Park
Abingdon
Oxford
OX14 4RN
Tel: +44 (0) 20 7017-6000
Fax: +44 (0) 20 7017-6699
Email: heidi.bishop@tandf.co.uk
Website: http://www.ashgate.com

Publishes: Nonfiction; *Areas:* Architecture; Arts; Business; Culture; Historical; Legal; Literature; Music; Philosophy; Politics; Religious; Sociology; *Markets:* Academic; Professional

Contact: Heidi Bishop, Senior Editor

Publishes books in the Social Sciences, Arts, and Humanities. See website for full submission guidelines.

Ashmolean Museum Publications
Ashmolean Museum
Beaumont Street
Oxford
OX1 2PH
Tel: +44 (0) 1865 278010
Email: publications@ashmus.ox.ac.uk
Website: http://www.ashmolean.org

Publishes: Nonfiction; *Areas:* Archaeology; Arts; Historical; *Markets:* Adult; Children's

Contact: Declan McCarthy

Publications mainly based on in-house collections. Publishes both adult and Children's on the subjects of European archeology and ancient history, European and Oriental arts, Egyptology and numismatics. No fiction, African / American / modern art, post-medieval history, ethnography, or unsolicited MSS.

Aureus Publishing Limited
Email: info@aureus.co.uk
Website: http://www.aureus.co.uk

Publishes: Nonfiction; *Areas:* Biography; Music; Sport; *Markets:* Academic; Adult

Publishes books on music, sport, biography and education.

Aurora Metro Press
67 Grove Avenue
Twickenham
TW1 4HX
Tel: +44 (0) 20 3261 0000
Email: submissions@aurorametro.com
Website: http://www.aurorametro.com

Publishes: Fiction; Nonfiction; Scripts; *Areas:* Arts; Biography; Cookery; Culture; Drama; Film; Humour; Literature; Music; Short Stories; Theatre; Translations; Women's Interests; *Markets:* Adult; Children's; Youth

Contact: Neil Gregory (Submissions Manager)

Publishes fiction, plays/theatre texts, and both general and specialist nonfiction books across theatre, film, music, literature, and popular culture. Send synopsis and complete ms by email only. For play submissions, if a production is scheduled then the full script must be sent at least 6 weeks before opening night.

Award Publications Limited
The Old Riding School
The Welbeck Estate
Worksop
Nottinghamshire
S80 3LR
Tel: +44 (0) 1909 478170
Fax: +44 (0) 1909 484632
Email: info@awardpublications.co.uk
Website: http://www.
awardpublications.co.uk

Publishes: Fiction; Nonfiction; Reference; *Markets:* Children's

Publishes children's fiction, nonfiction, and reference.

Barrington Stoke
18 Walker Street
Edinburgh
EH3 7LP
Tel: +44 (0) 131 225 4113
Fax: +44 (0) 131 225 4140
Email: info@barringtonstoke.co.uk
Website: http://www.barringtonstoke.co.uk

Publishes: Fiction; Nonfiction; Reference; *Markets:* Children's; Professional

Commissions books via literary agents only. No unsolicited material. Publishes books for "reluctant, dyslexic, disenchanted and under-confident" readers and their teachers.

Beercott Books
77 Welsh Road West
Southam
Warwickshire
Email: info@beercottbooks.co.uk
Website: https://beercottbooks.co.uk

Publishes: Reference; Scripts; *Areas:* Crafts; Theatre; *Markets:* Family; Professional

Contact: Simon Lucas

Small independent publisher specialising in craft and theatre related publications.

Bernard Babani (publishing) Ltd
The Grampians
Shepherds Bush Road
London
W6 7NF
Email: enquiries@babanibooks.com
Website: http://www.babanibooks.com

Publishes: Nonfiction; *Areas:* Technology; *Markets:* Adult

Publishes books on robotics, computing, and electronics. Always interested in hearing from potential authors. Send query by email with synopsis and details of your qualifications for writing on the topic.

BFI Publishing
Palgrave Macmillan Ltd
4 Crinan St
London
N1 9XW
Tel: +44 (0) 20 7418 5804
Email: j.steventon@palgrave.com
Website: http://www.palgrave.com/bfi

Publishes: Nonfiction; Reference; *Areas:* Film; Media; TV; *Markets:* Academic

Contact: Jenna Steventon, Senior Commissioning Editor and Head of Higher Education Humanities and BFI Publishing

Welcomes book proposals. Publishes film and television-related books and resources, both for schools and academic readerships, and more generally. See website for publishing proposal forms, and lists of editorial contacts to submit them to.

Birlinn Ltd
West Newington House
10 Newington Road
Edinburgh
EH9 1QS
Tel: +44 (0) 131 668 4371
Fax: +44 (0) 131 668 4466
Email: info@birlinn.co.uk
Website: http://www.birlinn.co.uk

Publishes: Fiction; Nonfiction; Poetry; Reference; *Areas:* Adventure; Architecture; Arts; Autobiography; Biography; Culture; Current Affairs; Finance; Historical; Humour; Legal; Medicine; Military; Nature; Politics; Sociology; Sport; Travel; *Markets:* Adult; Children's

Focuses on Scottish material: local, military, and Highland history; humour, adventure; reference, guidebooks, and folklore. Not currently accepting romantic fiction, science fiction, or short stories. Send query by post with SAE, synopsis, three sample chapters, and explanation of why you have chosen this publisher. No submissions by fax, email, or on disk. See website for full details.

Black & White Publishing Ltd
Nautical House
104 Commercial Street
Edinburgh

EH6 6NF
Tel: +44 (0) 01316 254500
Email: mail@blackandwhitepublishing.com
Website: http://www.
blackandwhitepublishing.com

Publishes: Fiction; Nonfiction; *Areas:*
Autobiography; Biography; Cookery; Crime;
Humour; Psychology; Romance; Sport;
Thrillers; Women's Interests; *Markets:*
Academic; Adult; Children's; Youth;
Treatments: Commercial

Contact: Campbell Brown; Alison McBride

Publisher of general fiction and nonfiction.
See website for an idea of the kind of books
normally published, and to submit via online
submission system. No poetry, short stories,
or work in languages other than English.

Black Dog Publishing London UK

10A Acton Street
London
WC1X 9NG
Tel: +44 (0) 20 7713 5097
Fax: +44 (0) 20 7713 8682
Email: info@blackdogonline.com
Website: http://blackdogonline.com

Publishes: Nonfiction; Reference; *Areas:*
Architecture; Arts; Beauty and Fashion;
Crafts; Culture; Design; Film; Music;
Nature; Photography; *Markets:* Adult;
Treatments: Contemporary

Publishes illustrated books with a fresh,
eclectic take on contemporary culture.
Originally focused on art and architecture,
but now includes subjects as varied as
design, fashion, music and environmental
concerns.

Blink Publishing

2.08 The Plaza
535 Kings Road
London
SW10 0SZ
Tel: +44 (0) 20 3770 8888
Email: info@blinkpublishing.co.uk
Website: http://www.blinkpublishing.co.uk

Publishes: Nonfiction; *Areas:*
Autobiography; Cookery; Crime; Culture;

Historical; Humour; Lifestyle; Military;
Music; Sport; Travel; *Markets:* Adult;
Treatments: Popular

Publishes illustrated and non-illustrated adult
nonfiction. No fiction. Send queries by email
with one-page synopsis and first three
chapters.

Bloodaxe Books Ltd

Eastburn
South Park
Hexham
Northumberland
NE46 1BS
Tel: +44 (0) 01434 611581
Email: editor@bloodaxebooks.com
Website: http://www.bloodaxebooks.com

Publishes: Poetry; *Markets:* Adult

Contact: Neil Astley, Managing/Editorial
Director

Submit poetry only if you have a track
record of publication in magazines. If so,
send sample of up to a dozen poems with
SAE, or email address for response if outside
the UK. No submissions by email or on disk.
Poems from the UK sent without return
postage will be recycled unread; submissions
by email will be deleted unread. No longer
accepting poets who have already published
a full-length collection with another
publisher. See website for full details.

Bloomsbury Spark

Email: BloomsburySparkUK@
bloomsbury.com
Website: http://www.bloomsbury.com/spark

Publishes: Fiction; *Areas:* Historical;
Mystery; Romance; Sci-Fi; Thrillers;
Markets: Children's; Youth; *Treatments:*
Contemporary

Global, digital imprint from a major
international publisher. Publishes ebooks for
teen, young adult, and new adult readers.
Willing to consider all genres, including
romance, contemporary, dystopian,
paranormal, sci-fi, mystery, and thrillers.
Accepts unsolicited mss between 25,000 and
60,000 words. Submit by email (see website
for specific email addresses for different

geographic locations) along with query and author bio. See website for full details.

Bodleian Library Publishing

Broad Street
Oxford
OX1 3BG
Tel: +44 (0) 1865 283850
Email: publishing@bodleian.ox.ac.uk
Website: https://www.bodleianshop.co.uk/bodleianlibrarypublishing

Publishes: Nonfiction; *Areas:* Arts; Historical; Literature; *Markets:* Academic; Adult

Publishes books relating to the library collections only.

Boydell & Brewer Ltd

Bridge Farm Business Park
Top Street
Martlesham
Suffolk
IP12 4RB
Tel: +44 (0) 1394 411320
Email: cpalmer@boydell.co.uk
Website: http://www.boydellandbrewer.com

Publishes: Nonfiction; *Areas:* Archaeology; Arts; Historical; Literature; Military; Music; Religious; *Markets:* Academic; Adult

Contact: Caroline Palmer (Medieval Studies); Michael Middeke (Modern History and Music); Peter Sowden (Maritime History)

Publishes nonfiction in the areas of medieval studies; music; early modern and modern history. Specialist areas include Arthurian studies; the history of religion; military history; and local history. Send proposals by post or by email. See website for specific contacts and individual email addresses.

Bradt Travel Guides

1st Floor IDC House
The Vale
Chalfont St Peter, Bucks
England
SL9 9RZ
Tel: +44 (0) 1753 893444
Fax: +44 (0) 1753 892333

Email: rachel.fielding@bradtguides.com
Website: http://www.bradtguides.com

Publishes: Nonfiction; *Areas:* Travel; *Markets:* Adult

Contact: Rachel Fielding, Commissioning Editor

Publishes travel guides to off-beat places. Send query by email with CV, details of any writing and travel experience, and proposal.

Nicholas Brealey Publishing

Hodder & Stoughton Ltd.
Carmelite House
50 Victoria Embankment
London
EC4Y 0DZ
Tel: +44 (0) 20 3122 6777
Email: educationenquiries@hodder.co.uk
Website: https://www.hodder.co.uk

Publishes: Nonfiction; *Areas:* Business; Culture; Finance; Psychology; Self-Help; Travel; *Markets:* Adult; Professional

Not accepting submissions as at March 2018.

Brilliant Publications

Unit 10, Sparrow Hall Farm
Edlesborough
Dunstable
Bedfordshire
LU6 2ES
Tel: +44 (0) 1525 222292
Fax: +44 (0) 1525 222720
Email: info@brilliantpublications.co.uk
Website: https://www.brilliantpublications.co.uk

Publishes: Nonfiction; *Markets:* Professional

Contact: Priscilla Hannaford

Independent educational publisher specialising in books for teachers. See FAQ section of website for instructions on submitting a new book proposal.

Bristol University Press

1-9 Old Park Hill
Bristol
BS2 8BB
Tel: +44 (0) 1179 545940

Email: pp-info@bristol.ac.uk
Website: http://bristoluniversitypress.co.uk

Publishes: Nonfiction; *Areas:* Business; Current Affairs; Finance; Legal; Nature; Politics; Sociology; *Markets:* Academic

Publishes scholarship and education in the social sciences. Send query with proposal by email.

Calisi Press
Tel: +44 (0) 1303 272216
Email: info@calisipress.com
Website: http://www.calisipress.com

Publishes: Fiction; *Areas:* Translations; Women's Interests; *Markets:* Adult

Contact: Franca Simpson

Publishes English translations of books by female Italian writers.

Candy Jar Books
Mackintosh House
136 Newport Road
Cardiff
CF24 1DJ
Tel: +44 (0) 29 2115 7202
Email: shaun@candyjarbooks.co.uk
Website: http://www.candyjarbooks.co.uk

Publishes: Fiction; Nonfiction; *Areas:* Biography; Fantasy; Historical; Military; Sci-Fi; TV; *Markets:* Adult; Children's; Youth

Contact: Shaun Russell (Head of Publishing)

Award-winning independent book publisher, publishing a wide variety of books, from nonfiction, general fiction and children's, through to a range of cult TV books. Submit by post or using online submission form. No children's picture books. See website for full guidelines.

Canongate Books
14 High Street
Edinburgh
EH1 1TE
Tel: +44 (0) 1315 575111
Email: support@canongate.co.uk
Website: http://www.canongate.net

Publishes: Fiction; Nonfiction; *Areas:* Autobiography; Biography; Culture; Historical; Humour; Politics; Science; Translations; Travel; *Markets:* Adult; *Treatments:* Literary

Publisher of a wide range of literary fiction and nonfiction, with a traditionally Scottish slant but becoming increasingly international. Publishes fiction in translation under its international imprint. No children's books, poetry, or drama. Send synopsis with three sample chapters and info about yourself. No submissions by fax, email or on disk.

Canopus Publishing Ltd
15 Nelson Parade
Bdeminster
Bristol
BS3 4HY
Tel: +44 (0) 7970 153217
Email: robin@canopusbooks.com
Website: http://www.canopusbooks.com

Publishes: Nonfiction; *Areas:* Science; Technology; *Markets:* Academic; Adult; *Treatments:* Popular

Contact: Robin Rees

Welcomes book proposals for both academic and popular branches of aerospace and astronomy. Send query by email with author bio, two-page summary outlining concept, coverage, and readership level. See website for more details.

Carcanet Press Ltd
4th Floor
Alliance House
Cross Street
Manchester
M2 7AP
Tel: +44 (0) 161 834 8730
Fax: +44 (0) 161 832 0084
Email: info@carcanet.co.uk
Website: http://www.carcanet.co.uk

Publishes: Nonfiction; Poetry; *Areas:* Biography; Literature; Translations; *Markets:* Academic; Adult; *Treatments:* Literary

Award-winning small press, publishing mainly poetry and academic material. Authors should familiarise themselves with the publisher's list, then, if appropriate, submit 6-10 pages of poetry or translations, with SAE. For other projects, send a full synopsis and covering letter, with sample pages, having first ascertained from the website that the kind of book proposed is suitable. No phone calls. No short stories, childrens prose/poetry or non-poetry related titles.

Carina UK

Harlequin
1 London Bridge Street
London
SE1 9GF
Email: CarinaUKSubs@hqnuk.co.uk
Website: https://www.millsandboon.co.uk

Publishes: Fiction; *Areas:* Adventure; Crime; Erotic; Fantasy; Gothic; Historical; Horror; Humour; Literature; Men's Interests; Mystery; Romance; Sci-Fi; Short Stories; Suspense; Thrillers; Westerns; Women's Interests; *Markets:* Adult; Children's; Family; Youth

Digital imprint from a major publisher, considering all genres of writing, whether novels, novellas, serials, or a series. Particularly interested in authors from the UK, Ireland, South Africa and India. Send submissions by email with any type of attachment.

Carlton Publishing Group

20 Mortimer Street
London
W1T 3JW
Tel: +44 (0) 20 7612 0400
Fax: +44 (0) 20 7612 0401
Email: submissions@carltonbooks.co.uk
Website: http://www.carltonbooks.co.uk

Publishes: Nonfiction; Reference; *Areas:* Architecture; Arts; Beauty and Fashion; Biography; Culture; Design; Entertainment; Film; Historical; Humour; Music; Sport; *Markets:* Adult; Children's; *Treatments:* Commercial; Mainstream; Popular

Publishes illustrated reference, sport, entertainment and children's books.

Synopses and ideas for suitable books are welcomed, but no unsolicited MSS, academic, fiction, or poetry. Send query by email only with short synopsis, author bio, market info, and up to two chapters up to a maximum of 20 pages. See website for full guidelines.

Chapman Publishing

4 Broughton Place
Edinburgh
EH1 3RX
Tel: +44 (0) 131 557 2207
Email: chapman-pub@blueyonder.co.uk
Website: http://www.chapman-pub.co.uk

Publishes: Fiction; Poetry; Scripts; *Areas:* Drama; Short Stories; *Markets:* Adult; *Treatments:* Literary

Contact: Joy Hendry

Note: No new books being undertaken as at April 2017. Check website for current status.

Publishes one or two books of short stories, drama, and (mainly) poetry by established and rising Scottish writers per year. No novels. Only considers writers who have previously been published in the press's magazine (see entry in magazines database). Only publishes plays that have been previously performed. No unsolicited MSS.

Churchwarden Publications Ltd

PO Box 420
WARMINSTER
BA12 9XB
Tel: +44 (0) 1985 840189
Fax: +44 (0) 1985 840243
Email: enquiries@churchwardenbooks.co.uk
Website: http://www.churchwardenbooks.co.uk

Publishes: Nonfiction; Reference; *Areas:* Religious; *Markets:* Professional

Contact: John Stidolph

Publisher of books and stationery for churchwardens and church administrators.

Cicerone Press

2 Police Square
Milnthorpe
Cumbria
LA7 7PY
Tel: +44 (0) 1539 562069
Email: info@cicerone.co.uk
Website: http://www.cicerone.co.uk

Publishes: Nonfiction; Reference; *Areas:*
Hobbies; Leisure; Travel; *Markets:* Adult

Considers synopses and ideas. Publishes
guidebooks for outdoor enthusiasts. No
poetry, fiction, or unsolicited MSS.

James Clarke & Co.

PO Box 60
Cambridge
CB1 2NT
Tel: +44 (0) 1223 366951
Fax: +44 (0) 1223 366951
Email: publishing@jamesclarke.co.uk
Website: http://www.jamesclarke.co

Publishes: Nonfiction; Reference; *Areas:*
Religious; *Markets:* Academic

Publishes nonfiction and reference for the
academic market on mainly theological
subject matter. Download new book proposal
form from website and return by post, fax, or
email. See website for full guidelines.

Classical Comics Limited

PO Box 177
Ludlow
SY8 9DL
Tel: +44 (0) 845 812 3000
Fax: +44 (0) 845 812 3005
Email: info@classicalcomics.com
Website: http://www.classicalcomics.com

Publishes: Fiction; *Areas:* Literature;
Markets: Children's

Contact: Gary Bryant (Managing Director);
Jo Wheeler (Creative Director)

Publishes graphic novel adaptations of
classical literature.

Co & Bear Productions

63 Edith Grove
London

SW10 0LB
Email: info@cobear.co.uk
Website: http://www.scriptumeditions.co.uk

Publishes: Nonfiction; *Areas:* Arts; Beauty
and Fashion; Design; Lifestyle; Nature;
Photography; *Markets:* Adult

Publishes illustrated books on interior
design, lifestyle, fashion and photography,
botanical art, natural history and exploration.

Comma Press

Studio 510a, 5th Floor
Hope Mill
113 Pollard Street
Manchester
M4 7JA
Tel: +44 (0) 7792 564747
Email: info@commapress.co.uk
Website: http://commapress.co.uk

Publishes: Fiction; *Areas:* Short Stories;
Markets: Adult

Short story publisher aiming to put the short
story at the heart of contemporary narrative
culture. Stories should be between 1,500 and
8,000 words. No micro-fiction or novellas.
See website for full submission guidelines.

Connections Book Publishing Ltd

St. Chad's House
148 King's Cross Road
London
WC1X 9DH
Tel: +44 (0) 20 7837 1968
Fax: +44 (0) 20 7837 2025
Email: info@connections-publishing.com
Website: http://www.connections-
publishing.com

Publishes: Nonfiction; Reference; *Areas:*
Health; Leisure; Lifestyle; Men's Interests;
New Age; Philosophy; Psychology;
Religious; Self-Help; Spiritual; Women's
Interests; *Markets:* Adult; Family; Youth;
Treatments: Light; Mainstream; Positive

Contact: Ian Jackson – Editorial Director

Specialises in New Age and spiritual.
Emphasis on oracles and self help approach.
Interest in martial arts and yoga as well as

new healing and physical well being techniques. No academic. Most authors are well known from previous success and widely published books.

Council for British Archaeology (CBA) Publishing

Council for British Archaeology
Beatrice de Cardi House
66 Bootham
York
YO30 7BZ
Tel: +44 (0) 1904 671417
Fax: +44 (0) 1904 671384
Email: webenquiry@archaeologyUK.org
Website: http://new.archaeologyuk.org/

Publishes: Nonfiction; *Areas:* Archaeology; *Markets:* Academic

Publisher of academic books on archaeology. Query by telephone in first instance.

Countryside Books

35 Kingfisher Court
Hambridge Road
Newbury
Berkshire
RG14 5SJ
Tel: +44 (0) 1635 43816
Fax: +44 (0) 1635 551004
Email: info@countrysidebooks.co.uk
Website: http://www.countrysidebooks.co.uk

Publishes: Nonfiction; *Areas:* Architecture; Historical; Leisure; Lifestyle; Military; Photography; Travel; *Markets:* Adult

Publishes nonfiction only, mostly regional books relating to specific English counties. Covers topics such as local history, walks, photography, dialect, genealogy, military and aviation, and some transport; but not interested in natural history books or personal memories. No fiction or poetry.

Cressrelles Publishing Co. Ltd

10 Station Road Industrial Estate
Colwall
Malvern
WR13 6RN
Tel: +44 (0) 1684 540154

Fax: +44 (0) 1684 540154
Email: simon@cressrelles.co.uk
Website: http://www.cressrelles.co.uk

Publishes: Nonfiction; Scripts; *Areas:* Drama; *Markets:* Academic; Adult

Contact: Simon Smith

Welcomes submissions. Publishes plays, theatre and drama textbooks, and local interest books. Accepts scripts by post or by email.

Crown House Publishing

Submissions
Crown Buildings
Bancyfelin
Carmarthen
SA33 5ND
Tel: +44 (0) 1267 211345
Fax: +44 (0) 1267 211882
Email: submissions@crownhouse.co.uk
Website: http://www.crownhouse.co.uk

Publishes: Nonfiction; *Areas:* Business; Health; Humour; Psychology; Self-Help; Spiritual; *Markets:* Academic; Adult; Children's; *Treatments:* Popular

Publishes books on Mind Body Spirit; Business Training and Development; Education Psychotherapy; Personal Growth; and Health and Wellbeing. Send email up to 300 words only describing your ideas in the first instance.

Crux Publishing

Email: hello@cruxpublishing.co.uk
Website: http://cruxpublishing.co.uk

Publishes: Fiction; Nonfiction; *Markets:* Adult

Founded to help authors publish (or republish) nonfiction works of the highest quality. Will also consider fiction if truly unique. Pursues a digital-first approach. See website for submission guidelines and more information.

CTS (Catholic Truth Society)

40 Harleyford Road
Vauxhall

London
SE11 5AY
Tel: +44 (0) 20 7640 0042
Fax: +44 (0) 20 7640 0046
Email: f.martin@cts-online.org.uk
Website: http://www.cts-online.org.uk

Publishes: Nonfiction; *Areas:* Religious; *Markets:* Adult

Contact: Fergal Martin (Publisher)

Publisher of Roman Catholic religious books. Publishes a range of books in this area, including Vatican documents and sources, as well as moral, doctrinal, liturgical, and biographical books. Welcomes appropriate ideas, synopses, and unsolicited MSS. Send query with 1-2 page synopsis or a sample text.

David Fickling Books

31 Beaumont Street
Oxford
OX1 2NP
Tel: +44 (0) 1865 339000
Website: http://www.
davidficklingbooks.com

Publishes: Fiction; Poetry; *Markets:* Children's; Youth

Publishes picture books, fiction for children and young adults, and poetry. Generally accepts submissions through literary agents only, except during specific open submission competitions. See website for details.

DB Publishing

29 Clarence Road
Attenborough
Nottingham
NG9 5HY
Tel: +44 (0) 1332 384235
Fax: +44 (0) 1332 292755
Email: submissions@jmdmedia.co.uk
Website: http://www.dbpublishing.co.uk

Publishes: Fiction; Nonfiction; *Areas:* Autobiography; Biography; Crime; Health; Historical; Sociology; Sport; Travel; *Markets:* Adult

Contact: Steve Caron

Considers all types of books, but focuses on local interest, sport, biography, autobiography and social history. Approach by email or phone – no submissions by post. See website for full guidelines.

De Montfort Literature

20-22 Wenlock Road
London
N1 7GU
Tel: +44 (0) 20 7205 2881
Email: info@demontfortliterature.com
Website: https://www.
demontfortliterature.com

Publishes: Fiction; *Markets:* Adult; Children's; Youth

Publisher founded by a hedge fund that successfully used data to predict (amongst other things) the bottom of the market in 2002, the 2008 crash, and Brexit. Now seeks to apply the same scientific approach to a new model of publishing based on predicting an author's chances of success. Where they find likely candidates, they will invest in the author by paying them an annual salary to become a full-time novelist. Applicants do not need to have already written a novel. The application process includes a psychometric test, an opportunity to discuss ideas, and a final interview. See website for full details.

Dedalus Ltd

Langford Lodge
St Judith's Lane
Sawtry
PE28 5XE
Tel: +44 (0) 1487 832382
Fax: +44 (0) 1487 832382
Email: info@dedalusbooks.com
Website: http://www.dedalusbooks.com

Publishes: Fiction; *Areas:* Literature; Translations; *Markets:* Adult; *Treatments:* Contemporary; Literary

Send query letter describing yourself along with SAE, synopsis, three sample chapters, and explanation of why you think this publisher in particular is right for you – essential to be familiar with and have read other books on this publisher's list before submitting, as most material received is entirely inappropriate. Welcomes submissions of suitable original fiction and is particularly interested in intellectually clever and unusual fiction, however undertakes only between one and three new projects a year. No email or disk submissions, or collections of short stories by unknown authors. Novels should be over 40,000 words – ideally over 50,000. Most books are translations.

Dino Books

3 Bramber Court
2 Bramber Road
London
W14 9PB
Tel: +44 (0) 20 7381 0666
Email: help@dinobooks.co.uk
Website: https://dinobooks.co.uk

Publishes: Nonfiction; *Areas:* Humour; Sport; *Markets:* Children's

Publishes nonfiction for children aged 9-12, that aim to entertain, educate, and "turn your way of thinking upside down".

Discovery Walking Guides Ltd

Email: ask.discovery@ntlworld.com
Website: http://www.dwgwalking.co.uk

Publishes: Nonfiction; *Areas:* Travel; *Markets:* Adult

Publishes walking guidebooks and maps. Welcomes proposals for new projects. Send query by email. No attachments.

Dodo Ink

Email: sam@dodoink.com
Website: http://www.dodoink.com

Publishes: Fiction; *Markets:* Adult; *Treatments:* Literary

Contact: Sam Mills

Independent UK publisher aiming to publish three novels per year, in paperback and digital formats. Publishes risk-taking, imaginative novels, that don't fall into easy marketing categories. Closed to submissions as at June 2017.

Dovecote Press

Stanbridge
Wimborne Minster
Dorset
BH21 4JD
Tel: +44 (0) 1258 840549
Email: online@dovecotepress.com
Website: http://www.dovecotepress.com

Publishes: Nonfiction; *Areas:* Architecture; Biography; Historical; Nature; *Markets:* Adult

Contact: David Burnett

Publishes books on architecture, local history, and natural history.

Dref Wen

28 Church Road
Whitchurch
Cardiff
CF14 2EA
Tel: +44 (0) 2920 617860
Fax: +44 (0) 2920 610507
Email: post@drefwen.com
Website: http://www.drefwen.com

Publishes: Fiction; Nonfiction; *Areas:* Autobiography; Travel; *Markets:* Academic; Adult; Children's

Publishes bilingual and Welsh language books for children, as well as Welsh and English educational books for those learning Welsh. Also moving into adult publishing, in particular autobiographies of Welsh personalities.

Duckworth Publishers

30 Calvin Street
London
E1 6NW
Tel: +44 (0) 20 7490 7300
Email: info@duckworth-publishers.co.uk
Website: http://www.ducknet.co.uk

Publishes: Fiction; Nonfiction; *Areas:* Arts; Autobiography; Biography; Crime; Criticism; Current Affairs; Design; Drama; Film; Finance; Historical; Horror; Humour; Literature; Music; Nature; Philosophy; Photography; Politics; Religious; Science; Sci-Fi; Sociology; Sport; Theatre; Thrillers; Translations; Travel; *Markets:* Adult;

Children's; *Treatments:* Commercial;
Literary

Britain's oldest active independent trade
publisher. Publishes nonfiction; literary
fiction; horrors and thrillers; and children's
books. Advises writers to seek representation
by a literary agent, but will accept proposals
directly by email. Include full synopsis,
author CV, and three sample chapters. See
website for full guidelines.

Dunedin Academic Press Ltd
Hudson House
8 Albany Street
Edinburgh
EH1 3QB

LONDON OFICE:
352 Cromwell Tower,
Barbican,
London
EC2Y 8NB
Tel: +44 (0) 1314 732397
Fax: +44 (0) 1250 770088
Email: mail@dunedinacademicpress.co.uk
Website: http://www.
dunedinacademicpress.co.uk

Publishes: Nonfiction; *Areas:* Anthropology;
Biography; Current Affairs; Finance; Health;
Historical; Legal; Medicine; Music; Nature;
Philosophy; Religious; Science; Sociology;
Markets: Academic; Professional

Publishes academic works, mainly at levels
from first year undergraduate to postgraduate
and research levels.

Dynasty Press
36 Ravensdon Street
Kennington
London
SE11 4AR
Tel: +44 (0) 7970 066894
Email: admin@dynastypress.co.uk
Website: http://www.dynastypress.co.uk

Publishes: Nonfiction; *Areas:* Biography;
Historical; *Markets:* Adult

Publishes books connected to royalty,
dynasties and people of influence.

Edinburgh University Press
The Tun – Holyrood Road
12 (2f) Jackson's Entry
Edinburgh
EH8 8PJ
Tel: +44 (0) 1316 504218
Fax: +44 (0) 1316 503286
Email: editorial@eup.ed.ac.uk
Website: http://www.euppublishing.com

Publishes: Nonfiction; Reference; *Areas:*
Archaeology; Architecture; Culture; Film;
Historical; Legal; Literature; Media;
Philosophy; Politics; Religious; Science;
Sociology; *Markets:* Academic

Publishes academic and scholarly nonfiction
and reference across the humanities and
social sciences.

Edward Elgar Publishing Ltd
The Lypiatts
15 Lansdown Road
Cheltenham
Glos
GL50 2JA
Tel: +44 (0) 1242 226934
Fax: +44 (0) 1242 262111
Email: info@e-elgar.com
Website: http://www.e-elgar.co.uk

Publishes: Nonfiction; *Areas:* Business;
Culture; Finance; Legal; Nature; Politics;
Sociology; *Markets:* Academic; Professional

Contact: [See website for contact details for
different areas]

Academic and professional publisher of
books and journals, with a strong focus on
the social sciences and legal fields. Actively
commissioning new titles. See website for
contact details and proposal forms.

The Emma Press Ltd
Email: queries@theemmapress.com
Website: http://theemmapress.com

Publishes: Fiction; Poetry; *Areas:* Short
Stories; *Markets:* Adult; Children's

Contact: Emma Wright

Publishes themed anthologies of poetry and
short stories. See website for themes of
current calls for submissions.

Encyclopedia Britannica (UK) Ltd

2nd Floor, Unity Wharf
Mill Street
London
SE1 2BH
Tel: +44 (0) 20 7500 7800
Fax: +44 (0) 20 7500 7878
Email: enquiries@britannica.co.uk
Website: https://britannica.co.uk

Publishes: Nonfiction; Reference; *Markets:* Academic; Adult; Family

Global digital educational publisher, publishing information and instructional products used in schools, universities, homes, libraries and workplaces throughout the world.

Enitharmon Press

10 Bury Place
London
WC1A 2JL
Tel: +44 (0) 20 7430 0844
Email: info@enitharmon.co.uk
Website: http://www.enitharmon.co.uk

Publishes: Fiction; Poetry; *Areas:* Arts; Criticism; Photography; *Markets:* Adult; *Treatments:* Literary

One of Britain's leading literary publishers, specialising in poetry and in high-quality artists' books and original prints. It is divided into two companies: the press, which publishes poetry and general literature in small-format volumes and anthologies, and the editions, which produces de luxe artists' books in the tradition of the livre d'artiste. No unsolicited mss.

Exley Publications

16 Chalk Hill
Watford
WD19 4BG
Tel: +44 (0) 1923 474480
Website: https://www.helenexley.com

Publishes: Nonfiction; *Markets:* Adult; *Treatments:* Popular

Publishes gift books.

Eye Books

Tel: +44 (0) 7973 861869
Email: dan@eye-books.com
Website: http://eye-books.com

Publishes: Nonfiction; *Areas:* Travel; *Markets:* Adult

Contact: Dan Hiscocks

Small independent publisher, publishing books about ordinary people doing extraordinary things. Often includes strong travel element. See website for detailed submission guidelines and online submission system.

Faber & Faber Ltd

Bloomsbury House
74-77 Great Russell Street
London
WC1B 3DA
Tel: +44 (0) 20 7927 3800
Fax: +44 (0) 20 7927 3801
Website: http://www.faber.co.uk

Publishes: Fiction; Nonfiction; Poetry; Scripts; *Areas:* Biography; Drama; Film; Music; Politics; Theatre; *Markets:* Adult; Children's

Originally published poetry and plays but has expanded into other areas. Has published some of the most prominent writers of the twentieth century, including several poet laureates. No longer accepting unsolicited MSS in any areas other than poetry. Submit 6 poems in first instance, with adequate return postage. Submissions of material other than poetry will neither be read nor returned. No submissions by email, fax, or on disk.

Faculty of 1000 Ltd

Middlesex House,
34-42 Cleveland Street,
London W1T 4LB
Email: info@f1000.com
Website: https://f1000.com

Publishes: Nonfiction; *Areas:* Science; *Markets:* Academic

Aims to transform the way science is communicated, by providing innovative solutions to rethink how research is shared, used and reused.

Findhorn Press Ltd
Delft Cottage
Dyke
Forres
IV36 2TF
Tel: +44 (0) 1309 690582
Email: submissions@findhornpress.com
Website: http://www.findhornpress.com

Publishes: Nonfiction; *Areas:* Health; New Age; Spiritual; *Markets:* Adult

Publishes books on mind, body, spirit, New Age and healing. Approach by email only. Send 1-2 page synopsis, word count, number of illustrations, table of contents, page describing intended readership, brief personal bio including any previous publications, and details on ways you can help promote your book. See website for more information.

Fingerpress UK
Email: firstwriter@fingerpress.co.uk
Website: http://www.fingerpress.co.uk

Publishes: Fiction; *Areas:* Historical; Sci-Fi; Thrillers; *Markets:* Adult; *Treatments:* Commercial

Note: Not accepting submissions as at May 2016 – check website for current status.

*** Please read the submissions page on our website before submitting anything... ***

Only open to submissions at certain times. Check website for current status. When open to submissions, this will be announced on our Facebook and Twitter pages.

We're an independent publisher based in London; we publish high quality Historical Fiction and Science Fiction. We're building a range of savvy, entertaining titles that are both thought-provoking and a good read. The ideal novel will have memorable characters with good plot development and pacing.

If your book isn't either Historical Fiction or Science Fiction, please don't submit it to us -

- many thanks for your understanding.

We look for:

* submissions of completed, professionally edited, commercial-grade novels

Please check out our sister website – a virtual reality Facebook for authors, publishers and readers.

Firefly
25 Gabalfa Road
Llandaff North
Cardiff
CF14 2JJ
Tel: +44 (0) 2920 218611
Email: janet.thomas@fireflypress.co.uk
Website: http://fireflypress.co.uk

Publishes: Fiction; *Markets:* Children's; Youth

Contact: Janet Thomas

Publishes fiction and nonfiction for children and young adults aged 5-19. Open to email or postal queries to nonfiction. Closed to fiction submissions as at June 2018, but plans to open to fiction submissions for one month starting September 1, 2018. Not currently publishing any picture books or colour illustrated book for any age group.

Fisherton Press
Email: general@fishertonpress.co.uk
Website: http://fishertonpress.co.uk

Publishes: Fiction; *Markets:* Children's

Contact: Eleanor Levenson

Closed to submissions as at April 2018. Check website for current status.

Aims to publish books for children that adults will also enjoy reading, whether for the first time or the hundredth. Send query with ideas or fully written or illustrated texts with short bio, by email.

Fitzrovia Press Limited
42 Monington Road
Glastonbury

Somerset
BA6 8HF
Tel: +44 (0) 20 7380 0749
Email: info@fitzroviapress.co.uk
Website: http://www.fitzroviapress.com

Publishes: Fiction; Nonfiction; *Areas:*
Philosophy; Spiritual; *Markets:* Adult

Contact: Ranchor Prime

Publishes fiction and nonfiction on
Hinduism, spirituality, and Eastern
philosophy. No unsolicited mss. Send query
with outline and sample chapter.

Flame Tree Publishing

6 Melbray Mews
London
SW6 3NS
Tel: +44 (0) 20 7751 9650
Fax: +44 (0) 20 7751 9651
Email: info@flametreepublishing.com
Website: http://www.
flametreepublishing.com

Publishes: Nonfiction; *Areas:* Cookery;
Culture; Lifestyle; Music; *Markets:* Adult;
Treatments: Popular

Publihses practical cookbooks, music,
popular culture and lifestyle books. Very
rarely accepts unsolicited mss or book
proposals.

Fleming Publications

134 Renfrew Street
Glasgow
G3 6ST
Email: info@ettadunn.com
Website: http://www.
flemingpublications.com

Publishes: Fiction; Nonfiction; Poetry;
Areas: Biography; Historical; Photography;
Self-Help; *Markets:* Adult

Contact: Etta Dunn

Publishes nonfiction, fiction, and poetry for
"mindful individuals".

Floris Books

2a Robertson Avenue
Edinburgh

EH11 1PZ
Tel: +44 (0) 1313 372372
Email: floris@florisbooks.co.uk
Website: http://www.florisbooks.co.uk

Publishes: Fiction; Nonfiction; *Areas:*
Architecture; Arts; Biography; Crafts;
Health; Historical; Literature; Philosophy;
Religious; Science; Self-Help; Sociology;
Spiritual; *Markets:* Adult; Children's; Youth

Publishes a wide range of books including
adult nonfiction, picture books and
children's novels. No poetry or verse, fiction
for people over the age of 14, or
autobiography, unless it specifically relates
to a relevant nonfiction subject area. No
submissions by email. See website for full
details of areas covered and submission
guidelines.

Fonthill Media Ltd

Millview House
Toadsmoor Road
Stroud
Gloucestershire
GL5 2TB

US OFFICE:
60 Thoreau Street #204
Concord, MA 01742
Email: submissions@fonthillmedia.com
Website: http://fonthillmedia.com

Publishes: Nonfiction; *Areas:* Archaeology;
Biography; Historical; Military; Sociology;
Sport; Travel; *Markets:* Adult

Independent publisher with offices in the UK
and US. Publishes nonfiction only. Send
query through website submissions form or
by email, providing your project's title,
description up to 200 words, description of
yourself up to 100 words, proposed word
count, and nature and number of
illustrations.

Footprint Handbooks

5 Riverside Court
Lower Bristol Road
Bath
BA2 3DZ
Tel: +44 (0) 1225 469141
Email: contactus@
morriscontentalliance.com

Website: http://www. footprinttravelguides.com

Publishes: Nonfiction; Reference; *Areas:* Travel; *Markets:* Adult

Publishes travel guides written by a small team of experts. See careers section of website for any opportunities.

Frances Lincoln Children's Books

74-77 White Lion Street
London
N1 9PF
Tel: +44 (0) 20 7284 9300
Fax: +44 (0) 20 7485 0490
Email: QuartoKidsSubmissions@
Quarto.com
Website: http://www.quartoknows.com/
Frances-Lincoln-Childrens-Books

Publishes: Fiction; Nonfiction; Poetry; *Areas:* Culture; *Markets:* Children's

Contact: Rachel Williams, Publisher; Janetta Otter-Barry, Publisher; Katie Cotton, Editor

Publishes picture books, multicultural books, poetry, picture books and information books. Submit by email. See website for full guidelines.

Frontinus

4 The Links
Cambridge Road
Newmarket
Suffolk
CB8 0TG
Tel: +44 (0) 1638 663456
Email: info@frontinus.org.uk
Website: http://www.frontinus.org.uk

Publishes: Nonfiction; *Areas:* Design; Technology; *Markets:* Academic; Professional

Publishes academic and professional nonfiction for engineers.

Galley Beggar Press

Email: submissions@galleybeggar.co.uk
Website: http://galleybeggar.co.uk

Publishes: Fiction; Nonfiction; *Areas:* Short Stories; *Markets:* Adult; *Treatments:* Literary

Publishes adult literary fiction and narrative nonfiction only. Open to submissions by email during specific submission windows. See website for full details.

Garnet Publishing

8 Southern Court
South Street
Reading
RG1 4QS
Tel: +44 (0) 118 959 7847
Fax: +44 (0) 118 959 0508
Email: info@garnetpublishing.co.uk
Website: http://www.garnetpublishing.co.uk

Publishes: Fiction; Nonfiction; *Areas:* Anthropology; Archaeology; Architecture; Arts; Autobiography; Biography; Cookery; Culture; Current Affairs; Historical; Literature; Media; Photography; Politics; Religious; Sociology; Translations; Travel; *Markets:* Academic; Adult; *Treatments:* Commercial; Literary; Mainstream; Niche

Contact: Arash Hejazi

An independent publishing company specialising in trade books, with a special interest in the Middle East. We publish in the fields of architecture, art, fiction, cookery and travel, and also in the areas of culture, heritage and history of the Middle East.

One imprint is a leading English-language publisher of academic books devoted to the Middle East Studies. Its authors are academic experts drawn from all over the world and the company has links with many major universities in the UK, the USA and Europe that have departments or faculties with Middle Eastern and Arab studies programmes.

Send query with brief cover letter, writer's bio, detailed synopsis, two sample chapters, and full contact details.

Geddes & Grosset

Gresham Publishing Company Limited
Academy Park
Building 4000

Glasgow
G51 1PR
Website: http://www.geddesandgrosset.co.uk

Publishes: Fiction; Nonfiction; Reference; *Areas:* Cookery; Health; Historical; Humour; Self-Help; Spiritual; *Markets:* Adult; Children's

Publishes dictionaries, bilingual books, English grammar and usage texts, Self-Help, Diet and Health, and Mind, Body and Spirit. Imprint focuses on Scottish titles.

GEY Books

Email: geybooks@gmail.com

Publishes: Fiction; Nonfiction; Poetry; *Areas:* Culture; Drama; Entertainment; Erotic; Fantasy; Men's Interests; Romance; Short Stories; Thrillers; Travel; *Markets:* Adult; *Treatments:* Contemporary; Experimental; Literary

Contact: Thomas Moore

We are interested in publishing writers who identify on the LGBTQIA spectrum. The work we publish represents the many complexities of human relationships within the crazy, brilliant and beautiful LGBTQIA community.

We are interested in publishing: Fiction, Non-fiction, Poetry, Photography, Art and Comics. We are open to all types of media so long as we can create a product out of the work.

We will only publish original and previously unpublished works.

As a standard we pay our authors 50% of profits made from all sales.

We will not accept a full submission in the first instance. Please send over a brief outline of the project attaching a small sample of the work no more then 2 sides of A4 in PDF form. We will not accept any submissions via any other form besides email or any attachments other then PDFs.

Gibson Square Books Ltd

Tel: +44 (0) 20 7096 1100
Fax: +44 (0) 20 7993 2214
Email: info@gibsonsquare.com
Website: http://www.gibsonsquare.com

Publishes: Nonfiction; *Areas:* Arts; Biography; Criticism; Culture; Current Affairs; Historical; Philosophy; Politics; Psychology; Travel; Women's Interests; *Markets:* Adult

Publishes books which contribute to a general debate. Send proposals by email. See website for full guidelines.

Gingko Library

4 Molasses Row
Plantation Wharf
London
SW11 3UX
Tel: +44 (0) 20 3637 9730
Email: gingko@gingkolibrary.com
Website: http://www.gingkolibrary.com

Publishes: Nonfiction; *Areas:* Architecture; Arts; Biography; Finance; Historical; Literature; Music; Philosophy; Politics; Religious; Science; Technology; *Markets:* Academic; Adult

Welcomes proposals for new, learned books that deal with topics pertaining to the Middle East and North Africa, or the Islamic world in general, whether they are academic monographs, edited volumes, or general interest (nonfiction) books. Send query by email.

GL Assessment

1st Floor Vantage London
Great West Road
Brentford
TW8 9AG
Tel: +44 (0) 20 8996 3333
Fax: +44 (0) 20 8742 8767
Email: info@gl-assessment.co.uk
Website: https://www.gl-assessment.co.uk

Publishes: Nonfiction; *Markets:* Academic

Publishes educational testing and assessment material.

Gomer Press

Llandysul Enterprise Park
Llandysul
Ceredigion
SA44 4JL
Tel: +44 (0) 1559 363092
Fax: +44 (0) 1559 363758
Email: gwasg@gomer.co.uk
Website: http://www.gomer.co.uk

Publishes: Fiction; Nonfiction; Poetry;
Reference; Scripts; *Areas:* Arts;
Autobiography; Biography; Culture; Drama;
Historical; Leisure; Literature; Music;
Nature; Religious; Sport; Theatre; Travel;
Markets: Academic; Adult; Children's;
Youth

Publishes fiction, nonfiction, plays, poetry,
language books, and educational material,
for adults and children, in English and in
Welsh. Query before making a submission.

Granta Books

12 Addison Avenue
London
W11 4QR
Tel: +44 (0) 20 7605 1360
Fax: +44 (0) 20 7605 1361
Email: info@grantabooks.com
Website: http://www.grantabooks.com

Publishes: Fiction; Nonfiction; *Areas:*
Autobiography; Biography; Criticism;
Culture; Historical; Nature; Politics;
Sociology; Travel; *Markets:* Adult;
Treatments: Literary; Serious

Publishes around 70% nonfiction / 30%
fiction. In nonfiction publishes serious
cultural, political and social history, narrative
history, or memoir. Rarely publishes
straightforward biographies. No genre
fiction. Not accepting unsolicited
submissions.

Gresham Books Ltd

The Carriage House
Ningwood Manor
Isle of Wight
PO30 4NJ
Tel: +44 (0) 1983 761389
Email: info@gresham-books.co.uk
Website: http://www.gresham-books.co.uk

Publishes: Nonfiction; *Areas:* Religious;
Markets: Academic; Adult; Children's

Contact: Paul Lewis

Publishes bespoke books for schools,
including hymn books, plus text books to
help teach British values.

Greystones Press

Email: editorial@greystonespress.com
Website: http://www.greystonespress.com

Publishes: Fiction; Nonfiction; *Areas:* Arts;
Historical; Literature; Music; Translations;
Markets: Adult; Youth

Closed to submissions as at November 2017.
See website for current status.

Independent start-up publishing adult fiction
and nonfiction in the areas of Art, History,
Literature, Music and Mythology (including
Fairy Tales and Folklore); Young Adult
(teenage) fiction; and translated European
fiction where there is a grant for translation
in the originating country or from a UK
institution. No illustrated books or memoirs.
Send query by email with synopsis and first
three chapters up to 10,000 words as
attachments.

Grub Street Publishing

4 Rainham Close
London
SW11 6SS
Tel: +44 (0) 20 7924 3966
Fax: +44 (0) 20 7738 1008
Email: post@grubstreet.co.uk
Website: http://www.grubstreet.co.uk

Publishes: Nonfiction; Reference; *Areas:*
Cookery; Historical; Military; *Markets:*
Adult

Publishes books on cookery and military
aviation history only. No fiction or poetry.
Accepts synopses and sample material by
email. See website for full submission
guidelines and specific email addresses for
different topics.

Guild of Master Craftsman (GMC) Publications Ltd

166 High Street
Lewes
BN7 1XU
Tel: +44 (0) 1273 477374
Fax: +44 (0) 1273 402866
Email: pubs@thegmcgroup.com
Website: http://www.gmcbooks.com

Publishes: Nonfiction; Reference; *Areas:* Architecture; Arts; Cookery; Crafts; Film; Gardening; Hobbies; How-to; Humour; Photography; TV; *Markets:* Adult; Children's

Publishes books on the above topics, plus woodworking, dolls houses, and miniatures. Also publishes magazines and videos. No fiction.

Halban Publishers

22 Golden Square
London
W1F 9JW
Tel: +44 (0) 20 7437 9300
Fax: +44 (0) 20 7437 9512
Email: books@halbanpublishers.com
Website: http://www.halbanpublishers.com

Publishes: Fiction; Nonfiction; *Areas:* Autobiography; Biography; Criticism; Historical; Literature; Philosophy; Politics; Religious; *Markets:* Adult

Contact: Peter Halban; Martine Halban

Independent publisher of fiction, memoirs, history, biography, and books of Jewish interest. Send query with synopsis by post or by email. No unsolicited MSS.

Harlequin Mills & Boon Ltd

Harlequin
1 London Bridge Street
London
SE1 9GF
Email: submissions@harlequin.com
Website: http://www.millsandboon.co.uk

Publishes: Fiction; *Areas:* Crime; Historical; Romance; *Markets:* Adult; *Treatments:* Commercial; Contemporary

Major publisher with extensive romance list and various romance imprints. Submit via online submission system.

Also includes digital imprint accepting submissions in any genre, and particularly interested in authors from rapidly expanding digital markets in the UK, Ireland, South Africa and India. See website for separate submission guidelines and specific email address for this imprint. Commercial fiction and crime imprint accepts submissions via literary agents only.

HarperCollins Publishers Ltd

The News Building
1 London Bridge Street
London
SE1 9GF

GLASGOW OFFICE:
103 Westerhill Road
Bishopbriggs
Glasgow
G64 2QT
Tel: +44 (0) 20 8741 7070
Fax: +44 (0) 20 8307 4440
Email: enquiries@harpercollins.co.uk
Website: http://www.harpercollins.co.uk

Publishes: Fiction; Nonfiction; Reference; *Areas:* Autobiography; Biography; Cookery; Crafts; Crime; Entertainment; Fantasy; Film; Gardening; Health; Historical; Leisure; Lifestyle; Media; Military; Science; Sci-Fi; Sport; Thrillers; *Markets:* Adult; Children's; *Treatments:* Literary

One of the UK's three largest publishers, with one of the broadest ranges of material published. All approaches must come through an agent. No unsolicited MSS.

Hart Publishing Ltd

Kemp House
Chawley Park
Cumnor Hill
Oxford
OX2 9PH
Tel: +44 (0) 1865 598648
Fax: +44 (0) 1865 727017
Email: sinead@hartpub.co.uk
Website: http://www.hartpub.co.uk

Publishes: Nonfiction; *Areas:* Legal; *Markets:* Academic; Professional

Contact: Sinead Moloney; Bill Asquith

Publisher or legal books and journals for the professional and academic markets. See website for submission guidelines and specific editor subject areas and contact details.

Haus Publishing

70 Cadogan Place
London
SW1X 9AH
Tel: +44 (0) 20 7838 9055
Fax: +44 (0) 20 7584 9501
Email: emma@hauspublishing.com
Website: http://www.hauspublishing.com

Publishes: Fiction; Nonfiction; *Areas:* Arts; Biography; Film; Historical; Music; Photography; Politics; Theatre; Travel; *Markets:* Adult; *Treatments:* Literary

Contact: Emma Henderson

Publishes non-academic biographies of historical figures, and literary travel accounts (not guides). No autobiographies, fiction for children or young adults, or biographies of living people. Send query by email only, with synopsis, author bio, sample chapter headings, and the first three chapters. If the book is not yet written, send a proposal and sample chapter of your writing. Allow 6-8 weeks for response.

Hawthorn Press

1 Lansdown Lane
Stroud
Gloucestershire
GL5 1BJ
Tel: +44 (0) 1453 757040
Fax: +44 (0) 1453 751138
Email: info@hawthornpress.com
Website: http://www.hawthornpress.com

Publishes: Nonfiction; *Areas:* Lifestyle; Self-Help; *Markets:* Adult

Publisher aiming to contribute to a more creative, peaceful and sustainable world through its publishing. Publishes mainly commissioned work, but will consider approaches. Send first two chapters with introduction, full table of contents/book plan, brief author biography and/or CV, and SAE. Allow at least 2–4 months for response. Accepts email enquiries, but full submissions should be made by post.

Hay House Publishers

33 Notting Hill Gate
London
W11 3JQ
Tel: +44 (0) 20 3675 2450
Fax: +44 (0) 20 3675 2451
Email: submissions@hayhouse.co.uk
Website: http://www.hayhouse.co.uk

Publishes: Nonfiction; *Areas:* Biography; Business; Current Affairs; Finance; Health; Lifestyle; Medicine; Men's Interests; Nature; Philosophy; Psychology; Religious; Self-Help; Sociology; Spiritual; Women's Interests; *Markets:* Adult; *Treatments:* Positive

Describes itself as the world's leading mind body and spirit publisher. Open to submissions from April 4, 2016. Accepts proposals as hard copy by post or by email, but prefers email approaches. See website for full submission guidelines.

Haynes Publishing

Sparkford
Near Yeovil
Somerset
BA22 7JJ
Tel: +44 (0) 1963 440635
Fax: +44 (0) 1963 440023
Email: bookseditorial@haynes.co.uk
Website: http://www.haynes.co.uk

Publishes: Nonfiction; Reference; *Areas:* How-to; Leisure; Sport; Technology; *Markets:* Adult

Contact: John H. Haynes OBE (Chairman)

Mostly publishes motoring and transport titles, including DIY service and repair manuals for cars and motorbikes, motoring in general (including Motor Sports), but also home, DIY, and leisure titles. Unsolicited MSS welcome, if on one of the above areas of interest.

Head of Zeus

Clerkenwell House
45-47 Clerkenwell Green
London
EC1R 0HT
Email: info@headofzeus.com
Website: http://www.headofzeus.com

Publishes: Fiction; Nonfiction; *Areas:*
Biography; Crime; Fantasy; Historical;
Mystery; Philosophy; Romance; Sci-Fi;
Short Stories; Sociology; Sport; Suspense;
Thrillers; *Markets:* Adult; Youth;
Treatments: Commercial; Literary

**Closed to submissions as at December
2017. Check website for current status.**

Publishes general and literary fiction, genre
fiction, and nonfiction. Submit via online
submission system.

Headline Publishing Group

Carmelite House
50 Victoria Embankment
London
EC4Y 0DZ
Tel: +44 (0) 20 3122 7222
Email: enquiries@headline.co.uk
Website: https://www.headline.co.uk

Publishes: Fiction; Nonfiction; *Areas:*
Autobiography; Biography; Cookery;
Gardening; Historical; Science; Sport; TV;
Markets: Adult; *Treatments:* Commercial;
Literary; Popular

Publishes hardback and paperback
commercial and literary fiction, as well as
popular nonfiction.

Hesperus Press Limited

28 Mortimer Street
London
W1W 7RD
Tel: +44 (0) 20 7436 0943
Email: info@hesperuspress.com
Website: http://www.hesperuspress.com

Publishes: Fiction; Nonfiction; Poetry;
Reference; *Areas:* Autobiography;
Biography; Crime; Culture; Erotic; Fantasy;
Historical; Literature; Romance; Sci-Fi;
Thrillers; Translations; Travel; *Markets:*

Adult; Children's; *Treatments:*
Contemporary; Literary; Traditional

Publishes the lesser known works of
classical authors, both in English and in
translation. No unsolicited MSS and no
submissions.

Hippopotamus Press

22 Whitewell Road
Frome
Somerset BA11 4EL
Tel: +44 (0) 1373 466653
Email: rjhippopress@aol.com

Publishes: Poetry; *Markets:* Adult;
Treatments: Literary

Contact: Roland John

Publishes first collections of poetry by poets
who have an established track-record of
publication in poetry magazines.

Hodder & Stoughton Ltd

Carmelite House
50 Victoria Embankment
London
EC4Y 0DZ
Tel: +44 (0) 20 3122 6777
Email: editorialwebenquiries@hodder.co.uk
Website: https://www.hodder.co.uk

Publishes: Fiction; Nonfiction; *Areas:*
Autobiography; Biography; Cookery;
Historical; Humour; Lifestyle; Spiritual;
Travel; *Markets:* Adult; *Treatments:*
Commercial; Literary

Large London-based publisher of nonfiction
and commercial and literary fiction.

Hodder Faith

Carmelite House
50 Victoria Embankment
London
EC4Y 0DZ
Tel: +44 (0) 20 3122 6777
Email: hodderfaith@hodder.co.uk
Website: http://www.hodderfaith.com

Publishes: Nonfiction; *Areas:* Religious;
Markets: Adult

Seeks to provide a platform for Christian views to be expressed across all denominations, races and ages.

Honno Welsh Women's Press

Honno
Unit 14, Creative Units
Aberystwyth Arts Centre
Aberystwyth
Ceredigion
SY23 3GL
Tel: +44 (0) 1970 623150
Fax: +44 (0) 1970 623150
Email: post@honno.co.uk
Website: http://www.honno.co.uk

Publishes: Fiction; Nonfiction; Poetry; *Areas:* Autobiography; Crime; Fantasy; Sci-Fi; Short Stories; Thrillers; Women's Interests; *Markets:* Adult; Children's; Youth; *Treatments:* Commercial; Literary

Contact: Caroline Oakley

Feminist Welsh publisher. Publishes work from women born in, living in, or significantly connected to Wales, only. Publishes fiction, autobiographical writing and reprints of classic titles in English and Welsh, as well as anthologies of poetry and short stories. Particularly looking for literary fiction, crime/thriller, commercial women's fiction, science fiction and fantasy. All submissions must be sent as hard copy; no email submissions. Send query with synopsis and first 50 pages. Not currently accepting children's, novellas, poetry, or short story collections by a single author.

Hopscotch

St Jude's Church
Dulwich Road
Herne Hill
London
SE24 0PB
Tel: +44 (0) 20 7501 6736
Fax: +44 (0) 20 7738 9718
Email: hopscotch@bebc.co.uk
Website: http://www.hopscotchbooks.com

Publishes: Nonfiction; *Areas:* Historical; Science; Technology; *Markets:* Professional

Publishes teaching resources for primary school teachers.

Hot Key Books

Bonnier Zaffre Ltd
80-81 Wimpole Street
London
W1G 9RE
Tel: +44 (0) 20 7490 3875
Email: enquiries@bonnierzaffre.co.uk
Website: http://hotkeybooks.com

Publishes: Fiction; Nonfiction; *Markets:* Children's; Youth

Publishes fiction and nonfiction for teens and young adults. Send complete ms with full synopsis by email only. Prefers Word and PDF files. Response only if interested.

House of Lochar

Isle of Colonsay
PA61 7YR
Tel: +44 (0) 1951 200232
Fax: +44 (0) 1951 200232
Email: sales@houseoflochar.com
Website: http://www.houseoflochar.com

Publishes: Fiction; Nonfiction; *Areas:* Biography; Historical; Literature; Travel; *Markets:* Adult; Children's; *Treatments:* Literary

Publishes fiction and nonfiction related to Scotland and / or Celtic themes, including history, fiction, transport, maritime, genealogy, Gaelic, and books for children. No poetry or books unrelated to Scottish or Celtic themes.

Hymns Ancient & Modern Ltd

3rd Floor, Invicta House
108-114 Golden Lane
London
EC1Y 0TG
Tel: +44 (0) 20 7776 7548
Fax: +44 (0) 20 7776 7556
Email: mary@hymnsam.co.uk
Website: http://www.hymnsam.co.uk

Publishes: Nonfiction; Reference; *Areas:* Biography; Humour; Music; Religious; Spiritual; *Markets:* Academic; Adult

Contact: Mary Matthews, Editorial Manager

Publishes religious books including hymn books, liturgical material, and schoolbooks.

No proposals for dissertations, fiction, poetry, drama, children's books, books of specialist local interest, or (generally) multi-authored collections of essays or symposium papers. Send query with contents page, synopsis, and first chapter with SAE.

Igloo Books Limited
Cottage Farm
Mears Ashby Road
Sywell
Northants
NN6 0BJ
Tel: +44 (0) 1604 741116
Fax: +44 (0) 1604 670495
Email: customerservice@igloobooks.com
Website: http://igloobooks.com

Publishes: Fiction; Nonfiction; Reference; *Areas:* Cookery; Hobbies; Lifestyle; *Markets:* Adult; Children's

Publishes nonfiction and gift and puzzle books for adults, and fiction, nonfiction, and novelty books for children.

Impress Books Limited
Innovation Centre
Rennes Drive
University of Exeter
Devon
EX4 4RN
Email: enquiries@impress-books.co.uk
Website: http://www.impress-books.co.uk

Publishes: Fiction; Nonfiction; *Areas:* Biography; Crime; Historical; Religious; *Markets:* Adult; *Treatments:* Contemporary; Literary

Interested in quality, thought-provoking titles for the enquiring general reader. Specialises in discovering and nurturing fresh voices in crime, historical and literary fiction.

Imprint Academic
PO Box 200
Exeter
EX5 5YX
Tel: +44 (0) 1392 851550
Fax: +44 (0) 1392 851178
Email: keith@imprint.co.uk
Website: http://www.imprint-academic.com

Publishes: Nonfiction; *Areas:* Criticism; Philosophy; Politics; Psychology; *Markets:* Academic; Adult

Contact: Keith Sutherland

Publisher of books on politics, psychology, and philosophy for both academic and general readership. Welcomes ideas and unsolicited MSS by email or by post, provided return postage is included.

Indigo Dreams Publishing
24 Forest Houses
Halwill
Beaworthy
Devon
EX21 5UU
Email: publishing@indigodreams.co.uk
Website: http://www.indigodreams.co.uk

Publishes: Poetry; *Markets:* Adult; *Treatments:* Literary

Contact: Ronnie Goodyer

Closed to pamphlet and collection submissions as at March 2018. Check website for current status.

Publishes poetry collections up to 60/70 pages and poetry pamphlets up to 36 pages. See website for submission guidelines.

Infinite Ideas
36 St Giles
Oxford
OX1 3LD
Tel: +44 (0) 1865 514888
Email: richard@infideas.com
Website: http://www.infideas.com

Publishes: Nonfiction; *Areas:* Autobiography; Biography; Business; Cookery; Culture; Current Affairs; Entertainment; Gardening; Hobbies; Lifestyle; Media; Politics; Self-Help; Travel; *Markets:* Professional; *Treatments:* Commercial; Contemporary; Progressive; Traditional

Contact: Richard Burton

Set up in 2004. We were on a mission to create a publishing business like no other. In a world that is teeming with books, good and bad (mainly bad), we set out to publish books of real value to the reader. Every page has something that might change readers' lives for the better, for ever.

160 plus books later, we like to think that we've achieved some of our ambitions. We've developed great book series.

We've worked with top brands including Marks and Spencer, Sainsbury's Champneys, Simple and Anne Summers who value our ability to produce great content in a beautiful package.

We've worked too with a number of new authors to help them get their masterpieces into the market.

We love great content, we love great books and we love great ideas.

Do feel free to get in touch to with us if you'd like to hear more. Send short synopsis by email.

IWM (Imperial War Museums)
IWM London
Lambeth Road
London
SE1 6HZ
Tel: +44 (0) 20 7416 5000
Email: publishing@iwm.org.uk
Website: http://www.iwm.org.uk/commercial/publishing

Publishes: Nonfiction; *Areas:* Historical; Military; *Markets:* Adult

Publishes books linked to its exhibitions and archives. Send query by email with brief outline and sample material.

J.A. Allen
The Stable Block
Crowood Lane
Ramsbury
Wiltshire
SN8 2HR
Tel: +44 (0) 1672 520280
Email: enquiries@crowood.com
Website: http://www.crowood.com

Publishes: Nonfiction; *Areas:* How-to; *Markets:* Adult

Contact: Lesley Gowers

Publishes books on horses and horsemanship. Send query by post, fax, or email. No unsolicited mss.

Jacaranda Books Art Music Ltd
27 Old Gloucester Street
London
WC1N 3AX
Email: office@jacarandabooksartmusic.co.uk
Website: http://www.jacarandabooksartmusic.co.uk

Publishes: Fiction; Nonfiction; *Areas:* Arts; Autobiography; Beauty and Fashion; Biography; Crime; Photography; Romance; *Markets:* Adult; *Treatments:* Contemporary

Contact: Valerie Brandes, Founder & Publisher

Not accepting submissions as at March 2018. Check website for current situation.

Publishes adult fiction and nonfiction, including crime, romance, illustrated books, biography, memoir, and autobiography. Particularly interested in books where the central character or theme relates to minority groups and/or has strong female protagonists. Also interested in original works from or about African, African-American, Caribbean and black British artists working in the fields of photography, fine art, fashion, and contemporary and modern art, and artists of calibre from the soul, blues, R&B and reggae traditions. Send query by email with writer CV, detailed synopsis, and two sample chapters. See website for full submission guidelines.

Jane's Information Group
Sentinel House
163 Brighton Road
Coulsdon
Surrey
CR5 2YH
Tel: +44 (0) 1344 328300

Fax: +44 (0) 20 8763 1006
Website: http://www.janes.com

Publishes: Nonfiction; Reference; *Areas:*
Military; *Markets:* Adult

Publisher of magazines, books, reference
works, online material, and yearbooks
related to defence, aerospace, security, and
transport topics.

Joffe Books Ltd

Email: submissions@joffebooks.com
Website: http://www.joffebooks.com

Publishes: Fiction; *Areas:* Crime; Mystery;
Suspense; Thrillers; *Markets:* Adult

Contact: Jasper Joffe

Publishes full-length crime fiction,
mysteries, and thrillers. No kids books, sci-
fi, nonfiction, conspiracy theories, or erotic.
Send query by email with complete ms as an
attachment, a synopsis in the body of the
email, and 100 words about yourself. Include
"submission" in the subject line. See website
for full guidelines.

John Murray (Publishers) Ltd

Carmelite House
50 Victoria Embankment
London
EC4Y 0DZ
Tel: +44 (0) 20 3122 6777
Website: https://www.hodder.co.uk

Publishes: Fiction; Nonfiction; *Markets:*
Adult

Accepts approaches through literary agents
only.

Josef Weinberger Ltd

12-14 Mortimer Street
London
W1T 3JJ
Tel: +44 (0) 20 7580 2827
Fax: +44 (0) 20 7436 9616
Email: general.info@jwmail.co.uk
Website: http://www.josef-weinberger.com

Publishes: Scripts; *Areas:* Theatre; *Markets:*
Adult

Publishes theatre scripts for musicals, plays,
pantomimes, operas, and operettas.

Kettillonia

Sidlaw House
South Street
NEWTYLE
Angus
PH12 8UQ
Tel: +44 (0) 1828 650615
Email: james@kettillonia.co.uk
Website: http://www.kettillonia.co.uk

Publishes: Fiction; Nonfiction; Poetry;
Areas: Historical; Humour; Literature; Short
Stories; *Markets:* Adult; *Treatments:*
Literary

Contact: James Robertson

Publisher of pamphlets containing original,
adventurous, neglected and rare Scottish
writing.

Kube Publishing

MCC, Ratby Lane
Markfield
Leicestershire
LE67 9SY
Tel: +44 (0) 1530 249230
Fax: +44 (0) 1530 249656
Email: info@kubepublishing.com
Website: http://www.kubepublishing.com

Publishes: Fiction; Nonfiction; Poetry;
Areas: Biography; Culture; Historical;
Lifestyle; Politics; Religious; Sociology;
Spiritual; *Markets:* Academic; Adult;
Children's; Youth

Independent publisher of general interest,
academic, and children's books on Islam and
the Muslim experience. Publishes nonfiction
for children, young people, and adults, but
fiction and poetry for children and teens
only. See website for full guidelines.

Lantana Publishing

Email: submissions@lantanapublishing.com
Website: http://www.lantanapublishing.com

Publishes: Fiction; Nonfiction; *Areas:*
Culture; *Markets:* Children's; *Treatments:*
Contemporary

Publishes picture books and narrative nonfiction focused on diversity for 4 to 8 year olds up to 500 words (prefers 200-400 words). Particularly interested in contemporary writing with modern-day settings, especially if they feature Black, Asian and Minority Ethnic families. Publishes almost exclusively authors of Black, Asian and Minority Ethnic backgrounds.

Laurence King Publishing Ltd
361-373 City Road
London
EC1V 1LR
Tel: +44 (0) 20 7841 6900
Fax: +44 (0) 20 7841 6910
Email: commissioning@laurenceking.com
Website: http://www.laurenceking.co.uk

Publishes: Nonfiction; *Areas:* Architecture; Arts; Beauty and Fashion; Design; Film; Historical; Photography; *Markets:* Academic; Adult

Publisher of books on the creative arts. Send proposal by email.

Lawrence & Wishart
Central Books Building
Freshwater Road
Chadwell Heath
RM8 1RX
Tel: +44 (0) 20 8597 0090
Email: submissions@lwbooks.co.uk
Website: http://www.lwbooks.co.uk

Publishes: Nonfiction; *Areas:* Culture; Current Affairs; Historical; Politics; *Markets:* Adult

Contact: Katharine Harris

Independent publisher of books on current affairs and political history and culture. Formed through a merger in the 1930s of the Communist Party's press and a liberal and anti-fascist publisher.

Legend Business
175-185 Gray's Inn Road
London
WC1X 8UE
Tel: +44 (0) 20 7812 0641

Email: submissions@legend-paperbooks.co.uk
Website: http://www.legendtimesgroup.co.uk/legend-business

Publishes: Nonfiction; *Areas:* Business; *Markets:* Professional

Publishes a wide-ranging list of business titles. Welcomes proposals and finished manuscripts. Submit synopsis and first three chapters through online submission system. See website for more details.

Legend Press
107-111 Fleet Street
London
EC4A 2AB
Tel: +44 (0) 20 7936 9941
Email: submissions@legend-paperbooks.co.uk
Website: http://www.legendpress.co.uk

Publishes: Fiction; *Areas:* Crime; Historical; *Markets:* Adult; *Treatments:* Commercial; Contemporary; Mainstream

Contact: Tom Chalmers

Publishes a diverse list of contemporary adult novels. No children's books, poetry or travel writing. See website for full submission guidelines and online submission system.

Lion Hudson Plc
Wilkinson House
Jordan Hill Road
Oxford
OX2 8DR
Tel: +44 (0) 1865 302750
Fax: +44 (0) 1865 302757
Email: SubmissionstoLionBooksMonarchLionFiction@LionHudson.com
Website: http://www.lionhudson.com

Publishes: Fiction; Nonfiction; Reference; *Areas:* Autobiography; Biography; Health; Religious; Spiritual; *Markets:* Adult; Children's; *Treatments:* Positive

Publishes books that reflect Christian values or are inspired by a Christian world view, including adult nonfiction / reference, and children's fiction and nonfiction. See website for specific submission guidelines for different imprints.

Little Tiger Press
1 The Coda Centre
189 Munster Road
London
SW6 6AW
Tel: +44 (0) 20 7385 6333
Fax: +44 (0) 20 7385 7333
Email: info@littletiger.co.uk
Website: http://www.littletigerpress.com

Publishes: Fiction; *Markets:* Children's

Not accepting submissions as at May 2018. Check website for current status.

Accepts unsolicited MSS up to 750 words. If inside UK include SAE for response (no postage vouchers/coupons); if from outside the UK include email address for response (no material returned). See website for full guidelines. No submissions by email or on disc.

Little, Brown Book Group
Carmelite House
50 Victoria Embankment
LONDON
EC4Y 0DZ
Tel: +44 (0) 20 3122 7000
Email: info@littlebrown.co.uk
Website: http://www.littlebrown.co.uk

Publishes: Fiction; Nonfiction; *Areas:* Autobiography; Biography; Crime; Entertainment; Fantasy; Historical; How-to; Humour; Literature; Sci-Fi; Thrillers; *Markets:* Adult; Youth; *Treatments:* Literary; Popular

Accepts proposals for how-to books from authors who have first-hand experience of their subjects. See website for specific email address. For all other book types, accepts submissions via agents only.

Lonely Planet
240 Blackfriars Road
London
SE1 8NW
Tel: +44 (0) 20 3771 5100
Fax: +44 (0) 20 3771 5101
Email: recruitingcontributors@lonelyplanet.com
Website: http://www.lonelyplanet.com

Publishes: Nonfiction; *Areas:* Travel; *Markets:* Adult

Publishes international travel guides. Send query by email with speculative CV or resume.

Luath Press Ltd
543/2 Castlehill
The Royal Mile
Edinburgh
EH1 2ND
Tel: +44 (0) 131 225 4326
Email: sales@luath.co.uk
Website: http://www.luath.co.uk

Publishes: Fiction; Nonfiction; Poetry; *Areas:* Arts; Beauty and Fashion; Biography; Crime; Current Affairs; Drama; Historical; Leisure; Lifestyle; Nature; Photography; Politics; Sociology; Sport; Thrillers; Travel; *Markets:* Adult; Children's; Youth

Contact: G.H. MacDougall, Managing Editor

Publishes a range of books, usually with a Scottish connection. Check upcoming publishing schedule on website, and – if you think your book fits – send query with SAE, synopsis up to 250 words, manuscript or sample chapters, author bio, and any other relevant material. See website for full submission guidelines. Approaches by email will not be considered.

Luna Press Publishing
149/4 Morrison Street
Edinburgh
EH3 8AG
Email: lunapress@outlook.com
Website: http://www.lunapresspublishing.com

Publishes: Fiction; *Areas:* Fantasy; Sci-Fi; Short Stories; *Markets:* Academic; Adult; *Treatments:* Dark

Publishes Science Fiction, Fantasy, and Dark Fantasy (including their sub-genres). Will consider short stories, novelettes, novellas, novels, graphic novels, academic material.

See website for submission guidelines.

Note: closed to all but academic works as at May 2018 – check website for current status.

Lund Humphries Limited
Office 3, Book House
261A City Road
London
EC1V 1JX
Tel: +44 (0) 20 7440 7530
Email: lclark@lundhumphries.com
Website: http://www.lundhumphries.com

Publishes: Nonfiction; *Areas:* Architecture; Arts; Design; Historical; *Markets:* Adult

Contact: Lucy Clark

Publishes books on art, art history, and design. See website for guidelines on submitting a proposal.

Management Books 2000 Ltd
36 Western Road
Oxford
OX1 4LG
Tel: +44 (0) 1865 600738
Email: info@mb2000.com
Website: http://www.mb2000.com

Publishes: Nonfiction; *Areas:* Business; Finance; Lifestyle; Self-Help; *Markets:* Adult

Send outline of book, including why it was written, where it would be sold and read, etc. synopsis or detailed contents page, and a couple of sample chapters. Publishes books on management, business, finance, and related topics. Welcomes new ideas.

Mandrake of Oxford
PO Box 250
Oxford
OX1 1AP
Email: mandrake@mandrake.uk.net
Website: http://mandrake.uk.net

Publishes: Fiction; Nonfiction; *Areas:* Arts; Crime; Culture; Erotic; Health; Horror; Lifestyle; Mystery; Philosophy; Sci-Fi; Self-Help; Spiritual; *Markets:* Adult

Send query by post or by email. May also include synopsis. See website for full guidelines, and for examples of the kind of material published.

Mantra Lingua Ltd
Global House
303 Ballards Lane
London
N12 8NP
Tel: +44 (0) 20 8445 5123
Fax: +44 (0) 20 8446 7745
Email: info@mantralingua.com
Website: http://www.mantralingua.com

Publishes: Fiction; Nonfiction; *Areas:* Translations; *Markets:* Children's

Multilingual educational publishers of nonfiction and picture books for children up to 12 years. 1,400 words maximum (800 for children up to 7). All books are print products which are sound enabled, playing back audio narrations or music, etc. Send submissions by email. See website for more details.

Kevin Mayhew Publishers
Buxhall
Stowmarket
Suffolk
IP14 3BW
Tel: +44 (0) 845 3881634
Fax: +44 (0) 1449 737834
Email: submissions@kevinmayhew.com
Website: http://www.kevinmayhew.com

Publishes: Nonfiction; *Areas:* Music; Religious; Spiritual; *Markets:* Academic; Adult; Children's

Contact: Manuscript Submissions Department

Publishes books relating to Christianity and music, for adults, children, schools, etc. Send query by email only, with first three chapters, full contents list, sales pitch, summary, market info, bio, and details of any previous publications. See website for full details.

The Merlin Press

99b Wallis Road
London
E9 5LN
Tel: +44 (0) 20 8533 5800
Email: info@merlinpress.co.uk
Website: http://www.merlinpress.co.uk

Publishes: Nonfiction; *Areas:* Historical;
Philosophy; Politics; *Markets:* Adult

Publisher based in London specialising in
history, philosophy, and politics.

Metro Publications Ltd

Po Box 6336
London
N1 6PY
Tel: +44 (0) 20 8533 7777
Fax: +44 (0) 20 8533 7777
Email: info@metropublications.com
Website: https://metropublications.com

Publishes: Nonfiction; *Areas:* Architecture;
Arts; Leisure; Travel; *Markets:* Adult

Publisher of guide books on many aspects of
London life.

Michael Joseph

80 Strand
London
WC2R 0RL
Tel: +44 (0) 20 7139 3000
Website: https://www.
penguinrandomhouse.co.uk/publishers/
michael-joseph/

Publishes: Fiction; Nonfiction; *Areas:*
Autobiography; Cookery; Crime; Lifestyle;
Thrillers; Women's Interests; *Markets:*
Adult; *Treatments:* Commercial

Publishes women's fiction, crime, thrillers,
cookery, memoirs and lifestyle books.
Accepts submissions through literary agents
only.

Michael Terence Publishing (MTP)

Two Brewers House
2A Wellington Street
Thame
OX9 3BN

Tel: +44 (0) 20 3582 2002
Email: admin@mtp.agency
Website: https://www.mtp.agency

Publishes: Fiction; Nonfiction; *Markets:*
Adult

Contact: Keith Abbott

A dynamic publisher offering quick
responses to MSS and queries with a fast
time to market for accepted works.
Submissions always welcome. Please send
your first 3 chapters, synopsis and a brief bio
by email or via our website.

Mirror Books

22nd Floor
One Canada Square
Canary Wharf
London
E14 5AP
Tel: +44 (0) 20 7293 3700
Email: mirrorbooks@trinitymirror.com
Website: https://mirrorbooks.co.uk

Publishes: Fiction; Nonfiction; *Areas:*
Autobiography; Crime; Drama; *Markets:*
Adult

Contact: Jo Sollis

Accepts submissions from new and existing
authors for fiction and nonfiction. Interested
in real life, memoir, crime, passion, and
human drama. Approach using online form
on website or by post, including three draft
chapters, the genre of your book, and your
target market. See website for more details.

Monsoon Books Pte Ltd

No.1 Duke of Windsor Suite
Burrough Court
Burrough on the Hill
Leics
LE14 2QS
Email: customerservice@
monsoonbooks.com.sg
Website: http://www.monsoonbooks.com.sg

Publishes: Fiction; Nonfiction; *Areas:*
Autobiography; Biography; Crime; Erotic;
Fantasy; Historical; Horror; Military;
Politics; Romance; Short Stories; Thrillers;
Travel; *Markets:* Adult; Children's; Youth

A Singapore-registered award-winning independent publisher of English-language books and ebooks on Asia, with its editorial office in the UK. Welcomes submissions with Asian (particularly Southeast Asian) themes from agents direct, or from published and unpublished authors via online submission system via website.

Myriad Editions
New Internationalist Publications
The Old Music Hall
106–108 Cowley Rd
Oxford
OX4 1JE
Tel: +44 (0) 1865 403345
Email: submissions@myriadeditions.com
Website: http://www.myriadeditions.com

Publishes: Fiction; Nonfiction; Reference; *Areas:* Politics; Women's Interests; *Markets:* Adult; *Treatments:* Literary

Publishes atlases, works or graphical nonfiction, and fiction. For fiction, enter annual competition or monitor website for open submission weeks available throughout the year. Also considers fiction by referral. For nonfiction, particularly interested in political, literary, and/or feminist. Send query by email.

National Museum Wales
Cathays Park
Cardiff
CF10 3NP
Tel: +44 (0) 300 111 2 333
Email: post@museumwales.ac.uk
Website: http://www.museumwales.ac.uk

Publishes: Nonfiction; *Areas:* Archaeology; Arts; Historical; Nature; Sociology; *Markets:* Academic; Adult; Children's

Publishes books based on the collections and research of the museum, aimed at adults, children, and schools. Publishes in both Welsh and English.

Natural History Museum Publishing
The Natural History Museum
Cromwell Road
London

SW7 5BD
Tel: +44 (0) 20 7942 5336
Email: publishing@nhm.ac.uk
Website: http://www.nhm.ac.uk/business-services/publishing.html

Publishes: Nonfiction; *Areas:* Arts; Nature; Science; *Markets:* Adult; *Treatments:* Popular

Publishes accessible, fully illustrated books about the natural world.

New Playwrights' Network (NPN)
10 Station Road Industrial Estate
Colwall
Herefordshire
WR13 6RN
Tel: +44 (0) 1684 540154
Email: simon@cressrelles.co.uk
Website: http://www.cressrelles.co.uk

Publishes: Scripts; *Areas:* Drama; Theatre; *Markets:* Adult

Contact: Simon Smith

Established in the 1970s to promote scripts by new writers. Send scripts by email or by post.

Nick Hern Books Ltd
The Glasshouse
49a Goldhawk Road
London
W12 8QP
Tel: +44 (0) 20 8749 4953
Fax: +44 (0) 20 8735 0250
Email: submissions@nickhernbooks.co.uk
Website: http://www.nickhernbooks.co.uk

Publishes: Nonfiction; Scripts; *Areas:* Film; Theatre; *Markets:* Adult; Professional

Publishes plays attached to significant professional productions in major theatres only. No unsolicited scripts. Also publishes books by theatre practitioners and for theatre practitioners. No critical, analytical or historical studies. Send proposals by email or by post.

Northcote House Publishers Ltd

Horndon House
Horndon
Tavistock
PL19 9NQ
Tel: +44 (0) 1822 810066
Fax: +44 (0) 1822 810034
Email: admin@writersandtheirwork.co.uk
Website: http://www.northcotehouse.co.uk

Publishes: Nonfiction; *Areas:* Criticism; Literature; *Markets:* Adult

Contact: Brian Hulme

Send proposal outlining contents, with sample chapters. Seeks well-thought-out approaches presented with strong marketing arguments. See website for full guidelines and forms.

Oberon Books

521 Caledonian Road
London
N7 9RH
Tel: +44 (0) 20 7607 3637
Fax: +44 (0) 20 7607 3629
Email: george@oberonbooks.com
Website: http://www.oberonbooks.com

Publishes: Nonfiction; Scripts; *Areas:* Drama; Theatre; *Markets:* Adult; Professional

Contact: George Spender, Senior Editor

Publishes play texts, and books on dance and theatre. Specialises in translations of European classics and contemporary plays, though also publishes edited performance versions of classics including Shakespeare. Play texts are usually published in conjunction with a production. Play scripts may be submitted by post or by email. Book proposals for trade and professional titles should include summary, table of contents, estimate word count, and sample chapter.

Octopus Publishing Group Limited

Carmelite House
50 Victoria Embankment
London
EC4Y 0DZ
Tel: +44 (0) 20 3122 6400
Email: info@octopusbooks.co.uk
Website: https://www.octopusbooks.co.uk

Publishes: Nonfiction; Reference; *Areas:* Antiques; Architecture; Arts; Beauty and Fashion; Cookery; Crafts; Culture; Design; Film; Gardening; Health; Historical; Humour; Lifestyle; Music; Psychology; Spiritual; Sport; Travel; *Markets:* Adult; Children's

Publisher with wide range of imprints dealing with a variety of nonfiction and reference subjects. See website for specific email addresses dedicated to each individual imprint.

Oleander Press

16 Orchard Street
Cambridge
CB1 1JT
Email: editor@oleanderpress.com
Website: http://www.oleanderpress.com

Publishes: Fiction; Nonfiction; Poetry; Reference; *Areas:* Biography; Historical; Horror; Literature; Travel; *Markets:* Adult; Children's

Contact: Jon Gifford

Publishes biography, Cambridge / local, children's, classic horror, language and literature, fiction, games and pastimes, modern poets, Arabia, and Libya. Looking for nonfiction – in particular children's nonfiction. Send submissions by email or by post.

Omnibus Press

14/15 Berners Street
London
W1T 3LJ
Tel: +44 (0) 20 7612 7400
Email: info@omnibuspress.com
Website: http://www.omnibuspress.com

Publishes: Nonfiction; *Areas:* Biography; Music; *Markets:* Adult

Publisher of music books, including song sheets and rock and pop biographies.

Oneworld Publications

10 Bloomsbury Street
London
WC1B 3SR
Tel: +44 (0) 20 7307 8900
Email: submissions@oneworld-publications.com
Website: http://www.oneworld-publications.com

Publishes: Fiction; Nonfiction; *Areas:* Anthropology; Arts; Biography; Business; Current Affairs; Historical; Literature; Nature; Philosophy; Politics; Psychology; Religious; Science; Self-Help; Translations; *Markets:* Adult; *Treatments:* Commercial; Literary; Popular

Not accepting fiction submissions as at July 2016, but hopes this will change in the near future. Check website for current status.

Nonfiction authors must be academics and/or experts in their field. Approaches for fiction must provide a clear and concise synopsis, outlining the novel's main themes. See website for full submission guidelines, and forms for fiction and nonfiction, which may be submitted by email.

Ouen Press

Email: submissions@ouenpress.com
Website: http://www.ouenpress.com

Publishes: Fiction; Nonfiction; *Areas:* Biography; Short Stories; Travel; *Markets:* Adult; *Treatments:* Contemporary

Publishes contemporary fiction, travel literature, short story collections and biography, if edgy. No genre, children's books, poetry, single short stories, guide books or recipe books. Send query by email only with outline, brief resume of your writing experience, and first 4,000 words, all in the body of the email. Do not include a cover letter. No attachments, or submissions by post. If no reponse within 60 days, assume rejection.

Oversteps Books

6 Halwell House
South Pool

Nr Kingsbridge
Devon
TQ7 2RX
Email: alwynmarriage@overstepsbooks.com
Website: http://www.overstepsbooks.com

Publishes: Poetry; *Markets:* Adult

Poetry publisher. Send email with copies of six poems that have been published in magazines or won competitions, along with details of dates or issue numbers and email addresses of the editors. Include poems and information in the body of your email. No submissions by post.

Pandora Press

144 Hemingford Road
London
N1 1DE
Tel: +44 (0) 20 7607 0823
Fax: +44 (0) 20 7609 2776
Email: ro@riversoram.com
Website: http://www.riversoram.com

Publishes: Nonfiction; Reference; *Areas:* Arts; Biography; Current Affairs; Health; Media; Politics; Women's Interests; *Markets:* Adult

Feminist press publishing general nonfiction, including arts, biography, current affairs, media, reference, and sexual politics.

PaperBooks

9 The Fairway
Northwood
Middlesex
HA6 3DZ
Email: submissions@legend-paperbooks.co.uk
Website: http://www.legend-paperbooks.co.uk

Publishes: Nonfiction; *Areas:* Autobiography; Cookery; Politics; Sociology; Travel; *Markets:* Adult

Former fiction publisher now relaunched as a nonfiction publisher. Publishes a wide range of nonfiction including cookery, memoir, travel, political and social writing. Send submissions online only, via form on website.

Pavilion Books Group Limited

43 Great Ormond Street
London
WC1N 3HZ
Tel: +44 (0) 20 7462 1500
Email: info@pavilionbooks.com
Website: http://www.pavilionbooks.com

Publishes: Nonfiction; *Areas:* Arts; Beauty
and Fashion; Cookery; Crafts; Culture;
Design; Gardening; Historical; Humour;
Lifestyle; *Markets:* Adult; Children's

Send query with SAE, outline, and sample
chapter, by post. Due to high volume of
submissions, no acknowledgement of receipt
is provided.

Pavilion Publishing

Rayford House
School Road
Hove
East Sussex
BN3 5HX
Tel: +44 (0) 1273 434943
Fax: +44 (0) 1273 227308
Email: info@pavpub.com
Website: http://www.pavpub.com

Publishes: Nonfiction; Reference; *Areas:*
Health; Sociology; *Markets:* Professional

Publishes books and resources for public,
private and voluntary workers in the health,
social care, education and community safety
sectors. Welcomes submissions from both
new and established authors, and
organisations that are developing training
materials.

Pen & Sword Books Ltd

47 Church Street
Barnsley
South Yorkshire
S70 2AS
Tel: +44 (0) 1226 734222
Fax: +44 (0) 1226 734438
Email: editorialoffice@pen-and-sword.co.uk
Website: http://www.pen-and-sword.co.uk

Publishes: Nonfiction; *Areas:* Antiques;
Archaeology; Autobiography; Biography;
Crime; Gardening; Health; Historical;
Hobbies; Lifestyle; Military; Nature;
Sociology; Sport; *Markets:* Adult

Contact: Lisa Hooson

Publishes across a number of areas including
military history, naval and maritime history,
aviation, local history, family history,
transport, discovery and exploration,
collectables and antiques, nostalgia and true
crime. In 2017, launched a new lifestyle
imprint which publishes books on areas such
as health and diet, hobbies and sport,
gardening and wildlife and space. Submit
proposal using form on website.

Periscope

8 Southern Court
South Street
Reading
Berkshire
RG1 4QS
Email: info@periscopebooks.co.uk
Website: http://www.periscopebooks.co.uk

Publishes: Fiction; Nonfiction; *Areas:*
Autobiography; Biography; Crime; Current
Affairs; Historical; Politics; Science;
Sociology; Translations; *Markets:* Adult;
Treatments: Literary

Send query by email with bio, synopsis, and
two sample chapters.

Phoenix Yard Books

65 King's Cross Road
London
WC1X 9LW
Tel: +44 (0) 20 7239 4968
Email: submissions@phoenixyardbooks.com
Website: http://www.phoenixyardbooks.com

Publishes: Fiction; Nonfiction; Poetry;
Markets: Children's; Youth; *Treatments:*
Literary

Contact: Emma Langley

Publishes picture books, fiction, poetry,
nonfiction and illustration for children aged
around three to thirteen. Considers books of
all genres, but leans more towards the
literary and of the fiction spectrum.
Particularly interested in character-based
series, and fiction appealing to boys aged 6-
9. Does not concentrate on young adult
fiction, but will consider older fiction as part
of epic series, sagas or trilogies. Accepts

queries through literary agents, foreign publishers, and literary translators only.

Pimpernel Press

22 Marylands Road
London
W9 2DY
Tel: +44 (0) 20 7289 7100
Email: jo@pimpernelpress.com
Website: http://www.pimpernelpress.com

Publishes: Nonfiction; *Areas:* Arts; Design; Gardening; *Markets:* Adult

Publishes books on art, design, houses, and gardens. Send submissions by post.

The Policy Press

1-9 Old Park Hill
Bristol
BS2 8BB
Tel: +44 (0) 1179 545940
Email: pp-info@bristol.ac.uk
Website: http://www.policypress.co.uk

Publishes: Nonfiction; *Areas:* Politics; Sociology; *Markets:* Academic; Professional

Publishes monographs, texts and journals for scholars internationally; reports for policy makers, professionals and researchers; and practice guides for practitioners and user groups. Aims to publish the latest policy research for the whole policy studies community, including academics, policy makers, practitioners and students. Welcomes proposals for books, reports, guides or journals. Author guidelines available on website.

Policy Studies Institute (PSI)

University of Westminster
35 Marylebone Road
London
NW1 5LS
Tel: +44 (0) 20 7911 7500
Fax: +44 (0) 20 7911 7501
Email: psi-admin@psi.org.uk
Website: http://www.psi.org.uk

Publishes: Nonfiction; *Areas:* Culture; Finance; Nature; Politics; Sociology; *Markets:* Academic; Adult; Professional

Has informed public policy since 1931, through the provision, dissemination and promotion of evidence-based research. Currently focused on energy and climate change; resource use and the circular economy; mobility and transport; the role of communities and business in delivering a sustainable future; cities, innovation and sustainability transitions; public behaviours, attitudes and policy; and policy and research evaluation.

Polity Press

65 Bridge Street
Cambridge
CB2 1UR
Tel: +44 (0) 1223 324315
Fax: +44 (0) 1223 461385
Email: editorial@politybooks.com
Website: http://www.polity.co.uk

Publishes: Nonfiction; Reference; *Areas:* Anthropology; Archaeology; Business; Crime; Culture; Finance; Health; Historical; Literature; Media; Medicine; Nature; Philosophy; Politics; Psychology; Religious; Sociology; Women's Interests; *Markets:* Adult

Contact: Appropriate commissioning editor (see website)

Describes itself as one of the world's leading publishers of social sciences and humanities. Welcomes synopses and ideas for books. See website for appropriate commissioning editor to contact, and details of what your proposal should include.

Profile Books

3 Holford Yard
Bevin Way
London
WC1X 9HD
Tel: +44 (0) 20 7841 6300
Fax: +44 (0) 20 7833 3969
Email: info@profilebooks.com
Website: https://profilebooks.com

Publishes: Nonfiction; *Areas:* Biography; Business; Culture; Current Affairs; Finance; Historical; Humour; Politics; Psychology; Science; *Markets:* Adult

Closed to submissions as at April 2018.
Check website for current status.

Award-winning small publisher noted for
author-friendly relations. Published the
number-one Christmas bestseller in 2003.
Recommends approaches be through a
literary agent, but will accept direct queries
by email (up to 250 words) with first 10
pages, with SUBMISSION and the title of
your work in the subject line. See website for
full guidelines.

Psychology Press

2 Park Square
Milton Park
Abingdon
Oxford
OX14 4RN
Tel: +44 (0) 1235 400400
Fax: +44 (0) 1235 400401
Email: russell.george@tandf.co.uk
Website: https://www.routledge.com/
psychology

Publishes: Nonfiction; *Areas:* Psychology;
Markets: Academic; Professional

Contact: Russell George

Publishes academic and professional books
and journals on psychology. Send query by
email to appropriate editor (see website for
specific addresses).

Quarto Publishing Group UK

The Old Brewery
6 Blundell Street
London
N7 9BH
Tel: +44 (0) 20 7700 6700
Fax: +44 (0) 20 7700 8066
Email: info@quarto.com
Website: http://www.quarto.com

Publishes: Nonfiction; *Areas:* Arts; Beauty
and Fashion; Cookery; Crafts; Design;
Entertainment; Gardening; Health;
Historical; Hobbies; How-to; Lifestyle;
Sport; *Markets:* Adult; Children's

Publisher of illustrated nonfiction books for
adults and children.

Quiller Publishing Ltd

Wykey House
Wykey
Shrewsbury
Shropshire
SY4 1JA
Tel: +44 (0) 1939 261616
Email: info@quillerbooks.com
Website: http://www.quillerpublishing.com

Publishes: Nonfiction; Reference; *Areas:*
Architecture; Biography; Business; Cookery;
Gardening; Humour; Sport; Travel; *Markets:*
Adult

Contact: Andrew Johnston

Publishes books for all lovers of fishing,
shooting, equestrian and country pursuits.
Accepts unsolicited MSS from authors. Send
submissions as hard copy only, with email
address for reply or SAE if return of ms is
required. Proposals may be sent by email.
Suggestions may be made by post, email, or
phone.

Rivers Oram Press

144 Hemingford Road
London
N1 1DE
Tel: +44 (0) 20 7607 0823
Fax: +44 (0) 20 7609 2776
Email: ro@riversoram.com
Website: http://www.riversoram.com

Publishes: Nonfiction; *Areas:* Culture;
Current Affairs; Historical; Politics;
Sociology; Women's Interests; *Markets:*
Adult

Publisher of social and political sciences,
including sexual politics, gender studies,
social history, cultural studies, and current
affairs.

Robert Hale Publishers

The Crowood Press
The Stable Block
Crowood Lane
Ramsbury
Wiltshire
SN8 2HR
Tel: +44 (0) 1672 520320
Fax: +44 (0) 1672 520280

Email: enquiries@crowood.com
Website: http://www.crowood.com

Publishes: Fiction; Nonfiction; Reference; *Areas:* Arts; Biography; Crime; Design; Health; Historical; Leisure; Lifestyle; Nature; Romance; Spiritual; Sport; Westerns; *Markets:* Adult; *Treatments:* Contemporary

Contact: Editorial Department

See website for full submission guidelines. Currently only accepting fiction submissions for the publisher's Western series. Send query with synopsis and complete ms (fiction) or sample chapter (nonfiction).

Ruby Tuesday Books

6 Newlands Road
Tunbridge Wells
Kent
TN4 9AT
Tel: +44 (0) 1892 557767
Email: shan@rubytuesdaybooks.com
Website: http://www.rubytuesdaybooks.com

Publishes: Nonfiction; *Areas:* Nature; Science; Technology; *Markets:* Academic; Children's

Publisher of nonfiction books for children, including books for schools.

Ryland Peters & Small

20-21 Jockey's Fields
London
WC1R 4BW
Tel: +44 (0) 20 7025 2200
Fax: +44 (0) 20 7025 2201
Email: enquiries@rps.co.uk
Website: http://www.rylandpeters.com

Publishes: Nonfiction; *Areas:* Cookery; Crafts; Gardening; Health; Lifestyle; *Markets:* Adult

Contact: David Peters (Managing Director); Alison Starling (Publishing Director)

Publishes highly illustrated books on homes and gardens, crafts, food and drink, health and well-being, weddings, and mother and baby. Also has a vibrant gift and stationery list. Welcomes synopses and ideas, but no unsolicited MSS.

Samuel French Ltd

24-32 Stephenson Way
London
NW1 2HD
Tel: +44 (0) 20 7387 9373
Email: submissions@samuelfrench.co.uk
Website: http://www.samuelfrench-london.co.uk

Publishes: Scripts; *Areas:* Drama; *Markets:* Adult

Publishes plays only. Send submissions by email only, following the guidelines on the website.

Schofield & Sims

Unit 11, The Piano Works
113-117 Farringdon Road
London
EC1R 3BX
Tel: +44 (0) 1484 607080
Fax: +44 (0) 1484 606815
Email: editorial@schofieldandsims.co.uk
Website: http://www.schofieldandsims.co.uk

Publishes: Nonfiction; *Areas:* Historical; Literature; Science; *Markets:* Academic; Children's

Publishes educational material for children at nursery, infants, and primary school, covering such topics as phonics, reading, maths, science, etc. Send manuscripts and ideas for educational resources by post or by email.

Science Museum Group

Email: wendy.burford@sciencemuseum.ac.uk
Website: https://group.sciencemuseum.org.uk

Publishes: Nonfiction; *Areas:* Science; Technology; *Markets:* Academic; Adult

Contact: Wendy Burford, Publishing Manager

Publishes books on science, technology, and engineering. Also museum guides. Send query by email.

Search Press Ltd

Wellwood
North Farm Road
Tunbridge Wells
Kent
TN2 3DR
Tel: +44 (0) 1892 510850
Fax: +44 (0) 1892 515903
Email: katie@searchpress.com
Website: http://www.searchpress.com

Publishes: Nonfiction; *Areas:* Arts; Crafts;
Hobbies; How-to; Leisure; *Markets:* Adult;
Children's

Contact: Katie French, Commissioning
Editor

Publishes books on fine art, textiles, general
crafts and children's crafts. Send query by
post or by email with summary, synopsis,
samples, and author information. See website
for full guidelines.

Serpent's Tail

3 Holford Yard
Bevin Way
London
WC1X 9HD
Tel: +44 (0) 20 7841 6300
Email: info@profilebooks.com
Website: http://www.serpentstail.com

Publishes: Fiction; Nonfiction; *Areas:*
Autobiography; Biography; Crime; Culture;
Current Affairs; Music; Politics; *Markets:*
Adult

**Closed to submissions as at April 2018.
See website for current status.**

Prefers to receive approaches through a
literary agent, but will also accept queries by
email (up to 250 words) with sample text (10
pages or the first chapter only). See website
for full submission guidelines. No Romance,
Science Fiction, YA or children's books, or
translations.

Responds to all queries, but may take up to
three months. If no response after 6 weeks,
email to request an update.

Sheldrake Press

PO Box 74852
London
SW12 2DX
Tel: +44 (0) 20 8675 1767
Fax: +44 (0) 20 8675 7736
Email: enquiries@sheldrakepress.co.uk
Website: http://www.sheldrakepress.co.uk

Publishes: Nonfiction; *Areas:* Architecture;
Cookery; Historical; Humour; Music;
Travel; *Markets:* Adult

Contact: Simon Rigge, Publisher

Publisher of illustrated nonfiction titles
covering travel, history, cookery, music,
humour, and stationery. No fiction.

Simon & Schuster UK Limited

1st Floor
222 Gray's Inn Road
London
WC1X 8HB
Tel: +44 (0) 20 7316 1900
Fax: +44 (0) 20 7316 0332
Email: enquiries@simonandschuster.co.uk
Website: http://www.simonandschuster.co.uk

Publishes: Fiction; Nonfiction; *Areas:*
Autobiography; Biography; Business;
Cookery; Health; Historical; Humour;
Politics; Science; Spiritual; Sport; Travel;
Markets: Adult; Children's; Youth;
Treatments: Commercial; Literary

Publisher of commercial and literary fiction
and nonfiction for adults and children,
including children's fiction and picture
books. No unsolicited MSS.

Singing Dragon

73 Collier Street
London
N1 9BE
Tel: +44 (0) 20 7833 2307
Email: hello@singingdragon.com
Website: http://singingdragon.com

Publishes: Nonfiction; *Areas:* Health;
Leisure; Medicine; Self-Help; Spiritual;
Markets: Academic; Adult; Professional

Publishes authoritative books on
complementary and alternative health, Tai

Chi, Qigong and ancient wisdom traditions for health, wellbeing, and professional and personal development, for parents, professionals, academics and the general reader. Welcomes ideas for new books. Send query by email with CV and completed proposal form (available on website).

Siri Scientific Press
Arrow Mill (Office 41)
Queensway
Rochdale
OL11 2YW
Email: books@siriscientificpress.co.uk
Website: http://siriscientificpress.co.uk

Publishes: Nonfiction; Reference; *Areas:* Science; *Markets:* Academic; Adult

Contact: Dave Penney

Publishes short run science books for the academic market (but also accessible to the general public) which are of scientific value, but which might not have a large enough market to be attractive to more mainstream publishers. Send query by email to discuss ideas, or arrange face-to-face meeting.

Snowbooks
Chiltern House
Thame Road
Haddenham
HP17 8BY
Tel: +44 (0) 1865 600995
Email: emma@snowbooks.com
Website: http://www.snowbooks.com

Publishes: Fiction; Nonfiction; *Areas:* Crafts; Crime; Fantasy; Historical; Horror; Leisure; Sci-Fi; Sport; Thrillers; *Markets:* Adult

Contact: Emma Barnes, Managing Director

Open to submissions of horror, science fiction, and fantasy novels over 70,000 words. Named joint Small Publisher of the Year at the 2006 British book Trade Awards. Friendly attitude towards authors and unsolicited approaches. See website for guidelines. Approach via web submission system only – postal submissions will neither be read nor returned, even if sent through an agent. £2 submission fee.

Speechmark Publishing Limited
5 Thomas More Square
St Katharine Docks
London
E1W 1YW
Tel: +44 (0) 1869 244644
Email: Ben.Hulme-Cross@speechmark.net
Website: http://www.speechmark.net

Publishes: Nonfiction; *Areas:* Health; Psychology; *Markets:* Academic; Professional

Contact: Ben Hulme-Cross

Publishes books, games, and other resources for use by professionals and students in the fields of special needs; speech & language therapy; mental health; groupwork; elderly care; and early development. Welcomes unsolicited MSS, synopses, and ideas. Download Author Submission Form from website.

Springer-Verlag London Ltd
6th Floor
236 Gray's Inn Road
WC1X 8HL
Tel: +44 (0) 20 3192 2000
Website: http://www.springer.com

Publishes: Nonfiction; *Areas:* Medicine; Science; Technology; *Markets:* Academic; Professional

Publishes books professional and academic books on science, technology, and medicine, particularly computing, chemistry, biosciences, medicine, maths, and engineering. No school books, science fiction, or fiction. Also publishes a range of journals.

St Pauls Publishing
by Westminster Cathedral
Morpeth Terrace
Victoria
London
SW1P 1EP
Tel: +44 (0) 20 7828 5582
Email: editor@stpauls.org.uk
Website: http://www.stpauls.org.uk

Publishes: Nonfiction; *Areas:* Religious; *Markets:* Adult

Publisher of religious material, including books on theology, scripture, and catechetics, as well as prayer books and religious biographies.

Stonewood Press

Submissions
Stonewood Press
97 Benefield Road
Oundle
PE8 4EU
Email: stonewoodpress@gmail.com
Website: http://www.stonewoodpress.co.uk

Publishes: Fiction; Poetry; *Areas:* Short Stories; *Markets:* Adult; *Treatments:* Contemporary

Contact: Martin Parker

Independent publisher dedicated to promoting new writing, with an emphasis on contemporary short stories and poetry. Send query with biography, publishing history, and either one story and a brief outline of the others in the collection, or up to 10 poems and details of how many other poems are in the collection. Submit by post only. No children's books, creative nonfiction, novels, or drama.

Stripes Publishing

1 The Coda Centre
189 Munster Road
London
SW6 6AW
Tel: +44 (0) 20 7385 6333
Email: editorial@stripespublishing.co.uk
Website: http://www.stripespublishing.co.uk

Publishes: Fiction; *Markets:* Children's

Publishes fiction for children aged 6-12 and teendagers. No books for adults, educational books, poetry, graphic novels, comics, multimedia, scripts, screenplays, short stories, nonfiction or picture books for babies and toddlers. No longer accepting submissions by post. Send queries by email only, with one-page synopsis and 1,000-word extract.

Summersdale Publishers Ltd

46 West Street
Chichester
West Sussex
PO19 1RP
Tel: +44 (0) 1243 771107
Fax: +44 (0) 1243 786300
Email: submissions@summersdale.com
Website: http://www.summersdale.com

Publishes: Nonfiction; *Areas:* Crime; Health; Humour; Lifestyle; Travel; *Markets:* Adult

Contact: Submissions Team

Publisher of books on travel, humour, health, and general nonfiction. No fiction, poetry, children's books, or autobiography. Send query with cover letter, synopsis, and two sample chapters, by post or by email.

Sunflower Books

Commissioning Editor
Sunflower Books
PO Box 36160
London
SW7 3WS
Email: info@sunflowerbooks.co.uk
Website: http://www.sunflowerbooks.co.uk

Publishes: Nonfiction; *Areas:* Leisure; Travel; *Markets:* Adult

Publishes walking guides only. Authors are advised to submit a proposal (hard copy by post only) before starting work on a book, as the format must match that of existing titles. No proposals by email.

Sweet Cherry Publishing

Unit E Vulcan Business Complex
Vulcan Road
Leicester
LE5 3EB
Email: submissions@sweetcherrypublishing.com
Website: http://www.sweetcherrypublishing.com

Publishes: Fiction; *Markets:* Children's

Contact: Abdul Thadha

Publishes books for children of all ages. Looking for talented new authors of children's series and collections. Send submissions by email or by post with SASE. See website for full submission guidelines.

I.B. Tauris & Co. Ltd
6 Salem Road
London
W2 4BU
Tel: +44 (0) 20 7243 1225
Fax: +44 (0) 20 7243 1226
Email: ibagherzade@ibtauris.com
Website: http://www.ibtauris.com

Publishes: Nonfiction; *Areas:* Architecture; Arts; Biography; Culture; Current Affairs; Design; Film; Historical; Media; Politics; Religious; Travel; *Markets:* Academic; Adult

Contact: Iradj Bagherzade, Publisher & Editorial Director

Publishes academic books on the latest research, student texts, and general nonfiction. No fiction, poetry, or children's. Send query with proposal outlining book's purpose and market, with synopsis, table of contents, two sample chapters, and author CV. Send proposal by email directly to appropriate editor (see website for details).

Think Publishing
Capital House
25 Chapel Street
London
NW1 5DH
Tel: +44 (0) 20 3771 7200
Fax: +44 (0) 20 7723 1035
Email: ian@thinkpublishing.co.uk
Website: http://www.thinkpublishing.co.uk

Publishes: Nonfiction; *Areas:* Gardening; Nature; *Markets:* Adult

Contact: Ian Mcauliffe

Publishes nonfiction in partnership with clients that are seeking to use books as a medium for their brand to reach new audiences and potentially provide a commercial revenue stream. Query by email in first instance.

Thistle Publishing
London
Email: info@thistlepublishing.co.uk
Website: http://www.thistlepublishing.co.uk

Publishes: Fiction; Nonfiction; *Markets:* Adult

London-based publisher of quality fiction and nonfiction. Welcomes submissions. For nonfiction, send synopsis, author profile, sample chapter, and brief chapter summaries; for fiction, send synopsis and three sample chapters.

Tiny Owl
1 Repton House
London
SW1V 2LD

Email: info@tinyowl.co.uk
Website: http://tinyowl.co.uk

Publishes: Fiction; *Markets:* Children's

Publisher of books for children.

Titan Books
Titan House
144 Southwark Street
London
SE1 0UP
Tel: +44 (0) 20 7620 0200
Email: editorial@titanemail.com
Website: http://www.titanbooks.com

Publishes: Fiction; Nonfiction; *Areas:* Entertainment; Film; Humour; Sci-Fi; Short Stories; TV; *Markets:* Adult; Youth

Contact: Commissioning Editor

Publisher of graphic novels, particularly with film or television tie-ins, and books related to film and TV. No unsolicited fiction or books for children, but will consider ideas for licensed projects they have already contracted. Send query with synopsis by post only. No email submissions.

Top That! Publishing
Marine House
Tide Mill Way
Woodbridge
Suffolk

IP12 1AP
Tel: +44 (0) 1394 386651
Email: josh@topthatpublishing.com
Website: http://topthatpublishing.com

Publishes: Fiction; Nonfiction; Reference;
Areas: Cookery; Humour; *Markets:* Adult;
Children's

Contact: Josh Simpkin-Betts

Publishes Activity Books, Character Books,
Cookery Books, Felt Books, Fiction,
Humour, Magnetic Books, Novelty Books,
Phonics Books, Picture Storybooks, Pop-Up
Books, Press Out & Play, Reference Books,
and Sticker Books. Does not currently
publish "regular" children's or adults fiction.
See online book catalogue for the kinds of
books published. If suitable for the list, send
submissions by email (preferred), ideally
under 1MB, or by post (mss not returned).
See website for full guidelines. Responds
within 8 weeks if interested. No
simultaneous submissions.

Trentham Books Limited
Institute of Education
University of London
20 Bedford Way
London
WC1H 0AL
Tel: +44 (0) 20 7911 5563
Email: g.klein@ioe.ac.uk
Website: http://www.trentham-books.co.uk

Publishes: Nonfiction; *Areas:* Design;
Science; Sociology; Technology; Women's
Interests; *Markets:* Academic

Contact: Dr Gillian Klein

Publishes academic and professional books.
No fiction, biography, or poetry. No
unsolicited MSS, but accepts queries by
email. See website for full guidelines and for
downloadable book proposal guidelines,
which you should fill in as thoroughly as
possible before submitting it by email.

Troika Books
Well House
Green Lane
Ardleigh
Essex

CO7 7PD
Tel: +44 (0) 1206 233 333
Email: info@troikabooks.com
Website: http://www.troikabooks.com

Publishes: Fiction; Poetry; *Markets:*
Children's

Contact: Martin West

Publishes picture books, fiction, and poetry
for children.

Trotman & Co. Ltd
21d Charles Street
Bath
BA1 1HX
Tel: +44 (0) 01225 584950
Email: dellao@trotman.co.uk
Website: http://www.trotman.co.uk

Publishes: Nonfiction; Reference; *Markets:*
Academic; Professional

Publishes books on careers, employment and
training resources, higher education guides,
teacher support material, etc. Send query by
email with brief summary, details of target
audience, and list of chapters / sections.

TSO (The Stationery Office)
Mandela Way
London
SE1 5SS
Tel: +44 (0) 20 7394 4200
Email: customer.services@tso.co.uk
Website: http://www.tso.co.uk

Publishes: Nonfiction; Reference; *Areas:*
Business; Current Affairs; Medicine;
Markets: Professional

One of the largest publishers by volume in
the UK, publishing more than 9,000 titles a
year in print and digital formats.

Twenty First Century Publishers Ltd
Email: tfcp@btinternet.com
Website: http://www.
twentyfirstcenturypublishers.com

Publishes: Fiction; *Areas:* Crime; Finance;
Historical; Psychology; Thrillers; *Markets:*
Adult

Publishes general fiction written thoughtfully and with insight, plot driven original works, and knowledgeably written financial thrillers, in English, French, and German. Send submissions by email, with a brief 1-2 page synopsis or overview in the body of the email, and the full ms, or as many chapters as you wish, in a file attachment.

Two Rivers Press

7 Denmark Road
Reading
RG1 5PA
Email: tworiverspress@gmail.com
Website: http://tworiverspress.com

Publishes: Nonfiction; Poetry; *Areas:* Arts; Culture; *Markets:* Adult; *Treatments:* Literary

Publishes poetry, art, culture, and local interest books, focusing on Reading and the surrounding area.

Ulric Publishing

PO Box 55
Church Stretton
Shropshire
SY6 6WR
Tel: +44 (0) 1694 781354
Email: enquiries@ulricpublishing.com
Website: http://www.ulricpublishing.com

Publishes: Nonfiction; *Areas:* Military; Technology; Travel; *Markets:* Adult

Publishes military and motoring history. Sister company provides publishing services to companies and individuals. Send synopsis (not exceeding two A4 pages) by email.

Unbound Press

Unit 18, Waterside
44-48 Wharf Road
London
N1 7UX
Tel: +44 (0) 20 7821 6561
Email: support@unbound.com
Website: https://unbound.com

Publishes: Fiction; Nonfiction; *Markets:* Adult

Crowdfunding publisher. Submit manuscripts via form on website.

Unicorn Publishing Group

Charleston Studio
Meadow Business Centre
Ringmer, Lewes
East Sussex
BN8 5RW
Tel: +44 (0) 7836 633377
Email: ian@unicornpublishing.org
Website: http://www.unicornpublishing.org

Publishes: Nonfiction; Reference; *Areas:* Arts; Biography; Culture; Historical; Military; *Markets:* Adult

Contact: Ian Strathcarron (Publisher)

Publishes books on the visual arts and cultural history, military history, and biographies and general history. Approach by email or by post.

University of Exeter Press

Reed Hall
Streatham Drive
Exeter
EX4 4QR
Tel: +44 (0) 1392 263066
Fax: +44 (0) 1392 263064
Email: uep@exeter.ac.uk
Website: http://www.exeterpress.co.uk

Publishes: Nonfiction; Reference; *Areas:* Archaeology; Culture; Film; Historical; Literature; Philosophy; Religious; Sociology; *Markets:* Academic

Contact: Simon Baker

Publisher of academic books. See website for guidelines on submitting a proposal.

University of Wales Press

10 Columbus Walk
Brigantine Place
Cardiff
CF10 4UP
Tel: +44 (0) 29 2049 6899
Email: press@press.wales.ac.uk
Website: http://www.uwp.co.uk

Publishes: Nonfiction; *Areas:* Culture; Historical; Literature; Media; Nature;

Philosophy; Politics; Religious; Sociology; *Markets:* Academic

Make contact by phone or by email at an early stage – preferably before book is written.

Valley Press
Woodend
The Crescent
Scarborough
YO11 2PW
Email: jamie@valleypressuk.com
Website: http://www.valleypressuk.com

Publishes: Fiction; Nonfiction; Poetry; *Areas:* Autobiography; Short Stories; Travel; *Markets:* Adult

Accepts submissions of poetry, fiction, and nonfiction, accompanied by SASE and submission form, which can be acquired by purchasing a book from the website.

Verso
6 Meard Street
London
W1F 0EG
Tel: +44 (0) 20 7437 3546
Fax: +44 (0) 20 7734 0059
Email: submissions@verso.co.uk
Website: http://www.versobooks.com

Publishes: Fiction; Nonfiction; *Areas:* Anthropology; Architecture; Arts; Autobiography; Biography; Culture; Film; Finance; Historical; Media; Philosophy; Politics; Sociology; *Markets:* Academic; Adult

"Radical" publisher of the political left. Publishes mainly nonfiction and does not consider unsolicited fiction submissions. For nonfiction, send proposal up to 15 pages, including overview, contents / chapter outline, author background, market info, and your timetable, by email only. No unsolicited MSS, or hard copy submissions. If no response within two months, assume rejection.

Wooden Books
8A Market Place
Glastonbury

BA6 8LT
Email: info@woodenbooks.com
Website: http://www.woodenbooks.com

Publishes: Nonfiction; *Areas:* Historical; Science; Spiritual; *Markets:* Adult

Publishes illustration-heavy books on such topics as ancient sciences, magic, mathematics, etc. Prospective authors will need to provide high quality illustrations. Essential to query before commencing work. Send query by email or by post. See website for full details.

W.W. Norton & Company Ltd
75-76 Wells Street
London
W1T 3QT
Tel: +44 (0) 20 7323 1579
Fax: +44 (0) 20 7436 4553
Email: office@wwnorton.co.uk
Website: http://wwnorton.co.uk

Publishes: Fiction; Nonfiction; Poetry; *Areas:* Adventure; Anthropology; Archaeology; Architecture; Autobiography; Biography; Business; Crafts; Crime; Current Affairs; Design; Drama; Film; Finance; Health; Historical; Hobbies; Humour; Legal; Leisure; Lifestyle; Literature; Medicine; Music; Nature; Philosophy; Politics; Psychology; Religious; Science; Self-Help; Sociology; Sport; Technology; Travel; Women's Interests; *Markets:* Academic; Adult; Professional

UK branch of a US publisher. No editorial office in the UK – contact the main office in New York (see separate listing).

Walker Books Ltd
87 Vauxhall Walk
London
SE11 5HJ
Tel: +44 (0) 20 7793 0909
Fax: +44 (0) 20 7587 1123
Email: editorial@walker.co.uk
Website: http://www.walkerbooks.co.uk

Publishes: Fiction; Nonfiction; *Markets:* Children's

Publishes fiction and nonfiction for children, including illustrated books. Does not accept full-length fiction manuscripts, but accepts illustrated picture-book stories and/or artwork samples via post or email.

Ward Lock Educational Ltd

BIC Ling Kee House
1 Christopher Road
East Grinstead
West Sussex
RH19 3BT
Tel: +44 (0) 1342 318980
Fax: +44 (0) 1342 410980
Email: wle@lingkee.com
Website: http://wle.lingkee.com

Publishes: Nonfiction; *Areas:* Drama; Literature; Music; Science; *Markets:* Academic; Children's; Professional

Publishes school text books and books for teachers, covering a range of school subjects at Key Stages 1-4 as well as resource materials.

Weidenfeld & Nicolson

3rd Floor, Carmelite House
50 Victoria Embankment
London
EC4Y 0DZ
Website: http://www.wnblog.co.uk

Publishes: Fiction; Nonfiction; *Areas:* Autobiography; Biography; Cookery; Current Affairs; Finance; Historical; Military; Travel; *Markets:* Adult; *Treatments:* Literary

Publishers of high quality, prize-winning fiction and nonfiction across a range of categories, including autobiography, business, cookery, economics, history and more.

Welsh Academic Press

PO Box 733
Caerdydd
Cardiff
CF14 7ZY
Tel: +44 (0) 29 2021 8187
Email: post@welsh-academic-press.com
Website: http://www.welsh-academic-press.com

Publishes: Nonfiction; *Areas:* Historical; Politics; *Markets:* Academic

Publishes academic monographs, reference works, text books and popular scholarly titles in the fields of education, history, political studies, Scandinavian and Baltic studies, contemporary work and employment, and medieval Wales. Complete questionnaire available on website.

Wild Goose Publications

The Iona Community
21 Carlton Court
Glasgow
G5 9JP
Tel: +44 (0) 1414 297281
Email: admin@iona.org.uk
Website: http://www.ionabooks.com

Publishes: Nonfiction; Poetry; *Areas:* Health; Politics; Religious; Sociology; Spiritual; *Markets:* Adult

Publishes books on Holistic Spirituality, Social Justice, Political and Peace Issues, Healing – Innovative Approaches to worship, Song and Material for Meditation and Reflection. Send query with synopsis and two or three sample chapters. Not a poetry publisher, but will sometimes include poems in its books. Samples of suitable poems may be sent to be held on file in case they are suitable for use in a future book.

WIT Press

Ashurst Lodge
Ashurst
Southampton
SO40 7AA
Tel: +44 (0) 23 8029 3223
Fax: +44 (0) 23 8029 2853
Email: witpress@witpress.com
Website: http://www.witpress.com

Publishes: Nonfiction; *Areas:* Architecture; Nature; Science; Technology; *Markets:* Academic; Adult

Contact: Professor C.A. Brebbia

Publisher of scientific and technical material in such fields as architecture, environmental engineering and bioengineering. Target market is generally postgraduate and above.

No school or college texts, or material not of a scientific or technical nature. Potential authors should contact the Chairman by email in the first instance (see website for specific email address).

Wordsworth Editions

8B, East Street
Ware
Hertfordshire
SG12 9HJ
Tel: +44 (0) 1920 465167
Fax: +44 (0) 1920 462267
Email: enquiries@wordsworth-editions.com
Website: http://www.wordsworth-editions.com

Publishes: Fiction; *Areas:* Adventure; Biography; Gothic; Mystery; Romance; Sci-Fi; *Markets:* Adult; Family; Professional; Youth; *Treatments:* Mainstream; Niche; Popular

Contact: Managing Director, Helen Trayler

Publishes out-of-copyright titles. No submissions of new material.

Zed Books Ltd

The Foundry
17 Oval Way
London
SE11 5RR
Tel: +44 (0) 20 3752 5830
Email: editorial@zedbooks.net
Website: http://www.zedbooks.co.uk

Publishes: Nonfiction; *Areas:* Anthropology; Architecture; Autobiography; Biography; Business; Culture; Current Affairs; Finance; Health; Historical; Media; Medicine; Nature; Politics; Sociology; *Markets:* Academic; Adult

Publishes academic works and books for a general audience. See website for information on submitting a proposal.

ZigZag Education

Unit 3
Greenway Business Centre
Doncaster Road
Bristol
BS10 5PY
Tel: +44 (0) 1179 503199
Fax: +44 (0) 1179 591695
Email: support@ZigZagEducation.co.uk
Website: http://www.zigzageducation.co.uk

Publishes: Nonfiction; *Areas:* Arts; Business; Design; Drama; Finance; Health; Historical; Legal; Leisure; Media; Music; Philosophy; Politics; Psychology; Religious; Science; Sociology; Sport; Technology; Travel; *Markets:* Academic; Children's; Professional; Youth

Educational publisher publishing photocopiable and digital teaching resources for schools and colleges. Register on publisher's author support website if interested in writing or contributing to resources.

Canadian Publishers

For the most up-to-date listings of these and hundreds of other publishers, visit https://www.firstwriter.com/publishers

*To claim your **free** access to the site, please see the back of this book.*

Brick Books

PO Box 404, Toronto Station C
Toronto, ON M6J 3P5
Tel: +1 (519) 657-8579
Email: brick.books@sympatico.ca
Website: http://www.brickbooks.ca

Publishes: Poetry; *Markets:* Adult

Contact: Barry Dempster

Publishes poetry by Canadian citizens or landed immigrants only. Considers submissions between January 1 and April 30 only. Prospective authors are advised to familiarise themselves with other books from the publisher before sending a complete ms by post. No multiple submissions. Response in 3-4 months.

Coteau Books

2517 Victoria Ave
Regina, SK S4P 0T2
Tel: +1 (306) 777-0170
Fax: +1 (306) 522-5152
Email: coteau@coteaubooks.com
Website: http://www.coteaubooks.com

Publishes: Fiction; Nonfiction; Poetry; Scripts; *Areas:* Autobiography; Culture; Drama; Fantasy; Historical; Humour; Literature; Media; Mystery; Short Stories; Spiritual; Sport; Travel; Women's Interests; *Markets:* Adult; Children's; Youth; *Treatments:* Literary; Mainstream

A literary press publishing novels, short fiction collections, poetry, drama, and nonfiction both creative and regional. Publishes work by Canadian citizens or permanent residents only. No multiple or simultaneous submissions, or unsolicited mss. Send query by post or by email with sample up to 20 pages.

Dragon Moon Press

Email: dmpsubmissions@gmail.com
Website: http://dragonmoonpress.com

Publishes: Fiction; Nonfiction; *Areas:* Fantasy; Horror; How-to; Romance; Sci-Fi; *Markets:* Adult; Youth

Publishes novel-length fantasy, science fiction, and gentle horror for adults and the upper end of the YA spectrum. No middle grade or children's, or short story collections. Particularly interested in traditional fantasy (quests / dragons rather than werewolves and vampires). Also publishes how-to titles on how to write / sell writing. See website for submission guidelines.

ECW Press

665 Gerrard Street East
Toronto, ON M4M 1Y2
Tel: +1 (416) 694-3348
Fax: +1 (416) 698-9906

Email: info@ecwpress.com
Website: http://www.ecwpress.com

Publishes: Fiction; Nonfiction; Poetry;
Areas: Autobiography; Biography; Business;
Culture; Finance; Health; Historical;
Humour; Literature; Mystery; Politics;
Religious; Sport; Suspense; TV; Women's
Interests; *Markets:* Adult; *Treatments:*
Commercial; Literary; Mainstream

Publishes only Canadian-authored fiction
and poetry. Non-fiction proposals accepted
from anywhere. Proposal should be made by
post and include: cover letter; biog; sample
of the manuscript (for poetry, 10-15 pages,
for fiction and nonfiction, 15-25 pages);
synopsis.

Fairleigh Dickinson University (FDU) Press

842 Cambie Street
Vancouver, BC
V6B 2P6
Tel: +1 (604) 648-4476
Fax: +1 (604) 648-4489
Email: fdupress@fdu.edu
Website: http://www.fdupress.org

Publishes: Nonfiction; *Areas:* Arts;
Biography; Film; Historical; Literature;
Music; Philosophy; Religious; Sociology;
Theatre; Women's Interests; *Markets:*
Academic

Contact: James Gifford, Director

Publishes nonfiction books in a variety of
scholarly fields. Send query by post or via
form on website describing the book and the
contribution it would make to the field.

Fernwood Publishing

32 Oceanvista Lane, Site 2A
Box 5
Black Point
NS B0J 1B0
Tel: +1 (902) 857-1388
Fax: +1 (902) 857-1328
Email: editorial@fernpub.ca
Website: http://www.fernwoodbooks.ca

Publishes: Nonfiction; Reference; *Areas:*
Anthropology; Archaeology; Business;
Criticism; Culture; Current Affairs; Finance;

Health; Historical; Literature; Medicine;
Nature; Philosophy; Politics; Sociology;
Sport; Translations; Women's Interests;
Markets: Academic; Adult

Contact: Errol Sharpe (Publisher); Wayne
Antony (Editor)

Social justice publisher. Publishes both for a
general and academic audience, including
reference books, for use in college and
university courses. Concentrates on social
sciences, humanities, gender studies, literary
criticism, politics, and cultural studies. Send
4-5 page proposal including tentative table of
contents; the theoretical framework of the
book, and how it relates to the subject
matter; market analysis; level (college /
university); and estimated length and
completion date. See website for full details.

Fitzhenry & Whiteside Ltd

195 Allstate Parkway
Markham, Ontario L3R 4T8
Tel: +1 (905) 477-9700
Fax: +1 (800) 260-9777
Email: godwit@fitzhenry.ca
Website: http://www.fitzhenry.ca

Publishes: Fiction; Nonfiction; *Markets:*
Adult; Children's; Youth

Contact: Sharon Fitzhenry (Adult); Cheryl
Chen (Children's)

Publishes fiction and nonfiction for adults,
children, and young adults. See website for
submission guidelines.

Formac Publishing Company Limited

5502 Atlantic Street
Halifax, Nova Scotia
B3H 1G4
Tel: +1 (902) 421-7022 ext. 28
Email: formaceditorial@formac.ca
Website: http://www.formac.ca

Publishes: Fiction; Nonfiction; *Areas:*
Biography; Cookery; Historical; Nature;
Politics; Travel; *Markets:* Adult; Children's

Contact: Heather Thomas

Publishes adult nonfiction in the areas of
Maritime regional, travel guides, history,

biography, natural history, Maritime Provinces politics and regional cookbooks and cookbooks with a fresh/healthy focus. Also classic Maritime fiction reprints. Also publishes fiction for children. Send query with outline, sample, and author CV. See website for full guidelines. Response only if interested.

Harlequin Dare

Email: CustomerService@Harlequin.com
Website: https://www.harlequin.com

Publishes: Fiction; *Areas:* Romance; Women's Interests; *Markets:* Adult; *Treatments:* Contemporary

Contact: Kathleen Scheibling

Imprint which aims to push the boundaries of sexual explicitness while keeping the focus on the developing romantic relationship. Submit novels up to 50,000 words via online submission system available on website.

Heritage House

103 – 1075 Pendergast Street
Victoria, BC, V8V 0A1
Email: heritage@heritagehouse.ca
Website: http://www.heritagehouse.ca

Publishes: Nonfiction; *Areas:* Adventure; Anthropology; Arts; Biography; Business; Crime; Culture; Historical; Humour; Military; Nature; Politics; Sport; Women's Interests; *Markets:* Adult; *Treatments:* Contemporary

Publishes books on the heritage and historical and contemporary culture of Canada. Submit complete ms or proposal by post only. See website for full guidelines.

Insomniac Press

520 Princess Avenue
London, ON N6B 2B8
Email: mike@insomniacpress.com
Website: http://www.insomniacpress.com

Publishes: Fiction; Nonfiction; Poetry; Reference; *Areas:* Business; Crime; Criticism; Culture; Finance; Gardening; Health; Humour; Legal; Lifestyle; Literature; Medicine; Music; Mystery; Politics;

Religious; Self-Help; Short Stories; Spiritual; Sport; Suspense; Travel; *Markets:* Adult; *Treatments:* Commercial; Experimental; Literary; Mainstream

Contact: Mike O'Connor

Particularly interested in creative nonfiction on business / personal finance; gay and lesbian studies; black canadian studies and others. No science fiction, cookbooks, romance, or children's books. Poetry list is booked up for the foreseeable future. Send query by email or post in first instance. Approaches by authors who have had work published elsewhere (e.g. short stories in magazines) will receive closer attention.

LexisNexis Canada

111 Gordon Baker Road, Suite 900
Toronto, ON, M2H 3R1
Tel: +1 (800) 668-6481
Email: productdevelopment@lexisnexis.ca
Website: https://www.lexisnexis.ca

Publishes: Nonfiction; Reference; *Areas:* Business; Finance; Legal; *Markets:* Professional

Publishes books for the professional legal, business, and accountancy markets. Send query by email. See website for full guidelines on submitting a proposal.

TouchWood Editions

103 – 1075 Pendergast Street
Victoria, BC V8V 0A1
Tel: +1 (250) 360-0829
Fax: +1 (250) 386-0829
Email: edit@touchwoodeditions.com
Website: http://www.touchwoodeditions.com

Publishes: Fiction; Nonfiction; *Areas:* Arts; Biography; Cookery; Culture; Gardening; Historical; Mystery; Nature; Suspense; Travel; *Markets:* Adult

Accepts submissions as hard copy by post and digitally by email. Publishes Canadian authors only. See website for full guidelines.

Vehicule Press

P.O.B. 42094 BP Roy
Montreal, Quebec H2W 2T3

Tel: +1 (514) 844-6073
Fax: +1 (514) 844-7543
Email: admin@vehiculepress.com
Website: http://www.vehiculepress.com

Publishes: Fiction; Nonfiction; Poetry;
Areas: Historical; Music; Religious;
Sociology; Translations; *Markets:* Adult

Publishes poetry, literary novels, novellas,
short story collections, and translations,
primarily from Canadian authors. Not
accepting poetry manuscripts as at April
2017. See website for current status, and full
fiction submission guidelines.

Irish Publishers

For the most up-to-date listings of these and hundreds of other publishers, visit https://www.firstwriter.com/publishers

*To claim your **free** access to the site, please see the back of this book.*

CJ Fallon
Ground Floor – Block B
Liffey Valley Office Campus
Dublin 22
Tel: 01 6166400
Fax: 01 6166499
Email: editorial@cjfallon.ie
Website: http://www.cjfallon.ie

Publishes: Nonfiction; Reference; Business; Finance; Historical; Literature; Music; Religious; Science; Technology; *Markets:* Academic; Children's; Professional; Youth

Publishes teaching resources written by teachers, for teachers. Send proposal to the Managing Editor in the first instance.

Cork University Press
Tel: +353 (0) 21 490 2980
Email: corkuniversitypress@ucc.ie
Website: http://www.
corkuniversitypress.com

Publishes: Nonfiction; *Areas:* Architecture; Arts; Cookery; Culture; Current Affairs; Drama; Film; Historical; Legal; Literature; Music; Philosophy; Politics; Self-Help; Sociology; Sport; Travel; Women's Interests; *Markets:* Academic

Publishes distinctive and distinguished scholarship in the broad field of Irish Cultural Studies.

The Educational Company of Ireland
Ballymount Road
Walkinstown
Dublin 12
Email: amolumby@edco.ie
Website: http://www.edco.ie

Publishes: Nonfiction; *Markets:* Academic; Adult; Children's; Professional

Contact: Aoibheann Molumby

Publishes textbooks and ancillary educational materials for the Primary and Post-Primary markets. Submit proposals by post or by email. See website for full guidelines.

Four Courts Press
7 Malpas Street
Dublin
D08 YD81
Tel: 353-1-453-4668
Email: info@fourcourtspress.ie
Website: http://www.fourcourtspress.ie

Publishes: Nonfiction; *Areas:* Archaeology; Architecture; Arts; Criticism; Historical; Legal; Literature; Philosophy; Religious; *Markets:* Academic

Academic press, originally focusing on theology, now also publishing books on history, art, literature, and law. Send query by email in first instance.

The Gallery Press
Loughcrew
Oldcastle
County Meath
Tel: +353 (0) 49 8541779
Fax: +353 (0) 49 8541779
Email: gallery@indigo.ie
Website: http://www.gallerypress.com

Publishes: Fiction; Nonfiction; Poetry;
Scripts; *Areas:* Theatre; *Markets:* Adult;
Treatments: Literary

Contact: Peter Fallon

Publishes poetry, drama, and prose by
Ireland's leading contemporary writers. See
website for submission guidelines. No
novels, historical romances, autobiographies,
biographies, children's books, etc. No
submissions by fax or email. Accepts work
from Irish or Irish-based authors only.

Gill Books
Hume Avenue
Park West
Dublin
D12 YV96
Tel: +353 (01) 500 9500
Email: dmarsh@gill.ie
Website: http://www.gillmacmillanbooks.ie

Publishes: Fiction; Nonfiction; Reference;
Areas: Biography; Cookery; Crafts; Crime;
Current Affairs; Historical; Hobbies;
Humour; Leisure; Lifestyle; Nature;
Spiritual; Sport; *Markets:* Adult; Children's

Contact: Deborah Marsh, Editorial
Administrator

Publishes adult nonfiction and children's
fiction and nonfiction. No adult fiction,
poetry, short stories or plays. Prefers
proposals by email, but will also accept
proposals by post. See website for full
submission guidelines.

The Lilliput Press
62-63 Sitric Road
Arbour Hill
Dublin 7
Tel: +353 (01) 671 16 47
Fax: +353 (01) 671 12 33

Email: editorial@lilliputpress.ie
Website: http://www.lilliputpress.ie

Publishes: Fiction; Nonfiction; Poetry;
Reference; Scripts; *Areas:* Architecture;
Arts; Autobiography; Biography; Business;
Cookery; Criticism; Culture; Current Affairs;
Drama; Historical; Literature; Music;
Nature; Philosophy; Photography; Politics;
Sociology; Sport; Travel; *Markets:* Adult;
Treatments: Literary; Popular

Contact: Submissions Editor

Publishes books broadly focused on Irish
themes. Send query by post with one-page
synopsis and complete ms or three sample
chapters. Include SASE if response required.
No submissions by email. See website for
full guidelines.

The O'Brien Press
12 Terenure Road East
Rathgar
Dublin 6
D06 HD27
Tel: +353-1-4923333
Fax: +353-1-4922777
Email: books@obrien.ie
Website: http://www.obrien.ie

Publishes: Fiction; Nonfiction; Reference;
Areas: Architecture; Arts; Autobiography;
Biography; Business; Cookery; Crafts;
Crime; Drama; Historical; Humour;
Lifestyle; Literature; Music; Nature;
Photography; Politics; Religious; Sport;
Travel; *Markets:* Adult; Children's; Youth

Mainly publishes children's fiction,
children's nonfiction and adult nonfiction.
Generally doesn't publish poetry, academic
works or adult fiction. Send synopsis and
two or three sample chapters. If fewer than
1,000 words, send complete ms. See website
for full guidelines.

Onstream Publications Ltd
Currabaha
Cloghroe
Blarney
Co. Cork
Tel: +353 21 4385798
Email: info@onstream.ie
Website: http://www.onstream.ie

Publishes: Fiction; Nonfiction; *Areas:* Cookery; Historical; Travel; *Markets:* Academic; Adult

Publisher of mainly nonfiction, although some fiction published. Also offers services to authors.

Somerville Press

Dromore
Bantry
Co. Cork
Tel: 353 (0) 28 32873
Fax: 353 (0) 28 328
Email: somervillepress@eircom.net
Website: http://www.somervillepress.com

Publishes: Fiction; Nonfiction; *Markets:* Adult

Publishes fiction and nonfiction, mainly of Irish interest.

Thomson Reuters Round Hall

13 Exchange Place
International Financial Services Centre
Dublin 1
Tel: 01 602 4832
Email: alana.gerring@thomsonreuters.com
Website: http://www.roundhall.ie

Publishes: Nonfiction; Reference; *Areas:* Legal; *Markets:* Academic; Professional

Contact: Alana Gerring, Publishing Manager

Publishes information on Irish law in the form of books, journals, periodicals, looseleaf services, CD-ROMs and online services. See website for submission guidelines.

University College Dublin (UCD) Press

UCD Humanities Institute Room H103
Belfield
Dublin 4

Tel: + 353 1 4716 4680
Email: ucdpress@ucd.ie
Website: http://www.ucdpress.ie

Publishes: Nonfiction; *Areas:* Criticism; Drama; Historical; Literature; Military; Music; Nature; Politics; Religious; Science; Sociology; *Markets:* Academic

Contact: Noelle Moran, Executive Editor

Peer-reviewed publisher of contemporary scholarship with a reputation for publications relating to historic and contemporary Ireland. Send synopsis with market description, a paragraph about the career and publications of the author(s), and two specimen chapters in hard copy (not email attachments). Will accept proposals up to 8 pages by email, but unlikely to consider a proposal without specimen material. See website for full guidelines.

Australian Publishers

For the most up-to-date listings of these and hundreds of other publishers, visit https://www.firstwriter.com/publishers

*To claim your **free** access to the site, please see the back of this book.*

Allen & Unwin

SYDNEY:
83 Alexander St
Crows Nest, NSW 2065

MELBOURNE:
406 Albert Street
East Melbourne, Vic 3002
Tel: +61 (0) 2 8425 0100
Fax: +61 (0) 2 9906 2218
Email: fridaypitch@allenandunwin.com
Website: https://www.allenandunwin.com

Publishes: Fiction; Nonfiction; Poetry;
Scripts; *Areas:* Arts; Autobiography;
Biography; Business; Crime; Culture;
Current Affairs; Fantasy; Finance; Health;
Historical; Humour; Lifestyle; Literature;
Media; Military; Music; Mystery; Nature;
Philosophy; Politics; Psychology; Religious;
Science; Self-Help; Sociology; Sport;
Travel; *Markets:* Academic; Children's;
Professional; Youth; *Treatments:*
Commercial; Literary; Popular

Publisher with offices in Australia, New
Zealand, and the UK. Accepts queries by
email. See website for detailed instructions.

Maverick Musicals & Plays

89 Bergann Road
Witta
QLD 4552
Tel: +61 (0) 7 5494 4007

Email: gail@maverickmusicals.com
Website: https://www.maverickmusicals.com

Publishes: Scripts; *Areas:* Drama; Music;
Markets: Children's; *Treatments:*
Contemporary

Publishes original high school musicals,
primary school musicals, and one act plays
and two act plays for schools and drama
groups.

Melbourne University Publishing Ltd

Level 1, 715 Swanston Street
Carlton
Victoria
3053
Tel: +61 (0) 3 9035 3333
Fax: +61 (0) 3 9342 0399
Email: mup-submissions@unimelb.edu.au
Website: https://www.mup.com.au

Publishes: Nonfiction; *Areas:* Arts;
Autobiography; Biography; Crime; Design;
Historical; Lifestyle; Literature; Politics;
Science; Sociology; Sport; *Markets:*
Academic; Adult

Publishes nonfiction only. No fiction,
children's literature, or poetry. Send
submissions by email only. See website for
full submission guidelines.

Playlab

PO Box 3701
South Brisbane
BC, 4101
Tel: +61 (0) 7 3220 2763
Fax: +61 (0) 7 3220 2764
Email: info@playlab.org.au
Website: http://www.playlab.org.au

Publishes: Scripts; *Markets:* Adult

Dedicated to the development and promotion
of new Australian playwriting.

SisterShip Press Pty Ltd

Email: sistershippress@gmail.com
Website: https://sistershippress.com

Publishes: Fiction; Nonfiction; Poetry;
Reference; *Areas:* Adventure;
Autobiography; Biography; Business;
Cookery; Crafts; Crime; Entertainment;
Fantasy; Film; Health; Hobbies; How-to;
Humour; Leisure; Lifestyle; Mystery;
Nature; Psychology; Romance; Science;
Self-Help; Short Stories; Technology;
Thrillers; Women's Interests; *Markets:*
Academic; Adult; Children's; Family;
Professional; Youth; *Treatments:*
Contemporary; In-depth; Light; Literary;
Mainstream; Niche; Popular; Positive;
Progressive; Satirical; Traditional

Contact: Jackie Parry and Shelley Wright

We are passionate about writing. We are
excited about books.

We (initially) are here for women; women
with finished manuscripts. A nautical theme
is our favourite but we are keen to read any
adventure/travel/inspirational story – fiction
or nonfiction. Technical books are also
invited. We have a team with vast experience
in all aspects of boating – professionally and
recreationally.

Read our FAQ on our website.

Publishers Subject Index

This section lists publishers by their subject matter, with directions to the section of the book where the full listing can be found.

You can create your own customised lists of publishers using different combinations of these subject areas, plus over a dozen other criteria, instantly online at https://www.firstwriter.com.

To claim your **free** access to the site, please see the back of this book.

Adventure
Birlinn Ltd (*UK*)
Carina UK (*UK*)
Cynren Press (*US*)
Dreamriver Press (*US*)
FalconGuides (*US*)
4RV Publishing (*US*)
Goosebottom Books LLC (*US*)
HarperCollins (*US*)
Heritage House (*Can*)
IDW Publishing (*US*)
JourneyForth (*US*)
Mountaineers Books (*US*)
Red Empress Publishing (*US*)
SisterShip Press Pty Ltd (*Aus*)
Sunstone Press (*US*)
Tumblehome Learning, Inc. (*US*)
W.W. Norton & Company Ltd (*UK*)
WaterBrook & Multnomah (*US*)
Wordsworth Editions (*UK*)
Anthropology
Abdo Publishing Co (*US*)
Algora Publishing (*US*)
Bucknell University Press (*US*)
Dreamriver Press (*US*)
Dunedin Academic Press Ltd (*UK*)
Eagle's View Publishing (*US*)
Elm Books (*US*)
Fernwood Publishing (*Can*)
Fordham University Press (*US*)
Garnet Publishing (*UK*)
Heritage House (*Can*)
Mage Publishers (*US*)
Oneworld Publications (*UK*)

Polity Press (*UK*)
Syracuse University Press (*US*)
Temple University Press (*US*)
Truman State University Press (*US*)
The University of Michigan Press (*US*)
University of Washington Press (*US*)
Verso (*UK*)
W.W. Norton & Company Ltd (*UK*)
Zed Books Ltd (*UK*)
Antiques
ACC Art Books Ltd (*UK*)
Astragal Press (*US*)
Krause Publications (*US*)
Oak Knoll Press (*US*)
Octopus Publishing Group Limited (*UK*)
Pelican Publishing Company (*US*)
Pen & Sword Books Ltd (*UK*)
Archaeology
Algora Publishing (*US*)
Amberley Publishing (*UK*)
Ashmolean Museum Publications (*UK*)
Boydell & Brewer Ltd (*UK*)
Council for British Archaeology (CBA) Publishing (*UK*)
Eagle's View Publishing (*US*)
Edinburgh University Press (*UK*)
Fernwood Publishing (*Can*)
Fonthill Media LLC (*US*)
Fonthill Media Ltd (*UK*)
Four Courts Press (*Ire*)
Garnet Publishing (*UK*)
LSU Press (*US*)
Mage Publishers (*US*)
National Museum Wales (*UK*)

Pen & Sword Books Ltd (*UK*)
Polity Press (*UK*)
Sunstone Press (*US*)
Truman State University Press (*US*)
University of Exeter Press (*UK*)
The University of Michigan Press (*US*)
W.W. Norton & Company Ltd (*UK*)

Architecture
ACC Art Books Ltd (*UK*)
ASCE Press (*US*)
Ashgate Publishing Limited (*UK*)
Birlinn Ltd (*UK*)
Black Dog Publishing London UK (*UK*)
Black Dome Press (*US*)
Bucknell University Press (*US*)
Carlton Publishing Group (*UK*)
Chronicle Books LLC (*US*)
Cork University Press (*Ire*)
Countryside Books (*UK*)
David R. Godine, Publisher (*US*)
Dovecote Press (*UK*)
Edinburgh University Press (*UK*)
Floris Books (*UK*)
Fordham University Press (*US*)
Four Courts Press (*Ire*)
Garnet Publishing (*UK*)
George Braziller, Inc. (*US*)
Gibbs Smith, Publisher (*US*)
Gingko Library (*UK*)
Guild of Master Craftsman (GMC) Publications
Ltd (*UK*)
Laurence King Publishing Ltd (*UK*)
The Lilliput Press (*Ire*)
Lund Humphries Limited (*UK*)
Mage Publishers (*US*)
Metro Publications Ltd (*UK*)
The O'Brien Press (*Ire*)
Octopus Publishing Group Limited (*UK*)
Pelican Publishing Company (*US*)
Princeton Architectural Press (*US*)
Quiller Publishing Ltd (*UK*)
Santa Monica Press (*US*)
Sheldrake Press (*UK*)
Sunstone Press (*US*)
I.B. Tauris & Co. Ltd (*UK*)
Truman State University Press (*US*)
University of Pittsburgh Press (*US*)
Verso (*UK*)
W.W. Norton & Company Ltd (*UK*)
WIT Press (*UK*)
Zed Books Ltd (*UK*)

Arts
Abdo Publishing Co (*US*)
ACC Art Books Ltd (*UK*)
Allen & Unwin (*Aus*)
Alma Classics (*UK*)
Ashgate Publishing Limited (*UK*)
Ashmolean Museum Publications (*UK*)
Aurora Metro Press (*UK*)
Beacon Press (*US*)
Birlinn Ltd (*UK*)
Black Dog Publishing London UK (*UK*)
Black Dome Press (*US*)

Bodleian Library Publishing (*UK*)
Boydell & Brewer Ltd (*UK*)
Bucknell University Press (*US*)
Carlton Publishing Group (*UK*)
Chronicle Books LLC (*US*)
Clarkson Potter (*US*)
Co & Bear Productions (*UK*)
Cork University Press (*Ire*)
The Crown Publishing Group (*US*)
David R. Godine, Publisher (*US*)
Dreamriver Press (*US*)
Duckworth Publishers (*UK*)
Enitharmon Press (*UK*)
Fairleigh Dickinson University (FDU) Press
(*Can*)
Fantagraphics (*US*)
Finney Company (*US*)
Floris Books (*UK*)
Fordham University Press (*US*)
Four Courts Press (*Ire*)
Garnet Publishing (*UK*)
George Braziller, Inc. (*US*)
Gibbs Smith, Publisher (*US*)
Gibson Square Books Ltd (*UK*)
Gingko Library (*UK*)
Gomer Press (*UK*)
Greenhaven Publishing (*US*)
Greystones Press (*UK*)
Guild of Master Craftsman (GMC) Publications
Ltd (*UK*)
Hal Leonard Performing Arts Publishing Group
(*US*)
Haus Publishing (*UK*)
Hendrick-Long Publishing Co. (*US*)
Heritage House (*Can*)
Heyday Books (*US*)
Hohm Press (*US*)
Interlink Publishing Group, Inc. (*US*)
Italica Press (*US*)
Jacaranda Books Art Music Ltd (*UK*)
Kaya Press (*US*)
Kent State University Press (*US*)
Laurence King Publishing Ltd (*UK*)
The Lilliput Press (*Ire*)
Luath Press Ltd (*UK*)
Lund Humphries Limited (*UK*)
Mage Publishers (*US*)
Mandrake of Oxford (*UK*)
McGraw-Hill Education (*US*)
McSweeney's Publishing (*US*)
Melbourne University Publishing Ltd (*Aus*)
Metro Publications Ltd (*UK*)
National Museum Wales (*UK*)
Natural History Museum Publishing (*UK*)
The O'Brien Press (*Ire*)
Octopus Publishing Group Limited (*UK*)
Oneworld Publications (*UK*)
Pandora Press (*UK*)
Pavilion Books Group Limited (*UK*)
Pelican Publishing Company (*US*)
Penguin Random House (*US*)
Pimpernel Press (*UK*)
Quarto Publishing Group UK (*UK*)

Red Wheel (*US*)
Robert Hale Publishers (*UK*)
Santa Monica Press (*US*)
Search Press Ltd (*UK*)
Southern Illinois University Press (*US*)
Sterling Publishing Co. Inc. (*US*)
Sunstone Press (*US*)
I.B. Tauris & Co. Ltd (*UK*)
Temple University Press (*US*)
TouchWood Editions (*Can*)
Truman State University Press (*US*)
Two Rivers Press (*UK*)
Unicorn Publishing Group (*UK*)
The University of Michigan Press (*US*)
University of Washington Press (*US*)
Verso (*UK*)
Walch Education (*US*)
WhiteFire Publishing (*US*)
ZigZag Education (*UK*)
Autobiography
Academy Chicago (*US*)
Allen & Unwin (*Aus*)
Allison & Busby Ltd (*UK*)
Alma Classics (*UK*)
Asabi Publishing (*US*)
Bancroft Press (*US*)
Beacon Press (*US*)
BearManor Media (*US*)
BenBella Books (*US*)
Birlinn Ltd (*UK*)
Black & White Publishing Ltd (*UK*)
Blink Publishing (*UK*)
Canongate Books (*UK*)
Chicago Review Press (*US*)
Coteau Books (*Can*)
The Crown Publishing Group (*US*)
Cynren Press (*US*)
DB Publishing (*UK*)
Dream of Things (*US*)
Dreamriver Press (*US*)
Dref Wen (*UK*)
Duckworth Publishers (*UK*)
ECW Press (*Can*)
Familius (*US*)
Fantagraphics (*US*)
Garnet Publishing (*UK*)
Gomer Press (*UK*)
Granta Books (*UK*)
Halban Publishers (*UK*)
HarperCollins (*US*)
HarperCollins Publishers Ltd (*UK*)
Headline Publishing Group (*UK*)
Health Communications, Inc. (*US*)
Hesperus Press Limited (*UK*)
Hodder & Stoughton Ltd (*UK*)
Honno Welsh Women's Press (*UK*)
Humanix Books (*US*)
Infinite Ideas (*UK*)
Jacaranda Books Art Music Ltd (*UK*)
Jolly Fish Press (*US*)
The Lilliput Press (*Ire*)
Lion Hudson Plc (*UK*)
Little, Brown Book Group (*UK*)

Mage Publishers (*US*)
Melbourne University Publishing Ltd (*Aus*)
Michael Joseph (*UK*)
MIrror Books (*UK*)
Monsoon Books Pte Ltd (*UK*)
The O'Brien Press (*Ire*)
PaperBooks (*UK*)
Pelican Publishing Company (*US*)
Pen & Sword Books Ltd (*UK*)
Penguin Random House (*US*)
Periscope (*UK*)
Robert D. Reed Publishers (*US*)
Serpent's Tail (*UK*)
Seven Stories Press (*US*)
Simon & Schuster UK Limited (*UK*)
SisterShip Press Pty Ltd (*Aus*)
Sunstone Press (*US*)
Triangle Square (*US*)
Truman State University Press (*US*)
University of Alaska Press (*US*)
The University of Michigan Press (*US*)
Valley Press (*UK*)
Verso (*UK*)
W.W. Norton & Company Ltd (*UK*)
Weidenfeld & Nicolson (*UK*)
Zed Books Ltd (*UK*)
Zumaya Publications (*US*)
Beauty and Fashion
ACC Art Books Ltd (*UK*)
Black Dog Publishing London UK (*UK*)
Carlton Publishing Group (*UK*)
Chronicle Books LLC (*US*)
Co & Bear Productions (*UK*)
Jacaranda Books Art Music Ltd (*UK*)
Laurence King Publishing Ltd (*UK*)
Luath Press Ltd (*UK*)
Octopus Publishing Group Limited (*UK*)
Pavilion Books Group Limited (*UK*)
Quarto Publishing Group UK (*UK*)
Biography
Abdo Publishing Co (*US*)
Allen & Unwin (*Aus*)
Allison & Busby Ltd (*UK*)
Alma Classics (*UK*)
Alpine Publications, Inc. (*US*)
Amberley Publishing (*UK*)
Asabi Publishing (*US*)
Aureus Publishing Limited (*UK*)
Aurora Metro Press (*UK*)
Bancroft Press (*US*)
Beacon Press (*US*)
BearManor Media (*US*)
BenBella Books (*US*)
Birlinn Ltd (*UK*)
Black & White Publishing Ltd (*UK*)
Black Dome Press (*US*)
Candy Jar Books (*UK*)
Canongate Books (*UK*)
Carcanet Press Ltd (*UK*)
Carlton Publishing Group (*UK*)
Chicago Review Press (*US*)
College Press Publishing (*US*)
The Crown Publishing Group (*US*)

Cynren Press (*US*)
David R. Godine, Publisher (*US*)
DB Publishing (*UK*)
Dovecote Press (*UK*)
Dreamriver Press (*US*)
Duckworth Publishers (*UK*)
Dunedin Academic Press Ltd (*UK*)
Dynasty Press (*UK*)
ECW Press (*Can*)
Faber & Faber Ltd (*UK*)
Fairleigh Dickinson University (FDU) Press (*Can*)
Fleming Publications (*UK*)
Floris Books (*UK*)
Fonthill Media LLC (*US*)
Fonthill Media Ltd (*UK*)
Fordham University Press (*US*)
Formac Publishing Company Limited (*Can*)
Forward Movement Publications (*US*)
Gallaudet University Press (*US*)
Garnet Publishing (*UK*)
George Braziller, Inc. (*US*)
Gibson Square Books Ltd (*UK*)
Gill Books (*Ire*)
Gingko Library (*UK*)
Gomer Press (*UK*)
Granta Books (*UK*)
Halban Publishers (*UK*)
HarperCollins (*US*)
HarperCollins Publishers Ltd (*UK*)
Haus Publishing (*UK*)
Hay House Publishers (*UK*)
Head of Zeus (*UK*)
Headline Publishing Group (*UK*)
Health Communications, Inc. (*US*)
Hendrick-Long Publishing Co. (*US*)
Heritage House (*Can*)
Hesperus Press Limited (*UK*)
Hodder & Stoughton Ltd (*UK*)
House of Lochar (*UK*)
Hymns Ancient & Modern Ltd (*UK*)
Impress Books Limited (*UK*)
Infinite Ideas (*UK*)
Jacaranda Books Art Music Ltd (*UK*)
Jolly Fish Press (*US*)
JourneyForth (*US*)
Judaica Press (*US*)
Kent State University Press (*US*)
Kube Publishing (*UK*)
The Lilliput Press (*Ire*)
Lion Hudson Plc (*UK*)
Little, Brown Book Group (*UK*)
Luath Press Ltd (*UK*)
Mage Publishers (*US*)
Melbourne University Publishing Ltd (*Aus*)
Monsoon Books Pte Ltd (*UK*)
The O'Brien Press (*Ire*)
Oleander Press (*UK*)
Omnibus Press (*UK*)
Oneworld Publications (*UK*)
Oregon State University Press (*US*)
Ouen Press (*UK*)
Pandora Press (*UK*)

Pelican Publishing Company (*US*)
Pen & Sword Books Ltd (*UK*)
Penguin Random House (*US*)
Periscope (*UK*)
Profile Books (*UK*)
Quiller Publishing Ltd (*UK*)
Red Moon Press (*US*)
Robert Hale Publishers (*UK*)
Santa Monica Press (*US*)
Serpent's Tail (*UK*)
Simon & Schuster UK Limited (*UK*)
SisterShip Press Pty Ltd (*Aus*)
Southern Illinois University Press (*US*)
St Pauls (*US*)
Sunstone Press (*US*)
Syracuse University Press (*US*)
I.B. Tauris & Co. Ltd (*UK*)
Temple University Press (*US*)
TouchWood Editions (*Can*)
Triangle Square (*US*)
Truman State University Press (*US*)
Unicorn Publishing Group (*UK*)
University of Alaska Press (*US*)
The University of Michigan Press (*US*)
University of Washington Press (*US*)
Verso (*UK*)
W.W. Norton & Company Ltd (*UK*)
Weidenfeld & Nicolson (*UK*)
Wordsworth Editions (*UK*)
Zed Books Ltd (*UK*)
Business
ACC Art Books Ltd (*UK*)
Allen & Unwin (*Aus*)
Ashgate Publishing Limited (*UK*)
BenBella Books (*US*)
Nicholas Brealey Publishing (*UK*)
Bristol University Press (*UK*)
Career Press (*US*)
CJ Fallon (*Ire*)
Crown House Publishing (*UK*)
The Crown Publishing Group (*US*)
ECW Press (*Can*)
Edward Elgar Publishing Inc. (*US*)
Edward Elgar Publishing Ltd (*UK*)
Fernwood Publishing (*Can*)
Fordham University Press (*US*)
Hanser Publications (*US*)
Harper Business (*US*)
HarperCollins (*US*)
Hay House Publishers (*UK*)
Heritage House (*Can*)
Humanix Books (*US*)
Infinite Ideas (*UK*)
Insomniac Press (*Can*)
International Wealth Success (IWS) Inc. (*US*)
Legend Business (*UK*)
LexisNexis Canada (*Can*)
The Lilliput Press (*Ire*)
Management Books 2000 Ltd (*UK*)
Maven House Press (*US*)
McGraw-Hill Education (*US*)
The O'Brien Press (*Ire*)
Oneworld Publications (*UK*)

O'Reilly Media (*US*)
PassKey Publications (*US*)
Pelican Publishing Company (*US*)
Polity Press (*UK*)
Profile Books (*UK*)
Quiller Publishing Ltd (*UK*)
Red Wheel (*US*)
Robert D. Reed Publishers (*US*)
Silver Lake Publishing, LLC (*US*)
Simon & Schuster UK Limited (*UK*)
SisterShip Press Pty Ltd (*Aus*)
Sunstone Press (*US*)
Temple University Press (*US*)
TSO (The Stationery Office) (*UK*)
The University of Michigan Press (*US*)
W.W. Norton & Company Ltd (*UK*)
Zed Books Ltd (*UK*)
ZigZag Education (*UK*)
Cookery
Abdo Publishing Co (*US*)
Andrews McMeel Publishing (*US*)
Aurora Metro Press (*UK*)
BenBella Books (*US*)
Black & White Publishing Ltd (*UK*)
Blink Publishing (*UK*)
Bull Publishing Company (*US*)
Chelsea Green Publishing, Inc. (*US*)
Chronicle Books LLC (*US*)
Clarkson Potter (*US*)
Cork University Press (*Ire*)
The Crown Publishing Group (*US*)
Dreamriver Press (*US*)
Familius (*US*)
Flame Tree Publishing (*UK*)
Formac Publishing Company Limited (*Can*)
Garnet Publishing (*UK*)
Geddes & Grosset (*UK*)
Gibbs Smith, Publisher (*US*)
Gill Books (*Ire*)
Grub Street Publishing (*UK*)
Guild of Master Craftsman (GMC) Publications
Ltd (*UK*)
HarperCollins (*US*)
HarperCollins Publishers Ltd (*UK*)
The Harvard Common Press (*US*)
Headline Publishing Group (*UK*)
Health Communications, Inc. (*US*)
Hendrick-Long Publishing Co. (*US*)
Hipso Media (*US*)
Hodder & Stoughton Ltd (*UK*)
Igloo Books Limited (*UK*)
Infinite Ideas (*UK*)
Interlink Publishing Group, Inc. (*US*)
The Lilliput Press (*Ire*)
Mage Publishers (*US*)
McSweeney's Publishing (*US*)
Michael Joseph (*UK*)
The O'Brien Press (*Ire*)
Octopus Publishing Group Limited (*UK*)
Onstream Publications Ltd (*Ire*)
Page Street Publishing Co. (*US*)
PaperBooks (*UK*)
Pavilion Books Group Limited (*UK*)

Pelican Publishing Company (*US*)
Penguin Random House (*US*)
Quarto Publishing Group UK (*UK*)
Quiller Publishing Ltd (*UK*)
Red Wheel (*US*)
Ryland Peters & Small (*UK*)
Sheldrake Press (*UK*)
Simon & Schuster UK Limited (*UK*)
SisterShip Press Pty Ltd (*Aus*)
Sunstone Press (*US*)
Top That! Publishing (*UK*)
TouchWood Editions (*Can*)
The University of Michigan Press (*US*)
Weidenfeld & Nicolson (*UK*)
Willow Creek Press, Inc. (*US*)
Crafts
Abdo Publishing Co (*US*)
ACC Art Books Ltd (*UK*)
American Quilter's Society (*US*)
Astragal Press (*US*)
Beercott Books (*UK*)
Black Dog Publishing London UK (*UK*)
C&T Publishing (*US*)
Chicago Review Press (*US*)
Chronicle Books LLC (*US*)
Divertir Publishing LLC (*US*)
Dreamriver Press (*US*)
Eagle's View Publishing (*US*)
Finney Company (*US*)
Floris Books (*UK*)
Gibbs Smith, Publisher (*US*)
Gill Books (*Ire*)
Guild of Master Craftsman (GMC) Publications
Ltd (*UK*)
HarperCollins Publishers Ltd (*UK*)
Interweave Press (*US*)
Kansas City Star Quilts (*US*)
The O'Brien Press (*Ire*)
Octopus Publishing Group Limited (*UK*)
Page Street Publishing Co. (*US*)
Pavilion Books Group Limited (*UK*)
Pelican Publishing Company (*US*)
Quarto Publishing Group UK (*UK*)
Ryland Peters & Small (*UK*)
Search Press Ltd (*UK*)
SisterShip Press Pty Ltd (*Aus*)
Snowbooks (*UK*)
Sterling Publishing Co. Inc. (*US*)
Sunstone Press (*US*)
W.W. Norton & Company Ltd (*UK*)
Crime
Allen & Unwin (*Aus*)
Allison & Busby Ltd (*UK*)
Asabi Publishing (*US*)
Black & White Publishing Ltd (*UK*)
Blink Publishing (*UK*)
Carina UK (*UK*)
Cynren Press (*US*)
DB Publishing (*UK*)
Duckworth Publishers (*UK*)
Gill Books (*Ire*)
Harlequin Mills & Boon Ltd (*UK*)
HarperCollins Publishers Ltd (*UK*)

Head of Zeus (*UK*)
Heritage House (*Can*)
Hesperus Press Limited (*UK*)
Honno Welsh Women's Press (*UK*)
Impress Books Limited (*UK*)
Insomniac Press (*Can*)
Jacaranda Books Art Music Ltd (*UK*)
Joffe Books Ltd (*UK*)
Legend Press (*UK*)
Little, Brown Book Group (*UK*)
Luath Press Ltd (*UK*)
Mandrake of Oxford (*UK*)
Melbourne University Publishing Ltd (*Aus*)
Michael Joseph (*UK*)
MIrror Books (*UK*)
Monsoon Books Pte Ltd (*UK*)
The O'Brien Press (*Ire*)
Pelican Publishing Company (*US*)
Pen & Sword Books Ltd (*UK*)
Periscope (*UK*)
Polis Books (*US*)
Polity Press (*UK*)
Robert Hale Publishers (*UK*)
Serpent's Tail (*UK*)
SisterShip Press Pty Ltd (*Aus*)
Snowbooks (*UK*)
Southern Illinois University Press (*US*)
Sterling Publishing Co. Inc. (*US*)
Summersdale Publishers Ltd (*UK*)
Sunstone Press (*US*)
Temple University Press (*US*)
Twenty First Century Publishers Ltd (*UK*)
W.W. Norton & Company Ltd (*UK*)
WhiteFire Publishing (*US*)
Zumaya Publications (*US*)
Criticism
Bucknell University Press (*US*)
David R. Godine, Publisher (*US*)
Duckworth Publishers (*UK*)
Enitharmon Press (*UK*)
Fence Books (*US*)
Fernwood Publishing (*Can*)
Four Courts Press (*Ire*)
Gibson Square Books Ltd (*UK*)
Granta Books (*UK*)
Halban Publishers (*UK*)
Imprint Academic (*UK*)
Insomniac Press (*Can*)
Kaya Press (*US*)
Kent State University Press (*US*)
The Lilliput Press (*Ire*)
Northcote House Publishers Ltd (*UK*)
Pelican Publishing Company (*US*)
Red Moon Press (*US*)
Truman State University Press (*US*)
University College Dublin (UCD) Press (*Ire*)
Culture
Abdo Publishing Co (*US*)
Allen & Unwin (*Aus*)
Allison & Busby Ltd (*UK*)
Asabi Publishing (*US*)
Ashgate Publishing Limited (*UK*)
Augsburg Fortress (*US*)

Aurora Metro Press (*UK*)
BenBella Books (*US*)
Birlinn Ltd (*UK*)
Black Dog Publishing London UK (*UK*)
Black Dome Press (*US*)
Blink Publishing (*UK*)
Blue River Press (*US*)
Nicholas Brealey Publishing (*UK*)
Bucknell University Press (*US*)
Canongate Books (*UK*)
Carlton Publishing Group (*UK*)
Charlesbridge Publishing (*US*)
Chicago Review Press (*US*)
Concordia Publishing House (*US*)
Cork University Press (*Ire*)
Coteau Books (*Can*)
Cynren Press (*US*)
Dreamriver Press (*US*)
Eagle's View Publishing (*US*)
ECW Press (*Can*)
Edinburgh University Press (*UK*)
Edward Elgar Publishing Ltd (*UK*)
Elm Books (*US*)
Fantagraphics (*US*)
Fernwood Publishing (*Can*)
Finney Company (*US*)
Flame Tree Publishing (*UK*)
Fordham University Press (*US*)
Frances Lincoln Children's Books (*UK*)
Gallaudet University Press (*US*)
Garnet Publishing (*UK*)
GEY Books (*UK*)
Gibson Square Books Ltd (*UK*)
Gomer Press (*UK*)
Granta Books (*UK*)
Hendrick-Long Publishing Co. (*US*)
Heritage House (*Can*)
Hesperus Press Limited (*UK*)
Heyday Books (*US*)
Hipso Media (*US*)
Infinite Ideas (*UK*)
Insomniac Press (*Can*)
Kaya Press (*US*)
Kube Publishing (*UK*)
Lantana Publishing (*UK*)
Lawrence & Wishart (*UK*)
Lee & Low Books (*US*)
The Lilliput Press (*Ire*)
LSU Press (*US*)
Mage Publishers (*US*)
Mandrake of Oxford (*UK*)
Octopus Publishing Group Limited (*UK*)
Oregon State University Press (*US*)
Paulist Press (*US*)
Pavilion Books Group Limited (*UK*)
Pinata Books (*US*)
Policy Studies Institute (PSI) (*UK*)
Polity Press (*UK*)
Profile Books (*UK*)
Quirk Books (*US*)
Red Empress Publishing (*US*)
Red Wheel (*US*)
Rivers Oram Press (*UK*)

Santa Monica Press (*US*)
Serpent's Tail (*UK*)
Syracuse University Press (*US*)
I.B. Tauris & Co. Ltd (*UK*)
Temple University Press (*US*)
TouchWood Editions (*Can*)
Two Rivers Press (*UK*)
Unicorn Publishing Group (*UK*)
University of Alaska Press (*US*)
University of Exeter Press (*UK*)
The University of Michigan Press (*US*)
University of Wales Press (*UK*)
University of Washington Press (*US*)
Verso (*UK*)
Wesleyan University Press (*US*)
WhiteFire Publishing (*US*)
Zed Books Ltd (*UK*)
Current Affairs
Abdo Publishing Co (*US*)
Allen & Unwin (*Aus*)
Beacon Press (*US*)
Birlinn Ltd (*UK*)
Bloomberg Press (*US*)
Bristol University Press (*UK*)
Clarity Press, Inc. (*US*)
Cork University Press (*Ire*)
Divertir Publishing LLC (*US*)
Dreamriver Press (*US*)
Duckworth Publishers (*UK*)
Dunedin Academic Press Ltd (*UK*)
Fernwood Publishing (*Can*)
Garnet Publishing (*UK*)
Gibson Square Books Ltd (*UK*)
Gill Books (*Ire*)
Greenhaven Publishing (*US*)
Hay House Publishers (*UK*)
Infinite Ideas (*UK*)
Lawrence & Wishart (*UK*)
The Lilliput Press (*Ire*)
Luath Press Ltd (*UK*)
Oneworld Publications (*UK*)
Pandora Press (*UK*)
Periscope (*UK*)
Profile Books (*UK*)
Rivers Oram Press (*UK*)
Serpent's Tail (*UK*)
Seven Stories Press (*US*)
Syracuse University Press (*US*)
I.B. Tauris & Co. Ltd (*UK*)
TSO (The Stationery Office) (*UK*)
W.W. Norton & Company Ltd (*UK*)
Weidenfeld & Nicolson (*UK*)
WhiteFire Publishing (*US*)
Zed Books Ltd (*UK*)
Design
Abdo Publishing Co (*US*)
ACC Art Books Ltd (*UK*)
ASCE Press (*US*)
Black Dog Publishing London UK (*UK*)
Carlton Publishing Group (*UK*)
Chronicle Books LLC (*US*)
Clarkson Potter (*US*)
Co & Bear Productions (*UK*)

Duckworth Publishers (*UK*)
Frontinus (*UK*)
Gibbs Smith, Publisher (*US*)
Laurence King Publishing Ltd (*UK*)
Lund Humphries Limited (*UK*)
Melbourne University Publishing Ltd (*Aus*)
Octopus Publishing Group Limited (*UK*)
O'Reilly Media (*US*)
Page Street Publishing Co. (*US*)
Pavilion Books Group Limited (*UK*)
Pimpernel Press (*UK*)
Princeton Architectural Press (*US*)
Quarto Publishing Group UK (*UK*)
Red Wheel (*US*)
Robert Hale Publishers (*UK*)
I.B. Tauris & Co. Ltd (*UK*)
Trentham Books Limited (*UK*)
W.W. Norton & Company Ltd (*UK*)
ZigZag Education (*UK*)
Drama
Aurora Metro Press (*UK*)
Chapman Publishing (*UK*)
Cork University Press (*Ire*)
Coteau Books (*Can*)
Cressrelles Publishing Co. Ltd (*UK*)
Dreamriver Press (*US*)
Duckworth Publishers (*UK*)
Faber & Faber Ltd (*UK*)
GEY Books (*UK*)
Gomer Press (*UK*)
Italica Press (*US*)
The Lilliput Press (*Ire*)
Luath Press Ltd (*UK*)
Maverick Musicals & Plays (*Aus*)
MIrror Books (*UK*)
New Playwrights' Network (NPN) (*UK*)
The O'Brien Press (*Ire*)
Oberon Books (*UK*)
Samuel French Ltd (*UK*)
Temple University Press (*US*)
University College Dublin (UCD) Press (*Ire*)
W.W. Norton & Company Ltd (*UK*)
Ward Lock Educational Ltd (*UK*)
WhiteFire Publishing (*US*)
ZigZag Education (*UK*)
Entertainment
Abdo Publishing Co (*US*)
Carlton Publishing Group (*UK*)
GEY Books (*UK*)
HarperCollins Publishers Ltd (*UK*)
Infinite Ideas (*UK*)
Little, Brown Book Group (*UK*)
Penguin Random House (*US*)
Quarto Publishing Group UK (*UK*)
Santa Monica Press (*US*)
SisterShip Press Pty Ltd (*Aus*)
Syracuse University Press (*US*)
Titan Books (*UK*)
WhiteFire Publishing (*US*)
Erotic
Asabi Publishing (*US*)
Carina UK (*UK*)
GEY Books (*UK*)

Hesperus Press Limited (*UK*)
Hipso Media (*US*)
Mandrake of Oxford (*UK*)
Melange Books, LLC (*US*)
Monsoon Books Pte Ltd (*UK*)
NBM Publishing (*US*)
Polis Books (*US*)
Fantasy
Allen & Unwin (*Aus*)
Allison & Busby Ltd (*UK*)
Baen Books (*US*)
BLVNP Incorporated (*US*)
Candy Jar Books (*UK*)
Carina UK (*UK*)
Coteau Books (*Can*)
Cuil Press (*US*)
Divertir Publishing LLC (*US*)
Dragon Moon Press (*Can*)
Ellysian Press (*US*)
Entangled Teen (*US*)
4RV Publishing (*US*)
GEY Books (*UK*)
Harken Media (*US*)
Harmony Ink Press (*US*)
HarperCollins (*US*)
HarperCollins Publishers Ltd (*UK*)
Head of Zeus (*UK*)
Hesperus Press Limited (*UK*)
Honno Welsh Women's Press (*UK*)
Jolly Fish Press (*US*)
Little, Brown Book Group (*UK*)
Luna Press Publishing (*UK*)
Martin Sisters Publishing (*US*)
Monsoon Books Pte Ltd (*UK*)
NBM Publishing (*US*)
Page Street Publishing Co. (*US*)
Penguin Random House (*US*)
Polis Books (*US*)
Red Empress Publishing (*US*)
SisterShip Press Pty Ltd (*Aus*)
Snowbooks (*UK*)
Sunstone Press (*US*)
WhiteFire Publishing (*US*)
World Weaver Press (*US*)
Zumaya Publications (*US*)
Fiction
Abdo Publishing Co (*US*)
Academy Chicago (*US*)
Albert Whitman & Company (*US*)
Allen & Unwin (*Aus*)
Allison & Busby Ltd (*UK*)
Alma Books Ltd (*UK*)
Alma Classics (*UK*)
American Quilter's Society (*US*)
Andersen Press Ltd (*UK*)
Andrews McMeel Publishing (*US*)
Arbordale Publishing (*US*)
Arthur A. Levine Books (*US*)
Asabi Publishing (*US*)
Augsburg Fortress (*US*)
Aurora Metro Press (*UK*)
Avatar Press (*US*)
Award Publications Limited (*UK*)

Baen Books (*US*)
Bancroft Press (*US*)
Barrington Stoke (*UK*)
Beacon Publishing Group (*US*)
BearManor Media (*US*)
Belle Lutte Press (*US*)
Beyond Words Publishing (*US*)
Birlinn Ltd (*UK*)
BkMk Press (*US*)
Black & White Publishing Ltd (*UK*)
Black Rose Writing (*US*)
Bloomsbury Spark (*UK*)
BLVNP Incorporated (*US*)
Calisi Press (*UK*)
Candy Jar Books (*UK*)
Canongate Books (*UK*)
Carina UK (*UK*)
Cave Hollow Press (*US*)
Cedar Fort (*US*)
Chapman Publishing (*UK*)
Charlesbridge Publishing (*US*)
Chicago Review Press (*US*)
Chronicle Books LLC (*US*)
Classical Comics Limited (*UK*)
Comma Press (*UK*)
Coteau Books (*Can*)
The Crown Publishing Group (*US*)
Crux Publishing (*UK*)
Cuil Press (*US*)
David Fickling Books (*UK*)
David R. Godine, Publisher (*US*)
DB Publishing (*UK*)
De Montfort Literature (*UK*)
Dedalus Ltd (*UK*)
Divertir Publishing LLC (*US*)
Dodo Ink (*UK*)
Down The Shore Publishing (*US*)
Dragon Moon Press (*Can*)
Dreamriver Press (*US*)
Dref Wen (*UK*)
Duckworth Publishers (*UK*)
ECW Press (*Can*)
Ellysian Press (*US*)
Elm Books (*US*)
The Emma Press Ltd (*UK*)
Enitharmon Press (*UK*)
Entangled Teen (*US*)
Faber & Faber Ltd (*UK*)
Familius (*US*)
Fantagraphics (*US*)
Farrar, Straus and Giroux Books for Younger Readers (*US*)
Fence Books (*US*)
Fingerpress UK (*UK*)
Firefly (*UK*)
First Second (*US*)
Fisherton Press (*UK*)
Fitzhenry & Whiteside Ltd (*Can*)
Fitzrovia Press Limited (*UK*)
Fleming Publications (*UK*)
Floris Books (*UK*)
Folded Word LLC (*US*)
Formac Publishing Company Limited (*Can*)

Four Way Books (*US*)
4RV Publishing (*US*)
Frances Lincoln Children's Books (*UK*)
The Gallery Press (*Ire*)
Galley Beggar Press (*UK*)
Garnet Publishing (*UK*)
Geddes & Grosset (*UK*)
George Braziller, Inc. (*US*)
GEY Books (*UK*)
Gill Books (*Ire*)
Gomer Press (*UK*)
Goosebottom Books LLC (*US*)
Granta Books (*UK*)
Greystones Press (*UK*)
Hachai Publishing (*US*)
Halban Publishers (*UK*)
Harken Media (*US*)
Harlequin American Romance (*US*)
Harlequin Dare (*Can*)
Harlequin Mills & Boon Ltd (*UK*)
Harmony Ink Press (*US*)
HarperCollins (*US*)
HarperCollins Publishers Ltd (*UK*)
Haus Publishing (*UK*)
Head of Zeus (*UK*)
Headline Publishing Group (*UK*)
Helicon Nine Editions (*US*)
Hendrick-Long Publishing Co. (*US*)
Henry Holt and Company (*US*)
Hesperus Press Limited (*UK*)
Heyday Books (*US*)
Hipso Media (*US*)
Hodder & Stoughton Ltd (*UK*)
Holiday House, Inc. (*US*)
Honno Welsh Women's Press (*UK*)
Hot Key Books (*UK*)
House of Lochar (*UK*)
IDW Publishing (*US*)
Igloo Books Limited (*UK*)
Illusio & Baqer (*US*)
Image Comics (*US*)
Impress Books Limited (*UK*)
Insomniac Press (*Can*)
Interlink Publishing Group, Inc. (*US*)
Italica Press (*US*)
Jacaranda Books Art Music Ltd (*UK*)
Joffe Books Ltd (*UK*)
John Murray (Publishers) Ltd (*UK*)
Jolly Fish Press (*US*)
JourneyForth (*US*)
Judaica Press (*US*)
Kaeden Books (*US*)
Kar-Ben Publishing (*US*)
Kathy Dawson Books (*US*)
Kaya Press (*US*)
Kettillonia (*UK*)
Kube Publishing (*UK*)
Lantana Publishing (*UK*)
Leapfrog Press (*US*)
Lee & Low Books (*US*)
Legend Press (*UK*)
The Lilliput Press (*Ire*)
Lion Hudson Plc (*UK*)

Little Pickle Press, Inc. (*US*)
Little Tiger Press (*UK*)
Little, Brown Book Group (*UK*)
Livingston Press (*US*)
Lost Horse Press (*US*)
LSU Press (*US*)
Luath Press Ltd (*UK*)
Luna Press Publishing (*UK*)
Mage Publishers (*US*)
Mandrake of Oxford (*UK*)
Mantra Lingua Ltd (*UK*)
Martin Sisters Publishing (*US*)
McSweeney's Publishing (*US*)
Melange Books, LLC (*US*)
Messianic Jewish Publishers (*US*)
Michael Joseph (*UK*)
Michael Terence Publishing (MTP) (*UK*)
MIrror Books (*UK*)
Monsoon Books Pte Ltd (*UK*)
Myriad Editions (*UK*)
NBM Publishing (*US*)
New Directions Publishing (*US*)
Nightboat Books (*US*)
NorthSouth Books (*US*)
The O'Brien Press (*Ire*)
Oceanview Publishing (*US*)
Oleander Press (*UK*)
Oneworld Publications (*UK*)
Onstream Publications Ltd (*Ire*)
Ouen Press (*UK*)
Page Street Publishing Co. (*US*)
Paulist Press (*US*)
Pelican Publishing Company (*US*)
Penguin Group (USA) Inc. (*US*)
Penguin Random House (*US*)
Periscope (*UK*)
Phoenix Yard Books (*UK*)
Pinata Books (*US*)
Pocol Press (*US*)
Polis Books (*US*)
Quirk Books (*US*)
Red Empress Publishing (*US*)
Red Moon Press (*US*)
Robert Hale Publishers (*UK*)
Saguaro Books, LLC (*US*)
Salvo Press (*US*)
Scholastic Library Publishing (*US*)
Scribner (*US*)
Serpent's Tail (*UK*)
Seven Stories Press (*US*)
Simon & Schuster UK Limited (*UK*)
SisterShip Press Pty Ltd (*Aus*)
Sky Pony Press (*US*)
Snowbooks (*UK*)
Somerville Press (*Ire*)
Southern Illinois University Press (*US*)
Star Bright Books (*US*)
Sterling Publishing Co. Inc. (*US*)
Stonewood Press (*UK*)
Stripes Publishing (*UK*)
Sunstone Press (*US*)
Sweet Cherry Publishing (*UK*)
Thistle Publishing (*UK*)

Thomas Dunne Books (*US*)
ThunderStone Books (*US*)
Tiny Owl (*UK*)
Titan Books (*UK*)
Top That! Publishing (*UK*)
TouchWood Editions (*Can*)
Triangle Square (*US*)
Troika Books (*UK*)
Tumblehome Learning, Inc. (*US*)
Twenty First Century Publishers Ltd (*UK*)
Unbound Press (*UK*)
University of Alaska Press (*US*)
The University of Michigan Press (*US*)
Valley Press (*UK*)
Vehicule Press (*Can*)
Verso (*UK*)
W.W. Norton & Company Ltd (*UK*)
Walker Books Ltd (*UK*)
WaterBrook & Multnomah (*US*)
Weidenfeld & Nicolson (*UK*)
WhiteFire Publishing (*US*)
Wordsworth Editions (*UK*)
World Weaver Press (*US*)
WorthyKids / Ideals (*US*)
Zumaya Publications (*US*)
Film
Aurora Metro Press (*UK*)
BearManor Media (*US*)
BFI Publishing (*UK*)
Black Dog Publishing London UK (*UK*)
Carlton Publishing Group (*UK*)
Chicago Review Press (*US*)
Chronicle Books LLC (*US*)
Cork University Press (*Ire*)
Duckworth Publishers (*UK*)
Edinburgh University Press (*UK*)
Faber & Faber Ltd (*UK*)
Fairleigh Dickinson University (FDU) Press
(*Can*)
Guild of Master Craftsman (GMC) Publications
Ltd (*UK*)
HarperCollins Publishers Ltd (*UK*)
Haus Publishing (*UK*)
Interlink Publishing Group, Inc. (*US*)
Laurence King Publishing Ltd (*UK*)
McGraw-Hill Education (*US*)
Nick Hern Books Ltd (*UK*)
Octopus Publishing Group Limited (*UK*)
Santa Monica Press (*US*)
SisterShip Press Pty Ltd (*Aus*)
Southern Illinois University Press (*US*)
I.B. Tauris & Co. Ltd (*UK*)
Temple University Press (*US*)
Titan Books (*UK*)
University of Exeter Press (*UK*)
Verso (*UK*)
W.W. Norton & Company Ltd (*UK*)
Wesleyan University Press (*US*)
Finance
Algora Publishing (*US*)
Allen & Unwin (*Aus*)
Bancroft Press (*US*)
Birlinn Ltd (*UK*)

Bloomberg Press (*US*)
Nicholas Brealey Publishing (*UK*)
Bristol University Press (*UK*)
Career Press (*US*)
Chelsea Green Publishing, Inc. (*US*)
CJ Fallon (*Ire*)
Clarity Press, Inc. (*US*)
Duckworth Publishers (*UK*)
Dunedin Academic Press Ltd (*UK*)
ECW Press (*Can*)
Edward Elgar Publishing Inc. (*US*)
Edward Elgar Publishing Ltd (*UK*)
Familius (*US*)
Fernwood Publishing (*Can*)
Fordham University Press (*US*)
Gingko Library (*UK*)
HarperCollins (*US*)
Hay House Publishers (*UK*)
Humanix Books (*US*)
Insomniac Press (*Can*)
International Wealth Success (IWS) Inc. (*US*)
LexisNexis Canada (*Can*)
Management Books 2000 Ltd (*UK*)
PassKey Publications (*US*)
Policy Studies Institute (PSI) (*UK*)
Polity Press (*UK*)
Profile Books (*UK*)
Robert D. Reed Publishers (*US*)
Silver Lake Publishing, LLC (*US*)
Sterling Publishing Co. Inc. (*US*)
Temple University Press (*US*)
Twenty First Century Publishers Ltd (*UK*)
The University of Michigan Press (*US*)
Verso (*UK*)
W.W. Norton & Company Ltd (*UK*)
Weidenfeld & Nicolson (*UK*)
Zed Books Ltd (*UK*)
ZigZag Education (*UK*)
Gardening
ACC Art Books Ltd (*UK*)
Ball Publishing (*US*)
Chelsea Green Publishing, Inc. (*US*)
Chicago Review Press (*US*)
David R. Godine, Publisher (*US*)
Dreamriver Press (*US*)
Finney Company (*US*)
Guild of Master Craftsman (GMC) Publications
Ltd (*UK*)
HarperCollins Publishers Ltd (*UK*)
Headline Publishing Group (*UK*)
Infinite Ideas (*UK*)
Insomniac Press (*Can*)
Octopus Publishing Group Limited (*UK*)
Pavilion Books Group Limited (*UK*)
Pelican Publishing Company (*US*)
Pen & Sword Books Ltd (*UK*)
Pimpernel Press (*UK*)
Quarto Publishing Group UK (*UK*)
Quiller Publishing Ltd (*UK*)
Ryland Peters & Small (*UK*)
Sterling Publishing Co. Inc. (*US*)
Sunstone Press (*US*)
Think Publishing (*UK*)

TouchWood Editions (*Can*)
Willow Creek Press, Inc. (*US*)
Gothic
Carina UK (*UK*)
HarperCollins (*US*)
Red Empress Publishing (*US*)
Wordsworth Editions (*UK*)
Zumaya Publications (*US*)
Health
Allen & Unwin (*Aus*)
American Counseling Association (*US*)
American Psychiatric Association Publishing (*US*)
Bancroft Press (*US*)
BenBella Books (*US*)
Beyond Words Publishing (*US*)
Blue River Press (*US*)
Bull Publishing Company (*US*)
Chronicle Books LLC (*US*)
Connections Book Publishing Ltd (*UK*)
Crown House Publishing (*UK*)
DB Publishing (*UK*)
Dreamriver Press (*US*)
Dunedin Academic Press Ltd (*UK*)
Eastland Press (*US*)
ECW Press (*Can*)
Familius (*US*)
Fernwood Publishing (*Can*)
Findhorn Press Ltd (*UK*)
Floris Books (*UK*)
Geddes & Grosset (*UK*)
Greenhaven Publishing (*US*)
HarperCollins Publishers Ltd (*UK*)
Hartman Publishing, Inc. (*US*)
Hay House Publishers (*UK*)
Health Communications, Inc. (*US*)
Health Professions Press (*US*)
Hipso Media (*US*)
Hohm Press (*US*)
Human Kinetics (*US*)
Humanix Books (*US*)
Insomniac Press (*Can*)
Lion Hudson Plc (*UK*)
Mandrake of Oxford (*UK*)
McGraw-Hill Education (*US*)
Octopus Publishing Group Limited (*UK*)
O'Reilly Media (*US*)
Pandora Press (*UK*)
Pavilion Publishing (*UK*)
Pelican Publishing Company (*US*)
Pen & Sword Books Ltd (*UK*)
Polity Press (*UK*)
Quarto Publishing Group UK (*UK*)
Red Wheel (*US*)
Robert D. Reed Publishers (*US*)
Robert Hale Publishers (*UK*)
Ryland Peters & Small (*UK*)
Seven Stories Press (*US*)
Simon & Schuster UK Limited (*UK*)
Singing Dragon (*UK*)
SisterShip Press Pty Ltd (*Aus*)
Southern Illinois University Press (*US*)
Speechmark Publishing Limited (*UK*)

Sterling Publishing Co. Inc. (*US*)
Summersdale Publishers Ltd (*UK*)
Sunstone Press (*US*)
Temple University Press (*US*)
Triangle Square (*US*)
W.W. Norton & Company Ltd (*UK*)
Wild Goose Publications (*UK*)
YMAA Publication Center, Inc. (*US*)
Zed Books Ltd (*UK*)
ZigZag Education (*UK*)
Historical
Abdo Publishing Co (*US*)
ACC Art Books Ltd (*UK*)
Algora Publishing (*US*)
Allen & Unwin (*Aus*)
Allison & Busby Ltd (*UK*)
Alma Books Ltd (*UK*)
Amberley Publishing (*UK*)
Asabi Publishing (*US*)
Ashgate Publishing Limited (*UK*)
Ashmolean Museum Publications (*UK*)
Astragal Press (*US*)
Augsburg Fortress (*US*)
Bancroft Press (*US*)
Beacon Press (*US*)
Birlinn Ltd (*UK*)
Black Dome Press (*US*)
Blink Publishing (*UK*)
Bloomsbury Spark (*UK*)
Bodleian Library Publishing (*UK*)
Boydell & Brewer Ltd (*UK*)
Bucknell University Press (*US*)
Candy Jar Books (*UK*)
Canongate Books (*UK*)
Carina UK (*UK*)
Carlton Publishing Group (*UK*)
Cedar Fort (*US*)
Charlesbridge Publishing (*US*)
Chicago Review Press (*US*)
CJ Fallon (*Ire*)
Clarity Press, Inc. (*US*)
College Press Publishing (*US*)
Cork University Press (*Ire*)
Coteau Books (*Can*)
Countryside Books (*UK*)
CQ Press (*US*)
Crabtree Publishing (*US*)
The Crown Publishing Group (*US*)
Cynren Press (*US*)
David R. Godine, Publisher (*US*)
DB Publishing (*UK*)
Divertir Publishing LLC (*US*)
Dovecote Press (*UK*)
Down The Shore Publishing (*US*)
Dreamriver Press (*US*)
Duckworth Publishers (*UK*)
Dunedin Academic Press Ltd (*UK*)
Dynasty Press (*UK*)
Eagle's View Publishing (*US*)
ECW Press (*Can*)
Edinburgh University Press (*UK*)
Elm Books (*US*)
Entangled Teen (*US*)

Fairleigh Dickinson University (FDU) Press (*Can*)
Fernwood Publishing (*Can*)
Fingerpress UK (*UK*)
Finney Company (*US*)
Fleming Publications (*UK*)
Floris Books (*UK*)
Fonthill Media LLC (*US*)
Fonthill Media Ltd (*UK*)
Fordham University Press (*US*)
Formac Publishing Company Limited (*Can*)
Four Courts Press (*Ire*)
Gallaudet University Press (*US*)
Garnet Publishing (*UK*)
Geddes & Grosset (*UK*)
Genealogical Publishing Company (*US*)
Gibson Square Books Ltd (*UK*)
Gill Books (*Ire*)
Gingko Library (*UK*)
Golden West Books (*US*)
Gomer Press (*UK*)
Goosebottom Books LLC (*US*)
Granta Books (*UK*)
Greenhaven Publishing (*US*)
Greystones Press (*UK*)
Grub Street Publishing (*UK*)
Hachai Publishing (*US*)
Halban Publishers (*UK*)
Harken Media (*US*)
Harlequin Mills & Boon Ltd (*UK*)
HarperCollins (*US*)
HarperCollins Publishers Ltd (*UK*)
Haus Publishing (*UK*)
Head of Zeus (*UK*)
Headline Publishing Group (*UK*)
Hendrick-Long Publishing Co. (*US*)
Heritage House (*Can*)
Hesperus Press Limited (*UK*)
Heyday Books (*US*)
Hodder & Stoughton Ltd (*UK*)
Hopscotch (*UK*)
House of Lochar (*UK*)
Humanix Books (*US*)
ICS Publications (*US*)
Impress Books Limited (*UK*)
Indiana Historical Society Press (*US*)
Interlink Publishing Group, Inc. (*US*)
Italica Press (*US*)
IWM (Imperial War Museums) (*UK*)
Jolly Fish Press (*US*)
JourneyForth (*US*)
Judaica Press (*US*)
Kent State University Press (*US*)
Kettillonia (*UK*)
Kube Publishing (*UK*)
Laurence King Publishing Ltd (*UK*)
Lawrence & Wishart (*UK*)
Legend Press (*UK*)
The Lilliput Press (*Ire*)
Little, Brown Book Group (*UK*)
LSU Press (*US*)
Luath Press Ltd (*UK*)
Lund Humphries Limited (*UK*)

Mage Publishers (*US*)
McGraw-Hill Education (*US*)
Melbourne University Publishing Ltd (*Aus*)
The Merlin Press (*UK*)
Monsoon Books Pte Ltd (*UK*)
National Museum Wales (*UK*)
New Directions Publishing (*US*)
Nomad Press (*US*)
The O'Brien Press (*Ire*)
Oak Knoll Press (*US*)
Octopus Publishing Group Limited (*UK*)
Oleander Press (*UK*)
Oneworld Publications (*UK*)
Onstream Publications Ltd (*Ire*)
Oregon State University Press (*US*)
Page Street Publishing Co. (*US*)
Paladin Press (*US*)
Pavilion Books Group Limited (*UK*)
Pelican Publishing Company (*US*)
Pen & Sword Books Ltd (*UK*)
Penguin Random House (*US*)
Periscope (*UK*)
Polity Press (*UK*)
Profile Books (*UK*)
Quarto Publishing Group UK (*UK*)
Quirk Books (*US*)
Red Empress Publishing (*US*)
Red Wheel (*US*)
Rivers Oram Press (*UK*)
Robert D. Reed Publishers (*US*)
Robert Hale Publishers (*UK*)
Santa Monica Press (*US*)
Schofield & Sims (*UK*)
Scribner (*US*)
Seven Stories Press (*US*)
Sheldrake Press (*UK*)
Simon & Schuster UK Limited (*UK*)
Snowbooks (*UK*)
Southern Illinois University Press (*US*)
Sunstone Press (*US*)
Syracuse University Press (*US*)
I.B. Tauris & Co. Ltd (*UK*)
Temple University Press (*US*)
Thomas Dunne Books (*US*)
Torah Aura Productions (*US*)
TouchWood Editions (*Can*)
Triangle Square (*US*)
Truman State University Press (*US*)
Twenty First Century Publishers Ltd (*UK*)
Unicorn Publishing Group (*UK*)
University College Dublin (UCD) Press (*Ire*)
University of Alaska Press (*US*)
University of Exeter Press (*UK*)
The University of Michigan Press (*US*)
University of Pittsburgh Press (*US*)
University of Wales Press (*UK*)
University of Washington Press (*US*)
Vehicule Press (*Can*)
Verso (*UK*)
Wooden Books (*UK*)
W.W. Norton & Company Ltd (*UK*)
WaterBrook & Multnomah (*US*)
Weidenfeld & Nicolson (*UK*)

Welsh Academic Press (*UK*)
Wesleyan University Press (*US*)
WhiteFire Publishing (*US*)
Zed Books Ltd (*UK*)
ZigZag Education (*UK*)
Zumaya Publications (*US*)

Hobbies

Abdo Publishing Co (*US*)
Alpine Publications, Inc. (*US*)
American Quilter's Society (*US*)
C&T Publishing (*US*)
Cicerone Press (*UK*)
Divertir Publishing LLC (*US*)
Eagle's View Publishing (*US*)
Familius (*US*)
Genealogical Publishing Company (*US*)
Gill Books (*Ire*)
Guild of Master Craftsman (GMC) Publications
Ltd (*UK*)
Igloo Books Limited (*UK*)
Infinite Ideas (*UK*)
Interweave Press (*US*)
Kansas City Star Quilts (*US*)
Krause Publications (*US*)
Pelican Publishing Company (*US*)
Pen & Sword Books Ltd (*UK*)
Quarto Publishing Group UK (*UK*)
Search Press Ltd (*UK*)
Seaworthy Publications (*US*)
SisterShip Press Pty Ltd (*Aus*)
Sterling Publishing Co. Inc. (*US*)
W.W. Norton & Company Ltd (*UK*)

Horror

Asabi Publishing (*US*)
Carina UK (*UK*)
Dragon Moon Press (*Can*)
Duckworth Publishers (*UK*)
Ellysian Press (*US*)
Jolly Fish Press (*US*)
Mandrake of Oxford (*UK*)
Monsoon Books Pte Ltd (*UK*)
NBM Publishing (*US*)
Oleander Press (*UK*)
Pocol Press (*US*)
Polis Books (*US*)
Snowbooks (*UK*)
WhiteFire Publishing (*US*)
Zumaya Publications (*US*)

How-to

American Quilter's Society (*US*)
Bloomberg Press (*US*)
Bull Publishing Company (*US*)
Career Press (*US*)
Chelsea Green Publishing, Inc. (*US*)
Dragon Moon Press (*Can*)
Dreamriver Press (*US*)
Eagle's View Publishing (*US*)
Ferguson Publishing (*US*)
Genealogical Publishing Company (*US*)
Gryphon House, Inc. (*US*)
Guild of Master Craftsman (GMC) Publications
Ltd (*UK*)
Haynes Publishing (*UK*)

Health Communications, Inc. (*US*)
Health Professions Press (*US*)
Hipso Media (*US*)
International Wealth Success (IWS) Inc. (*US*)
J.A. Allen (*UK*)
Krause Publications (*US*)
Little, Brown Book Group (*UK*)
MC Press (*US*)
Paladin Press (*US*)
Quarto Publishing Group UK (*UK*)
Search Press Ltd (*UK*)
Silver Lake Publishing, LLC (*US*)
SisterShip Press Pty Ltd (*Aus*)
Sterling Publishing Co. Inc. (*US*)
Sunstone Press (*US*)
Willow Creek Press, Inc. (*US*)

Humour

Allen & Unwin (*Aus*)
American Quilter's Society (*US*)
Andrews McMeel Publishing (*US*)
Aurora Metro Press (*UK*)
Bancroft Press (*US*)
BearManor Media (*US*)
Birlinn Ltd (*UK*)
Black & White Publishing Ltd (*UK*)
Blink Publishing (*UK*)
BLVNP Incorporated (*US*)
Canongate Books (*UK*)
Carina UK (*UK*)
Carlton Publishing Group (*UK*)
Chronicle Books LLC (*US*)
Coteau Books (*Can*)
Crown House Publishing (*UK*)
The Crown Publishing Group (*US*)
Cynren Press (*US*)
David R. Godine, Publisher (*US*)
Dino Books (*UK*)
Divertir Publishing LLC (*US*)
Duckworth Publishers (*UK*)
ECW Press (*Can*)
Familius (*US*)
Fantagraphics (*US*)
Folded Word LLC (*US*)
4RV Publishing (*US*)
Geddes & Grosset (*UK*)
Gibbs Smith, Publisher (*US*)
Gill Books (*Ire*)
Guild of Master Craftsman (GMC) Publications
Ltd (*UK*)
Harken Media (*US*)
Heritage House (*Can*)
Hipso Media (*US*)
Hodder & Stoughton Ltd (*UK*)
Hymns Ancient & Modern Ltd (*UK*)
Insomniac Press (*Can*)
Jolly Fish Press (*US*)
Kettillonia (*UK*)
Little, Brown Book Group (*UK*)
McSweeney's Publishing (*US*)
NBM Publishing (*US*)
New Directions Publishing (*US*)
The O'Brien Press (*Ire*)
Octopus Publishing Group Limited (*UK*)

Pavilion Books Group Limited (*UK*)
Pelican Publishing Company (*US*)
Penguin Random House (*US*)
Polis Books (*US*)
Profile Books (*UK*)
Quiller Publishing Ltd (*UK*)
Quirk Books (*US*)
Red Wheel (*US*)
Robert D. Reed Publishers (*US*)
Santa Monica Press (*US*)
Sheldrake Press (*UK*)
Simon & Schuster UK Limited (*UK*)
SisterShip Press Pty Ltd (*Aus*)
Sterling Publishing Co. Inc. (*US*)
Summersdale Publishers Ltd (*UK*)
Sunstone Press (*US*)
Titan Books (*UK*)
Top That! Publishing (*UK*)
W.W. Norton & Company Ltd (*UK*)
WhiteFire Publishing (*US*)

Legal
Ashgate Publishing Limited (*UK*)
Birlinn Ltd (*UK*)
Bristol University Press (*UK*)
Bucknell University Press (*US*)
Clarity Press, Inc. (*US*)
Cork University Press (*Ire*)
Dunedin Academic Press Ltd (*UK*)
Edinburgh University Press (*UK*)
Edward Elgar Publishing Inc. (*US*)
Edward Elgar Publishing Ltd (*UK*)
Fordham University Press (*US*)
Four Courts Press (*Ire*)
Hart Publishing Ltd (*UK*)
Insomniac Press (*Can*)
LexisNexis Canada (*Can*)
McGraw-Hill Education (*US*)
Pelican Publishing Company (*US*)
Silver Lake Publishing, LLC (*US*)
Southern Illinois University Press (*US*)
Sunstone Press (*US*)
Temple University Press (*US*)
Thomson Reuters Round Hall (*Ire*)
The University of Michigan Press (*US*)
W.W. Norton & Company Ltd (*UK*)
ZigZag Education (*UK*)

Leisure
Appalachian Mountain Club Books (*US*)
Career Press (*US*)
Cicerone Press (*UK*)
Connections Book Publishing Ltd (*UK*)
Countryside Books (*UK*)
Cynren Press (*US*)
Finney Company (*US*)
Gill Books (*Ire*)
Gomer Press (*UK*)
HarperCollins Publishers Ltd (*UK*)
Haynes Publishing (*UK*)
Human Kinetics (*US*)
Interlink Publishing Group, Inc. (*US*)
Luath Press Ltd (*UK*)
Metro Publications Ltd (*UK*)
Mountaineers Books (*US*)

Pelican Publishing Company (*US*)
Robert Hale Publishers (*UK*)
Search Press Ltd (*UK*)
Seaworthy Publications (*US*)
Singing Dragon (*UK*)
SisterShip Press Pty Ltd (*Aus*)
Snowbooks (*UK*)
Sunflower Books (*UK*)
Temple University Press (*US*)
Venture Publishing, Inc. (*US*)
W.W. Norton & Company Ltd (*UK*)
WhiteFire Publishing (*US*)
Willow Creek Press, Inc. (*US*)
ZigZag Education (*UK*)

Lifestyle
Allen & Unwin (*Aus*)
Andrews McMeel Publishing (*US*)
Augsburg Fortress (*US*)
Bancroft Press (*US*)
Beacon Press (*US*)
BenBella Books (*US*)
Beyond Words Publishing (*US*)
Black Dome Press (*US*)
Blink Publishing (*UK*)
Blue Mountain Arts, Inc. (*US*)
Career Press (*US*)
Chelsea Green Publishing, Inc. (*US*)
Chicago Review Press (*US*)
Chronicle Books LLC (*US*)
Clarkson Potter (*US*)
Co & Bear Productions (*UK*)
Concordia Publishing House (*US*)
Connections Book Publishing Ltd (*UK*)
Countryside Books (*UK*)
Cynren Press (*US*)
Dreamriver Press (*US*)
Familius (*US*)
Ferguson Publishing (*US*)
Flame Tree Publishing (*UK*)
Gill Books (*Ire*)
HarperCollins Publishers Ltd (*UK*)
The Harvard Common Press (*US*)
Hawthorn Press (*UK*)
Hay House Publishers (*UK*)
Health Communications, Inc. (*US*)
Hipso Media (*US*)
Hodder & Stoughton Ltd (*UK*)
Hohm Press (*US*)
Igloo Books Limited (*UK*)
Infinite Ideas (*UK*)
Insomniac Press (*Can*)
Kube Publishing (*UK*)
Luath Press Ltd (*UK*)
Management Books 2000 Ltd (*UK*)
Mandrake of Oxford (*UK*)
Melbourne University Publishing Ltd (*Aus*)
Michael Joseph (*UK*)
The O'Brien Press (*Ire*)
Octopus Publishing Group Limited (*UK*)
Page Street Publishing Co. (*US*)
Pavilion Books Group Limited (*UK*)
Pelican Publishing Company (*US*)
Pen & Sword Books Ltd (*UK*)

Quarto Publishing Group UK (*UK*)
Red Wheel (*US*)
Robert D. Reed Publishers (*US*)
Robert Hale Publishers (*UK*)
Ryland Peters & Small (*UK*)
Silver Lake Publishing, LLC (*US*)
SisterShip Press Pty Ltd (*Aus*)
Sterling Publishing Co. Inc. (*US*)
Summersdale Publishers Ltd (*UK*)
Temple University Press (*US*)
Torah Aura Productions (*US*)
W.W. Norton & Company Ltd (*UK*)
WorthyKids / Ideals (*US*)
Literature
Algora Publishing (*US*)
Allen & Unwin (*Aus*)
Alma Books Ltd (*UK*)
Alma Classics (*UK*)
Ashgate Publishing Limited (*UK*)
Aurora Metro Press (*UK*)
Beacon Press (*US*)
BL VNP Incorporated (*US*)
Bodleian Library Publishing (*UK*)
Boydell & Brewer Ltd (*UK*)
Bucknell University Press (*US*)
Carcanet Press Ltd (*UK*)
Carina UK (*UK*)
CJ Fallon (*Ire*)
Classical Comics Limited (*UK*)
Cork University Press (*Ire*)
Coteau Books (*Can*)
David R. Godine, Publisher (*US*)
Dedalus Ltd (*UK*)
Dreamriver Press (*US*)
Duckworth Publishers (*UK*)
Duquesne University Press (*US*)
ECW Press (*Can*)
Edinburgh University Press (*UK*)
Fairleigh Dickinson University (FDU) Press
(*Can*)
Fence Books (*US*)
Fernwood Publishing (*Can*)
Floris Books (*UK*)
Folded Word LLC (*US*)
Fordham University Press (*US*)
Four Courts Press (*Ire*)
Gallaudet University Press (*US*)
Garnet Publishing (*UK*)
George Braziller, Inc. (*US*)
Gingko Library (*UK*)
Gomer Press (*UK*)
Greenhaven Publishing (*US*)
Greystones Press (*UK*)
Halban Publishers (*UK*)
Hesperus Press Limited (*UK*)
Heyday Books (*US*)
Hohm Press (*US*)
House of Lochar (*UK*)
Insomniac Press (*Can*)
Interlink Publishing Group, Inc. (*US*)
Kaya Press (*US*)
Kent State University Press (*US*)
Kettillonia (*UK*)

The Lilliput Press (*Ire*)
Little, Brown Book Group (*UK*)
LSU Press (*US*)
Mage Publishers (*US*)
Melbourne University Publishing Ltd (*Aus*)
Northcote House Publishers Ltd (*UK*)
The O'Brien Press (*Ire*)
Oak Knoll Press (*US*)
Oleander Press (*UK*)
Oneworld Publications (*UK*)
Oregon State University Press (*US*)
Pelican Publishing Company (*US*)
Polity Press (*UK*)
Red Moon Press (*US*)
Santa Monica Press (*US*)
Schofield & Sims (*UK*)
Sterling Publishing Co. Inc. (*US*)
Syracuse University Press (*US*)
Temple University Press (*US*)
Truman State University Press (*US*)
University College Dublin (UCD) Press (*Ire*)
University of Exeter Press (*UK*)
The University of Michigan Press (*US*)
University of Wales Press (*UK*)
W.W. Norton & Company Ltd (*UK*)
Ward Lock Educational Ltd (*UK*)
Wesleyan University Press (*US*)
WhiteFire Publishing (*US*)
Media
Allen & Unwin (*Aus*)
BFI Publishing (*UK*)
Coteau Books (*Can*)
Edinburgh University Press (*UK*)
Fordham University Press (*US*)
Garnet Publishing (*UK*)
HarperCollins Publishers Ltd (*UK*)
Infinite Ideas (*UK*)
LSU Press (*US*)
Pandora Press (*UK*)
Polity Press (*UK*)
I.B. Tauris & Co. Ltd (*UK*)
Temple University Press (*US*)
The University of Michigan Press (*US*)
University of Wales Press (*UK*)
Verso (*UK*)
Zed Books Ltd (*UK*)
ZigZag Education (*UK*)
Medicine
Abdo Publishing Co (*US*)
Beacon Press (*US*)
Birlinn Ltd (*UK*)
Bucknell University Press (*US*)
Bull Publishing Company (*US*)
Dreamriver Press (*US*)
Dunedin Academic Press Ltd (*UK*)
Eastland Press (*US*)
Familius (*US*)
Fernwood Publishing (*Can*)
Fordham University Press (*US*)
Greenhaven Publishing (*US*)
Hay House Publishers (*UK*)
Health Communications, Inc. (*US*)
Health Professions Press (*US*)

Hipso Media (*US*)
Human Kinetics (*US*)
Insomniac Press (*Can*)
Pelican Publishing Company (*US*)
Polity Press (*UK*)
Silver Lake Publishing, LLC (*US*)
Singing Dragon (*UK*)
Springer-Verlag London Ltd (*UK*)
TSO (The Stationery Office) (*UK*)
W.W. Norton & Company Ltd (*UK*)
YMAA Publication Center, Inc. (*US*)
Zed Books Ltd (*UK*)
Men's Interests
Carina UK (*UK*)
Connections Book Publishing Ltd (*UK*)
Cynren Press (*US*)
GEY Books (*UK*)
Hay House Publishers (*UK*)
Health Communications, Inc. (*US*)
Military
Abdo Publishing Co (*US*)
Algora Publishing (*US*)
Allen & Unwin (*Aus*)
Allison & Busby Ltd (*UK*)
Amberley Publishing (*UK*)
Birlinn Ltd (*UK*)
Blink Publishing (*UK*)
Boydell & Brewer Ltd (*UK*)
Candy Jar Books (*UK*)
Clarity Press, Inc. (*US*)
Countryside Books (*UK*)
Fonthill Media LLC (*US*)
Fonthill Media Ltd (*UK*)
Grub Street Publishing (*UK*)
HarperCollins Publishers Ltd (*UK*)
Hendrick-Long Publishing Co. (*US*)
Heritage House (*Can*)
IWM (Imperial War Museums) (*UK*)
Jane's Information Group (*UK*)
LSU Press (*US*)
Monsoon Books Pte Ltd (*UK*)
Paladin Press (*US*)
Pen & Sword Books Ltd (*UK*)
Sunstone Press (*US*)
Ulric Publishing (*UK*)
Unicorn Publishing Group (*UK*)
University College Dublin (UCD) Press (*Ire*)
Weidenfeld & Nicolson (*UK*)
Music
Algora Publishing (*US*)
Allen & Unwin (*Aus*)
Arc Publications (*UK*)
Ashgate Publishing Limited (*UK*)
Aureus Publishing Limited (*UK*)
Aurora Metro Press (*UK*)
Black Dog Publishing London UK (*UK*)
Blink Publishing (*UK*)
Boydell & Brewer Ltd (*UK*)
Carlton Publishing Group (*UK*)
Chicago Review Press (*US*)
Chronicle Books LLC (*US*)
CJ Fallon (*Ire*)
Cork University Press (*Ire*)

Duckworth Publishers (*UK*)
Dunedin Academic Press Ltd (*UK*)
Faber & Faber Ltd (*UK*)
Fairleigh Dickinson University (FDU) Press
(*Can*)
Flame Tree Publishing (*UK*)
Fordham University Press (*US*)
Gingko Library (*UK*)
Gomer Press (*UK*)
Greenhaven Publishing (*US*)
Greystones Press (*UK*)
Hal Leonard Performing Arts Publishing Group
(*US*)
Haus Publishing (*UK*)
Hymns Ancient & Modern Ltd (*UK*)
Insomniac Press (*Can*)
Interlink Publishing Group, Inc. (*US*)
The Lilliput Press (*Ire*)
LSU Press (*US*)
Mage Publishers (*US*)
Maverick Musicals & Plays (*Aus*)
Kevin Mayhew Publishers (*UK*)
McGraw-Hill Education (*US*)
The O'Brien Press (*Ire*)
Octopus Publishing Group Limited (*UK*)
Omnibus Press (*UK*)
Pelican Publishing Company (*US*)
Serpent's Tail (*UK*)
Sheldrake Press (*UK*)
Sterling Publishing Co. Inc. (*US*)
Sunstone Press (*US*)
Triangle Square (*US*)
University College Dublin (UCD) Press (*Ire*)
The University of Michigan Press (*US*)
Vehicule Press (*Can*)
W.W. Norton & Company Ltd (*UK*)
Ward Lock Educational Ltd (*UK*)
Wesleyan University Press (*US*)
ZigZag Education (*UK*)
Mystery
Academy Chicago (*US*)
Allen & Unwin (*Aus*)
Allison & Busby Ltd (*UK*)
American Quilter's Society (*US*)
Asabi Publishing (*US*)
Bancroft Press (*US*)
Bloomsbury Spark (*UK*)
BL VNP Incorporated (*US*)
Carina UK (*UK*)
Coteau Books (*Can*)
Cynren Press (*US*)
Divertir Publishing LLC (*US*)
ECW Press (*Can*)
Elm Books (*US*)
4RV Publishing (*US*)
Harken Media (*US*)
Harmony Ink Press (*US*)
HarperCollins (*US*)
Head of Zeus (*UK*)
Hipso Media (*US*)
Insomniac Press (*Can*)
Joffe Books Ltd (*UK*)
Jolly Fish Press (*US*)

JourneyForth (*US*)
Mandrake of Oxford (*UK*)
NBM Publishing (*US*)
Oceanview Publishing (*US*)
Page Street Publishing Co. (*US*)
Penguin Random House (*US*)
Polis Books (*US*)
Quirk Books (*US*)
Red Empress Publishing (*US*)
Salvo Press (*US*)
Scribner (*US*)
SisterShip Press Pty Ltd (*Aus*)
Sterling Publishing Co. Inc. (*US*)
Sunstone Press (*US*)
Thomas Dunne Books (*US*)
TouchWood Editions (*Can*)
WaterBrook & Multnomah (*US*)
WhiteFire Publishing (*US*)
Wordsworth Editions (*UK*)
Zumaya Publications (*US*)
Nature
Algora Publishing (*US*)
Allen & Unwin (*Aus*)
Alpine Publications, Inc. (*US*)
Appalachian Mountain Club Books (*US*)
Beacon Press (*US*)
Birlinn Ltd (*UK*)
Black Dog Publishing London UK (*UK*)
Black Dome Press (*US*)
Bristol University Press (*UK*)
Charlesbridge Publishing (*US*)
Chelsea Green Publishing, Inc. (*US*)
Co & Bear Productions (*UK*)
David R. Godine, Publisher (*US*)
Dawn Publications (*US*)
Dovecote Press (*UK*)
Down The Shore Publishing (*US*)
Dreamriver Press (*US*)
Duckworth Publishers (*UK*)
Dunedin Academic Press Ltd (*UK*)
Edward Elgar Publishing Ltd (*UK*)
Encante Press, LLC (*US*)
FalconGuides (*US*)
Fernwood Publishing (*Can*)
Finney Company (*US*)
Folded Word LLC (*US*)
Formac Publishing Company Limited (*Can*)
Gill Books (*Ire*)
Gomer Press (*UK*)
Granta Books (*UK*)
Greenhaven Publishing (*US*)
Hay House Publishers (*UK*)
Heritage House (*Can*)
Heyday Books (*US*)
Hohm Press (*US*)
JourneyForth (*US*)
The Lilliput Press (*Ire*)
LSU Press (*US*)
Luath Press Ltd (*UK*)
Mountaineers Books (*US*)
National Museum Wales (*UK*)
Natural History Museum Publishing (*UK*)
The O'Brien Press (*Ire*)

Oneworld Publications (*UK*)
Oregon State University Press (*US*)
Page Street Publishing Co. (*US*)
Pelican Publishing Company (*US*)
Pen & Sword Books Ltd (*UK*)
Policy Studies Institute (PSI) (*UK*)
Polity Press (*UK*)
Red Wheel (*US*)
Robert Hale Publishers (*UK*)
Ruby Tuesday Books (*UK*)
SisterShip Press Pty Ltd (*Aus*)
Sterling Publishing Co. Inc. (*US*)
Sunstone Press (*US*)
Temple University Press (*US*)
Think Publishing (*UK*)
TouchWood Editions (*Can*)
Triangle Square (*US*)
Truman State University Press (*US*)
University College Dublin (UCD) Press (*Ire*)
University of Alaska Press (*US*)
The University of Michigan Press (*US*)
University of Wales Press (*UK*)
University of Washington Press (*US*)
Venture Publishing, Inc. (*US*)
W.W. Norton & Company Ltd (*UK*)
Willow Creek Press, Inc. (*US*)
WIT Press (*UK*)
Zed Books Ltd (*UK*)
New Age
Chelsea Green Publishing, Inc. (*US*)
Connections Book Publishing Ltd (*UK*)
Dreamriver Press (*US*)
Findhorn Press Ltd (*UK*)
Red Wheel (*US*)
Sterling Publishing Co. Inc. (*US*)
Nonfiction
Abdo Publishing Co (*US*)
Academy Chicago (*US*)
ACC Art Books Ltd (*UK*)
ACTA Publications (*US*)
Albert Whitman & Company (*US*)
Algora Publishing (*US*)
Allen & Unwin (*Aus*)
Allison & Busby Ltd (*UK*)
Allyn and Bacon / Merrill Education (*US*)
Alma Books Ltd (*UK*)
Alpine Publications, Inc. (*US*)
Amberley Publishing (*UK*)
American Counseling Association (*US*)
American Psychiatric Association Publishing (*US*)
American Quilter's Society (*US*)
Andrews McMeel Publishing (*US*)
Appalachian Mountain Club Books (*US*)
Appletree Press Ltd (*UK*)
Arbordale Publishing (*US*)
Arthur A. Levine Books (*US*)
Asabi Publishing (*US*)
ASCE Press (*US*)
Ashgate Publishing Limited (*UK*)
Ashmolean Museum Publications (*UK*)
Association for Supervision and Curriculum Development (ASCD) (*US*)

Astragal Press (*US*)
Augsburg Fortress (*US*)
Aureus Publishing Limited (*UK*)
Aurora Metro Press (*UK*)
Award Publications Limited (*UK*)
Baker Publishing Group (*US*)
Ball Publishing (*US*)
Bancroft Press (*US*)
Barrington Stoke (*UK*)
Beacon Hill Press of Kansas City (*US*)
Beacon Press (*US*)
Beacon Publishing Group (*US*)
BearManor Media (*US*)
BenBella Books (*US*)
Bernard Babani (publishing) Ltd (*UK*)
Beyond Words Publishing (*US*)
BFI Publishing (*UK*)
Birlinn Ltd (*UK*)
BkMk Press (*US*)
Black & White Publishing Ltd (*UK*)
Black Dog Publishing London UK (*UK*)
Black Dome Press (*US*)
Black Rose Writing (*US*)
Blink Publishing (*UK*)
Bloomberg Press (*US*)
Blue Mountain Arts, Inc. (*US*)
Blue River Press (*US*)
Bodleian Library Publishing (*UK*)
Boydell & Brewer Ltd (*UK*)
Bradt Travel Guides (*UK*)
Nicholas Brealey Publishing (*UK*)
Brewers Publications (*US*)
Brilliant Publications (*UK*)
Bristol University Press (*UK*)
Bucknell University Press (*US*)
Bull Publishing Company (*US*)
Butte Publications, Inc. (*US*)
C&T Publishing (*US*)
Candy Jar Books (*UK*)
Canongate Books (*UK*)
Canopus Publishing Ltd (*UK*)
Capstone Professional (*US*)
Carcanet Press Ltd (*UK*)
Career Press (*US*)
Carlton Publishing Group (*UK*)
Carson-Dellosa Publishing Company, Inc. (*US*)
CATO Institute (*US*)
Cedar Fort (*US*)
Charlesbridge Publishing (*US*)
Chelsea Green Publishing, Inc. (*US*)
Chicago Review Press (*US*)
Chronicle Books LLC (*US*)
Churchwarden Publications Ltd (*UK*)
Cicerone Press (*UK*)
CJ Fallon (*Ire*)
Clarity Press, Inc. (*US*)
James Clarke & Co. (*UK*)
Clarkson Potter (*US*)
Co & Bear Productions (*UK*)
College Press Publishing (*US*)
Concordia Publishing House (*US*)
Connections Book Publishing Ltd (*UK*)
Cork University Press (*Ire*)

Coteau Books (*Can*)
Council for British Archaeology (CBA) Publishing (*UK*)
Countryside Books (*UK*)
CQ Press (*US*)
Crabtree Publishing (*US*)
Cressrelles Publishing Co. Ltd (*UK*)
The Crossroad Publishing Company (*US*)
Crown House Publishing (*UK*)
The Crown Publishing Group (*US*)
Crux Publishing (*UK*)
CSLI Publications (*US*)
CTS (Catholic Truth Society) (*UK*)
Cynren Press (*US*)
David R. Godine, Publisher (*US*)
Dawn Publications (*US*)
DB Publishing (*UK*)
Dino Books (*UK*)
Discovery Walking Guides Ltd (*UK*)
Divertir Publishing LLC (*US*)
Dovecote Press (*UK*)
Down The Shore Publishing (*US*)
Dragon Moon Press (*Can*)
Dream of Things (*US*)
Dreamriver Press (*US*)
Dref Wen (*UK*)
Duckworth Publishers (*UK*)
Dunedin Academic Press Ltd (*UK*)
Duquesne University Press (*US*)
Dynasty Press (*UK*)
Eagle's View Publishing (*US*)
Eastland Press (*US*)
ECW Press (*Can*)
Edinburgh University Press (*UK*)
The Educational Company of Ireland (*Ire*)
Edward Elgar Publishing Inc. (*US*)
Edward Elgar Publishing Ltd (*UK*)
Elm Books (*US*)
Encante Press, LLC (*US*)
Encyclopedia Britannica (UK) Ltd (*UK*)
Exley Publications (*UK*)
Eye Books (*UK*)
Faber & Faber Ltd (*UK*)
Faculty of 1000 Ltd (*UK*)
Fairleigh Dickinson University (FDU) Press (*Can*)
FalconGuides (*US*)
Familius (*US*)
Farrar, Straus and Giroux Books for Younger Readers (*US*)
Fence Books (*US*)
Ferguson Publishing (*US*)
Fernwood Publishing (*Can*)
Findhorn Press Ltd (*UK*)
Finney Company (*US*)
Fitzhenry & Whiteside Ltd (*Can*)
Fitzrovia Press Limited (*UK*)
Flame Tree Publishing (*UK*)
Fleming Publications (*UK*)
Floris Books (*UK*)
Folded Word LLC (*US*)
Fonthill Media LLC (*US*)
Fonthill Media Ltd (*UK*)

Footprint Handbooks (*UK*)
Fordham University Press (*US*)
Formac Publishing Company Limited (*Can*)
Forward Movement Publications (*US*)
Four Courts Press (*Ire*)
4RV Publishing (*US*)
Frances Lincoln Children's Books (*UK*)
Franciscan Media Books (*US*)
Frontinus (*UK*)
Gallaudet University Press (*US*)
The Gallery Press (*Ire*)
Galley Beggar Press (*UK*)
Garnet Publishing (*UK*)
Geddes & Grosset (*UK*)
Genealogical Publishing Company (*US*)
George Braziller, Inc. (*US*)
GEY Books (*UK*)
Gibbs Smith, Publisher (*US*)
Gibson Square Books Ltd (*UK*)
Gill Books (*Ire*)
Gingko Library (*UK*)
GL Assessment (*UK*)
Golden West Books (*US*)
Gomer Press (*UK*)
Goosebottom Books LLC (*US*)
Granta Books (*UK*)
Great Potential Press, Inc. (*US*)
Greenhaven Publishing (*US*)
Gresham Books Ltd (*UK*)
Greystones Press (*UK*)
Grub Street Publishing (*UK*)
Gryphon House, Inc. (*US*)
Guild of Master Craftsman (GMC) Publications
Ltd (*UK*)
Hachai Publishing (*US*)
Hal Leonard Performing Arts Publishing Group
(*US*)
Halban Publishers (*UK*)
Hanser Publications (*US*)
Harper Business (*US*)
HarperCollins (*US*)
HarperCollins Publishers Ltd (*UK*)
Hart Publishing Ltd (*UK*)
Hartman Publishing, Inc. (*US*)
The Harvard Common Press (*US*)
Haus Publishing (*UK*)
Hawthorn Press (*UK*)
Hay House Publishers (*UK*)
Haynes Publishing (*UK*)
Head of Zeus (*UK*)
Headline Publishing Group (*UK*)
Health Communications, Inc. (*US*)
Health Professions Press (*US*)
Hendrick-Long Publishing Co. (*US*)
Hendrickson Publishers (*US*)
Henry Holt and Company (*US*)
Heritage House (*Can*)
Hesperus Press Limited (*UK*)
Heyday Books (*US*)
Hipso Media (*US*)
Hodder & Stoughton Ltd (*UK*)
Hodder Faith (*UK*)
Hohm Press (*US*)

Holiday House, Inc. (*US*)
Honno Welsh Women's Press (*UK*)
Hopscotch (*UK*)
Hot Key Books (*UK*)
House of Lochar (*UK*)
Human Kinetics (*US*)
Humanix Books (*US*)
Hymns Ancient & Modern Ltd (*UK*)
ICS Publications (*US*)
Igloo Books Limited (*UK*)
Impress Books Limited (*UK*)
Imprint Academic (*UK*)
Incentive Publications (*US*)
Indiana Historical Society Press (*US*)
Infinite Ideas (*UK*)
Information Today, Inc. (*US*)
Insomniac Press (*Can*)
Interlink Publishing Group, Inc. (*US*)
International Wealth Success (IWS) Inc. (*US*)
Interweave Press (*US*)
Italica Press (*US*)
IWM (Imperial War Museums) (*UK*)
J.A. Allen (*UK*)
Jacaranda Books Art Music Ltd (*UK*)
Jane's Information Group (*UK*)
John Murray (Publishers) Ltd (*UK*)
JourneyForth (*US*)
Judaica Press (*US*)
Judson Press (*US*)
Kaeden Books (*US*)
Kansas City Star Quilts (*US*)
Kar-Ben Publishing (*US*)
Kaya Press (*US*)
Kent State University Press (*US*)
Kettillonia (*UK*)
Kirkbride Bible Company (*US*)
Krause Publications (*US*)
Kube Publishing (*UK*)
Lantana Publishing (*UK*)
Laurence King Publishing Ltd (*UK*)
Lawrence & Wishart (*UK*)
Lawrence Hill Books (*US*)
Leapfrog Press (*US*)
Lee & Low Books (*US*)
Legend Business (*UK*)
LexisNexis Canada (*Can*)
The Lilliput Press (*Ire*)
Lion Hudson Plc (*UK*)
Little Pickle Press, Inc. (*US*)
Little, Brown Book Group (*UK*)
Lonely Planet (*UK*)
Loyola Press (*US*)
LSU Press (*US*)
Luath Press Ltd (*UK*)
Lund Humphries Limited (*UK*)
Mage Publishers (*US*)
Management Books 2000 Ltd (*UK*)
Mandrake of Oxford (*UK*)
Mantra Lingua Ltd (*UK*)
Martin Sisters Publishing (*US*)
Maven House Press (*US*)
Kevin Mayhew Publishers (*UK*)
MC Press (*US*)

McGraw-Hill Education (*US*)
McSweeney's Publishing (*US*)
Melbourne University Publishing Ltd (*Aus*)
The Merlin Press (*UK*)
Messianic Jewish Publishers (*US*)
Metro Publications Ltd (*UK*)
Michael Joseph (*UK*)
Michael Terence Publishing (MTP) (*UK*)
MIrror Books (*UK*)
Monsoon Books Pte Ltd (*UK*)
Mountaineers Books (*US*)
Myriad Editions (*UK*)
National Museum Wales (*UK*)
Natural History Museum Publishing (*UK*)
Nick Hern Books Ltd (*UK*)
Nightboat Books (*US*)
No Starch Press, Inc. (*US*)
Nomad Press (*US*)
Northcote House Publishers Ltd (*UK*)
The O'Brien Press (*Ire*)
Oak Knoll Press (*US*)
Oberon Books (*UK*)
Octopus Publishing Group Limited (*UK*)
Oleander Press (*UK*)
Omnibus Press (*UK*)
Oneworld Publications (*UK*)
Onstream Publications Ltd (*Ire*)
Oregon State University Press (*US*)
Ouen Press (*UK*)
O'Reilly Media (*US*)
Page Street Publishing Co. (*US*)
Paladin Press (*US*)
Pandora Press (*UK*)
PaperBooks (*UK*)
PassKey Publications (*US*)
Paulist Press (*US*)
Pavilion Books Group Limited (*UK*)
Pavilion Publishing (*UK*)
Pelican Publishing Company (*US*)
Pen & Sword Books Ltd (*UK*)
Penguin Group (USA) Inc. (*US*)
Penguin Random House (*US*)
Periscope (*UK*)
Philosophy Documentation Center (*US*)
Phoenix Yard Books (*UK*)
Pimpernel Press (*UK*)
Pocol Press (*US*)
The Policy Press (*UK*)
Policy Studies Institute (PSI) (*UK*)
Polity Press (*UK*)
Princeton Architectural Press (*US*)
Profile Books (*UK*)
Psychology Press (*UK*)
Quarto Publishing Group UK (*UK*)
Quiller Publishing Ltd (*UK*)
Quirk Books (*US*)
Red Moon Press (*US*)
Red Wheel (*US*)
Rivers Oram Press (*UK*)
Robert D. Reed Publishers (*US*)
Robert Hale Publishers (*UK*)
Ruby Tuesday Books (*UK*)
Ryland Peters & Small (*UK*)

SAE International (*US*)
Santa Monica Press (*US*)
Schofield & Sims (*UK*)
Scholastic Library Publishing (*US*)
Science Museum Group (*UK*)
Scribner (*US*)
Search Press Ltd (*UK*)
Seaworthy Publications (*US*)
Serpent's Tail (*UK*)
Seven Stories Press (*US*)
Sheldrake Press (*UK*)
Silver Lake Publishing, LLC (*US*)
Simon & Schuster UK Limited (*UK*)
Singing Dragon (*UK*)
Siri Scientific Press (*UK*)
SisterShip Press Pty Ltd (*Aus*)
Sky Pony Press (*US*)
Snowbooks (*UK*)
Somerville Press (*Ire*)
Southern Illinois University Press (*US*)
Speechmark Publishing Limited (*UK*)
Springer-Verlag London Ltd (*UK*)
St Pauls (*US*)
St Pauls Publishing (*UK*)
Star Bright Books (*US*)
Sterling Publishing Co. Inc. (*US*)
Summersdale Publishers Ltd (*UK*)
Sunflower Books (*UK*)
Sunstone Press (*US*)
Syracuse University Press (*US*)
I.B. Tauris & Co. Ltd (*UK*)
Temple University Press (*US*)
Think Publishing (*UK*)
Thistle Publishing (*UK*)
Thomas Dunne Books (*US*)
Thomson Reuters Round Hall (*Ire*)
ThunderStone Books (*US*)
Titan Books (*UK*)
Top That! Publishing (*UK*)
Torah Aura Productions (*US*)
TouchWood Editions (*Can*)
Trentham Books Limited (*UK*)
Triangle Square (*US*)
Trotman & Co. Ltd (*UK*)
Truman State University Press (*US*)
TSO (The Stationery Office) (*UK*)
Two Rivers Press (*UK*)
Ulric Publishing (*UK*)
Unbound Publishing (*UK*)
Unicorn Publishing Group (*UK*)
University College Dublin (UCD) Press (*Ire*)
University of Alaska Press (*US*)
University of Exeter Press (*UK*)
The University of Michigan Press (*US*)
University of Pittsburgh Press (*US*)
University of Wales Press (*UK*)
University of Washington Press (*US*)
Valley Press (*UK*)
Vehicule Press (*Can*)
Venture Publishing, Inc. (*US*)
Verso (*UK*)
Wooden Books (*UK*)
W.W. Norton & Company Ltd (*UK*)

Walch Education (*US*)
Walker Books Ltd (*UK*)
Ward Lock Educational Ltd (*UK*)
WaterBrook & Multnomah (*US*)
Weidenfeld & Nicolson (*UK*)
Welsh Academic Press (*UK*)
Wesleyan University Press (*US*)
Wild Goose Publications (*UK*)
Willow Creek Press, Inc. (*US*)
WIT Press (*UK*)
WorthyKids / Ideals (*US*)
YMAA Publication Center, Inc. (*US*)
Zed Books Ltd (*UK*)
ZigZag Education (*UK*)
Zumaya Publications (*US*)

Philosophy
Algora Publishing (*US*)
Allen & Unwin (*Aus*)
Ashgate Publishing Limited (*UK*)
Bucknell University Press (*US*)
CATO Institute (*US*)
Connections Book Publishing Ltd (*UK*)
Cork University Press (*Ire*)
The Crossroad Publishing Company (*US*)
Cynren Press (*US*)
Dreamriver Press (*US*)
Duckworth Publishers (*UK*)
Dunedin Academic Press Ltd (*UK*)
Duquesne University Press (*US*)
Edinburgh University Press (*UK*)
Fairleigh Dickinson University (FDU) Press (*Can*)
Fernwood Publishing (*Can*)
Fitzrovia Press Limited (*UK*)
Floris Books (*UK*)
Fordham University Press (*US*)
Four Courts Press (*Ire*)
Gibson Square Books Ltd (*UK*)
Gingko Library (*UK*)
Halban Publishers (*UK*)
Hay House Publishers (*UK*)
Head of Zeus (*UK*)
Imprint Academic (*UK*)
The Lilliput Press (*Ire*)
Mandrake of Oxford (*UK*)
The Merlin Press (*UK*)
Oneworld Publications (*UK*)
Paulist Press (*US*)
Philosophy Documentation Center (*US*)
Polity Press (*UK*)
Red Wheel (*US*)
Scribner (*US*)
Southern Illinois University Press (*US*)
Triangle Square (*US*)
University of Exeter Press (*UK*)
The University of Michigan Press (*US*)
University of Pittsburgh Press (*US*)
University of Wales Press (*UK*)
Verso (*UK*)
W.W. Norton & Company Ltd (*UK*)
WhiteFire Publishing (*US*)
YMAA Publication Center, Inc. (*US*)
ZigZag Education (*UK*)

Photography
ACC Art Books Ltd (*UK*)
Black Dog Publishing London UK (*UK*)
Chronicle Books LLC (*US*)
Co & Bear Productions (*UK*)
Countryside Books (*UK*)
David R. Godine, Publisher (*US*)
Duckworth Publishers (*UK*)
Enitharmon Press (*UK*)
Fleming Publications (*UK*)
Fordham University Press (*US*)
Garnet Publishing (*UK*)
Guild of Master Craftsman (GMC) Publications Ltd (*UK*)
Haus Publishing (*UK*)
Interlink Publishing Group, Inc. (*US*)
Jacaranda Books Art Music Ltd (*UK*)
Laurence King Publishing Ltd (*UK*)
The Lilliput Press (*Ire*)
Luath Press Ltd (*UK*)
The O'Brien Press (*Ire*)
O'Reilly Media (*US*)
Pelican Publishing Company (*US*)
Santa Monica Press (*US*)
Southern Illinois University Press (*US*)
Sterling Publishing Co. Inc. (*US*)
Sunstone Press (*US*)
Temple University Press (*US*)
WhiteFire Publishing (*US*)

Poetry
Alice James Books (*US*)
Allen & Unwin (*Aus*)
Alma Classics (*UK*)
Andrews McMeel Publishing (*US*)
Arc Publications (*UK*)
Arrowhead Press (*UK*)
Bear Star Press (*US*)
Birlinn Ltd (*UK*)
BkMk Press (*US*)
Bloodaxe Books Ltd (*UK*)
Blue Mountain Arts, Inc. (*US*)
Brick Books (*Can*)
Carcanet Press Ltd (*UK*)
Chapman Publishing (*UK*)
Coteau Books (*Can*)
David Fickling Books (*UK*)
David R. Godine, Publisher (*US*)
Divertir Publishing LLC (*US*)
Down The Shore Publishing (*US*)
ECW Press (*Can*)
Elm Books (*US*)
The Emma Press Ltd (*UK*)
Enitharmon Press (*UK*)
Faber & Faber Ltd (*UK*)
Fence Books (*US*)
Fleming Publications (*UK*)
Floating Bridge Press (*US*)
Folded Word LLC (*US*)
Four Way Books (*US*)
Frances Lincoln Children's Books (*UK*)
FutureCycle Press (*US*)
The Gallery Press (*Ire*)
George Braziller, Inc. (*US*)

GEY Books (*UK*)
Gomer Press (*UK*)
Helicon Nine Editions (*US*)
Hesperus Press Limited (*UK*)
Heyday Books (*US*)
Hippopotamus Press (*UK*)
Honno Welsh Women's Press (*UK*)
Indigo Dreams Publishing (*UK*)
Insomniac Press (*Can*)
Italica Press (*US*)
Kaya Press (*US*)
Kettillonia (*UK*)
Kube Publishing (*UK*)
Leapfrog Press (*US*)
The Lilliput Press (*Ire*)
Lost Horse Press (*US*)
LSU Press (*US*)
Luath Press Ltd (*UK*)
Luna Bisonte Prods (*US*)
Mage Publishers (*US*)
McSweeney's Publishing (*US*)
New Directions Publishing (*US*)
Nightboat Books (*US*)
Oleander Press (*UK*)
Oversteps Books (*UK*)
Pelican Publishing Company (*US*)
Penguin Random House (*US*)
Phoenix Yard Books (*UK*)
Red Moon Press (*US*)
Sibling Rivalry Press, LLC (*US*)
SisterShip Press Pty Ltd (*Aus*)
Southern Illinois University Press (*US*)
Stonewood Press (*UK*)
Sunstone Press (*US*)
Troika Books (*UK*)
Two Rivers Press (*UK*)
University of Alaska Press (*US*)
University of Pittsburgh Press (*US*)
Valley Press (*UK*)
Vehicule Press (*Can*)
W.W. Norton & Company Ltd (*UK*)
Wave Books (*US*)
WhiteFire Publishing (*US*)
Wild Goose Publications (*UK*)
Politics
Abdo Publishing Co (*US*)
Algora Publishing (*US*)
Allen & Unwin (*Aus*)
Ashgate Publishing Limited (*UK*)
Beacon Press (*US*)
BenBella Books (*US*)
Birlinn Ltd (*UK*)
Bristol University Press (*UK*)
Bucknell University Press (*US*)
Canongate Books (*UK*)
CATO Institute (*US*)
Chelsea Green Publishing, Inc. (*US*)
Chicago Review Press (*US*)
Clarity Press, Inc. (*US*)
Cork University Press (*Ire*)
CQ Press (*US*)
The Crown Publishing Group (*US*)
Divertir Publishing LLC (*US*)

Dreamriver Press (*US*)
Duckworth Publishers (*UK*)
ECW Press (*Can*)
Edinburgh University Press (*UK*)
Edward Elgar Publishing Ltd (*UK*)
Encante Press, LLC (*US*)
Faber & Faber Ltd (*UK*)
Fernwood Publishing (*Can*)
Fordham University Press (*US*)
Formac Publishing Company Limited (*Can*)
Garnet Publishing (*UK*)
Gibson Square Books Ltd (*UK*)
Gingko Library (*UK*)
Granta Books (*UK*)
Greenhaven Publishing (*US*)
Halban Publishers (*UK*)
Haus Publishing (*UK*)
Heritage House (*Can*)
Humanix Books (*US*)
Imprint Academic (*UK*)
Infinite Ideas (*UK*)
Insomniac Press (*Can*)
Interlink Publishing Group, Inc. (*US*)
Kube Publishing (*UK*)
Lawrence & Wishart (*UK*)
Lawrence Hill Books (*US*)
The Lilliput Press (*Ire*)
Luath Press Ltd (*UK*)
McGraw-Hill Education (*US*)
Melbourne University Publishing Ltd (*Aus*)
The Merlin Press (*UK*)
Monsoon Books Pte Ltd (*UK*)
Myriad Editions (*UK*)
The O'Brien Press (*Ire*)
Oneworld Publications (*UK*)
Paladin Press (*US*)
Pandora Press (*UK*)
PaperBooks (*UK*)
Pelican Publishing Company (*US*)
Penguin Random House (*US*)
Periscope (*UK*)
The Policy Press (*UK*)
Policy Studies Institute (PSI) (*UK*)
Polity Press (*UK*)
Profile Books (*UK*)
Rivers Oram Press (*UK*)
Serpent's Tail (*UK*)
Seven Stories Press (*US*)
Silver Lake Publishing, LLC (*US*)
Simon & Schuster UK Limited (*UK*)
Southern Illinois University Press (*US*)
Sunstone Press (*US*)
Syracuse University Press (*US*)
I.B. Tauris & Co. Ltd (*UK*)
Temple University Press (*US*)
Thomas Dunne Books (*US*)
Triangle Square (*US*)
University College Dublin (UCD) Press (*Ire*)
University of Alaska Press (*US*)
The University of Michigan Press (*US*)
University of Wales Press (*UK*)
Verso (*UK*)
W.W. Norton & Company Ltd (*UK*)

Welsh Academic Press (*UK*)
Wild Goose Publications (*UK*)
Zed Books Ltd (*UK*)
ZigZag Education (*UK*)

Psychology
Algora Publishing (*US*)
Allen & Unwin (*Aus*)
American Psychiatric Association Publishing (*US*)
Black & White Publishing Ltd (*UK*)
Nicholas Brealey Publishing (*UK*)
Bucknell University Press (*US*)
Bull Publishing Company (*US*)
Connections Book Publishing Ltd (*UK*)
Crown House Publishing (*UK*)
Dreamriver Press (*US*)
Duquesne University Press (*US*)
Gallaudet University Press (*US*)
Gibson Square Books Ltd (*UK*)
Hay House Publishers (*UK*)
Health Communications, Inc. (*US*)
Health Professions Press (*US*)
Human Kinetics (*US*)
Imprint Academic (*UK*)
McGraw-Hill Education (*US*)
Octopus Publishing Group Limited (*UK*)
Oneworld Publications (*UK*)
Pelican Publishing Company (*US*)
Polity Press (*UK*)
Profile Books (*UK*)
Psychology Press (*UK*)
Red Wheel (*US*)
Robert D. Reed Publishers (*US*)
Scribner (*US*)
SisterShip Press Pty Ltd (*Aus*)
Speechmark Publishing Limited (*UK*)
Temple University Press (*US*)
Twenty First Century Publishers Ltd (*UK*)
The University of Michigan Press (*US*)
W.W. Norton & Company Ltd (*UK*)
WhiteFire Publishing (*US*)
ZigZag Education (*UK*)

Radio
BearManor Media (*US*)

Reference
Award Publications Limited (*UK*)
Barrington Stoke (*UK*)
Beercott Books (*UK*)
BFI Publishing (*UK*)
Birlinn Ltd (*UK*)
Black Dog Publishing London UK (*UK*)
Bloomberg Press (*US*)
Career Press (*US*)
Carlton Publishing Group (*UK*)
Churchwarden Publications Ltd (*UK*)
Cicerone Press (*UK*)
CJ Fallon (*Ire*)
James Clarke & Co. (*UK*)
Connections Book Publishing Ltd (*UK*)
CQ Press (*US*)
Edinburgh University Press (*UK*)
Encyclopedia Britannica (UK) Ltd (*UK*)
Ferguson Publishing (*US*)

Fernwood Publishing (*Can*)
Footprint Handbooks (*UK*)
Geddes & Grosset (*UK*)
Gill Books (*Ire*)
Gomer Press (*UK*)
Greenhaven Publishing (*US*)
Grub Street Publishing (*UK*)
Guild of Master Craftsman (GMC) Publications Ltd (*UK*)
Hanser Publications (*US*)
HarperCollins (*US*)
HarperCollins Publishers Ltd (*UK*)
Haynes Publishing (*UK*)
Health Professions Press (*US*)
Hendrickson Publishers (*US*)
Hesperus Press Limited (*UK*)
Hymns Ancient & Modern Ltd (*UK*)
Igloo Books Limited (*UK*)
Insomniac Press (*Can*)
Interlink Publishing Group, Inc. (*US*)
Jane's Information Group (*UK*)
Kirkbride Bible Company (*US*)
Krause Publications (*US*)
LexisNexis Canada (*Can*)
The Lilliput Press (*Ire*)
Lion Hudson Plc (*UK*)
Myriad Editions (*UK*)
The O'Brien Press (*Ire*)
Octopus Publishing Group Limited (*UK*)
Oleander Press (*UK*)
Pandora Press (*UK*)
Pavilion Publishing (*UK*)
Penguin Random House (*US*)
Philosophy Documentation Center (*US*)
Polity Press (*UK*)
Quiller Publishing Ltd (*UK*)
Robert Hale Publishers (*UK*)
Santa Monica Press (*US*)
Scholastic Library Publishing (*US*)
Silver Lake Publishing, LLC (*US*)
Siri Scientific Press (*UK*)
SisterShip Press Pty Ltd (*Aus*)
Sterling Publishing Co. Inc. (*US*)
Sunstone Press (*US*)
Thomson Reuters Round Hall (*Ire*)
Top That! Publishing (*UK*)
Trotman & Co. Ltd (*UK*)
TSO (The Stationery Office) (*UK*)
Unicorn Publishing Group (*UK*)
University of Exeter Press (*UK*)
The University of Michigan Press (*US*)
Willow Creek Press, Inc. (*US*)

Religious
Abdo Publishing Co (*US*)
ACTA Publications (*US*)
Algora Publishing (*US*)
Allen & Unwin (*Aus*)
Ashgate Publishing Limited (*UK*)
Augsburg Fortress (*US*)
Baker Publishing Group (*US*)
Beacon Hill Press of Kansas City (*US*)
Beacon Press (*US*)
Boydell & Brewer Ltd (*UK*)

Bucknell University Press (*US*)
Cedar Fort (*US*)
Churchwarden Publications Ltd (*UK*)
CJ Fallon (*Ire*)
James Clarke & Co. (*UK*)
College Press Publishing (*US*)
Concordia Publishing House (*US*)
Connections Book Publishing Ltd (*UK*)
The Crossroad Publishing Company (*US*)
CTS (Catholic Truth Society) (*UK*)
Divertir Publishing LLC (*US*)
Dreamriver Press (*US*)
Duckworth Publishers (*UK*)
Dunedin Academic Press Ltd (*UK*)
Duquesne University Press (*US*)
ECW Press (*Can*)
Edinburgh University Press (*UK*)
Fairleigh Dickinson University (FDU) Press
(*Can*)
Floris Books (*UK*)
Fordham University Press (*US*)
Forward Movement Publications (*US*)
Four Courts Press (*Ire*)
4RV Publishing (*US*)
Franciscan Media Books (*US*)
Garnet Publishing (*UK*)
Gingko Library (*UK*)
Gomer Press (*UK*)
Gresham Books Ltd (*UK*)
Hachai Publishing (*US*)
Halban Publishers (*UK*)
HarperCollins (*US*)
Hay House Publishers (*UK*)
Health Communications, Inc. (*US*)
Hendrickson Publishers (*US*)
Hodder Faith (*UK*)
Hohm Press (*US*)
Hymns Ancient & Modern Ltd (*UK*)
ICS Publications (*US*)
Impress Books Limited (*UK*)
Insomniac Press (*Can*)
JourneyForth (*US*)
Judaica Press (*US*)
Judson Press (*US*)
Kar-Ben Publishing (*US*)
Kirkbride Bible Company (*US*)
Kube Publishing (*UK*)
Lillenas Drama Resources (*US*)
Lion Hudson Plc (*UK*)
Loyola Press (*US*)
Martin Sisters Publishing (*US*)
Kevin Mayhew Publishers (*UK*)
Messianic Jewish Publishers (*US*)
The O'Brien Press (*Ire*)
Oneworld Publications (*UK*)
Paulist Press (*US*)
Pelican Publishing Company (*US*)
Polity Press (*UK*)
Red Wheel (*US*)
Scribner (*US*)
St Pauls (*US*)
St Pauls Publishing (*UK*)
Sunstone Press (*US*)

Syracuse University Press (*US*)
I.B. Tauris & Co. Ltd (*UK*)
Temple University Press (*US*)
Torah Aura Productions (*US*)
Triangle Square (*US*)
Truman State University Press (*US*)
University College Dublin (UCD) Press (*Ire*)
University of Exeter Press (*UK*)
The University of Michigan Press (*US*)
University of Wales Press (*UK*)
Vehicule Press (*Can*)
W.W. Norton & Company Ltd (*UK*)
WaterBrook & Multnomah (*US*)
WhiteFire Publishing (*US*)
Wild Goose Publications (*UK*)
WorthyKids / Ideals (*US*)
ZigZag Education (*UK*)
Romance
American Quilter's Society (*US*)
Black & White Publishing Ltd (*UK*)
Bloomsbury Spark (*UK*)
BLVNP Incorporated (*US*)
Carina UK (*UK*)
Cuil Press (*US*)
Divertir Publishing LLC (*US*)
Dragon Moon Press (*Can*)
Ellysian Press (*US*)
Elm Books (*US*)
Entangled Teen (*US*)
4RV Publishing (*US*)
GEY Books (*UK*)
Harlequin American Romance (*US*)
Harlequin Dare (*Can*)
Harlequin Mills & Boon Ltd (*UK*)
Harmony Ink Press (*US*)
HarperCollins (*US*)
Head of Zeus (*UK*)
Hesperus Press Limited (*UK*)
Jacaranda Books Art Music Ltd (*UK*)
Melange Books, LLC (*US*)
Monsoon Books Pte Ltd (*UK*)
Penguin Random House (*US*)
Polis Books (*US*)
Red Empress Publishing (*US*)
Robert Hale Publishers (*UK*)
SisterShip Press Pty Ltd (*Aus*)
Sunstone Press (*US*)
WaterBrook & Multnomah (*US*)
WhiteFire Publishing (*US*)
Wordsworth Editions (*UK*)
World Weaver Press (*US*)
Zumaya Publications (*US*)
Science
Abdo Publishing Co (*US*)
Algora Publishing (*US*)
Allen & Unwin (*Aus*)
American Psychiatric Association Publishing
(*US*)
Arbordale Publishing (*US*)
ASCE Press (*US*)
Astragal Press (*US*)
Beacon Press (*US*)
BenBella Books (*US*)

Black Dome Press (*US*)
Bucknell University Press (*US*)
Canongate Books (*UK*)
Canopus Publishing Ltd (*UK*)
Charlesbridge Publishing (*US*)
Chelsea Green Publishing, Inc. (*US*)
Chicago Review Press (*US*)
CJ Fallon (*Ire*)
Crabtree Publishing (*US*)
Dreamriver Press (*US*)
Duckworth Publishers (*UK*)
Dunedin Academic Press Ltd (*UK*)
Edinburgh University Press (*UK*)
Encante Press, LLC (*US*)
Faculty of 1000 Ltd (*UK*)
Finney Company (*US*)
Floris Books (*UK*)
Fordham University Press (*US*)
Gingko Library (*UK*)
Greenhaven Publishing (*US*)
Hanser Publications (*US*)
HarperCollins Publishers Ltd (*UK*)
Headline Publishing Group (*UK*)
Hendrick-Long Publishing Co. (*US*)
Hopscotch (*UK*)
Human Kinetics (*US*)
Humanix Books (*US*)
Kaeden Books (*US*)
McGraw-Hill Education (*US*)
Melbourne University Publishing Ltd (*Aus*)
Natural History Museum Publishing (*UK*)
Nomad Press (*US*)
Oneworld Publications (*UK*)
Oregon State University Press (*US*)
O'Reilly Media (*US*)
Page Street Publishing Co. (*US*)
Pelican Publishing Company (*US*)
Penguin Random House (*US*)
Periscope (*UK*)
Profile Books (*UK*)
Quirk Books (*US*)
Ruby Tuesday Books (*UK*)
Schofield & Sims (*UK*)
Science Museum Group (*UK*)
Scribner (*US*)
Simon & Schuster UK Limited (*UK*)
Siri Scientific Press (*UK*)
SisterShip Press Pty Ltd (*Aus*)
Springer-Verlag London Ltd (*UK*)
Sterling Publishing Co. Inc. (*US*)
Temple University Press (*US*)
Trentham Books Limited (*UK*)
Tumblehome Learning, Inc. (*US*)
University College Dublin (UCD) Press (*Ire*)
University of Alaska Press (*US*)
University of Pittsburgh Press (*US*)
Wooden Books (*UK*)
W.W. Norton & Company Ltd (*UK*)
Walch Education (*US*)
Ward Lock Educational Ltd (*UK*)
WIT Press (*UK*)
ZigZag Education (*UK*)

Sci-Fi
Allison & Busby Ltd (*UK*)
Baen Books (*US*)
Bloomsbury Spark (*UK*)
BL VNP Incorporated (*US*)
Candy Jar Books (*UK*)
Carina UK (*UK*)
Cuil Press (*US*)
Divertir Publishing LLC (*US*)
Dragon Moon Press (*Can*)
Duckworth Publishers (*UK*)
Ellysian Press (*US*)
Elm Books (*US*)
Entangled Teen (*US*)
Fingerpress UK (*UK*)
4RV Publishing (*US*)
Harken Media (*US*)
Harmony Ink Press (*US*)
HarperCollins (*US*)
HarperCollins Publishers Ltd (*UK*)
Head of Zeus (*UK*)
Hesperus Press Limited (*UK*)
Honno Welsh Women's Press (*UK*)
IDW Publishing (*US*)
Jolly Fish Press (*US*)
Little, Brown Book Group (*UK*)
Luna Press Publishing (*UK*)
Mandrake of Oxford (*UK*)
Martin Sisters Publishing (*US*)
NBM Publishing (*US*)
Penguin Random House (*US*)
Polis Books (*US*)
Quirk Books (*US*)
Snowbooks (*UK*)
Sunstone Press (*US*)
Titan Books (*UK*)
WaterBrook & Multnomah (*US*)
WhiteFire Publishing (*US*)
Wordsworth Editions (*UK*)
World Weaver Press (*US*)
Zumaya Publications (*US*)
Scripts
Allen & Unwin (*Aus*)
Alma Classics (*UK*)
Aurora Metro Press (*UK*)
Beercott Books (*UK*)
Chapman Publishing (*UK*)
Coteau Books (*Can*)
Cressrelles Publishing Co. Ltd (*UK*)
Faber & Faber Ltd (*UK*)
The Gallery Press (*Ire*)
Gomer Press (*UK*)
Italica Press (*US*)
Josef Weinberger Ltd (*UK*)
Lillenas Drama Resources (*US*)
The Lilliput Press (*Ire*)
Maverick Musicals & Plays (*Aus*)
New Playwrights' Network (NPN) (*UK*)
Nick Hern Books Ltd (*UK*)
Oberon Books (*UK*)
Playlab (*Aus*)
Samuel French Ltd (*UK*)

Self-Help
ACTA Publications (*US*)
Allen & Unwin (*Aus*)
Allison & Busby Ltd (*UK*)
BenBella Books (*US*)
Blue Mountain Arts, Inc. (*US*)
BLVNP Incorporated (*US*)
Nicholas Brealey Publishing (*UK*)
Bull Publishing Company (*US*)
Career Press (*US*)
Cedar Fort (*US*)
Connections Book Publishing Ltd (*UK*)
Cork University Press (*Ire*)
Crown House Publishing (*UK*)
Divertir Publishing LLC (*US*)
Dreamriver Press (*US*)
Familius (*US*)
Ferguson Publishing (*US*)
Fleming Publications (*UK*)
Floris Books (*UK*)
Geddes & Grosset (*UK*)
HarperCollins (*US*)
Hawthorn Press (*UK*)
Hay House Publishers (*UK*)
Health Communications, Inc. (*US*)
Health Professions Press (*US*)
Hipso Media (*US*)
Infinite Ideas (*UK*)
Insomniac Press (*Can*)
International Wealth Success (IWS) Inc. (*US*)
Jolly Fish Press (*US*)
Judaica Press (*US*)
Management Books 2000 Ltd (*UK*)
Mandrake of Oxford (*UK*)
Martin Sisters Publishing (*US*)
Oneworld Publications (*UK*)
O'Reilly Media (*US*)
Paulist Press (*US*)
Pelican Publishing Company (*US*)
Red Wheel (*US*)
Robert D. Reed Publishers (*US*)
Singing Dragon (*UK*)
SisterShip Press Pty Ltd (*Aus*)
St Pauls (*US*)
W.W. Norton & Company Ltd (*UK*)
Short Stories
Allison & Busby Ltd (*UK*)
Aurora Metro Press (*UK*)
BkMk Press (*US*)
BLVNP Incorporated (*US*)
Carina UK (*UK*)
Cedar Fort (*US*)
Chapman Publishing (*UK*)
Comma Press (*UK*)
Coteau Books (*Can*)
Divertir Publishing LLC (*US*)
Down The Shore Publishing (*US*)
Elm Books (*US*)
The Emma Press Ltd (*UK*)
Fence Books (*US*)
Four Way Books (*US*)
Galley Beggar Press (*UK*)
George Braziller, Inc. (*US*)

GEY Books (*UK*)
Head of Zeus (*UK*)
Helicon Nine Editions (*US*)
Hipso Media (*US*)
Honno Welsh Women's Press (*UK*)
Insomniac Press (*Can*)
Judaica Press (*US*)
Kettillonia (*UK*)
Leapfrog Press (*US*)
Livingston Press (*US*)
Lost Horse Press (*US*)
Luna Press Publishing (*UK*)
Mage Publishers (*US*)
Martin Sisters Publishing (*US*)
Melange Books, LLC (*US*)
Monsoon Books Pte Ltd (*UK*)
New Directions Publishing (*US*)
Ouen Press (*UK*)
Pocol Press (*US*)
SisterShip Press Pty Ltd (*Aus*)
Stonewood Press (*UK*)
Sunstone Press (*US*)
Titan Books (*UK*)
Valley Press (*UK*)
WhiteFire Publishing (*US*)
World Weaver Press (*US*)
Zumaya Publications (*US*)
Sociology
Abdo Publishing Co (*US*)
Algora Publishing (*US*)
Allen & Unwin (*Aus*)
Alma Classics (*UK*)
Ashgate Publishing Limited (*UK*)
Beacon Press (*US*)
BenBella Books (*US*)
Birlinn Ltd (*UK*)
Bristol University Press (*UK*)
Bucknell University Press (*US*)
CATO Institute (*US*)
Clarity Press, Inc. (*US*)
Cork University Press (*Ire*)
Crabtree Publishing (*US*)
DB Publishing (*UK*)
Dreamriver Press (*US*)
Duckworth Publishers (*UK*)
Dunedin Academic Press Ltd (*UK*)
Duquesne University Press (*US*)
Edinburgh University Press (*UK*)
Edward Elgar Publishing Inc. (*US*)
Edward Elgar Publishing Ltd (*UK*)
Fairleigh Dickinson University (FDU) Press
(*Can*)
Fernwood Publishing (*Can*)
Floris Books (*UK*)
Fonthill Media LLC (*US*)
Fonthill Media Ltd (*UK*)
Fordham University Press (*US*)
Gallaudet University Press (*US*)
Garnet Publishing (*UK*)
Granta Books (*UK*)
Greenhaven Publishing (*US*)
Hay House Publishers (*UK*)
Head of Zeus (*UK*)

Kube Publishing (*UK*)
The Lilliput Press (*Ire*)
Luath Press Ltd (*UK*)
McGraw-Hill Education (*US*)
Melbourne University Publishing Ltd (*Aus*)
National Museum Wales (*UK*)
Nomad Press (*US*)
PaperBooks (*UK*)
Pavilion Publishing (*UK*)
Pelican Publishing Company (*US*)
Pen & Sword Books Ltd (*UK*)
Periscope (*UK*)
The Policy Press (*UK*)
Policy Studies Institute (PSI) (*UK*)
Polity Press (*UK*)
Rivers Oram Press (*UK*)
Syracuse University Press (*US*)
Temple University Press (*US*)
Trentham Books Limited (*UK*)
University College Dublin (UCD) Press (*Ire*)
University of Exeter Press (*UK*)
The University of Michigan Press (*US*)
University of Wales Press (*UK*)
Vehicule Press (*Can*)
Venture Publishing, Inc. (*US*)
Verso (*UK*)
W.W. Norton & Company Ltd (*UK*)
Walch Education (*US*)
Wild Goose Publications (*UK*)
Zed Books Ltd (*UK*)
ZigZag Education (*UK*)
Spiritual
ACTA Publications (*US*)
Beyond Words Publishing (*US*)
Career Press (*US*)
Cedar Fort (*US*)
Chelsea Green Publishing, Inc. (*US*)
Concordia Publishing House (*US*)
Connections Book Publishing Ltd (*UK*)
Coteau Books (*Can*)
The Crossroad Publishing Company (*US*)
Crown House Publishing (*UK*)
Cynren Press (*US*)
Divertir Publishing LLC (*US*)
Dreamriver Press (*US*)
Duquesne University Press (*US*)
Findhorn Press Ltd (*UK*)
Fitzrovia Press Limited (*UK*)
Floris Books (*UK*)
Forward Movement Publications (*US*)
Geddes & Grosset (*UK*)
Gill Books (*Ire*)
Hay House Publishers (*UK*)
Health Communications, Inc. (*US*)
Hodder & Stoughton Ltd (*UK*)
Hymns Ancient & Modern Ltd (*UK*)
ICS Publications (*US*)
Insomniac Press (*Can*)
Kube Publishing (*UK*)
Lion Hudson Plc (*UK*)
Loyola Press (*US*)
Mandrake of Oxford (*UK*)
Kevin Mayhew Publishers (*UK*)

Octopus Publishing Group Limited (*UK*)
Red Wheel (*US*)
Robert D. Reed Publishers (*US*)
Robert Hale Publishers (*UK*)
Simon & Schuster UK Limited (*UK*)
Singing Dragon (*UK*)
St Pauls (*US*)
Sterling Publishing Co. Inc. (*US*)
Sunstone Press (*US*)
Wooden Books (*UK*)
WaterBrook & Multnomah (*US*)
Wild Goose Publications (*UK*)
YMAA Publication Center, Inc. (*US*)
Sport
Abdo Publishing Co (*US*)
Allen & Unwin (*Aus*)
Amberley Publishing (*UK*)
Aureus Publishing Limited (*UK*)
Bancroft Press (*US*)
BenBella Books (*US*)
Birlinn Ltd (*UK*)
Black & White Publishing Ltd (*UK*)
Blink Publishing (*UK*)
Blue River Press (*US*)
Bull Publishing Company (*US*)
Carlton Publishing Group (*UK*)
Chicago Review Press (*US*)
Cork University Press (*Ire*)
Coteau Books (*Can*)
DB Publishing (*UK*)
Dino Books (*UK*)
Duckworth Publishers (*UK*)
ECW Press (*Can*)
Fernwood Publishing (*Can*)
Finney Company (*US*)
Fonthill Media LLC (*US*)
Fonthill Media Ltd (*UK*)
Gill Books (*Ire*)
Gomer Press (*UK*)
HarperCollins Publishers Ltd (*UK*)
Haynes Publishing (*UK*)
Head of Zeus (*UK*)
Headline Publishing Group (*UK*)
Heritage House (*Can*)
Human Kinetics (*US*)
Insomniac Press (*Can*)
Interlink Publishing Group, Inc. (*US*)
JourneyForth (*US*)
Krause Publications (*US*)
The Lilliput Press (*Ire*)
Luath Press Ltd (*UK*)
Melbourne University Publishing Ltd (*Aus*)
The O'Brien Press (*Ire*)
Octopus Publishing Group Limited (*UK*)
Page Street Publishing Co. (*US*)
Pelican Publishing Company (*US*)
Pen & Sword Books Ltd (*UK*)
Quarto Publishing Group UK (*UK*)
Quiller Publishing Ltd (*UK*)
Robert Hale Publishers (*UK*)
Santa Monica Press (*US*)
Simon & Schuster UK Limited (*UK*)
Snowbooks (*UK*)

Sterling Publishing Co. Inc. (*US*)
Sunstone Press (*US*)
Syracuse University Press (*US*)
Temple University Press (*US*)
Thomas Dunne Books (*US*)
University of Alaska Press (*US*)
The University of Michigan Press (*US*)
W.W. Norton & Company Ltd (*UK*)
Willow Creek Press, Inc. (*US*)
YMAA Publication Center, Inc. (*US*)
ZigZag Education (*UK*)

Suspense
Carina UK (*UK*)
Divertir Publishing LLC (*US*)
ECW Press (*Can*)
4RV Publishing (*US*)
HarperCollins (*US*)
Head of Zeus (*UK*)
Insomniac Press (*Can*)
Joffe Books Ltd (*UK*)
Jolly Fish Press (*US*)
New Directions Publishing (*US*)
Penguin Random House (*US*)
Polis Books (*US*)
Scribner (*US*)
Thomas Dunne Books (*US*)
TouchWood Editions (*Can*)
WaterBrook & Multnomah (*US*)
WhiteFire Publishing (*US*)

Technology
Abdo Publishing Co (*US*)
ASCE Press (*US*)
Astragal Press (*US*)
Bernard Babani (publishing) Ltd (*UK*)
Canopus Publishing Ltd (*UK*)
CJ Fallon (*Ire*)
Dreamriver Press (*US*)
Finney Company (*US*)
Frontinus (*UK*)
Gingko Library (*UK*)
Hanser Publications (*US*)
Haynes Publishing (*UK*)
Hopscotch (*UK*)
Information Today, Inc. (*US*)
MC Press (*US*)
McGraw-Hill Education (*US*)
No Starch Press, Inc. (*US*)
O'Reilly Media (*US*)
Paladin Press (*US*)
Ruby Tuesday Books (*UK*)
SAE International (*US*)
Science Museum Group (*UK*)
SisterShip Press Pty Ltd (*Aus*)
Springer-Verlag London Ltd (*UK*)
Temple University Press (*US*)
Trentham Books Limited (*UK*)
Ulric Publishing (*UK*)
W.W. Norton & Company Ltd (*UK*)
WIT Press (*UK*)
ZigZag Education (*UK*)

Theatre
Aurora Metro Press (*UK*)
Beercott Books (*UK*)

Duckworth Publishers (*UK*)
Faber & Faber Ltd (*UK*)
Fairleigh Dickinson University (FDU) Press (*Can*)
The Gallery Press (*Ire*)
Gomer Press (*UK*)
Haus Publishing (*UK*)
Josef Weinberger Ltd (*UK*)
McGraw-Hill Education (*US*)
New Playwrights' Network (NPN) (*UK*)
Nick Hern Books Ltd (*UK*)
Oberon Books (*UK*)
Southern Illinois University Press (*US*)
Sunstone Press (*US*)
The University of Michigan Press (*US*)

Thrillers
Allison & Busby Ltd (*UK*)
Asabi Publishing (*US*)
Bancroft Press (*US*)
Black & White Publishing Ltd (*UK*)
Bloomsbury Spark (*UK*)
Carina UK (*UK*)
Duckworth Publishers (*UK*)
Entangled Teen (*US*)
Fingerpress UK (*UK*)
4RV Publishing (*US*)
GEY Books (*UK*)
HarperCollins Publishers Ltd (*UK*)
Head of Zeus (*UK*)
Hesperus Press Limited (*UK*)
Honno Welsh Women's Press (*UK*)
Joffe Books Ltd (*UK*)
Jolly Fish Press (*US*)
Little, Brown Book Group (*UK*)
Luath Press Ltd (*UK*)
Michael Joseph (*UK*)
Monsoon Books Pte Ltd (*UK*)
Oceanview Publishing (*US*)
Polis Books (*US*)
Salvo Press (*US*)
SisterShip Press Pty Ltd (*Aus*)
Snowbooks (*UK*)
Thomas Dunne Books (*US*)
Twenty First Century Publishers Ltd (*UK*)
WhiteFire Publishing (*US*)
Zumaya Publications (*US*)

Translations
Algora Publishing (*US*)
Alma Classics (*UK*)
Arc Publications (*UK*)
Aurora Metro Press (*UK*)
Calisi Press (*UK*)
Canongate Books (*UK*)
Carcanet Press Ltd (*UK*)
David R. Godine, Publisher (*US*)
Dedalus Ltd (*UK*)
Duckworth Publishers (*UK*)
Fernwood Publishing (*Can*)
Folded Word LLC (*US*)
Garnet Publishing (*UK*)
George Braziller, Inc. (*US*)
Greystones Press (*UK*)
Hesperus Press Limited (*UK*)

ICS Publications (*US*)
Interlink Publishing Group, Inc. (*US*)
Italica Press (*US*)
Mage Publishers (*US*)
Mantra Lingua Ltd (*UK*)
New Directions Publishing (*US*)
Nightboat Books (*US*)
Oneworld Publications (*UK*)
Periscope (*UK*)
Red Empress Publishing (*US*)
Red Moon Press (*US*)
Seven Stories Press (*US*)
Syracuse University Press (*US*)
Truman State University Press (*US*)
University of Alaska Press (*US*)
Vehicule Press (*Can*)
Travel
Abdo Publishing Co (*US*)
ACC Art Books Ltd (*UK*)
Allen & Unwin (*Aus*)
Allison & Busby Ltd (*UK*)
Amberley Publishing (*UK*)
Appalachian Mountain Club Books (*US*)
Birlinn Ltd (*UK*)
Blink Publishing (*UK*)
Blue River Press (*US*)
Bradt Travel Guides (*UK*)
Nicholas Brealey Publishing (*UK*)
Canongate Books (*UK*)
Chicago Review Press (*US*)
Chronicle Books LLC (*US*)
Cicerone Press (*UK*)
Cork University Press (*Ire*)
Coteau Books (*Can*)
Countryside Books (*UK*)
Cynren Press (*US*)
DB Publishing (*UK*)
Discovery Walking Guides Ltd (*UK*)
Dref Wen (*UK*)
Duckworth Publishers (*UK*)
Edward Elgar Publishing Inc. (*US*)
Encante Press, LLC (*US*)
Eye Books (*UK*)
FalconGuides (*US*)
Finney Company (*US*)
Folded Word LLC (*US*)
Fonthill Media LLC (*US*)
Fonthill Media Ltd (*UK*)
Footprint Handbooks (*UK*)
Formac Publishing Company Limited (*Can*)
Garnet Publishing (*UK*)
George Braziller, Inc. (*US*)
GEY Books (*UK*)
Gibson Square Books Ltd (*UK*)
Golden West Books (*US*)
Gomer Press (*UK*)
Granta Books (*UK*)
HarperCollins (*US*)
Haus Publishing (*UK*)
Hesperus Press Limited (*UK*)
Hipso Media (*US*)
Hodder & Stoughton Ltd (*UK*)
House of Lochar (*UK*)

Infinite Ideas (*UK*)
Insomniac Press (*Can*)
Interlink Publishing Group, Inc. (*US*)
Italica Press (*US*)
The Lilliput Press (*Ire*)
Lonely Planet (*UK*)
Luath Press Ltd (*UK*)
Metro Publications Ltd (*UK*)
Monsoon Books Pte Ltd (*UK*)
Mountaineers Books (*US*)
The O'Brien Press (*Ire*)
Octopus Publishing Group Limited (*UK*)
Oleander Press (*UK*)
Onstream Publications Ltd (*Ire*)
Ouen Press (*UK*)
PaperBooks (*UK*)
Pelican Publishing Company (*US*)
Penguin Random House (*US*)
Quiller Publishing Ltd (*UK*)
Santa Monica Press (*US*)
Seaworthy Publications (*US*)
Sheldrake Press (*UK*)
Simon & Schuster UK Limited (*UK*)
Sterling Publishing Co. Inc. (*US*)
Summersdale Publishers Ltd (*UK*)
Sunflower Books (*UK*)
Sunstone Press (*US*)
I.B. Tauris & Co. Ltd (*UK*)
TouchWood Editions (*Can*)
Truman State University Press (*US*)
Ulric Publishing (*UK*)
The University of Michigan Press (*US*)
Valley Press (*UK*)
W.W. Norton & Company Ltd (*UK*)
Weidenfeld & Nicolson (*UK*)
ZigZag Education (*UK*)
TV
BearManor Media (*US*)
BFI Publishing (*UK*)
Candy Jar Books (*UK*)
Chronicle Books LLC (*US*)
ECW Press (*Can*)
Guild of Master Craftsman (GMC) Publications
Ltd (*UK*)
Headline Publishing Group (*UK*)
Syracuse University Press (*US*)
Titan Books (*UK*)
Westerns
Carina UK (*UK*)
Harlequin American Romance (*US*)
HarperCollins (*US*)
Hendrick-Long Publishing Co. (*US*)
JourneyForth (*US*)
Robert Hale Publishers (*UK*)
Sunstone Press (*US*)
Zumaya Publications (*US*)
Women's Interests
Algora Publishing (*US*)
Allison & Busby Ltd (*UK*)
Aurora Metro Press (*UK*)
Beacon Press (*US*)
Beyond Words Publishing (*US*)
Black & White Publishing Ltd (*UK*)

Bull Publishing Company (*US*)
Calisi Press (*UK*)
Carina UK (*UK*)
Chicago Review Press (*US*)
Connections Book Publishing Ltd (*UK*)
Cork University Press (*Ire*)
Coteau Books (*Can*)
The Crossroad Publishing Company (*US*)
Cynren Press (*US*)
ECW Press (*Can*)
Fairleigh Dickinson University (FDU) Press (*Can*)
Fernwood Publishing (*Can*)
Fordham University Press (*US*)
Gibson Square Books Ltd (*UK*)
Harlequin Dare (*Can*)
Hay House Publishers (*UK*)
Health Communications, Inc. (*US*)
Heritage House (*Can*)
Hohm Press (*US*)

Honno Welsh Women's Press (*UK*)
Lawrence Hill Books (*US*)
Michael Joseph (*UK*)
Myriad Editions (*UK*)
Pandora Press (*UK*)
Polis Books (*US*)
Polity Press (*UK*)
Quirk Books (*US*)
Red Empress Publishing (*US*)
Red Wheel (*US*)
Rivers Oram Press (*UK*)
SisterShip Press Pty Ltd (*Aus*)
Southern Illinois University Press (*US*)
Sunstone Press (*US*)
Syracuse University Press (*US*)
Temple University Press (*US*)
Thomas Dunne Books (*US*)
Trentham Books Limited (*UK*)
The University of Michigan Press (*US*)
W.W. Norton & Company Ltd (*UK*)

Get Free Access to the firstwriter.com Website

To claim your free access to the firstwriter.com website simply go to the website at https://www.firstwriter.com/subscribe and begin the subscription process as normal. On the second page, enter the required details (such as your name and address, etc.) then for "Voucher / coupon number" enter the following promotional code:

- **GB71-2FXG**

This will reduce the cost of creating a subscription by up to $15 / £10 / €15, making it free to create a monthly, quarterly, or combination subscription. Alternatively, you can use the discount to take out an annual or life subscription at a reduced rate.

Continue the process until your account is created. Please note that you will need to provide your payment details, even if there is no up-front payment. This is in case you choose to leave your subscription running after the free initial period, but there is no obligation for you to do so.

When you use this code to take out a free subscription you are under no obligation to make any payments whatsoever and you are free to cancel your account before you make any payments if you wish.

If you need any assistance, please email support@firstwriter.com.

If you have found this book useful, please consider leaving a review on the website where you bought it.

What you get

Once you have set up access to the site you will be able to benefit from all the following features:

Databases

All our databases are updated almost every day, and include powerful search facilities to help you find exactly what you need. Searches that used to take you hours or even days in print books or on search engines can now be done in seconds, and produce more accurate and up-to-date information. Our agents database also includes independent reports from at least three separate sources, showing you which are the top agencies and helping you avoid the scams that are all over the internet. You can try out any of our databases before you subscribe:

Search dozens of **current competitions**

Search **over 2,300 magazines**

---

*Claim your free access to **www.firstwriter.com**: See p.389*

Search **over 750 literary agencies**

Search **over 1,900 book publishers** that **don't** charge fees

PLUS advanced features to help you with your search:

- Save searches and save time – set multiple search parameters specific to your work, save them, and then access the search results with a single click whenever you log in. You can even save multiple different searches if you have different types of work you are looking to place.
- Add personal notes to listings, visible only to you and fully searchable – helping you to organise your actions.
- Set reminders on listings to notify you when to submit your work, when to follow up, when to expect a reply, or any other custom action.
- Track which listings you've viewed and when, to help you organise your search – any listings which have changed since you last viewed them will be highlighted for your attention!

Daily email updates

As a subscriber you will be able to take advantage of our email alert service, meaning you can specify your particular interests and we'll send you automatic email updates when we change or add a listing that matches them. So if you're interested in agents dealing in romantic fiction in the United States you can have us send you emails with the latest updates about them – keeping you up to date without even having to log in.

User feedback

Our agent, publisher, and magazine databases all include a user feedback feature that allows our subscribers to leave feedback on each listing – giving you not only the chance to have your say about the markets you contact, but giving a unique authors' perspective on the listings.

Save on copyright protection fees

If you're sending your work away to publishers, competitions, or literary agents, it's vital that you first protect your copyright. As a subscriber to firstwriter.com you can do this through our site and save 10% on the copyright registration fees normally payable for protecting your work internationally through the Intellectual Property Rights Office.

Monthly newsletter

When you subscribe to firstwriter.com you also receive our monthly email newsletter – described by one publishing company as "the best in the business" – including articles, news, and interviews for writers. And the best part is that you can continue to receive the newsletter even after you stop your paid subscription – at no cost!

Terms and conditions

The promotional code contained in this publication may be used by the owner of the book only to create one subscription to firstwriter.com at a reduced cost, or for free. It may not be used by or disseminated to third parties. Should the code be misused then the owner of the book will be liable for any costs incurred, including but not limited to payment in full at the standard

---

rate for the subscription in question. The code may be used at any time until the end of the calendar year named in the title of the publication, after which time it will become invalid. The code may be redeemed against the creation of a new account only – it cannot be redeemed against the ongoing costs of keeping a subscription open. In order to create a subscription a method of payment must be provided, but there is no obligation to make any payment. Subscriptions may be cancelled at any time, and if an account is cancelled before any payment becomes due then no payment will be made. Once a subscription has been created, the normal schedule of payments will begin on a monthly, quarterly, or annual basis, unless a life Subscription is selected, or the subscription is cancelled prior to the first payment becoming due. Subscriptions may be cancelled at any time, but if they are left open beyond the date at which the first payment becomes due and is processed then payments will not be refundable.

11351353R00217

Printed in Great Britain
by Amazon